PCI

Hardware and Software

Architecture and Design

Second Edition

Edward Solari and George Willse

Annabooks

San Diego

PCI Hardware and Software

by

Edward Solari and George Willse

Second Edition

PUBLISHED BY

Annabooks
11838 Bernardo Plaza Court, Suite 102
San Diego, CA 92128
USA

619-673-0870

Printed in the United States of America

ISBN 0-929392-28-0

Second Edition

Third Printing, March 1995

Dedications

As with my previous books

The patience and understanding by my wife (who never sees me when I undertake a project like this) is greatly appreciated.

The education, discipline, and dedication imparted to me by my mother and father has once again proved invaluable in this project.

Finally, working with George Willse on this and other projects has been a great pleasure. His dedication to a quality product is refreshing.

Ed

To Brigitte -
For all the encouragement, late night company, and being my best friend. I could not have done this without you by my side.

To Travis and Tyler -
For letting me use "your" computer and software to write my part of this book. I am so proud of you.

To my Mother, Father and Mother-in-Law -
For all your love and support.

And to Ed -
For giving me the opportunity to work on this project with you. But more importantly, for being a great friend over the years.

George

Contents

Preface

The major cause of low performance in computer systems is the time it takes to execute memory and I/O functions related to peripheral devices such as LAN, SCSI, and motion video. Low bus bandwidth adversely impacts data processing and screen output. In recent years, two independent approaches have been taken to solve this low bandwidth obstacle. First, peripheral device vendors have implemented new architectures to increase the data transfer rates between their devices and other system components. The second approach is the movement of peripheral devices from lower to higher performance buses.

The Peripheral Component Interconnect (PCI) Bus is the latest bus architecture to address the performance issues associated with personal computers. The PCI Bus solves the bandwidth problem by providing a data path capable of accessing up to 264 megabytes of data per second. In addition to being optimized for high bandwidth, the PCI Bus also addresses cache coherency and multiple bus master support. The PCI Bus component and add-in card interface is also processor independent. Both present and future processors of different architectures are fully supported.

The features of the PCI Bus architecture also extend into the software realm. PCI devices incorporate registers that contain device-specific information. This information enables System BIOSs and operating system level software to automatically configure PCI Bus components and add-in cards. Automatic device configuration eliminates the need for hardware jumpers and software configuration utilities. In addition, this feature reduces the possibility of system resource conflicts that can occur when two or more devices are assigned the same resource.

The major goal of this book is to document in one location both the hardware and software architectures of the PCI Bus. This book is based on the PCI Local Bus Specification Rev. 2.0, PCI BIOS Specification Rev. 2.1, and additional information not incorporated in either (and only available in this book). This enables the reader to quickly access ALL the information necessary to ensure the proper design of a PCI based system or add-in card. The book is divided into three sections. Chapters 1 and 2 are introductory and provide a very general overview of the PCI Bus hardware and software. Chapters 3 through 15 are dedicated to the detailed specification and discussion of PCI Bus hardware. Finally, Chapters 16 through 20 are dedicated to the detailed specification and discussion of PCI Bus software.

Both we and Annabooks are interested in the continuing evolution, clarification, and corrections to this book. Please direct any related inputs to Annabooks.

We would like to make special note of the assistance rendered by Norman Rasmussen and Brad Hosler ... two of the key PCI experts on the planet. They dedicated excessive hours of their own time to this project. Their diligent review, comments, corrections, and insights were invaluable during the preparation of this book. The authors are tremendously indebted to Norman and Brad for their help.

We would also like to thank Mike Bailey (PCI SIG Steering Committee Chairman) for permission to extract and use portions of the aforementioned PCI specifications, and William Samaris for his help with the electrical specifications.

Ed Solari and George Willse
Oregon

CHAPTER 1

ISA SYSTEM ARCHITECTURAL OVERVIEW

This chapter consists of the following subchapters:

1.0 ISA SYSTEM ARCHITECTURE

The architecture of ISA compatible systems can be viewed as four individual layers. Each layer has a defined interface between itself and the other layers. Utilizing this layered architecture permits each layer to be developed and modified independently of the others. It also translates into portability for the upper software layers.

> Even though not specifically mentioned, the architectural concepts described for an ISA system also apply to EISA and Micro Channel systems.

> The term "system" represents the entire hardware and software required to create an ISA compatible personal computer. The term "platform" represents the physical collection of hardware on a single Fiberglas board. The platform contains connectors to support the attachment of add-in cards.

1.1 LAYER 1—PLATFORM HARDWARE

At the innermost layer of the architecture lies the platform hardware. This hardware consists of the platform with its integrated components and add-in cards that expand platform features. The simplest architecture of a ISA compatible platform is outlined in Figure 1-1. The HOST CPU, cache, and memory (HDRAM) all reside on the HOST bus. The HOST bus is attached to an ISA bus (or EISA or Micro-Channel, depending on the platform) via a BRIDGE. The ISA bus contains ISA bus connectors and ISA compatible resources.

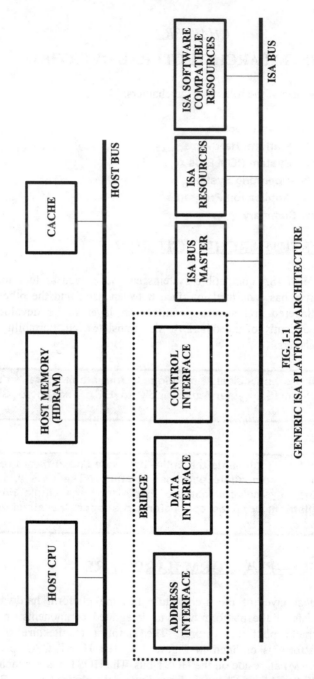

Figure 1-1: Generic ISA Platform Architecture

HOST BUS

The HOST bus supports the highest performance resources on the platform and is separated from the ISA bus. Newer platforms allow the HOST CPU to continue execution (with the cache and HDRAM) when the ISA bus is executing a bus cycle. The HOST bus is proprietary to the platform, but in most personal computers resembles the Intel 386, 486, or Pentium. The ISA bus provides a general purpose bus that is of lower performance but provides a wealth of add-in functions as a defacto standard. As will be discussed in Chapter 2, a third bus (PCI) has been added to newer personal computer platforms. This local bus blends the high performance of the HOST bus with the flexibility to attach a variety of functions with its standardized and documented protocol.

BRIDGE

The BRIDGE provides the link between the HOST and ISA buses. The three major components are: ADDRESS, DATA, and CONTROL Interfaces.

The ADDRESS Interface translates the address memory space of the HOST bus (typically 32 bits or more) to the address space of the ISA bus (24 bits). In the case of the I/O address space, the conversion from HOST bus to ISA bus is from 16 to 10 address bits, respectively.

The DATA Interface matches the data size of the HOST bus (typically 32 bits or more) to the data size of the ISA bus (8 or 16 bits). This interface includes byte swapping and the execution of the multiple cycles (in conjunction with the CONTROL Interface). Multiple cycle support includes (for example) a 32 data bit access on the HOST bus to be translated to two 16 data bit cycles on the ISA bus. The DATA Interface may also post write DATA (under certain conditions) to allow the cycles on the two buses to complete at different times.

The CONTROL Interface translates the HOST bus protocol to the ISA bus protocol and vice versa. In the case of multiple cycles, the CONTROL Interface will generate the additional bus cycles required.

ISA RESOURCES

ISA Software Compatible Resources are required for compatibility with the ISA software. The ISA software requires certain resources with predefined registers to reside at specific addresses. The defacto resources required are: Interrupt Controller, Keyboard, Mouse, Video, Floppy Disk, Hard Disk, Refresh and DMA Controllers, and the Real Time Clock.

Also attached to the ISA bus are the ISA bus masters and ISA resources. The ISA bus master can arbitrate (via the DMA Controller) to own the ISA bus and access ISA bus resources or the HOST memory. The ISA resource can consist of both memory and I/O types.

1.2 LAYER 2—SYSTEM ROM BIOS

The System ROM BIOS, or Basic Input Output System, sits at the layer directly above the platform hardware. The run-time function of the System ROM BIOS is to provide a two-step interface between the layers of software above itself and the platform hardware below it. The System ROM BIOS receives requests from the upper layers of software to manipulate the platform hardware.

Because the System ROM BIOS communicates directly with the platform hardware it is not usually portable between different computers. This is due in part to the difference in chip sets, microprocessor types, and bus architectures used in different computers. The software layers above the System ROM BIOS can remain hardware independent by using the System ROM BIOS software to communicate with the platform hardware. The mechanism for this communication is through the use of software interrupts and is described in detail in Chapter 16, *System Resources*.

1.3 LAYER 3—OPERATING SYSTEM

The third layer in the software architecture of an ISA compatible system is the operating system. The most common operating system for ISA compatible systems is DOS. DOS consists of three major components: the DOS BIOS, the DOS Kernel, and the DOS Command Processor. These fundamental segments of the operating system reside in three different system files.

DOS BIOS

The DOS BIOS services the platform hardware-dependent components of the system. These functions include device drivers for the system date and time (CLOCK), serial port input or auxiliary interface (AUX), keyboard and video display (CON), line printer output (PRN), and the disk drives that are accessed by the A, B, and C disk drive specifiers. The DOS BIOS software is in a file that usually is named IO.SYS, IBMIO.SYS or IBMBIO.COM.

DOS KERNEL

The DOS Kernel services the platform hardware-independent components of the system. These functions include character input and output, file management, the execution of other software programs, and real-time clock services. As with the System ROM BIOS services, programmers also use software interrupts to access the DOS Kernel functions. The DOS Kernel is typically found in a file called IBMDOS.COM or MSDOS.SYS.

DOS COMMAND PROCESSOR

The DOS Command Processor is the software module that provides the user interface to the operating system. It is a program controlled by DOS that accepts the user's command line input, parses it, and then executes the commands. These commands usually include loading and executing other software programs. The DOS Command Processor is found in a file named COMMAND.COM.

1.4 LAYER 4—APPLICATION PROGRAMS

Application Programs are the software programs the user loads and executes under the control of DOS. These include word processors, graphics packages, games, and telecommunications programs.

1.5 CHAPTER SUMMARY

Since the first versions of DOS (MS-DOS 1.0 and PC-DOS 1.0) were introduced in 1981, the operating system has increased in power and flexibility. With each new version, the three software layers described above were enhanced to accommodate new hardware features such as larger disk drives, networking and more powerful microprocessors. With the more complex functionality of the systems came a major emphasis on simplifying user interfaces for the software programs contained in each of the layers. However, as will be seen, little has been done to enhance the ease of integration and use of the first layer of the ISA compatible systems, the platform hardware itself.

CHAPTER 2

PCI SYSTEM ARCHITECTURAL OVERVIEW

This chapter consists of the following subchapters:

2.0   Introduction
2.1   Overview of Plug and Play Architecture
2.2   PCI Platform Hardware Architecture
2.3   PCI Software and the
        Plug and Play Architecture
2.4   Chapter Summary

2.0 INTRODUCTION

A major strength of any computer system is its expansion capability. This is the ability to add new components to the system, typically through the use of expansion bus add-in cards, to increase the existing machine's functional capabilities. This concept, in conjunction with an open system architecture approach, is without a doubt the cornerstone behind the astonishing success of the IBM and compatible personal computers.

Despite its success, however, there are two cardinal omissions in the original design of the IBM personal computer that have plagued the computer industry.

The first omission is that no formal hardware design specification was provided for the design of both the system platforms and the ISA expansion bus add-in cards. This lack of a uniform specification produced two major consequences. The first consequence affects the designers and manufactures of computer hardware: untold man-hours of reverse-engineering have been spent by various vendors over the years to produce the system components. The second consequence affects the consumer: the lack of a uniform hardware specification often results in an incompatibility between the system components. This in turn makes it difficult if not impossible to install and configure many hardware components in a computer system.

The second outstanding omission in the design of the original IBM personal computer is the lack of an architecture that coordinates the integration of the hardware and software components of the system. Currently, installing and configuring new components such that the computer system remains resource conflict-free is very troublesome. For example, assigning DMA, IRQ, memory, and I/O Port resources to older ISA expansion bus add-in cards and system platforms usually requires the reading of hardware manuals as well as the manipulation of jumpers or switches. Newer add-in cards and system platforms require the installer to run software setup utilities to configure the add-in cards for use in the system.

Neither of the above methods ensures a system that is resource conflict-free. The reason is that in order to assign unused resources to a previously uninstalled add-in card, the installer or the add-in card installation utility must be cognizant of all the system resources currently consumed by the system. This is impossible under the current methodology. Compounding the problem is the fact that expansion bus add-in cards may require specific resources already consumed by other devices in the system.

In addition, even when the system hardware is configured correctly, there is no consistent interface that permits the software at the device driver/operating system level to reliably determine what devices are installed and what system resources these devices are consuming. This is particularly critical in those systems that permit hot insertion and removal of devices (such as PCMCIA) or hot docking of a mobile computer. Strict system resource management is required in such instances to ensure that system resources are allocated and deallocated in a conflict-free manner when devices are added or removed from the system.

LEGACY DEVICES AND CARDS

Devices that fall into the class of not being fully identifiable and configurable without user intervention (other than simply installing the device) such as those discussed above are referred to as LEGACY devices. ISA expansion bus add-in cards that are built with LEGACY devices are referred to as LEGACY cards. A major goal of the PCI Local Bus and its device class was to overcome the pitfalls inherited by system components designed according to the LEGACY architecture model. However, designing and implementing a new bus and device class are not enough to overcome the LEGACY of early devices. A new software methodology that coordinates the hardware configuration process at the System BIOS, device driver and operating system levels is also required. This methodology, which exploits the hardware and software power of PCI and other device classes, is known as the Plug and Play architecture.

SUMMARY

The major emphasis of this book is to aid in this goal with respect to the PCI architecture. However, prior to discussing actual specifics of the PCI hardware and software architectures, it is important to have an understanding of the general principles of the Plug and Play architecture.

2.1 OVERVIEW OF PLUG AND PLAY ARCHITECTURE

In 1993 an industry-wide group was formed. The common objective of this group is to resolve the deficiencies of the ISA bus architecture and to advance the usability of the personal computer. When this objective is achieved, the personal computer industry will possess an architecture for system configuration that encompasses all of the hardware and software components in the system. When this architecture is fully implemented in a given system, nothing will be required of the user except to add or remove the system hardware and software components. The system will automatically detect any hardware or software change and configure itself accordingly after any type of system reset. In addition, software executing at the operating system level will dynamically adapt to the new working environment without having to turn the system off first. To reach this level of integration, a set of design requirements was established for Plug and Play system hardware and software.

PLUG AND PLAY SYSTEM DESIGN REQUIREMENTS

A set of design requirements for a Plug and Play is being specified to aid in the development of Plug and Play systems. These requirements encompass both the system hardware and software. Below is a summary of the current list of requirements for Plug and Play, as specified in the document *The Plug and Play Framework: Advancing the PC Architecture Backgrounder, September 1993, Microsoft Corporation*:

EASE OF INSTALLATION AND CONFIGURATION OF NEW DEVICES

For Plug and Play to be viable, software at all levels from the System BIOS to operating systems and device drivers require information about the devices in a system. This information includes the identity of the device's function, what services the device provides, and the system resources the device needs in order to function. For example, a graphics device will identify itself as such. In addition, if the video device requires a block of memory for a video frame buffer or a hardware interrupt, it should communicate this information to the controlling software.

With this information, software at the System BIOS level or higher can automatically detect the presence of the device. The software can assign system resources to the device while maintaining a computer system that is free of system resource conflicts. Operating system level software can also detect the presence of the device and automatically load its device drivers if required. The user simply has to install the device and perform a one-time load of the software associated with the device into the system. Thereafter the operating system will automatically detect the presence of the Plug and Play device and load its drivers without user intervention.

SEAMLESS DYNAMIC CONFIGURATION CHANGES

Another design requirement is to permit the hot insertion or removal of devices from a system. This includes add-in cards as well as the docking of a mobile computer. The operating system level software in conjunction with the System BIOS can configure the system automatically without requiring the user to power down the system.

There are many considerations to be addressed for this goal to be realized. For instance software must be written to dynamically detect the system status change. Applications must be told about the change in order to start or stop using the device based on its insertion or removal. And again, system resources are required to be allocated or deallocated while keeping the system resources conflict-free.

For example, assume a printer was just added to the system. The software would detect this change without manual user notification, assign system resources such as an available parallel port to the device, load any required printer drivers, and then notify all active applications that a new printer is available for printing documents.

BACKWARD COMPATIBILITY

As mentioned above, non Plug and Play systems and peripherals cannot communicate information about what functions they perform or what their requirements are to successfully function in a system. This is unquestionably the greatest problem to overcome in the implementation of any Plug and Play system.

The existing method of dealing with the problem involves some user intervention. Software programs such as the computer's system's Setup (or Configuration) Utility are in some cases being modified to allow the user to input information about LEGACY devices. This information is stored in the computer system and is used in the power-up and run-time configuration of the system components.

In addition, some companies such as Intel Corporation have developed software utilities to aid in configuring systems with LEGACY add-in devices. These utilities allow the user to determine a working configuration for LEGACY devices in the system prior to adding the device to the system. These programs take into account both Plug and Play devices as well as LEGACY devices. Depending on the system, this information may or may not be stored in the computer system and then used in the power-up and run-time configuration of the system components.

EXTENSIBILITY

The Plug and Play architecture must accommodate both existing classes of devices as well as future classes. PCI, along with ISA, EISA, and Micro Channel are types of existing device classes. The ACCESS bus is an example of a new device class.

OPEN ARCHITECTURE

To fully realize the architectural goals of Plug and Play, both the computer software and hardware communities must agree to a defined set of interface specifications. These specifications have to be extensible to existing and future bus and device architectures.

This is a difficult (but not impossible) goal to achieve for several reasons. First, there are several different parties involved, each with their own market interests at heart. Creating a new standard that crosses so many boundaries at so many different technical levels does not come without paying the price of time to market and the redefining of some components that comprise the Plug and Play architecture.

There is also confusion about the existing design specifications. For example, many vendors of PCI devices have entered the market place with non-compliant components. This is fueling confusion in the market as to what is compliant at the device hardware level as well as the different levels of software.

Another major factor is that Plug and Play hardware has been introduced into the market prior to the full implementation of the software architecture. For example, PCI based Plug and Play systems are readily available for purchase. There is a danger that certain undesirable software "features" that exist now in the interim of finalizing the Plug and Play architecture specifications may become defacto standards. This could result in unwanted baggage, both for hardware and software designers.

ECONOMICAL

Plug and Play should be financially attractive to the market place. The cost of implementation should be minimal and the benefits maximized to provide the marketplace a competitive product. This means that hardware complexity must decrease. This in turn decreases the component cost of the device. In addition, hardware flexibility must increase. This allows the software to take full advantage of Plug and Play. To this end, design guidelines and standardized

11

software and hardware interfaces must be defined and adhered to by all participating parties.

2.2   PCI PLATFORM HARDWARE ARCHITECTURE

GENERIC PCI PLATFORM ARCHITECTURE

Figure 2-1 outlines the simplest generic platform architecture with three buses. The HOST bus is the high performance link between the primary platform resources. For a PC the HOST bus is an INTEL x86 type bus. The LEGACY bus is a medium to low performance bus that allows multiple functions to be attached to the platform. A PC LEGACY bus includes the ISA, EISA, and Micro Channel buses. The medium to high performance local bus in this model is the PCI bus.

Each bus has its own unique purpose in a PC architecture. The HOST bus provides a high speed link between the HOST CPU, HOST MEMORY (typically dynamic RAM called HDRAM), and the cache (high speed static RAM). Typically these buses are lightly loaded and have very short backplanes (signal line length) to minimize bus losses (transmission line effects). The LEGACY bus provides complimentary resources to the primary resources on the HOST bus. It can contain other CPUs (bus masters), additional memory, and I/O. It allows for longer backplanes with connectors to support add-in cards. In a PC architecture, the I/O space also contains the PC-compatible DMA, interrupt, and keyboard/mouse controllers. It also contains the real time clock, video interface, and, for EISA and Micro Channel, the configuration registers. The PCI bus provides additional complimentary resources to the HOST bus. Like the I/O buses, it contains other CPUs (bus masters), memory (typically dynamic RAM called PDRAM), and I/O. In the vernacular of the PCI, the memory and I/O resources are called "targets".

Some of the resources on the HOST and LEGACY buses can migrate to the PCI bus. For example, early PCs had the video interface on the LEGACY bus. Some of the newer PCs have moved the video to the PCI bus to improve performance. The HOST memory could also be placed on the PCI bus to be more equally shared between the HOST CPU and bus masters. The migration of resources between buses requires that address locations and software related functional attributes remain compatible to PC software.

Circuitry used to link these different buses are called BRIDGEs. BRIDGEs will be discussed in more detail later, but the primary purpose is to interface one bus protocol to another. The protocol includes the definition of the bus control signal lines, and data and address sizes. When a BRIDGE interfaces identical

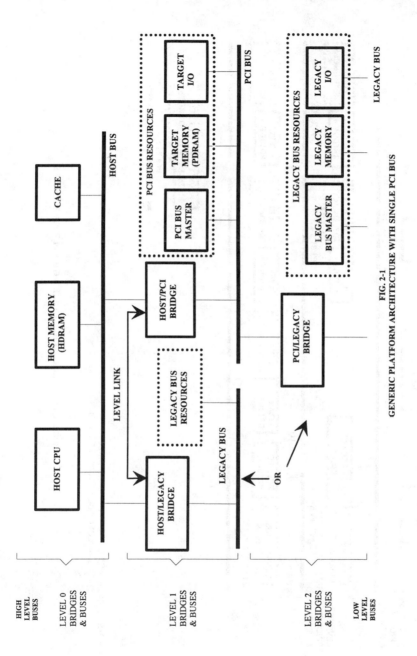

FIG. 2-1
GENERIC PLATFORM ARCHITECTURE WITH SINGLE PCI BUS

Figure 2–1: Generic Platform Architecture with Single PCI Bus

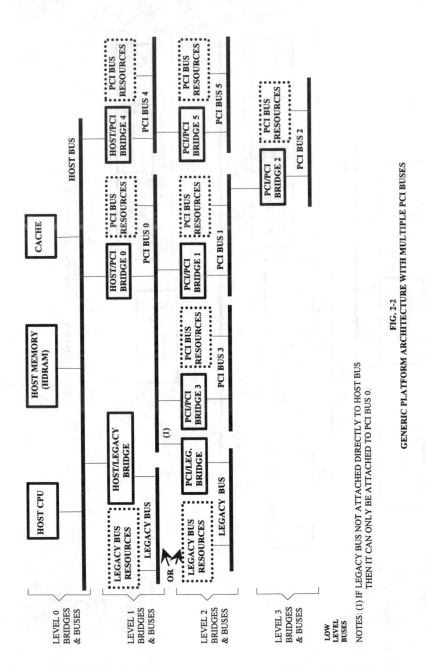

FIG. 2-2
GENERIC PLATFORM ARCHITECTURE WITH MULTIPLE PCI BUSES

NOTES: (1) IF LEGACY BUS NOT ATTACHED DIRECTLY TO HOST BUS
THEN IT CAN ONLY BE ATTACHED TO PCI BUS 0.

Figure 2-2: Generic Platform Architecture with Multiple PCI Buses

buses, the BRIDGE primarily limits the loading of each bus. As outlined in Figure 2-1, BRIDGEs link different bus levels.

The focal point of the architecture is the HOST bus; consequently, the linkage of the I/O and PCI buses to the HOST bus is important. The HOST CPU is the primary bus master, it usually has the highest performance, and it services the interrupts and platform errors. The LEGACY and PCI buses can be connected directly to the HOST bus via a single BRIDGE level and are defined as LEVEL 1 buses. The LEGACY bus could also be placed "under" the PCI bus and be defined as a LEVEL 2 bus. Accesses between the HOST and a LEVEL 2 LEGACY bus must use the LEVEL 1 PCI bus. In some platforms, it is important for a LEVEL 1 PCI bus to communicate directly with a LEVEL 1 LEGACY bus; consequently, a LEVEL LINK is possible between the BRIDGEs. A LEVEL LINK is not part of the PCI bus protocol and is platform dependent.

As outlined in Figure 2-2, additional PCI buses can be added to LEVEL 1. Also, LEVEL 2 PCI buses can added to LEVEL 1 PCI buses, LEVEL 3 PCI buses can added to LEVEL 2 PCI buses, and so forth. As in Figure 2-1, the LEGACY bus can be connected to the HOST bus or the primary PCI bus (PCI bus 0) and may be a LEVEL LINK. Figure 2-2 also outlines the naming convention for the BRIDGEs according to the PCI protocol. The "number" of the BRIDGE and of the lower level PCI bus immediately attached to it is the same. One of the LEVEL 1 HOST/PCI BRIDGEs is selected as "number 0" and the associated lower level PCI bus is "number 0". One of the LEVEL 2 PCI/PCI BRIDGEs is selected as "number 1", and the associated lower level PCI bus is "number 1". The next sequential numbers are assigned to PCI/PCI BRIDGEs that connect to LOWER LEVEL buses before numbers are assigned to PCI/PCI BRIDGEs on the same LEVEL. In this example, the "number 2" is assigned to the next lower level PCI bus and "number 3" is assigned to a PCI/PCI BRIDGE attached to a LEVEL 1 bus. If a PCI/PCI BRIDGE had been attached to a LEVEL 3 bus (PCI bus 2) or a LEVEL 2 bus (PCI bus 1), the number 3 would have been assigned that PCI/PCI BRIDGE instead.

Once all of the PCI buses associated with PCI/PCI BRIDGE 0 have been assigned numbers, the next HOST/PCI BRIDGE on LEVEL 1 is assigned the next sequential number (Number 4 in this example).

The numbering protocol applies to BRIDGEs that connect to PCI buses and the associated PCI buses. BRIDGEs and buses associated with non-PCI buses are not numbered.

In order to limit the complexity of the architecture discussion, the platform outlined in Figure 2-3 will be used. The principles discussed relative to the architecture in Figure 2-3 are applicable to Figures 2-1, 2-2, and extensions.

> In Figures 2-1 to 2-3, the cache is shown as external to the HOST CPU. It is possible for an additional cache to be internal to the HOST CPU. The internal and external caches are behind the HOST/PCI BRIDGE; consequently, the PCI bus cache protocol is the same for both.

> By convention, buses on the same LEVEL are called "peer buses" and buses on different levels are called "hierarchical buses". Peer PCI buses can access each other through two PCI/PCI BRIDGEs with a common PCI bus. A PCI bus that is peer to a LEGACY bus can access it with a LEVEL LINK and vice versa. Hierarchical buses on adjacent bus levels can directly access each other through a single BRIDGE. Hierarchical buses not on adjacent levels can access each other via multiple BRIDGEs and PCI buses.

SOURCE AND DESTINATION BUSES

To describe bus protocol across a BRIDGE, we use the following naming convention for "source" and "destination". The PCI source bus is the one that contains the PCI bus master and the PCI destination bus is the one that contains the target. For example, in Figure 2-3 a PCI bus master on PCI bus 0 (which could be HOST/PCI BRIDGE 0) is accessing a PCI resource (target) on PCI bus 1 via PCI/PCI BRIDGE 1. In this example, PCI bus 0 is the source bus and PCI bus 1 is the destination bus. Another example, in Figure 2-3 a PCI bus master on PCI bus 1 is accessing a PCI resource (target) on PCI bus 0 via PCI/PCI BRIDGE 1. Here, PCI bus 1 is the source bus and PCI bus 0 is the destination bus.

BUS OWNERSHIP

At any given time a bus may be owned by a bus resource called the bus master. Ownership allows the bus master to be the only resource executing bus cycles. A bus master may be an intelligent resource that resides on the bus or may be a BRIDGE acting on behalf of a bus master on another bus. The operation of the bus is the same whether the bus master resides directly on the bus or it is the BRIDGE representing a bus master.

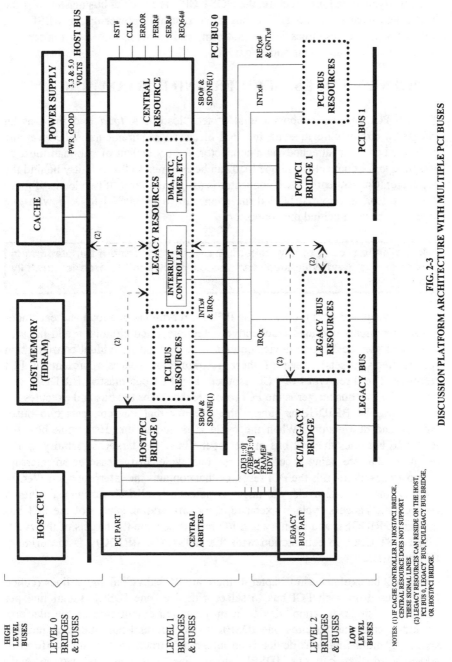

Figure 2-3: Discussion Platform Architecture with Multiple PCI Buses

17

In the typical PCI architecture, the HOST CPU is a special bus master. It is the initial bus master of the HOST bus after platform power-up or RESET, it initializes all the resources in the platform, and it is the only bus master that services platform interrupts and errors.

PCI RESOURCES, DEVICES, AND BUS LOADING

Each PCI bus can support a total of ten "loads". A *load* is defined as an integrated circuit chip meeting the PCI electrical requirements. Whenever the integrated circuit is attached via a connector, the equivalent of one load must be assigned to the connector and one load can be assigned to the circuitry behind the connector. Consequently, each connector is assigned a limit of two loads. If more than one load is required behind the connector, a PCI/PCI BRIDGE with one load must be used behind the connector.

> More than ten loads at any frequency can be supported if the platform is properly designed, validated, and the effect of add-in cards is carefully considered.

Each integrated circuit chip on the PCI bus represents one load and each add-in card represents two loads. Collectively, the integrated circuits or add-in cards are called "devices". Each device contains one to eight individual configuration spaces (register sets). Each of these configuration spaces represents a PCI resource. The three types of PCI resources are: PCI bus master, BRIDGE, and target. The PCI bus master is the PCI resource that owns the bus and executes the bus cycle. The BRIDGE is simply the circuitry that interconnects two buses (source and destination). When the cycle is ported to the destination bus, the BRIDGE becomes the PCI bus master of the bus. The target is memory or I/O resources that are being accessed by the bus cycle. In the case of an interrupt acknowledge cycle, it is the PCI resource that contains the interrupt controller. In the case of a special cycle, the target is potentially all PCI resources. When a configuration access cycle is executed, the configuration spaces of the PCI bus masters, BRIDGEs, and memory and I/O targets become the targets of the cycle. The HOST CPU, in conjunction with the HOST/PCI BRIDGE, is the primary PCI bus master.

As will be explained in Chapter 4, there are 21 individual signal lines (called IDSEL) used on each PCI bus to select a device (one IDSEL signal line per device). A "single-function" device is an integrated circuit chip on the platform or add-in card that requires one IDSEL signal line and has one configuration space. A "multi-function" device is an integrated circuit chip on the platform or add-in card that has one IDSEL signal line, but contains two to eight configuration spaces. The FUNCTION Number in the configuration access cycle is used to select one of the configuration spaces contained within a device.

> If a PCI resource drives 10 loads (the limit at 33 MHz CLK signal line), and each load is an integrated circuit (device) with eight configuration spaces (multi-function), the PCI bus can support eighty configuration spaces. In this example only 10 IDSEL signal lines of the 21 possible were used. If a lower CLK signal line frequency is used, more loads (devices) can be supported.

CENTRAL RESOURCE

The central resource on the platform contains support circuitry not "assigned" to other platform resources. It typically contains the RESET circuitry (RST# signal line), the clock driver (CLK signal line), the error reporting circuitry (to communicate error to the HOST CPU, monitor PERR# and SERR# signal lines, and drive the SERR# signal line), and the support of memory access cycle address snoop if a cache controller is not in the HOST/PCI BRIDGE (SBO# and SDONE signal lines). Though not shown in Figure 2-3, it may also monitor and drive other PCI bus signal lines.

CENTRAL ARBITER

The central arbiter consists of platform circuitry that can be viewed as two distinct parts: PCI and LEGACY bus compliant. The PCI-compliant portion defines unique arbitration signal line pairs (REQ# = request bus ownership and GNT# = grant bus ownership) to each of the PCI resources that can potentially own the PCI bus (PCI bus master) (see Figure 2-3). The exact algorithm to determine the next PCI bus master is not defined by the PCI bus specification. However, whichever algorithm is selected it should include "fairness" to all platform bus masters. "Fairness" can mean many things, but essentially should insure that the amount of time a bus master must wait for the bus is appropriate. For example, high priority bus masters should obtain the bus relatively quickly. However, two or three high priority bus masters should not be awarded their respective buses at the detriment of lower priority buses. Lower priority buses must not be "starved"; they must not be denied sufficient bus ownership time or be forced to wait extremely long periods of time to obtain bus ownership.

The LEGACY bus compliant portion of the central arbiter is actually part of the PCI/LEGACY BRIDGE and its protocol is defined according to the protocol of the LEGACY bus. For example: if the LEGACY bus is ISA, arbitration for

ISA bus ownership is via the DMA controller in the PCI/LEGACY BRIDGE, which must also support arbitration for refresh. If the LEGACY bus is EISA, arbitration for EISA bus ownership is via arbitration circuitry in the BRIDGE that accounts for unique arbitration signal line pairs (EISA-defined), bus time-out, refresh, and bus preemption. The LEGACY bus compliant portion can interface with the PCI compliant portion of the central arbiter via REQ# and GNT# signal lines (as shown in Figure 2-3) or can use other non-PCI bus signal lines between the PCI and LEGACY compliant portions of the central arbiter.

> In the above discussion, the central arbiter was divided between PCI and LEGACY bus compliant portions, with the latter in the PCI/LEGACY BRIDGE. It is possible to build a central arbiter that contains both PCI and LEGACY bus compliant portions in the same physical location.

Finally, the central arbiter may have to act as the Park master. The PCI bus protocol insures that the float time of the signal lines is minimized. For most signal lines, this is achieved by being driven by a resource at all times or driven to a logical "1" by pull-up resistors. The AD[31::0], C/BE#[3::0], and PAR signal lines do not fall under any of these categories; consequently, they must be driven (parked) by a PCI resource when bus cycles are not executed. On some architectures, this resource may be the central arbiter.

DEADLOCK ISSUES

By definition, deadlock is a fatal platform condition. Deadlock occurs when a bus resource is being accessed by two bus masters and one bus master cannot complete the access to a resource until the other bus master accesses the same bus resource. The second bus master cannot access the bus resource because it is being accessed by the first bus master. The PCI bus protocol provides mechanisms to prevent deadlock conditions within the PCI bus. Platforms that contain PCI and LEGACY buses (like ISA or EISA) must have carefully designed BRIDGEs to prevent deadlock conditions.

The PCI bus protocol prevents deadlocks by supporting bus termination without data access, commonly called "back off". The actual PCI bus protocols to achieve back off will be explained in Chapters 7 and 8, but the concept can be understood from the following example: assume that the HOST CPU is using a PCI memory resource (called PDRAM) on PCI bus 0 (see Figure 2-3) and the PDRAM is cached by a write-back cache on the HOST bus. If the HOST CPU writes data to the cache, the PDRAM does not have correct data until the PDRAM is updated. Prior to updating the PDRAM, a PCI bus master on PCI bus 0 tries to read the same cache line in the PDRAM, but obviously the read access cycle cannot be completed because the data has not been updated. A deadlock condition would occur if the PCI bus master could not finish the read access cycle with valid data because the cache controller in the HOST/PCI BRIDGE must gain access to the PDRAM in order to update it. The PCI bus protocol allows the cache controller in the HOST/PCI BRIDGE to request the PCI bus master to complete the cycle without reading data from the PDRAM (back off) and to try the access at another time (according to the PCI protocol, this is called Retry termination and is requested by the PDRAM). The cache controller can now obtain access to the PDRAM and copy the cache line in the write-back cache to the PDRAM. When the PCI bus master repeats the read access cycle, the data in the PDRAM is correct and the cycle is allowed to complete with data being read from the PDRAM.

The above situation is completely different when the PCI bus master is actually a PCI/LEGACY BRIDGE. The PCI/LEGACY BRIDGE is acting on behalf of the LEGACY bus master; consequently, it is restricted by the LEGACY bus master protocol. For LEGACY buses like ISA or EISA, once an access cycle has begun it must be completed with the actual accessing of data. If the LEGACY bus master (with a non-back off protocol) is accessing the PDRAM via the PCI/LEGACY BRIDGE with the conditions outlined in the previous section, a deadlock condition will result. The PCI/LEGACY BRIDGE could be designed to actually back off its PCI read access and supply wait states to the LEGACY bus cycle. The LEGACY bus access can be completed when the PCI/LEGACY BRIDGE repeats the PCI access cycle after the PDRAM has been updated. Unfortunately, LEGACY buses like ISA and EISA require that the LEGACY bus cycle be completed within a specific time. Unless the PCI/LEGACY BRIDGE knows that it can successfully repeat the PCI access cycle within a specific time (dependent on the central arbiter) LEGACY bus errors will occur. Another solution to this problem would be to disallow PCI resources which are accessible by LEGACY bus masters to be cached.

A similar deadlock condition occurs when write data is posted in BRIDGEs attached to PCI bus 0. Until the buffers are written to the PDRAM (flushed), accesses to PDRAM cannot be completed. As with the cache example, the PCI /LEGACY BRIDGE can add wait states to the LEGACY bus cycle. The LEGACY bus access cycle can be completed when the PCI/LEGACY BRIDGE repeats the PCI access cycle after the PDRAM has been updated.

A deadlock condition can also occur when the PDRAM is locked by a PCI bus master according to the PCI bus protocol. Under the PCI bus protocol, the PDRAM can only be accessed by the PCI bus master that locked it (see subchapters 4.0 and 6.3, respectively, for more information). Accesses to a locked PDRAM by other PCI bus masters results in a back off. A deadlock condition will occur if PCI bus master is a PCI/LEGACY BRIDGE acting on behalf of the LEGACY bus master because back off is not supported on LEGACY buses like ISA and EISA. Consequently, either the LEGACY bus master does not access the locked PDRAM or the PCI/LEGACY BRIDGE must wait until all PCI memory resources are unlocked prior to obtaining ownership of the PCI bus and granting LEGACY bus ownership to a LEGACY bus resource. Another opportunity would be to lock only a small portion of the PCI resource (16 bytes is the minimum) and thus the LEGACY bus master can access other non-locked portions of the PCI resource.

> Notice that the PCI/LEGACY BRIDGE does not know what resources will be accessed when it awards LEGACY bus ownership to a LEGACY bus resource. There is no guarantee that the LEGACY bus master will access only LEGACY bus resources. The PCI/LEGACY BRIDGE does not know that an access is to a PCI bus resource until the LEGACY bus access cycle has begun, which according to ISA and EISA protocols can only be completed with successfully accessing data.

> A LEGACY bus master that does not support a "back off" cannot access a resource that is behind a PCI/PCI BRIDGE. If such a LEGACY bus was attached (via a PCI/LEGACY BRIDGE) to PCI bus 1 in Figure 2-3, it could access PCI resources on PCI bus 1 but not on PCI bus 0.

LIVELOCK ISSUES

By definition, a livelock is not a fatal platform condition.

Livelock is when PCI bus cycles can continue but with lower performance. An example is when a target executes a Disconnect termination because it was not available to complete the access in a reasonable amount of time. If the PCI bus master immediately accesses the same target, the target may still not be ready and respond with a Retry termination. Further "immediate accesses" may also result in Retry terminations which are effectively preventing other PCI bus master ownership of the bus. Another example: assume PCI resource (A) has both target and PCI bus master attributes. Assume that PCI bus master (A) does not allow access to its associated target (A) until the successful completion (no Retry, Disconnect, or Target Abort termination) of the access cycle it had tried. Assume that PCI bus master (A) begins an access cycle that results in a Retry termination. Under this protocol, if PCI bus master (B) accesses target (A), a Retry termination is also executed. At a later time, PCI bus master (A) is able to complete its access cycle successfully. Subsequently, PCI bus master (B) can then successfully complete its access to target (A). Functionally, the access cycles were completed, but the performance of PCI bus master (B) was lowered by the protocol of PCI bus master (A).

The PCI bus protocol avoids livelocks whenever possible. The two examples above would not occur in an actual PCI platform. Relative to the first example, according to the actual PCI bus protocol, the execution of a Disconnect (also Retry or Target Abort) termination requires the present PCI bus master to relinquish bus ownership. Another PCI bus master can then become bus owner and execute a bus cycle. Relative to the second example, the PCI bus protocol does not allow a PCI bus resource with PCI bus master and target attributes that are interdependent. The PCI bus master cannot prevent access to its associated target because its access cycle was not successfully completed.

Another interesting livelock example is when the post-write buffers in a HOST/PCI BRIDGE are flushed. As data is written from the write buffers to the PCI bus the HOST CPU may continue writing to the buffers. As the HOST/PCI BRIDGE is emptying the buffers, the HOST CPU is filing them. Unless the BRIDGE is specifically designed to address this situation, it will empty all the data originally in the buffers, and will continue the access cycle with the new data written by the HOST CPU. Consequently, the PCI bus is owned by the HOST/PCI BRIDGE for a longer period of time than was necessary to flush the original data in the buffers. Other PCI bus masters are delayed in obtaining bus ownership and thus bus performance among multiple PCI bus masters is decreased.

INTERRUPT SIGNAL LINES

The interrupt structure of the PCI bus must be used in conjunction with Intel 8259 interrupt controllers to be fully compatible with personal computer software. Other architectures can use other interrupt controllers. ISA bus requirements define an edge triggered interrupt line with a low to high transition to request interrupt service via the 8259. Even though the interrupt request on an ISA bus is defined as edge triggered signal line, the interrupt input must remain asserted (logical "1") until the software has begun the interrupt service routine. EISA bus requirements define both an edge triggered input (for compatibility to ISA compatible add-in cards) and a level (logical "0") sensitive input to the interrupt controller circuit to allow interrupts to be shared via open collector outputs.

The concept of level sensitive interrupts has been applied to the PCI bus interrupt structure. Four interrupt signal lines have been defined (INTA#, INTB#, INTC#, and INTD#, collectively called INTx# signal lines). The INTx# signal lines are attached to Intel 8259 compatible circuitry via platform circuitry. The exact circuitry varies depending on the architecture of the platform. Compatibility to the ISA, EISA, and Micro Channel software does place some restraints on which personal computer (PC) compatible interrupts should be attached the INTx# signal lines. The most obvious PC compatible interrupts are the four defined as bus interrupts (IRQ 9 to 11 and 15) and the one attached to the second parallel port (IRQ5). Any combination of the PCI INTx# signal lines can be combined or individually attached in any arrangement to the PC compatible interrupt lines. The exact implementation is the responsibility of the platform architect.

There are several protocol requirements for implementing the INTx# signal lines:

> The three device types defined on a PCI bus are PCI bus master, target, and BRIDGE; collectively they are called *PCI resources.*

- Several devices (each with individual configuration registers) can be attached to each INTx# signal line; this is defined as interrupt sharing.

- A device is wire-ORed to an INTx# signal line.

- Once a device has asserted an INTx# signal line, it must keep it asserted until instructed to deassert by the appropriate interrupt service routine.

- A "single-device" integrated circuit chip on the platform or add-in card (see definitions in the Glossary) that requires only one interrupt must use the INTA# signal line. Each integrated circuit chip or add-in card with at least one device that requires an interrupt service must use the INTA# signal line before any of the other interrupt signal lines can be used. The additional devices in an integrated circuit chip or an add-in card can also use INTA# or use any one of the other INTx# signal lines (INTB#, INTC#, and INTD#).

- Each individual device can only request service (assert) on one of the INTx# single lines. It can never request service on two or more INTx# signal lines.

> The interrupt acknowledge cycle protocol on the PCI bus is only one cycle that returns the interrupt vector. It is the responsibility of the HOST/PCI BRIDGE or similar circuitry to convert the dual cycle 8259 compatible interrupt acknowledge cycle on the HOST bus to a SINGLE cycle PCI interrupt acknowledge cycle. It also is the responsibility of the PCI resource that contains the 8259 to convert the SINGLE cycle PCI interrupt acknowledge cycle into the dual cycle required by the 8259.

SIDEBAND SIGNAL LINES

The PCI bus specification allows signal lines to be defined between two or more PCI resources that are proprietary to these resources. These are defined as "sideband". Sideband signal lines are not part of the PCI bus specification; consequently the sideband signal lines can only be defined for PCI resources on the same physical bus plane. That is, sideband signal lines cannot traverse a PCI connector. Similarly, sideband signal lines cannot be attached between two PCI buses (cannot traverse a PCI/PCI BRIDGE).

2.3 PCI SOFTWARE AND THE PLUG AND PLAY ARCHITECTURE

INTRODUCTION

The PCI Local Bus hardware and software is the first architecture that technologically incorporates true Plug and Play into ISA compatible computers. All compliant PCI devices can easily be identified, along with the functions they provide. Also, PCI compliant devices identify their individual system resource requirements. These system resources can be dynamically assigned with no user intervention.

In addition to the hardware capabilities of PCI devices, a new software methodology that coordinates the hardware configuration process at the System BIOS, device driver, and operating system levels is also required. This methodology exploits the hardware and software power of the PCI device class to bring Plug and Play capability to ISA compatible computers.

Figure 2-4 contains a view of a software architecture that encompasses software at all levels from the System BIOS to the operating system and device drivers. This architecture is capable of configuring PCI and other device classes in true Plug and Play fashion. While other solutions may exist, System BIOS vendors in particular that choose to implement the architecture presented are provided a great deal of flexibility for implementing a Plug and Play System BIOS. Refer to this figure as each component of the architecture is discussed below. Note that to be less confusing, non-PCI Plug and Play device classes are not specified by name. They are referred to as *other*.

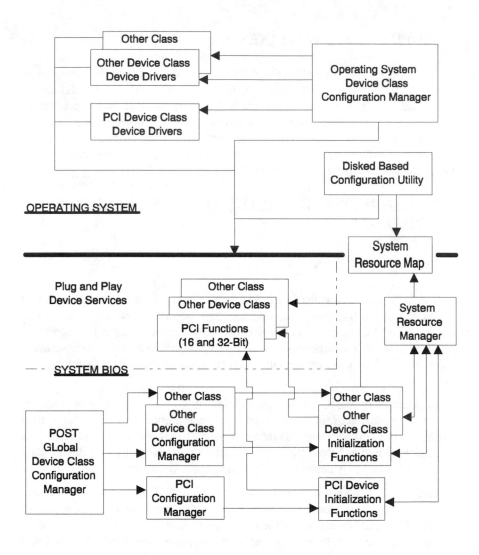

Figure 2-4: Plug and Play System

DEVICE CLASS MANAGEMENT

The System BIOS software is the first code executed when the computer system is powered on. One of its major functions is to test and configure devices. This function is accomplished during the execution of the System BIOS Power-

On Self Test (POST). It is at this time that PCI devices are detected and configured along with the non-PCI components of the system.

A major goal of the design of the Plug and Play System BIOS code is to be as unobtrusive as possible with the industry standard System BIOSs such as those developed by IBM, AMI, Phoenix Technologies and Award Software. These BIOSs already perform device initialization and testing. Consequently, the most reasonable approach for initializing and testing PCI devices is to align these functions with those of the existing BIOSs. At this point, the problem becomes two-fold: first, while all System BIOS vendors perform basically the same tasks during the POST, the sequence in which the tasks are performed may vary significantly. For example, some vendors shadow and cache the System BIOS very early in the POST while other vendors may delay this function until just prior to bootstrapping an operating system. The second problem is that the functions provided by PCI devices may overlap with those supplied by non-PCI devices in the system. A VGA compatible video card installed on the ISA bus and a VGA compatible PCI video card may be installed in the same system at the same time. Both of these cards utilize identical industry compatible I/O ports. Which device has precedence during the boot sequence as well as when the device gets tested and initialized is of critical importance to maintaining a system that is resource conflict-free and guaranteed to boot. To solve these problems, a function known as the POST Global Device Class Configuration Manager is implemented.

POST GLOBAL DEVICE CLASS CONFIGURATION MANAGER

The POST Global Device Class Configuration Manager is responsible for the overall testing and initializing of all Plug and Play device classes. The POST Global Device Class Configuration Manager can be viewed as a global dispatcher for initializing and testing Plug and Play devices. As Figure 2-1 shows, the System BIOS invokes the POST Global Device Class Configuration Manager. The POST Global Device Class Configuration Manager in turn invokes each individual Plug and Play device class configuration manager. Exactly when the POST Global Device Class Configuration Manager is invoked is System BIOS dependent. Also, the order in which each Plug and Play device class configuration manager is invoked is System BIOS dependent. The POST Global Device Class Configuration Manager is platform independent. It can work in any modified System BIOS.

PCI CONFIGURATION MANAGER

The PCI Configuration Manager is responsible solely for the initialization of PCI devices in the system. This includes identifying each PCI device in the system as well as identifying the individual functions provided by each device. In addition, the PCI Configuration Manager is responsible for determining the system resources each PCI device requests, obtaining the required resources from the System Resource Manager, and then assigning those resources to each PCI device. The PCI Configuration Manager is also platform independent. However, to accomplish its tasks, the PCI Configuration Manager requires access to platform dependent hardware. For example, the way in which PCI devices are programmed is platform specific. Device initialization functions are provided for each Plug and Play device class to permit access to the platform dependent hardware.

PCI DEVICE INITIALIZATION FUNCTIONS

PCI Device Initialization Functions allow the PCI device class platform independent software to access the platform dependent hardware. This minimizes the amount of Plug and Play software that has to be created for each new platform to those components that are unique to the platform. The PCI Device Initialization Functions access each PCI device to first determine the system resources required by each device, assign system resources to each PCI device and, depending on the function provided, initialize and test each PCI device.

SYSTEM RESOURCE MAP

The System Resource Map contains an encoded description of which system resources are currently consumed by devices in the system. Both the System BIOS System Resource Manager and certain run-time utilities can use the System Resource Map to monitor exactly which system resources have been allocated. Knowing which system resources have been allocated permits the easy identification of free system resources when an allocation request is serviced.

The medium that stores the System Resource Map depends on the implementation of the Plug and Play architecture. In addition, the specific information stored in the System Resource Map is platform specific.

NON-VOLATILE MEMORY STORAGE

In some systems, the System Resource Map is stored in non-volatile memory such as Flash memory or battery backed-up CMOS RAM. The information in the non-volatile memory is accessible by the System BIOS during system initialization and by Plug and Play configuration utilities during run-time operation. Having the System Resource Map contents accessible to the System BIOS prior to booting greatly increases the opportunity to configure the system so that no system resource conflicts occur.

DISK-BASED STORAGE

In some systems, the System Resource Map is stored in a special file on a floppy or hard disk. The file is created and maintained by a Plug and Play configuration utility. The disadvantage of this method is that the information is not available during the system initialization that occurs prior to bootstrapping the operating system.

When this method is used, the System BIOS must build a dynamic system resource map each time the system is RESET. At the end of the system automatic configuration process the map is discarded. This implementation forces the system initialization software to make assumptions as to the what resources are consumed by certain LEGACY devices that may be installed in the system. Incorrect assumptions may lead to system resource conflicts that can result in improper system operation.

SYSTEM RESOURCE MAP CONTENTS

The minimum implementation of a System Resource Map can be as basic as storing a bit-map of what hardware interrupts (IRQs) have been consumed by devices. On the other hand, the System Resource Map can be very exhaustive. Enhanced System Resource Maps may contain information such as the location and type of device that consumes a specific resource.

This information is especially important for Plug and Play disked based configuration utilities that have the ability to configure system resources for both LEGACY and Plug and Play devices at run-time. With this information, the software can make recommendations as to how to reconfigure the system to accommodate devices that may only be configured with a restricted set of system resources. For instance, the two standard ISA LEGACY serial port devices can only be assigned one of two different hardware interrupt lines. In contrast, a compliant PCI device can be assigned any hardware interrupt line and still function. Software can detect that a PCI device has been assigned the hardware interrupt line required by the ISA LEGACY device. It can deallocate the interrupt line from the PCI device, allocate the interrupt line to the ISA LEGACY device, and then allocate a different hardware interrupt line to the PCI device. This process is known as system resource balancing.

SUMMARY

To increase the possibility of a system free of resource conflicts, locate the System Resource Map in non-volatile memory on the platform. This permits access to its contents during all phases of system operation. The amount and type of information stored has a direct impact on dynamically configuring the system as well as successfully achieving system resource balancing.

> With 8-slot ISA systems, 4K of non-volatile RAM is recommended; 8K of non-volatile RAM is recommended for 8 slot EISA systems.

BIOS SYSTEM RESOURCE MANAGER

The BIOS System Resource Manager is available only to pre-boot software. The System Resource Manager relieves each device class initialization function of having to maintain a list of free and consumed system resources. The System Resource Manager centralizes the task of allocating (assigning) and deallocating (freeing) system resources. This function is crucial for achieving a resource conflict-free system.

Device class initialization functions can request that system resources be allocated or deallocated for their devices. In the case of allocating a system resource, the System Resource Manager will attempt to allocate resources that are free and not currently allocated to another device. One exception for PCI is hardware interrupts. PCI hardware interrupts are a shareable system resource.

> Non-shareable system resources should only be assigned to one device. It is up to the discretion of the System Resource Manager how to assign shareable system resources.

Once the System Resource Manager either allocates or deallocates the system resource, the device class initialization function making the request is responsible for configuring the Plug and Play device according to the type of request. As an example, when a PCI device requests that a hardware interrupt be allocated to it, the hardware specific code is responsible for physically connecting the hardware interrupt line allocated by the System Resource Manager to the requesting device.

As stated in the previous section, the location of the System Resource Map has a direct impact on device configuration. If the System Resource Map is stored in non-volatile memory in the system, the System Resource Manager can use the information to configure the system with a high confidence level. When the System Resource Map is not available to the System Resource Manager, a dynamic map that contains the system resource consumption must be built during system initialization. This information is limited because many of the resources consumed by LEGACY devices cannot be detected.

Note that it is possible to dynamically configure Plug and Play devices such as PCI without requiring the user to execute the system Setup Utility. This is accomplished by doing the following:

1. During system initialization, the System Resource Manager is informed by the System BIOS what specific resources it can reliably detect that the platform consumes.

2. All dynamically-configurable devices that are configured prior to POST must obtain their system resource assignments from the System Resource manager.

Note that functions such as setting the system time and date do require the user to execute a program such as the system Setup Utility in order to accomplish the task.

PCI PLUG AND PLAY DEVICE SERVICES

As Figure 2-4 shows, the PCI Device Initialization Functions that are available only during POST utilize PCI Plug and Play device services. These services are available for use during the POST and at run-time to software components such as an operating system. See *Chapter 19: PCI System BIOS Software Interface*, for a list of the defined PCI Plug and Play device services and how they are accessed. The PCI functions are typically used to read and write PCI device registers.

OPERATING SYSTEM DEVICE CLASS CONFIGURATION MANAGER

The operating system is responsible for the run-time portion of the Plug and Play architecture. Like the System BIOS, it relies on special interfaces to accomplish the task of dynamically configuring the system such that there are no system resource conflicts.

A Plug and Play enabled operating system has the ability to dynamically configure the system in much the same way as the System BIOS. To do so, it must also have access to the platform hardware. To generically run on different types of hardware, the operating system also relies on the Plug and Play Device Services provided by the PCI and other device classes.

The Operating System Device Class Configuration Manager is decidedly more complex than its System BIOS counterpart. This is because of the nature of managing the run-time operation of the system in conjunction with the dynamics of Plug and Play. For example, in the case of hot-insertion, a device may be added to the system at any time. The Plug and Play operating system must detect the change in the system configuration, dynamically allocate system resources to the device if required, and load any device drivers associated with the device—all without user intervention.

PCI DEVICE DRIVERS

Operating system level device drivers provide application software with a common interface to the machine-dependent features of a system. Device drivers such as those that support PCI devices are written specifically for the hardware that they control. For instance, there are many PCI VGA compatible video devices. The VGA compatible functions that these devices provide are common to all VGA devices. However, there is no common method for accessing and configuring these devices at the hardware level. Without device drivers, applications programmers would be required to embed device-specific code to support each device in their software program. Code size and the constant introduction of new devices makes this process unfeasible.

The operating system is required to load device drivers. When a device driver is loaded it usually determines the hardware configuration for its device and configures its environment accordingly. In the case of a PCI VGA device that supports a linear frame buffer, the associated device driver must interrogate the PCI component to determine the base address and length of the frame buffer that was allocated to the device. It does this by utilizing the appropriate Plug and Play Device Services. Once the device driver has determined the assigned resources of its device, it can configure the device and its own software for optimum performance.

DISK BASED CONFIGURATION UTILITY

Disk-based configuration utilities allow users to easily configure a system that is system resource conflict free. This is a valuable tool when attempting to configure one or more ISA LEGACY devices in a system. These utilities allow the user to describe LEGACY devices to be used in the system prior to installation. In turn, these utilities make recommendations as to how the LEGACY devices should be configured to ensure that the system is resource conflict free. The utilities take into account those resources consumed by the platform as well as those that may be consumed by Plug and Play devices. They also take into account the valid subset of system resources that a LEGACY device may utilize. The disk-based configuration utilities may store the configuration of a system in a disk based file and/or a block of non-volatile memory on the platform. This aspect is machine and software dependent.

2.4 CHAPTER SUMMARY

In an ideal computer system, the System BIOS and operating system level software automatically configure all devices so that no system resource conflicts exist. This includes devices located on the platform as well as those devices added via add-in cards. The successful operation of an add-in card in the ideal system requires no user intervention other than the physical installation of the card itself. In addition, the automatic configuration of the system also accounts for the removal of an add-in card; this insures that no system resource conflicts exist after the add-in card is extracted as well as optimizing the system for performance.

However, the possibility of system resource conflicts is greatly increased when a PCI based system is integrated with a LEGACY based system such as ISA. Because LEGACY devices are not dynamically configurable, the configuration software must obtain the LEGACY configuration information. In almost all cases this is accomplished with the aid of the user. Utilities are available to help in this task and make it easier for the user to configure a system.

The PCI Local Bus standard permits the design of a computer system that is fully capable of being automatically configured. For this to be achieved an architecture that encompasses all aspects of the hardware and software of a system must be implemented. Interfaces must be crisply defined and strictly adhered to. This architecture is referred known as Plug and Play. While only a high level overview of the architecture is presented in this chapter, it can readily be seen that the task of providing users with a Plug and Play system is extremely complex and requires the participation of both hardware and software vendors to ensure success.

The remainder of this book addresses the fundamental hardware and software concepts of a PCI based computer system. The power of the PCI Local Bus hardware and software is explored in great detail. This will give the reader a thorough working knowledge of the PCI Local Bus standard.

> Note that the discussion is limited to the Intel x86 architecture and the Intel 82430 PCI chip set. However, the guidelines and concepts presented are readily adaptable to other system types.

CHAPTER 3

GENERIC PCI HARDWARE OPERATION

This chapter consists of the following subchapters:

3.0   Generic PCI Bus Cycles
3.1   Bridges and Interbus Operations

3.0   GENERIC PCI BUS CYCLES

INTRODUCTION

The PCI bus specification defines the interaction between two PCI resources: the PCI bus master and target. The PCI bus master may be a processor or a BRIDGE that represents a processor on another bus. The target may be a memory or I/O resource in addition to a BRIDGE that ports the interaction to resources on other buses. As with other bus specifications, the PCI specification defines a protocol for the PCI bus master to read and write (access) data from and to a target, respectively. Also, similar to other bus specifications, a memory and an I/O address space is defined.

The PCI bus specification defines other bus cycles that are more sophisticated than the simple access of memory or I/O resources. It also defines access cycles to a configuration address space to identify and establish hardware requirements of PCI resources. In addition, it defines a special cycle to broadcast a message to all PCI resources and an interrupt acknowledge cycle to return the interrupt vector to the platform CPU.

All bus protocols support "SINGLE" read and write memory access cycles. SINGLE is defined as one access of a memory resource. Some bus protocols support "BURST" read and write memory access cycles. BURST is defined as multiple read and writes during one access cycle. These bus protocols do not provide "insight" on how the memory resource affects the aforementioned BURST access cycles, except that the addressing is incremental relative to a base address. The PCI bus protocol provides the memory resource with additional "insight" on how the bus cycles could be executed. The PCI bus specification defines BURST memory read access cycles with multiple cache lines and byte attributes. The execution of the appropriate BURST access cycle indicates to the memory resource that perhaps multiple cache lines or multiple bytes may be accessed in order to allow the memory resource to prepare. It also defines a BURST memory write access cycle cache protocol to indicate to the memory resource that an entire cache line will be overwritten to eliminate copy-back protocols for write-back caches.

Other important attributes of the PCI bus specification are *caching of the PCI memory* targets, memory target *locking,* and *bus cycle termination and retry.* The PCI protocol also supports SINGLE and BURST cycles for executing I/O access cycles, and special and interrupt acknowledge cycles. It also supports parity protection over the address, data, and control signal lines. The PCI bus specification supports 32 data and 32 address bits for memory, I/O, and configuration access cycles, and special and interrupt acknowledge cycles. It also supports 64 address bits for memory and I/O cycles. Finally, it supports 64 data bit memory access cycles and also theoretically for the I/O access cycles. This book assumes the use of only 32 address bits.

The PCI bus protocol is defined as synchronous. All of the signal line and bus activity is referenced to the rising edge of a bus clock (CLK signal line) except for the SERR# (system error), RST# (RESET), and INT# (interrupt) signal lines.

DRAWING PROTOCOL

A more detailed protocol is outlined in Chapter 6. For the purposes of discussing the generic bus cycles, the following protocol is adopted:

- The protocol for individual signal lines driven by a single PCI resource during the bus cycle and driven to a logical "1" by pull-up resistors some of the time is exemplified by the FRAME#, IRDY#, and TRDY# signal lines in Figure 3-0. The FRAME# (also STOP# and DEVSEL# [not shown]) signal line changes from logical "1" (deasserted) to a logical "0" (asserted) at only one transition point during the bus cycle, and remains asserted for the remainder of the cycle. The IRDY# and TRDY# signal lines may toggle between logical "1" (deasserted) to logical "0" (asserted) at one or several points during the bus cycle. The FRAME# and IRDY# signal lines are driven by the PCI bus master during the bus cycle. The TRDY#, DEVSEL#, and STOP# signal lines are driven by the target during the bus cycle.

- The AD signal lines typify the protocol for signal lines not driven by pull-up resistors. The "A" and "D" between the parallel lines indicate that address and data are driven onto the signal lines, respectively. Non-labeled areas with parallel lines represent signal lines driven to a stable level—but do not always contain valid information. The non-labeled areas with the single horizontal line represent a tri-stated level; consequently, the signal lines are floating. Although not shown in Figure 3.0, C/BE# and PAR signal lines also adhere to this protocol.

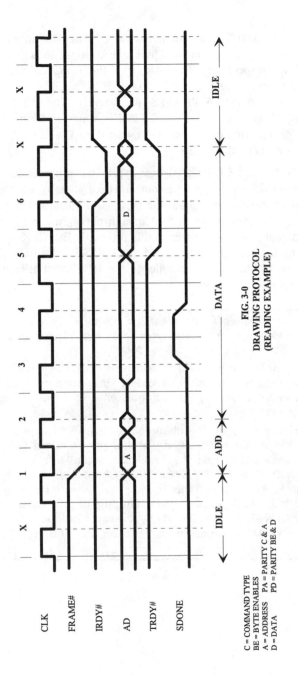

CLK
FRAME#
IRDY#
AD
TRDY#
SDONE

C = COMMAND TYPE
BE = BYTE ENABLES   PA = PARITY C & A
A = ADDRESS   PD = PARITY BE & D
D = DATA

FIG. 3-0
DRAWING PROTOCOL
(READING EXAMPLE)

Figure 3–0: Drawing Protocol (Reading Example)

The C/BE# signal lines are marked with "C" and "BE" to indicate when COMMAND type and that valid byte lane information is driven onto the signal lines, respectively. The PAR signal line is marked with "PA" and "PD" for parity over the AD and C/BE# signal lines during the ADDRESS and DATA PHASES, respectively. The C/BE#, AD, and PAR signal lines are driven by the PCI bus master during a write bus cycle. For a portion of the read bus cycle, the AD and PAR signal lines are also driven by the target.

■ The SDONE and CLK signal lines typify the protocol for individual signal lines driven by a single source. These signal lines change from asserted to deasserted without the periods of float or being driven to logical "1" by pull-up resistors. Although not shown in Figure 3.0, the SBO# signal line also adheres to this protocol. The CLK signal line is driven by the central resource, and the SDONE and SBO# signal lines are driven by the cache controller in the HOST/PCI BRIDGE, or the central resource.

In the figures in Chapter 3 not all of the signal lines of the PCI bus protocol are used. These figures only provide a general idea of the bus cycle protocol. See Chapters 5 and 6 for details.

The LOCK# signal line in Figure 3-15 is driven by the LOCK master (one of the PCI bus masters) and changes logical state once or twice during a bus cycle. When not driven by the lock master, it is driven to logical "1" by a pull-up resistor.

For the rest of this chapter, the changing states of the signal lines are referenced to the numbered CLK signal line period when the FRAME# signal line is asserted during the first CLK signal line period. Under conditions of ADDRESS/DATA STEPPING (Chapter 4) and PRE-DRIVE (Chapter 6) the FRAME# signal line may not be asserted during the first signal line period; consequently, the changing of the signal lines are shifted to later CLK signal line periods by the same number of CLK signal line periods the FRAME# signal line is asserted after the first CLK signal line period.

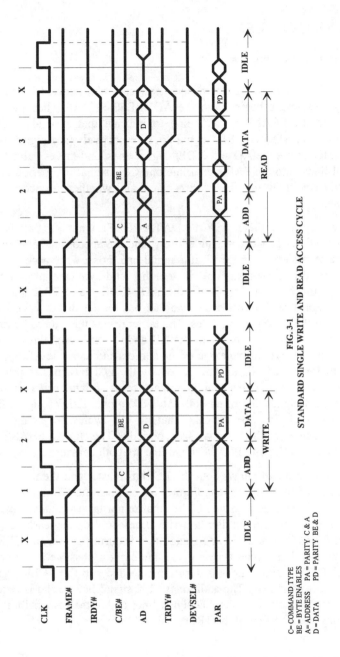

C= COMMAND TYPE
BE = BYTE ENABLES   PA = PARITY C & A
A= ADDRESS   PD = PARITY BE & D
D = DATA

FIG. 3-1
STANDARD SINGLE WRITE AND READ ACCESS CYCLE

Figure 3-1: Standard Single Write and Read Access Cycle

ACCESS CYCLES

SINGLE ACCESS CYCLE

Memory, I/O, and configuration address spaces are selected by the access cycle. An access cycle begins with the ADDRESS PHASE when the PCI bus master asserts the FRAME# signal line to indicate that a valid address and command exist on AD and C/BE# signal lines, respectively (see Figure 3-1). The PCI bus master drives the AD and C/BE# signal lines, and drives valid parity for these signal lines onto the PAR signal line one CLK signal line period later. The COMMAND type indicates the address space and whether the access cycle is read or write.

The access cycle continues with the DATA PHASE when the data is actually accessed. All PCI targets decode the address, and the appropriate one claims the access cycle by asserting the DEVSEL# signal line. For a write access cycle, the PCI bus master drives the data to be written, the valid byte lane information, and the parity of these signal lines onto the AD, C/BE#, and PAR signal lines, respectively. For a read access cycle, the PCI bus master drives valid byte lane information on the C/BE# signal lines. The target drives the data to be read onto the AD signal lines, and the parity of the AD and C/BE# signal lines onto to the PAR signal line. Due to multiplexing of the address and data, the AD signal lines are tri-stated for a CLK signal line period by the PCI bus master prior to the target driving data onto these signal lines. The access of data occurs on the rising edge of the CLK signal line when both the IRDY# and TRDY# signal lines are asserted. The IDLE PHASE indicates that no bus cycles are being executed during the respective CLK signal line periods. The IDLE PHASE occurs whenever the FRAME# and IRDY# signal line are both deasserted.

The PCI bus protocol allows both the PCI bus master and the target to delay the completion of the access cycle. Figure 3-1 outlines the STANDARD access cycle that occurs when neither the PCI bus master nor target request any delay in the completion of the cycle. For a write access cycle, the earliest possible assertion of the IRDY# and TRDY# signal lines is during the second CLK signal line clock period. For a read access cycle, the earliest possible assertion of the IRDY# and TRDY# signal lines is during the second and third CLK signal line clock periods, respectively. The additional CLK signal line period is required to change the driving source of the AD signal lines and is the responsibility of the target to delay the assertion of the TRDY# signal line.

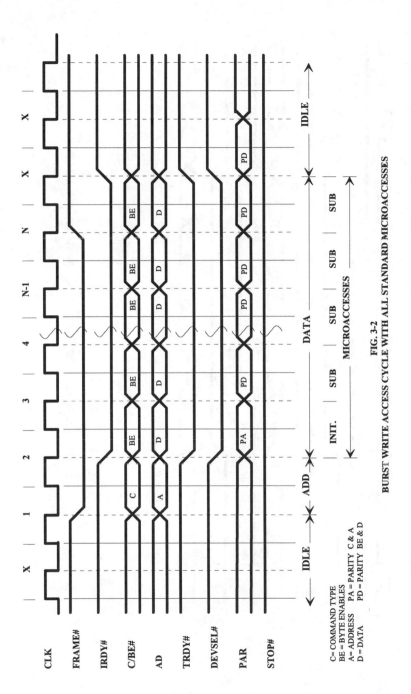

FIG. 3-2
BURST WRITE ACCESS CYCLE WITH ALL STANDARD MICROACCESSES

C= COMMAND TYPE
BE = BYTE ENABLES   PA = PARITY C & A
A= ADDRESS   PD = PARITY BE & D
D = DATA

Figure 3-2: Burst Write Access Cycle with all Standard Microaccesses

41

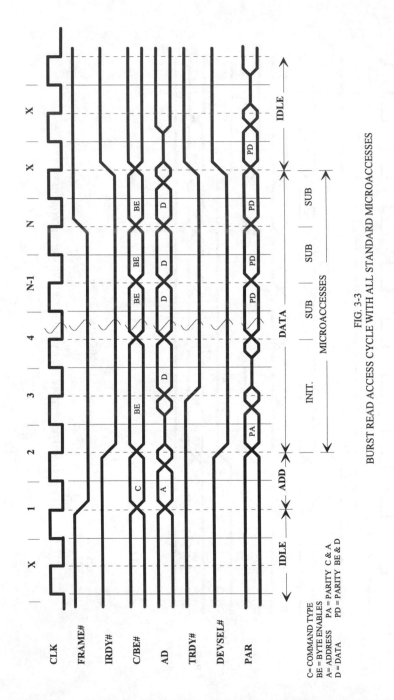

FIG. 3-3
BURST READ ACCESS CYCLE WITH ALL STANDARD MICROACCESSES

C = COMMAND TYPE
BE = BYTE ENABLES   PA = PARITY C & A
A = ADDRESS   PD = PARITY BE & D
D = DATA

Figure 3-3: Burst Read Access Cycle with all Standard Microaccesses

The AD signal lines are translated into the IDSEL signal lines for configuration access cycles. See *Chapter 6: Detailed Bus Cycle Operation*, for details.

BURST ACCESS CYCLES

Figure 3-1 outlines STANDARD SINGLE access cycles, which access data only once during the cycle. The PCI bus protocol also supports BURST access cycles as outlined in Figures 3-2 and 3-3. Unlike other bus protocols, the PCI bus does not use unique commands or signal lines to execute a BURST access cycle. The assertion and deassertion of the FRAME# and IRDY# signal lines transforms a SINGLE access cycle into a BURST access cycle. During the ADDRESS PHASE, the protocol of the signal lines are the same for both the SINGLE and BURST access cycles. During the DATA PHASE, the IRDY# signal line is asserted when the PCI bus master is ready to access the data.

If the FRAME# signal line is deasserted simultaneously with the assertion of the IRDY# signal lines for the first access, access is completed as a SINGLE access cycle. If the FRAME# signal line remains asserted after the assertion of the IRDY# signal line for the first access, the cycle continues as a BURST access cycle. The BURST access cycle continues until the FRAME# signal line is deasserted when IRDY# signal line is asserted. The DATA PHASE of a BURST access cycle consists of a series of microaccesses. Each microaccess consists of data access when the IRDY# and TRDY# signal lines are both asserted. The first microaccess is defined as the "initial microaccess" (INITI) and remaining microaccesses are defined as "subsequent microaccesses" (SUB). The base address of the initial microaccess is established during the ADDRESS PHASE. The addresses for the subsequent microaccesses are incremental relative to the base address.

The entire BURST access cycle is either all reads or all writes. The COMMAND type driven onto the C/BE# signal lines during the ADDRESS PHASE establishes the direction of data flow for all microaccesses.

STANDARD VERSUS READY ACCESS CYCLES

Most bus protocols support extensions to the cycle length of the minimum access cycle by the resource being accessed. The minimum access cycle is called STANDARD and the extended access cycle is called READY. The accessed resource on the typical bus extends the STANDARD access cycle by deasserting a signal line defined as "ready". The assertion of the ready signal line allows the access cycle to be completed.

The PCI bus has adapted a similar protocol and has expanded it; both the resource executing the bus cycle (PCI bus master) and the resource being accessed (target) can extend the bus cycle. The STANDARD SINGLE access cycle outlined in Figure 3-1 is executed when the IRDY# and TRDY# signal lines are both asserted at the beginning of the DATA PHASE. For a write access cycle, the earliest possible assertion of the IRDY# and TRDY# signal lines is during the second CLK signal line clock period. For a read access cycle, the earliest possible assertion of the IRDY# and TRDY# signal lines is during the second and third CLK signal line clock periods, respectively. Figures 3-4 and 3-5 outline the write and read READY SINGLE access cycles, respectively. Either the PCI bus master (via the IRDY# signal line) or the target (via the TRDY# signal line) or both can extend the cycle length. The data access occurs on the rising edge of the CLK signal line when the IRDY# and TRDY# signal lines are both asserted.

> During the DATA PHASE, the C/BE# signal lines are always driven with valid byte lane information while the AD and PAR signal lines may be driven to invalid values until the PCI bus master and target are ready to complete the access.

Each microaccess of a BURST access cycle can be individually executed as STANDARD or READY using the same protocol as the STANDARD or READY SINGLE access cycles, respectively. Figures 3-2 and 3-3 execute all of the microaccesses with the STANDARD protocol. The protocol of the initial microaccess is the same as the STANDARD SINGLE access cycle. The subsequent microaccesses follow the STANDARD protocol because both IRDY# and TRDY# signal lines are asserted to allow a data access on each rising edge of the CLK signal line.

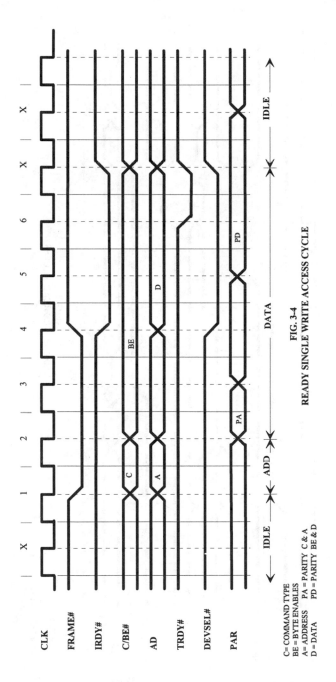

C = COMMAND TYPE
BE = BYTE ENABLES   PA = PARITY C & A
A = ADDRESS   PD = PARITY BE & D
D = DATA

FIG. 3-4
READY SINGLE WRITE ACCESS CYCLE

Figure 3-4: Ready Single Write Access Cycle

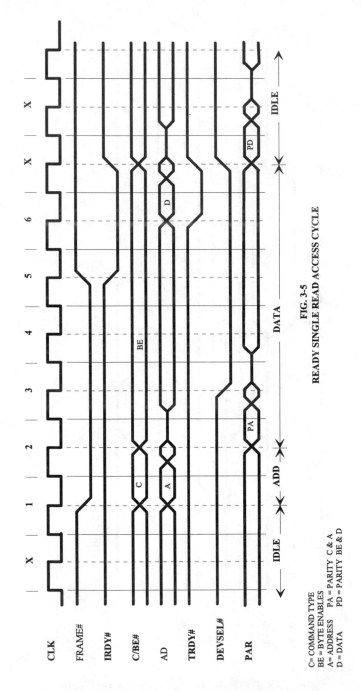

FIG. 3-5
READY SINGLE READ ACCESS CYCLE

C = COMMAND TYPE
BE = BYTE ENABLES   PA = PARITY C & A
A = ADDRESS   PD = PARITY BE & D
D = DATA

Figure 3-5: Ready Single Read Access Cycle

Figures 3-6 and 3-7 outline BURST access cycles with a mixture of READY and STANDARD microaccesses. The mixture of READY and STANDARD microaccesses in these figures are examples; any microaccess can use either the READY or STANDARD protocol. In Figure 3-6, the initial microaccess and first subsequent microaccess is extended by the PCI bus master and target, respectively. The initial microaccess would have been STANDARD if the PCI bus master asserted the IRDY# signal line during the second CLK signal line period. The first subsequent microaccess would have been STANDARD if the target did not deassert the TRDY# signal line during the fourth CLK signal line period. The second subsequent microaccess is STANDARD due to the continued assertion of the IRDY# and TRDY# signal lines during the sixth CLK signal line period.

In Figure 3-7 the initial microaccess and first subsequent microaccess is extended by the target and PCI bus master, respectively. The initial microaccess would have been STANDARD if the target asserted the TRDY# signal line during the third CLK signal line period. The first subsequent microaccess would have been STANDARD if the PCI bus master did not deassert the IRDY# signal line during the fifth CLK signal line period. The second subsequent microaccess is STANDARD due the continued assertion of the IRDY# and TRDY# signal lines during the seventh CLK signal line period.

> For all access cycles, the byte lane information on the C/BE# signal lines during the DATA PHASE indicates which AD signal lines contain valid data information. It is not required that any of the byte lanes contain any valid data.

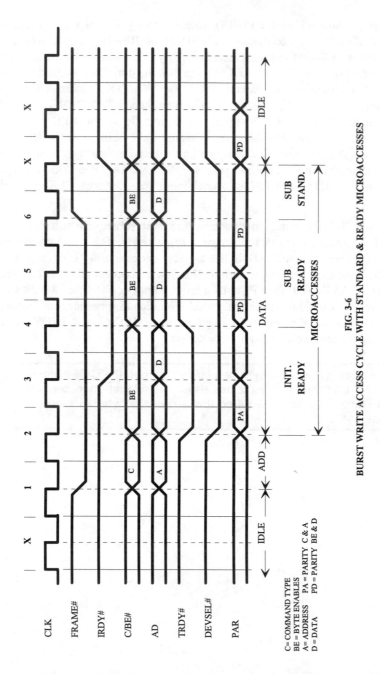

FIG. 3-6
BURST WRITE ACCESS CYCLE WITH STANDARD & READY MICROACCESSES

C = COMMAND TYPE
BE = BYTE ENABLES
A = ADDRESS   PA = PARITY C & A
D = DATA   PD = PARITY BE & D

Figure 3-6: Burst Write Access Cycle with Standard and Ready Microaccesses

48

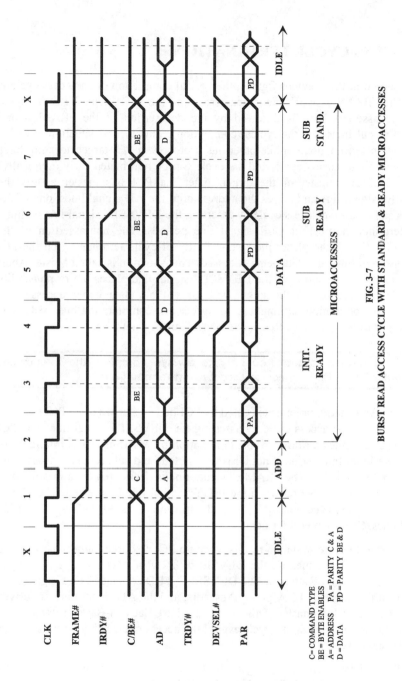

C = COMMAND TYPE   PA = PARITY C & A
BE = BYTE ENABLES   PD = PARITY BE & D
A = ADDRESS
D = DATA

FIG. 3-7
BURST READ ACCESS CYCLE WITH STANDARD & READY MICROACCESSES

Figure 3-7: Burst Read Access Cycle with Standard and Ready Microaccesses

ACCESS CYCLE TERMINATION

As shown in the previous figures, the typical completion of an access cycle is when the FRAME# signal line is deasserted and the IRDY# and TRDY# signal lines are asserted. This is followed by the deassertion of the FRAME# and IRDY# signal lines (for the typical completion). This typical situation is called Completion termination. Unlike other bus protocols, a PCI target does not have to respond to an access cycle, and the cycle can be terminated early (atypically) by the PCI bus master or the target. After the PCI bus master asserts the FRAME# signal line and drives the address onto the AD signal lines, one of the targets can claim the access cycle by asserting the DEVSEL# signal line within a predetermined number of CLK signal line periods. The non-assertion of the DEVSEL# signal line places the responsibility of cycle termination on the PCI bus master without any data being accessed. This situation is called Master Abort termination. The assertion of the DEVSEL# signal line places the responsibility of cycle termination on the target with or without data being accessed. In addition to Completion termination, the target can complete the bus cycle with three types of terminations: Retry, Disconnect, and Target Abort.

> A well designed target should try to always complete the bus cycle without a Retry, Disconnect, or Target Abort termination.

A Master Abort termination is executed by PCI bus master when no PCI resource (target) claims the access cycle by asserting the DEVSEL# signal line. The PCI bus master executes a Master Abort termination by asserting (for a minimum of one CLK signal line period if not already asserted) and subsequently deasserting the IRDY# signal line. The FRAME# signal line is deasserted for a minimum of one CLK signal line period when the IRDY# signal line is asserted. The Master Abort termination is completed with the deassertion of the FRAME# and IRDY# signal lines. See Chapter 8 for details.

A Master Abort termination results when no PCI resource (target) has claimed the bus cycle. Consequently, the DEVSEL#, TRDY#, STOP#, and AD signal lines are not driven by a target. The DEVSEL#, TRDY#, and STOP# signal lines are driven to a logical "1" by pull-up resistors, and the AD signal lines are driven only by the PCI bus master. This allows the Fast Back-to-Back protocol to be applied to the subsequent bus cycle even if the access cycle being terminated was a read access cycle.

A Retry, Disconnect, and Target Abort termination is executed by the target by asserting the STOP# signal line after it has claimed the access cycle by asserting the DEVSEL# signal line. The Retry termination occurs when no data has been accessed during the cycle but the target can be accessed at a later time. The Disconnect termination occurs when data has been accessed during the cycle but further accesses during the cycle are not possible. The target can be accessed at a later time. The Target Abort occurs regardless of whether data has been accessed, the target cannot be accessed at a later time, and if data had been accessed it may not be valid. Once the target has requested one of these terminations, the PCI bus master must still complete the access cycle as outlined above. The IRDY# signal line must be asserted for a minimum of one CLK signal line period when the FRAME# signal line is deasserted. Subsequently, the FRAME# and IRDY# signal lines are both deasserted. See *Chapter 8: Master and Target Termination*, for details.

A Retry, Disconnect, and Target Abort termination requires the central arbiter to deassert the REQ# signal line. The protocol requires the REQ# signal line to be deasserted a minimum of two CLK signal line periods relative to the end of the bus cycle that was completed by the termination. As a result of this protocol, an IDLE PHASE occurs between sequential bus cycles; consequently, the Fast Back-to-Back protocol cannot be applied to the subsequent bus cycle, even if the access cycle being terminated was a *write* access cycle.

CACHE SUPPORT ON THE PCI BUS PROTOCOL

As outlined in Chapter 2, the example platform in Figure 2-3 assumes that a single cache resource resides on the HOST bus behind the HOST/PCI BRIDGE. The cache controller is located in the HOST/PCI BRIDGE, and in this discussion it is assumed that both the HOST and PCI memory resources are cached. The cache resource can be either a write-through or write-back cache. Each memory access cycle requires that the address on the AD signal lines is compared (snooped) to the addresses of the entries in the cache to determine a match (cache hit). The cache controller in the HOST/PCI BRIDGE drives the SDONE and SBO# signal lines to indicate the completion of the snoop and whether a cache hit has occurred. The asserted SDONE signal line indicates that the snoop has completed. If the cache resource is a write-through cache, the deasserted SBO# signal line always remains deasserted. If the cache resource is a write-back cache, a deasserted SBO# signal line indicates that the cache hit is to an unmodified/valid or invalid cache line. Consequently, the target will assert the TRDY# signal line when it samples the SDONE and SBO# signal lines asserted and deasserted, respectively (see Figures 3-8, 3-9, 3-10, and 3-11).

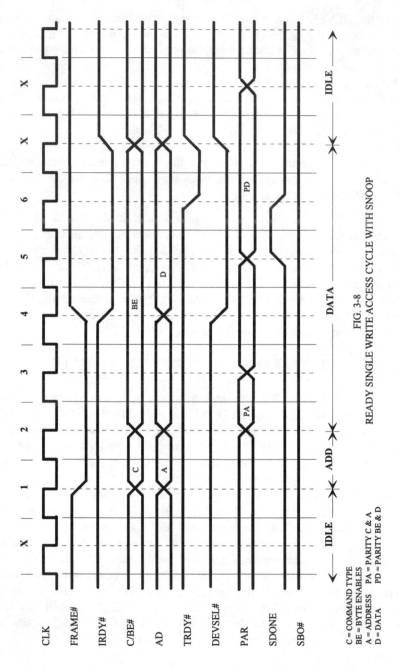

Figure 3-8: Ready Single Write Access Cycle with Snoop

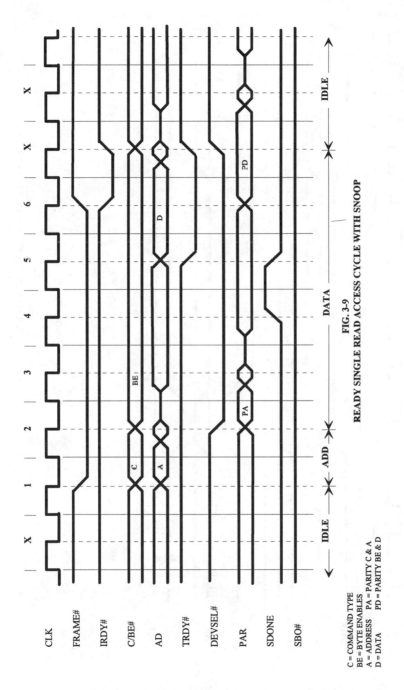

FIG. 3-9
READY SINGLE READ ACCESS CYCLE WITH SNOOP

C = COMMAND TYPE
BE = BYTE ENABLES
A = ADDRESS   PA = PARITY C & A
D = DATA   PD = PARITY BE & D

Figure 3-9: Ready Single Read Access Cycle with Snoop

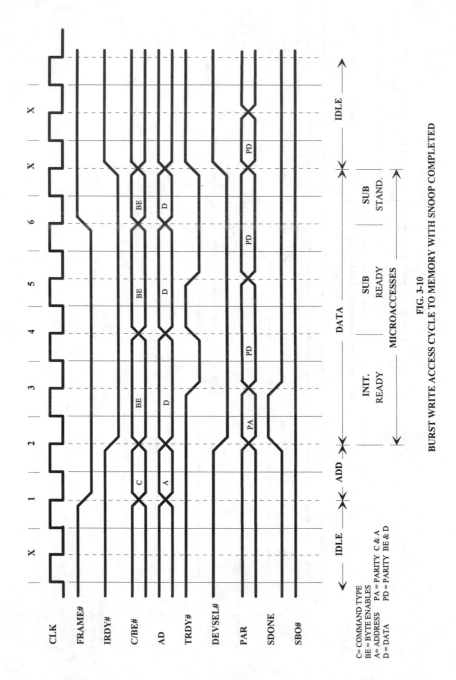

FIG. 3-10
BURST WRITE ACCESS CYCLE TO MEMORY WITH SNOOP COMPLETED

Figure 3-10: Burst Write Access Cycle with Snoop Completed

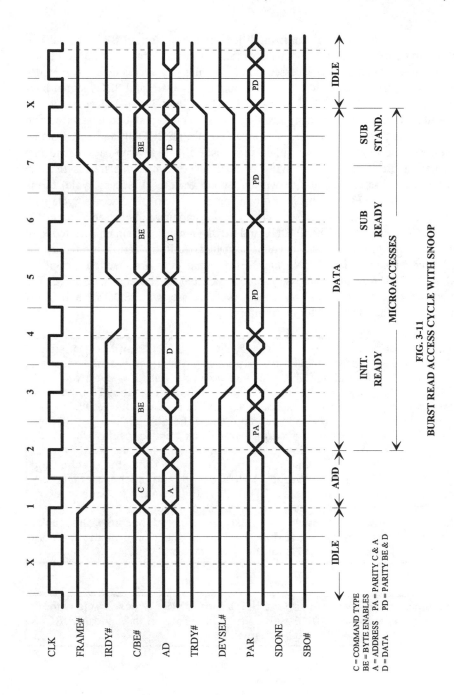

FIG. 3-11
BURST READ ACCESS CYCLE WITH SNOOP

Figure 3-11: Burst Read Access Cycle with Snoop

If the write-back cache line is modified/valid, the asserted SBO# signal line indicates a cache hit and the contents of the PCI memory resource (target) is not correct and data cannot be accessed during the memory access cycle. A memory target must terminate the access cycle if both the SDONE and SBO# signal lines are asserted (see Figures 3-12-A, 3-12-B, 3-13-A, and 3-13-B). The target will execute a Retry termination by keeping the TRDY# signal line deasserted and asserting the STOP# signal line. The assertion of both SDONE and SBO# signal lines indicates that a snoop resulted in a cache hit of a write-back cache line marked modified/valid. For a write or read access cycle, this means that the cache line in the cache must be written (snoop write-back access cycle) to the target prior to the PCI bus master completing the write or read access cycle with the target (an exception is the memory write and invalidate; see *Chapter 7: Cache Support on PCI*. The SDONE and SBO# signal lines remain asserted until the snoop write-back access cycle is executed. A Retry termination must be executed whenever the SDONE and SBO# signal lines are asserted during the ADDRESS PHASE of an access cycle to a cacheable PCI memory resource. The execution of a snoop write-back access cycle deasserts the SDONE and SBO# signal lines. See Chapter 7 for more information.

Typically during a BURST access cycle, the SDONE and SBO# signal lines are asserted or deasserted, respectively, for the initial microaccess, and apply to the subsequent microaccesses as well. However, during a BURST access cycle the cache boundary may be crossed. The memory target must be aware of this boundary and not assert the TRDY# signal line until the cache controller has completed the address snoop (SDONE signal line asserted) and a snoop write-back access cycle will not be required (SBO# signal line deasserted). Otherwise the target must execute a Disconnect without data termination and the cache line boundary will not be crossed. If the cache and cacheable memory resource are behind the same BRIDGE (isolated from the PCI bus master), it may never be necessary to execute a Disconnect without data termination when the cache boundary is crossed because the cache controller can obtain correct data from either the cache or the memory resource. See Subchapter 7.3 for more information.

It is possible to complete either a SINGLE or BURST access cycle without the assertion of the SDONE signal line. This protocol is called ADDRESS STACKING and is explained in Chapter 7.

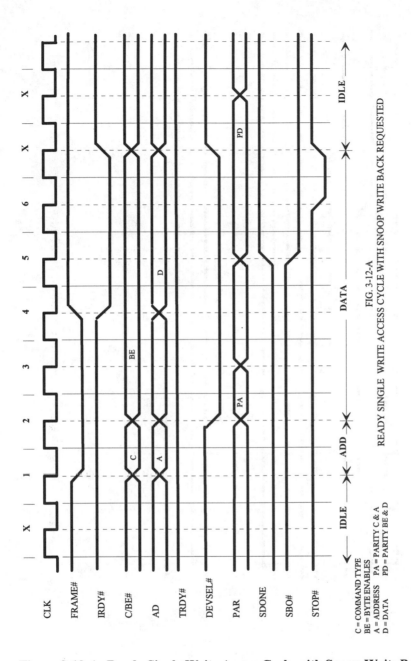

C = COMMAND TYPE
BE = BYTE ENABLES
A = ADDRESS   PA = PARITY C & A
D = DATA   PD = PARITY BE & D

FIG. 3-12-A
READY SINGLE WRITE ACCESS CYCLE WITH SNOOP WRITE BACK REQUESTED

Figure 3-12-A: Ready Single Write Access Cycle with Snoop Write Back Requested

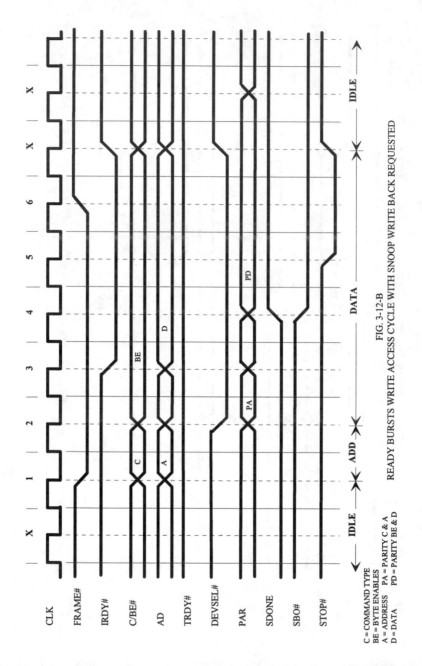

Figure 3-12-B: Ready Bursts Write Access Cycle with Snoop Write Back Requested

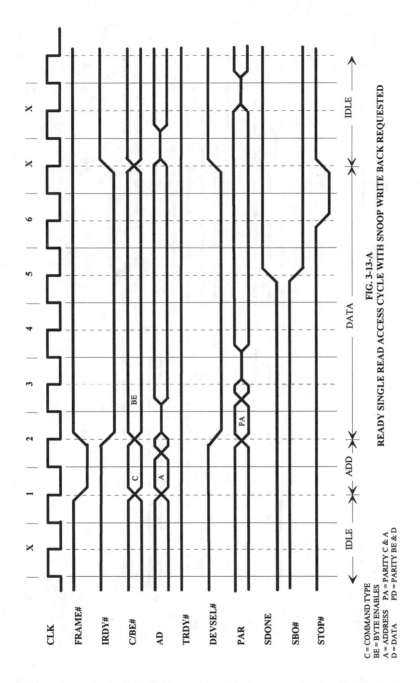

Figure 3-13-A: Ready Single Read Access Cycle with Snoop Write Back
Requested

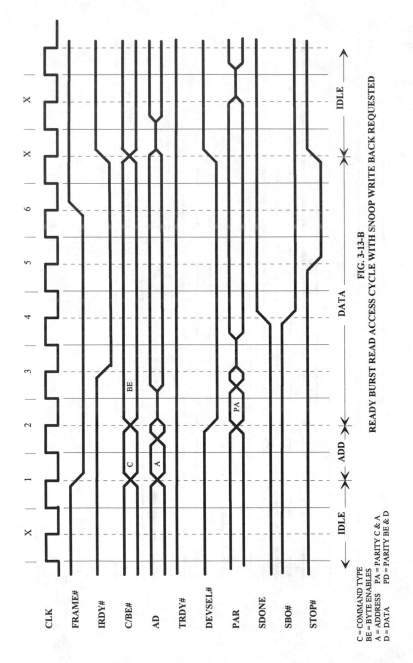

FIG. 3-13-B
READY BURST READ ACCESS CYCLE WITH SNOOP WRITE BACK REQUESTED

C = COMMAND TYPE
BE = BYTE ENABLES
A = ADDRESS   PA = PARITY C & A
D = DATA   PD = PARITY BE & D

Figure 3-13-B: Ready Burst Read Access Cycle with Snoop Write Back Requested

64 DATA BIT PCI BUS MASTERS AND TARGETS

The generic access cycles described above apply to both 32 and 64 data bit cycles. The 32 data bit PCI bus protocol implements the AD[31::0], C/BE#[3::0] and PAR signal lines. The 64 data bit extension of the PCI bus protocol adds the AD[63::32], C/BE#[7::4], and PAR64 signal lines. The operation of the AD[63::32] and C/BE#[7::4] signal lines is almost identical to the operation of the AD[31::0] and C/BE#[3::0] signal lines.

The ability to actually execute 64 data-bit accesses requires that both the PCI bus master and the target support 64 data bits as indicated by asserted REQ64# and ACK64# signal lines, respectively. The REQ64# signal line is asserted during the ADDRESS PHASE (same timing protocol as the FRAME# signal line) to indicate that the PCI bus master wants to read or write 64 data bits per access. The ACK64# signal line is asserted during the DATA PHASE (same timing protocol as the DEVSEL# signal line) to indicate that it does support 64 data bit accesses. See *Chapter 6: Detailed Bus Cycle Operation*, for details.

DUAL ADDRESS

The PCI bus protocol also supports a 64-bit address space. The typical access cycle defines 32 address bits on the AD[31::0] signal lines when the FRAME# signal line is first asserted during the ADDRESS PHASE. If the DUAL ADDRESS command encoding is driven onto the C/BE# signal lines during the ADDRESS PHASE, the length of the ADDRESS PHASE is doubled (see Figure 3-14). The second CLK signal line period of the longer ADDRESS PHASE allows the upper order 32 address bits to be driven onto the AD[31::0] signal lines. Also, the COMMAND type (memory versus I/O, read versus write, etc.) are driven onto the C/BE#[3::0] signal lines during this second CLK signal line period of the ADDRESS PHASE. Figure 3-14 uses read access cycles as examples, although the protocol is the same for a write access cycle. See Chapter 6: *Detailed Bus Cycle Operation* for details.

> If the PCI bus master asserts the REQ64# signal line, the upper order address and COMMAND type information on the AD[31::0] and C/BE#[3::0] signal lines are mirrored on the AD[63::32] and C/BE#[7::4] signal lines, respectively.

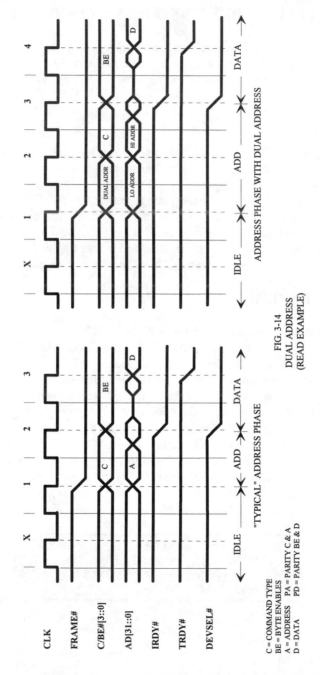

Figure 3-14: DUAL ADDRESS (Read Example)

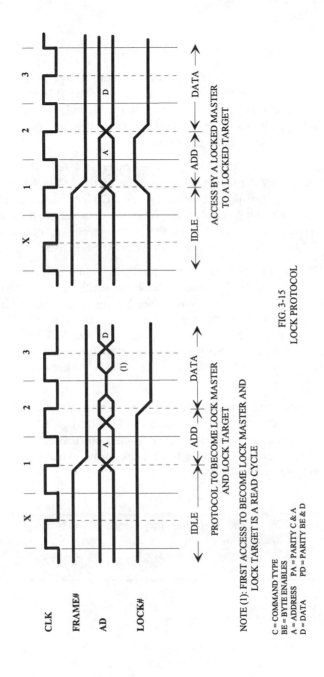

FIG. 3-15
LOCK PROTOCOL

Figure 3-15: Lock Protocol

63

LOCK

A PCI bus master can lock any PCI memory resource (target) that supports the LOCK# signal line. A locked target means that only the PCI bus master that locked it (Lock master) can access it, and can eventually unlock it. Other PCI bus masters cannot access a locked target. If an access is attempted by the non-Lock master, the target executes a Retry termination.

A PCI bus master can lock a target if no other PCI resource is presently locked (as indicated by the continued deassertion of the LOCK# signal line by pull-up resistors). At any given time, only one PCI bus master can be Lock master and only one target can be locked. When no Lock master presently exists on the bus, a PCI bus master begins the access cycle to lock a target by deasserting the LOCK# signal line during the ADDRESS PHASE.

If the LOCK# signal line is asserted by the PCI bus master during the second CLK signal line period, the PCI bus master becomes the Lock master and the target is locked if data is successfully read (see Figure 3-15). The LOCK# signal line must remain asserted for the remainder of the access cycle and after the access cycle is completed for the PCI bus master to remain Lock master. The continued assertion of the LOCK# signal line after the access cycle by Lock master indicates to other PCI bus masters that a Lock master and locked target already exist.

The Lock master accesses a locked target by deasserting the LOCK# signal during the ADDRESS PHASE (see Figure 3-15). The LOCK# signal line is asserted for the remainder of the access cycle if the Lock master wants to remain Lock master. The Lock master ceases to be Lock master when the LOCK# and FRAME# signal lines are both deasserted.

> When a DUAL ADDRESS is executed, the length of the ADDRESS PHASE is doubled. This has no effect on the LOCK# signal line protocol. The transition of the LOCK# signal line must be during the second CLK signal line period.

SPECIAL CYCLES

The PCI bus protocol defines a version of a write cycle called *special cycle*. The special cycle operates with the same protocol as a write access cycle (SINGLE or BURST) except none of the PCI resources (targets) claims the cycle. The DEVSEL#, TRDY#, and STOP# signal lines remain driven to a logical "1" by pull-up resistors. The special cycle allows data to be "broadcast" (simultaneously written) to all PCI bus resources on a specific bus. The source of a special cycle is a PCI bus master on the PCI bus, or a bridge to the PCI bus. A PCI bus master can directly execute a special cycle to the PCI resources on the same bus. When a special cycle is to be executed to PCI resources not on the same PCI bus as the PCI bus master or not directly attached to a BRIDGE, then the request for a PCI/PCI BRIDGE to execute a special cycle is conveyed by a type 1 configuration access cycle.

When a special cycle is executed, no PCI resource (target) can claim the bus cycle. Consequently, the DEVSEL#, TRDY#, STOP#, and AD signal lines are not driven by a target. The DEVSEL#, TRDY#, and STOP#, signal lines are driven to a logical "1" by pull-up resistors and the AD signal lines are only driven by the PCI bus master.

The protocol of special cycles requires an IDLE PHASE (FRAME# and IRDY# signal lines deasserted) between the special cycle and any subsequent bus cycle; consequently, Fast Back-to-Back protocol can not be applied.

INTERRUPT ACKNOWLEDGE CYCLES

The PCI bus protocol defines a version of a read cycle called *interrupt acknowledge cycle*. The interrupt acknowledge cycle operates with the same protocol as a read access cycle (SINGLE or BURST). The only PCI resource that can respond to this bus cycle is the one that contains the interrupt controller. As outlined in Chapter 2, this PCI resource must be attached to PCI bus 0. The interrupt controller can reside in a PCI resource on PCI Bus 0. the PCI/LEGACY BRIDGE on PCI bus 0, or in a resource on the LEGACY bus. The HOST/PCI BRIDGE, on behalf of the HOST CPU, is the only platform resource that can execute an interrupt acknowledge cycle on PCI bus 0. If the interrupt controller is on the LEGACY bus, a version of the interrupt acknowledge cycle will also be executed, according to the protocol of the LEGACY bus.

It is also possible for the interrupt controller to reside on the HOST bus or on a LEGACY bus that is directly attached to the HOST bus with a HOST/LEGACY BRIDGE. In these situations, no interrupt acknowledge cycle will be executed on PCI bus 0.

The protocol of the interrupt acknowledge cycle is that of a read bus cycle; so, the subsequent bus cycle cannot be executed with the Fast Back-to-Back protocol. If the interrupt acknowledge cycle ends with a Master Abort termination, the subsequent bus cycle can be executed with the Fast Back-to-Back protocol. A Master Abort termination results when no PCI resource (target) has claimed the bus cycle. The DEVSEL#, TRDY#, STOP#, and AD signal lines, therefore, are not driven by a target. The DEVSEL#, TRDY#, and STOP# signal lines are only driven by pull-up resistors. This allows the Fast Back-to-Back protocol to be applied to the following bus cycle.

The completion of an interrupt acknowledge cycle with a Retry, Disconnect, or Target Abort termination requires the PCI bus master to deassert its REQ# signal line. The protocol requires the REQ# signal line to be deasserted a minimum of two CLK signal line periods relative to the end of the bus cycle that was completed by these terminations. As a result of this protocol, an IDLE PHASE occurs between sequential bus cycles; consequently, the Fast Back-to-Back protocol cannot be applied.

3.1 BRIDGES AND INTERBUS OPERATIONS

INTRODUCTION

There are many architectural details that could be discussed relative to the interbus operations and the diversity of BRIDGEs between the different bus levels. The diversity is so great that this type of discussion would be a book in itself. Because the focus of this book is the PCI bus protocol, an extensive discussion of most other buses is inappropriate; however, a brief overview is appropriate and important. First, a general discussion of PCI bus protocols relative to BRIDGEs is presented, followed by a brief case-by-case discussion of interbus operation.

General PCI bus protocols relative to BRIDGEs are as follows:

- As outlined in Chapter 4, a BRIDGE can only COMBINE memory write access cycles (for memory, memory write and invalidate, and memory mapped I/O). Also, a BRIDGE can only MERGE memory write (and memory write and invalidate, but not for memory mapped I/O) access cycles.

- Only memory write (and memory mapped I/O write, and memory write and invalidate) access cycles can be posted in the BRIDGE. Posting of the data associated with these bus cycles allows the BRIDGE to complete the bus cycle on the source bus and complete the bus cycle on the destination bus at a later time.

- As outlined in Subchapters 4.0, 8.2, and Chapter 14, the BRIDGE (acting as the target) must execute a Retry termination on the source bus if it cannot complete a SINGLE access cycle or interrupt acknowledge cycle, or the initial microaccess of a BURST access cycle or interrupt acknowledge cycle within sixteen CLK signal line periods after the

FRAME# signal line is asserted (see "16 clock" rule in Subchapters 4.0, 8.2, and Chapter 14). A BRIDGE can port the bus cycle from the source to destination buses and hope that a response from the destination bus will allow the BRIDGE to respond to the source bus according to the "16 clock" rule and achieve Immediate Completion (IC). During IC, the BRIDGE (as target) inserts waits by deasserting the TRDY# signal line until it is ready to complete the bus cycle without Retry termination. It completes the bus cycle with Completion, Completion without Timeout, Disconnect, or Target Abort. Master Abort termination is also a version of IC. For a memory write access cycle that is postable (memory write, memory write and invalidate, and memory mapped I/O) the BRIDGE can post the data from the source bus and complete the access cycle at a later time on the destination bus, therefore achieving compliance to the "16 clock" rule. Read access cycles and interrupt acknowledge cycles are not postable, and achieving compliance to the "16 clock" rule is more difficult. One solution is for the BRIDGE to implement the protocol outlined below.

■ As outlined above, the BRIDGE (acting as a target) must execute a Retry termination if it cannot complete a write bus cycle according to the "16 clock" rule. The Retry termination requirement does not apply to a special cycle because it is a target termination protocol and there is no specific target in a Retry termination. See Subchapter 4.0 and Chapter 14 for more information.

■ The "16 clock" rule does not apply to configuration access cycles during non-runtime (i.e., initialization) or when EEPROM is being read to the shadow DRAM. The "16 clock" rule also does not apply to special cycles.

As outlined above, an Immediate Completion by the BRIDGE (acting as a target) is possible with posted data writes or by inserting wait states (TRDY# signal line) until the destination bus completes the read bus cycle and ports the completion of the bus cycle on the destination bus to the source bus. When the BRIDGE implements the "16 clock" rule, the BRIDGE may not be able to execute a read bus cycle (memory read, memory read line, and memory read multiple access cycles, all I/O access cycles, configuration access cycles, and interrupt acknowledge cycles) on the destination bus in compliance to the "16 clock" rule on the source bus. The BRIDGE can be compliant to the "16 clock" rule on the source bus for ONLY non-postable bus cycles by executing a Retry termination if it cannot complete the SINGLE bus cycle or the initial microaccess of a BURST bus cycle according to the "16 clock" rule. When the BRIDGE cannot meet the "16 clock" rule it can latch address, COMMAND type, byte enables, REQ64#, and so forth (in anticipation of the repeat of the "exact same" bus cycle) of the bus cycle on the source bus, execute Retry termination on the source bus, and continue the bus cycle on the destination bus. The PCI bus master is required to repeat the "exact same" bus cycle on the source bus and the BRIDGE will continue to execute Retry termination until the associated bus cycle on the destination bus has completed without Retry termination (according to the protocol of a bus cycle completed with Retry termination). The BRIDGE will terminate the next subsequent repeat of the "exact same" bus cycle on the source bus with the same termination on the destination bus (Completion, Completion with Timeout, Disconnect, Master Abort, or Target Abort termination). A Retry termination on the destination bus is ported to the source bus as a Retry termination and requires continued repeating of the "exact same" bus cycle.

If the BRIDGE adopts the above protocol, the BRIDGE must follow the conditions outlined in the "Immediate and Delayed Transaction" section of Subchapter 4.1.

The protocols outlined above can also be applied to targets that are not BRIDGEs interconnecting HOST/PCI, PCI/PCI, and PCI/LEGACY buses. In essence, the PCI interface to the circuitry in the target is similar to a BRIDGE. For example, a DRAM controller interfaces the PCI bus to the DRAM bus.

The following paragraphs provide a case-by-case discussion of interbus operation. This discussion is broken into six cases: HOST bus to PCI bus, PCI bus to HOST bus, high level PCI bus to lower level PCI bus, low level PCI bus to higher level PCI bus, PCI bus to LEGACY bus, and LEGACY bus to PCI bus.

There are several basic issues that affect interbus operation and that are discussed in each of the six cases:

1. The ability for the bus master on one bus to access a memory or I/O resource of another bus.

2. Differing data size between buses.

3. The posting of memory write data in BRIDGEs.

4. The matching of I/O access cycles between buses.

5. The protocol for configuration access, special, and interrupt acknowledge cycles ported from one bus to another through a BRIDGE.

6. The existence of a cache on the bus and whether the memory resource on the bus is cached.

> For the purposes of this discussion, the architecture in Figure 2-3 is assumed. Only HOST CPUs and PCI bus masters can execute incomplete accesses with cycle termination (a cycle begins but only part or none of the data is successfully accessed). The cache resides on the HOST bus, and DRAM on both the HOST bus (HDRAM) and PCI bus (PDRAM) are cached. Memory on PCI bus 1 or the LEGACY bus is not cached. Pre-fetching of data is not supported by any of the targets in these examples; consequently, data merging is not possible. Finally, all of the BRIDGEs can post write data to the memory address space.

> If I/O registers are mapped to the memory address space, it is assumed that all of the protocols for a memory access cycle apply. The protocols for the I/O address space do not apply to these registers.

Case—HOST Bus to PCI Bus 0: The typical HOST/PCI BRIDGE (defined as BRIDGE in the following paragraphs) operation for the HOST CPU accessing resources on a LEVEL 1 PCI bus 0 (defined as "PCI bus" in the following paragraphs) is as follows:

1. The address of the memory or I/O access cycle requested by the HOST CPU is compared to the address range in the BRIDGE. If the address is within the range, the access cycle is claimed by the BRIDGE and an access cycle on the PCI bus is attempted. If the PCI bus is presently owned by another PCI bus master, the BRIDGE either terminates the HOST bus access cycle or inserts wait states in the HOST bus access cycle. If the HOST bus access cycle is terminated, the HOST CPU can retry the access at a later time. If the BRIDGE inserts waits states, the central arbiter must deassert the GNT# signal line to the PCI bus master to limit the number of wait states required. The HOST CPU in conjunction with the BRIDGE appears as a PCI bus master to the resources on the PCI bus.

2. The data size of the HOST bus access executed by the HOST CPU may not match the data size of the PCI bus. If the HOST data size is smaller (or equal), only the smaller (or equal) data size is accessed on the PCI bus (assuming no pre-fetching). If the HOST data size is larger, the HOST bus access cycle must be broken into multiple PCI bus access cycles by the BRIDGE. The completion of the multiple PCI bus access cycles will equal the completion of a single HOST bus access cycle.

3. For a HOST CPU memory access to the PCI bus, write data can be posted into the BRIDGE and the HOST bus cycle immediately completed. The data will be written to the PCI bus at a later time. Prior

to the execution of a read access cycle to the PCI bus by the HOST CPU, the posted data must first be written to the PCI target. For an I/O access cycle, write data cannot be posted in the BRIDGE. The restriction on the I/O access cycle reflects the fact that an I/O resource may control other bus functions. For example, the interrupt in an I/O resource must be disabled before the interrupt input to the HOST CPU is unmasked. If the write data to the I/O resource is posted, the HOST CPU interrupt input may be unmasked before the I/O interrupt is disabled.

4. The addressing order of a PCI bus I/O BURST access cycle must match the addressing order of a HOST bus BURST access cycle executed by the HOST CPU. Multiple SINGLE HOST bus I/O access cycles cannot be combined into a single BURST PCI bus I/O access cycle, or vice versa.

5. An access to the PCI configuration address space only begins by the HOST CPU executing a series of HOST bus I/O cycles to access the configuration registers in the HOST/BRIDGE or to enable the HOST/BRIDGE to execute a configuration access cycle on the PCI bus to a PCI resource. If the PCI resource is not on a LEVEL 1 bus, PCI/PCI BRIDGEs will port the configuration access cycles to lower-LEVEL buses. The PCI configuration space is not defined for a LEGACY bus.

The interrupt acknowledge cycle only begins on the HOST bus (by the HOST CPU) and is ported to PCI bus 0 by the HOST/PCI BRIDGE if the interrupt controller resource is on the PCI bus 0 (directly on the PCI bus, in the PCI/LEGACY BRIDGE, or on the LEGACY bus). No interrupt acknowledge cycle is executed on PCI bus 0 if the interrupt resource is attached to the HOST bus.

The special cycle can begin by the HOST CPU executing a series of HOST bus I/O cycles to access registers in the HOST/PCI BRIDGE or a PCI bus master executing it on the PCI bus. If the special cycle is to be executed on a PCI bus not attached to the HOST/PCI BRIDGE or the PCI bus master, it is ported to other PCI buses as configuration access cycles type 1 by PCI/PCI BRIDGEs. When the HOST CPU is the source of the special cycle, it is ported from HIGHER to LOWER LEVEL BRIDGEs. When a PCI bus master is the source of the special cycle, it is ported to HIGHER or LOWER LEVEL buses. A special cycle is not defined for the LEGACY bus.

6. HOST CPU accesses to cache may not always cause an immediate PCI bus access cycle to be executed. If the valid cache line is a copy of a cache line in the HDRAM, no PCI bus cycle is executed. If the valid

cache line is a copy of a cache line in the PDRAM, the cache controller in the BRIDGE must determine the appropriate PCI bus access cycle. For a write-through cache, the cache controller in the BRIDGE will execute a PCI write access cycle when the HOST CPU writes to the cache. HOST CPU access to write-back cache types requires the cache controller in the BRIDGE to execute PCI read and write access cycles to support cache coherency with PCI memory resources that are cached.

Case—PCI Bus to HOST Bus: Typical HOST/PCI BRIDGE (defined as "BRIDGE" in the following paragraphs) operation for a PCI bus master on a LEVEL 1 PCI bus 0 (defined as "PCI bus" in the following paragraphs) accessing resources on the HOST bus is as follows:

1. The address of the memory access cycle requested by the PCI bus master is compared to the address range of the BRIDGE. If the address is within the range, the access cycle is claimed by the BRIDGE and an access cycle on the HOST bus is attempted. If the HOST CPU is presently executing a HOST bus cycle, the BRIDGE either terminates (Retry termination) the PCI bus access cycle or inserts wait states in the PCI bus access cycle. If the PCI bus access cycle is completed with Retry termination, the PCI bus master must repeat the access at a later time. By convention, the typical HOST bus does not have I/O resources.

2. The data size of the PCI bus access executed by the PCI bus master may not match the data size of the HOST bus. If the PCI bus data size is smaller (or equal), only the smaller (or equal) data size is accessed on the HOST bus (assuming no pre-fetching). If the PCI bus data size is larger, the PCI bus access cycle must be broken into multiple HOST bus access cycles. The completion of the multiple HOST bus access cycles will equal the completion of a single PCI bus access cycle.

3. A PCI bus master memory write access to HDRAM write data can be posted in the BRIDGE and the PCI bus cycle immediately completed. The data will be written to the HDRAM at a later time. Prior to the execution of a read access cycle to the HOST bus by a PCI bus master, the posted data must first be written to the HDRAM.

4. A typical PC platform does not have any I/O resources on the HOST bus; consequently, PCI I/O access cycles do not result in a HOST bus cycle.

5. An access to the PCI configuration address space can only begin by the HOST CPU executing a series of HOST bus I/O cycles to access the configuration registers in the HOST/BRIDGE or to enable the HOST/BRIDGE to execute a configuration access cycle on the PCI bus

to a PCI resource. If the PCI resource is not on a LEVEL 1 bus, then PCI/PCI BRIDGEs will port the configuration access cycles to lower-LEVEL buses. The PCI configuration space is not defined for a LEGACY bus.

The interrupt acknowledge cycle only begins on the HOST bus (by the HOST CPU) and is ported to PCI bus 0 by the HOST/PCI BRIDGE if the interrupt controller resource is on the PCI bus 0 (directly on the PCI bus, in the PCI/LEGACY BRIDGE, or on the LEGACY bus). No interrupt acknowledge cycle is executed on PCI bus 0 if the interrupt resource is attached to the HOST bus.

If the special cycle is to be executed on a PCI bus not attached to the HOST/PCI BRIDGE or the PCI bus master, it is ported to other PCI buses as configuration access cycles type 1 by PCI/PCI BRIDGEs. When the HOST CPU is the source of the special cycle, it is ported from HIGHER to LOWER LEVEL buses. When a PCI bus master is the source of the special cycle, it must be ported to HIGHER or LOWER LEVEL buses. A special cycle is not defined for the LEGACY bus.

6.   The address of the memory access cycle requested by the PCI bus master is compared to the address range of the BRIDGE. If the address is within the range of the HOST bus memory (HDRAM), the access cycle is claimed by the BRIDGE and an access cycle on the HOST bus is attempted. If the address is also within the range of a valid cache line in the cache, the cache controller in the BRIDGE has additional options. The existence of both the HDRAM and cache "behind" the BRIDGE allows the cache controller to access the data with the cache or the HDRAM. If the address is not within the range of a valid cache line in the cache, the BRIDGE accesses the HDRAM on behalf of the PCI bus master.

Case—High Level PCI Bus to Lower Level PCI Bus: Typical PCI/PCI BRIDGE (defined as "BRIDGE" in the following paragraphs) operation for PCI bus master on a LEVEL 1 PCI bus (PCI bus 0) accessing resources on a LEVEL 2 PCI bus (PCI bus 1) is as follows:

1.   The address of the memory or I/O access cycle requested by the PCI bus master on PCI bus 0 is compared to the address range of the BRIDGE. If the address is within the range, the access cycle is claimed by the BRIDGE and an access cycle on PCI bus 1 is attempted. If a PCI bus master is not presently executing a bus cycle on PCI bus 1, PCI bus 1 ownership can be awarded to the BRIDGE and the access cycle can begin. If PCI bus 1 is presently owned by another PCI bus master, the BRIDGE has two possible options: (1) the BRIDGE can terminate the

PCI bus 0 access cycle (Retry termination) and the PCI bus master on PCI bus 0 must repeat the access at a later time. The BRIDGE, in conjunction with the central arbiter, should deassert the signal line that awarded PCI bus 1 to the PCI bus master (GNT# signal line) to force it to relinquish the bus so a subsequent repeat of the access by a PCI bus master on PCI bus 0 will be ported to PCI bus 1. (2) the BRIDGE inserts wait states on the PCI bus 0 access cycle (deassertion of the TRDY# signal line). The BRIDGE, in conjunction with the central arbiter, should deassert the signal line that awarded PCI bus 1 to the PCI bus master (GNT# signal line) to limit the number of waits states required. When the present PCI bus 1 owner relinquishes the bus, the BRIDGE can begin an access cycle on PCI bus 1.

2. The data size of the PCI bus access executed on PCI bus 1 master may not match the data size of the PCI bus 0. If the PCI bus 0 data size is smaller (or equal), only the smaller (or equal) data size is accessed on PCI bus 1 bus (assuming no pre-fetching). If the PCI bus 0 data size is larger, it must be broken into multiple PCI bus 1 access cycles. The completion of the multiple PCI bus 1 access cycles will equal the completion of a single PCI bus 0 access cycle.

3. For a PCI bus 0 write access cycle, the data can be posted in the BRIDGE and the PCI bus 0 access cycle is immediately completed; the data will be written to PCI bus 1 at a later time. Prior to the execution of a read access cycle to PCI bus 0 by a PCI bus master on PCI bus 1, the posted data must first be written to the PCI target. For an I/O access cycle, write data cannot be posted in the BRIDGE. The restriction on the I/O access cycle reflects the fact that an I/O resource may control other bus functions.

4. The addressing order of a PCI bus 1 I/O BURST access cycle must match the addressing order of the PCI bus 0 bus BURST access cycle executed by the PCI bus master. Multiple SINGLE PCI bus 0 I/O access cycles cannot be combined into a single BURST PCI bus 1 I/O access cycle, and vice versa.

5. An access to the PCI configuration address space can only begin by the HOST CPU executing a series of HOST bus I/O cycles to access the configuration registers in the HOST/BRIDGE or to enable the HOST/BRIDGE to execute a configuration access cycle on the PCI bus to a PCI resource. If the PCI resource is not on a LEVEL 1 bus, then PCI/PCI BRIDGEs will port the configuration access cycles to lower-LEVEL buses. The PCI configuration space is not defined for a LEGACY bus.

The interrupt acknowledge cycle can only begin on the HOST bus (by the HOST CPU) and is ported to PCI bus 0 by the HOST/PCI BRIDGE if the interrupt controller resource is on the PCI bus 0 (directly on the PCI bus, in the PCI/LEGACY BRIDGE, or on the LEGACY bus). No interrupt acknowledge cycle is executed on PCI bus 0 if the interrupt resource is attached to the HOST bus.

If the special cycle is to be executed on a PCI bus not attached to the HOST/PCI BRIDGE or the PCI bus master, then it is ported to other PCI buses as configuration access cycles type 1 by PCI/PCI BRIDGEs. When the HOST CPU is the source of the special cycle, it is ported from HIGHER to LOWER LEVEL buses. When a PCI bus master is the source of the special cycle, it is ported to HIGHER or LOWER LEVEL buses. A special cycle is not defined for the LEGACY bus.

6. The memory resources on PCI bus 1 are not cached; consequently, the cache on the HOST bus is not involved with an access by the PCI bus master on PCI bus 0 to memory on PCI bus 1. However, the cache controller in the HOST/PCI BRIDGE must still snoop the address and assert the SDONE# signal line.

Case—Low Level PCI Bus to Higher Level PCI Bus: Typical PCI/PCI BRIDGE (defined as BRIDGE in the following paragraphs) operation for a PCI bus master on a LEVEL 2 PCI bus (PCI bus 1) accessing resources on a LEVEL 1 PCI bus (PCI bus 0) is as follows:

1. The address of the memory or I/O access cycle requested by the PCI bus master on PCI bus 1 is compared to the address range of the BRIDGE. If the address is within the range, the access cycle is claimed by the BRIDGE and an access cycle on PCI bus 0 is attempted. If a PCI bus master is not presently executing a bus cycle on PCI bus 0, PCI bus 0 ownership can be awarded to the BRIDGE and the access cycle can begin. If PCI bus 0 is presently owned by another PCI bus master, the BRIDGE has two possible options: (1) the BRIDGE can terminate the PCI bus 1 access cycle (Retry termination) and the PCI bus master on PCI bus 1 must repeat the access at a later time. The BRIDGE, in conjunction with the central arbiter, should deassert the signal line that awarded PCI bus 0 to the PCI bus master (GNT# signal line) to force it to relinquish the bus so a subsequent repeat of the access cycle by a PCI bus master on PCI bus 1 will be ported to PCI bus 0. (2) the BRIDGE inserts wait states on the PCI bus 1 access cycle (desertion of the TRDY# signal line). The BRIDGE, in conjunction with the central arbiter, should deassert the signal line that awarded PCI bus 0 to the PCI bus master (GNT# signal line) to limit the number of waits states

required. When the present PCI bus 0 owner relinquishes the bus, the BRIDGE can begin an access cycle on PCI bus 0.

2. The data size of the PCI bus access executed on PCI bus 0 master may not match the data size of the PCI bus 1. If the PCI bus 1 data size is smaller (or equal), only the smaller (or equal) data size is accessed on PCI bus 0 bus (assuming no pre-fetching). If the PCI bus 1 data size is larger, it must be broken into multiple PCI 0 bus access cycles. The completion of the multiple PCI bus 0 access cycles will equal the completion of a single PCI bus 1 access cycle.

3. For a PCI bus 1 write access cycle, the data can be posted in the BRIDGE and the PCI bus 1 access cycle is immediately completed; the data will be written to PCI bus 0 at a later time. Prior to the execution of a read access cycle to PCI bus 1 by a PCI bus master on PCI bus 0, the posted data must first be been written to the PCI target. For a I/O access cycle, write data cannot be posted in the BRIDGE. The restriction on the I/O access cycle reflects the fact that an I/O resource may control other bus functions.

4. The addressing order of a PCI bus 0 I/O BURST access cycle must match the addressing order of the PCI bus 1 bus BURST access cycle executed by the PCI bus master. Multiple SINGLE PCI bus 1 I/O access cycles cannot be combined into a single BURST PCI bus 0 I/O access cycle, and vice versa.

5. An access to the PCI configuration address space only begins by the HOST CPU executing a series of HOST bus I/O cycles to access the configuration registers in the HOST/BRIDGE or to enable the HOST/BRIDGE to execute a configuration access cycle on the PCI bus to a PCI resource. If the PCI resource is not on a LEVEL 1 bus, then PCI/PCI BRIDGEs will port the configuration access cycles to lower-LEVEL buses. The PCI configuration space is not defined for a LEGACY bus.

    The interrupt acknowledge cycle only begins on the HOST bus (by the HOST CPU) and is ported to PCI bus 0 by the HOST/PCI BRIDGE if the interrupt controller resource is on the PCI bus 0 (directly on the PCI bus, in the PCI/LEGACY BRIDGE, or on the LEGACY bus). No interrupt acknowledge cycle is executed on PCI bus 0 if the interrupt resource is attached to the HOST bus.

    If the special cycle is to be executed on a PCI bus not attached to the HOST/PCI BRIDGE or the PCI bus master, it is ported to other PCI buses as a configuration access cycle type 1 by PCI/PCI BRIDGEs. When the HOST CPU is the source of the special cycle, it is ported from

HIGHER to LOWER LEVEL buses. When a PCI bus master is the source of the special cycle, it is ported to HIGHER or LOWER LEVEL buses. A special cycle is not defined for the LEGACY bus.

6. The memory resources on PCI bus 0 are possibly cached; consequently, the cache controller in the HOST/BRIDGE must do an address snoop for a memory access on PCI bus 0 by the BRIDGE. A cache hit to a write-through cache line in the PDRAM allows the access cycle to be completed and a cache hit to a write-back cache (modified/valid) line in the PDRAM will result in the PCI bus 0 access cycle. Consequently, the BRIDGE may have to execute a Retry termination to the PCI bus master on PCI bus 1.

Case—PCI Bus to LEGACY Bus: Typical PCI/LEGACY BRIDGE (defined as BRIDGE in the following paragraphs) operation for PCI bus master on a LEVEL 1 PCI bus 0 (defined as PCI bus in the following paragraphs) accessing resources on a LEGACY bus is as follows:

1. The address of the memory or I/O access cycle requested by the PCI bus master is compared to the address range of the BRIDGE. If the address is within range, the access cycle is claimed by the BRIDGE and an access cycle on the LEGACY bus is attempted. If a bus master is not presently executing a LEGACY bus cycle, LEGACY bus ownership can be awarded to the BRIDGE and the access cycle can begin. If the LEGACY bus is presently owned by another bus master, the BRIDGE has two possible options: (1) the BRIDGE can terminate the PCI access cycle (Retry termination) and the PCI bus master can retry the access at a later time. The BRIDGE, in conjunction with the central arbiter, should pre-empt the bus ownership of the LEGACY bus according to the protocol of the bus. A subsequent retry by a PCI bus master to the LEGACY bus will be serviced. (2) the BRIDGE inserts wait states on the PCI bus (deassertion of the TRDY# signal line). The BRIDGE, in conjunction with the central arbiter, should pre-empt bus ownership of the LEGACY bus. When the present LEGACY bus owner relinquishes the bus, the BRIDGE can begin an access cycle. Option (2) is most unlikely due to the "16 clock" rule.

> If the LEGACY bus has a weak preemption protocol like the ISA bus, the BRIDGE should terminate the accesses by the PCI bus (Retry termination). The weak preemption protocol of the ISA bus does not force the ISA bus master to relinquish the bus; consequently, the insertion of wait sates on the PCI bus access cycle may extend indefinitely.

2. The data size of the PCI bus access executed on the PCI bus master may not match the data size of the LEGACY bus. If the PCI bus access cycle data size is smaller (or equal), only the smaller data size is accessed on the LEGACY bus (assuming no pre-fetching). If the PCI bus access cycle data size is larger, the access must be broken into multiple LEGACY bus access cycles. The completion of the multiple LEGACY bus cycles will equal the completion of a single PCI bus access cycle.

3. For a PCI bus write access cycle, the data can be posted in the BRIDGE and the PCI bus access cycle is immediately completed. The data will be written to the LEGACY bus at a later time. Prior to the execution of any access cycle to the LEGACY bus by a PCI bus master on PCI bus 0 or by another LEGACY bus master, the posted data must first be been written to the LEGACY resource. For an I/O access cycle, write data cannot be posted in the BRIDGE. The restriction on the I/O access cycle reflects the fact that an I/O resource may control other bus functions.

4. The addressing order of a LEGACY I/O BURST access cycle must match the order of the PCI bus BURST access cycle executed by the PCI bus master. Multiple SINGLE PCI bus I/O access cycles cannot be combined into a single BURST LEGACY bus I/O access cycle, and vice versa.

5. An access to the PCI configuration address space only begins by the HOST CPU executing a series of HOST bus I/O cycles to access the configuration registers in the HOST/BRIDGE or to enable the HOST/BRIDGE to execute a configuration access cycle on the PCI bus to a PCI resource. The PCI configuration space is not defined for a LEGACY bus.

    The interrupt acknowledge cycle only begins on the HOST bus (by the HOST CPU) and is ported to PCI bus 0 by the HOST/PCI BRIDGE if the interrupt controller resource is on the PCI bus 0 (directly on the PCI bus, in the PCI/LEGACY BRIDGE, or on the LEGACY bus). No interrupt acknowledge cycle is executed on PCI bus 0 if the interrupt resource is attached to the HOST bus without porting through the PCI bus.

    If the special cycle is to be executed on a PCI bus not attached to the HOST/PCI BRIDGE or the PCI bus master, it is ported to other PCI buses as configuration access cycles type 1 by PCI/PCI BRIDGEs. When a PCI bus master is the source of the special cycle, it is ported to HIGHER or LOWER LEVEL PCI buses. A special cycle is not defined for the LEGACY bus.

6. The memory resources on a LEGACY bus are not cached; so, the cache on the HOST bus is not involved with an access by the PCI bus master to the LEGACY bus. However, the cache controller in the HOST/PCI BRIDGE must still snoop the address and assert the SDONE# signal line.

Case— LEGACY Bus to PCI Bus: Typical PCI/LEGACY BRIDGE (defined as BRIDGE in the following paragraphs) operation for bus master on the LEGACY bus (defined as LEGACY master) accessing resources on a LEVEL 1 PCI bus 0 (defined as PCI bus) is as follows:

1. The address of the memory or I/O access cycle requested by the LEGACY master is compared to the address range of the BRIDGE. If the address is within the range, the access cycle is claimed by the BRIDGE and an access cycle on the PCI bus is attempted. If a PCI bus master is not presently executing a bus cycle on the PCI bus, PCI bus ownership can be awarded to the BRIDGE and the access cycle can begin. If the PCI bus is presently owned by a PCI bus master, the BRIDGE must insert wait states in the access cycle of the LEGACY master. The assertion of wait states is typically the only option because LEGACY buses (like ISA and EISA) do not have a retry protocol and once a LEGACY bus access cycle begins it must be completed. The BRIDGE, in conjunction with the central arbiter, should deassert the signal line that awarded the PCI bus to the PCI bus master (GNT# signal line) to limit the number of wait states required. When the present PCI bus owner relinquishes the bus, the BRIDGE can begin an access cycle on the PCI bus.

   The typical LEGACY bus protocol cannot extend cycles with wait states indefinitely for the access cycle to complete. When the LEGACY bus master begins an access cycle, it is not known by the bus if the access is to the LEGACY bus or the PCI bus. If the access is to a PCI bus resource, PCI bus must be immediately available to insure completion within a reasonable period of time. Under these considerations, the central arbiter must insure that no other PCI resource owns the PCI bus when it awards the LEGACY bus to the LEGACY bus master.

   Another consideration is the LOCK protocol of the PCI bus, which allows a PCI bus resource to be locked, with the PCI bus master that locked the resource being the only PCI bus master that can access it (except for snoop write-back access cycle). Consequently, the BRIDGE in conjunction with the central arbiter must insure that PCI resources that can potentially be accessed by the LEGACY bus master are not locked. See the *Lock* section for details.

2. The data size of the LEGACY bus access cycle being executed may not match the data size of the PCI bus. If the LEGACY bus access cycle data size is smaller (or equal), only the smaller (or equal) data size is accessed on the PCI bus (assuming no pre-fetching). If the LEGACY bus access cycle data size is larger, the PCI bus access cycle must be broken into multiple PCI bus access cycles. The completion of the multiple PCI bus access cycles will equal the completion of a single LEGACY bus access cycle.

3. For a LEGACY bus write access cycle, the data can be posted in the BRIDGE and the LEGACY bus access cycle is immediately completed. The data will be written to the PCI bus at a later time. Prior to the execution of a read access cycle to the PCI bus by the LEGACY bus master, the posted data must first be written to the PCI target. For a I/O access cycle, write data cannot be posted in the BRIDGE. The restriction on the I/O access cycle reflects the fact that an I/O resource may control other bus functions.

4. The addressing order of a PCI bus I/O BURST access cycle must match the order of the LEGACY bus BURST access cycle executed by the LEGACY bus master. Multiple SINGLE LEGACY bus I/O access cycles cannot be combined into a single BURST PCI bus I/O access cycle, and vice versa. These restrictions do not apply to a memory access cycles to memory resources or to a memory-mapped I/O resources.

5. LEGACY bus master cannot execute configuration access cycles.

    LEGACY bus master cannot service interrupts; only the platform CPU services interrupts.

    LEGACY bus master cannot execute special bus cycles.

6. The LEGACY bus does not support cache protocol.

CHAPTER 4

FUNCTIONAL INTERACTION BETWEEN PCI RESOURCES

This chapter consists of the following subchapters:

4.0 GENERAL CONSIDERATIONS

INTRODUCTION

As outlined in Chapter 2, the PCI bus supports both PCI bus masters and targets. In platforms with multiple buses that are bridged to a PCI bus, the BRIDGE can operate as a PCI resource on behalf of resources of other buses. Bus masters are those resources that obtain bus ownership and determine the type of cycle to be executed on a bus. PCI bus masters include PCI bus resources that become bus owners, the HOST CPU via a BRIDGE, and owners of other buses via a BRIDGE. The targets are those PCI resources addressed by the PCI bus master, HOST memory via a BRIDGE, and resources on other buses via BRIDGEs.

The PCI bus, compared to a more common bus like ISA, has a unique architecture. Some of the unique attributes are as follows:

- The address and data are multiplexed onto the same signal lines (AD), and the command and data size information are multiplexed onto the same signal lines (C/BE#). Consequently, the access cycle is divided into ADDRESS and DATA PHASES. During the ADDRESS PHASE the address and command are presented. During the DATA PHASE the data and active byte lanes are presented.

■ The address space is a full 32 bits with an option to extend it to 64 bits on a cycle-to-cycle basis.

■ The data width of the bus is defined as 32 data bits with an option to extend it to 64 data bits on a cycle-to-cycle basis.

■ The basic bus cycle to access PCI resources is a BURST access cycle. The BURST access cycle allows multiple data accesses during the cycle. When a BURST access cycle accesses the resource only once in the cycle it is defined as a SINGLE access cycle.

■ Between bus cycles the signal lines are driven to a logical "1" by pull-up resistors or to a stable level by a PCI bus master or central resource.

■ There are several other bus activities besides bus cycles to access memory, I/O, and configuration address spaces. These other activities include a non-specific message broadcast to all PCI targets (Special cycle) and an interrupt acknowledge cycle. Other bus attributes support cache coherency, limitation of a bus master's ownership of the bus, and target lock.

■ Parity is supported across the address, data, and control signal lines. Also, a more complete error reporting structure is defined.

■ There is no byte swapping between byte lanes on the bus. PCI bus masters and targets must support a full 32 data bit interface. There are unique requirements for the optional 64 data bit extension.

■ A bus cycle can be terminated with or without a data access.

■ In addition to the target, the PCI bus master can prolong the completion of the access cycle. The completion of the access requires a handshake between the bus master and the target.

■ The CLK signal line periods between bus cycles vary depending on bus ownership, the previous cycle, the type of bus cycle, and the targets involved in the access.

■ There is no central DMA controller that transfers data between PCI memory and I/O targets.

■ Except for the SERR#, RST#, and INT# signal lines, the PCI signal lines are synchronous with the CLK signal line.

■ There is no refresh cycle across the PCI bus.

The remainder of this chapter will address 32 and 64 data bit PCI resources. The first portion will concentrate on 32 data bit PCI resources and the latter will provide the incremental information relevant to the 64 data bit extension.

ACCESS CYCLES VERSUS OTHER BUS CYCLES

As outlined in the above introduction, there are several types of bus cycles executed on the PCI bus. In the following discussion, the interaction of the PCI resources will be described in terms of "access" cycles, "special" cycles, and "interrupt acknowledge" cycles. The access cycles imply that the PCI bus master accesses data with a target. The access cycles are: memory read and write, I/O read and write, configuration read and write, Memory Read Multiple, Memory Read Line, and Memory/Write and Invalidate. The special cycle broadcasts a message to all targets on the same bus (the special cycle cannot be ported through a BRIDGE to another bus). The interrupt acknowledge cycle returns an interrupt vector to the HOST CPU. Collectively, the access, special, and interrupt acknowledge cycles are called bus cycles. A PCI resource only has to support the configuration access cycles; all other bus cycles are optional.

As outlined in Chapter 3 and summarized below, the PCI bus protocol seamlessly switches from a SINGLE access cycle to a BURST access cycle. A SINGLE access cycle provides one specific address for a SINGLE access of data. It begins with the assertion of the FRAME# signal line in the ADDRESS PHASE. If the FRAME# signal line is asserted when the IRDY# signal line is asserted with the first data access during the DATA PHASE, the SINGLE access cycle becomes a BURST access cycle. Within the BURST access cycle protocol, each of the data accesses during the DATA PHASE is called a microaccess. The address provided in the ADDRESS PHASE is used for the initial microaccess in the DATA PHASE. Addresses for subsequent microaccesses in the DATA PHASE are based on the address provided in the ADDRESS PHASE. During the ADDRESS PHASE the AD signal lines contain the address of the target. During the DATA PHASE, these signal lines contain the accessed data. The type of access is encoded onto a binary pattern (command) driven onto the C/BE# signal lines during the ADDRESS PHASE. During the DATA PHASE, these signal lines identify the byte lanes on the AD signal lines to be accessed. A SINGLE access cycle means that a single byte (8 data bits), word (16 data bits), triple byte (24 data bits), or double word (32 data bits) is accessed via the AD[31::0] signal lines.

The special cycle can be executed with a SINGLE or BURST write cycle protocol. The PCI bus master can be any PCI resource. The target can be any of the PCI bus resources on the same bus as the PCI bus master or via PCI/PCI

BRIDGEs to PCI resources on other buses. It is only defined as a 32 data bit cycle; that is, the cycle is executed only with the AD[31::0], C/BE#[3::0], and PAR signal lines.

The interrupt acknowledge cycle can only be executed with a SINGLE or BURST read access cycle protocol. It is executed by the HOST/PCI BRIDGE on behalf of the HOST CPU to a LEVEL 1 PCI bus. The target is the PCI bus resource that contains the interrupt controller. It is only defined as 32 data bit cycle; that is, the cycle is executed only with the AD[31::0] and C/BE#[3::0] and PAR signal lines.

BYTE LANE OPERATION

The PCI bus specification dynamically identifies the data size of each bus cycle. The central resource does not swap data between byte lanes; thus all AD[31::0] signal lines must be supported by all PCI resources. The AD[31::0] signal lines contain four byte lanes (AD[7::0] signal lines comprise the first byte lane, AD[15::8] signal lines are the second byte lane, and so forth.). The protocol for byte lane operation on the PCI bus backplane is as follows:

- Any combination of asserted and deasserted C/BE#[3::0] signal lines are allowed, including all deasserted. These signal lines are valid or driven to a stable level for the entire DATA PHASE of a bus cycle.

- No byte lane swapping occurs between the byte lanes of the AD[31::0] signal lines.

- A bus cycle does not always mean that data is read or written. During the DATA PHASE the C/BE#[3::0] signal lines indicate which byte lanes contain valid data. If none of the C/BE#[3::0] signal lines are asserted, no data is driven onto the AD[31::0] signal lines during the bus cycle. Under this condition, the target of the access cycle can immediately assert a TRDY# signal line, but immediate assertion is not required. No bus cycle error is indicated unless a parity error occurs.

> An exception to a target not driving read data when all C/BE# signal lines are deasserted is when a cached line in a PCI memory resource is accessed. Similarly, when a cache line in a PCI memory resource is accessed and only some of the C/BE# signal lines are asserted, all read data is driven onto the bus as if all C/BE# signal lines are asserted. See *Chapter 7: Cache Support on PCI*, for details.

- During the DATA PHASE, the AD[31::0] signal lines that do not have valid data (according to the C/BE#[3::0] signal lines) must be driven to a stable level. For a non-64 data bit access, the AD[63::32] and C/BE#[7::4] signal lines are driven to a logical "1" by pull-up resistors.

> The requirements for valid parity generation and checking over the AD[31::0] lines apply even when no data is accessed (i.e., C/BE#[3::0] are deasserted).

- The C/BE#[3::0] signal lines for a given microaccess of a BURST bus cycle can enable different bytes relative to previous and subsequent microaccesses. The byte lanes do not have to be continuous. This applies to byte lanes identified within a specific bus cycle or byte lanes identified from one bus cycle to another.

- When byte lanes (AD[31::0] signal lines) are not driven with valid data per the assertion of the associated C/BE#[3::0] signal lines, they must be driven to a stable level throughout the bus cycle by the PCI bus master. When byte lanes (AD[63::32] signal lines) are not driven with valid data per the assertion of the C/BE#[7::4] signal lines, they do not have to be driven to a stable level throughout the bus cycle by the PCI bus master because pull-up resistors will drive them to a logical "1".

> The 32 data bits reflect a block of data addressed. It does not mean that an actual 32 data bits are accessed.

PARK

The PCI bus defines a protocol that is not found in many other buses, such as ISA. Although most buses allow signal lines to float when no bus cycles are executed, the PCI bus specification defines a protocol that prevents the floating of signal lines by "parking" the signal line at a PCI resource. When the PCI bus master (REQ# and GNT# signal lines are both asserted) is between cycles, the bus is IDLE (FRAME# and IRDY# signal lines both deasserted). The AD[31::0], C/BE#[3::0], FRAME#, IRDY#, and PAR signal lines are driven to stable levels by the PCI bus master. The LOCK# signal line is asserted by the Lock master or driven to a logical "1" by a pull-up resistor. The other signal lines are driven by other resources, or are driven to logical "1" by pull-up resistors or to stable levels by the central resource. When the REQ# and GNT# signal lines of a PCI resource are both deasserted (by definition it is not a PCI bus master or Park master), it must not drive any signal lines (except for the LOCK# signal line and, if appropriate, the SERR# signal line). The central arbiter must assert the GNT# signal line of a PCI resource to request that it become Park master and drive the AD[31::0], C/BE#[3::0], and PAR signal lines to a stable level. The other signal lines are driven by other resources, or are driven to logical "1" by pull-up resistors or to stable levels by the central resource. By definition, a PCI bus resource with its associated REQ# signal line deasserted and GNT# signal line asserted is a Park master. See *Chapter 9: Bus Ownership*, for details.

> The Park master may be any platform resource selected by the central arbiter. If all GNT# signal lines are deasserted, the central arbiter or possibly the central resource becomes the Park master.

> When a 32 data bit PCI bus master becomes a Park master it drives the AD[31::0], C/BE#[3::0], and PAR signal lines to a stable level. The AD[63::32], C/BE#[7::4], and PAR64 signal lines are driven to a logical "1" by pull-up resistors.

POSTING OF WRITE DATA

> The following discussion is applicable to both the interface circuitry between the PCI bus and internal chip circuitry of a PCI resource and the BRIDGE between two PCI buses. The interface circuitry is in many ways a simple bridge. Similarly, the protocol of a PCI to PCI BRIDGE is a complicated interface between buses. In order to convey key concepts the following terms will be used: Primary bus, Secondary bus, and "bridge". As this discussion is applied to a PCI resource (chip) the Primary bus is the PCI bus, the Secondary bus is the internal circuitry, and the "bridge" is the interface circuitry. As this discussion is applied to a PCI to PCI BRIDGE on a platform, the Primary bus is a PCI bus on one side of the BRIDGE, the Secondary bus is another PCI bus on the other side of the BRIDGE, the "bridge" is the PCI to PCI BRIDGE. When the discussion is applied to a PCI to PCI BRIDGE, it must be remembered that there are other protocol and architectural issues not discussed here.

> In the following discussion, only access cycles beginning on the Primary bus and porting to the Secondary bus are under consideration. See the subsequent "ORDERING" section for the relationship of access cycles flowing both ways simultaneously.

Posting is defined as placing memory write data into a "bridge" buffer and completing the access cycle on the Primary bus before the access cycle is completed on the Secondary bus. Consequently, a write access cycle executed in the memory address space can be completed on the Primary bus before the associated access cycle is completed on the Secondary bus The order of data writes on the Secondary bus must maintain the data order written from the Primary bus. Posting can only occur for both memory write and memory write and invalidate access cycles.

Data associated with I/O and configuration write access cycles cannot be posted in the "bridge" buffer. These cycles begin on the Primary bus and cannot be completed on the Primary bus until the associated cycle is completed on the Secondary bus. If any write memory data is posted in the "bridge", the "bridge" must terminate all of the I/O and configuration write access cycles with Retry termination until all the posted data in the "bridge" is written to the Secondary bus. Also, special cycles cannot be posted because they complete on the bus they originate on and are not ported through the "bridge". The special cycles are only addressing internal registers in the "bridge".

If a memory read, MRM, MRL, configuration read, or I/O read access cycle occurs on the Primary bus to a resource on the Secondary bus, the read access cycle cannot be executed on the Secondary bus until all the posted memory write data is written to the Secondary bus. Read access cycles are completed with Retry termination on the Primary bus until no posted write data remains in the "bridge".

Bus cycles originating on the Secondary bus are ported to the Primary bus without any consideration of the posted data porting from the Primary bus to the Secondary bus or the Primary bus cycles that have been completed with Retry termination.

"16 CLOCK" RULE

The "16 clock" rule is discussed in detail in Subchapter 8.2. Simply stated, the rule requires that a target execute a Retry termination when the data cannot be accessed (STOP# and TRDY# signal lines asserted and deasserted, respectively) within sixteen CLK signal line periods from the assertion of the FRAME# signal line. The "16 clock" rule must be executed by the target or BRIDGE (as target) for all bus cycles.

The "16 clock" rule is not executed for a configuration access cycle during initialization or when expansion ROM is copied to memory. The "16 clock" rule does not apply to special cycles.

"8 CLOCK RULE"

The "8 clock" rule is discussed in detail in Subchapter 14.0. Simply stated, the rule requires that a target execute a Disconnect termination when the data cannot be accessed (STOP# signal line asserted) within eight CLK signal line periods from the simultaneous assertion of the IRDY# and TRDY# signal lines during the subsequent microaccesses of BURST cycles. The "8 clock" rule must be executed by the target or BRIDGE (as target) for all bus cycles except for special cycles.

> The "8 clock" rule cannot be executed for special bus cycles.

IMMEDIATE AND DELAYED TRANSACTIONS

> The following discussion is applicable to both the interface circuitry between the PCI bus and internal chip circuitry of a PCI resource and the BRIDGE between two PCI buses. The interface circuitry is in many ways a simple bridge. Similarly, the protocol of a PCI to PCI BRIDGE is a complicated interface between buses. In order to convey key concepts the following terms will be used: Primary bus, Secondary bus, and "bridge". As this discussion is applied to a PCI resource (chip) the Primary bus is the PCI bus, the Secondary bus is the internal circuitry, and the "bridge" is the interface circuitry. As this discussion is applied to a PCI to PCI BRIDGE on a platform, the Primary bus is a PCI bus on one side of the BRIDGE, the Secondary bus is another PCI bus on the other side of the BRIDGE, the "bridge" is the PCI to PCI BRIDGE. When the discussion is applied to a PCI to PCI BRIDGE, it must be remembered that there are other protocol and architectural issues not discussed here.

> In the following discussion, only access cycles beginning on the Primary bus and porting to the Secondary bus are under consideration. See the subsequent "ORDERING" section for the relationship of access cycles flowing both ways simultaneously.

When a PCI bus cycle is executed on the Primary bus, the "bridge" can either post memory write data in a "bridge" buffer or port memory read access cycles, I/O access cycles, etc. immediately to the Secondary bus. When the "bridge" is interface circuitry in a PCI chip, it is possible to port a memory write bus cycle without posting. The bus cycle on the Primary bus is not completed until the posting is completed or the Secondary bus cycle has completed. This protocol is defined as Immediate Transaction. When a PCI bus cycle is executed, the "bridge" may not be able to immediately complete the Primary bus cycle with accessed data. In order to minimize bus latency and maximize bus bandwidth, the "bridge" must terminate the bus cycle until the data is prepared to be accessed at a later time. The protocol to access the data at a later time is defined as Delayed

Transaction. The Delayed Transaction protocol is divided into two components: Delayed Request and Delayed Completion. The Delayed Transaction is completed with the execution of the Delayed Completion component. Delayed Transaction can be applied to all bus cycles except for the special bus cycle. See Subchapter 3.1 for more information.

As outlined above, the Delayed Transaction can be applied to a memory write or memory write and invalidate, but it is more appropriate to post memory write data in the "bridge". The Delayed Transaction can also be applied to single DATA PHASE read memory, I/O read and write, and configuration read and write access cycles, as well as single DATA PHASE interrupt acknowledge cycles. Finally, Delayed Transaction can also be applied to multiple DATA PHASE (BURST) memory read (to a prefetchable address space), MRM, and MRL access cycles.

The PCI bus master cannot distinguish a Retry termination due to a Delayed Transaction from a Retry termination for other reasons.

The Delayed Request occurs when a Primary bus cycle is completed with a Retry termination. The Retry termination may result from the "16 clock" rule or when the "bridge" knows that the data cannot be accessed within a reasonable amount of time. The Delayed Request protocol includes "latching" of cycle information (command type, byte enables, REQ64#, etc.). Once the "bridge" has determined to invoke a Delayed Transaction, it must "latch" the bus cycle information and execute a Retry termination (if possible, without waiting for time associated with the "16 clock" rule). For a read bus cycle, the "bridge" does not have to wait until the IRDY# signal line to request a Retry termination For a write bus cycle, the "bridge" must wait for the IRDY# signal line to be asserted before requesting Retry termination. The "bridge" will continue to execute the Primary bus cycle on the Secondary bus.

When a Primary bus cycle has completed with a Retry termination, the PCI bus master must repeat the "exact same" bus cycle. The Delayed Completion component of Delayed Transaction occurs when the "bridge" is ready to complete the Delayed Transaction by completing the repeated "exact same" Primary bus cycle with the same completion of the associated cycle on the Secondary bus (Disconnect, Completion, Completion with Timeout, Target Abort, or Master Abort termination). If the "bridge" is not ready to complete the "exact same" Primary bus cycle, then it will execute a Retry termination (without relatching bus cycle information) and the PCI bus master will repeat the "exact same" bus cycle. Once Delayed Completion has occurred the PCI bus master does not repeat the "exact same" bus cycle.

The PCI bus master may execute other Primary bus cycles to the "bridge" and other PCI resources between repeating the "exact same" bus cycle. Also, other PCI bus masters may execute Primary bus cycles to the "bridge" and other PCI resources between repeats of the "exact same" bus cycle. The completion of these "other" Primary bus cycles is not required prior to the completion of the repeated "exact same" bus cycle.

> The "exact same" bus cycle means that command type, byte enables, REQ64#, etc., are the same.

When a "bridge" is participating in a Delayed Transaction, there is a unique side effect to be considered. It is possible that when the PCI bus master (labeled "A") is repeating the aforementioned "exact same" Primary bus cycle another PCI bus master (Labeled "B") may coincidentally execute the "exact same" Primary bus cycle and the "bridge" may coincidentally be ready to complete the Delay Transaction at this time. Under this condition, the "bridge" believes that the Delayed Completion has occurred and PCI bus master (B) has completed its bus cycle. PCI bus master (A) still believes that a Delayed Transaction is pending and will continue to repeat the "exact same" Primary bus cycle. On the first repeat after PCI bus master (B) completing its bus cycle, the "bridge" will either be ready to complete the bus cycle (i.e., completing the Delayed Transaction of PCI bus master (A)) or will execute a Retry termination. The execution of Retry termination will continue the Delayed Transaction protocol for PCI bus master (A) and re-establish the Delayed Transaction for the "bridge".

> The above discussion focuses on a BRIDGE between PCI buses. The concepts outlined above also apply to the interface between the PCI bus and circuitry internal to the PCI resource.

SUMMARY OF "16 CLOCK" RULE, "8 CLOCK" RULE, AND DELAYED TRANSACTION

In summary, the "16 clock" rule APPLIES to the SINGLE bus cycles and initial microaccess of BURST bus cycles of the following:

- Memory access cycles
- All I/O access cycles
- Configuration access cycles during run time (i.e., when not during initialization or when expansion ROM is copied to memory)
- Interrupt acknowledge cycles

In summary, the "8 clock" rule APPLIES to subsequent microaccesses of BURST bus cycles of the following:

- Memory access cycles
- All I/O access cycles
- Configuration access cycles
- Interrupt acknowledge cycles

In summary, the Delayed Transaction APPLIES to the SINGLE bus cycles of the following:

- Memory access cycles
- I/O access cycles
- Configuration access cycles
- Interrupt acknowledge cycles

In summary, the Delayed Transaction APPLIES to the BURST bus cycles of the following:

- Only for MRL access cycles, MRM access cycles, and memory read (if the memory target is within a prefetchable address range).

ORDERING

The following discussion is applicable to both the interface circuitry between the PCI bus and internal chip circuitry of a PCI resource and the BRIDGE between two PCI buses. The interface circuitry is in many ways a simple bridge. Similarly, the protocol of a PCI to PCI BRIDGE is a complicated interface between buses. In order to convey key concepts the following terms will be used: Primary bus, Secondary bus, and "bridge". As this discussion is applied to a PCI resource (chip) the Primary bus is the PCI bus, the Secondary bus is the internal circuitry, and the "bridge" is the interface circuitry. As this discussion is applied to a PCI to PCI BRIDGE on a platform, the Primary bus is a PCI bus on one side of the BRIDGE, the Secondary bus is another PCI bus on the other side of the BRIDGE, the "bridge" is the PCI to PCI BRIDGE. When the discussion is applied to a PCI to PCI BRIDGE, it must be remembered that there are other protocol and architectural issues not discussed here.

When a "bridge" has posted write data or is executing a Delayed Transaction, a "new" Primary bus memory write data cycle can be completed with Retry termination (with or without Delayed transaction) or the associated data can be posted and the cycle completed on the Primary bus. Similarly, a "new" Primary bus cycle (read or non-memory writes) must be completed with a Retry termination and the "bridge" may or may not apply Delayed Transaction. If Delayed Transaction or data posting is not applied to the "new" Primary bus cycle (read or non-memory writes), the Retry termination simply means that the PCI bus master must repeat the "exact same" Primary bus cycle. There are no Secondary bus cycles being executed associated with the Primary bus cycles. If Delayed Transaction or data posting is applied to the "new" Primary bus cycle, the order of the Secondary bus cycles (associated to these Primary bus cycles) to be executed by the "bridge" must adhere to the following rules:

> The following discussion assumes that the "bridge" allows bus cycles to flow from the Primary bus to the Secondary bus through one path and from the Secondary bus to the Primary bus through another path simultaneously. The bus cycle flow through these two paths are independent. All protocols applicable to bus cycles from the Primary bus to the Secondary bus also apply to bus cycles from the Secondary bus to the Primary bus.

- Memory write data posted in the "bridge" data buffer must be written to the Secondary bus in the EXACT ORDER received from the Primary bus. If a write cycle on the Secondary bus is completed with Retry or Disconnect without data termination, the associated data retained in the buffer and bus cycles for other data in the buffer cannot be executed on the Secondary bus. Data in the buffer is not removed until successfully written (Disconnect with data, Completion, Completion with Timeout) to the target on the Secondary bus or the associated destination bus cycles complete with Master Abort or Target Abort. If the Secondary bus is reset, the "bridge" data buffer by definition is empty when the bus begins bus cycles. Similarly, if the Primary bus is reset, by definition the Secondary bus is reset.

- Primary bus cycles completed with Delayed Request or Immediate Transaction cannot be executed on the Secondary bus until the posted data buffer (Primary to Secondary bus) in the "bridge" is empty.

- It is possible for the "bridge" to place the Delayed Requests from the Primary bus in a bus cycle buffer. The Delayed Requests in the bus cycle buffer must be executed on the Secondary bus in the same order executed in the Primary bus. For example, Primary bus cycles ordered A, B, and C are executed on the Secondary bus in the same order. There is no requirement that once a Secondary bus cycle has attempted the Delayed Transaction in the order received from the Primary bus that the associated bus cycles will complete in the same order. Consequently, completion of the Delayed Requests on the Secondary bus may be in any order. For example, once the order of A, B, and C is attempted, the actual completion may be B, C, A.

■ A Delayed Request executed on the Secondary bus must remain in the "bridge" bus cycle buffer until successful completion (Completion, Completion without Timeout), Master Abort, or Target Abort is executed. If the secondary bus is reset, the "bridge" bus cycle buffer by definition is empty when the bus begins bus cycles. Similarly, if the Primary bus is reset, by definition the Secondary bus is reset.

■ Delayed Completions resulting from completed Secondary bus cycles can be placed in a "bridge" completion buffer waiting for the repeat of the associated Primary bus that completed with Retry termination. The order of Delayed Completion in the completion buffer must be maintained. A repeated Primary bus cycle must be completed with a Retry termination if its associated Delayed Completion is not the highest order in the completion buffer. The flow of Delayed Completions back to the Primary bus is not affected by the existence of posted data or bus cycles in the "bridge" for bus cycles from Primary bus to Secondary bus.

■ When a memory write access cycle on the Primary bus (writing to a resource on the Secondary bus) is completed with an Immediate Transaction, the posted data or immediate execution of the bus cycle on the Secondary bus has priority (not required) over any Delayed Requests (bus cycle buffer) or Delayed Completions (completion buffer). It does not have priority over posted write data from the Primary to the Secondary bus.

■ When an interrupt acknowledge bus cycle on the Primary bus (reading from a resource on the Secondary bus) is completed with an Immediate Transaction, the immediate execution of the bus cycle on the Secondary bus has priority (not required) over any Delayed Requests (bus cycle buffer) or Delayed Completions (completion buffer). It does not have priority over posted write data from the Primary to the Secondary bus.

> The above protocols do not apply to special cycles. Special cycles do not port through "bridges"; when one is executed on the Primary bus it is only writing data to targets specific to the immediate PCI bus (Primary bus).

SIGNAL LINE DRIVERS DURING BUS CYCLES WITH 32 DATA BIT RESOURCES

During memory and I/O access cycles, the interrupt acknowledge cycle, and the special cycle, the signal lines are owned by different PCI bus resources. A PCI resource owns the signal line when it is the only resource (other than pull-up resistors) that can drive the signal line during a portion of the cycle. The protocol is as follows:

- FRAME#, IRDY#, and C/BE#[3::0], and REQ# signal lines are owned by the PCI bus master.

- During a write access or special cycle, the PCI bus master owns the AD[31::0] and PAR signal lines.

- During a read access or interrupt acknowledge cycle, the PCI bus master owns the AD[31::0] and PAR signal lines during the ADDRESS PHASE. The target owns these signal lines during the DATA PHASE.

- During an access or interrupt acknowledge cycle, the TRDY#, DEVSEL#, and STOP# signal lines are owned by the target. During a special cycle, these signal lines are not owned by the target because no target is addressed. They are driven to logical "1" by pull-up resistors.

During a configuration access cycle, the ownership of the signal lines is defined as above. The only difference is that the IDSEL signal lines are defined.

The remaining signal lines are owned according to the following protocol:

- The CLK and RST# signal lines are owned by platform resources.

- The GNT# signal lines are owned by the central arbiter.

- The LOCK# signal line is owned by the Lock master.

- The SDONE and SBO# signal lines are owned by the cache controller in the HOST/PCI BRIDGE, or other platform resources if the platform does not have a cache controller.

4.1 MEMORY AND I/O ACCESS CYCLES

> This is a brief introduction. See Subchapter 4.5: *32 Data Bit PCI Bus Master to 32 Data Bit Target* for more detail.

As outlined in Subchapter 4.0, only memory write access cycles (including memory write and invalidate) can be posted and all I/O access cycles cannot be posted. Also, Delayed Transaction can be applied to memory and I/O access cycles. Only some of the memory read access cycles can have a BURST cycle with Delayed Transaction. All I/O access cycles can only use a SINGLE cycle with Delayed Transaction. The "16 clock" rule applies to all memory and I/O access cycles. See Subchapter 4.0 for more information.

ADDRESS DECODING FOR A MEMORY OR I/O ACCESS CYCLE

The address decoding protocol for access cycles is more extensive than other buses. Most bus protocols allow a bus master to begin an access cycle and assume that a bus resource will respond to the address. A PCI bus resource can claim the access cycle and become the target by asserting the DEVSEL# signal line. In that the address must be checked by all potential targets, the decoding protocol is defined as distributed.

It is not required that all targets decode the AD[31::02] signal lines (and AD[63::32] signal lines under the 64 bit extension) and claim the access cycle in the same number of CLK signal line periods. As shown in Figure 4-1, the fastest possible decode will respond one CLK signal line period after the FRAME# signal line is first sampled asserted (identifies valid address on the AD signal lines). The sampling point of the DEVSEL# signal line for a "FAST" decode is one CLK signal line period after the FRAME# signal line is sampled asserted. There are two additional DEVSEL# signal line sample points that follow at one CLK signal line period intervals, defined as "MEDIUM" and "SLOW". These three sampling points reflect a POSITIVE DECODING protocol. If the DEVSEL# signal line is not asserted at any of the POSITIVE DECODING sample points, a single PCI resource can claim the access cycle through SUBTRACTIVE DECODING by asserting the DEVSEL# signal line after the POSITIVE DECODING sample points. An example of a PCI resource that would use SUBTRACTIVE DECODING is a bus-to-bus BRIDGE. The resources on the PCI bus that contain the PCI bus master that began the access cycle have the right of first refusal with POSITIVE DECODING. The bus "behind" the BRIDGE will have an opportunity to claim the access cycle via the BRIDGE with SUBTRACTIVE DECODING. Subtractive decoding is particularly for targets with fragmented address space. If no PCI resource claims the access cycle, a Master Abort termination is executed. See *Chapter 8: Master and Target Termination* for more information.

For the I/O address space, AD[01::00] must be decoded in addition to the aforementioned address signal lines.

When a RESERVED command is executed, no PCI resource may assert the DEVSEL# signal line for either POSITIVE or SUBTRACTIVE decoding.

The three POSITIVE DECODING sample points (FAST, MEDIUM, and SLOW) of the DEVSEL# signal line to claim the access cycle are delayed by one CLK signal line (relative to the first rising edge of the CLK signal line when FRAME# signal line is asserted) period if DUAL ADDRESS is executed. See the DUAL ADDRESS section for details.

All bus cycles (except DUAL ADDRESS) can begin with ADDRESS/DATA/STEPPING and the configuration access cycle can begin with a PRE-DRIVE PHASE which results in the FRAME# signal line being asserted later in the cycle (not during #1 CLK period as shown in Figure 4-1). Consequently, the decoding sampling points must be referenced to the first rising edge of the CLK signal line when FRAME# signal line is asserted. See *6.0 General Considerations*, for details.

Targets that support MEDIUM DECODING will indicate this information in their STATUS Register. If all of the PCI resources that are potential targets support a MEDIUM DECODE, the target that implements SUBTRACTIVE DECODING can assert the DEVSEL# signal line at the MEDIUM DECODING sample point. Consequently, the targets implementing "early" SUBTRACTIVE DECODING by asserting the DEVSEL# signal line at the MEDIUM DECODING sample point must "wait" (non-support of MEDIUM DECODING) until the SLOW DECODING sample point when the TARGET Back-to-Back bus cycle protocol is implemented.

Similarly, as previously mentioned, the execution of DUAL ADDRESS will "automatically" delay the POSITIVE DECODING sample points by one CLK signal line period. The aforementioned "non-support" of the MEDIUM DECODING for SUBTRACTIVE DECODING does not apply when the TARGET Back-to-Back protocol is executed with a DUAL ADDRESS. In other words, when a DUAL ADDRESS is executed with TARGET Back-to-Back protocol, a target implementing SUBTRACTIVE DECODING can assert the DEVSEL# signal line at the MEDIUM DECODING sample point when it and all other targets support FAST DECODING as indicated in their STATUS Registers.

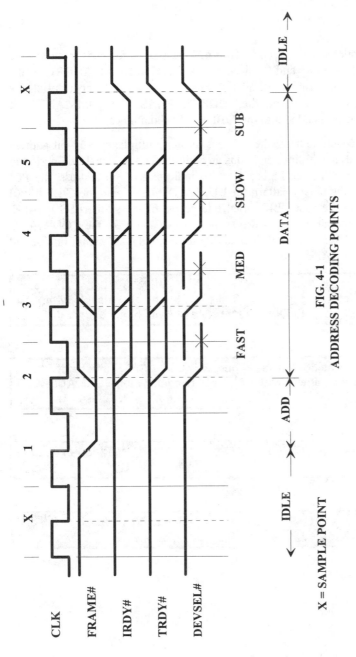

FIG. 4-1
ADDRESS DECODING POINTS

X = SAMPLE POINT

Figure 4-1: ADDRESS Decoding Points

97

DUAL ADDRESS

The PCI bus supports both 32 and 64-bit address spaces for both memory and I/O addresses. For memory and I/O access cycles without DUAL ADDRESS, the AD[31::0] signal lines contain 32 address bits (30 bits for memory) during the ADDRESS PHASE. Also, during the ADDRESS PHASE the COMMAND type of the access cycle is encoded into the C/BE#[3::0] signal lines.

To support a 64-bit address, the PCI bus master multiplexes a 64-bit address onto the AD[31::0] signal lines and adds an additional CLK signal line period to the ADDRESS PHASE (see Figure 4-2). To indicate a 64-bit address, the PCI bus master drives the binary pattern for DUAL ADDRESS onto the C/BE#[3::0] signal lines during the first CLK signal line period of the ADDRESS PHASE. The PCI bus master subsequently drives the binary pattern for the COMMAND type onto the C/BE#[3::0] signal lines during the second CLK signal line period of the ADDRESS PHASE.

> A PCI bus master that supports a 64-bit address space and only addresses the lower 4 gigabytes must execute an access cycle without a DUAL ADDRESS. By definition upper order address bits are logical "0".

> A PCI resource that does not support DUAL ADDRESS must not assert the DEVSEL# signal line to claim the access cycle when DUAL ADDRESS is executed.

> PCI bus masters cannot use ADDRESS/DATA STEPPING when executing a DUAL ADDRESS.

> DUAL ADDRESS is not defined for configuration address space or special and interrupt acknowledge cycles.

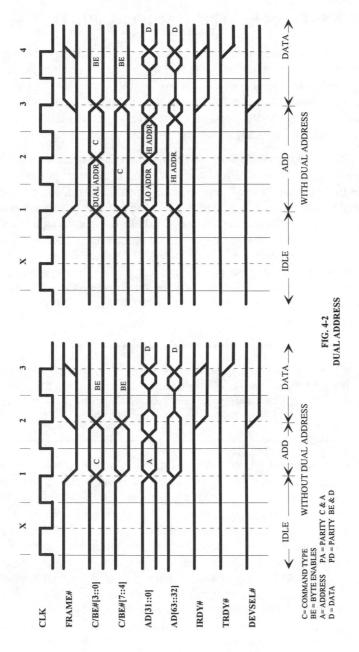

Figure 4-2: DUAL ADDRESS

ADDRESS/DATA STEPPING AND PRE-DRIVE

The majority of figures in this book assume that the CLK signal line periods are numbered (#) 1 to N with the FRAME# signal line asserted during CLK signal line period #1. There are two protocols in which the FRAME# signal line will not be asserted during CLK signal line period #1: ADDRESS/DATA STEPPING and PRE-DRIVE. Under these protocols the FRAME# signal line is not asserted during the #1 CLK signal line period.

ADDRESS/DATA STEPPING (A/D) allows the PCI bus master to drive some of the signal lines (AD, PAR, PAR64, and IDSEL) at different points within the bus cycle to lower the cost of implementing the PCI bus. Consider the three examples outlined in Figure 4-3. Without A/D the AD signal lines are all driven at the same point at the beginning of the cycle. This requires strong drivers for an integrated circuit and extra ground pins. These requirements may affect die size and package size, and therefore the cost. The A/D protocol allows the AD signal lines to be driven at different points; i.e., staggered. These signal lines can implement the A/D protocol because they are qualified by the FRAME# signal line during the ADDRESS PHASE, and the IRDY# and TRDY# signal lines during the DATA PHASE.

> Though not graphically shown in this section, the PAR and PAR64 signal lines follow the timing and qualification protocol of the AD signal lines, except delayed by a one CLK signal line period. Thus, the PAR and PAR64 signal lines can also implement the A/D protocol. Similarly, the IDSEL signal lines follow the timing and qualification of the AD signal lines and can implement the A/D protocol.

The first example in Figure 4-3 outlines the beginning of a bus cycle without the use of A/D. All of the AD signal lines (along with other signal lines) are simultaneously driven and the FRAME# signal line asserted during the #1 CLK signal line period. In the second example, the AD signal lines are driven at different times. Subgroups of the AD signal lines can be driven at different times. In this example, the AD[15::0] and AD[31::16] signal lines are driven to stable levels, and subsequently with valid address information at different times. The assertion of the FRAME# signal line is delayed until the #3 CLK signal line period to allow the AD signal lines to contain valid address information. During the DATA PHASE, the driving of write data onto the AD signal lines can also be performed at different times by delaying the assertion of the IRDY# signal line. Though not shown, read data can also be driven at different times by the target by delaying the assertion of the TRDY# signal line.

There are several important points about A/D to be considered:

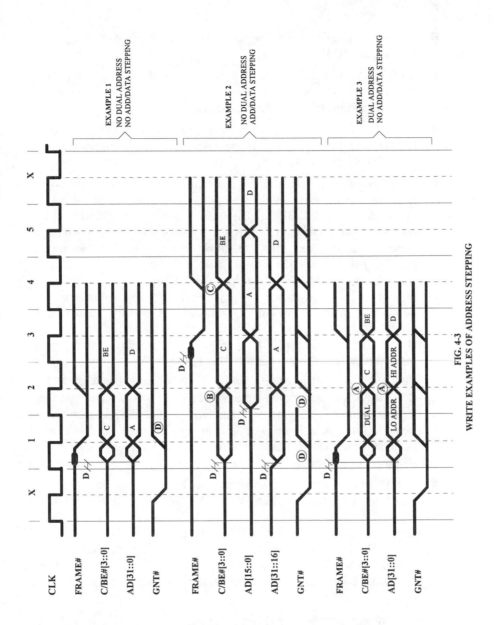

Figure 4-3: Write Examples of ADDRESS/DATA STEPPING

- The signal lines that can use the A/D protocol are AD[63::0], PAR, PAR64, and IDSEL.

- In addition to reducing the number of signal lines simultaneously driven, the A/D protocol also allows the signal line drivers to be smaller and thus take more time to reach a stable level.

- A/D requires that the decoding sampling points (FAST, MEDIUM, SLOW, and SUBTRACTIVE) are referenced to the assertion of the FRAME# signal line.

- When the FRAME# signal line is asserted later in the cycle, other signal lines can also be driven at different points. In Example 2 of Figure 4-3, the FRAME# and C/BE# signal lines are driven at different points relative to the assertion of the FRAME# signal line. The range to drive these or similar signal lines are shown in the example. Even though these signal lines can be driven later in the cycle with the delayed assertion of the FRAME# signal line, there is still a requirement that the drivers are powerful enough to meet the driving requirements at other points later in the cycle. For example, the C/BE# signal lines can be driven later in the cycle at Point B (Circle B in Figure 4-3), but the change from COMMAND type to byte enables must occur instantaneously at Point C (Circle C) in Figure 4-3.

- The A/D protocol cannot be used by the PCI bus master when DUAL ADDRESS is executed. Example 3 in Figure 4-3 outlines the problem with applying the A/D protocol when DUAL ADDRESS is executed. At Point A (Circle A in Figure 4-3) ALL of the AD[31::0] signal lines must simultaneously change between low address to high address, thus requiring a powerful driver.

- The PCI bus master that implements A/D risks losing bus ownership while delaying the assertion of the FRAME# signal line after the associated GNT# signal line is asserted. In Example 1 in Figure 4-3, the deassertion of the associated GNT# signal line at Point D (Circle D) still allows the PCI bus master to begin the bus cycle. In Example 2 in Figure 4-3, the deassertion of the associated GNT# signal line at Points D (Circle D) forces the PCI bus master not to begin the cycle and relinquish the bus.

Another consideration is the pre-drive protocol, which applies to only the configuration access cycle. As with the A/D protocol, the FRAME# signal line is not asserted until a later point in the cycle. The difference is the delay in asserting the FRAME# signal lines that is needed to allow the IDSEL signal lines to reach a stable level. See *Chapter 6: Detailed Bus Cycle Operation*, for details.

Unless otherwise indicated, the figures in this book assume ADDRESS/DATA STEPPING and PRE-DRIVE (for the configuration access cycle) are not implemented; consequently, the FRAME# signal line is asserted during the #1 CLK signal line period.

COMBINING

For the following discussion the "individual write access cycles" are executed on the source bus and the "single BURST write access cycle" is executed on the destination bus.

Any HOST/PCI and PCI/PCI BRIDGE can combine individual SINGLE and BURST write access cycles (individual write access cycles) to the PCI memory address space into a single BURST write access cycle. The addressing order of the single BURST write access cycle must be linearly increasing and equal to the addressing order of the individual write access cycles. The value of the C/BE# signal lines of the microaccesses of the single BURST write access cycle must match the value of the C/BE# signal lines during the DATA PHASE for the DWORDS or QWORDS of the individual write access cycles. For example, the individual write access cycles that address DWORDS 0, 1, 2, and 3 (in this order) can be combined into a single BURST write access cycle that maintains this order in the microaccesses. Similarly, if the individual write access cycles that address DWORDS 0, 1, and 3 (in this order) can be combined into a single BURST write access cycle with following microaccesses: initial microaccess is DWORD 0, the first subsequent microaccess is DWORD 1, the second subsequent microaccess has all of the associated C/BE#[3::0] signal lines deasserted, and the third subsequent microaccess is DWORD 3. If the individual write access cycles address DWORDS 3, 0, 1 (in this order), combining is not allowed (if allowed, the resultant single BURST write access cycle cannot maintain the exact addressing order with linear addressing). Finally, individual write access cycles with all C/BE# signal lines deasserted during the DATA PHASE must be ported to the destination bus, either combined or individually.

An individual BURST write access cycle or a series of individual SINGLE write access cycles that execute a cache wrap or other non-linear address sequence cannot be combined. The combining of individual write access with non-linear addressing versus a linear addressing would require the BRIDGE to have extensive information on all memory targets.

The data size of the individual write access cycles and the single BURST write access cycle must be the same to be combined. The REQ64# signal line must be deasserted for all the individual write access cycles of DWORDS and the single BURST write access cycle of DWORDS. Similarly, the REQ64# signal line must be asserted for all the individual write access cycles of QWORDS and the single BURST write access cycle of QWORDS.

The PCI protocol allows any HOST/PCI or PCI/PCI BRIDGE to combine individual write access cycles according to the protocol outlined above. A PCI memory resource that cannot support the addressing order of the resultant single BURST write access cycle simply executes a Disconnect termination to force the BRIDGE to port the individual write access cycles in the original sequence of individual SINGLE and BURST write access cycles. A PCI memory resource is not optimally designed if it must execute a Disconnect termination of ANY single BURST write access cycle.

Combining is recommended when write posting.

Merging and combining are recommended when write posting.

Memory read access, I/O access, configuration access cycles, and interrupt acknowledge cycles cannot be combined. Memory mapped I/O access cycles can be combined. Also, combining cannot be applied to special cycles because the PCI/PCI BRIDGE can only port a request for a special cycle from PCI bus to PCI bus with a Type 1 configuration access cycle.

Any PCI resource with the Prefetchable Bit in its Base Address Register set must support combining.

COLLAPSING

For the following discussion, the "individual write access cycles" are executed on the source bus and the "single BURST write access cycle" is executed on the destination bus.

HOST/PCI and PCI/PCI BRIDGEs cannot collapse data. Consider individual write access cycles (on the source bus) where the bytes, WORDS, DWORD, or QWORDS of data are placed in the BRIDGE's buffer and prior to writing the buffer to the destination bus "new" data within the address range of the buffer arrives from the source bus. Collapsing occurs when the "new" data over-writes the data in the buffer and then the buffer is written to the destination bus.

Memory read access, I/O access, configuration access cycles, and interrupt acknowledge cycles cannot be collapsed. Memory mapped I/O access cycles cannot be collapsed. Also, collapsing cannot be applied to special cycles because the PCI/PCI BRIDGE can only port a request for a special cycle from PCI bus to PCI bus with a Type 1 configuration access cycle.

PREFETCHING

For the following discussion, the "individual write access cycles" are executed on the source bus and the "single BURST write access cycle" is executed on the destination bus.

When the PCI bus master is executing a memory read multiple (MRM) or memory read line (MRL) access cycle, the PCI memory resource (memory target) can operate with a prefetching protocol. Also, memory targets (not I/O) can operate with a prefetching protocol when the Prefetchable Bit is set in its Base Address Register. A read access cycle of a memory target operating with prefetching protocol results in all of the bytes returned independent of the value of the C/BE# signal lines; for a 32 data bit access this is four bytes (ACK64# signal line deasserted). For a 64 data bit access this is eight bytes (ACK64# signal line asserted). Prefetching is only allowed when all of the following conditions are met:

- The target is a memory resource with the Prefetchable Bit set in its Base Address Register and a Range Register, or MRM or MRL access cycle, is being executed.

- A read access cycle is executed.

- The returning of all bytes does not have any negative side effects.

When read access cycles to the PCI memory address space ports through HOST/PCI or PCI/PCI BRIDGEs, prefetching by the BRIDGE is allowed if all of the above conditions (bullets) are met.

MERGING

For the following discussion, the "individual write access cycles" are executed on the source bus and the "single BURST write access cycle" is executed on the destination bus.

A HOST/PCI or PCI/PCI BRIDGE porting multiple individual SINGLE or BURST write access cycles addressing memory targets with the Prefetchable Bit set can merge these bus cycles. Byte merging is defined as an optional function of a BRIDGE by which memory data bytes, WORDS, multiple bytes (3, 5, 6, and 7 bytes), or DWORDS written in ANY order by multiple individual write access cycles can be merged into a SINGLE write access cycle of DWORD or QWORD by a BRIDGE. The following conditions are required for data to be merged:

- The target is a memory resource with the Prefetchable Bit set in its Base Address Register. When this bet is set the target must support byte merging.

- The entire address range of the merged SINGLE write access cycle does not have to be written to by the multiple individual write access cycles. For example, if the sequence of the multiple individual write access cycles addresses bytes 3, 1, 0, and 2 with the associated C/BE# signal lines asserted, the BRIDGE can merge this into a single DWORD write access cycle. The BRIDGE will not merge this into two WORD write access cycles. Consider another example: the sequence of the multiple individual write access cycles addresses bytes 3, 1, and 2 with the C/BE# signal lines associated with bytes 3 and 2 asserted, and the C/BE# signal line associated with byte 1 deasserted. The BRIDGE will execute a single DWORD write access cycle with the C/BE# signal lines associated with bytes 3 and 2 asserted, and the C/BE# signal lines associated with bytes 1 and 0 deasserted. Consider another example: the sequence of the multiple individual write access cycles addresses bytes 3, 1, 1, 2, and 0 with the C/BE# signal lines associated with these bytes asserted and the other C/BE# signal lines deasserted. The BRIDGE will first execute two single byte write access cycles. The first access cycle will write byte 3 of the original sequence with the C/BE# signal line associated with byte 3 asserted and the other C/BE# signal lines deasserted. The second access cycle will write the first byte 1 of the original sequence with the C/BE# associated with byte 1 asserted and the other C/BE# signal lines deasserted. The BRIDGE will then execute a single DWORD write access cycle with the C/BE# signal lines associated with bytes 1, 2, and 0 asserted and the C/BE# signal line associated with byte 3 deasserted. As final example, consider the sequence of the multiple individual write access cycles addressed bytes 3, 1, and 2 with the associated C/BE# signal lines deasserted and the REQ64# signal line deasserted. The BRIDGE will execute a single DWORD write access cycle with all the C/BE# signal lines deasserted and the REQ64# signal line deasserted.

- The merged data cannot include collapsed data. See the discussion of collapsed data in the previous section.

The concept of merging can be extended from bytes to cache lines. When a series of bytes, WORDS, multiple bytes, DWORDS, or QWORDS write access cycles are executed in any order, they can be merged into a write of a single cache line provided three conditions are met:

1.   Any of the bytes, WORDS, multiple bytes, DWORDS, or QWORDS are written only once.

2.   The associated memory address space is cacheable.

3.   The BRIDGE doing cache merging contains the cache controller (HOST/PCI BRIDGE) or has explicit knowledge of the cacheable memory address range.

Merging is recommended when write posting.

Merging and combining are recommended when write posting.

Inside of a BRIDGE, combining improves platform performance more than merging. However, if the BRIDGE is merging mis-aligned bytes into a SINGLE memory write, merging can reduce destination bus cycles by a factor of two. There is no real performance improvement for merging data within a single cache line.

Memory read access, I/O access, configuration access cycles, and interrupt acknowledge cycles cannot be merged. Memory mapped I/O access cycles cannot be merged. Also, merging cannot be applied to special cycles because the PCI/PCI BRIDGE can only port a request for a special cycle from PCI bus to PCI bus with a Type 1 configuration access cycle.

LOCK

The PCI architecture supports locking of memory targets (not I/O) on the PCI bus. During any access cycle to a memory target, the resource is locked for the duration of the cycle. Other PCI bus masters cannot access the target because they do not own the bus. Also, non-PCI bus resources behind the target (such as a second CPU that accesses via the second port of a dual port memory) cannot access the target during a PCI access cycle. The PCI bus specification allows the target lock to extend beyond the completion of the bus cycle. The locking of a specific target after the completion of the access cycle simply means it can only be accessed by a specific PCI bus master or by a snoop write-back access cycle. See Subchapter 6.3 for further information on locking a multiported target.

> **A PCI target must be "lockable" if it is platform memory which contains executable memory.**

Only a memory target can be locked, and is locked in a 16 byte block on 16 byte address boundaries. Any lock of a byte within the 16 byte block results in the lock of the entire block. For a target to become locked, the PCI bus master must successfully execute a read access cycle.

> **The PCI bus specification requires a minimum of 16 bytes (aligned on 16 byte address multiples) to be locked at a time. The target can optionally lock a larger portion up to a maximum of its entire address space. The 16 byte block or continuous multiple block portion of the target (HDRAM or PDRAM) that is locked is the only portion of the target that follows the lock protocol when accessed by the Lock master, by the HOST CPU accessing HDRAM, or the other processors via dual port memory (HDRAM or PDRAM). Accesses by other PCI bus masters (not Lock master), by HOST CPU accessing HDRAM, or other processors via dual port memory (HDRAM or PDRAM) to non-locked portions of the target MAY be affected by the lock protocol if the target had locked more than the portion required.**

The Lock Function (LF) is defined as a target that remains locked between access cycles coupled with a PCI bus master which controls the LOCK# signal line. Only one PCI bus master at a time can own the Lock Function, and is known as the Lock master. the Lock master allows other PCI bus masters to own the bus and execute access cycles to targets that have not been locked.

There are two types of LF that can be owned by the Lock master: PCI RESOURCE LOCK (PRL) and COMPLETE BUS LOCK (CBL). The PRL means that a target is locked and the central arbiter can award bus ownership to both the Lock master and the other PCI bus masters. CBL means that the central arbiter will only award bus ownership to the Lock master. CBL is the prerogative of the central arbiter and is unknown to the Lock master; consequently, the operation of the bus access cycles are unaffected by which type of LF is active.

> **PC compatible software is written without consideration of multiple PCI bus masters. CBL may be useful in maintaining compatibility.**

The LF can be owned by only one PCI bus master at a time. After RESET, the LF is not owned by any PCI bus master and none of the targets are locked. Once a PCI bus master is granted bus ownership by an asserted GNT# signal line it has the opportunity to own the LF during an access to a memory target. If the LF was owned by a previous PCI bus master, the PCI bus master must wait until the present Lock master relinquishes control of the LF.

> **If a PCI bus master plans to obtain ownership of the LF, it may not request bus ownership until the LF is not owned by another PCI bus master.**

How a PCI memory resource is attached to the PCI bus and whether it contains executable code also affects the application of the LOCK protocol. There are several situations to be considered:

The first situation is when the memory is located on the HOST bus (HOST DRAM = HDRAM). If the HDRAM contains executable code or is simply platform memory, LOCK FUNCTION (LF) must be supported by HDRAM in conjunction with the HOST/PCI BRIDGE. When the HDRAM is locked by the HOST/PCI BRIDGE, the HOST CPU, other processors on the HOST bus, and other processors that have a dual port access to the HDRAM SHOULD treat the locked HDRAM as non-accessible.

However, not all platforms can guarantee that the LF from the PCI bus will be honored by the HOST CPU or the other aforementioned processors. In platforms that have MORE than a single HOST CPU (on the HOST bus) a PCI bus master accessing the HDRAM software device drivers may have to implement the LF with software and not rely on implementation by the hardware (LOCK# signal line).

The second situation is when executable memory is attached to the PCI bus without the HOST/PCI BRIDGE. The DRAM is attached to the PCI bus (PDRAM) with the minimum amount of interface circuitry. The interface circuitry is required to support the LF for access from the PCI bus. Other processors that have access to the PDRAM via a dual port address (not via the PCI bus) MUST also respect the LF of the PCI bus as indicated by the interface circuitry and not access the PDRAM when it is a locked PCI target.

The third situation is when non-executable memory (simple PCI memory resource) is attached to the PCI bus without the HOST/PCI BRIDGE. The DRAM is attached to the PCI bus (PDRAM) with the minimum amount of interface circuitry. The interface circuitry is not required to support the LF. If the LF is not supported, access to the PDRAM from the PCI bus and other processors (via dual port) are unrestricted. If the LF is supported, the protocol outlined above for executable memory (PDRAM) applies to access from the PCI bus and other processors that have access to the PDRAM (via a dual port).

For a PCI bus master to become Lock master the target must remain locked after the completion of the access cycle. For a target to remain locked after the access cycle all of the following must occur:

- The LOCK# signal line must be deasserted at the first CLK rising edge of the ADDRESS PHASE and asserted at the subsequent CLK signal line rising edge during a read access cycle to a memory resource.

- The PCI bus master must successfully complete the entire memory read access cycle to the target. The access cycle is not successfully completed if a Master Abort, Retry, or Target Abort termination is executed.

See *Chapter 6: Detailed Bus Cycle Operation*, for details.

The Lock Function (LF) can only be owned by the Lock master; consequently, a locked target can only be accessed by the one PCI bus master that is the Lock master. If a PCI bus master that is not Lock master accesses a locked target a Retry termination will be executed. The execution of the Retry termination does not unlock the target and the PCI bus master that is the Lock master retains the LF. One condition exists when a locked target can be accessed by PCI bus master that is not the Lock master without a Retry termination being executed. A snoop write-back access cycle is allowed to access a locked target without affecting the lock status of the target and the Lock master's ownership of the Lock Function. The snoop write-back access cycle is identified by the deassertion of the SDONE and SBO# signals lines during the ADDRESS PHASE. See *Chapter 7: Cache Support on PCI*, for details.

> The Lock master can only access the locked target, and no other target.

> The snoop write-back access cycle condition also requires the central arbiter to award bus ownership to the cache resource that is executing the snoop write-back cycle during a COMPLETE BUS LOCK.

A target remains locked until the Lock master unlocks it, or an access by the Lock master results in a Target Abort or Master Abort termination. When the LOCK# and FRAME# signal lines are both deasserted, the target is unlocked and the Lock master must relinquish the LF. A Target Abort or Master Abort termination when the Lock master is accessing a locked target will force the following: the Lock master will immediately deassert the LOCK# signal line;

subsequent deassertion of the FRAME# signal line results in the Lock master relinquishing the LF and target unlocking.

If a PCI bus master that is *not* the Lock master accesses a locked target that results in a Target Abort or Master Abort termination, the target remains locked and the Lock master retains the LF. It is assumed that a subsequent access of the locked target by the Lock master will repeat the target or Master Abort termination. A Target Abort or Master Abort during the Lock master access to the locked target will force the Lock master to relinquish the Lock Function (relinquish control of the LOCK# signal line and unlock the target). This protocol prevents the Lock master from having to know the address range of the locked target and monitor the access cycles of other PCI bus masters.

4.2 CONFIGURATION ACCESS CYCLES

This is a brief introduction. See Subchapter 4.5: *32 Data Bit PCI Bus Master to 32 Data Bit Target* for details.

A configuration access cycle originates with the HOST CPU and is ported from PCI bus to PCI bus with the BRIDGEs acting as the PCI bus master for each respective bus. A PCI bus master (BRIDGE) of a specific LEVEL bus can only access the configuration space of a lower LEVEL bus—not a higher-LEVEL bus.

As outlined in Subchapter 4.0, configuration write access cycles cannot be posted. Delayed Transaction can be applied to configuration access cycles, but only as SINGLE access cycles. The "16 clock" rule only applies during run time; the "8 clock" rule applies all of the time.

Please see Subchapter 4.1 on how ADDRESS/DATA STEPPING and PRE-DRIVE operate; this protocol applies to the configuration access cycle. As outlined in Subchapter 4.1, COMBINING, COLLAPSING, PREFETCHING, and MERGING cannot be applied to configuration access cycles.

Address decoding (i.e., claiming the cycle by asserting the DEVSEL# signal lines) for configuration access cycles is the same as for memory and I/O access cycles with the following exceptions:

- 64 bit extension is not defined for the configuration access cycle — the AD[63::32] signal lines are never part of the decode.

- DUAL ADDRESS is not executed with configuration access cycles — a PCI resource does not claim the configuration access cycle if DUAL ADDRESS is executed.

- The AD[31::11] signal lines are reserved and not used for decoding.
- The AD[01::00] signal lines are used for decoding.
- The IDSEL signal line of the resource must be asserted.

The PCI bus specification supports configuration registers for each PCI resource (PCI bus master, target, or BRIDGE. defined as "device"). Even though the configuration access cycle follows the basic protocol of a memory or I/O access cycle, there are some differences.

The definition of a configuration cycle places the following unique protocol requirements on this type of bus cycle:

- Each device that is accessed by a configuration access cycle has 256 byte registers.

- Each PCI bus can have 21 individual devices with configuration registers through the use of the AD[31::11] signal lines as IDSEL signal lines.

- The configuration access cycle executes read and write access cycles with the same protocol as memory or I/O access cycles. The configuration access cycle can be executed as a SINGLE or BURST cycle.

- There are two types of configuration access cycles; Types 0 and 1. Type 0 must be claimed by a device on the same bus that the configuration access cycle is being executed. Type 1 can only be claimed by a PCI/PCI BRIDGE.

- A BRIDGE can only execute a Type 1 configuration access cycle to access a PCI resource on a lower LEVEL bus via another BRIDGE.

- A PCI bus master on one PCI bus can only execute a Type 1 configuration access cycle to access a PCI resource, via the BRIDGE, on another bus that is at a lower level.

- Only a SINGLE Type 1 configuration access cycle can be converted by a PCI/PCI BRIDGE to a SINGLE special cycle. Conversion of BURST Type 1 configuration access cycles to a BURST special cycle is not allowed. The BURST Type 1 configuration access cycle must be converted to a series of SINGLE special cycles by the PCI/PCI BRIDGE. Consequently, BURST special cycles can only be executed by a HOST/PCI BRIDGE.

- The Fast Back-to-Back protocol that is defined for a memory or I/O access cycle applies to the configuration access cycle. See Subchapter 6.10: *Access-Cycle-to-Access-Cycle Operation* for details.

■ The BRIDGE completes the configuration access cycle with the same protocol as an access cycle including Completion, Completion with Timeout, Master Abort, Retry, Disconnect, and Target Abort terminations. *Chapter 8: Master and Target Termination* for details.

4.3 SPECIAL CYCLES

This is a brief introduction. See Subchapter *4.5: 32 Data Bit PCI Bus Master to 32 Data Bit Target* for details.

A special cycle request originates with the HOST CPU or a PCI bus master on one of the lower LEVEL PCI buses. The request is ported from the HOST CPU to lower LEVEL PCI buses with the BRIDGEs acting as the PCI bus master for each respective bus. A PCI bus master of a specific PCI bus can execute a special cycle to PCI resources on the same bus or request a special cycle on another bus. The request for special cycles is ported from a specific PCI bus to other higher or lower LEVEL PCI buses via Type 1 configuration access cycles, with BRIDGEs acting as the PCI bus master for each respective bus.

As outlined in Subchapter 4.0, special cycles cannot be posted. Delayed Transaction cannot be applied to special bus cycles. The "16 clock" and "8 clock" rules do not apply to special cycles.

Please see Subchapter 4.1 on how ADDRESS/DATA STEPPING operates; this protocol applies to the special cycle. As outlined in Subchapter 4.1, COMBINING, COLLAPSING, PREFETCHING, and MERGING cannot be applied to special cycles.

There is no address decoding (i.e., claiming the cycle by asserting the DEVSEL# signal lines) for special cycles.

The PCI bus specification allows for "physical" signal lines (called sidebands) that are not defined by the PCI bus specification to be connected between PCI resources. The PCI resources must be on the same circuit card because sideband signal lines are not defined on the PCI connector. The purpose of the sideband signal lines is to allow specific information to be conveyed between PCI resources.

Similarly, the special cycle allows PCI bus masters to broadcast messages to all resources on the PCI bus. These messages can convey PCI bus master status and can also act as "logical" sideband signal lines. The concept of "logical" sideband signal line is to use the special cycle to convey specific information to

113

all PCI resources. The special cycle provides the PCI bus master the opportunity to broadcast information to all PCI resources without the use of physical sideband signal lines. This information can be of any type, including the setting of flip flops in real time. It is the responsibility of each PCI resource to determine if the information is relevant to the resource and how it will be used. The resource MUST immediately use the information. The completion of the special cycle guarantees that the information to be acted on immediately.

The definition of a special cycle places unique protocol requirements on this type of bus cycle:

- The special cycle is broadcast to all PCI bus resources; consequently, no individual target can claim a special cycle by asserting the DEVSEL# signal line.

- No PCI resources claim the special cycle; consequently, the TRDY# signal line is not asserted and the length of the cycle is controlled by the PCI bus master via the IRDY# signal line.

- A special cycle can only do data writes. No data reads are possible.

- A special cycle can only occur on the same bus as the PCI bus master that is executing the cycle. A BRIDGE cannot port a special cycle from one bus to another.

- A PCI bus master can cause the BRIDGE(s) to execute a special cycle on any other PCI bus by executing a special version of a configuration access cycle type 1 to the BRIDGE(s).

- The special cycle is executed with the protocol of a SINGLE or BURST access cycle. See Subchapter *6.1: 32 Data Bit PCI Bus Master to 32 Data Bit Target*, for more information.

- A special cycle guarantees a minimum of five CLK signal line periods between valid data and the beginning of the subsequent bus cycle. An IDLE PHASE is required between a special cycle and the subsequent bus cycle; consequently, the Fast Back-to-Back protocol is not supported. See Subchapter *6.10: Access-Cycle-to-Access-Cycle Operation*, for details.

- The PCI bus master completes the special cycle with a Master Abort termination (which includes Completion termination). The Retry, Disconnect, Completion with Timeout, and Target Abort terminations cannot be executed with special cycles. See *Chapter 8: Master and Target Termination*, for details.

- Only SINGLE Type 1 configuration access cycles can be converted by a PCI/PCI BRIDGE to SINGLE special cycles. Conversion of a BURST Type 1 configuration access cycle to a BURST special cycle is not allowed. A BURST Type 1 configuration access cycle must be converted to a series of SINGLE special cycles by the PCI/PCI BRIDGE. Consequently, BURST special cycles can only be executed by a HOST/PCI BRIDGE.

> It is optional for a PCI bus master to have the capability to execute a special cycle. A HOST/PCI BRIDGE may support the special cycle to allow the HOST CPU to broadcast to PCI resources, but it is not required.

4.4 INTERRUPT ACKNOWLEDGE CYCLES

> This is a brief introduction. See Subchapter 4.5: *32 Data Bit PCI Bus Master to 32 Data Bit Target* for details.

> An interrupt acknowledge cycle originates with the HOST CPU and is ported to PCI bus 0 by the HOST/PCI BRIDGE. A typical platform will place the interrupt controller in a PCI resource on PCI bus 0. This PCI resource can be a "non-BRIDGE" component or a PCI/LEGACY BRIDGE. If the interrupt controller is on the LEGACY bus, the PCI/LEGACY BRIDGE will represent it on PCI bus 0.
>
> The interrupt controller may be contained in a HOST bus resource, a HOST/LEGACY BRIDGE , or on a LEGACY bus attached to the HOST/LEGACY bus BRIDGE. In this architecture, no interrupt acknowledge cycle is executed on PCI Bus 0.

As outlined in Subchapter 4.0, interrupt acknowledge cycles cannot be posted. Delayed Transactions can be applied to interrupt acknowledge cycles, but only as SINGLE bus cycles. The "16 clock" and "8 clock" rules apply to interrupt acknowledge cycles.

Please see Subchapter 4.1 on how ADDRESS/DATA STEPPING operates; this protocol applies to the interrupt acknowledge cycle. As outlined in Subchapter 4.1, COMBINING, COLLAPSING, PREFETCHING, and MERGING cannot be applied to interrupt acknowledge cycles.

There is no address decoding (i.e., claiming the cycle by asserting the DEVSEL# signal lines) for interrupt acknowledge cycles.

The PCI bus specification supports discrete interrupt request signal lines (INTx#) that are not defined by bus cycle protocol. The purpose of the INTx# signal lines is to allow specific PCI resources to request service from the HOST CPU. In response to a request for service, the HOST CPU, in conjunction with the HOST/PCI BRIDGE, executes an interrupt acknowledge cycle. It is the responsibility of the interrupt controller to place the appropriate interrupt vector onto the AD[31::0] signal lines during the DATA PHASE of the interrupt acknowledge cycle.

The definition of an interrupt acknowledge cycle places the following unique protocol requirements on this type of bus cycle:

- The interrupt acknowledge cycle is executed without an address; consequently, the PCI resource that contains the interrupt controller "claims" the cycle by asserting the DEVSEL# signal line.

- The PCI resource that claimed the interrupt acknowledge cycle uses the TRDY# signal line to lengthen the cycle. Like access cycles, the TRDY# signal line, in conjunction with the IRDY# signal driven by the PCI bus master (HOST/PCI BRIDGE), controls the length of the cycle.

- An interrupt acknowledge cycle can only perform data reads. No data writes are possible.

- The interrupt acknowledge cycle follows the protocol of a read access cycle. Therefore, the Fast Back-to-Back protocol cannot be applied to a subsequent bus cycle. See *Subchapter 6.10: Access-Cycle-to-Access Cycle Operation*, for details.

- The interrupt acknowledge cycle is executed with the protocol of a SINGLE or BURST access cycle. See *Subchapter 6.1: 32 Data Bit PCI Bus Master to 32 Data Bit Target*, for details.

- The PCI bus master (BRIDGE) completes the interrupt acknowledge cycle with the same protocol as an access cycle including Completion, Master Abort, Retry, Disconnect, and Target Abort terminations. See *Chapter 8: Master and Target Termination*, for details.

- The interrupt acknowledge cycle does not support the execution of the Completion with Timeout termination. See Chapter 8 for details.

4.5   32 DATA BIT PCI BUS MASTER TO 32 DATA BIT TARGET

MEMORY ACCESS CYCLE

See Subchapter *4.1: Memory and I/O Access Cycles* for related information.

A PCI bus master requests a 32 data bit access with the continued deassertion of the REQ64# signal line during the ADDRESS PHASE (deasserted by a pull-up resistor on the bus backplane). The target acknowledges executing a 32 data bit access cycle with the continued deassertion of the ACK64# signal line during the DATA PHASE. The AD[63::32], C/BE#[7::4], and PAR64 signal lines are driven to logical "1" by pull-up resistors; consequently, the PAR64 signal line does not have valid parity information. Once the size of the respective access cycle participants is established it remains unchanged during the remainder of the access cycle.

A memory access cycle *can* be executed with DUAL ADDRESS.

The signal line protocol during the ADDRESS and DATA PHASES are the same for the SINGLE and BURST memory access cycles. The PCI bus master executes a successful memory access cycle as SINGLE versus BURST by the activity of the FRAME# and IRDY# signal lines. As outlined in Chapter 3 and detailed in Chapter 6, the simultaneous deassertion of the FRAME# signal line and assertion of the IRDY# signal line during the first data access of the DATA PHASE results in a SINGLE memory access cycle. The simultaneous assertion of both the FRAME# and IRDY# signal lines during the first data access in the DATA PHASE results in a BURST memory access cycle.

During the ADDRESS PHASE of the access cycle, the AD[31::2] signal lines select a 32 data bit double word, and the C/BE#[3::0] signal lines contain the encoded information of the COMMAND type. The 0110 ([3::0]) or 0111 ([3::0]) encoding indicates a memory read or a memory write access cycle, respectively. The execution of a SINGLE or BURST memory access cycle is not identified in the encoded information contained in the C/BE#[3::0] signal lines. The AD[1::0] signal lines during the ADDRESS PHASE are used to qualify the addressing order of the access cycle. When the AD[1::0] signal lines are both logical "0", the addressing order for the BURST access cycle is linear. For a SINGLE access cycle the AD[31::2] signal lines during the ADDRESS PHASE select the 32 data bits (double words) to be accessed during the DATA PHASE. For a BURST access cycle, the AD[31::2] signal lines during the ADDRESS PHASE select the base address of the 32 data bits (double words) to be accessed during the DATA PHASE. The initial microaccess of a BURST access cycle will access the double word selected by the AD[31::2] signal lines during the ADDRESS PHASE. The subsequent microaccesses will select the next double word located at the next sequential address (increasing) according to a linear addressing protocol.

The PAR signal line is driven by the PCI bus master and reflects the parity of the C/BE#[3::0] and AD[31::0] signal lines during the ADDRESS PHASE. The PAR signal line is driven with valid information with the same protocol as the

AD signal lines, but with a one CLK signal line period delay. For a memory access cycle, the entire address must be supplied by the PCI bus master. Similarly, the C/BE#[3::0] signal must be driven by the PCI bus master with the complete COMMAND type encoding.

During the ADDRESS PHASE, the target latches and decodes the AD[31::2] signal lines to determine if it will respond by asserting the DEVSEL# signal line; consequently, all AD[31::2] signal lines must be driven with valid information. Once the DEVSEL# signal line is asserted, it remains asserted until the completion of the access cycle.

There are two other interpretations of the AD[1::0] signal lines during the ADDRESS PHASE: Reserved and Cache Line Wrap (CLW). When the AD[0] signal line is logical "1" the burst order is defined as Reserved. The target will allow a SINGLE access cycle to be executed, but will prevent the continuation of a BURST access cycle by requesting a Disconnect with data termination with the first data access or Disconnect without data termination with the second data access (first subsequent microaccess). When the AD[1::0] signal lines have a binary pattern of "10" (AD[1] = "1" and AD[0] = "0") the BURST access cycle addressing order is CLW. The CLW simply means that the initial microaccess of a BURST access cycle is to the address specified by the AD signal lines. If the address is in the "middle" of a cache line, then the initial microaccess begins there and the next subsequent microaccess of the BURST access cycle is to the next higher address in the cache line until the end of the cache line is encountered. Additional subsequent microaccesses address the beginning of the cache line and continue until the address of the initial microaccess is reached. At this point the subsequent microaccess is to the same "middle" location in the cache line with the next higher order addresses as the cache line of the initial microaccess.

The reserved encoding may be defined in the future by the PCI Special Interest Group. The term "middle" of the cache line represents any location in the cache line, not necessarily the actual middle.

If a target does not support the Cache Line Size register, the PCI bus master cannot access it with a Cache Line Wrap or Reserve burst order. If either of these burst modes is attempted, the target must execute a DISCONNECT with data termination on the first access or a DISCONNECT without data termination on the first subsequent microaccess.

The switch from a SINGLE to a BURST access cycle is controlled by the PCI bus master. Consequently, all memory targets are required to check the burst order encoded on the AD[1::0] signal lines during the ADDRESS PHASE. If the target cannot support the burst order requested, it must execute a Disconnect with data termination with the completion of the first access or a Disconnect without data termination with the second data access (first subsequent microaccess) which results in a SINGLE access cycle, *Chapter 8: Master and Target Termination* for details.

The Rev. 2.0 of the PCI bus specification states that if the AD[0] signal line equals a logical "1" (deasserted) and the AD[1] signal line equals a logical "0" (asserted), the addressing order of the BURST access cycle follows the Intel 86 and Pentium cache filling order. This protocol is no longer supported or applicable to the PCI bus specification. This binary pattern is now reserved.

During the DATA PHASE of a SINGLE or BURST access cycle, the C/BE#[3::0] signal lines will identify which bytes within the selected 32 data bits (double words) will be accessed. For a BURST memory access cycle, the C/BE#[3::0] signal lines identify the bytes within the 32 data bits (double word) selected by each microaccess. It is possible that a different set of bytes are selected for each microaccess within the BURST access cycle. As previously outlined in the "byte lane operation" section, the valid bytes lanes for a given access or between accesses do not have to be continuous.

For the DATA PHASE of a read or write access cycle, the PAR signal line is driven by the target or PCI bus master, respectively. It reflects the parity over ALL the C/BE#[3::0] and AD[31::0] signal lines. The byte lanes not valid (according to the C/BE#[3::0] signal lines) must be driven to a stable level, and parity is still computed on these unused lines.

For both SINGLE and BURST access cycles, it is possible for none of the C/BE#[3::0] signal lines to be asserted during the DATA PHASE, and thus none of the associated byte lanes are valid. Under this condition the target should immediately assert the TRDY# signal line.

If target is not able to support non-continuous byte accesses, it must execute a Target Abort termination. See *Chapter 8: Master and Target Termination* for details.

The completion of an access cycle requires the simultaneous deassertion of the FRAME# signal line and assertion of the TRDY# signal, followed by the simultaneous deassertion of the FRAME# and IRDY# signal lines. Exceptions to these requirements occur due to termination (see Chapter 8, referenced above, for details) or Fast Back-to-Back protocol (see *Chapter 6: Detailed Bus Cycle Operation* for details).

SPECIAL CACHEABLE PCI MEMORY CONSIDERATIONS RELATIVE TO SDONE AND SBO# SIGNAL LINES

A cacheable PCI memory resource (PDRAM) must monitor the SDONE signal line driven by the cache controller in the HOST/PCI BRIDGE. The monitoring of the SDONE signal line is required for two reasons: (1) If the previous memory access was completed prior to the assertion of the SDONE signal line, the present memory access may not be immediately completed. If the present access is to a cacheable PDRAM, it cannot be completed (TRDY# signal line not asserted) until the SDONE# signal line is asserted to indicate the completion of address snooping for the previous memory access cycle. This protocol allows for completion of the access without waiting for the completion of the cache snoop. It requires snoop circuitry in the cache controller and PDRAM to latch two addresses, one for the previous and one for the present memory access cycle. The latching of addresses for a non-cacheable memory resource is required because the snoop must be performed for all addresses. (2) The SDONE signal line is monitored in conjunction with the SBO# signal line by cacheable PDRAM. The cacheable PDRAM of the present access cycle must execute a Retry termination when both of these signal lines are asserted. See *Chapter 7: Cache Support on PCI*, for information.

The memory resource of the present access may not be the same as the previous access cycle; therefore, all cacheable PDRAM must monitor the SDONE and SBO# signal lines for the previous memory access cycles in anticipation of becoming the target for the present memory access cycle.

The above protocol ELIMINATES the need for the cacheable PDRAM to know the address ranges of all cacheable PDRAM. It does require that the SDONE signal line is asserted for accesses to both cacheable and non-cacheable memory resources.

The above protocol does not affect special and interrupt acknowledge cycles, access cycles for non-cacheable memory resources, I/O resources, or configuration resources. Consequently, these resources do not have to monitor the SDONE and SBO# signal lines, and the associated bus cycles execute independently from the condition of the SDONE and SBO# signal lines.

Another important consideration about the SDONE and SBO# signal lines is when cacheable PDRAM knows if the cache resource is write-through or write-back. If the PCI bus master executes a read access cycle to a PDRAM entry that is copied in a write-back cache as a modified/valid cache line, the completion of the access cycle to the PDRAM (assertion of the IRDY# and TRDY# signal lines) prior to the completion of the snoop (assertion of the SDONE signal line) *is not allowed* because the data is invalid. If the cacheable PDRAM is cached by a write-back cache resource, it cannot assert the TRDY# signal line until the snoop is complete. If the snoop indicates that the cache line in the cache was modified/valid (SBO# signal line asserted), the target must execute a Retry termination. See *Chapter 7: Cache Support on PCI*, for details.

If the PCI bus master reads a PDRAM cache line entry that is a copy of a valid write-through cache line, the entry is correct and can be completed prior to the assertion of the SDONE signal line. If the PDRAM does not "know" if it is cached by write-through cache, the PDRAM must assume a write-back cache.

Also, consider when the PCI bus master executes a write access cycle to a cacheable PDRAM entry that is stored in a write-back cache as a modified/valid cache line and the access cycle completes prior to the completion of the snoop. The snoop will subsequently complete with the assertion of the SDONE and SBO# signal lines, which indicates that the data written to the PDRAM will be overwritten by the pending snoop write-back access cycle. If the cacheable PDRAM is designed to allow the subsequent snoop write-back access cycle to over write the associated cache line without loss of the data written just prior to snoop completion, the cache line entry in the cacheable PDRAM is correct. If it is not designed to operate in such a fashion, it cannot assert the TRDY# signal line until the snoop completes with the SBO# signal line deasserted. If the snoop completes with the SBO# signal line asserted, the target must execute a Retry termination unless it supports *over write*. See Subchapter 7.3 for more information.

If the PCI bus master reads a PDRAM cache line entry that is a copy of a valid write-through cache line, the entry is correct and can be completed prior to the assertion of the SDONE signal line. If the PDRAM does not "know" if it is cached by write-through cache, the PDRAM must assume a write-back cache.

During read access cycles, cacheable or prefetchable PCI memory resources have special interpretation of the C/BE# signal lines. If the PCI memory resource knows it is cacheable or prefetchable, it must drive all of the byte lanes with valid data independently from the C/BE# signal lines asserted. If the memory does not know that it resides in a cacheable address space, the PCI bus master must assert all of the C/BE# signal lines (if it knows the cacheability map) to read all of the cache data. The cacheable PCI memory resource must return the entire cache line or, if the entire cache line is not accessed, only the first data requested.

SPECIAL CACHEABLE PCI MEMORY CONSIDERATIONS RELATIVE TO CACHE LINE BOUNDARIES

The BURST access cycle can potentially access any amount of data; therefore, cache line boundaries can be crossed. The cache address snoop and the subsequent state of the SDONE and SBO# signal lines are determined during the initial microaccess of a cache line. The result of the address snoop and the state of the SDONE and SBO# signal lines relative to the initial microaccess applies to the subsequent microaccesses of the cache line in a BURST access cycle. During a BURST access cycle, the crossing of a cache boundary to a new cache line may result in an address snoop with different results for the SBO# signal line state than the cache line prior to the boundary. Consequently, the BURST access cycle the SDONE and SBO# signal lines must be monitored by the target at cache line boundaries. See *Chapter 7: Cache Support on PCI*, for details.

The above restrictions on crossing a cache boundary *do not* apply if the cache and cached memory are integrated as a single PCI resource. For example, the HOST bus DRAM (HDRAM) and cache are both behind the HOST/PCI BRIDGE. The cache and memory controllers in the HOST/PCI BRIDGE can determine in advance of crossing the boundary whether an address snoop for the subsequent cache line would result in a SDONE and SBO# signal line states that differ with the state of the cache line presently being accessed. Consequently, the cache controller can select correct data from either the HDRAM or cache and the value of the SDONE and SBO# signal lines (i.e., no snoop write back access cycle needed) can apply for multiple cache lines. The memory target must not be monitoring the SDONE signal line or the cache controller must toggle the SDONE signal line at a cache line boundary to take advantage of this architecture.

MEMORY READ MULTIPLE (MRM) ACCESS CYCLE

The MRM access cycle operates with the same protocol as a non-MRM SINGLE or BURST read access memory cycle, including the support of DUAL ADDRESS. During ADDRESS PHASE, the C/BE#[3::0] signal lines contain the encoded information of the COMMAND type. The 1100 ([3::0]) encoding indicates an MRM access cycle. The MRM access cycle indicates to the cacheable PCI memory resource (PDRAM) that multiple cache lines will be read. In theory, an MRM can be executed as a series of MRM SINGLE read access memory cycles; but in practice, the reading of the cache lines should be performed with a series of MRM BURST read access memory cycles within cache line boundaries.

The MRM access cycle provides the best PCI bus performance for reading multiple cache lines. Support of the Cache Line Size Register is not required for this COMMAND type, but if supported it should be used as an indicator for the optimum use of the MRM access cycle. As a default, 32 data bytes (for 32 data bit PCI buses) or 64 data bytes (for 64 data bit PCI buses) should be used.

A non-MRM access cycle is defined as a memory read access cycle with an encoding on the C/BE# signal lines of 0110 ([3::0]) during the ADDRESS PHASE.

Even though the MRM access cycle indicates that multiple cache lines will be read, an MRM BURST read access cycle can only cross a cache boundary under the conditions outlined in the *Special Cacheable PCI Memory Considerations Relative to Cache Line Boundaries* section. The use of the MRM access cycle allows the memory resource to do advance memory reads of entire cache lines and to pipeline the data. The proper use of this access cycle will improve system performance.

If the cacheable PCI memory resource (PDRAM) supports MRM and the PCI bus master completes an MRM access cycle on a non-cache boundary, the cycle completes without an error related to accessing less than an entire cache line. The buffers in the PDRAM that contain the prefetched cache lines must be cleared. The intention of the MRM is to provide the memory resource "advance information" such that additional cache lines will be accessed. Consequently, the use of an MRM access cycle for one cache line (or less) should be avoided. If the PCI bus master uses the MRM command, it is responsible that no adverse side effects will occur when the memory target does not support this command or when prefetched cached lines are "cleared".

If the cacheable PCI memory resource (PDRAM) does not support MRM and the PCI bus master executes an MRM access cycle, the target executes the access as a memory read or an MRL access cycle. It still appears to the PCI bus as an MRM access cycle because of the COMMAND type during the ADDRESS PHASE. The performance of the bus would be less because a cache line prefetch does not occur.

The PCI memory resource does not have to be cached for the MRM access cycle to be relevant. The MRM access cycle simply allows the PCI memory resource to prefetch data in a fixed block. The block of data is simply defined in terms of cache lines.

The execution of the MRM access cycle to a PCI resource that is a BRIDGE is defined differently. A BRIDGE should read an amount of data on the destination bus equal to a cache line of the source bus. The BRIDGE should try to stay one cache line ahead in its accesses of the destination bus.

The cache protocol and the operation of the SDONE and SBO# signal lines for an MRM are the same as the non-MRM read access cycle.

MEMORY READ LINE (MRL) ACCESS CYCLE

The MRL access cycle operates with the same protocol as the non-MRL SINGLE or BURST read access memory cycle, including the support of DUAL ADDRESS. During ADDRESS PHASE, the C/BE#[3::0] signal lines contain the encoded information of the COMMAND type. The 1110 ([3::0]) encoding indicates an MRL access cycle. The MRL access cycle indicates to the memory resource (target) that three or more 32 data bits (double words) will be read. In theory, an MRL can be executed as a series of MRL SINGLE read access memory cycles, but in practice the reading of multiple double words should be performed with a series of MRL BURST read access memory cycles within cache line boundaries.

A non-MRL access cycle is defined as a memory read access cycle with an encoding on the C/BE# signal lines of 0110 ([3::0]) during the ADDRESS PHASE.

An MRL BURST read access cycle can only cross a cache boundary under conditions outlined in the *Special Cacheable PCI Memory Considerations Relative to Cache Line Boundaries* section. The use of the MRL access cycle allows the memory resource to perform advance memory reads of double words and to pipeline the data. Proper use of this access cycle will improve system performance.

If the memory target supports MRL, and the PCI bus master completes an MRL or non- MRL read access cycle by accessing only two or fewer, less 32 data bits (double words), the cycle is successfully completed without an error related to accessing fewer than three double words. The buffers in the target that contain the prefetched data must be cleared.

If the PCI memory resource (PDRAM) does not support MRL, and the PCI bus master executes an MRL access cycle, the cycle completes as a non-MRL read access cycle. It still appears to the PCI bus as an MRL access cycle because of the COMMAND type during ADDRESS PHASE. Access performance would be poorer because the prefetch of the data does not occur.

The cache protocol and the operation of the SDONE and SBO# signal lines for an MRL are the same as the non-MRL read access cycle.

MEMORY WRITE AND INVALIDATE (MWI) CYCLE

The MWI access cycle operates with the same protocol as a non-MWI BURST memory write access cycle, including the support of DUAL ADDRESS. During the ADDRESS PHASE, the C/BE#[3::0] signal lines contain the encoded information of the COMMAND type. The 1111 ([3::0]) encoding indicates an MWI access cycle. The MWI access cycle indicates to the cacheable PCI memory resource (PDRAM) that an entire cache line will be written. An MWI can only be executed as single MWI BURST write access memory cycle within a cache line boundary. Support of the Cache Line Size Register is required for this COMMAND type.

If the PCI bus master is not going to write the entire cache line in a single BURST access cycle, it *cannot* use the MWI command. The MWI command can only be used with linear addressing order, and cannot be used with the Cache Line Wrap protocol.

It is possible that a PCI bus master will begin execution of the MWI access cycle with the intention to write an entire cache line, but the target may terminate the access cycle (Retry, Disconnect, or Target Abort termination) prior to the PCI bus master writing the entire cache line. In this situation no error is generated. The access cycle must be immediately terminated.

A non-MWI access cycle is defined as a memory write access cycle with an encoding on the C/BE# signal lines of 0111 ([3::0]) during the ADDRESS PHASE.

The use of the MWI access cycle allows the cache controller in the HOST/PCI BRIDGE to mark a modified/valid cache line in a write-back cache invalid (after a cache hit) without executing a snoop write-back access cycle to the PDRAM. The benefit of the MWI access cycle is that the snoop write-back access cycle is not executed and thus system performance is improved. The cache controller in the HOST/PCI BRIDGE only asserts the SDONE signal lines and does not assert the SBO# signal line. Optionally, the cache controller in the PCI BRIDGE can execute the snoop write-back access cycle by asserting the SBO# signal line when the SDONE signal line is asserted. See Chapter 7 *Cache Support on PCI*, for details.

When the MWI is executed as a BURST access cycle, a cache boundary in a write-back cache cannot be crossed unless all of the following conditions are met:

- The entire cache line addressed at the beginning of the BURST access cycle must be written by the PCI bus master.

- Whenever the cache boundary is crossed, the entire new cache line must also be written by the PCI bus master.

If all of the these conditions are not met, the cache controller in the HOST/PCI BRIDGE must assert the SERR# signal line.

If the PDRAM does *not* support MWI and the PCI bus master executes an MWI access cycle, the cycle completes as an MWI access cycle. All of the MWI access cycle protocols relative to the SDONE and SBO# signal lines still apply.

If the PDRAM supports MWI, and the PCI bus master executes a non-MWI access cycle, the cycle completes as a non-MWI write access cycle.

I/O ACCESS CYCLES

A PCI bus master requests a 32 data bit access by deasserting the REQ64# signal line during the ADDRESS PHASE. The target can only respond by executing a 32 data bit access cycle (ACK64# signal line deasserted). The AD[63::32], C/BE#[7::4], and PAR64 signal lines are driven to a logical "1" by pull-up resistors; consequently, the PAR64 signal line does not have valid parity information. Once the size of the respective access cycle participants is established it remains unchanged during the remainder of the access cycle.

An I/O access cycle CAN be executed with DUAL ADDRESS.

The signal line protocol during the ADDRESS and DATA PHASES are the same for the SINGLE and BURST I/O access cycles. The PCI bus master executes a successful I/O access cycle as SINGLE versus BURST by the deassertion of the FRAME# signal line. As outlined in Chapter 3 and detailed in Chapter 6, the deassertion of the FRAME# signal line during the first data access of the DATA PHASE results in a SINGLE I/O access cycle. The continued assertion of the FRAME# signal line after the first data access of the DATA PHASE results in a BURST I/O access cycle.

As discussed below, the present PCI bus specification supports SINGLE I/O access cycles. A BURST I/O access cycle is possible under certain conditions.

During the ADDRESS PHASE of the access cycle, the AD[31::0] signal lines identify a specific 8 data bit byte and the C/BE#[3::0] signal lines contain the encoded information of the COMMAND type. The 0010 ([3::0]) or 0011 ([3::0]) encoding indicates an I/O read or an I/O write access cycle, respectively. The execution of a SINGLE or BURST I/O access cycle is not identified in the encoded information contained in the C/BE#[3::0] signal lines. The support of the AD[1::0] signal lines are according to a traditional addressing scheme which allows a PCI I/O resource (target) with a one byte size address space to claim the cycle by asserting the DEVSEL# signal line. If the target can respond with more than one byte, the AD[01::00] signal lines address the least significant byte in the access. The AD[1::0] signal lines only contain address information during the ADDRESS PHASE. The AD[1::0] signal lines contain data during the DATA PHASE.

The PAR signal line during the ADDRESS PHASE is driven by the PCI bus master and reflects the parity over the C/BE#[3::0] and AD[31::0] signal lines. The PAR signal line is driven with valid information with the same protocol as the AD signal lines but with a one CLK signal line period delay. For an I/O access cycle the entire address must be supplied. Similarly, the C/BE#[3::0] signal must be driven by the PCI bus master with the complete COMMAND type encoding.

During ADDRESS PHASE, the target decodes the AD[31::0] signal lines to determine if it will claim the access cycle by asserting the DEVSEL# signal line. Consequently, all AD[31::0] signal lines must be driven with valid information. Once the DEVSEL# signal line is asserted, it remains asserted until the completion of the access cycle, except for a Target Abort termination.

During the DATA PHASE of a SINGLE or BURST access cycle, the C/BE#[3::0] signal lines will identify which bytes will be accessed. For a BURST I/O access cycle, the C/BE#[3::0] signal lines identify the bytes selected by each microaccess. The C/BE#[3::0] signal lines during the DATA PHASE of a SINGLE access cycle or the initial microaccess of a BURST access cycle must also match the bytes that were addressed by the AD[1::0] signal lines during the ADDRESS PHASE. The allowed protocol for the AD[1::0] signal lines during the ADDRESS PHASE and the C/BE#[3::0] signal lines during the DATA PHASE is as follows:

AD[1]	AD[0]	C/BE#[3]	C/BE#[2]	C/BE#[1]	C/BE#[0]
0	0	X	X	X	0
0	1	X	X	0	1
1	0	X	0	1	1
1	1	0	1	1	1
X	X	1	1	1	1

Table 4-1. Relationship of AD signal lines (ADDRESS PHASE) with C/BE# signal lines (DATA PHASE) for I/O access cycle (SINGLE bus cycle or initial microaccess of BURST bus cycle)

X = Don't care (asserted or deasserted)
1 = 3.3 or 5 volts (deasserted for C/BE#[3::0] signal lines)
0 = 0 volts (asserted for C/BE#[3::0] signal lines)

A target that has adopted the above protocol must monitor the AD[1::0] signal lines during ADDRESS PHASE and compare their values with the C/BE#[3::0] signal lines during DATA PHASE of a SINGLE bus cycle or initial microaccess of BURST bus cycle. If the values do not support the same byte address, the target must execute a Target Abort termination. This protocol allows one to four different targets to own mutually-exclusive portions of the 32 data bits (double words) being addressed by the access cycle. This protocol DOES NOT apply if one target owns an entire double word. This protocol also does not apply to PCI/PCI or PCI/LEGACY BRIDGEs because there is no complete knowledge of resources on the destination PCI bus or the LEGACY bus, respectively.

Rev 2.0 of the PCI bus specification did not provide a "clear" protocol for BURST access cycles. Rev. 2.1 defines a BURST I/O access cycle protocol. 64 data bit I/O targets can be implemented, but there is no benefit to requiring the increased complexity and it is therefore strongly recommended that 64 data bit I/O targets are not implemented. For the purposes of this book, I/O targets are only 32 data bits in size. If a 64 data bit I/O target is implemented, the 64 data bit protocol applied to memory targets would also apply to I/O targets.

As outlined above, the initial microaccess of a BURST I/O access cycle must have the C/BE#[3::0] signal lines in the DATA PHASE that agree with the AD[01::00] signal lines in the ADDRESS PHASE. The value of the C/BE#[3::0] signal lines in the subsequent microaccesses of the DATA PHASE do not have to agree with the AD[01::00] signal lines in the ADDRESS PHASE per Table 4-1.

Only a linear incrementing address sequence is allowed for a BURST I/O access cycle. It is possible that a different set of bytes are selected for each microaccess within the BURST access cycle. As previously outlined in the "Byte Lane Operation" section, valid byte lanes for a given access or between accesses do not have to be continuous.

The switch from a SINGLE to a BURST access cycle is controlled by the PCI bus master. If the target cannot support BURST access cycles, it must execute a Disconnect with data termination on completion of the first access or Disconnect without data termination after completion of the first access. The aforementioned Target Abort is executed instead if the byte enables do not agree with address. See *Chapter 6: Master and Target Determination*, for details.

> For both SINGLE and BURST I/O access cycles, it is possible for none of the C/BE#[3::0] signal lines to be asserted during the DATA PHASE of a SINGLE access cycle or the initial microaccess of a BURST access cycle.

An I/O target re-mapped to the memory address space can support up to 32 or 64 data bits and can operate with the same protocol as any non-cacheable memory resource.

For the DATA PHASE of a read or write access cycle, the PAR signal line is driven by the target or PCI bus master, respectively. It reflects the parity over ALL of the C/BE#[3::0] and AD[31::0] signal lines. The byte lanes not valid according to the C/BE#[3::0] signal lines must be driven to a stable level, and parity is still computed on these unused lines.

The completion of an access cycle requires the simultaneous deassertion of the FRAME# signal line and assertion of the TRDY# signal, followed by the simultaneous deassertion of the FRAME# and IRDY# signal lines. Exceptions to these requirements occur due to termination (see *Chapter 8: Master and Target Termination*, for details) or Fast Back-to-Back protocol (*Chapter 6: Detailed Bus Operation*, for details).

CONFIGURATION ACCESS CYCLE

See Subchapter *4.2: Configuration Access Cycles* for related information.

> A PCI bus master of a specific LEVEL bus can only access the configuration space of a lower LEVEL bus but not a higher LEVEL bus. A configuration access cycle originates with the HOST CPU and is ported from PCI bus to PCI bus with the BRIDGEs acting as the PCI bus master for each respective bus.

> The term "device" used in the following section is collectively the configuration space (register sets) of the PCI resources. These PCI resources can be PCI bus masters (with configuration registers as a target), targets, or BRIDGEs. A device can have one to eight configuration spaces.

The signal line protocol during the ADDRESS and DATA PHASES of a configuration access cycle is the same as a memory or I/O access cycle, and both SINGLE and BURST configuration access cycles are supported. During ADDRESS PHASE, the AD[7::2] signal lines select a double word (32 data bits) within a 256 byte address space of the configuration space. C/BE#[3::0] signal lines contain the COMMAND type: 1010 ([3::0]) or 1011 ([3::0]) encoding indicates a configuration read or configuration write access cycle, respectively. The use of the AD[7::2] signal lines during the ADDRESS PHASE indicates that only 64 double words are available per configuration space. For a SINGLE access cycle , the AD[7::2] signal lines during the ADDRESS PHASE select the double words to be accessed during the DATA PHASE. For a BURST access cycle, the AD[7::2] signal lines during the ADDRESS PHASE select the base address of the double words to be accessed during the initial microaccess. The subsequent microaccesses will select the next double word located at the next sequential address (increasing) using a linear addressing protocol. The number contained within the AD[7::2] signal lines during the ADDRESS PHASE is defined as the REGISTER Number being accessed.

The PAR signal line is driven by the PCI bus master and reflects the parity of the C/BE#[3::0] and AD[31::0] signal lines during the ADDRESS PHASE. The PAR signal line is driven with valid information with the same protocol as the AD signal lines but with a one CLK signal line period delay. For a configuration access cycle, all the AD[31::0] signal lines must be driven to a stable level by the PCI bus master. Similarly, the C/BE#[3::0] signal must be driven by the PCI bus master with the complete COMMAND type encoding.

During the DATA PHASE of the configuration access cycle, the C/BE#[3::0] signal lines will identify which bytes within the selected 32 data bit (double words) will be accessed. For a BURST memory access cycle, the C/BE#[3::0] signal lines identify the bytes within the 32 data bit (double word) selected by each microaccess. It is possible that a different set of bytes are selected for each microaccess within the BURST access cycle. As previously outlined in the "Byte Lane Operation" section, the valid byte lanes for a given access or between accesses do not have to be continuous.

For the DATA PHASE of a read or write access cycle, the PAR signal line is driven by the device or PCI bus master, respectively. It reflects the parity over ALL the C/BE#[3::0] and AD[31::0] signal lines. The byte lanes not valid according to the C/BE#[3::0] signal lines must be driven to a stable level, and parity is still computed on these unused lines.

The completion of an access cycle requires the simultaneous deassertion of the FRAME# signal line and assertion of the TRDY# signal, followed by the simultaneous deassertion of the FRAME# and IRDY# signal lines. Exceptions to these requirements occur either due to termination (see *Chapter 8: Master and Target Termination*, for details) or Fast Back-to-Back protocol (see *Chapter 6: Detailed Bus Cycle Operation*, for details).

During ADDRESS PHASE, the AD[1::0] signal lines are used to select the configuration access cycle type: Type 0 is selected when the AD[1::0] signal lines both = logical "0". Type 1 is selected when the AD[0] signal line = logical "1" and the AD[1] signal line = logical "0". Type 0 is used to select (in conjunction with an asserted IDSEL) the configuration space of a device on the PCI bus when the configuration access cycle is being executed (source bus). Type 1 is used to port the configuration access cycle through a PCI/PCI BRIDGE to a PCI resource behind the BRIDGE (destination bus). The PCI/PCI BRIDGE converts the Type 1 configuration access cycle on the source PCI bus to a Type 0 configuration access cycle on the destination bus.

During the ADDRESS PHASE of a Type 0 configuration access cycle, the AD[31::11] signal lines are defined as reserved and the AD[10::8] signal lines contain the FUNCTION Number, (see Figure 4-4). The definition of these signals lines are as follows:

- *Reserved*: Must be driven to a stable level by the PCI bus master and must contain the IDSEL pattern. The parity for these signal lines is included in the PAR signal line.

- *Function number*: Used to select one of eight possible configuration spaces within the device.

During the ADDRESS PHASE of a Type 0 configuration access cycle, the AD[31::11] signal lines are individually mapped to the IDSEL signal lines to select one of twenty-one PCI resources (devices) on the bus. The BRIDGE provides programmable registers which allow the HOST CPU to select the configuration access cycle of a device on the lower LEVEL bus by programming the IDSEL number into these registers. When the bus master begins a configuration access cycle, the IDSEL signal lines reflect the encoded value of these programmable registers. The assertion of the IDSEL signal line must result in the associated device to claim the access cycle by asserting the DEVSEL# signal line. The device of a Type 0 configuration access cycle cannot be on another bus connected by the BRIDGE; consequently, negative decoding is not supported. If a BRIDGE claims a Type 0 configuration access cycle, it is for the purpose of accessing the configuration registers within the BRIDGE and by definition is defined as the device. If the configuration access cycle is not claimed, a Master Abort termination is executed.

> The mapping of the IDSEL signal lines to the AD[31::11] signal lines is one possible implementation. The IDSEL signal lines essentially function as chip selects and can be implemented by any platform circuitry that allows for selection of individual IDSEL signal lines.

During the ADDRESS PHASE of a Type 1 configuration access cycle, the AD[31::24] signal lines are defined as reserved, the AD[23::16] signal lines contain the BUS Number, the AD[15::11] signal lines contain the Device

Number, and the AD[10::8] signal lines contain the FUNCTION Number. (see Figure 4-5).

■ RESERVED: The AD[31::24] are driven to a logical "0" by the PCI bus master. Parity for these signal lines is included in the PAR signal line.

■ BUS Number: Determines which one of a possible 256 buses is selected. The buses are numbered from 0 to 255 with the protocol outlined in Chapter 1.

■ Device Number: This selects 1 of 32 devices on the bus identified by the BUS Number. (Note: The IDSEL tied to the AD[31::11] signal lines allows up to 21 devices.)

■ FUNCTION Number: Used to select one of eight possible configuration spaces (register sets) on each device.

During the ADDRESS PHASE of a Type 1 configuration access cycle, the AD[23::16] signal lines contain the BUS Number and the AD[15::11] signal lines contain the Device Number. The BRIDGE on the PCI bus executing the Type 1 configuration access cycle claims the cycle if the BUS Number matches a bus behind the BRIDGE. If the BUS Number behind this BRIDGE is directly attached to the BRIDGE (defined as "destination bus"), the Type 1 configuration access cycle is repeated as a Type 0 configuration access cycle on the destination bus with the binary pattern of the Device Number encoded onto the IDSEL (AD[31::11]) signal lines on the destination bus. If the BUS Number behind this BRIDGE is not directly attached to the BRIDGE (defined as *non-destination bus*), the Type 1 configuration access cycle is repeated as a Type 1 configuration access cycle (unchanged) on the non-destination bus. Once the Type 0 configuration access cycle is executed on a destination bus behind a BRIDGE, the FUNCTION Number and REGISTER Number apply to the device that claimed the cycle.

The result of the above protocol allows each PCI bus to have 21 devices, each device has up to 8 selectable configuration spaces and contains 64 double words.

A device that claims a Type 0 configuration access cycle falls into two classes: a Single or Multi-Function Device. A Single-Function Device uses only the asserted IDSEL signal line to determine if it is accessed. A Multi-Function Device uses the asserted IDSEL signal line plus the Function Number in the AD[10::8] signal lines to determine if it is accessed. A Multi-Function Device must also claim the Type 0 configuration access cycle if the FUNCTION Number is [000] = AD[10::8].

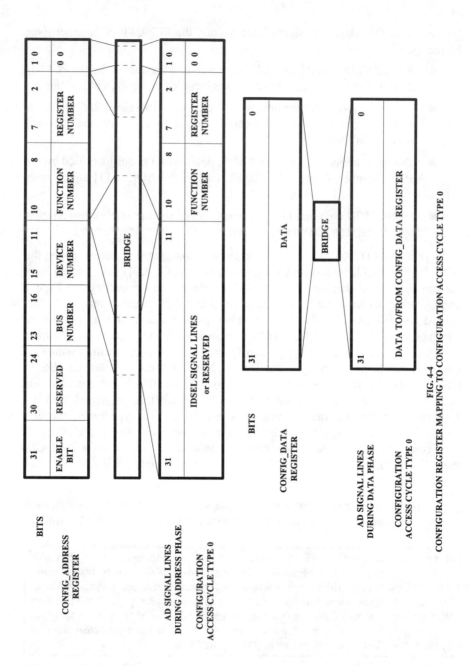

Figure 4-4: Configuration Register Mapping to Configuration Access Cycle Type 0

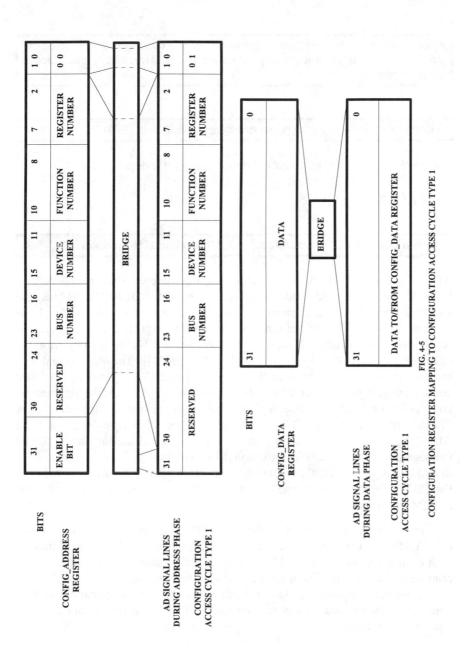

Figure 4-5: Configuration Register Mapping to Configuration Access Cycle Type 1

A configuration access cycle supports the execution of Completion, Completion with Timeout, Retry, Disconnect, Master Abort, and Target Abort terminations.

A configuration access cycle *cannot* be executed with DUAL ADDRESS.

See Subchapter *4.1: Memory and I/O Access Cycles*, for details.

SPECIAL CYCLES

See Subchapter *4.3: Special Bus Cycles*, for related information.

AD[31::0] and C/BE#[3::0] signal lines have the same protocol as that defined for a SINGLE or BURST access cycle. During the ADDRESS PHASE, the AD[31::0] signal lines are driven by the PCI bus master to a stable level but contain no valid address information because no specific PCI resource is addressed. The C/BE#[3::0] signal lines contain the binary pattern with the COMMAND type of a special cycle ([3::0] = [0001]). The PAR signal line contains parity information over the AD[31::0] and C/BE#[3::0] signal lines; consequently, a parity error during the ADDRESS PHASE can be reported by any platform resource by asserting the SERR# signal line. During the DATA PHASE, the C/BE#[3::0] signal lines indicate the valid byte lanes, and the AD[31::0] signal lines contain the special cycle encoded message and optional message-dependent data. The PAR signal line contains parity information over the AD[31::0] and C/BE#[3::0] signal lines; consequently, a parity error during the DATA PHASE can be reported by any platform resource by asserting the SERR# signal line.

The information contained within the AD[31::0] signal lines during the DATA PHASE consists of two parts. The AD[15::0] signal lines are encoded with the message type. The AD[31::16] signal lines contain an optional data field relative to the message. The message type is defined by the PCI Special Interest Group steering committee. Any encoding that has been approved by this committee can be used by any manufacturer. The present list of four message types is shown below:

AD[15::0]	Message Type
0000h	SHUTDOWN
0001h	HALT
0002h	x86 architecture spec. (reserved for Intel)
0003h to FFFFh	Reserved

During the DATA PHASE, AD[15::0] signal lines contain the message type; consequently, C/BE#[3::0] signal lines are all logical "0" (asserted) to indicate valid byte lanes. The AD[31::16] signal lines contain optional message-dependent data; the message type defines whether these signal lines have valid information.

Because the special cycle completes with the Master Abort termination protocol, it is not possible to have a Master Abort termination as defined for other bus cycles (e.g., a memory access cycle). When a PCI bus master executes a special cycle, it terminates it with the Master Abort termination, but does not set the Received Master Abort bit in its Status Register.

Because a special cycle does not address a specific target to claim the cycle, Retry, Disconnect, Completion with Timeout, and Target Abort terminations cannot be executed with a special cycle.

A special cycle cannot be executed with DUAL ADDRESS.

INTERRUPT ACKNOWLEDGE CYCLES

See Subchapter 4.4: *Interrupt Acknowledge Cycles*, for related information.

The AD[31::0] and C/BE#[3::0] signal lines have the same protocol as that defined for a SINGLE or BURST access cycle. During the ADDRESS PHASE, the AD[31::0] signal lines are driven by the PCI bus master to a stable level, but contain no valid address information. The C/BE#[3::0] signal lines contain the binary pattern with the COMMAND type of an interrupt acknowledge cycle ([3::0] = [0000]). The PAR signal line contains parity information over the

AD[31::0] and C/BE#[3::0] signal lines; consequently, a parity error during the ADDRESS PHASE can be reported by any PCI resource by asserting the SERR# signal line. During the DATA PHASE, the C/BE#[3::0] signal lines indicate the valid byte lanes and the AD[31::0] signal lines contain the interrupt vector. The PAR signal line contains parity information over the AD[31::0] and C/BE#[3::0] signal lines; consequently, a parity error during the DATA PHASE can be reported by the PCI bus master (BRIDGE) by asserting the PERR# signal line.

> An 8259 interrupt-compatible vector requires only 8 data bits on the AD[7::0] signal lines.

> An interrupt acknowledge cycle supports the execution of Completion, Retry, Disconnect, Master Abort, and Target Abort terminations.

> An interrupt acknowledge cycle does not support execution of the Completion with Timeout termination.

> An interrupt acknowledge cycle cannot be executed with DUAL ADDRESS.

> Rev 2.0 of the PCI bus specification defines the size of the interrupt vector read from the PCI resource that contains the interrupt controller to be one byte (eight bits) in size is an example relative to Intel architectures. Consequently, the C/BE#[3::0] signal lines have a fixed binary pattern ([3::0] = [1110]). Larger data sizes with the appropriate C/BE#[3::0] asserted can also be used.

4.6 64 DATA BIT EXTENSION

INTRODUCTION

The PCI bus specification supports both 32 and 64 data bit bus sizes. A 32 data bit implementation of the PCI bus specification is all that is required to be compliant. The 64 data bit extension is optional and 32 and 64 data bit resources can coexist on the same bus. The 64 data bit extension allows 32 data bit PCI bus masters to access 64 data bit targets, 64 data bit PCI bus masters to access 32 data bit targets, and 64 data bit PCI bus masters to access 64 data bit targets.

The support of the 64 data bit extension is accomplished with the addition of the AD[63::32], C/BE#[7::4], REQ64#, ACK64#, and PAR64 signal lines on the bus backplane. All of the access cycle protocol outlined for platforms with the 32 data bit-only PCI buses also apply to platforms with the 64 data bit extension. The 64 data bit extension does not apply to either configuration access cycles or Special and Interrupt Acknowledge bus cycles. See *Chapter 13: Connector, Platform and Add-in Card Design, and Mechanical Considerations*, for details.

A SINGLE access cycle or a microaccess of a BURST access cycle with 32 data bit resources means that a single byte (8 data bits), word (16 data bits), triple bytes (24 data bits), or double words (32 data bits) are accessed via the AD[31::0] signal lines. A SINGLE access cycle or a microaccess of a BURST access cycle with 64 data bit resources means that a single byte to quadruple words (64 data bits) can be accessed in 8 data bit increments via the AD[63::0] signal lines.

32 AND 64 DATA BIT PCI BUS MASTER AND PCI TARGETS

The PCI bus protocol supports 32 and 64 data bit PCI bus masters. The additional signal lines required to support 64 data bit PCI bus masters are not required on all PCI bus backplanes; consequently, the 64 data bit PCI bus masters must determine if they reside on a 32 or 64 data bit bus. Platforms that support a 64 data bit PCI bus backplane do not require that any PCI resource is a 64 data bit resource. For a PCI bus master to determine if it can request a 64 data bit access cycle, it must monitor the REQ64# signal line during RESET. If the REQ64# and RST# signal lines are both asserted, the PCI bus master resides on a 64 data bit bus and can request a 64 data bit access, otherwise only 32 data bit accesses can requested. See *Chapter 11: RESET, Power, and Signal Line Initialization*, for details.

> **Targets do not have to monitor the REQ64# signal line during RESET.**

Due to the mixture of 64 data bit and non-64 data bit resources on 32 and 64 data bit buses, the PCI bus masters and targets must rely on the handshake of the REQ64# and ACK64# signal lines. A PCI bus master that samples the REQ64# signal line asserted during RESET asserts the REQ64# signal line during the ADDRESS PHASE to request a 64 data bit access cycle. The access cycle proceeds as a 64 data bit cycle if the target asserts the ACK64# signal line during the DATA PHASE in response to the asserted REQ64# signal line during the ADDRESS PHASE.

> Only the memory address space supports 64 data bit accesses; consequently, only 64 data bit memory targets must monitor and drive the REQ64# and ACK64# signal lines, respectively.

> 32 data bit PCI bus masters do not monitor (during RESET) or drive (during access cycles) the REQ64# signal line, or monitor the ACK64# signal line during access cycles. PCI targets that do not execute 64 data bit accesses do not monitor or drive the REQ64# or ACK64# signal lines during access cycles, respectively.

SIGNAL LINE DRIVERS DURING BUS CYCLES WITH 64 DATA BIT RESOURCES

During an access cycle, signal lines are owned by different PCI bus resources. A PCI resource "owns" the signal line when it is the only resource (other than pull-up resistors) that can drive the signal line during a portion of the cycle. The protocol is as follows:

- FRAME#, IRDY#, and C/BE#[7::0], IDSEL, REQx#, and REQ64# signal lines are owned by the PCI bus master.

- During a write access or special cycle, the PCI bus master owns the AD[63::0], PAR, and PAR64 signal lines.

- During a read access cycle, the PCI bus master owns the AD[63::0], PAR, and PAR64 signal lines during the ADDRESS PHASE. The target owns these signal lines during the DATA PHASE.

- The TRDY#, DEVSEL#, STOP#, ACK64# signal lines are owned by the target.

Ownership of the remaining signal lines are defined according to the following protocol:

- The CLK and RST# signal lines are owned by platform resources.

- The GNT# signal lines are owned by the central arbiter.

- The LOCK# signal line is owned by the Lock master.

- The SDONE and SBO# signal lines are owned by the cache controller in the HOST/PCI BRIDGE, or other platform resources if the platform does not have a cache controller.

DUAL ADDRESS

The DUAL ADDRESS protocol outlined in Subchapter 4.0 for 32 data bit resources applies to 64 data bit resources. As previously outlined, a 32 data bit PCI bus master can provide 64 address bits under the DUAL ADDRESS protocol without the use of the AD[63::32] signal lines. If the PCI bus master resides on a 64 data bit bus, requests a 64 data bit access (REQ64# signal line asserted during the ADDRESS PHASE), and executes a DUAL ADDRESS, the AD[63::32] signal lines contain the upper order address bit and the C/BE#[7::4] signal lines contain the encoding for the COMMAND type.

BYTE LANE OPERATION

As outlined in Subchapter 4.0, the data size of each bus cycle is dynamically identified by the C/BE# signal lines. As with the 32 data bit protocol, the central resource does not swap data between byte lanes. The AD[63::32] signal lines contain four byte lanes. (AD[39::32] signal lines is the first byte lane, AD[47::40] signal lines are the second byte lane, and so forth.) The optional 64 data bit extension defines an additional 32 data bits (AD[63::32] signal lines) for memory access cycles. The protocol for byte lane operation for the 64 data bit extension is the same as for the 32 data bit with the following additions:

■ No byte lane swapping occurs between the byte lanes of the AD[63::32] signal lines. Similarly, the central resource does not provide byte swapping between the byte lanes of the AD[31::0] and the AD[63::32] signal lines.

■ If a 64 data bit PCI bus master accesses a 32 data bit memory target, the 32 data bit target can only reside on the AD[31::0] signal lines, and the 64 data bit PCI bus master must internally swap the data between the AD[63::32] and AD[31::0] signal lines.

■ During the DATA PHASE of a write access cycle, the AD[63::32] signal lines that do not have valid data (according to the C/BE#[7::4] signal lines) must be driven to a stable level. For the DATA PHASE of a read access cycle, the AD[63::32] signal lines that do not have valid data (according to the C/BE#[7::4] signal lines) are driven to a stable level by the target. For a non-64 data bit target, the AD[63::32] and C/BE#[7::4] signal lines are driven to a logical "1" by pull-up resistors.

> The requirements for valid parity generation and checking over the AD[63::32] signal lines apply even when no data is accessed.

- The C/BE# signal lines for a given microaccess of a BURST bus cycle can enable different bytes relative to previous and subsequent microaccesses. The byte lanes do not have to be continuous. This applies to byte lanes identified within a specific bus cycle or byte lanes identified from one bus cycle to another.

- When byte lanes (AD[31::0] signal lines) are not driven with valid data according to the assertion of the associated C/BE#[3::0] signal lines, they must be driven to a stable level throughout the bus cycle by the PCI bus master. When byte lanes (AD[63::32] signal lines) are not driven with valid data according to the associated C/BE#[7::4] signal lines, they do not have to be driven to a stable level throughout the bus cycle by the PCI bus master because pull-up resistors will drive them to a logical "1".

> The 64 data bits reflects a block of data addressed. It does not mean that an actual 64 data bits is accessed.

PARK

The park protocol for 64 data bit PCI bus masters is the same as for a 32 data bit PCI bus master. When a 32 data bit PCI bus master becomes a Park master it drives the AD[31::0], C/BE#[3::0], and PAR signal lines to a stable level. The AD[63::32], C/BE#[7::4], and PAR64 signal lines are driven to a logical "1" by pull-up resistors. When a 64 data bit PCI bus master becomes a Park master it also drives the AD[31::0], C/BE#[3::0], and PAR signal lines to a stable level. The AD[63::32], C/BE#[7::4], and PAR64 signal lines are driven to a logical "1" by pull-up resistors.

4.7 32 DATA BIT PCI BUS MASTER TO 64 DATA BIT TARGET

MEMORY ACCESS CYCLE

A PCI bus master requests a 32 data bit access by the continued deassertion the REQ64# signal line during the ADDRESS PHASE. The target can only respond by executing a 32 data bit access cycle (ACK64# signal line deasserted). REQ64# and ACK64# signal lines are deasserted by pull-up resistors on the bus backplane. AD[63::32], C/BE#[7::4], and PAR64 signal lines are driven to a logical "1" by pull-up resistors; consequently, the PAR64 signal line does not have valid parity information. Once the size of the respective access cycle participants is established it remains unchanged during the remainder of the access cycle.

Only a PCI memory resource (target) can be defined as a 32 or a 64 data bit resource. All memory access cycles executed by a 32 data bit PCI bus master (REQ64# signal line deasserted) are independent of target data size (ACK64# signal line asserted or deasserted) and only execute 32 data bit access cycles.

For a 64 data bit target, the memory access cycles (including MRM, MRL and MWI) and DUAL ADDRESS operation, LOCK operation, and cache are supported with the same protocol as access cycles between a 32 data bit PCI bus master and a 32 data bit target.

I/O AND CONFIGURATION ACCESS CYCLES, INTERRUPT ACKNOWLEDGE CYCLES, AND SPECIAL CYCLES

These bus cycles are executed only with 32 data bit targets and the REQ64# and ACK64# signal lines must remain deasserted.

64 data bit I/O targets can be implemented, but there is no benefit to requiring the increased complexity and it is therefore strongly recommended that 64 data bit I/O targets are not implemented. For the purposes of this book, I/O targets are only 32 data bits in size. If a 64 data bit I/O target is implemented, the 64 data bit protocol applied to memory targets would also apply to I/O targets.

4.8 64 DATA BIT PCI BUS MASTER TO 64 DATA BIT TARGET

MEMORY ACCESS CYCLE

A PCI bus master or memory resource (target) is defined as a 64 data bit resource when the REQ64# or ACK64# signal lines are asserted, respectively. The PCI bus master requests a 64 data bit access cycle by asserting the REQ64# signal line during the ADDRESS PHASE and the target acknowledges a 64 data bit access cycle by asserting the ACK64# signal line during the DATA PHASE. The timing protocol of the FRAME# and REQ64# signal lines are the same, as well as the timing protocol of the DEVSEL# and ACK64# signal lines. The major difference between a 32 data bit and a 64 data bit access is that the AD[63::32], C/BE#[7::4], and PAR64 signal lines are used. The C/BE#[7::4] and AD[63::32] signal lines operate with the same protocol as the C/BE#[3::0] and

AD[31::0] signal lines. The PAR64 signal line has valid parity information over the C/BE#[7::4] and AD[63::32] signal lines in the same fashion as the PAR signal line has valid parity information over the C/BE#[3::0] and AD[31::0] signal lines.

The addressing protocol of a 64 data bit BURST access cycle is the same as for a 32 data bit BURST access cycle, except that the address increments are 64 data bits (QWORDS). (The AD[2] signal line must be logical "0" during the ADDRESS PHASE.) The addressing order of the 64 data bit BURST access cycle is defined by the AD[1::0] signal lines in the same fashion as a 32 data bit BURST access cycle. The execution protocol of the 64 data bit SINGLE and BURST access cycles is the same as for 32 data bit SINGLE and BURST access cycles except the AD[31::2] signal lines identify a 64 data bit QWORDS. (The AD[2] signal line is logical "0" during the ADDRESS PHASE.)

During the ADDRESS PHASE when a 32 data bit PCI bus master (REQ64# signal line deasserted) begins an access cycle, the AD[63::32], C/BE#[7::4], and the PAR64 signal lines are driven to a logical "1" by pull-up resistors. The PAR64 signal line does not contain any valid parity information. When a 64 data bit PCI bus master (REQ64# signal line asserted) begins an access cycle without DUAL ADDRESS it drives the AD[63::32] and C/BE#[7::4] signal lines to a stable level without any valid information. If a 64 data bit PCI bus master (REQ64# signal line asserted) begins an access cycle with DUAL ADDRESS, it drives the upper order address and COMMAND type onto the AD[63::32] and C/BE#[7::4] signals, respectively. For either situation, the PAR64 signal line will contain valid parity information over these signal lines during the ADDRESS PHASE with a one CLK signal line period delay.

> See *Chapter 6: Detailed Bus Cycle Operation,* for details.

For a 64 data bit target, the memory access cycles (including MRM, MRL, and MWI), DUAL ADDRESS operation, LOCK operation, and cache) are supported with the same protocol as access cycles between a 32 data bit PCI bus master and a 32 data bit target

I/O AND CONFIGURATION ACCESS CYCLES, INTERRUPT ACKNOWLEDGE CYCLES, AND SPECIAL CYCLES

These bus cycles are executed only with 32 data bit targets and the REQ64# and ACK64# signal lines must remain deasserted.

64 data bit I/O targets can be implemented, but there is no benefit to requiring the increased complexity and it is therefore strongly recommended that 64 data bit I/O targets are not implemented. For the purposes of this book, I/O targets are only 32 data bits in size. If a 64 data bit I/O target is implemented, the 64 data bit protocol applied to memory targets would also apply to I/O targets.

4.9   64 DATA BIT PCI BUS MASTER TO 32 DATA BIT TARGET

MEMORY ACCESS CYCLE

A PCI bus master and memory resource (target) is defined as a 64 and 32 data bit resource when the REQ64# and ACK64# signal lines are asserted and deasserted, respectively. The PCI bus master requests a 64 data bit access cycle by asserting the REQ64# signal line during the ADDRESS PHASE. A 32 data bit target responds without asserting the ACK64# signal line; a pull-up resistor on the bus backplane will deassert the ACK64# signal line during the DATA PHASE. The major difference between a PCI bus master request for a 64 data bit access to a 32 data bit target versus a 64 data bit target is the operation of the AD[63::32], C/BE#[7::4], and PAR64 signal lines during the DATA PHASE. During the ADDRESS PHASE the AD[63::32], C/BE#[7::4], and PAR64 signal lines operate with the same protocol as outlined in the previous section for a 64 data bit access cycle. After the completion of the initial microaccess during the DATA PHASE, the AD[63::32], C/BE#[7::4], and PAR64 signal lines can be driven to logical "1" by pull-up resistors OR can be driven to logical "1" or a stable level by the PCI bus master for the remainder of the BURST access cycle.

When a PCI bus master requests a 64 data bit access to a 32 data bit target, a SINGLE access cycle cannot be executed. As explained in Chapter 6, a request for a 64 data bit SINGLE access cycle must be broken down into a BURST access cycle with two 32 data bit microaccesses.

> If the 64 data bit access cycle (REQ64# signal line asserted) completes with Disconnect with data termination during the initial microaccess or Disconnect without data termination during the first subsequent microaccess with a 32 data bit target (ACK64# signal line deasserted), only the lower four bytes of the eight bytes (QWORD) of the 64 data bits has been accessed. The PCI bus master must subsequently execute an access cycle as a 32 data bit PCI bus master (REQ64# signal line deasserted) to access the upper four bytes of the original eight bytes (QWORD).

Except as outlined above, the addressing protocol of a 64 data bit PCI bus master BURST access cycle to a 32 data bit target is the same as for a 32 data bit PCI bus master BURST access cycle to a 32 data bit target. Similarly, except as outlined above, a PCI bus master request for a 64 data bit access to a 32 data bit target, the memory access cycles (including MRM, MRL, and MWI), DUAL ADDRESS operation, LOCK operation, and cache are with the same protocol as access cycles between a 32 data bit PCI bus master and a 32 data bit target.

> See *Chapter 6: Detailed Bus Cycle Operation*, for detailed information.

I/O AND CONFIGURATION ACCESS CYCLE, INTERRUPT ACKNOWLEDGE CYCLE, AND SPECIAL CYCLE

These bus cycles are executed only with 32 data bit targets and the REQ64# and ACK64# signal lines must remain deasserted.

> 64 data bit I/O targets can be implemented, but there is no benefit to requiring the increased complexity and it is therefore strongly recommended that 64 data bit I/O targets are not implemented. For the purposes of this book, I/O targets are only 32 data bits in size. If a 64 data bit I/O target is implemented, the 64 data bit protocol applied to memory targets would also apply to I/O targets.

4.10 INTERACTION OF CONFIGURATION ACCESS CYCLES, BRIDGES, AND REGISTERS

As previously outlined in this chapter, configuration access cycles are executed on the PCI bus to provide access to the configuration space of the PCI resources. The BRIDGEs between buses play an important role in the execution of configuration access cycles.

Traditional CPU and LEGACY buses define only memory and I/O address spaces. In the case of the x86 family of Intel CPUs (HOST CPU), no configuration access cycles are defined. For LEGACY buses such as EISA, the equivalent of the configuration space is accessed via the I/O address space. In the PCI bus protocol, the configuration access cycle is executed by a PCI bus master. The HOST CPU is the initiator of a configuration access cycle. The combination of the HOST CPU and the HOST/PCI BRIDGE is defined as the PCI bus master that is executing a configuration access cycle on a LEVEL 1 PCI bus. In order to port a configuration access cycle from one bus (source bus) to another (destination bus), a set of registers in the PCI/PCI BRIDGE in addition to a bus cycle protocol is defined. The following configuration access cycle discussion is broken into two cases: CASE 1—The HOST CPU executing I/0 HOST bus cycles to the HOST/PCI BRIDGE to generate configuration access cycles on a LEVEL 1 PCI bus, and CASE 2—The configuration access cycle on one PCI bus must be ported to another PCI bus.

The PCI Local Bus Specifications Rev. 2.0 and 2.1 define two "configuration mechanisms", #1 and #2. Configuration mechanism #2 was used on very early PCI bus implementations. All present and future implementations of the PCI bus should exclusively use configuration mechanism #1. The following discussion assumes that only configuration mechanism #1 is supported. For information on configuration mechanism #2, see the PCI Local Bus Specification.

Accesses to the CONFIG_ADDRESS Register must be in the form of 32 data bits (DWORD). An access to the CONFIG_ADDRESS Register of any other data size results in access being passed to the I/O address space of the PCI bus without affecting the CONFIG_ADDRESS Register. Accesses to the CONFIG_DATA Register can be 8 data bits (byte), 16 data bits (WORD), or 32 data bits (DWORD). The data size of configuration access cycles reflect the data size of the access to the CONFIG_DATA Register.

CASE 1

The HOST CPU accesses two registers within the HOST/PCI BRIDGE: CONFIG_ADDRESS (at I/O address 0CF8h) and CONFIG_DATA (at I/O address 0CFCh). The protocols of these two registers are summarized in Figures 4-4 and 4-5.

The bits in the CONFIG_ADDRESS Register and how they are translated to a type 0 configuration access cycle for a configuration space of a PCI resource directly attached to a LEVEL 1 PCI bus is as follows (see Figure 4-4):

- Bits 1 and 0 are defined as "00" and are ported directly to the AD[1::0] signal lines of a type 0 configuration space access cycle during the ADDRESS PHASE. A "0" is returned for these bits if the register is read.

- Bits 7 to 2 are defined as the REGISTER Number and are ported directly to the AD[7::2] signal lines of a type 0 configuration access cycle during the ADDRESS PHASE. The REGISTER Number selects the 32 data bits (double word) to be accessed within the configuration space.

- Bits 10 to 8 are defined as the FUNCTION Number and are ported directly to the AD[10::8] signal lines of a type 0 configuration access cycle during the ADDRESS PHASE. The FUNCTION Number selects one of the possible eight configuration spaces within the selected device.

- Bits 15 to 11 are defined as the Device Number and are decoded by the HOST/PCI BRIDGE into the IDSEL signal lines. The IDSEL signal lines are attached one-to-one to the AD[31:11] signal lines of a type 0 configuration access cycle during the ADDRESS PHASE. Only one IDSEL signal line can be asserted. The correlation between the IDSEL number (AD[31::11] signal lines) and the Device number is not fixed by the PCI bus specification. For example, Device Number 0 may be attached to AD[17] or AD[19] or AD[20] signal lines, etc. Another example: Device Number 0 to 16 can be assigned to signal lines AD[17] to AD[31]. If Device Numbers 17 to 31 are accessed, the HOST/PCI BRIDGE will execute the configuration access cycle with the IDSEL (AD signal lines) deasserted resulting in a MASTER Abort termination. When a MASTER Abort termination occurs under this condition, the Master-Abort bit is not set in the STATUS Register.

- Bits 23 to 16 are defined as the BUS Number and are NOT ported directly to the AD signal lines of a type 0 configuration access cycle during the ADDRESS PHASE. Their use will be explained in a later part of this section.

- Bits 30-24 are defined as reserved and are NOT ported directly to the AD signal lines of a type 0 configuration access cycle during the ADDRESS PHASE. A 0 is returned for these bits if the register is read.

- Bit 31 is defined as the ENABLE BIT and is NOT ported directly to the AD signal lines of a type 0 configuration access cycle during the ADDRESS PHASE. The HOST CPU sets this bit to a logical "1" to activate the configuration access cycle mechanism. When this bit is set to "1" any read or write of the CONFIG_DATA register results in a configuration access cycle. If this bit is "0", any accesses by the HOST

CPU to the I/O address of the CONFIG_DATA register (0CFCh) is ported through the HOST/PCI BRIDGE as an access to the PCI bus I/O address space.

The bits in the CONFIG_DATA register and how they are translated to a configuration access cycle for a configuration space in a PCI resource directly attached to a LEVEL 1 PCI bus is as follows:

■ Bits 31 to 0 are defined as data and are ported (read or write) directly to the AD[31::0] signal lines of a type 0 configuration access cycle during the DATA PHASE. They reflect data in the configuration space within the device selected.

The HOST CPU is the only bus master that begins the execution of the configuration access cycle. The CONFIG_ADDRESS and CONFIG_DATA registers are only defined for HOST/PCI BRIDGEs. A PCI bus master on a LEVEL 1 or lower PCI bus cannot begin the execution of the configuration access cycle. Consequently, the PCI/PCI BRIDGEs only port the type 1 configuration access cycle on the source bus to a type 1 or type 0 on the destination bus.

CASE 2

In the above discussion, it was assumed that the configuration space being accessed was in a PCI resource that resided on a LEVEL "1" PCI bus. When the HOST CPU reads or writes the CONFIG_DATA register (when the ENABLE BIT of the CONFIG_ADDRESS Register is set [DWORD]) a type 0 configuration access cycle is executed on the PCI bus. If the configuration space being accessed was in a PCI resource not on a LEVEL 1 PCI bus, the HOST/PCI BRIDGE must execute a type 1 configuration access cycle on the LEVEL 1 PCI bus. The method by which a HOST/PCI BRIDGE determines where the PCI resource resides will be discussed later. The type 1 configuration access cycle can only be claimed by a PCI/PCI BRIDGE on the PCI bus. The PCI/PCI BRIDGE will port the configuration access cycle (as either type 0 or type 1) to the next lower LEVEL bus.

The bits in the CONFIG_ADDRESS Register and how they are translated to a type 1 configuration access cycle for a configuration space not directly attached to a LEVEL 1 PCI bus is as follows (see Figure 4-5):

■ Bits 1 and 0 are defined as "00" and are not ported directly to the AD[1::0] signal lines of a type 1 configuration space access cycle during the ADDRESS PHASE. The BRIDGE places the binary pattern of "01" onto the AD[1::0] signal lines to identify a type 1 configuration access cycle. A logical "0" is returned for these bits if the register is read.

■ Bits 7 to 2 are defined as the REGISTER Number and are ported directly to the AD[7::2] signal lines of a type 1 configuration access cycle during the ADDRESS PHASE. The REGISTER Number selects the 32 data bit (double word) to be accessed within the configuration space.

■ Bits 10 to 8 are defined as the FUNCTION Number and are ported directly to the AD[10::8] signal lines of a type 1 configuration access cycle during the ADDRESS PHASE. The FUNCTION Number selects one of the possible eight configuration spaces within the selected device.

■ Bits 15 to 11 are defined as the Device Number and are ported directly to AD[15::11] signal lines of a type 1 configuration access cycle during ADDRESS PHASE. The Device Number selects one of the possible 32 devices on a PCI bus. Due to the availability of only 21 IDSEL signal lines, all 32 possible devices do not exist on the PCI bus. If the Device Number is selecting an IDSEL signal line not supported by the BRIDGE, a type 0 configuration access cycle is executed. No PCI resource will claim the cycle, so it will be terminated with Master Abort termination. The BRIDGE should discard the writes and return all "1"s on a read.

■ Bits 23 to 16 are defined as the BUS Number and are ported directly to the AD[23::16] signal lines of a type 1 configuration access cycle during the ADDRESS PHASE. The BUS Number selects one of the possible 256 PCI buses in a platform.

■ Bits 30-24 are defined as reserved and are ported directly to the AD [30::24] signal lines of a type 1 configuration access cycle during the ADDRESS PHASE. The associated signal lines will be driven to stable level but contain no valid information. A logical "0" is returned for these bits if the register is read.

■ Bit 31 is defined as the ENABLE BIT and is NOT ported directly to the AD signal lines of a type 1 configuration access cycle during the ADDRESS PHASE. The BRIDGE drives the AD[31] signal line with a logical "0". The HOST CPU sets this bit to a logical "1" to activate the configuration access cycle mechanism. When this bit is set to "1" any read or write of the CONFIG_DATA register results in a configuration access cycle. If this bit is "0", any accesses by the HOST CPU to the I/O address of the CONFIG_DATA register (0CFCh) is ported through the HOST/PCI BRIDGE as an access to the PCI bus I/O address space.

The bits in the CONFIG_DATA register and how they are translated to a type 1 configuration access cycle for a configuration space not directly attached to a LEVEL 1 PCI bus are as follows:

- Bits 31 to 0 are defined as data, and are ported (read or write) directly to the AD[31::0] signal lines of a type 1 configuration access cycle during the DATA PHASE. They reflect data in the configuration space within the device selected.

In the above two cases, the HOST/PCI BRIDGE was executing a type 0 or type 1 configuration access cycle to a LEVEL 1 PCI bus. The type 0 configuration access cycle is executed on the LEVEL 1 PCI bus if the PCI resource with the addressed configuration space (PCI bus master, BRIDGE, or target) resides on the specific LEVEL 1 PCI bus. The type 1 configuration access cycle is executed on the LEVEL 1 PCI bus if PCI resource with the addressed configuration space (PCI bus master, BRIDGE, or target) *does not* reside on the specific LEVEL 1 PCI bus. The PCI/PCI BRIDGE on the LEVEL 1 PCI bus will claim the type 1 configuration access cycle if the appropriate BUS Number is behind it. If the BUS Number is immediately attached to the PCI/PCI BRIDGE, a type 0 configuration access cycle is executed. If the BUS Number is not immediately attached to the PCI/PCI BRIDGE, a type 1 configuration access cycle is claimed by the next lower PCI/PCI BRIDGE. As the type 1 configuration access cycle is ported to lower and lower bus LEVELs, the associated PCI/PCI BRIDGEs are only passing through the information contained in the type 1 configuration access cycle's AD signal lines during the ADDRESS and DATA PHASES.

In order for each BRIDGE to determine if the type 1 configuration access cycles should be claimed and ported as a type "0" or type "1" configuration access cycle to the next lower bus, two additional registers are required in each BRIDGE: BUS Number (BN) and SUBORDINATE BUS Number (SBN). (See Figure 4-6.) The BN register identifies which PCI bus is immediately attached to the BRIDGE and the SBN register identifies the highest-numbered PCI bus behind the BRIDGE. The protocol for using these registers is as follows:

For a HOST/PCI BRIDGE:

- If the BUS Numbers in the BN register and Bits 16 to 23 in the CONFIG_ADDRESS Register match, the associated HOST/PCI BRIDGE claims the HOST bus cycle and a type 0 configuration access cycle is executed on the destination bus.

- If the BUS Number in the SBN register is greater than or equal to the BUS Number in Bits 16 to 23 in the CONFIG_ADDRESS Register match, the associated HOST/PCI BRIDGE claims the HOST bus cycle and a type 1 configuration access cycle is executed on the destination bus.

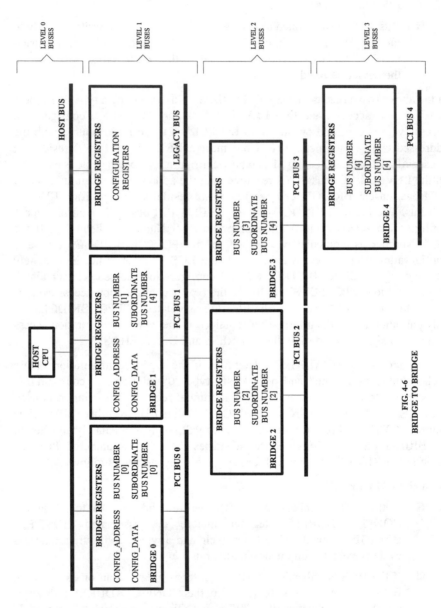

Figure 4-6: Bridge to Bridge

For a PCI/PCI BRIDGE:

- If the BUS Numbers in the AD[23::16] signal lines during the ADDRESS PHASE of a type 1 configuration access cycle on the source bus and the BN register match, the associated PCI/PCI BRIDGE claims the source bus type 1 configuration access cycle and executes a type 0 configuration access cycle on the destination bus.

- If the BUS Number in the AD[23::16] signal lines during the ADDRESS PHASE of a type 1 configuration access cycle on the source bus is less than or equal to the BUS Number in the SBN register match and greater than secondary bus numbers, the associated PCI/PCI BRIDGE claims the source bus type 1 configuration access cycle and executes a type 1 configuration access cycle on the destination bus.

See *Subchapter4.11: Interaction of Special Cycles, Bridges, and Registers*, for unique use of the BUS, FUNCTION, DEVICE, and REGISTER Numbers in the CONFIG_Address Register.

In Figure 4-6, there is more than one HOST/PCI BRIDGE; consequently, there are multiple CONFIG_ADDRESS and CONFIG_DATA at the same addresses. The platform must assign one of the BRIDGEs as the one responsible for handshaking (primary) with the HOST CPU and the other BRIDGEs must snoop the data written to the CONFIG_Address Register in the primary BRIDGE. The ENABLE BIT should only be enabled in the BRIDGE that is the link to the PCI bus being accessed.

A HOST or PCI bus BRIDGE that does not have any peer BRIDGEs does not need the SB and SBN registers. In Figure 4-6, PCI/PCI BRIDGE 4 does not need these registers. If only one HOST/PCI BRIDGE resided on the HOST bus, these registers would not be needed in the one HOST/PCI BRIDGE. This is because by definition the destination is PCI bus 0 and all other PCI buses must be below PCI bus 0.

Notice in Figure 4-6 that the HOST LEGACY BRIDGE also may have a set of configuration registers. These are not the same as PCI and are specific to the protocol of the LEGACY bus.

4.11 INTERACTION OF SPECIAL CYCLES, BRIDGES, AND REGISTERS

> The PCI Local Bus Specifications Rev. 2.0 and 2.1 define two "Configuration Mechanisms", #1 and #2. Configuration #2 was used on very early PCI bus implementations. All present and future implementations of the PCI bus should exclusively use Configuration Mechanism #1. The following discussion assumes that only Configuration Mechanism #1 is supported relative to special cycles. For information on Configuration Mechanism #2, read the PCI Local Bus Specification.

When the BUS Number in the CONFIG_ADDRESS Register matches the number of the BRIDGE, writing to the CONFIG_DATA register results in a special cycle on the destination PCI bus directly attached to the BRIDGE. If they do not match, writing to the CONFIG_DATA register (when the ENABLE BIT is set) results in a type 1 configuration access cycle.

The special cycle will be executed when all of the following conditions are met:

- The aforementioned BUS and BRIDGE numbers match.

- The bits of the Device Number in the CONFIG_ADDRESS Register are all logical "1"s.

- The bits of the FUNCTION Number in the CONFIG_ADDRESS Register are all logical "1"s.

- The bits of the REGISTER Number in the CONFIG_ADDRESS Register are all logical "0"s.

- The ENABLE BIT CONFIG_ADDRESS Register is set to a logical "1"

- DATA is written to the CONFIG_DATA register. If data is read under these conditions, the result is undefined. One possibility is for the BRIDGE to execute a type "0" configuration access cycle. This will result in a Master Abort because no PCI resource will respond and thus the data returned to the HOST CPU are all logical "1"*s*.

- Only SINGLE Type 1 configuration access cycles can be converted by a PCI/PCI BRIDGE to a SINGLE special cycle. Conversion of BURST Type 1 configuration access cycles to BURST special cycles is not allowed. A BURST Type 1 configuration access cycle must be converted to a series of SINGLE special cycles by the PCI/PCI BRIDGE. Consequently, BURST special cycles can only be executed by a HOST/PCI BRIDGE.

CHAPTER 5

SIGNAL LINE DEFINITION

This chapter consists of the following subchapters:

5.0 INTRODUCTION

The following discussions describe the definition of the signal lines on the PCI bus. The operation of the signal lines will vary depending on the type of bus cycle, the data size of the bus master, whether the DUAL ADDRESS is being executed, whether the bus is IDLE (no bus cycles and not parked), and when the bus is RESET or parked. The different types of bus cycles include access (memory, I/O and configuration), special, and interrupt acknowledge cycles. The data size of a PCI resource can be either 32 or 64 data bits. When the bus is IDLE, the signal lines are driven to a stable level by the present PCI bus owner, Park master, or by pull-up resistors. The signal lines are driven to specific values when RESET or parked.

The signal lines are all referenced to the rising edge of the CLK signal line (see Chapter 12 for more information) with the following exceptions:

- The RESET signal line is asynchronous to the CLK signal line. See Chapter 11 for more information.

- The SERR# signal line is asserted synchronous and deasserted asynchronous to the CLK signal line. See a latter portion of this chapter and Chapter 10 for more information.

- The INTx# signal lines are asynchronous to the CLK signal line.

The PCI bus protocol does not require that every resource support all of the possible PCI bus signal lines. PCI bus masters and targets that reside on the platform (not via the connector) require 47 and 45 signal lines, respectively. The

PERR# and SERR# signal lines do not have to be supported by resources that do not attach to the platform via a connector. However, the PERR# and SERR# signal lines must be supported by each connector and by platforms that support connectors. Additionally, the PRSNT[1::2]# pins must also be supported for platforms that support connectors. These pins are not signal lines per the bus protocol; consequently, they will not be discussed in this chapter (see Chapter 11 for more information). Finally, a platform must support all of the REQ# and GNT# signal line pairs required for the support of PCI bus masters.

> The PCI Mobile Design Guide also defines an optional signal line called CLKRUN#. This signal line is not required for a non-mobile environment. Please see the PCI Mobile Design Guide for more information.

The **REQUIRED** signal lines must be supported by all PCI bus masters and targets. The exception are the REQ# and GNT# (bus ownership arbitration) signal lines which are only required for PCI bus masters. The **OPTIONAL** signal lines can be supported individually by PCI bus masters and targets.

The signal lines also have different electrical characteristics. These characteristics will be discussed in detail in Chapter 12. In summary, the **ELECTRICAL ATTRIBUTES** of the signal lines are as follows:

- Input: Driven into the PCI resource and never tri-stated.

- Output: Driven by the PCI resource and never tri-stated.

- Bi-directional tri-state: Driven into and driven by the PCI resource. The signal line can also be tri-stated.

- Bi-directional drive tri-state: driven into and driven by the PCI resource. The signal line can also be tri-stated. When the PCI resource has driven this signal line low it must drive it high for one CLK signal line period prior to tri-state.

- Open drain: driven by the PCI resource as an output, and is an open drain device to allow for a wire-OR sharing of the signal line. The central resource is the only circuitry that receives it as an input.

The format of each entry is as follows:

Signal Name (Short)	Signal Name (Long)	Req./Opt.	I/O Pin Attributes	Resistors

Signal name (short):   The name used in the text
Signal name (long):   Full name
Req./Opt.:   Distinguishes between required and an optional signal lines.

I/O pin attributes: Identifies the electrical attributes of the pins outlined above.

Resistors: Identifies the pull-up resistor value the platform provides to 3.3 or 5 volts. Resistors are mounted on the platform unless otherwise noted.

The use of the "#" suffix with the signal line name indicates that it is asserted with a logical "0" at 0 volts. A signal line without the "#" suffix is asserted when at a logical "1" at 3.3 or 5 volts.

BRIEF DESCRIPTION

This line will contain a brief description of the signal line(s), followed by a description of the following conditions:

RESET: Describes signal line operation during RESET and when the bus is parked. The RESET condition is when the RST# signal line is asserted.

PARK: The park condition is when the bus is parked under one of the following conditions: A PCI bus master is the Park master with its associated REQ# and GNT# signal lines deasserted and asserted, respectively, or the central arbiter is the Park master when all REQ# and GNT# signal lines are deasserted.

IDLE PHASE: Describes the signal line operation between bus cycles when the PCI bus master retains ownership of the bus (associated REQ# and GNT# signal lines are both asserted).

ADDRESS, DATA PHASES: Describes the signal line operation during the ADDRESS and DATA PHASE of bus cycles.

In this and other chapters the phrase "driven to a logical '1' by pull-up resistor(s)" means that the signal line(s) reach a stable level by being pulled to logical "1" by the resistor(s). It does not represent an *active* driving of the signal line(s) to a logical "1".

5.1 ADDRESS, DATA, AND ASSOCIATED SIGNAL LINES

The AD[31::0] signal lines multiplex addresses and data. The C/BE#[3::0], FRAME#, and PAR signal lines are used to interpret and validate the signal lines that carry the addresses and data.

AD[31::0]	Address and DATA	Req.	Bi-Directional Tri-state	No Pull-up Resistors

These signal lines contain the address and data bits for the bus cycles.

This section covers AD[31::0] where used by a 32 data bit bus master (REQ64# deasserted by pull-up resistor). See *Subchapter 5.6: 64 Data Bit Signal Lines* for the case using a 64 data bit bus master.

RESET

Driven to stable level (logical "0" ... not logical "1") by central resource.

PARK

Driven to a stable level by Park master (logical "0" ... not logical "1" if central resource is PARK master).

IDLE PHASE

Driven to a stable level by PCI bus master.

ADDRESS PHASE

MEMORY AND I/O

For the memory address space, the AD[32::2] signal lines address a double word and the AD[1::0] signal lines provide the BURST sequence address order. For the I/O address space, the AD[31::0] signal lines contain the address of the least significant byte.

CONFIGURATON ACCESS CYCLE

The AD[31::0] signals are divided into several groups. The definition of the signal lines in each group is dependent on the type of configuration access cycle. For details, see *Subchapters 4.2: Configuration Access Cycles* and *4.5: 32 Data Bit PCI Bus Master to 32 Data Bit Target*.

SPECIAL AND INTERRUPT ACKNOWLEDGE CYCLES

The AD[31::0] signal lines are driven to a stable level but contain no valid information.

DATA PHASE

MEMORY, I/O, AND CONFIGURATION

The least significant data is on signal lines AD[7::0] with the most significant data in signal lines AD[31::24].

Only those AD signal lines indicated as valid by the C/BE#[3::0] signal lines have valid data. Those that are indicated as invalid do not contain data but must be driven to a stable level. For a write access cycle, the bus master is responsible for driving the AD[31::0] signal lines, and for a read access cycle the target is responsible for driving the AD[31::0] signal lines. Under certain write-back cache and prefetchable memory conditions, all of the AD signal lines have valid read data independent of the C/BE# signal lines.

SPECIAL CYCLE

The AD[15::0] signal lines contain the message type. The AD[31::16] signal lines are driven to a stable level or contain an optional data field related to the message.

INTERRUPT ACKNOWLEDGE CYCLE

The AD[31::0] signal lines contain the interrupt vector.

See *Subchapter 5.6: 64 Data Bit Signal Line* section for information on the protocol of the AD[63::32] signal lines with 32 data bit PCI bus resources, and AD[31::0] and AD[63::32] signal lines with 64 data bit PCI resources.

C/BE#[3::0]	Bus Command and Byte Enables	Req.	Bi-Directional Tri-state	No Pull-up Resistors

These signal lines contain the COMMAND type for the bus cycle and the valid byte lanes of the ad signal lines.

This section covers C/BE#[3::0] where used by a 32 data bit bus master (REQ64# deasserted by pull-up resistor). See *Section 5.6: 64 Data Bit Signal Lines*, for the case using a 64 data bit bus master.

RESET

Driven to a stable level (logical "0" ... not logical "1") by central resource.

PARK

Driven to a stable level by Park master (logical "0" ... not logical "1" if central resource is PARK master).

IDLE PHASE

Driven to a stable level by PCI bus master.

ADDRESS PHASE

MEMORY, I/O, AND CONFIGURATION

These signal lines contain the COMMAND type for the access cycle and DUAL ADDRESS.

SPECIAL CYCLE

These signal lines contain the COMMAND type for a special cycle.

INTERRUPT ACKNOWLEDGE

These signal lines contain the COMMAND type for an interrupt acknowledge cycle.

DATA PHASE

MEMORY ACCESS, CONFIGURATION ACCESS, AND SPECIAL CYCLES.

The C/BE#[3::0] signal lines indicate which byte lanes of the AD[31::0] signal lines contain valid data.

I/O ACCESS CYCLE

The C/BE#[3::0] signal lines indicate which byte lanes of the AD[31::0] signal lines contain valid data. The byte lanes identified by the C/BE#[3::0] signal lines valid must agree with the byte address specified by the AD[1::0] signal lines during ADDRESS PHASE

INTERRUPT ACKNOWLEDGE CYCLE

The C/BE#[3::0] signal lines indicate which byte lanes of the AD[31::0] signal lines contain valid interrupt vector information.

The COMMAND type encoding of the C/BE#[3::0] signal lines (and C/BE#[7::4] signal lines for 64 data bit PCI bus masters when DUAL ADDRESS is executed) during the ADDRESS PHASE of a bus cycle is as follows:

C/BE# [3 2 1 0] Command Type

([7 6 5 4])

0 0 00	Interrupt Acknowledge Cycle
0 0 0 1	Special Cycle
0 0 1 0	I/O Read Access Cycle
0 0 1 1	I/O Write Access Cycle
0 1 0 0	Reserved
0 1 0 1	Reserved
0 1 1 0	Memory Read Access Cycle
0 1 1 1	Memory Write Access Cycle
1 0 0 0	Reserved
1 0 0 1	Reserved
1 0 1 0	Configuration Read Access Cycle
1 0 1 1	Configuration Write Access Cycle
1 1 0 0	Memory Read Multiple Access Cycle
1 1 0 1	DUAL ADDRESS Access Cycle
1 1 1 0	Memory Read Line Access Cycle
1 1 1 1	Memory Write And Invalidate Access Cycle

See *Section 5.6: 64 Data Bit Signal Lines* for information on the protocol of the C/BE#[7::4] signal lines with 32 data bit PCI resources, and the C/BE#[3::0] and C/BE#[7::4] signal lines with 64 data bit PCI resources.

PAR	Parity	Req.	Bi-Directional Tri-state	No Pull-up Resistor

This signal line provides even parity across the AD and C/BE# signal lines

This section covers PAR where used by a 32 data bit bus master (REQ64# deasserted by pull-up resistor). See *Section 5.6: 64 Data Bit Signal Lines*, for the case using a 64 data bit bus master.

RESET

Driven to a stable level (logical "0" ... not logical "1") by central resource.

PARK

Driven to a stable state by the Park master (logical "0" ... not logical "1" if central resource is PARK master).

IDLE PHASE

Driven to a stable level by the PCI bus master.

This signal line lags the AD signal lines by one CLK signal line period. Consequently, what is defined for the ADDRESS and DATA PHASES below is actually one CLK signal period later.

161

ADDRESS PHASE

MEMORY ACCESS, I/O ACCESS, CONFIGURATION ACCESS, INTERRUPT ACKNOWLEDGE, AND SPECIAL CYCLES

The PAR signal line is driven by the PCI bus master to provide even parity over the AD[31::0] and C/BE#[3::0] signal lines. The total number of "1"s over these signal lines including the PAR signal line is an even number.

DATA PHASE

MEMORY ACCESS, I/O ACCESS, CONFIGURATION ACCESS, INTERRUPT ACKNOWLEDGE, AND SPECIAL CYCLES

The PAR signal line is driven to provide even parity over the AD[31::0] and C/BE#[3::0] signal lines. The total number of "1"s over these signal lines including the PAR signal line is an even number. For a write access cycle the PAR signal line is driven by the PCI bus master. For a read access cycle the PAR signal line is driven by the target.

See *Section 5.6: 64 Data Bit Signal Lines* for information on the protocol of the C/BE#[7::4] signal lines with 32 data bit PCI resources, and the PAR64 and PAR signal lines with 64 data bit PCI resources.

5.2   CYCLE CONTROL SIGNAL LINES

FRAME#	Frame	Req.	Bi-Directional Drive Tri-state	Pull-up Resistor

This signal line identifies the beginning of a bus cycle.

RESET

Driven to a logical "1" (deasserted) by a pull-up resistor.

PARK

Driven to a logical "1" (deasserted) by a pull-up resistor.

IDLE PHASE

Driven to a logical "1" (deasserted) by PCI bus master.

ADDRESS AND DATA PHASE

MEMORY ACCESS, I/O ACCESS, AND INTERRUPT ACKNOWLEDGE CYCLES

The PCI bus master asserts the FRAME# signal line to identify the ADDRESS PHASE and therefore the beginning of an access cycle. The asserted FRAME# signal line during the ADDRESS PHASE indicates that the AD and C/BE# signal lines contain valid address and COMMAND type information, respectively. When a DUAL ADDRESS is not executed, the minimum asserted pulse width is one CLK signal line period. When a DUAL ADDRESS is executed, the minimum asserted pulse width is two CLK signal line periods.

The PCI bus master uses the FRAME# signal lines during the DATA PHASE to control the length of the cycle. If the FRAME# signal line is deasserted simultaneously with the first assertion of the IRDY# signal line, a SINGLE access cycle is executed. If the FRAME# signal line is deasserted after the first assertion of the IRDY# signal line, a BURST access cycle is executed.

> During an access cycle, the IRDY# signal line must be asserted simultaneously or prior to the deassertion of the FRAME# signal line.

An access cycle is complete, even if a Retry, Disconnect, Master Abort, or Target Abort termination is executed, when the FRAME# and IRDY# signal lines are simultaneously sampled deasserted (IDLE PHASE). Prior to the IDLE PHASE the IRDY# signal line must be asserted for minimum of one CLK signal line period. The one exception is the execution of Fast Back-to-Back access cycles. Under Fast Back-to-Back protocol an access cycle completes with the simultaneous deassertion and assertion of the FRAME# and TRDY# signal lines, respectively. By convention, the IRDY# signal line is required to be asserted for one CLK signal line period when the FRAME# signal line is deasserted at the completion of the cycle.

CONFIGURATION ACCESS CYCLE

The PCI bus master asserts the FRAME# signal line to identify the ADDRESS PHASE and therefore the beginning of the an access cycle. The asserted FRAME# signal line during the ADDRESS PHASE indicates that the AD[31::0] contain valid IDSEL and address information. Also, the C/BE#[3::0] signal lines contain valid COMMAND type information. The minimum asserted pulse width is one CLK signal line period.

The PCI bus master uses the FRAME# signal lines during the DATA PHASE to control the length of the cycle. If the FRAME# signal line is deasserted simultaneously with the first assertion of the IRDY# signal line, a SINGLE access cycle is executed. If the FRAME# signal line is asserted with the first assertion of the IRDY# signal line, a BURST access cycle is executed.

> During a configuration access cycle the IRDY# signal line must be asserted simultaneously or prior to the deassertion of the FRAME# signal line.

A configuration access cycle is complete even if a Retry, Disconnect, Master Abort, or target termination is executed, when the FRAME# and IRDY# signal lines are simultaneously sampled deasserted (IDLE PHASE). Prior to the IDLE PHASE the IRDY# signal line must be asserted for a minimum of one CLK signal line period.

SPECIAL CYCLE

The FRAME# signal line is defined with the same protocol as defined for the memory and I/O access cycles with a few exceptions. Fast Back-to-Back protocol cannot be applied.

IRDY#	Initiator Ready	Req.	Bi-Directional Drive Tri-state	Pull-up Resistor

This signal line indicates when the PCI bus master (initiator) is ready to complete the bus cycle.

RESET

Driven to a logical "1" (deasserted) by a pull-up resistor.

PARK

Driven to a logical "1" (deasserted) by a pull-up resistor.

IDLE PHASE

Driven to a logical "1" (deasserted) by PCI bus master.

ADDRESS PHASE

Driven to a logical "1" (deasserted) by PCI bus master or a pull-up resistor.

DATA PHASE

MEMORY ACCESS, I/O ACCESS, CONFIGURATION ACCESS, AND INTERRUPT ACKNOWLEDGE CYCLES

The PCI bus master asserts the IRDY# signal line to indicate that it is ready to complete the access. For a write access cycle, it indicates that the bus master has driven valid data onto the AD signal lines. For a read access cycle or interrupt acknowledge cycle, it indicates that the PCI bus master is ready to retrieve data or interrupt vector from the AD signal lines.

By convention, both the IRDY# and TRDY# signal lines must be asserted to complete the access cycle. The deassertion of the either of these signal lines prior to the completion of the access cycles results in the automatic insertion of wait states with a resolution of one CLK signal line period.

During an access cycle, the IRDY# signal line must be asserted simultaneously or prior to the deassertion of the FRAME# signal line.

Once the IRDY# signal line is asserted it remains asserted for each data access until TRDY# (and/or STOP# signal line) signal line is asserted. When a Retry, Disconnect without data, Master Abort, or Target Abort termination is executed, the IRDY# signal line must be asserted a minimum of one CLK signal line period prior to the simultaneous deassertion of the FRAME# and IRDY# signal lines to complete the cycle.

SPECIAL CYCLE

The IRDY# signal line operates with the same protocol as outlined for the memory, I/O and configuration access cycles, except that the TRDY# signal line is not asserted during a special cycle.

TRDY#	Target Ready	Req.	Bi-Directional Drive Tri-state	Pull-up Resistor

This signal line indicates when the accessed PCI resource (target) is ready to complete the bus cycle.

RESET

Driven to a logical "1" (deasserted) by a pull-up resistor.

PARK

Driven to a logical "1" (deasserted) by a pull-up resistor.

IDLE PHASE

Driven to a logical "1" (deasserted) by a pull-up resistor.

ADDRESS PHASE

Driven to a logical "1" (deasserted) by a pull-up resistor.

DATA PHASE

**MEMORY ACCESS, I/O ACCESS, CONFIGURATION ACCESS, AND
INTERRUPT ACKNOWLEDGE CYCLES**

The target asserts the TRDY# signal line to indicate that the target is ready to
complete the access or interrupt acknowledge cycle. For a read access cycle, it
indicates that the target has driven valid data onto the AD signal lines. For an
interrupt acknowledge cycle, it indicates that the target has driven a valid
interrupt vector onto the AD signal lines. For a write access cycle, it indicates
that the target is ready to retrieve data from the AD signal lines.

By convention, both the IRDY# and TRDY# signal lines must be asserted to
complete the access or interrupt acknowledge cycle. The deassertion of either of
these signal lines prior to the completion of the access or interrupt acknowledge
cycle results in the automatic insertion of wait states with a resolution of one
CLK signal line period.

> **During a read access cycle, the TRDY# signal line must be asserted one
> CLK signal line period later than earliest possible point to allow the AD
> signal lines to be tri-stated by the bus master.**

> **The DEVSEL# signal line must be asserted simultaneously with or prior
> to the assertion of the TRDY# signal line.**
>
> **Once asserted, the TRDY# signal line remains asserted for each data
> access or interrupt acknowledge cycle until the IRDY# signal line is
> asserted.**

> **During Fast Back-to-Back access cycles, the assertion of the TRDY#
> signal line must be one CLK signal line period later (minimum) than the
> earliest possible point for a FAST decode versus a non-Fast Back-to-Back
> access cycle condition. Please see the *Fast Back-to-Back* portion of
> Section 6.10 for details.**

SPECIAL CYCLE

This signal line remains deasserted throughout the special cycle.

DEVSEL#	Device Select	Req.	Bi-Directional Drive Tri-state	Pull-up Resistor

This signal line indicates when a PCI resource (target) has decoded the address on the ad signal lines and claims the bus cycle.

RESET

Driven to a logical "1" (deasserted) by a pull-up resistor.

PARK

Driven to a logical "1" (deasserted) by a pull-up resistor.

IDLE PHASE

Driven to a logical "1" (deasserted) by a pull-up resistor.

ADDRESS PHASE

Driven to a logical "1" (deasserted) by a pull-up resistor.

DATA PHASE

MEMORY ACCESS, I/O ACCESS, CONFIGURATION ACCESS, AND INTERRUPT ACKNOWLEDGE CYCLES

The target asserts the DEVSEL# signal line to indicate it has decoded the address on the AD signal lines and will participate in (claim) the access cycle. For an interrupt acknowledge cycle, the assertion of the DEVSEL# signal line indicates that it is the PCI resource that requested service. The PCI bus master must monitor the DEVSEL# signal line to determine if a target has claimed the cycle or if a Master Abort termination will be executed. The PCI BRIDGE resource that utilizes SUBTRACTIVE DECODING must monitor the DEVSEL# signal line to determine if it should claim the cycle if not claimed by other PCI resources on the bus.

The DEVSEL# signal line must be asserted simultaneously with or prior to the assertion of the TRDY#, STOP#, and PERR# signal lines by the target. The DEVSEL# signal line is asserted simultaneously with the ACK64# signal if a 64 data bit access is acknowledged.

Once asserted, the DEVSEL# signal line remains asserted until the completion of the DATA PHASE except when a Target Abort occurs.

167

During Fast Back-to-Back access cycles, the assertion of the DEVSEL# signal line must be one CLK signal line period later (minimum) than the earliest possible point for a FAST decode versus a non Fast Back-to-Back access cycle condition. Please see the *Fast Back-to-Back* portion of Section 6.10 for details.

SPECIAL CYCLE

This signal line remains deasserted throughout the special cycle.

STOP#	Stop	Req.	Bi-Directional Drive Tri-state	Pull-up Resistor

This signal line indicates that the accessed PCI resource (target) wants to end the bus cycle without the PCI bus master completing any or all accesses.

RESET

Driven to a logical "1" (deasserted) by a pull-up resistor.

PARK

Driven to a logical "1" (deasserted) by a pull-up resistor.

IDLE PHASE

Driven to a logical "1" (deasserted) by a pull-up resistor.

ADDRESS PHASE

Driven to a logical "1" (deasserted) by a pull-up resistor.

DATA PHASE

MEMORY ACCESS, I/O ACCESS, CONFIGURATION ACCESS, INTERRUPT ACKNOWLEDGE CYCLES

The target asserts the STOP# signal line to inform the PCI bus master that the current cycle must be immediately terminated. The STOP# signal line is used in conjunction with the TRDY# and DEVSEL# signal lines to request a Retry, Disconnect, or Target Abort termination. The PCI bus master completes the cycle with the protocol of the requested termination.

The DEVSEL# signal line must be asserted simultaneously with or prior to the assertion of the STOP# signal line.

Once asserted, the STOP# signal line remains asserted until the completion of the DATA PHASE.

During Fast Back-to-Back cycles the assertion of the STOP# signal line must be one CLK signal line period later (minimum) than the earliest possible point for a FAST decode versus a non Fast Back-to-Back cycle condition. Please see the *Fast Back-To-Back* portion of Section 6.10 for details.

SPECIAL CYCLE

This signal line remains deasserted throughout the special cycle.

IDSEL	Initialization Device Select	Req.	Input (1)	No Pull-up Resistor

Note (1): The **AD[31::11]** signal lines are used for the **IDSEL** signal lines for each PCI resource. To the resource, this is always an input pin.

These lines are driven by the PCI bus master to select the configuration space of a specific PCI resource.

In this book, the IDSEL signal lines are driven from the AD signal lines. Platform resources may also drive the IDSEL signal lines by any method independent of the AD signal lines. It is assumed that most every implementation will use the AD signal lines; consequently, this book will only assume this method.

RESET

Driven to a stable level by central resource.

PARK

Driven to a stable level by Park master.

IDLE PHASE

Driven to a stable level by PCI bus master.

ADDRESS PHASE

CONFIGURATION

Used to select one of the PCI bus resource's configuration registers when the AD[1::0] signal lines = [0::0].

MEMORY ACCESS, I/O ACCESS, SPECIAL ACCESS, AND INTERRUPT ACKNOWLEDGE CYCLES

These signal lines have no meaning during these bus cycles.

DATA PHASE

CONFIGURATION ACCESS, MEMORY ACCESS, I/O ACCESS, SPECIAL, AND INTERRUPT ACKNOWLEDGE CYCLES

These signal lines have no meaning during these bus cycles.

5.3 BUS CONTROL SIGNAL LINES

CLK	PCI Clock	Req.	Input (1)	No Pull-up Resistor

Note (1): Driven by central resource.

This signal line is the PCI bus clock that synchronizes all PCI bus events.

RESET

Always driven by the central resource.

PARK

Always driven by the central resource.

IDLE, ADDRESS, AND DATA PHASES

MEMORY ACCESS, I/O ACCESS, CONFIGURATION ACCESS, SPECIAL, AND INTERRUPT ACKNOWLEDGE CYCLES

The CLK signal line is driven by the central resource and acts as the synchronous reference point for all PCI bus signal line transitions. All signal lines are sampled on the rising edge of the CLK signal line except for the RST#, IRQ A to D#, and the deassertion of the SERR# signal lines.

The frequency of the CLK signal line can be dynamically changed during bus cycles. The change of frequency must provide clean clock edges and the minimum low and high CLK signal line specifications must be maintained. If the CLK signal line frequency is reduced to 0 MHz, the state of the signal line must be low. PCI compatible components can restrict the CLK signal line to a single frequency if the component will only be used on the platform.

Other specifications of the CLK signal relative frequency tolerance over temperature must comply with the minimum low and high pulse times. See *Chapter 12: Signal Line Timing and Electrical Requirements*, for more information.

Note: If the M66EN signal line is a logical "0", the CLK signal line's maximum frequency is 33 MHz. If the M66EN signal line is a logical "1", the CLK signal line's maximum frequency is 66 MHz.

M66EN	66 MHz ENABLE	Opt.	Input/Output)	Pull-Up Resistor 5K to Vcc

Rev. 2.1 of the PCI bus specification has defined one of the reserved pins as M66EN to allow a 66 MHz PCI bus. In a 33 MHz PCI bus or add-on card this pin is grounded. In a 66 MHz PCI bus this pin is pulled to V_{cc} with a 5K resistor

and is bussed to every chip and add-on connector. When a 33 MHz chip or add-on card is installed in a 66 MHz PCI bus, the M66EN is pulled to ground. This informs the central resource and any 66 MHz chips and add-on cards that the bus must operate at 33 MHz.

When a 66 MHz chip or add-on card is installed in a 66 MHz PCI bus, the M66EN is either a logical "1" or "0". Logical "1" (via a pull-up resistor) indicates that all PCI resources will operate at 66 MHz. Logical "0" (ground) indicates that at least one PCI resource is 33 MHz only; consequently, the bus must operate at 33 MHz.

Note: 66 MHz is only defined for 3.3 volt operation.

RST#	RESET	Req.	Input (1)	No Pull-up Resistor

Note (1): Driven by central resource.

This signal line indicates a RESET of all PCI resources.

RESET

Driven to a logical "0" (asserted) by central resource.

PARK

Driven to a logical "1" (deasserted) by central resource.

IDLE, ADDRESS, AND DATA PHASES

MEMORY ACCESS, I/O ACCESS, CONFIGURATION ACCESS, SPECIAL, AND INTERRUPT ACKNOWLEDGE CYCLES

Driven to a logical "1" (deasserted) by central resource.

LOCK#	Lock	Opt.	Bi-Directional Drive Tri-state	Pull-up Resistor

This signal line indicates that a PCI bus master has locked a PCI resource for its exclusive access.

RESET

Driven to a logical "1" (deasserted) by a pull-up resistor.

PARK

Driven to a logical "1" (deasserted) by a pull-up resistor or to a logical "0" (asserted) by Lock master.

IDLE, ADDRESS, AND DATA PHASES

MEMORY ACCESS CYCLE

The LOCK# signal line is asserted by a PCI bus master to lock a specific memory target on the PCI bus. The locking of a memory target simply means that only one PCI bus master (called Lock master) can access the locked resource (target). Any PCI bus master can become the Lock master of a given target.

An access to a locked resource (target) by a PCI bus master that is not the Lock master results in a Retry termination of the access cycle. There is one exception: if the cache controller in the HOST/PCI BRIDGE is executing a snoop write-back access cycle to the locked target, the cycle is allowed to successfully complete without a Retry termination.

I/O ACCESS, CONFIGURATION ACCESS, SPECIAL, AND INTERRUPT ACKNOWLEDGE CYCLES

Only a memory target can be locked; consequently, this signal line is ignored for these bus cycles.

5.4   ERROR REPORTING SIGNAL LINES

PERR#	Parity Error	Req.	Bi-Directional Drive Tri-state	Pull-up Resistor

This signal line indicates a data parity error in the **AD**, **C/BE#**, **PAR**, and **PAR64** signal lines during the DATA PHASE.

RESET

Driven to a logical "1" (deasserted) by a pull-up resistor.

PARK

Driven to a logical "1" (deasserted) by a pull-up resistor.

IDLE PHASE

Driven to a logical "1" (deasserted) by a pull-up resistor.

ADDRESS PHASE

MEMORY ACCESS, I/O ACCESS, CONFIGURATION ACCESS, SPECIAL, AND INTERRUPT ACKNOWLEDGE CYCLES

This signal line is not defined for the ADDRESS PHASE. Assertion of this signal line is reflective of the DATA PHASE of the preceding access cycle.

DATA PHASE

MEMORY ACCESS, I/O ACCESS, CONFIGURATION ACCESS, AND INTERRUPT ACKNOWLEDGE CYCLES

The PERR# signal line reports parity errors detected over the AD, C/BE#, PAR, and PAR64 signal lines during the DATA PHASE. The PCI bus master will drive this signal line during a read access or interrupt acknowledge cycle, and the target will drive this signal line during a write access cycle. The PERR# signal line must be asserted for each data access (IRDY# and TRDY# signal lines asserted) for a minimum of one CLK signal line period whenever a parity error occurs. To report a parity error, the PERR# signal line must be asserted two CLK signal line periods after the data is accessed. If a BURST access cycle is being executed, the PERR# signal line is asserted for multiple CLK signal line periods provided a parity error occurred on adjacent microaccesses.

The PERR# signal line is monitored by the central resource (and PCI bus master during write bus cycles) and parity errors can be reported by several means including the assertion of the SERR# signal line.

> The DEVSEL# signal line must be asserted two CLK signal line periods prior to the assertion of the PERR# signal line.

SPECIAL CYCLE

The PERR# signal line cannot be used to report parity errors on the AD[31::0], C/BE#[3::0], and PAR signal lines during the DATA PHASE of SPECIAL bus cycles. The SPECIAL bus cycles broadcast data to all target resources; consequently, no single target resource can claim the PERR# signal line.

SERR#	System Error	Req.	Open Drain (1)	Pull-up Resistor

Note (1): This signal line is only an input to central resource.

This signal line indicates an address parity error in the AD, C/BE#, PAR, and PAR64 signal lines during the ADDRESS PHASE. also used for catastrophic PCI bus errors.

> SERR# is synchronous to the CLK signal line when asserted. However, the rise time of the open collector provides an asynchronous characteristic to this signal line. Consequently, this book defines this as an asynchronous signal line to emphasize the deassertion protocol.

The SERR# signal line is asserted synchronously with the CLK signal line for one CLK signal line period and is then tri-stated. The open drain characteristic allows the central resource and multiple PCI resources to simultaneously assert this signal line. The deassertion of this signal lines relies on a pull-up resistor and not on a short active pulse; consequently, the deassertion is asynchronous to the CLK signal line. Once the SERR# signal line is asserted it is considered active until sampled deasserted for two consecutive CLK signal line periods. The SERR# signal line can be asserted by the central resource or any of the PCI resources for any error condition. The platform's reaction to an asserted SERR# signal line is not specified by the PCI bus specification. However, a resource that asserts the SERR# signal line must assume that the HOST CPU NMI (non maskable interrupt) will be asserted.

RESET

Driven to a logical "1" (deasserted) by a pull-up resistor.

PARK

Driven to a logical "1" (deasserted) by a pull-up resistor.

IDLE PHASE

Driven to a logical "1" (deasserted) by a pull-up resistor.

ADDRESS PHASE

MEMORY AND I/O ACCESS CYCLES, CONFIGURATION ACCESS, SPECIAL, AND INTERRUPT ACKNOWLEDGE CYCLES

The SERR# signal line reports parity errors detected over the AD, C/BE#, PAR, and PAR64 signal lines during the ADDRESS PHASE. It can be asserted by the target resources involved in the access cycle. Also, the SERR# signal line may be asserted during the ADDRESS PHASE by any PCI resource for any error condition.

DATA PHASE

MEMORY ACCESS, I/O ACCESS, CONFIGURATION ACCESS, AND INTERRUPT ACKNOWLEDGE CYCLES

This signal line is not defined for the DATA PHASE directly. Assertion of this signal line reflects other unrelated bus errors or the assertion of the PERR# signal line.

SPECIAL CYCLE

The SERR# signal line reports parity errors detected over the AD[31::0], C/BE#[3::0], and PAR signal lines during the DATA PHASE of SPECIAL CYCLES. The PERR# signal line cannot be used to report this error during SPECIAL CYCLES because a target resource cannot claim the access cycle.

5.5 CACHE CONTROL SIGNAL LINES

The existence of a cache in a PCI compatible system is optional. The implementation of a cacheable memory resource on a PCI bus requires the monitoring of the two signal lines described in this section. The cache controller must operate SDONE signal line for a write-through cache and both the SDONE and SBO# signal lines for a write-back cache.

> If a cache does not exist in the system or is disabled, the SDONE signal line must still be toggled by central resource. See *Chapter 7: Cache Support on PCI*, for details.

> For the purpose of the following discussion, an enabled cache controller in the system is assumed.

SDONE	Snoop Done	Opt.	Input/Output (1)	No Pull-up Resistor (2)

Note (1): This signal line is an input to all cacheable PCI memory resources; it is an output from the cache controller in the HOST/PCI BRIDGE or central resource if there is no cache controller in the platform. *Note (2):* On platforms without cache, this signal line will be driven to logical "1" by a pull-up resistor.

This signal line is driven by the cache controller to indicate that an address snoop of the cache has been completed.

RESET

Driven to a logical "0" (deasserted) by the cache controller in HOST/PCI BRIDGE or central resource if there is no cache controller in the platform.

PARK

Driven to a stable level by the cache controller in HOST/PCI BRIDGE or central resource if there is no cache controller in the platform.

IDLE PHASE

Driven to a stable level by the cache controller in HOST/PCI BRIDGE or central resource if there is no cache controller in the platform.

ADDRESS AND DATA PHASES

MEMORY ACCESS CYCLE

The SDONE signal line is asserted to indicate the completion of an address snoop of a cache. The purpose of the snoop is to determine if the address of the memory access matches an address of a valid cache line in the cache. The SDONE signal is driven only by the cache controller in the PCI interface circuit. As outlined in Chapter 1, the Discussion Platform Architecture assumes that a cache resides on the HOST bus; consequently, the PCI interface is the HOST/PCI BRIDGE. For a write-through or a write-back cache, the SDONE signal line only indicates the completion of the snoop of the contents of the cache. For a write-back cache the SDONE signal line is also used as a qualifier for the SBO# signal line. The SBO# signal lines indicates the access resulted in a cache hit of a modified/valid cache line in a write-back cache.

The SDONE signal line is an output for the cache controller in the PCI interface. The SDONE signal line is an input for both non-cacheable and cacheable memory (DRAM) resources on the PCI bus.

I/O ACCESS, CONFIGURATION ACCESS, SPECIAL, AND INTERRUPT ACKNOWLEDGE CYCLES

Only a memory target can be cached; consequently, this signal line is ignored for these bus cycles.

SBO#	Snoop Back Off	Opt.	Input/Output (1)	No Pull-up Resistor (2)

Note (1): This signal line is an input to all cacheable PCI memory resources; it is an output from the cache controller in the HOST/PCI BRIDGE or central resource if there is no cache controller in the platform. *Note (2):* On platforms without cache, this signal line will be driven to logical "1" by a pull-up resistor

This signal line is driven by the cache controller to indicate that a cache hit to a modified/valid cache line of a write-back cache has occurred.

RESET

Driven to a logical "1" (deasserted) by the cache controller in HOST/PCI BRIDGE or central resource if there is no cache controller in the platform.

PARK

Driven to a stable level by the cache controller in HOST/PCI BRIDGE or central resource if there is no cache controller in the platform.

IDLE PHASE

Driven to a stable level by the cache controller in HOST/PCI BRIDGE or central resource if there is no cache controller in the platform.

ADDRESS, DATA, AND IDLE PHASES

MEMORY ACCESS CYCLE

The SBO# signal line is asserted to indicate a cache hit to a modified/valid cache line in a write-back cache. The SBO# signal line is driven only by the cache controller in the PCI interface circuit for a write-back cache. As outlined in Chapter 1, the Discussion Platform Architecture assumes that a cache resides on the HOST bus; consequently, the PCI interface is the HOST/PCI BRIDGE. For a write-through cache this signal line is not used and is tied to logical "1". The SBO# signal line is valid only when the SDONE signal line is asserted. Once the SBO# signal line is asserted due to a cache hit, both it and the SDONE signal line must remain asserted until the snoop write-back access cycle is executed.

The SBO# signal line is an output for the cache controller in the PCI interface. The SBO# signal line is an input for the cacheable memory (DRAM) resources on the PCI bus.

I/O ACCESS, CONFIGURATION ACCESS, SPECIAL, AND INTERRUPT ACKNOWLEDGE CYCLES

Only a memory target can be cached; consequently, this signal line is ignored for these bus cycles.

5.6 64 DATA BIT SIGNAL LINES

The PCI bus supports 32 data bits as the standard data width. Accesses to memory resources have been extended to support a 64 bit data width. In addition to the REQ64# and ACK64# signal lines, a 64 data bit access also requires the AD[63::32], C/BE#[7::4], and PAR64 signal lines.

AD[63::32]	ADDRESS and DATA	Opt.	Bi-Directional Tri-state	Pull-up Resistors

When PCI 64 data bit resources are attached to a 32 data bit bus or slot they must insure that 64 data bit related signal lines do not oscillate. Each PCI resource can drive the AD[63::32] signal lines as outputs (stable level), or if an input, can be biased to a stable level. These and other solutions are allowed, provided the input leakage current specification is not violated. External resistors on an add-in card are not allowed. PCI resources attached to a 64 data bit bus or slot rely on pull-up resistors in the central resource to drive these signal lines to a logical "1".

AD[63::32] WITH A 32 DATA BIT PCI BUS MASTER (REQ64# DEASSERTED BY PULL-UP RESISTOR)

RESET

Driven to a logical "1" by pull-up resistors.

PARK

Driven to a logical "1" by pull-up resistors.

IDLE PHASE

Driven to a logical "1" by pull-up resistors.

ADDRESS PHASE

MEMORY, I/O, CONFIGURATION, SPECIAL, AND INTERRUPT ACKNOWLEDGE CYCLES

These signal lines are driven to a logical "1" by pull-up resistors.

DATA PHASE

MEMORY, I/O, CONFIGURATION, SPECIAL, AND INTERRUPT ACKNOWLEDGE CYCLES

These signal lines are driven to a logical "1" by pull-up resistors.

AD[63::32] WITH A 64 DATA BIT PCI BUS MASTER (REQ64# ASSERTED)

RESET

Driven to a logical "1" by pull-up resistors.

PARK

Driven to a logical "1" by pull-up resistors.

IDLE PHASE

Driven to a logical "1" by pull-up resistors. Optionally, if a 64 data bit PCI bus master owns the bus, it can drive these signal lines to a logical "1".

ADDRESS PHASE

MEMORY ACCESS CYCLES

These signal lines are driven to a stable level by the PCI bus master when DUAL ADDRESS is not executed. Alternatively, the PCI bus master does not have to drive these signal lines and can rely on the pull-up resistors. When the DUAL ADDRESS is executed, these signal lines are driven by the PCI bus master with the upper order address bits for a 64-bit address space.

I/O ACCESS, CONFIGURATION ACCESS, SPECIAL, AND INTERRUPT ACKNOWLEDGE CYCLES

An access, special, or interrupt acknowledge cycle is not defined differently for a 64 data bit PCI bus master. Consequently, the asserted REQ64# signal line is ignored and these signal lines operate as previously defined for a 32 data bit PCI bus master.

DATA PHASE

MEMORY ACCESS CYCLE

The least significant data byte is on signal lines AD[39::32] with the most significant data byte on signal lines AD[63::56]. The data being accessed is the upper order double word (i.e., AD[2] signal line = logical "0" during ADDRESS PHASE). If the ACK64# signal line is asserted, these signal lines contain valid data. For a write access cycle, these signal lines are driven by the PCI bus master. For a read access cycle, these signal lines are driven by the target.

If the ACK64# signal line is deasserted, these signal lines may or may not contain valid information. These signal lines contain valid data during the initial microaccess of a BURST access cycle. During subsequent write microaccesses the PCI bus master can drive these signal lines to a stable level or logical "1". For a read access cycle, these signal lines are driven to a logical "1" by pull-up resistors.

If the ACK64# signal line is asserted, only those AD signal lines indicated as valid by the C/BE#[7::4] signal lines have valid data. Those that are indicated as invalid do not contain data but must be driven to a stable level. For a write access cycle, the PCI bus master is responsible for driving the AD[63::32] signal lines, and for a read access cycle the target is responsible for driving the AD[63::32] signal lines. Under certain write-back cache and prefetchable memory conditions all of the AD signal lines have valid read data independent of the C/BE# signal lines.

I/O ACCESS, CONFIGURATION ACCESS, SPECIAL, AND INTERRUPT ACKNOWLEDGE CYCLES

An access, special, or interrupt acknowledge cycle is not defined differently for a 64 data bit PCI bus master. Consequently, the asserted REQ64# signal line is ignored and these signal lines operate as previously defined for a 32 data bit PCI bus master.

ALSO CONSIDER.

AD[31::0] WITH A 64 DATA BIT PCI BUS MASTER (REQ64# ASSERTED)

RESET

Driven to a stable level (logical "0" ... not logical "1") by central resource.

PARK

Driven to a stable level by Park master (logical "0" ... not logical "1" if central resource is Park master).

IDLE PHASE

Driven to a stable level by PCI bus master.

ADDRESS PHASE

MEMORY ACCESS CYCLE

For the memory address space, the AD[31::3] signal lines address a double word and the AD[1::0] signal lines provide the BURST sequence address order. The AD[2] signal line is driven to a logical "0".

I/O ACCESS, CONFIGURATION ACCESS, SPECIAL, AND INTERRUPT ACKNOWLEDGE CYCLES

An access by a 64 data bit bus master is not defined for these address spaces. Consequently, the asserted REQ64# signal line is ignored and these signal lines operate as previously defined for a 32 data bit PCI bus master.

DATA PHASE

MEMORY ACCESS CYCLE

The least significant data is on signal lines AD[7::0] with the most significant data on signal lines AD[31::24].

Only those AD signal lines indicated as valid by the C/BE#[3::0] signal lines have valid data. Those that are indicated as invalid do not contain data but must be driven to a stable level. For a write access cycle the bus master is responsible for driving the AD[31::0] signal lines and for a read access cycle the target is responsible for driving them.

I/O ACCESS, CONFIGURATION ACCESS, SPECIAL, AND INTERRUPT ACKNOWLEDGE CYCLES

An access by a 64 data bit bus master is not defined for these address spaces. Consequently, the asserted REQ64# signal line is ignored and these signal lines operate as previously defined for a 32 data bit PCI bus master.

C/BE#[7::4]	Bus Command and Byte Enables	Opt.	Bi-Directional Tri-state	Pull-up Resistors

When PCI 64 data bit resources are attached to a 32 data bit bus or slot they must insure that 64 data bit related signal lines do not oscillate. Each PCI resource can drive the C/BE#[7::4] signal lines as outputs (stable level), or if an input, can be biased to a stable level. These and other solutions are allowed, provided that the input leakage current specification is not violated. External resistors on an add-in card are not allowed. PCI resources attached to a 64 data bit bus or slot rely on pull-up resistors in the central resource to drive them to a logical "1".

C/BE#[7::4] SIGNAL LINES WITH A 32 DATA BIT PCI BUS MASTER (REQ64# DEASSERTED BY PULL-UP RESISTOR).

RESET

Driven to a logical "1" by pull-up resistors.

PARK

Driven to a logical "1" by pull-up resistors.

IDLE PHASE

Driven to a logical "1" by pull-up resistors.

ADDRESS PHASE

MEMORY ACCESS, I/O ACCESS, CONFIGURATION ACCESS, SPECIAL, AND INTERRUPT ACKNOWLEDGE CYCLES

Driven to a stable logical "1" by pull-up resistors.

DATA PHASE

MEMORY ACCESS, I/O ACCESS, CONFIGURATION ACCESS, SPECIAL, AND INTERRUPT ACKNOWLEDGE CYCLES

Driven to a stable logical "1" by pull-up resistors.

C/BE#[7::4] SIGNAL LINES WITH A 64 DATA BIT PCI BUS MASTER (REQ64# ASSERTED)

RESET

Driven to a logical "1" by pull-up resistors.

PARK

Driven to a logical "1" by pull-up resistors.

IDLE PHASE

Driven to a logical "1" by pull-up resistors. Optionally, if a 64 data bit PCI bus master owns the bus it can drive these signal lines to a logical "1".

ADDRESS PHASE

MEMORY ACCESS CYCLE

These signal lines are driven to a stable level by the PCI bus master when a DUAL ADDRESS is not executed. Alternatively, the PCI bus master does not have to drive these signal lines and can rely on the pull-up resistors. When the DUAL ADDRESS is executed these signal lines are driven by the PCI bus master and contain the COMMAND type of the access cycle.

I/O ACCESS, CONFIGURATION ACCESS, SPECIAL, AND INTERRUPT ACKNOWLEDGE CYCLES

An access, special, or interrupt acknowledge cycle is not defined differently for a 64 data bit PCI bus master. Consequently, the asserted REQ64# signal line is ignored and these signal lines operate as previously defined for a 32 data bit PCI bus master.

DATA PHASE

MEMORY ACCESS CYCLE

The C/BE#[7::4] signal lines indicate which byte lanes of the AD[63::32] signal lines contain valid data. If the ACK64# signal line is asserted, these signal lines contain valid byte lane information.

If the ACK64# signal line is deasserted, these signal lines may or may not contain valid information. These signal lines contain valid byte lane information during the initial microaccess of a BURST access cycle. During subsequent microaccesses, the PCI bus master can drive these signal lines to a stable level or logical "1".

I/O ACCESS, CONFIGURATION ACCESS, SPECIAL, AND INTERRUPT ACKNOWLEDGE CYCLES

An access, special, or interrupt acknowledge cycle is not defined differently for a 64 data bit PCI bus master. Consequently, the asserted REQ64# signal line is ignored and these signal lines operate as previously defined for a 32 data bit PCI bus master.

ALSO CONSIDER:

C/BE#[3::0] WITH A 64 DATA BIT PCI BUS MASTER (REQ64# ASSERTED).

RESET

Driven to a stable level (logical "0" ... not logical "1") by central resource.

PARK

Driven to a stable state by Park master (logical "0" ... not logical "1" if central resource is Park master).

IDLE PHASE

Driven to a stable level by PCI bus master.

ADDRESS PHASE

MEMORY ACCESS CYCLE

These signal lines contain the COMMAND type for the access cycle including DUAL ADDRESS.

I/O ACCESS, CONFIGURATION ACCESS, SPECIAL, AND INTERRUPT ACKNOWLEDGE CYCLES

An access, special, or interrupt acknowledge cycle is not defined differently for a 64 data bit PCI bus master. Consequently, the asserted REQ64# signal line is ignored and these signal lines operate as previously defined for a 32 data bit PCI bus master.

DATA PHASE

MEMORY ACCESS CYCLE

The C/BE#[3::0] signal lines indicate which byte lanes of the AD[31::0] signal lines contain valid data.

I/O ACCESS, CONFIGURATION ACCESS, SPECIAL, AND INTERRUPT ACKNOWLEDGE CYCLES

An access, special, or interrupt acknowledge cycle is not defined differently for a 64 data bit PCI bus master. Consequently, the asserted REQ64# signal line is ignored and these signal lines operate as previously defined for a 32 data bit PCI bus master.

PAR64	Parity 64	Opt.	Bi-Directional Tri-state	Pull-up Resistor

PCI 64 data bit resources that are attached to only a 32 data bit bus or slot must insure that 64 data bits related signal lines do not oscillate. Each PCI resource can drive the ACK64# signal line as an output (stable level), or if an input, can be biased to a stable level. These and other solutions are allowed, provided that the input leakage current specification is not violated. External resistors on an add-in card are not allowed. The PCI resources that are attached to a 64 data bit bus or slot rely on pull-up resistors in the central resource to drive these signal lines to a logical "1".

PAR64 WITH A 32 DATA BIT PCI BUS MASTER (REQ64# DEASSERTED BY PULL-UP RESISTOR).

RESET

Driven to a logical "1" by a pull-up resistor.

PARK

Driven to a logical "1" by a pull-up resistor.

IDLE PHASE

Driven to a logical "1" by a pull-up resistor.

ADDRESS PHASE

MEMORY ACCESS, I/O ACCESS, CONFIGURATION ACCESS, SPECIAL, AND INTERRUPT ACKNOWLEDGE CYCLES

This signal line is driven to a logical "1" by a pull-up resistor.

DATA PHASE

MEMORY ACCESS, I/O ACCESS, CONFIGURATION ACCESS, SPECIAL, AND INTERRUPT ACKNOWLEDGE CYCLES

This signal line is driven to a logical "1" by a pull-up resistor.

PAR64 WITH A 64 DATA BIT PCI BUS MASTER (REQ64# ASSERTED)

RESET

Driven to a logical "1" by a pull-up resistor.

PARK

Driven to a logical "1" by a pull-up resistor.

IDLE PHASE

Driven to a logical "1" by a pull-up resistor. Optionally, if a 64 data bit PCI bus master owns the bus it can drive this signal line to a logical "1".

> This signal line lags the AD signal lines by one CLK signal line period. Consequently, what is defined for the ADDRESS and DATA PHASES below is actually one CLK signal period later.

185

ADDRESS PHASE

MEMORY ACCESS CYCLES

The PAR64 signal line is driven to a stable level by the PCI bus master when a DUAL ADDRESS is not executed. Alternatively, the PCI bus master does not have to drive this signal line and can rely on the pull-up resistor. When the DUAL ADDRESS is executed, the PAR64 signal line is driven by the PCI bus master to provide even parity over the AD[63::32] and C/BE#[7::3] signal lines. The total number of "1"s over these signal lines including the PAR signal line is an even number.

I/O ACCESS, CONFIGURATION ACCESS, SPECIAL, AND INTERRUPT ACKNOWLEDGE CYCLES

An access, special, or interrupt acknowledge cycle is not defined differently for a 64 data bit PCI bus master. Consequently, the asserted REQ64# signal line is ignored and these signal lines operate as previously defined for a 32 data bit PCI bus master.

DATA PHASE

MEMORY ACCESS CYCLE

The PAR64 signal line is driven to provide even parity over the AD[63::32] and C/BE#[7::4] signal lines. The total number of "1"s over these signal lines including the PAR64 signal line is an even number.

If the ACK64# signal line is asserted, the PAR64 signal line provides valid parity information. For a write access cycle it is driven by the PCI bus master. For a read access cycle it is driven by the target.

If the ACK64# signal line is deasserted, the PAR64 signal line may or may not contain provide valid parity information. The PAR64 signal line is driven by the PCI bus master with valid parity during the initial microaccess of a BURST write access cycle. During subsequent write microaccesses, the PCI bus master can drive this signal line to a stable level or logical "1" (stable with or without valid parity). For a read access cycle, the PAR64 signal line is driven to a logical "1" by a pull-up resistor.

I/O ACCESS, CONFIGURATION ACCESS, SPECIAL, AND INTERRUPT ACKNOWLEDGE CYCLES

An access, special, or interrupt acknowledge cycle is not defined differently for a 64 data bit PCI bus master. Consequently, the asserted REQ64# signal line is ignored and these signal lines operate as previously defined for a 32 data bit PCI bus master.

ALSO CONSIDER:

PAR 64 SIGNAL LINES WITH A 64 DATA BIT PCI BUS MASTER (REQ64# ASSERTED)

RESET

Driven to a stable level (logical "0" ... not logical "1") by central resource.

PARK

Driven to a stable level by Park master (logical "0" ... not logical "1" if central resource is Park master).

IDLE PHASE

Driven to a stable level by PCI bus master.

> This signal line lags the AD signal lines by one CLK signal line period. Consequently, what is defined for the ADDRESS and DATA PHASES below is actually one CLK signal period later.

ADDRESS PHASE

MEMORY ACCESS CYCLE

The PAR signal line is driven by the PCI bus master to provide even parity over the AD[31::0] and C/BE#[3::0] signal lines. Therefore the total number of "1"s over these signal lines including the PAR signal line is an even number.

I/O ACCESS, CONFIGURATION ACCESS, SPECIAL, AND INTERRUPT ACKNOWLEDGE CYCLES

An access, special, or interrupt acknowledge cycle is not defined differently for a 64 data bit PCI bus master. Consequently, the asserted REQ64# signal line is ignored and these signal lines operate as previously defined for a 32 data bit PCI bus master.

DATA PHASE

MEMORY ACCESS CYCLE

The PAR signal line is driven to provide even parity over the AD[31::0] and C/BE#[3::0] signal lines. The total number of "1"s over these signal lines including the PAR signal line is an even number. For a write access cycle the PAR signal line is driven by the PCI bus master. For a read access cycle, the PAR signal line is driven by the target.

I/O ACCESS, CONFIGURATION ACCESS, SPECIAL, AND INTERRUPT ACKNOWLEDGE CYCLES

An access, special, or interrupt acknowledge cycle is not defined differently for a 64 data bit PCI bus master. Consequently, the asserted REQ64# signal line is ignored and these signal lines operate as previously defined for a 32 data bit PCI bus master.

REQ64#	Request 64 Data Bit Access	Opt.	Bi-Directional Drive Tri-state	Pull-up Resistor

This signal line indicates that the PCI bus master can execute 64 data bit bus cycles.

RESET

Driven to a logical "1" (deasserted) by a pull-up resistor.

PARK

Driven to a logical "1" (deasserted) by a pull-up resistor.

IDLE PHASE

Driven to a logical "1" (deasserted) by 64 data bit PCI bus master or driven to a logical "1" (deasserted) by a pull-up resistor when a 32 data bit PCI bus master owns the bus.

ADDRESS PHASE

MEMORY ACCESS CYCLE

The REQ64# signal line is asserted by the PCI bus master to request a 64 data bit access cycle. Its timing is identical to the FRAME# signal line.

I/O ACCESS, CONFIGURATION ACCESS, SPECIAL, AND INTERRUPT ACKNOWLEDGE CYCLES

An access, special, or interrupt acknowledge cycle is not defined differently for a 64 data bit PCI bus master; consequently, this signal line is ignored.

DATA PHASE

MEMORY ACCESS CYCLES

The assertion of the REQ64# signal line requests a 64 data bit access during the ADDRESS PHASE. Once this signal line is asserted it remains asserted throughout the DATA PHASE. Its timing protocol is identical to the FRAME# signal line.

I/O ACCESS, CONFIGURATION ACCESS, SPECIAL, AND INTERRUPT ACKNOWLEDGE CYCLES

An access, special, or interrupt acknowledge cycle is not defined differently for a 64 data bit PCI bus master; consequently, this signal line is ignored.

ACK64#	Acknowledge 64 Data Bit Access	Opt.	Bi-Directional Drive Tri-state	Pull-up Resistor

PCI 64 data bit resources that are attached to only a 32 data bit bus or slot must insure that 64 data bits related signal lines do not oscillate. Each PCI resource can drive the ACK64# signal line as an output (stable level), or if an input, can be biased to a stable level. These and other solutions are allowed, provided that the input leakage current specification is not violated. External resistors on an add-in card are not allowed. The PCI resources that are attached to a 64 data bit bus or slot rely on pull-up resistors in the central resource to drive these signal lines to a logical "1".

This signal line indicates that the accessed PCI resource (target) supports 64 data bit bus cycles.

RESET

Driven to a logical "1" (deasserted) by a pull-up resistor.

PARK

Driven to a logical "1" (deasserted) by a pull-up resistor.

IDLE PHASE

Driven to a logical "1" (deasserted) by a pull-up resistor.

ADDRESS PHASE

MEMORY ACCESS CYCLE

Driven to a logical "1" (deasserted) by a pull-up resistor.

I/O ACCESS, CONFIGURATION ACCESS, SPECIAL, AND INTERRUPT ACKNOWLEDGE CYCLES

An access, special, or interrupt acknowledge cycle is not defined differently for a 64 data bit PCI bus master; consequently, this signal line is ignored. It is driven to a logical "1" (deasserted) by a pull-up resistor.

DATA PHASE

MEMORY ACCESS CYCLE

The ACK64# signal line is asserted by the target to indicate that the target can support a 64 data bit access cycle. The ACK64# signal line can only be asserted in response to the assertion of the REQ64# signal line during the ADDRESS PHASE. Once the ACK64# signal line asserted it remains asserted for the entire DATA PHASE. Its timing is identical to the DEVSEL# signal line.

I/O ACCESS, CONFIGURATION ACCESS, SPECIAL, AND INTERRUPT ACKNOWLEDGE CYCLES

An access, special, or interrupt acknowledge cycle is not defined differently for a 64 data bit PCI bus master; consequently, this signal line is ignored.

5.7 ARBITRATION SIGNAL LINES

REQx#	Request	Req.	Bi-Directional Tri-state (1)	No Pull-up Resistor (2)

Note (1): A PCI bus master uses this signal line only as an output. The signal line is defined as a bi-directional driver to take advantage of a standard PCI buffer that has tri-state attributes. *Note (2):* To prevent the REQx# signal lines from floating, the central arbiter must attach a weak pull-up resistor to each line.

Each PCI resource that can become PCI bus master has an individual REQx# signal line to request ownership of the PCI bus.

RESET

Tri-stated and floating. The central arbiter must ignore the REQx# signal line when the RST# signal line is asserted.

PARK

Does not apply to a specific cycle. These signal lines operate independently of bus cycles. PCI resource will assert when bus ownership is requested.

IDLE PHASE

Does not apply to a specific cycle. These signal lines operate independently of bus cycles. PCI resource will assert when bus ownership is requested.

ADDRESS PHASE

MEMORY ACCESS, I/O ACCESS, CONFIGURATION ACCESS, SPECIAL, AND INTERRUPT ACKNOWLEDGE CYCLES

Does not apply to a specific cycle. These signal lines operate independently of bus cycles. PCI resource will assert when bus ownership is requested.

DATA PHASE

MEMORY ACCESS, I/O ACCESS, CONFIGURATION ACCESS, SPECIAL, AND INTERRUPT ACKNOWLEDGE CYCLES

Does not apply to a specific cycle. These signal lines operate independently of bus cycles. PCI resource will assert when bus ownership is requested.

GNTx#	Grant	Req.	Bi-Directional Tri-state[1]	No Pull-up Resistor

Note: [1]The PCI bus master uses this signal line only as an input. The signal line is defined as a bi-directional driver to take advantage of a standard PCI buffer that has tri-state attributes.

Each PCI resource that can become PCI bus master has an individual GNTx# signal line to allow the central arbiter to communicate to the PCI resource that it now owns the bus.

RESET

Tri-stated and floating. Each PCI bus master must ignore its associated GNT# signal line when the RST# signal line is asserted.

PARK

Does not apply to a specific cycle. These signal lines operate independently of bus cycles. Central arbiter will assert to indicate ownership.

IDLE PHASE

Does not apply to a specific cycle. These signal lines operate independently of bus cycles. Central arbiter will assert to indicate ownership.

ADDRESS PHASE

MEMORY ACCESS, I/O ACCESS, CONFIGURATION ACCESS, SPECIAL, AND INTERRUPT ACKNOWLEDGE CYCLES

Does not apply to a specific cycle. These signal lines operate independently of bus cycles. Central arbiter will assert to indicate ownership.

DATA PHASE

MEMORY ACCESS, I/O ACCESS, CONFIGURATION ACCESS, SPECIAL, AND INTERRUPT ACKNOWLEDGE CYCLES

Does not apply to a specific cycle. These signal lines operate independently of bus cycles. Central arbiter will assert to indicate ownership.

5.8 INTERRUPT ACKNOWLEDGE SIGNAL LINES

INTx#	Interrupt	Opt.	Open Drain	Pull-up Resistor

These signal lines indicate a PCI resource needs service by the platform CPU. The platform CPU responds by executing an interrupt acknowledge cycle. Four interrupt signal lines are defined: INTA#, INTB#, INTC# and INTD#.

When an INTx# signal line is asserted, it remains asserted until the software device driver clears the interrupt request.

RESET

Driven to a logical "1" (deasserted) by a pull-up resistor..

PARK

Does not apply to a specific cycle. These signal lines operate independently of bus cycles. PCI resource will assert when interrupt service is requested.

IDLE PHASE

Does not apply to a specific cycle. These signal lines operate independently of bus cycles. PCI resource will assert when interrupt service is requested.

ADDRESS PHASE

MEMORY ACCESS, I/O ACCESS, CONFIGURATION ACCESS, SPECIAL, AND INTERRUPT ACKNOWLEDGE CYCLES

Does not apply to a specific cycle. These signal lines operate independently of bus cycles. PCI resource will assert when interrupt service is requested.

DATA PHASE

MEMORY ACCESS, I/O ACCESS, CONFIGURATION ACCESS, SPECIAL, AND INTERRUPT ACKNOWLEDGE CYCLES

Does not apply to a specific cycle. These signal lines operate independently of bus cycles. PCI resource will assert when interrupt service is requested.

5.9 JTAG SIGNAL LINES

These are not defined as part of the PCI bus protocol and are optional for PCI compliant integrated circuits (resources). The purpose of these signal lines is to support boundary scan in a PCI resource according to the IEEE Standard 1149.1. If a PCI resource supports boundary scan according to this standard, the TCK, TDI, TDO and TMS signal lines must be supported. Optional to the support of the IEEE Standard 1149.1 is the support of the TRST# signal line.

TCK	Test Clock	Opt.	Input	No Pull-up Resistor (2)

TCK is the J-TAG clock to reference the instructions and data in/out of the test signal lines.

TDI	Test DATA Input	Opt.	Input	No Pull-up Resistor (1)

TDI is the input port for the serial shifting of J-TAG instructions and data.

TDO	Test DATA Output	Opt.	Output	No Pull-up Resistor

TDO is the output port for the serial shifting of J-TAG instructions and data.

TMS	Test Mode Select	Opt.	Input	No Pull-up Resistor (1)

TMS is the input port to control the state of the TAP controller in the PCI resource.

TRST#	Test RESET	Opt.	Input	No Pull-up Resistor (2)

TRST# is the input port to initialize the TAP controller in the PCI resource.

Note (1): When boundary scan is not implemented on the platform (or independently on an add-in card), these signal lines should be independently connected and each driven to logical "1" by 5K pull-up resistors. *Note (2):* When boundary scan is not implemented on the platform (or independently on an add-in card), these signal lines should be independently connected and each driven to logical "0" by 5K pull-down resistors

The J-TAG signal lines are not active when the PCI resource is operating PCI bus cycles, but must meet the 3.3 and 5 volt electrical requirements, are part of the PCI connector specification, and are not required to have the same drive requirements of other PCI bus signal lines. The TCK, TMS, and TRST# signal lines of the PCI resources are all connected to common drivers. The TDI signal line of one PCI resource is connected to the TDO of another resource, and so forth in a daisy chain fashion. In addition to the IEEE standard, the *PCI System Design Guide*, and the *PCI Local Bus Specification Rev. 2.0* suggests the following use of J-TAG test rings:

- Only use the test ring on the expansion board during manufacturing test.

- Create a test ring on the main platform and link with the test ring on the expansion boards.

- Integrated circuits can support hierarchical IEEE 1149.1 multi-drop addressability.

CHAPTER 6

DETAILED BUS CYCLE OPERATION

This chapter consists of the following subchapters:

6.0 GENERAL CONSIDERATIONS

INTRODUCTION:

As discussed in Chapter 3, there are several types of bus cycles: access, special, and interrupt acknowledge. The access cycle is further defined in terms of memory, I/O and configuration. This chapter will discuss the detailed operation of these bus cycles for 32 and 64 data bit PCI bus masters and targets.

A unique aspect of the PCI bus is that addresses and data are multiplexed onto the same signal lines: AD[31::0]. Under the 64 data bit extension option, addresses and data are also multiplexed onto the AD[63::32] signal lines. During a read access cycle, an extra CLK signal line period must be added after the ADDRESS PHASE and at the beginning of the DATA PHASE portion of the cycle to change the resource driving the bus. This added CLK signal period allows the ASIC driving the address to tri-state the AD[63::0] signal lines before another ASIC (for example, the target) drives data onto the AD signal lines. Special and interrupt acknowledge cycles are write and read, respectively. Consequently, only the interrupt acknowledge cycle has the extra CLK signal line period.

It is assumed in this book that the address and write data are driven by the same ASIC; consequently, there is no additional CLK signal line period required. If the address and write data are provided from different ASICs, an additional CLK signal line period must be added as in the case of a read cycle.

The memory, I/O, and configuration address spaces can be addressed with SINGLE or BURST access cycles. Each access cycle can be executed as STANDARD or READY, sequential access cycles can optionally be executed with Fast Back-to-Back, any access cycle can be prematurely terminated, and both the PCI bus master and the target can control the length of the cycle. Each access cycle consists of three phases: ADDRESS, DATA, and IDLE. The ADDRESS PHASE is one CLK signal line period in length at the beginning of the cycle and provides the address of the target of access cycle. If a DUAL ADDRESS executes, the ADDRESS PHASE will be two CLK signal line periods in length. The DATA PHASE can last for several CLK signal line periods and is the portion of the access cycle where data is accessed. Between each access cycle, when Fast Back-to-Back is not executed, the PCI bus enters the IDLE PHASE.

Rev. 2.0 of the PCI specification does not specifically define the addressing protocol for a BURST I/O access cycle, but Rev. 2.1 does define such a protocol. See *Chapter 4: Functional Interaction Between PCI Resources* for details.

The special cycle does not have an address space associated with it. It is a "broadcast" SINGLE or BURST write cycle to all PCI resources. Each SINGLE access or microaccess (BURST access cycle) can be executed as STANDARD or READY. The special cycle is a minimum of five CLK signal line periods with only the PCI bus master controlling the length of the cycle with the IRDY# signal line. Each special cycle consists of three phases: ADDRESS, DATA, and IDLE. The ADDRESS PHASE is one CLK signal line period in length at the beginning of the cycle without a target address. The DATA PHASE can last for several CLK signal line periods and is the portion of the special cycle where information is broadcast. The IDLE PHASE occurs between bus cycles unless the Fast Back-to-Back protocol is executed. The Fast Back-to-Back protocol can be used under certain conditions when a special cycle is one of the bus cycles in the back-to-back sequence. (See *Subchapter 6.10: Access-Cycle-to-Access-Cycle Operation*, for details.) Note: a DUAL ADDRESS cannot be executed as part of a special cycle.

The interrupt acknowledge cycle does not have an address space associated with it. It is a SINGLE or BURST read access cycle to the platform resource that contains the interrupt controller. Each SINGLE access or microaccess (BURST access cycle) can be executed as STANDARD or READY. The length of the interrupt acknowledge cycle is controlled by the PCI bus master (BRIDGE) and the target with the IRDY# and TRDY# signal lines, respectively. Each interrupt acknowledge cycle consists of three phases: ADDRESS, DATA, and IDLE (optional). The ADDRESS PHASE is one CLK signal line period in length at the beginning of the cycle without a target address. The DATA PHASE is the portion of the interrupt acknowledge cycle where the interrupt vector is read. The IDLE PHASE occurs between bus cycles unless the Fast Back-to-Back protocol is executed. The Fast Back-to-Back protocol can only be used under certain conditions when the interrupt acknowledge cycle is one of the bus cycles in the back-to-back sequence (see *Subchapter 6.10: Access-Cycle -to-Access-Cycle Operation,* for details). Note: a DUAL ADDRESS cannot be executed as part of an interrupt acknowledge cycle.

> This book uses the convention of STANDARD and READY bus cycles. STANDARD cycles mean that no wait states are required by either the PCI bus master or target. Both resources are able to complete the bus cycle in the shortest period for a particular bus cycle. READY cycles mean that wait states are required by either the PCI bus master or the target or both. The waits states are defined in increments of the CLK signal line period. The PCI bus master and target request wait states by asserting the IRDY# and TRDY# signal lines, respectively.

We will address 32 and 64 data bit PCI resources for the remainder of this chapter. First we will concentrate on 32 data bit PCI resources and then will examine the 64 data bit extension.

SIGNAL LINE OWNERSHIP DURING BUS CYCLES WITH 32 DATA BIT RESOURCES

During memory and I/O access cycles, interrupt acknowledge cycles, and special cycles, the signal lines are owned by different PCI bus resources. A PCI resource owns a signal line when it is the only resource (other than pull-up resistors) that can drive the signal line during a portion of the cycle. The protocol is as follows:

- The FRAME#, IRDY#, C/BE#[3::0], and REQ# signal lines are owned by the PCI bus master.

- During a write access or special cycle, the PCI bus master owns the AD[31::0] and PAR signal lines.

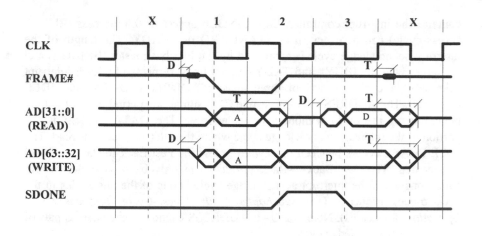

Figure 6-0: Signal Line Protocol Example

■ During a read access cycle or interrupt acknowledge cycle, the PCI bus master owns the AD[31::0] and PAR signal lines during the ADDRESS PHASE. The target owns these signal lines during the DATA PHASE

■ During an access cycle or interrupt acknowledge cycle, the TRDY#, DEVSEL#, and STOP# signal lines are owned by the target. During a special cycle, these signal lines are not owned by the target because no target is addressed.

During a configuration access cycle, the protocol is the same as listed above with the following exceptions:

■ The IDSEL signal lines are driven by a platform resource that is programmed by the PCI bus master. Typically it is the BRIDGE, acting as a PCI bus master, that drives the IDSEL signal lines via the AD signal lines.

■ The "target" in the above section is defined as the "device" according to the configuration access cycle protocol. The device is defined as any PCI resource that has configuration registers, and includes PCI bus masters, targets, and BRIDGEs.

The remaining signal lines for all bus cycles are owned according to the following protocol:

■ The CLK and RST# signal lines are owned by the central resource.

■ The GNT# signal lines are owned by the central arbiter.

■ The LOCK# signal line is owned by the Lock master.

■ The SDONE and SBO# signal lines are owned by the cache controller in the HOST/PCI BRIDGE, or the central resource if the platform does not have a cache controller.

■ The INTx# signal lines are owned by various PCI resources.

■ The REQ64#, ACK64#, PAR64, C/BE#[7::4], and AD[63::32] are driven to logical "1" by pull-up resistors.

For further information, see *Subchapters 6.2: Signal Line Protocol for 32 Data Bit Bus Cycles*, *6.4: 64 Data Bit Extension*, and *6.7: Signal Line Protocol for 64 Data Bit Bus Cycles*.

SIGNAL LINE PROTOCOL CONSIDERATIONS

The detailed figures in this and other chapters conform to the signal line protocol outlined in Figure 6-0 and is as follows:

NOTE: Figure 6-0 provides an example of the signal line protocol for individual signal lines and does not represent actual or specific bus cycles.

■ The FRAME# signal line typifies the protocol for individual signal lines driven by multiple sources. The signal line changes from logical "1" driven by a pull-up resistor to being driven by the PCI bus master and vice versa by the timing marks labeled "D" and "T", respectively. D represents driving and T represents tri-stating. Asserted and deasserted signal lines are the lower and upper single lines, respectively.

■ The AD[31::0] signal lines typify the protocol for signal lines not driven by pull-up resistors. For the read example, the AD[31::0] signal lines are driven by another PCI bus master prior to the access cycle; consequently, the signal lines are tri-stated (timing mark "T") and driven (timing mark "D"). The "A" and "D" between the parallel lines indicate address and data are driven onto the signal lines, respectively. The unlabeled areas between the parallel lines indicate that the signal lines are driven to a stable level but do not always contain valid information. In the read example, the signal lines are tri-stated by the PCI bus master in the second CLK signal line period in preparation for the target driving these signal lines in the third CLK signal line period. At the completion of the read access cycle, the target tri-states the AD[31::0] signal lines after the third CLK signal line period in preparation for the new PCI bus master to subsequently bring these signal lines to a stable level. The single horizontal lines that are neither asserted nor deasserted indicate that the signal lines are floating.

■ The AD[63::32] signal lines typify the protocol for the group of signal lines driven by pull-up resistors. In the write example, the signal lines prior to and after the access cycle are driven to a logical "1" by pull-up resistors. The signal line changes from logical "1" driven by a pull-up resistor to being driven by the PCI bus master and vice versa by the timing marks labeled "D" and "T", respectively. The "D" represents "driving" and the "T" represents tri-stating. The write example has no change of signal line ownership ("D" and "T") but does show the valid periods of address and data marked "A" and "D". The unlabeled areas between the parallel lines indicate that the signal lines are driven to a stable level but do not always contain valid information.

■ The SDONE signal line typifies the protocol for individual signal lines driven by a single source. The signal line changes between asserted and deasserted without the periods of float or being driven to a logical "1" by pull-up resistors. As will be explained in Chapter 7, the SDONE signal line can be driven by the cache controller in the HOST/PCI BRIDGE or by the central resource. There is no change of signal line ownership from bus cycle to bus cycle.

Other considerations related to signal line protocol are ADDRESS/DATA STEPPING and PRE-DRIVE. These protocols were discussed in Chapter 4 and result in the assertion of the FRAME# signal line later in the bus cycle. For ease of understanding, these protocols are treated as extensions of the typical bus cycles; consequently, unless otherwise noted, all drawings in this book do not include ADDRESS/DATA STEPPING or PRE-DRIVE protocols. Thus the FRAME# signal line is asserted during the first (#1) CLK signal line period of the bus cycle.

DUAL ADDRESS

The PCI bus supports both 32 and 64-bit address spaces for memory and I/O address spaces. The typical memory access cycle supports 30 address bits encoded into the AD[31::2] signal lines with BURST sequence information encoded into the AD[1::0] signal lines (see Figures 6-1 to 6-2 and 6-14-A to B). The typical I/O access cycle supports 32 address bits encoded into the AD[31::0] signal lines. Also, during the ADDRESS PHASE, the COMMAND type of the access cycle is encoded into the C/BE#[3::0] signal lines. For a SINGLE access cycle not executing a DUAL ADDRESS the minimum pulse width for an asserted FRAME# signal line is one CLK period.

To support a 64-bit address, the PCI bus master multiplexes the address onto the AD[31::0] signal lines with the following protocol:

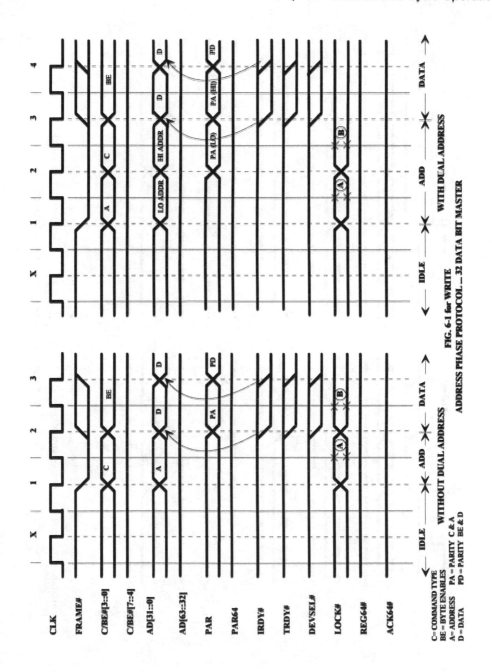

Figure 6-1: ADDRESS PHASE Protocol for Write, 32 Data Bit Master

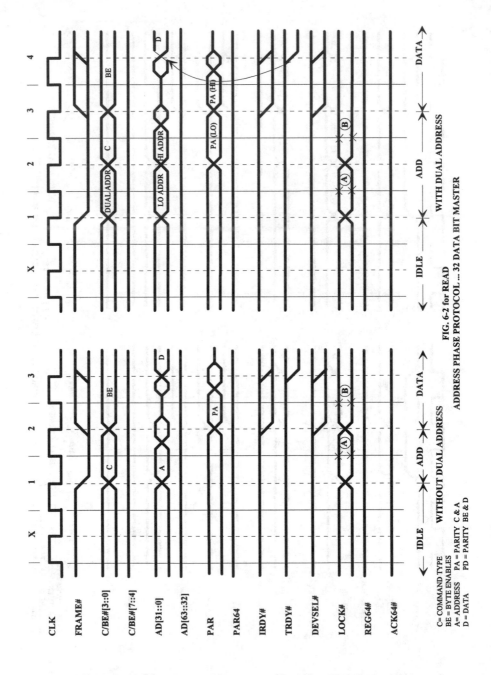

Figure 6-2: ADDRESS PHASE Protocol for Read, 32 Data Bit Master

- The PCI bus master drives the DUAL ADDRESS encoding (C/BE#[3::0] = [1011]) at the beginning of the ADDRESS PHASE (see Figures 6-1, 6-2, and 6-14-A and B). Simultaneously, the PCI bus master places the low order address onto the AD[31::2] signal lines for a memory access and the AD[31::0] signal lines for an I/O access.

- The DUAL ADDRESS encoding at the beginning of the ADDRESS PHASE requires the PCI bus master to subsequently drive the COMMAND type onto the C/BE#[3::0] signal lines during the second CLK signal line period of the ADDRESS PHASE. Simultaneously, the AD[31::0] signal lines are driven with the high order 32 address bits.

The net effect of the two above items results in an ADDRESS PHASE that is two CLK signal line periods in length. For a SINGLE access cycle with DUAL ADDRESS, the minimum pulse width for an asserted FRAME# signal line is two CLK signal line periods.

A PCI bus master that supports the 64-bit address space and only addresses the lower four gigabytes *cannot* execute access cycles with DUAL ADDRESS. By definition, the upper order address bits are logical "0".

PCI bus masters that use ADDRESS/DATA STEPPING cannot use the DUAL ADDRESS protocol.

The 64-bit address space (DUAL ADDRESS) is not defined for the configuration access cycle, special cycle, and interrupt acknowledge cycles. In the case of special cycles and interrupt acknowledge cycles, there is no address involved in the protocol.

In Figures 6-1, 6-2, and 6-14-A and B, the signal lines with parity and data are shown driven immediately with valid information. This was done for simplicity in these drawings. See the previous section, *Signal Line Protocol Considerations*, for details.

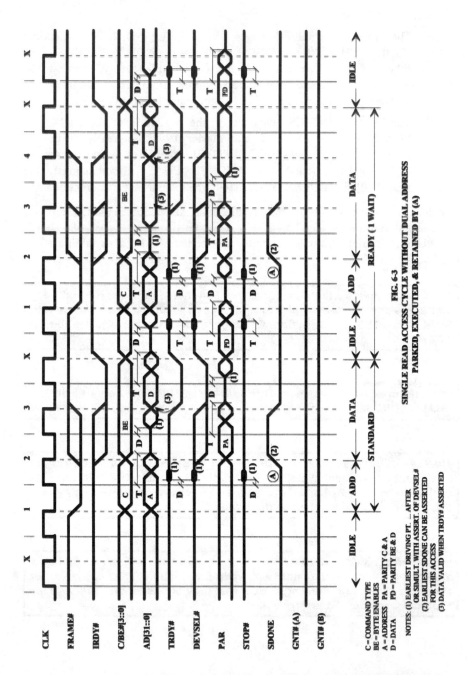

**Figure 6-3: Single Read Access Cycle without DUAL ADDRESS Parked,
Executed, and Retained by (A)]**

6.1 32 DATA BIT PCI BUS MASTER TO 32 DATA BIT TARGET

SINGLE READ ACCESS CYCLE

A SINGLE read access cycle begins with the PCI bus master asserting the FRAME# signal line, driving valid COMMAND type information onto the C/BE#[3::0] lines, and a valid address onto the AD[31::0] signal lines (see Figure 6-3). This activity comprises the ADDRESS PHASE of the access cycle.

Immediately following the ADDRESS PHASE is the DATA PHASE. At the beginning of the DATA PHASE the PCI bus master drives valid byte enable information onto the C/BE#[3::0] signal lines and tri-states the AD[31::0] signal lines (see Figure 6-3). Also during this transition period, the TRDY#, DEVSEL#, and STOP# signal lines are driven by the target.

For a STANDARD read access cycle the IRDY# and DEVSEL# signal lines must be asserted in the second or third CLK signal line periods. The AD[31::0] signal lines must be tri-stated by the PCI bus master at the beginning of the second CLK signal line period. The tri-state of these signal lines allows the target to drive them at the beginning of the third CLK signal line period. The TRDY# signal line cannot be asserted until the third CLK signal line period for a read access cycle. The STANDARD read access cycle is continued until the IRDY# and TRDY# are both asserted at the end of the third CLK signal line period, and the IRDY#, TRDY#, and DEVSEL# signal lines are subsequently deasserted. Also, at this time the AD[31::0] signal lines are tri-stated by the target, and the C/BE#[3::0] signal lines do not have valid byte enable information. One CLK signal line period later, the AD[31::0] signal lines are driven by the PCI bus master for the next access cycle. The access cycle is completed when the FRAME# and IRDY# signal lines are both deasserted.

Ideally, all SINGLE read access cycles should be STANDARD for maximum system performance; however, in reality not all resources can operate at maximum bus speed. Consequently, the PCI bus also defines a protocol called READY to accommodate slower resources. For a READY read access cycle, the DEVSEL# signal line must be asserted within the first four CLK signal line rising edges of the DATA PHASE; if not, a Master Abort termination will be executed. The AD[31::0] signal lines must be tri-stated by the PCI bus master at the beginning of the second CLK signal line period. The tri-state of these signal lines allows the target to drive them at the beginning of the third CLK signal line period. The READY read access cycle continues until the IRDY# and TRDY# signal lines are both sampled asserted on a rising edge of the CLK signal line. The IRDY# signal lines can be asserted as early as the second CLK signal line period. The TRDY# signal line cannot be asserted until the third CLK signal line period for a read access cycle. The access cycle continues until the IRDY# and TRDY# signal lines are both asserted. Subsequently, the IRDY#, TRDY#, and DEVSEL# signal lines are subsequently deasserted. Also, at this time the AD[31::0] signal lines are tri-stated by the target, and the C/BE#[3::0] signal lines do not have valid information. One CLK signal line period later, the AD[31::0] signal lines are driven by the PCI bus master for a new access cycle. The access cycle completes when the FRAME# and IRDY# signal lines are both deasserted.

The PAR signal line provides even parity for the C/BE#[3::0] and AD[31::0] signal lines. The value of the PAR signal line reflects the value of these signal lines one CLK signal line period earlier. The points in the cycle where the PAR signal line are tri-stated and driven are same as the AD[31::0] signal lines but delayed by one CLK signal line period.

The SDONE signal line is asserted for every access cycle to a PCI memory resource. In Figure 6-3 it is shown asserted for one CLK signal line period at the earliest point in the access cycle. The SDONE signal line can be asserted at later points in the access cycle. For more general and detailed information, see *Chapter 4: Functional Interaction Between PCI Resources.*

SINGLE WRITE ACCESS CYCLE

A SINGLE write access cycle begins in the same fashion as the read access cycle (see Figure 6-4). Unlike the read access cycle shown in Figure 6-3, some of the signal lines in Figure 6-4 are initially parked at a PCI bus master. Prior to the ADDRESS PHASE the Park master tri-states some of the signal lines and the PCI bus master will execute the access cycle by driving these signal lines.

Immediately following the ADDRESS PHASE is the DATA PHASE. At the beginning of the DATA PHASE the PCI bus master drives valid byte enable information onto the C/BE#[3::0] signal lines, and drives the AD[31::0] signal lines (see Figure 6-4). Valid data is not always available at the very beginning of the DATA PHASE. Also, during this period the TRDY#, DEVSEL#, and STOP# signal lines are driven by the target but may not be immediately asserted. The STOP# signal line may or may not be asserted during the DATA PHASE.

For a STANDARD write access cycle, the IRDY#, TRDY#, and DEVSEL# signal lines must be asserted in the second CLK signal line period. The STANDARD write access cycle is continued with the IRDY# and TRDY# both asserted at the end of the second CLK signal line period, and the IRDY#, TRDY#, and DEVSEL# signal lines subsequently deasserted. Also, during the completion of the access cycle the AD[31::0] and the C/BE#[3::0] signal lines do not contain valid information. The access cycle completes when the FRAME# and IRDY# signal lines both deasserted.

For a READY write access cycle, the DEVSEL# must be asserted within the first four CLK signal line rising edges of the DATA PHASE; if not, a Master Abort termination will be executed. The READY write access cycle continues until the IRDY# and TRDY# signal lines are both asserted. The IRDY# and TRDY# signal lines can be asserted as early as the second CLK signal line period. Subsequently, the IRDY#, TRDY#, and DEVSEL# signal lines are deasserted. Also, during the completion of the access cycle the AD[31::0] and C/BE#[3::0] signal lines do not have valid information. The access cycle is completed when the FRAME# and IRDY# signal lines are both deasserted.

The PAR signal line provides even parity for the C/BE#[3::0] and AD[31::0] signal lines. The value of the PAR signal line reflects the value of these signal lines one CLK signal line period earlier. The points in the cycle where the PAR signal line are tri-stated and driven are the same as the AD[31::0] signal lines but delayed by one CLK signal line period.

BURST READ AND WRITE ACCESS CYCLES

BURST access cycles allow the PCI bus master to access the target as a sequence of microaccesses. The access cycle begins with the PCI bus master asserting the FRAME# signal line, driving valid control cycle information onto the C/BE#[3::0] signal lines, and driving valid address onto the AD[31::0] signal lines (see Figures 6-5 and 6-6). This activity comprises the ADDRESS PHASE for the entire BURST access cycle, and establishes the base address for all microaccesses. Just prior to the ADDRESS PHASE, the PCI bus master begins driving these signal lines if the bus was not parked at the PCI bus master that will execute the access cycle.

Immediately following the ADDRESS PHASE is the DATA PHASE. At the beginning of the DATA PHASE, the PCI bus master drives valid byte enable cycle information onto the C/BE#[3::0] signal lines, and drives data onto the AD[31::0] signal lines for a write access cycle, or tri-states the AD[31::0] signal lines for a read access cycle (see Figures 6-5 and 6-6). Also, during this period the TRDY#, DEVSEL#, STOP# signal lines are driven by the target.

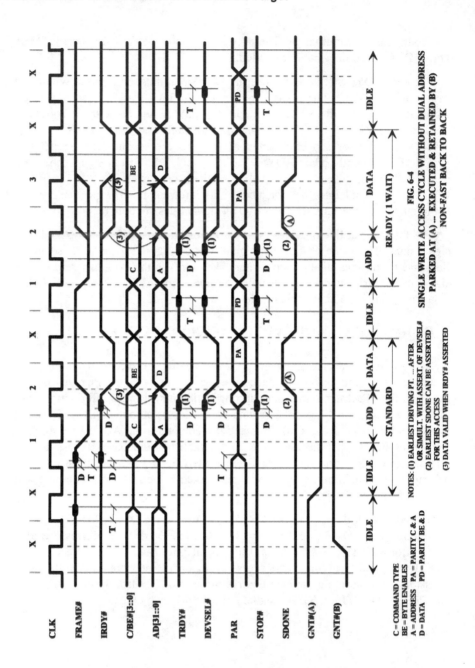

Figure 6-4: Single Write Access Cycle without DUAL ADDRESS Parked at A, Executed and Retained by (B), Non-Fast Back-to-Back

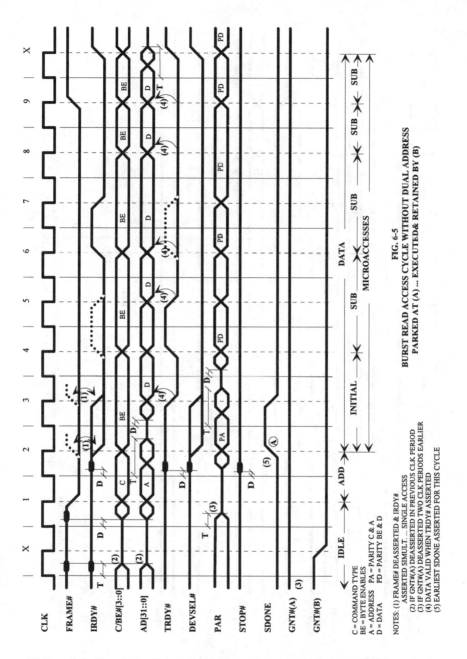

CLK

FRAME#

IRDY#

C/BE#[3::0]

AD[31::0]

TRDY#

DEVSEL#

PAR

STOP#

SDONE

GNT#(A)

GNT#(B)

C = COMMAND TYPE
BE = BYTE ENABLES
A = ADDRESS   PA = PARITY C & A
D = DATA   PD = PARITY BE & D

NOTES: (1) FRAME# DEASSERTED & IRDY#
ASSERTED SIMULT. ... SINGLE ACCESS
(2) IF GNT#(A) DEASSERTED IN PREVIOUS CLK PERIOD
(3) IF GNT#(A) DEASSERTED TWO CLK PERIODS EARLIER
(4) DATA VALID WHEN TRDY# ASSERTED
(5) EARLIEST SDONE ASSERTED FOR THIS CYCLE

FIG. 6-5
BURST READ ACCESS CYCLE WITHOUT DUAL ADDRESS
PARKED AT (A) ... EXECUTED& RETAINED BY (B)

Figure 6-5: Burst Read Access Cycle without DUAL ADDRESS Parked at (A), Executed and Retained by (B)

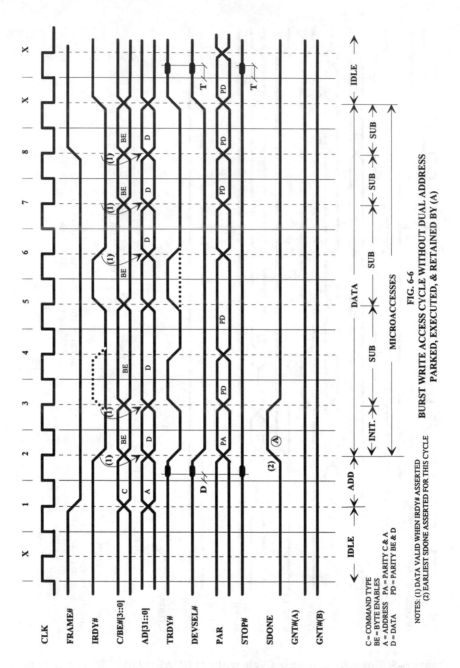

Figure 6-6: Burst Write Access Cycle without DUAL ADDRESS Parked at (A), Executed and Retained by (A)

> *Microaccess* is a naming convention that identifies the individual data accesses within a BURST access cycle. The *initial microaccess* begins at the end of the ADDRESS PHASE and ends when the IRDY# and TRDY# signal lines are first both asserted. *Subsequent microaccesses* begin with the end of the previous microaccess and end when the IRDY# and TRDY# signal lines are both asserted. See *Chapter 3: Generic PCI Hardware Operation*, for details.

Unlike the SINGLE access cycle in which the entire cycle is STANDARD or READY, the BURST access cycle can consist of microaccesses with or without added wait states. The existence of a wait state is determined for each microaccess on a case by case basis and can be requested by either the PCI bus master or target.

The protocol to distinguish between a SINGLE access cycle and a BURST access is the value of the FRAME# signal line when the IRDY# signal line is asserted. If the FRAME# signal line is deasserted at the first assertion of the IRDY# signal line, the access cycle is completed as a SINGLE access cycle. Otherwise, the cycle proceeds as a BURST access cycle and must execute at least two microaccesses.

> If the IRDY# signal line is asserted, the FRAME# signal line must be deasserted to insure a SINGLE access cycle. This is because the TRDY# signal line can be asserted at any time.

When the access cycle is established as a BURST access cycle, the data will be accessed according to the following protocol:

- The data will be accessed on each rising edge of the CLK signal line when the IRDY# and TRDY# signal lines are both asserted. DATA access will not occur on a rising edge of the CLK signal line when either the IRDY# or TRDY# signal line is deasserted.

- The values of the AD[31::0] signal lines establish the base address of the initial microaccesses (see Figures 6-5 and 6-6). All subsequent microaccesses reflect the incremental address of four bytes from the previous microaccess for the linear addressing modes. For other address modes the order will be different. See *Chapter 4: Functional Interaction Between PCI Resources* for details.

- The COMMAND type of the BURST access cycle is established by the C/BE#[3::0] during the ADDRESS PHASE of the initial microaccess. The type of access remains the same for the entire BURST access cycle.

- The values of the C/BE#[3::0] signal lines during the DATA PHASE reflect the byte lanes that are being accessed by the associated microaccess. For the initial microaccess, the C/BE#[3::0] signal line value changes to the first byte lane value at the transition from the ADDRESS and DATA PHASES. For the subsequent microaccesses, the values of the C/BE#[3::0] signal lines may change when the IRDY# and TRDY# signal lines are both asserted for the completion of the present microaccess.

■   The BURST access cycle is completed when the FRAME# signal line is deasserted and the IRDY# and TRDY# signal lines are both asserted; subsequently, the FRAME# and IRDY# signal lines are both deasserted.

The FRAME# signal line cannot be deasserted until the second to last data is accessed, but must be deasserted before the last data is accessed.

The BURST access cycle usually accesses data entirely within a single target, but the PCI bus master may not know the actual boundary of a specific target. Consequently, one microaccess would be to one target and the next microaccess to another. The PCI bus protocol requires that when the target boundary is crossed, the BURST access cycle must be terminated as outlined in the following example:

The PCI bus master is accessing target (A) with a BURST access cycle with increasing linear addressing. It accesses data at address (X), with microaccess (N). Microaccess (N+1) accesses data in target (B) at address (X+1). Target (B) has not claimed the BURST access cycle (assertion of the DEVSEL# signal line) and target (A) must execute a Disconnect with data termination. The PCI bus master has successfully accessed data at address (X+1) in target (B) when the termination is executed. Consequently, when the PCI bus master accesses target (B) with a new access cycle, it must begin with accessing data at address (X+2). The above protocol assumes that the memory at X+1 is not cacheable memory. If it is cacheable memory, the access must complete per the cache line protocol outlined in Subchapter 7.3

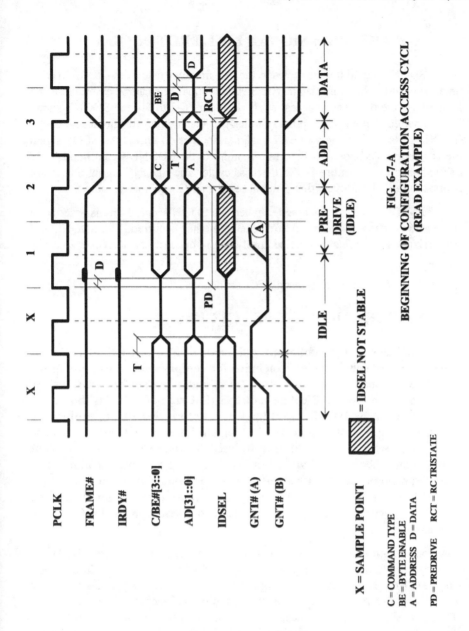

Figure 6-7-A: Beginning of Configuration Access Cycle (Read Example)

SDONE AND SBO# SIGNAL LINE PROTOCOL

The SDONE signal line indicates to the PCI memory resources (PDRAM) that the address snoop has completed. The SDONE signal line can be asserted during the access cycle or after the access cycle. In Figure 6-3 to 6-6 the SDONE signal line is asserted at the earliest point (Circle A in the figures) for the access cycle. SDONE is asserted for only one CLK signal line period unless the SBO# signal line is asserted. As shown in Figures 6-5 and 6-6, the SDONE signal line is only asserted once for the entire BURST access cycle. The SDONE signal line is not asserted for a PCI bus cycle that is not accessing a PCI memory resource.

If the SBO# signal line is asserted when the SDONE signal line is asserted, a snoop address cache hit to a modified/cache line has occurred. The SDONE and SBO# signal lines remain asserted until the snoop write-back access cycle is executed.

See *Chapter 7: Cache Support on PCI* for details.

CONFIGURATION ACCESS CYCLES

IMPORTANT: The following discussion about PRE-DRIVE for configuration access cycles is included for completeness in explaining the PCI Local Bus Specification Rev. 2.0. Simulations performed since the writing of the bus specification indicates that the timing delay due to the extra load of the IDSEL signal lines does not cause a timing problem; a resistor between AD and IDSEL signal lines is not required. The following discussion should only be used to understand platforms that may have been built according to the original specification. The configuration access cycles should follow the same protocol as a memory or I/O access cycle. PCI resources that become targets should have no problem decoding the address relative to the assertion of the FRAME# signal line.

A configuration access cycle begins with the PCI bus master (BRIDGE) asserting the FRAME# signal line, driving valid COMMAND type information onto the C/BE#[3::0] lines and driving the AD[31::0] signal lines to a stable level (see Figure 6-7-A). For a Type 0 configuration access cycle, individual AD[31::11] signal lines are attached to the individual IDSEL signal lines that are attached to each device. During the ADDRESS PHASE, only one of the IDSEL (therefore AD[31::11]) signal lines is asserted to select only one device. According to the PCI Local Bus Specification Rev. 2.0, the additional load on each of these AD signal lines may cause timing problems; consequently, the individual IDSEL signal line may have to be attached to the individual AD signal lines with a resistor. If attached via resistors, the IDSEL signal lines are not driven to a stable level as quickly as the AD signal lines. Consequently, the ADDRESS PHASE may not begin until the second CLK signal line period of the configuration access cycle. The additional CLK signal line period before the ADDRESS PHASE allows the PCI bus master (BRIDGE) to pre-drive the IDSEL signal lines (via the AD[31::11] signal lines), and to overcome the resistor and capacitor effects (RC time constant). The amount of time for the IDSEL signal line to reach a stable level is identified by "PD". In the case of a configuration read access cycle (or when a PCI bus master relinquishes the bus), the IDSEL signal lines will take longer to tri-state, and the time is identified by "RCT".

In the above discussion, the configuration read access cycle outlined in Figure 6-7-A was used to exemplify the pre-drive protocol. In this example, one CLK signal line was inserted between the beginning of the configuration access cycle and the ADDRESS PHASE for the PRE-DRIVE PHASE. A PRE-DRIVE PHASE is *not* required if the type of driver buffer, load of backplane, etc., are such that resistors are not used to link the AD and IDSEL signal lines. Conversely, a PRE-DRIVE PHASE of more than one CLK signal line period may be required for the PRE-DRIVE PHASE to overcome the resistor and capacitor effects for buses with greater loads. When a PRE-DRIVE PHASE is not used, the configuration access cycles operate with the same protocol as memory or I/O access cycles. The same issues apply to a configuration write access cycle.

The PRE-DRIVE PHASE is indistinguishable from an IDLE PHASE; consequently, the FRAME# signal line is the only indicator when the configuration access cycle begins.

Other key considerations about the configuration access cycle are as follows:

- Immediately following the ADDRESS PHASE is the DATA PHASE. The DATA PHASE protocol for SINGLE or BURST configuration access cycle is the same as a memory or I/O SINGLE or BURST access cycle.

- The sampling points of the DEVSEL# signal line for "FAST", "MEDIUM", and "SLOW" POSITIVE DECODINGs and SUBTRAC- TIVE DECODING are displaced (relative to the beginning of the cycle) by the number of CLK signal line periods in the PRE-DRIVE PHASE. The protocol for the sampling points relative to the assertion of the FRAME# signal line is the same as for the memory or I/O access cycles.

■ The assertion of the FRAME# signal line occurs later in the configuration access cycle than in the memory or I/O access cycles and thus the tri-stating of signal lines by the previous target occurs earlier relative to the driving of these signal lines by the present target. This situation does not change the protocol for the back-to-back bus cycles and Fast Back-to-Back bus cycles for configuration access cycles relative to other bus cycles. The protocols are still defined relative to the assertion of the FRAME# signal line.

■ The place where the PCI bus master that wishes to execute a configuration access cycle can first drive the signal lines is defined relative to the assertion of the associated GNT# signal line (see Figure 6-7-A). This is the same protocol as for other bus cycles. As with other bus cycles, the associated GNT# signal line be must asserted on the rising edge of the CLK signal line just prior to the assertion of the FRAME# signal lines. Unlike other bus cycles, the PCI bus master may have already begun the PRE-DRIVE PHASE when the associated GNT# signal line is deasserted. If the associated GNT# signal line is deasserted at Point A (Circle A in Figure 6-7-A), the configuration access cycle cannot be executed (The FRAME# signal line cannot be asserted).

A Type 1 configuration access cycle does not have to provide valid IDSEL signal lines; therefore, the pre-drive protocol *does not* apply to Type 1.

SPECIAL CYCLES

A special cycle begins with the PCI bus master asserting the FRAME# signal line, driving valid COMMAND type information onto the C/BE#[3::0] lines and the AD[31::0] signal lines to a stable level (see Figure 6-7-B). This activity comprises the ADDRESS PHASE of the special cycle.

Immediately following the ADDRESS PHASE is the DATA PHASE. The DATA PHASE protocol for a SINGLE or BURST special access cycle is the same as a memory or I/O SINGLE or BURST access cycle. At the beginning of the DATA PHASE, the PCI bus master drives valid byte enable information onto the C/BE#[3::0] signal lines, and provides the encode message type and optional message dependent data (defined as primary data, see Figure 6-7-B). Unlike an access cycle, the TRDY#, DEVSEL#, and STOP# signal lines remain deasserted throughout the DATA PHASE.

The minimum length of a special bus cycle is five CLK signal line periods.

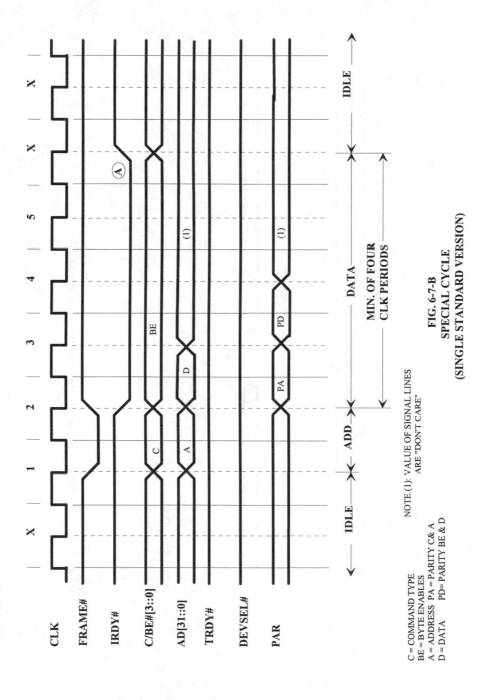

NOTE (1): VALUE OF SIGNAL LINES
ARE "DON'T CARE"

C = COMMAND TYPE
BE = BYTE ENABLES
A = ADDRESS   PA = PARITY C& A
D = DATA   PD= PARITY BE & D

FIG. 6-7-B
SPECIAL CYCLE
(SINGLE STANDARD VERSION)

Figure 6-7-B: Special Cycle (Single Standard Version)

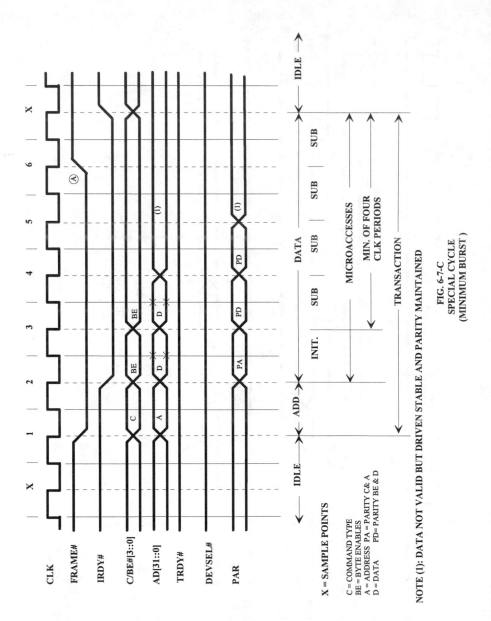

Figure 6-7-C: Special Cycle (Minimum Burst)

For a STANDARD SINGLE special cycle the IRDY# signal line must be asserted in the second CLK signal line period, which ensures that the IRDY# signal line is asserted for four CLK signal line periods. Without the support of the TRDY# signal line, the protocol for the SINGLE special cycle is as follows:

- The AD[31::0] signal lines contain valid data only when the IRDY# signal line is first asserted.

- For a READY single special cycle, the IRDY# signal line remains deasserted beyond the fifth CLK signal line period. The IRDY# signal line must be asserted a minimum of four CLK signal line periods.

- To maintain minimum length of a special cycle, the IRDY# signal line is not deasserted until after the fifth CLK signal line period at Point A (Circle A in Figure 6-7-B). The special cycle completes when the FRAME# and IRDY# signal lines both deassert.

Special cycles that require PCI resources to do a more elaborate response than setting a flip flop may require the PCI bus master to execute a READY SINGLE special cycle. For a READY SINGLE special cycle, the protocol outlined in the above bullets apply. The READY SINGLE special cycle allows the IRDY# signal line to be asserted later than the second CLK signal line period and longer than four CLK signal line periods; consequently, it remains asserted beyond Point A (Circle A in Figure 6-7-B). According to the READY SINGLE write access protocol, the FRAME# signal line is deasserted during the last CLK signal line period. The special cycle completes when the FRAME# and IRDY# signal lines are both deasserted.

The special cycle can also be executed following the BURST write access cycle protocol (exclusive of the assertion of the TRDY#, STOP#, and DEVSEL# signal lines). The non-assertion of the TRDY# signal line requires a slightly different interpretation of the microaccesses. When the IRDY# signal line is first asserted (initial microaccess) the special cycle primary data is available. The subsequent rising edge of the CLK signal line (subsequent microaccesses) provide secondary data associated with the primary data (provided the primary data indicated that more data would be available, and the amount). The minimum length of a special bus cycle is six CLK signal line periods; consequently, a minimum BURST special access cycle provides the primary data and one sample point for the secondary data (see Figure 6-7-C). Not all of the secondary data bytes available at the sample points must be valid; the sample points with valid secondary data is determined by the assertion of the C/BE#[3::0] signal lines during the subsequent microaccesses. If the PCI bus master wants to provide additional secondary data or additional time for PCI resources to respond to a special cycle request, it can continue the BURST access cycle with the assertion of the FRAME# and IRDY# signal lines past Point A (Circle A in Figure 6-7-C). Wait states can be added to each microaccess by deasserting the IRDY# signal line when the FRAME# signal line is asserted. According to the BURST write access cycle protocol, the FRAME# signal line is deasserted and the IRDY# signal line is asserted during the last CLK signal line period. The special cycle completes when the FRAME# and IRDY# signal lines both deassert.

The PAR signal line provides even parity for the C/BE#[3::0] and AD[31::0] signal lines. The value of the PAR signal line reflects the value of these signal lines one CLK signal line period earlier. The points in the cycle where the PAR signal line are tri-stated and driven are same as the AD[31::0] signal lines but delayed by one CLK signal line period.

Fast-Back-to-Back protocol between a special cycle and a subsequent bus cycle is not supported. The special cycle must always be followed by an IDLE PHASE.

The STANDARD SINGLE special cycle provides a minimum of five CLK signal line periods between valid data and the beginning of the subsequent bus cycle (assertion of the FRAME# signal line). The READY SINGLE special cycle provides additional time to implement the data by the continued assertion of the IRDY# signal line (remember the primary data is valid only when the IRDY# signal line is first asserted). The BURST special cycle provides a minimum of five CLK signal line periods between valid last secondary data and the beginning of the subsequent bus cycle. If more time is required for implementing the primary or secondary data, the PCI bus master must execute additional subsequent microaccesses with the continued assertion of the IRDY# signal line. The number of valid subsequent microaccesses is defined in the primary data or message and must be present in the first set of valid (IRDY# signal line asserted) subsequent microaccesses. The continued assertion of the IRDY# signal line for subsequent microaccesses (after all of the secondary data has been written) is the method by which additional wait states can be added before the completion of the cycle. Consequently, data for the subsequent microaccesses is only valid when the IRDY# signal is first asserted for each subsequent microaccess.

The special cycle completes according to the Master Abort termination protocol because the DEVSEL# signal line is not asserted.

INTERRUPT ACKNOWLEDGE CYCLES

An interrupt acknowledge cycle executes with the protocol of a SINGLE or BURST bus cycle and begins with the PCI bus master (BRIDGE) asserting the FRAME# signal line, driving valid COMMAND type information onto the C/BE#[3::0] lines and the AD[31::0] signal lines to a stable level. This activity comprises the ADDRESS PHASE of the interrupt acknowledge cycle.

Immediately following the ADDRESS PHASE is the DATA PHASE. The DATA PHASE protocol for a SINGLE or BURST interrupt acknowledge cycle is the same as a memory or I/O SINGLE or BURST access cycle. At the beginning of the DATA PHASE, the PCI bus master drives valid byte enable information onto the C/BE#[3::0] signal lines and tri-states the AD[31::0] signal lines (see Figures 6-3 and 6-5). The PCI resource that contains the interrupt controller claims the interrupt acknowledge cycle by asserting the DEVSEL# signal line. This PCI resource (target) can also use the STOP# and TRDY# signal lines as needed.

For a STANDARD SINGLE interrupt acknowledge cycle, the IRDY# and DEVSEL# signal lines must be asserted in the second or third CLK signal line period. The AD[31::0] signal lines must be tri-stated by the PCI bus master at the beginning of the second CLK signal line period. The tri-state of these signal lines allows the PCI resource (target) to drive them at the beginning of the third CLK signal line period. The TRDY# signal line cannot be asserted until the third CLK signal line period for an interrupt acknowledge cycle. The STANDARD SINGLE interrupt acknowledge cycle is continued until the IRDY# and TRDY# are both asserted at the end of the third CLK signal line period, and the IRDY#, TRDY#, and DEVSEL# signal lines are subsequently deasserted. Also at this time, the AD[31::0] signal lines are tri-stated by the PCI resource (target), and the C/BE#[3::0] signal lines do not have valid byte enable information. One CLK signal line period later the AD[31::0] signal lines are driven by the PCI bus master for the next access cycle. The access cycle is completed when the FRAME# and IRDY# signal lines are both deasserted.

Ideally, all interrupt acknowledge cycles should be STANDARD for maximum system performance; however, in reality not all resources can operate at maximum bus speed. Consequently, the PCI bus also defines a protocol to accommodate slower resources called READY. For a READY SINGLE interrupt acknowledge cycle, the DEVSEL# signal line must be asserted within the first four CLK signal line rising edges of the DATA PHASE; otherwise, a Master Abort termination will be executed. The AD[31::0] signal lines must be tri-stated by the PCI bus master at the beginning of the second CLK signal line period. The tri-state of these signal lines allows the target to drive them at the beginning of the third CLK signal line period. The READY SINGLE interrupt acknowledge cycle continues until the IRDY# and TRDY# signal lines are both sampled asserted on a rising edge of the CLK signal line. The IRDY# signal lines can be asserted as early as the second CLK signal line period. The earliest the TRDY# signal line can be asserted is the third CLK signal line period for a interrupt acknowledge cycle. The cycle continues until the IRDY# and TRDY# signal lines are both asserted. Subsequently, the IRDY#, TRDY#, and DEVSEL# signal lines are subsequently deasserted. Also, at this time the AD[31::0] signal lines are tri-stated by the PCI resource (target), and the C/BE#[3::0] signal lines do not have valid information. One CLK signal line period later the AD[31::0] signal lines are driven by the PCI bus master for a new bus cycle. The cycle completes when the FRAME# and IRDY# signal lines are both deasserted. The interrupt acknowledge cycle can also be executed using the BURST read access cycle protocol. It is unclear at this time if support of a BURST interrupt acknowledge cycle is useful, given the "normal" interrupt controller.

The PAR signal line provides even parity for the C/BE#[3::0] and AD[31::0] signal lines. The value of the PAR signal line reflects the value of these signal lines one CLK signal line period earlier. The points in the cycle where the PAR signal line are tri-stated and driven are same as the AD[31::0] signal lines but delayed by one CLK signal line period.

6.2   SIGNAL LINE PROTOCOL FOR 32 DATA BIT BUS CYCLES

Subchapter 6.0 outlined ownership of the signal lines during a bus cycle. Chapter 8 details the change of signal line ownership, and signal line driving and tri-stating when Completion, Retry, Disconnect, Master Abort, or Target Abort terminations are executed. Chapter 9 covers the change of signal line ownership, and signal line driving and tri-stating between changes of bus ownership. Chapter 10 explains the signal line ownership, and signal line driving and tri-stating of the SERR# and PERR# signal lines. The following lists the signal line protocol for signal lines during the bus cycle with Completion termination and between bus cycles when the PCI bus master retains bus ownership:

> In the following discussion, the terms "drive or tri-state" are different than the terms "assert or deassert". The former identifies when the signal line buffers are enabled or disabled. The latter reflects when signal lines change their logical state.

The signal line protocol outlined below defines cycle completion when the FRAME# and TRDY# signal lines are simultaneously deasserted and asserted, respectively. Cycle completion is slightly different under conditions of special cycle and Master Abort, Retry, Disconnect, and Target Abort terminations. The more formal description of cycle completion is outlined in Completion termination, Chapter 8.

- When a PCI bus master retains bus ownership, it drives the FRAME# and IRDY# signal lines to a logical "1" between bus cycles.

- When the PCI bus master retains bus ownership, it drives C/BE#[3::0] and AD[31::0] signal lines to a stable level between bus cycles, and, with a one CLK signal line period lag, the PAR signal line to a stable level between bus cycles.

- Once the FRAME# signal line is asserted, it is not deasserted until after or simultaneously with the assertion of the IRDY# signal line. During the bus cycles, the FRAME# and IRDY# signal lines are always driven by the PCI bus master.

- Once the FRAME# signal line is asserted and then deasserted, it remains deasserted until the completion of the bus cycle.

- Once the FRAME# signal line is asserted, the PCI bus master drives the C/BE#[3::0] signal lines with valid information for the remainder of the bus cycle.

- During a write bus cycle (access and special), the PCI bus master drives the AD[31::0] and PAR signal lines with valid information or to a stable state. For the ADDRESS PHASE, these signal lines are driven with valid addresses and parity. For the DATA PHASE these signal lines are driven to a stable level when the IRDY# signal line is deasserted, and are driven with valid information when the IRDY# signal line is asserted. A lag of one CLK signal line period applies to the PAR signal line.

- During a read bus cycle (access and interrupt acknowledge), the PCI bus master drives the AD[31::0] and PAR signal lines with valid information during the ADDRESS PHASE. The PCI bus master tri-states the AD[31::0] signal lines relative to the first CLK signal line rising edge when FRAME# is asserted and DUAL ADDRESS is not asserted, or the second CLK signal line rising edge when FRAME# is first asserted when DUAL ADDRESS is asserted. For the DATA PHASE, the target drives the AD[31::0] and PAR signal lines to a stable level when the TRDY# signal line is deasserted, and with valid information when the TRDY# signal line is asserted. At the end of the DATA PHASE, the PCI bus master will drive the AD[31::0] signal lines one CLK signal line period after the TRDY# and FRAME# signal lines are simultaneously sampled asserted and deasserted, respectively. The same protocol applies to the PAR signal line with a one CLK signal line period delay.

The signal line protocol for the other signal lines during the bus cycle and between bus cycles relative to the target is as follows:

- At the beginning of the bus cycle, the target begins driving the DEVSEL# signal line upon completion of the address decode. The earliest point without DUAL ADDRESS is immediately after the FRAME# signal line is first sampled asserted. The earliest point with DUAL ADDRESS is one CLK signal line period after the FRAME# signal line is first sampled asserted.

- The DEVSEL# signal line remains asserted until the completion of the cycle when the FRAME# and TRDY# signal lines are simultaneously sampled deasserted and asserted, respectively. One exception to this protocol is when a Target Abort is executed. See *Chapter 8: Master and Target Termination* for details.

- The FRAME# signal line must be deasserted simultaneously with the assertion of the IRDY# signal line to indicate that this is the last access of a BURST or SINGLE access cycle.

- At the beginning of the bus cycle, the target begins driving the TRDY# and optionally the STOP# signal lines simultaneously with or after driving the DEVSEL# signal line.

- Deassertion of the DEVSEL# signal line prior to cycle completion must be simultaneous with the assertion of the STOP# signal line (Target Abort termination).

- If the STOP# signal line is asserted for a Disconnect with data termination, it must be simultaneous with the assertion of the TRDY# signal line.

- Once the STOP# or TRDY# signal lines are asserted they cannot be deasserted until the completion of the cycle.

- During a read bus cycle (access and interrupt acknowledge), the PCI bus master drives the AD[31::0] and PAR signal lines with valid information during the ADDRESS PHASE. The earliest a target can drive the AD[31::0] signal lines is relative to the second or third CLK signal line rising edge from first assertion of the FRAME# signal when DUAL ADDRESS (access cycle only)is not or is executed, respectively. For the DATA PHASE, the target drives the AD[31::0] signal lines to a stable level when the TRDY# signal line is deasserted, and drives these signal lines with valid information when the TRDY# signal line is asserted. At the end of the DATA PHASE, the target will tri-state the AD[31::0] signal lines when the TRDY# and FRAME# signal lines are simultaneously sampled asserted and deasserted, respectively. The AD signal lines protocol applies to the PAR signal line with a one CLK signal line period delay. Optionally, the STOP# signal line can be asserted during the bus cycle by the target. *See Chapter 8: Master and Target Termination* for details.

■ Data is only accessed when the IRDY# and TRDY# signal lines are both asserted. The one exception is the special cycle.

■ Once the IRDY# or TRDY# signal lines are asserted they cannot be deasserted until the completion of the SINGLE bus cycle or the microaccess of the BURST bus cycle.

■ At the completion of the bus cycle, the target tri-states the TRDY#, DEVSEL#, and STOP# (if driven) signal lines one CLK signal line period after the FRAME# and TRDY# signal lines are simultaneously sampled deasserted and asserted, respectively. Until driven by another target, these signal lines are driven to logical "1" by pull-up resistors.

■ At the end of a bus cycle (access and interrupt acknowledge), the target tri-states the AD[31::0] signal lines immediately after the FRAME# and TRDY# signal lines are simultaneously sampled deasserted and asserted, respectively. Until driven by the PCI bus master these signal lines float.

■ At the end of a read bus cycle, the target tri-states the PAR signal line one CLK signal line period after the FRAME# and TRDY# signal lines are simultaneously deasserted and asserted, respectively. Until driven by the PCI bus master the PAR signal line floats.

The protocol for the remaining signal lines for all bus cycles is as follows:

■ The CLK and RST# signal lines are driven to valid levels by the central resource. For a typical bus cycle, the CLK signal line oscillates and the RST# signal line is deasserted.

■ The GNT# signal lines are driven to valid levels by the central arbiter.

■ The LOCK# signal line is driven to valid levels by the Lock master.

■ The SDONE and SBO# signal lines are deasserted and asserted by the cache controller in the HOST/PCI BRIDGE when cache is supported on the platform. If cache is not supported, these signal lines are deasserted and the SDONE signal line is toggled by the central resource if cacheable PCI memory is installed.

■ An INTx# signal line is asserted when a PCI resource needs interrupt service.

■ The REQ64#, ACK64#, PAR64, C/BE#[7::4], and AD[63::32] are driven to a logical "1" by pull-up resistors.

For further information, see Subchapters 6.0: General Considerations, 6.4: 64 Data Bit Extension, and 6.7: Signal Line Protocol for 64 Data Bit Bus Cycles.

6.3   LOCK ACCESS CYCLE

INTRODUCTION

The Lock Function (LF) is defined as a target that has been locked, and the LOCK# signal line is controlled by a PCI bus master. Only one PCI bus master at a time can own the Lock Function, and it is known as the Lock master. The Lock master allows other PCI bus masters to own the bus and execute access cycles to targets that are not presently locked. The target remains locked by the Lock master until it unlocks the target or until an access by the Lock master to the locked target results in a Target Abort or Master Abort termination. *See Subchapter 4.1: Memory and I/O Access Cycles* for more information.

Only memory targets can be locked and are locked in 16 byte blocks on 16 byte address boundaries. Any lock of a byte within the 16 byte block results in the lock of the entire block. A locked target can only be accessed by a specific PCI bus master (Lock master) or by a snoop write-back access cycle by a PCI bus master that may or may not be the Lock master. Any other access to a locked target results in the execution of a Retry termination by the target.

The PCI bus specification requires a minimum of 16 bytes (aligned on 16 byte address multiples) to be locked at a time. The target can optionally lock a larger portion up to a maximum of its entire address space. The 16 byte block or continuous multiple block portion of the target (HDRAM or PDRAM) that is locked is the only portion of the target that follows the lock protocol when accessed by the Lock master, by the HOST CPU accessing HDRAM, or other processors via dual port memory (HDRAM or PDRAM). Accesses by other PCI bus masters (not Lock master) by HOST CPU accessing HDRAM, or other processors via dual port memory (HDRAM or PDRAM) to non-locked portions of the target MAY be affected by the lock protocol if the target had locked more than the portion required.

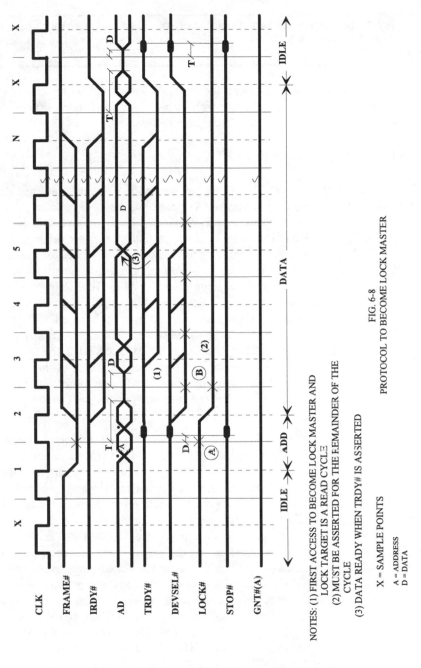

NOTES: (1) FIRST ACCESS TO BECOME LOCK MASTER AND
LOCK TARGET IS A READ CYCLE

(2) MUST BE ASSERTED FOR THE REMAINDER OF THE
CYCLE

(3) DATA READY WHEN TRDY# IS ASSERTED

X = SAMPLE POINTS

A = ADDRESS
D = DATA

FIG. 6-8
PROTOCOL TO BECOME LOCK MASTER

Figure 6-8: Protocol to Become Lock Master

227

> Once a PCI resource is locked (target), *only* the Lock master can access the locked PCI resource. The Lock master can ONLY access the locked PCI resource.

There are four basic considerations for the Lock Function: *Establishment of Lock, Continuance of Lock, Release of Target Lock and Lock Function Ownership,* and *Unsuccessful Access Cycle Termination.*

ESTABLISHMENT OF LOCK

Lock Function (LF) is established by the sequence of events outlined in Figure 6-8, showing the PCI bus master (A) becoming the Lock master. After PCI bus master (A) becomes the bus owner, it accesses the target it wants to lock. The LOCK# signal line has been deasserted by a pull-up resistor prior to the access. At the beginning of the access, PCI bus master (A) continues to deassert the LOCK# signal line during the ADDRESS PHASE, and then asserts it prior to the subsequent CLK signal line rising edge after the ADDRESS PHASE. The selected target of the access, according to a decode of the AD[31::2] (AD[63::2] signal lines for 64 data bit) signal lines, must respond by asserting the DEVSEL# signal line. The lock of the target and the establishment of PCI bus master (A) becoming Lock master is completed by a successful data access when the IRDY# and TRDY# signal lines are both asserted. An unsuccessful access of the target prevents it from becoming locked and bus master (A) from becoming Lock master. See *Unsuccessful Access Cycle Termination,* after the next section, for details.

The sequence of sampling a deasserted LOCK# signal line at Point A during the ADDRESS PHASE and sampling it asserted at Point B (Circle A and B in Figure 6-8) is the protocol to create a Lock master and to lock the target. Once the LOCK# signal line is asserted at Point B, it must remain asserted for the duration of the access cycle. If the target is a multiported resource (HDRAM accessible by HOST CPU or other processors on the HOST bus or dual port, or PDRAM accessible by processors via dual port), the HOST CPU and other processors cannot access the resource during the access cycle. Consequently, a successful access cycle results in a Lock master and a locked target *during* and *after* the cycle. If the LOCK# signal line had not been asserted at Point B, the present PCI bus master cannot become the Lock master and the target is not locked after completion of the access cycle. If the LOCK# signal line is deasserted at Point B, it must remain deasserted for the duration of the access cycle. If the target is a multiported resource (HDRAM accessible by HOST CPU or other processors on the HOST bus or dual port, or PDRAM accessible by processors via dual port), the HOST CPU and other processors can access the resource during the access cycle.

The first access cycle used to establish PCI bus master ownership of an LF (become Lock master) and the target to be locked must be a read access cycle to a memory target.

The ability for a PCI bus master to begin an access and attempt to become Lock master is dependent upon the LF being available (LOCK# deasserted) and the associated GNT# signal line asserted. As outlined in Chapter 9, a PCI bus master can also begin an access without its associated REQ# signal line asserted and thus can become Lock master.

The execution of a DUAL ADDRESS does not change the sampling points for the LOCK# signal line (Circle A and B in Figures 6-1-A and B, 6-14-A and B, and Figure 6-8); Point B is always the one CLK signal line period after the FRAME# signal line is first sampled asserted.

All targets that can be locked must latch the value of the LOCK# signal line during the ADDRESS PHASE at Point A and optionally Point B (circles A and B in Figures 6-1-A and B, 6-14-A and B, and 6-8). This requirement is needed because the decode to validate access may take several CLK signal line periods. Point B is optional because the value of the LOCK# signal line at Point B must be retained for the duration of the access cycle. The multiport memory target will sample the LOCK# signal line at Point B to determine if it is locked. If the LOCK# signal line is asserted at Point B, no other processor can access the target. It is locked and can only be accessed by the PCI bus master (Lock master). If the LOCK# signal line is deasserted at Point B, other processors can access the target; it is not locked and can be accessed by both the PCI bus master and other processors accessing through non-PCI bus ports. It is a "multiport memory target" resource that can be accessed by means other than the PCI bus.

CONTINUANCE OF LOCK FUNCTION OWNERSHIP

The Lock master does not have to retain bus ownership to remain Lock master and for the target to remain locked. In Figure 6-8, the PCI bus master (A) retains the LF after the completion of the access cycle by the continued assertion the LOCK# signal line. As shown in Figure 6-9, the asserted LOCK# signal line during the ADDRESS PHASE when PCI bus master (B) (not Lock master) accesses the target does not meet the criteria for becoming Lock master or locking the target by the PCI bus master (B). If the decode of the address selects a locked target and the locked target had sampled the LOCK# signal line asserted at Point A (Circle A in Figure 6-9), the locked target must execute a Retry termination. The target remains locked and the Lock master retains the LF. The one exception to this protocol is a snoop write-back access cycle as previously discussed. The snoop write-back access cycle is identified by assertion of both the SDONE and SBO# signal lines. See *Chapter 7: Cache Support on PCI* for details.

When the Lock master becomes the PCI bus master, the locked target can be accessed. Operation of the LOCK# signal is similar to the protocol that locked the target and established the Lock master. As shown in Figure 6-10, access to a locked target by the Lock master requires the sampling of a deasserted LOCK# signal line by the target at Point A (Circle A in Figure 6-10). If the LOCK# signal line is sampled asserted at Point B (the rising edge of the third CLK signal line period Circle B in Figure 6-10), the target remains locked and the Lock master remains Lock master during the entire access cycle. If the LOCK# signal line is deasserted at Point B (Circle B in Figure 6-10 and shaded box below), the target ceases to be locked by the LF and the Lock master ceases to be the Lock master whenever both the FRAME# and LOCK# signal line are both deasserted during or at the end of the bus cycle.

The Lock master must not deassert the LOCK# signal line at Point B (Circle B in Figure 6-10). It must wait until the end of the access cycle. If it deasserted the LOCK# signal line at Point B and the target executes a Retry or Disconnect termination, the access of the final data of the locked operation cannot occur during the same lock period of the target as the other data.

As noted, the execution of a DUAL ADDRESS does not affect the sampling points outlined in Figure 6-10.

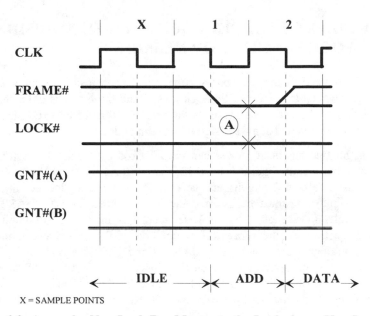

X = SAMPLE POINTS

Figure 6-9: Access by Non-Lock Bus Master to the Locked or a Non-Locked Target

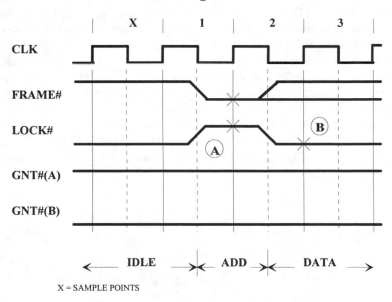

X = SAMPLE POINTS

Figure 6-10: Access by the Locked Master to the Locked Target

RELEASE OF TARGET LOCK AND RELINQUISHING
OF LOCK FUNCTION OWNERSHIP

As introduced in the previous section, the Lock master relinquishes Lock Function ownership (ceases to be Lock master and the target is unlocked at the completion of the cycle) whenever both the LOCK# and FRAME# signal lines are sampled deasserted at a CLK signal line rising edge.

A target that has been locked can be unlocked by the Lock master by the procedure outlined in Figures 6-11, 6-12, and 6-13. As shown in Figure 6-11, the Lock master is completing its last access to the presently locked target. The LOCK# signal line must be asserted during the entire DATA PHASE of the access cycle in case of Retry or Disconnect termination, as outlined in the previous section. At the successful completion of the access cycle, the Lock master simultaneously deasserts the LOCK# and IRDY# signal lines. Because FRAME# must be deasserted one clock prior to the deassertion of the IRDY# signal line, the LF is immediately relinquished by the PCI bus master and the target is unlocked when the FRAME# and LOCK# are both sampled asserted.

If the Lock master wants to unlock one target and immediately access another target to lock, at least one IDLE PHASE must occur. During this IDLE PHASE, the FRAME# and LOCK# signal lines are simultaneously sampled deasserted and thus the Lock master relinquishes LF ownership and the target is unlocked at Point A (Circle A in Figure 6-11). The FRAME# and LOCK# signal lines must be simultaneously deasserted prior to asserting the FRAME# signal line for the next access; consequently, a Fast Back-to-Back LOCK ACCESS CYCLE cannot be executed. This is not an issue if the target to be immediately accessed is not to be locked during that access. The deassertion of the LOCK# signal line beginning at Point A (Circle A in Figure 6-11) will eventually coincide with a deasserted FRAME# signal line in one of the subsequent access cycles. However, the preferred protocol is to have an IDLE PHASE between the two bus cycles.

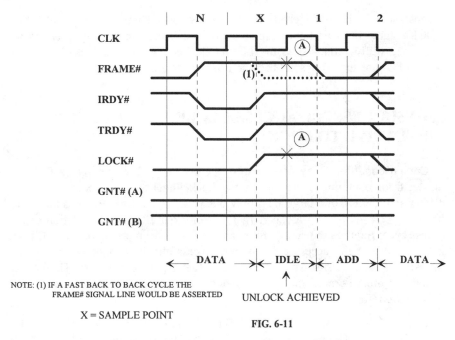

NOTE: (1) IF A FAST BACK TO BACK CYCLE THE
FRAME# SIGNAL LINE WOULD BE ASSERTED

UNLOCK ACHIEVED

X = SAMPLE POINT

FIG. 6-11

Figure 6-11: Lock Master Unlocking Target

The Lock master can relinquish the LF and the target can be unlocked when the Lock master does not own the bus. The Lock master relinquishing the LF and the unlocking of a locked target when the Lock master or another PCI bus master is not accessing the locked target is considered in greater detail in Figures 6-12 and 6-13. In Figure 6-12 the LOCK# signal line is sampled asserted at Point A during the ADDRESS PHASE (Circle A in Figure 6-12) when PCI bus master (B) (not the Lock master) is accessing a non-locked target. The continued assertion of the LOCK# signal line at Point B (Circle B in Figure 6-12) does not affect the locked target or the retention of the LF by the Lock master. The deassertion of the LOCK# signal line at Point B (Circle B in Figure 6-12) results in the relinquishing of the LF by the Lock master and the unlocking of the locked target when the FRAME# signal line is eventually deasserted. In Figure 6-13, the Lock master has deasserted the LOCK# signal line prior to Point A (Circle A in Figure 6-13) of the ADDRESS PHASE during the access cycle executed by another PCI bus master to a non-locked target. The Lock master does not relinquish the LF and the locked target is not unlocked until the FRAME# and LOCK# signal lines are both sampled deasserted. The assertion of the LOCK# signal line at point A (Circle A in Figure 6-13) does not cause another PCI bus master to become Lock master because a successful read access cycle has yet to be completed and the LOCK# signal line is deasserted at Point B and the duration of the bus cycle (Circle B in Figure 6-13). The existing Lock master retains the LF and the locked target remains locked until the FRAME# and LOCK# signal lines are both sampled deasserted. Thus, the existing Lock master has successfully relinquished the LF, the locked target is unlocked, and the present PCI bus master has not become Lock master.

UNSUCCESSFUL ACCESS CYCLE TERMINATION RELATIVE TO LOCK

Certain conditions may occur during the access cycle to prevent a PCI bus master from obtaining ownership of the Lock Function (LF) (becoming Lock master and locking of a target). As previously discussed, for a PCI bus master to become Lock master and for the target to be locked after the completion of the access cycle requires the successful reading of data from a memory target. Data is not read and the access cycle is not successfully completed if one of the following occur: Master Abort, Retry, or Target Abort termination. The LOCK signal line must be immediately deasserted. See *Chapter 8: Master and Target Termination*, for details.

Once a PCI bus master owns the LF (PCI bus master is Lock master and a target has been locked), the execution Retry termination has no effect on retaining ownership of the LF, but Master and Target Abort termination does affect LF ownership. If the non-Lock master is accessing the locked target, the execution of a Master or Target Abort termination does not affect the Lock master's retaining ownership of the LF. If the Lock master is accessing the locked target, the execution of a Master or Target Abort termination *forces* the Lock master to relinquish ownership of the LF. See Chapter 8, referenced above, for details.

The other access cycle termination types (DISCONNECT and Completion with Timeout) have no affect on a PCI bus master obtaining or retaining the LF and therefore keeping the target locked.

As previously discussed, if the locked target is cached by a write-back cache resource and a read hit to a modified/valid cache line occurs, a snoop write-back access cycle will be executed. The locked target can determine that a snoop write-back access cycle is occurring by the assertion of the SDONE and SBO# signal lines during the ADDRESS PHASE. The locked target will not execute a Retry termination when accessed by a non-Lock master executing a snoop write-back access cycle. This situation also requires the central arbiter to award bus ownership to the cache resource that is executing the snoop write-back cycle during a COMPLETE BUS LOCK. The execution of the snoop write-back access cycle does not force the Lock master to relinquish ownership of the LF and the target remains locked.

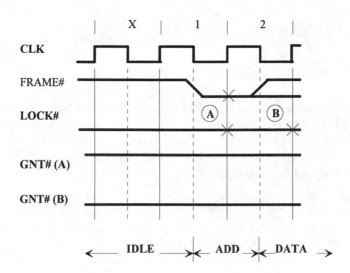

X = SAMPLE POINT

Figure 6-12: Access by Non-Lock Master to Non-Locked Target, Lock Master Keeps LOCK# Signal Line Asserted

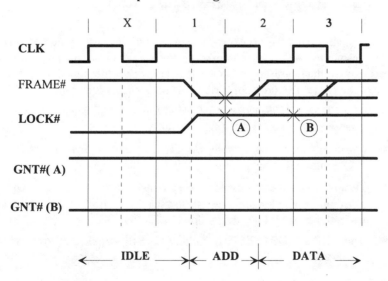

X = SAMPLE POINT

Figure 6-13: Access by Non-Lock Bus Master to Non-Locked Target, Lock Master Deasserts LOCK# Signal Line

235

6.4   64 DATA BIT EXTENSION

INTRODUCTION

As outlined in Chapter 4, the PCI bus specification is both a 32 and 64 data bit bus specification. A 32 data bit implementation of the PCI bus specification is all that is required to be compliant. The 64 data bit extension is optional, and 32 and 64 data bit resources can coexist on the same bus. A 32 data bit PCI bus master can access a 64 data bit target and vice versa.

The support of the 64 data bit extension is accomplished with the addition of the AD[63::32], C/BE#[7::4], REQ64#, ACK64#, and PAR64 signal lines. All of the access cycle protocol outlined for platforms with the 32 data bit PCI buses also apply to platforms with the 64 data bit extension. Note: 64 data bit extension does not apply to I/O access cycles, configuration access cycles, and special and interrupt Acknowledge cycles.

See *Chapter 4: Functional Interaction Between PCI Resources* for details.

SIGNAL LINE OWNERSHIP DURING BUS CYCLES WITH 64 DATA BIT RESOURCES

During memory and I/O access cycles, the signal lines are owned by different PCI bus resources. A PCI resource owns the signal lines when it is the only resource (other than pull-up resistors) that can drive the signal line during a portion of the cycle. The protocol for 64 data bit accesses is as follows:

- The FRAME#, IRDY#, and C/BE#[7::0], REQ#, and REQ64# signal lines are owned by the PCI bus master.

- During a write access cycle, the PCI bus master owns the AD[63::0], PAR, and PAR64 signal lines.

- During a read access cycle, the PCI bus master owns the AD[63::0], PAR, and PAR64 signal lines during the ADDRESS PHASE. The target owns these signal lines during the DATA PHASE.

- The TRDY#, DEVSEL#, STOP#, ACK64# signal lines are owned by the target.

The remaining signal lines are owned according to the following protocol:

- The CLK and RST# signal lines are owned by the central resource.

- The GNT# signal lines are owned by the central arbiter.

- The LOCK# signal line is owned by the Lock master.

- The SDONE and SBO# signal lines are owned by the cache controller in the HOST/PCI BRIDGE or the central resource if the platform does not have a cache controller.

- The INTx# signal lines are owned by various PCI resources.

The I/O access, configuration access, interrupt acknowledge, and special cycles are defined as 32 data bit cycles. Please see *Subchapter 6.0: General Considerations*, for details about these cycles.

> 64 data bit I/O targets can be implemented, but there is no benefit to requiring the increased complexity and it is therefore strongly recommended that 64 data bit I/O targets are not implemented. For the purposes of this book, I/O targets are only 32 data bits in size. If a 64 data bit I/O target is implemented, the 64 data bit protocol applied to memory targets would also apply to I/O targets.

For further information, see Subchapters 6.0, referenced above, *6.2: Signal Line Protocol for 32 Data Bit Bus Cycles*, and *6.7: Signal Line Protocol for 64 Data Bit Bus Cycles*.

> The protocol for ACCESS CYCLE to ACCESS CYCLE operation and LOCK ACCESS CYCLE when 64 data bit resources are involved are the same as outlined in the previous sections for 32 data bit resources. There are additional considerations about the DUAL ADDRESS protocol relative to the 64 data bit extension as outlined below.

DUAL ADDRESS

The protocol outlined in Subchapter 6.0 for 32 data bit resources provides 64 address bits without the use of AD[63::32] signal lines. If the PCI bus master resides on a 64 data bit bus (REQ64# signal line asserted during RESET), and requests a 64 data bit access (REQ64# signal line asserted during the ADDRESS PHASE), the additional information must be provided for a DUAL ADDRESS. When a DUAL ADDRESS is not requested, AD[63::32] and C/BE#[7::4] signal lines are driven to a stable level during the ADDRESS PHASE but contain no valid information. PAR64 is also driven in the subsequent CLK signal line period to the ADDRESS PHASE with valid parity. When a DUAL ADDRESS is requested, AD[63::32] and C/BE#[7::4] signal lines are driven during the ADDRESS PHASE with the upper order address bits and the COMMAND type , respectively (see Figures 6-1, 6-2, and 6-14-A and B). PAR64 is also driven in the second CLK signal line period of the ADDRESS PHASE and the subsequent CLK signal line period with valid parity.

6.5   32 DATA BIT PCI BUS MASTER TO 64 DATA BIT TARGET

MEMORY ACCESS CYCLE

A 32 data bit access by the PCI bus master to a 64 data bit target can be executed with SINGLE and BURST access cycles using the same protocol as outlined for a 32 data bit target. All access cycles executed by a 32 data bit PCI bus master are the same independent of the data size of the target. Since the 64 data bit target cannot assert the ACK64# signal line, it appears to the PCI bus master as a 32 data bit target.

A PCI bus master requests a 32 data bit access by the deassertion of the REQ64# signal line during the ADDRESS PHASE. The target does not respond by asserting the ACK64# signal line. The REQ64# and ACK64# signal lines are kept deasserted by pull-up resistors. The AD[63::32], C/BE#[7::4], and PAR64 signal lines are driven to a logical "1" by pull-up resistors for the entire access cycle; consequently, the PAR64 signal line does not have valid parity information.

A 64 data bit target access cycle with DUAL ADDRESS operates with the same protocol as outlined for 32 data bit PCI bus masters accessing a 32 data bit target.

I/O AND CONFIGURATION ACCESS CYCLES, INTERRUPT ACKNOWLEDGE CYCLES, AND SPECIAL CYCLES

These bus cycles are executed only with 32 data bit resources. The deassertion of the ACK64# signal line makes the target appear as a 32 data bit resource. The protocol for these access cycles is the same as a 32 data bit PCI bus master accessing a 32 data bit target.

64 data bit I/O targets can be implemented, but there is no benefit to requiring the increased complexity and it is therefore strongly recommended that 64 data bit I/O targets are not implemented. For the purposes of this book, I/O targets are only 32 data bits in size. If a 64 data bit I/O target is implemented, the 64 data bit protocol applied to memory targets would also apply to I/O targets.

6.6   64 DATA BIT PCI BUS MASTER TO 64 DATA BIT TARGET

Note—Figure 6-15 referenced in this section does not show the SDONE and SBO# signal lines. The protocol of these signal lines is independent of data size. Information about these signal lines is shown in Figures 6-3 to 6-5 and is applicable to Figure 6-15.

MEMORY ACCESS CYCLES

A PCI bus master or a target is a defined as a 64 data bit resource when the REQ64# or ACK64# signal lines are asserted, respectively. The PCI bus master requests a 64 data bit access cycle by asserting the REQ64# signal line, and the PCI target acknowledges a 64 data bit access cycle by asserting the ACK64# signal line. The REQ64# and ACK64# signal lines are driven to a logical "1" by pull-up resistors when not driven by the PCI bus master and target resource, respectively. The execution of a 32 or 64 data bit access cycle is determined on a cycle-by-cycle basis. During the ADDRESS PHASE, the REQ64# signal line is asserted and the AD[31::0], C/BE#[3::0], and PAR signal lines operate with the same protocol as a 32 data bit access cycle (see Figure 6-15). During the DATA PHASE, the ACK64# signal line is asserted, and the AD[31::0], C/BE#[3::0], and PAR signal lines operate with the same protocol as a 32 data bit access cycle. Also, during the DATA PHASE, the operation of the C/BE#[7::4], AD[63::32], and PAR64 signal lines operate with the same protocol as the C/BE#[3::0], AD[31::0], and PAR signal lines in a 32 data bit access cycle.

Figure 6-15 outlines the SINGLE read access cycle for a 64 data bit PCI bus master accessing a 64 data bit memory resource (target). The concepts outlined for a SINGLE read access cycle are the same for SINGLE write, and BURST read and write access cycles. As outlined above, the protocol for all signal lines during 64 and 32 data bit accesses are the same except for the AD[63::32], C/BE#[7::4], REQ64#, ACK64#, and PAR64 signal lines.

The 64 data bit extension to the PCI bus protocol is optional. The operation of the AD[63::32], C/BE#[7::4], REQ64#, ACK64#, and PAR64 signal lines are slightly more complicated than the signal lines associated with 32 data bit bus cycles. Their unique operation during an access cycle are outlined below.

In the following discussion, the activity of the PAR and PAR64 signal lines are referenced to the ADDRESS and DATA PHASES. In actuality, the PAR and PAR64 signal lines are delayed by one CLK signal line period; consequently, they do not exactly align with the ADDRESS and DATA PHASES as implied.

For a 64 data bit access, without DUAL ADDRESS, the protocol of the AD[63::32], C/BE#[7::4], REQ64#, ACK64#, and the PAR64 signal lines is as follows:

- The REQ64# signal line is asserted during the ADDRESS PHASE and deasserted at the end of the DATA PHASE by the PCI bus master with the same timing profile as the FRAME# signal line.

- The ACK64# signal line is asserted and deasserted by the target with the same timing profile as the DEVSEL# signal line during the DATA PHASE.

- During the ADDRESS PHASE, the AD[63::32] and C/BE#[7::4] signal lines are driven to a stable level by the PCI bus master. Due to the assertion of the REQ64# signal line, the PAR64 signal line contains valid parity information.

- Due to the assertion of the REQ64# signal line during the ADDRESS PHASE, the PCI bus master drives the C/BE#[7::4] signal lines during the DATA PHASE with the valid byte lane information for the AD[63::32] signal lines. This compliments the C/BE#[3::0] signal lines containing valid byte lane information for the AD[31::0] signal lines.

- During the DATA PHASE of a read access cycle (see Figure 6-15), the AD[63::32] and PAR64 signal lines are tri-stated by the PCI bus master and driven by the target with the same time profile as the AD[31::0] and PAR signal lines, respectively. The target drives these signal lines with valid data and parity information simultaneously with or subsequent to the assertion of the DEVSEL# and ACK64# signal lines. Prior to being driven by the target, the AD[63::32] and PAR64 signal lines are driven to a logical "1" by pull-up resistors.

- During the DATA PHASE of a write access cycle, the AD[63::32] and PAR64 signal lines are driven by the PCI bus master with the same timing profile as the AD[31::0] and PAR signal lines, respectively.

For a 64 data bit access with DUAL ADDRESS, the protocol of the AD[63::32], C/BE#[7::4], REQ64#, ACK64#, and the PAR64 signal lines is as follows:

- The REQ64# signal line is asserted during the ADDRESS PHASE and deasserted at the end of the DATA PHASE by the PCI bus master with the same timing profile as the FRAME# signal line.

- The ACK64# signal line is asserted and deasserted by the target with the same timing profile as the DEVSEL# signal line during the DATA PHASE.

- The ADDRESS PHASE is two CLK signal line periods in length (see Figure 6-14-A and B).

- During the ADDRESS PHASE, the assertion of the REQ64# signal line requires the PCI bus master to drive the AD[63::32] signal lines with valid upper order addresses (see Figure 6-14-A and B). Also, the PCI bus master drives the C/BE#[7::4] and PAR64 signal lines with COMMAND type and valid parity information, respectively.

- Due to the assertion of the REQ64# signal line during the ADDRESS PHASE, the PCI bus master drives the C/BE#[7::4] signal line during the DATA PHASE with the valid byte lane information for the AD[63::32] signal lines. This compliments the C/BE#[3::0] signal lines containing valid byte lane information for the AD[31::0] signal lines.

- During the DATA PHASE of a read access cycle (see Figure 6-14-A), the AD[63::32] and PAR64 signal lines are tri-stated and driven by the target with the same timing profile as the AD[31::0] and PAR signal lines, respectively. The target drives these signal lines with valid data and parity information simultaneously with or subsequent to the assertion of the DEVSEL# and ACK64# signal lines.

- During the DATA PHASE of a write access cycle (see Figure 6-14-A), the AD[63::32] and PAR64 signal lines are driven by the PCI bus master with the same timing profile as the AD[31::0] and PAR signal lines, respectively.

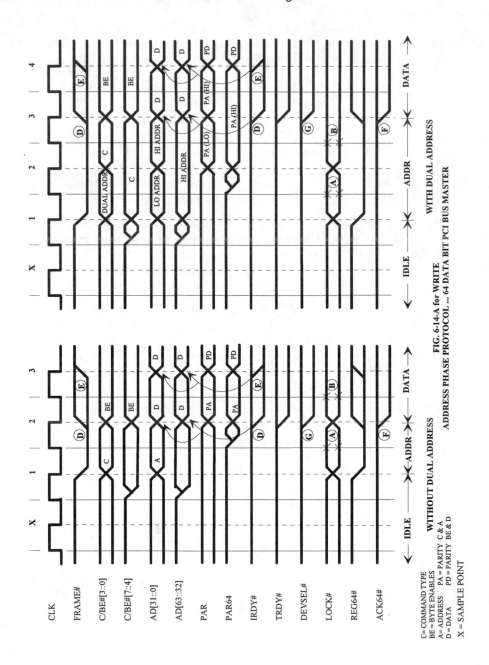

Figure 6-14-A: ADDRESS PHASE Protocol for Write, 64-Data Bit PCI Bus Master

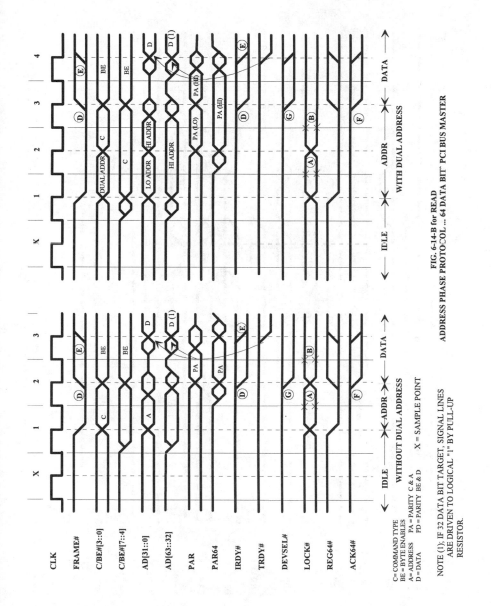

CLK
FRAME#
C/BE#[3::0]
C/BE#[7::4]
AD[31::0]
AD[63::32]
PAR
PAR64
IRDY#
TRDY#
DEVSEL#
LOCK#
REG64#
ACK64#

C = COMMAND TYPE
BE = BYTE ENABLES
A = ADDRESS   PA = PARITY C & A
D = DATA   PD = PARITY BE & D

X = SAMPLE POINT

NOTE (1); IF 32 DATA BIT TARGET, SIGNAL LINES
ARE DRIVEN TO LOGICAL "1" BY PULL-UP
RESISTOR.

FIG. 6-14-B for READ
ADDRESS PHASE PROTOCOL ... 64 DATA BIT PCI BUS MASTER

Figure 6-14-B: ADDRESS PHASE Protocol for Read, 64-Data Bit PCI Bus Master

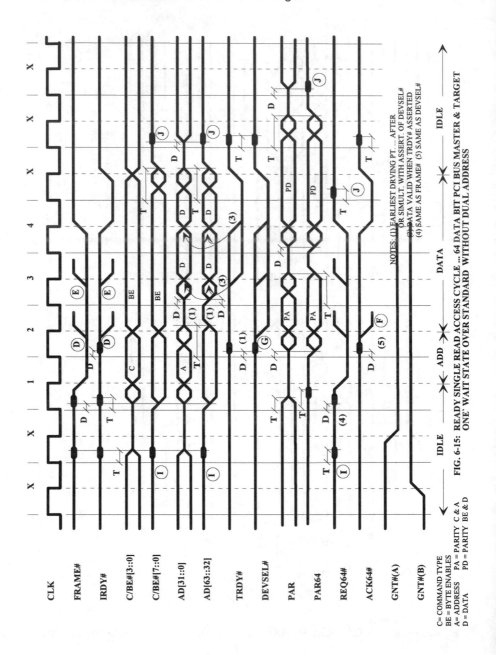

Figure 6-15: Ready Signal Read Access Cycle, 64 Data Bit PCI Bus Master and Target, One Wait State Over Standard without DUAL ADDRESS

The addressing protocol of a 64 data bit BURST access cycle is the same as for a 32 data bit BURST access cycle except the address increments are in 64 data bit increments (QWORDS) (AD[2] signal line is logical "0" during the ADDRESS PHASE). The order of the BURST access cycle is defined by the AD[1::0] in the same fashion as a 32 data bit access cycle.

I/O AND CONFIGURATION ACCESS CYCLES, INTERRUPT ACKNOWLEDGE CYCLES, AND SPECIAL CYCLES

These bus cycles are not defined for a 64 data bit access cycle and must be executed as 32 data bit access cycles. If the REQ64# or ACK64# signal lines are asserted during one of these bus cycles, they are ignored.

> 64 data bit I/O targets can be implemented, but there is no benefit to requiring the increased complexity and it is therefore strongly recommended that 64 data bit I/O targets are not implemented. For the purposes of this book, I/O targets are only 32 data bits in size. If a 64 data bit I/O target is implemented, the 64 data bit protocol applied to memory targets would also apply to I/O targets.

6.7 SIGNAL LINE PROTOCOL FOR 64 DATA BIT BUS CYCLES

Subchapter 6.4 outlines the ownership of the signal lines during a bus cycle. Chapter 8 details the change of signal line ownership and signal line driving and tri-stating when Completion, Retry, Disconnect, Master Abort, or Target Abort terminations are executed. Chapter 9 explains the change of signal line ownership and signal line driving and tri-stating between changes of bus ownership. Chapter 10 covers the signal line ownership and signal line driving and tri-stating of the SERR# and PERR# signal lines. The signal line protocol for the other signal lines during the bus cycle with Completion termination and between bus cycles when the PCI bus master retains bus ownership is as follows:

> In the following discussion, the terms *drive* or *tri-state* are different from *assert* or *deassert*. The former identifies when the signal line buffers are enabled or disabled. The latter reflects when signal lines change their logical state.

> The signal line protocol outlined below defines cycle completion when the FRAME# and TRDY# signal lines are simultaneously deasserted and asserted, respectively. Cycle completion is slightly different under conditions of special cycle and Master Abort, Retry, Disconnect, and Target Abort terminations. The more formal description of cycle completion is detailed under Completion with Timeout termination, in Chapter 8.

- All of the signal lines used by a 32 data bit PCI bus master that are used by a 64 data bit PCI bus master with the same protocol have been previously outlined in *6.2 Signal Line Protocol for 32 Data Bit Bus Cycles.*

- When a 64 data bit PCI bus master retains bus ownership, it can optionally drive the C/BE#[7::4], AD[63::32], REQ64#, and PAR64 signal lines to a logical "1" between bus cycles. If it optionally decides to tri-state these signal lines between bus cycles, the protocol is as follows:

  ⇒ The C/BE#[7::4], REQ64#, and AD[63::32] signal lines are tri-stated immediately after the FRAME# and TRDY# signal lines are simultaneously sampled deasserted and asserted, respectively.

  ⇒ The PAR64 signal line is tri-stated one CLK signal line period after the assertion of the FRAME# and TRDY# signal lines are simultaneously sampled deasserted and asserted respectively.

  ⇒ If tri-stated, these signal lines are driven to a logical "1" by pull-up resistors as identified by Point J (Circle J in Figures 6-15, 6-16 and 6-17) when bus ownership changes.

- The REQ64# signal line is asserted during the ADDRESS PHASE and deasserted at the end of the DATA PHASE by the PCI bus master with the same timing profile as the FRAME# signal line.

- During the entire bus cycle, the PCI bus master drives the C/BE#[7::4] signal lines with valid or stable information.

- During a write access cycle, the PCI bus master drives the AD[63::32] and PAR64 signal lines with the same protocol as the AD[31::0] and PAR signal lines, respectively (with some exceptions with DUAL ADDRESS.

- During the ADDRESS PHASE of a read access cycle, the PCI bus master drives the AD[63::32] and PAR64 signal lines with the same protocol as the AD[31::0] and PAR signal lines, respectively (with some exceptions with DUAL ADDRESS).

The signal line protocol for the other signal lines during the bus cycle and between bus cycles relative to the target is as follows:

■ All of the signal lines used by a 32 data bit target are used by a 64 data bit target with the same protocol have been previously outlined in *Subchapter 6.2 Signal Line Protocol for 32 Data Bit Bus Cycles.*

■ The ACK64# signal line is asserted and deasserted by the target with the same timing profile as the DEVSEL# signal line.

■ During a read access cycle, the PCI bus master drives the AD[63::32] and PAR64 signal lines with valid information during the ADDRESS PHASE with the same protocol as the AD[31::0] and PAR signal lines, respectively. For the DATA PHASE, the target drives the AD[63::32] and PAR64 signal lines with the same protocol as the AD[31::0] and PAR signal lines, respectively (with some exceptions for 32 data bit targets).

■ At the end of a read access cycle, a 64 data bit target tri-states the AD[63::32] signal lines immediately after the FRAME# and TRDY# signal lines are simultaneously sampled deasserted and asserted, respectively. Until driven by a 64 data bit PCI bus master, these signal lines are driven to a logical "1" by pull-up resistors. Optionally, the 64 data bit PCI bus master, if not a Park master, can drive these signal lines to a logical "1" one CLK signal line period after the FRAME# and TRDY# signal lines are simultaneously sampled deasserted and asserted, respectively.

■ At the end of a read access cycle, a 64 data bit target tri-states the PAR64 signal line one CLK signal line period after the FRAME# and TRDY# signal lines are simultaneously sampled deasserted and asserted, respectively. Until driven by a 64 data bit PCI bus master, this signal line is driven to a logical "1" by a pull-up resistor. Optionally, the 64 data bit PCI bus master, if not Park master, can drive this signal line to a logical "1" one CLK signal line period after the FRAME# and TRDY# signal lines are simultaneously sampled deasserted and asserted, respectively.

The I/O access, configuration access, interrupt acknowledge, and special cycles are defined as 32 data bit cycles. See *Subchapter 6.2: Signal Line Protocol for 32 Data Bit Bus Cycles*, for details about these cycles. For more information about other related topics, see *Subchapters 6.0: General Considerations, 6.2,* referenced above, and *6.4: 64 Data Bit Extension.*

6.8   64 DATA BIT PCI BUS MASTER TO 32 DATA BIT TARGET

Figures 6-16 and 6-17, referenced in this section, do not show SDONE and SBO# signal lines. The protocol of these signal lines is independent of data size. Information about these signal lines is shown in Figures 6-3 through 6-5 and is applicable to Figures 6-16 and 6-17.

MEMORY ACCESS CYCLES

A PCI bus master and a target are defined as 64 and 32 data bit resources when the REQ64# and ACK64# signal lines are asserted and deasserted, respectively. The PCI bus master requests a 64 data bit access cycle by asserting the REQ64# signal line and the PCI target acknowledges support of a 32 data bit access by not asserting the ACK64# signal line (deasserted by pull-up resistor).

The access of a 64 data bit PCI bus master to a 32 data bit target is determined on a cycle-by-cycle basis. During the ADDRESS PHASE, the REQ64# signal line is asserted, and the AD[31::0], C/BE#[3::0], and PAR signal lines operate with the same protocol as a 32 data bit PCI bus master executing a 32 data bit access cycle (see Figures 6-16 and 6-17). During the ADDRESS PHASE, the REQ64# signal line is asserted and the AD[31::0], C/BE#[3::0], and PAR signal lines operate with the same protocol as in a 32 data bit access cycle (see Figures 6-16 and 6-17). Also, during the DATA PHASE, the operation of the C/BE#[7::4], AD[63::32], and PAR64 signal lines operate with the same protocol as the C/BE#[3::0], AD[31::0], and PAR signal lines in a 32 data bit access cycle. Also, during the DATA PHASE, the ACK64# signal line remains deasserted to indicate that a 32 data bit access will be executed for the entire cycle.

In the following discussion, the activity of the PAR and PAR64 signal lines are referenced to the ADDRESS and DATA PHASES. In actuality, the PAR and PAR64 signal lines are delayed by one CLK signal line period; consequently, they do not exactly align with the ADDRESS and DATA PHASES as implied.

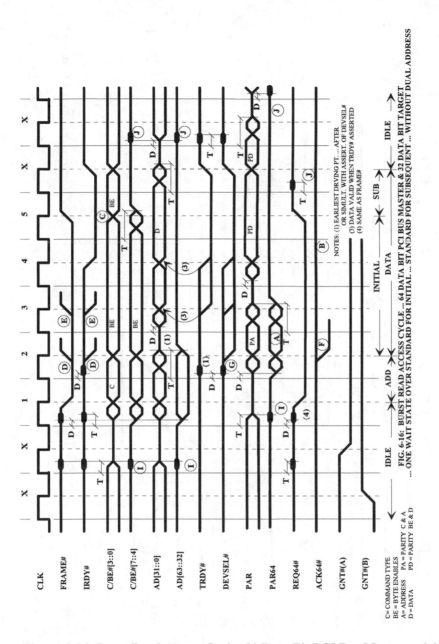

Figure 6-16: Burst Read Access Cycle, 64-Data Bit PCI Bus Master and 32 Data Bit Target, One Wait State Over Standard for Initial, Standard for Subsequent, without DUAL ADDRESS

249

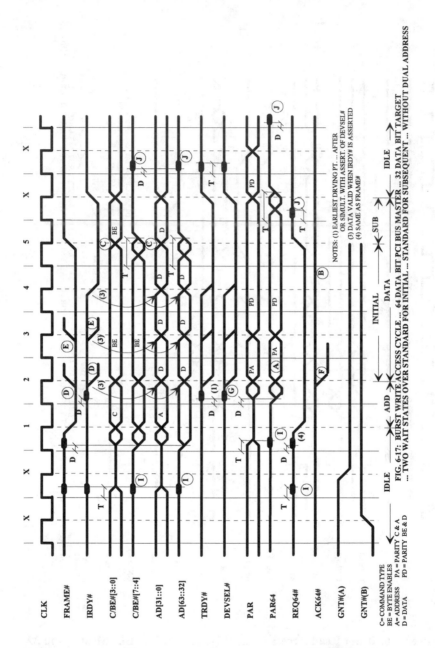

Figure 6-17: Burst Write Access Cycle, 64-Data Bit PCI Bus Master, 64 Data Bit Target, Two Wait States Over Standard for Initial, Standard for Subsequent, without DUAL ADDRESS

As will be outlined below, a 64 data bit PCI bus master does not usually access a 32 data bit target using a SINGLE access cycle. Normally, a 64 data bit SINGLE access cycle requested by the PCI bus master becomes a BURST access of two 32 data bit microaccesses. If the 64 data bit PCI bus master knows in advance (via configuration address space) that the target supports 64 data bit accesses, then it executes a single 64 data bit access cycle.

For a 64 data bit PCI bus master's access to a 32 data bit target without DUAL ADDRESS, the protocol of the AD[63::32], C/BE#[7::4], REQ64#, ACK64#, and PAR64 signal lines is as follows:

- The REQ64# signal line is asserted during the ADDRESS PHASE and deasserted at the end of the DATA PHASE by the PCI bus master with the same timing profile as the FRAME# signal line.

- The ACK64# signal line remains deasserted throughout the access cycle.

- During the ADDRESS PHASE, the AD[63::32], and C/BE#[7::4] signal lines are driven to a stable level by the PCI bus master. Due to the assertion of the REQ64# signal lines the PAR64 signal line contains valid parity information.

- Due to the assertion of the REQ64# signal line during the ADDRESS PHASE, the PCI bus master drives the C/BE#[7::4] signal lines during the DATA PHASE with the valid byte lane information for the initial microaccess (see Figures 6-16 and 6-17). After the completion of the initial microaccess, the C/BE#[7::4] signal lines are driven by the PCI bus master to a logical "1". Prior to the completion of the initial microaccess, the target has been identified as 32 data bits in size (TRDY# and DEVSEL# signal lines are asserted, and ACK64# signal line is deasserted). The byte information on the C/BE#[7::4] signal lines during the initial microaccess is repeated on the C/BE#[3::0] signal lines at Point C during the first of the subsequent microaccesses (Circle C in Figures 6-16 and 6-17).

The above bullet states that the PCI bus master drives C/BE#[7::4] signal lines to a logical "1". Optionally, the PCI bus master can drive these signal lines to any stable level or tri-state them. The latter results in pull-up resistors driving them to a logical "1".

- During the DATA PHASE of a read access cycle (see Figure 6-16), the AD[63::32] and PAR64 signal lines are tri-stated and driven to a logical

"1" by pull-up resistors. The PAR64 signal line does not contain valid parity information due to the deasserted ACK64# signal line.

■ During the initial microaccess of the DATA PHASE of a write access cycle (see Figure 6-17), the AD[63::32] and PAR64 signal lines are driven with valid information by the PCI bus master with the same timing profile as the AD[31::0] and PAR signal lines, respectively. After the completion of the initial microaccess, the AD[63::32] and PAR64 signal lines are driven by the PCI bus master to a logical "1"; consequently, the PAR64 signal line does not contain valid parity information due to the deasserted ACK64# signal line. Prior to the completion of the initial microaccess, the target has been identified as 32 data bits in size (TRDY# and DEVSEL# signal lines are asserted, and ACK64# signal line is deasserted). The valid information on the AD[63::32] and PAR64 signal lines during the initial microaccess is repeated on the AD[31::0] and PAR signal lines during the first subsequent microaccess, respectively.

> The above bullet states that the PCI bus master drives AD[63::32] and PAR64 signal lines to a logical "1". Optionally, the PCI bus master can drive these signal lines to any stable level or tri-state them. The latter results in pull-up resistors driving them to a logical "1". In any case the PAR64 signal line does not contain valid parity information.

> For the read access cycle, the AD[63::32], C/BE#[7::4], and PAR64 signal lines are driven to a logical "1" by pull-up resistors during the DATA PHASE of the initial and the first subsequent microaccess. When the BURST access cycle contains additional subsequent microaccesses, pull-up resistors hold these signal lines at logical "1".

> For the write access cycle, the AD[63::32], C/BE#[7::4], and PAR64 signal lines are driven with valid information by the PCI bus master during the initial microaccess during the DATA PHASE. The operation of these signal lines during the first subsequent microaccess has been outlined above. If the BURST access cycle contains other subsequent microaccesses, the PCI bus master can drive these signal lines to any stable level or tri-state them. The latter results in pull-up resistors driving them to a logical "1". In any case, the PAR64 signal line does not contain valid parity information.

For a 64 data bit PCI bus master's access to the 32 data bit target with DUAL ADDRESS, the protocol of the AD[63::32], C/BE#[7::4], REQ64#, ACK64#, and the PAR64 signal lines is as follows:

- The REQ64# signal line is asserted during the ADDRESS PHASE and deasserted at the end of the DATA PHASE by the PCI bus master with the same timing profile as the FRAME# signal line.

- The ACK64# signal line remains deasserted throughout the access cycle.

- The ADDRESS PHASE is two CLK signal line periods in length (see Figures 6-14-A and B).

- During the ADDRESS PHASE, due to the assertion of the REQ64# signal line, the AD[63::32] signal lines are driven by the PCI bus master with a valid upper order address (see Figure 6-14-A and B). The PCI bus master also drives the C/BE#[7::4] and PAR64 signal lines with the COMMAND type and the parity information, respectively.

- Due to the assertion of the REQ64# signal line during the ADDRESS PHASE, the PCI bus master drives the C/BE#[7::4] signal lines during the DATA PHASE with the valid byte lane information for the initial microaccess. After the completion of the initial microaccess, the C/BE#[7::4] signal lines are driven by PCI bus master to a logical "1". Prior to the completion of the initial microaccess, the target has been identified as 32 data bits in size (TRDY# and DEVSEL# signal lines are asserted, and ACK64# signal line is deasserted). The byte information on the C/BE#[7::4] signal lines during the initial microaccess is repeated on the C/BE#[3::0] signal lines at Point C during the first of the subsequent microaccesses (Circle C in Figures 6-16 and 6-17).

> The above bullet says that the PCI bus master drives the C/BE#[7::4] signal lines to a logical "1". Optionally, the PCI bus master can drive these signal lines to any stable level or tri-state them. The latter results in pull-up resistors driving them to logical "1".

- During the DATA PHASE of a read access cycle (see Figure 6-16), the AD[63::32] and PAR64 signal lines are tri-stated and driven to a logical "1" by pull-up resistors. The PAR64 signal line does not contain valid parity information due to the deasserted ACK64# signal line.

- During the initial microaccess of the DATA PHASE of a write access cycle (see Figure 6-17), the AD[63::32] and PAR64 signal lines are driven with valid information by the PCI bus master with the same timing profile as the AD[31::0] and PAR signal lines, respectively. After the completion of the initial microaccess, the AD[63::32] and PAR64 signal lines are driven by the PCI bus master to a logical "1"; consequently, the PAR64 signal line does not contain valid parity information due to the deasserted ACK64# signal line. Prior to the completion of the initial microaccess, the target has been identified as 32 data bits in size (TRDY# and DEVSEL# signal lines are asserted, and ACK64# signal line is deasserted). The valid information on the AD[63::32] and PAR64 signal lines during the initial microaccess is repeated on the AD[31::0] and PAR signal lines during the subsequent microaccess, respectively.

> The above bullet states that the PCI bus master drives AD[63::32] and PAR64 signal lines to a logical "1". Optionally, the PCI bus master can drive these signal lines to any stable level or tri-state them. The latter results in pull-up resistors driving them to a logical "1". In any case the PAR64 signal line does not contain valid parity information.

> For the read access cycle, the AD[63::32], C/BE#[7::4], and PAR64 signal lines are driven to a logical "1" by pull-up resistors during the DATA PHASE of the initial and the first subsequent microaccesses. When the BURST access cycle contains additional subsequent microaccesses, these signal lines remain at the logical "1" by pull-up resistors.

> For the write access cycle, the AD[63::32], C/BE#[7::4], and PAR64 signal lines are driven with valid information by the PCI bus master during the initial microaccess during the DATA PHASE. The operation of these signal lines during the first subsequent microaccess has been outlined above. If the BURST access cycle contains other subsequent microaccesses, the PCI bus master can drive these signal lines to any stable level or tri-state them. The latter results in pull-up resistors driving them to a logical "1". In any case, the PAR64 signal line does not contain valid parity information.

The addressing protocol of a 64 data bit PCI bus master's request to a 32 data bit target BURST access cycle is the same as for a 32 data bit BURST access cycle. The address increments are 32 data bit (double word) increments. The order of the burst is defined by the AD[1::0] in the same fashion as a 32 data bit access cycle.

The above assumes that the PCI bus master is requesting a 64 data bit SINGLE access cycle. The 32 data bit target responded by allowing the SINGLE 64 data bit access cycle to turn into a BURST access cycle with an initial and subsequent microaccesses of 32 data bits each. If the PCI bus master was requesting a 64 data bit BURST access cycle, the 64 data bit initial microaccess becomes a 32 data bit initial and subsequent microaccess. The BURST access cycle continues with 32 data bit microaccesses. Alternatively, the target can execute a Disconnect with data termination with the data access of the SINGLE access cycle or the initial microaccess of the BURST access cycle. Under this protocol the PCI bus master MUST continue the access later as a 32 data bit PCI bus master (REQ64# signal line deasserted).

I/O AND CONFIGURATION ACCESS CYCLES, INTERRUPT ACKNOWLEDGE CYCLES, AND SPECIAL CYCLES

These bus cycles are not defined for 64 data bit access cycles and must be executed as 32 data bit access cycles. If the REQ64# or ACK64# signal lines are asserted during one of these access cycles, they are ignored.

> 64 data bit I/O targets can be implemented, but there is no benefit to requiring the increased complexity and it is therefore strongly recommended that 64 data bit I/O targets are not implemented. For the purposes of this book, I/O targets are only 32 data bits in size. If a 64 data bit I/O target is implemented, the 64 data bit protocol applied to memory targets would also apply to I/O targets.

6.9 SPECIAL CONSIDERATIONS FOR A 64 DATA BIT PCI BUS MASTER TO A 32 DATA BIT TARGET

A PCI bus master asserts the REQ64# signal line at the beginning of the access cycle without any assurance that the ACK64# signal line will be asserted. The target does not have to acknowledge a 64 data bit access (Point F) until the assertion of the DEVSEL# signal line at Point G (Circles F and G in Figures 6-14 A and B, and Figures 6-15 to 6-17). The protocol of a SINGLE access cycle allows the FRAME# and IRDY# signal lines to be deasserted and asserted at Point D, respectively (Circle D in Figures 6-14-A and B, and Figures 6-15 to 6-17). The deassertion of the FRAME# signal line and the assertion of the IRDY# signal lines at any point prior to Point F will prevent the proper completion of the access cycle if the ACK64# signal line is not asserted. If the ACK64# signal line remains deasserted at Point B (Circle B in Figures 6-16 and

6-17) when the TRDY# and IRDY# signal lines are both asserted, a SINGLE access cycle will become a BURST access cycle because two 32 data bit (double words) must be accessed. The PCI bus master cannot deassert the FRAME# signal line until it is determined if the ACK64# signal line is asserted or remains deasserted; consequently, the FRAME# signal line must remain asserted until the DEVSEL# signal line is asserted. The timing protocol of the DEVSEL# and ACK64# signal lines are the same; consequently, the DEVSEL# signal line can be used as a qualifier of the ACK64# signal and indicator when the FRAME# signal line can be deasserted. Points G and E (Circles G and E in Figures 6-14 A and B, and Figures 6-16 and 6-17) are the earliest assertion and deassertion points for the DEVSEL# and FRAME# signal lines, respectively.

If the ACK64# signal line is asserted when the DEVSEL# signal line is asserted, a SINGLE access cycle will be executed; consequently, the FRAME# and IRDY# signal line can be immediately deasserted and asserted at Point E (Circle E in Figures 6-14-A and B, and Figures 6-16 and 6-17), respectively. The protocol of the FRAME# signal line requires it to be deasserted simultaneously with the assertion of the IRDY# signal line to execute a SINGLE access cycle. If the ACK64# signal line is deasserted when the DEVSEL# signal line is asserted, the FRAME# signal line must remain asserted to allow a BURST access cycle to be executed.

Once the first access is completed, the data size of the target is known; consequently, the requirements outlined above for the FRAME# signal line about the DEVSEL# signal line does not apply for the subsequent microaccesses of a BURST access cycle.

If the PCI bus master knows the target size is 64 data bits, the above protocol of the FRAME# signal line deassertion and IRDY# signal line assertion after the assertion of the DEVSEL# and ACK64# signal lines is not required. This will allow the cycle to be executed as a single 64 data bit access cycle in the minimum amount of time. Otherwise, the length of the cycle is longer due to the PCI bus master waiting for the assertion of the DEVSEL# signal line to determine when it can deassert the FRAME# signal line. The PCI bus master knows the size of the target via the device specific configuration space.

If the DUAL ADDRESS is executed, points D, E, F, and G (circles D, E, F, and G in Figures 6-14-A and B) are delayed by one CLK signal line period.

6.10 BUS-CYCLE -TO-BUS-CYCLE OPERATION

INTRODUCTION

As shown in Figures 6-3 to 6-6 and Figures 6-15 to 6-17, the individual SINGLE and BURST access cycles are preceded and followed by IDLE PHASE*S*. IDLE PHASES occur whenever both the FRAME# and IRDY# signal lines are both deasserted. During the IDLE PHASES, the FRAME#, IRDY#, C/BE#[3::0], AD[31::0], and PAR signal lines are driven by a PCI bus master, and the C/BE#[7::4], AD[63::32], PAR64 (optional for 64 data bit), TRDY#, DEVSEL#, STOP#, and PERR# signal lines are driven by pull-up resistors. The PCI bus specification outlines a protocol to change the resources responsible for driving the aforementioned signal lines. In addition, under certain circumstances IDLE PHASES do not occur between the individual SINGLE and BURST access cycles. The following will first describe how the aforementioned signal lines are driven by different resources from access cycle to access cycle when IDLE is achieved. It will then describe how Fast Back-to-Back access cycles occur without IDLE PHASES, and how the signal lines are driven by different resources during Fast Back-to-Back access cycles.

> The LOCK signal line is driven by the Lock master when other PCI bus masters own the bus; consequently, there is not always a change of ownership between the access cycles.

> In the following discussions, the term "access" cycle refers to memory, I/O, and configuration. These are distinguished from interrupt acknowledge and special cycles.

SIGNAL LINE DRIVING NON-FAST BACK-TO-BACK

ACCESS CYCLES

Figure 6-3 outlines two SINGLE read access cycles when a single PCI bus master (A) owns the PCI bus before and after the execution of the two access cycles. The FRAME#, IRDY#, and C/BE#[3::0] signal lines are driven by the current PCI bus master throughout the execution of these two access cycles because its associated GNT# signal line remains asserted. The AD[31::0] and PAR signal lines are driven by both the PCI bus master and the target. During the IDLE PHASE prior to the first access cycle, the AD[31::0] signal lines are driven by the current PCI bus master. Once the access cycle has started (FRAME#

257

signal line asserted), the PCI bus master must tri-state the AD[31::0] signal lines at the end of the ADDRESS PHASE in preparation for the target driving these signal lines with read data at the beginning of the DATA PHASE. The AD[31::0] signal lines are tri-stated by the target at the end of the first access cycle when the FRAME# and TRDY# signal lines are simultaneously deasserted and asserted, respectively. Subsequently, the AD[31::0] signal lines are driven by the current PCI bus master when the FRAME# and IRDY# are both deasserted because its associated GNT# signal line remains asserted.

The PAR signal lines operate in exactly the same fashion as the AD[31::0] signal lines with a one CLK signal line period lag.

Figure 6-3 also outlines the protocol for the portion of the read access cycles when the TRDY#, DEVSEL#, and STOP# signal lines are driven by the target. Whenever these signal lines are not driven by a target, they are driven by the pull-up resistors on the bus backplane. The target will drive the TRDY#, DEVSEL#, and STOP# signal lines at the beginning of the DATA PHASE of the first access cycle. The target tri-states these signal lines when the FRAME# and IRDY# are both deasserted.

The tri-state and drive protocol of the second access cycle in Figure 6-3 is identical to the first access because IDLE is achieved between the two access cycles. The protocol is the same subsequent to the second access cycle even though a third access cycle will not immediately begin.

Figure 6-4 outlines two SINGLE write access cycles when a single PCI bus master (A) owns the PCI bus during and after the execution of two access cycles, but not before the first access cycle. The FRAME#, IRDY#, C/BE#[3::0], AD[31::0], PAR signal lines are driven by the current PCI bus master (B) while the GNT# (B) signal line is asserted. When the GNT# (B) signal line is deasserted, the aforementioned signal lines are tri-stated in anticipation of PCI bus master (A) driving these signal lines. Because the IDLE PHASE was achieved by PCI bus master (B) a CLK signal line period is inserted between the deassertion and assertion of the GNT# (B) and GNT# (A) signal lines, respectively. Until the GNT# (A) signal line is asserted, the FRAME# and IRDY# signal lines are driven by pull-up resistors, and the C/BE#[3::0], AD[31::0], and PAR signal lines are allowed to float. Once the GNT# (A) signal line is asserted, these signal lines are driven by the PCI bus master (A). The PCI bus master (A) executes the two write access cycles in the same fashion as the two read access cycles outlined in Figure 6-3. The only difference is that the AD[31::0] signal lines are not driven by the target.

The protocol for the portion of the write access cycles when the TRDY#, DEVSEL#, and STOP# signal lines are driven by the target are outlined in Figure

6-4. The protocol is the same as for the read access cycles as outlined in Figure 6-3.

Both Figures 6-3 and 6-4 outline the tri-state and drive protocol of the signal lines prior to, during, and after the two access cycles. Obviously, this protocol applies for multiple sequential access cycles. Figure 6-18 outlines the general case when more than one IDLE PHASE occurs between access cycles when the PCI bus master remains the same. During the IDLE PHASE the FRAME#, IRDY#, C/BE#, AD[31::0], and PAR signal lines are driven by the PCI bus master associated with the asserted GNT# signal line. The TRDY#, DEVSEL#, and STOP# signal lines are driven by pull-up resistors. The PAR signal line is driven by the target during some portion of the IDLE PHASE subsequent to a read access cycle.

The unmarked portions of the C/BE#, AD, PAR, and PAR64 signal lines in Figures 6-18 to 6-25 are driven to a stable level—but without valid information—during the IDLE PHASE (though not shown separately, for *reads*, the PAR64 is driven to a logical "1" by a pull-up resistor). As previously mentioned, the PAR and PAR64 signal lines always lag by one CLK signal line period. As outlined in the *Signal Line Protocol* section, the AD[63::32], C/BE#[7::4], and PAR64 signal lines are driven to a logical "1" by either the PCI bus master or pull-up resistors. Consequently, for these signal lines, the shaded areas would appear as logical "1". Similarly, in these figures when the signal line is drawn with a single horizontal line to indicate *floating*, these signal lines are driven to a logical "1" by either the PCI bus master or pull-up resistors.

Figures 6-18 to 6-25 do not include the SDONE, SBO#, and LOCK# signal lines. Because the operation of these signal lines transcends a specific bus cycle, their inclusion is not important to understanding Fast Back-to-Back cycle operation. Figures 6-18 to 6-25 show the data and parity (*D* and *PD*) are valid for the entire cycle. As outlined in previous figures in this chapter, the assertion of the IRDY# and TRDY# signal lines qualifies when the AD, PAR, and PAR64 signal lines are valid. Consequently, the indication of valid data and parity is for simplification of Figures 6-18 to 6-25. Refer to previous figures for specific information about valid data and parity.

Figures 6-19 to 6-21 outline the tri-state and drive protocol for the signal lines between access cycles when the ownership of the bus will change. Figure 6-19 outlines the protocol when the GNT# (A) signal line is deasserted prior to the completion of the last access cycle of the PCI bus master (A) but prior to an IDLE PHASE. The simultaneous sampling at Point A of deasserted FRAME#

and GNT#(A) signal lines, and asserted of the IRDY# and TRDY# signal lines indicates the completion of the access cycle and the end of bus ownership by PCI bus master (A). The FRAME#, C/BE#, and AD signal lines are immediately tri-stated at Point A. For a read access cycle, the target will tri-state the AD signal lines, and one CLK signal line period later the PAR signal line. For a write access cycle, the PAR and PAR64 signal lines are tri-stated by the PCI bus master (A) one CLK signal line period later. The IRDY# signal line is tri-stated one CLK signal line period after Point A. In this example, the GNT# signal line (B) is asserted prior to IDLE being achieved by the last access cycle of PCI bus master (A). The simultaneous sampling of the asserted GNT# (B) signal line and the IDLE ACHIEVED (FRAME# and IRDY# signal lines deasserted) at Point B allows the PCI bus master (B) to immediately drive the FRAME#, C/BE#, and AD signal lines (Circle B in Figure 6-19). The PCI bus master (B) drives the IRDY# signal line one CLK signal line period later, and the PAR (and PAR64 for 64 data bit accesses cycles) signal line two CLK signal line periods later to avoid signal line contention with the PCI bus master (A). The TRDY#, DEVSEL#, STOP#, PAR, and PAR64 signal lines are tri-stated and driven with the same protocol used when bus ownership has not changed.

In Figure 6-19, the GNT#(A) signal line is deasserted prior to IDLE ACHIEVED FRAME# and IRDY# signal lines deasserted) occurring; consequently, the GNT#(B) signal line can be asserted immediately or at Point C (Circle C in Figure 6-19). The resulting bus cycle is the same for either point where the GNT#(B) signal line is asserted. See *Chapter 9: Bus Ownership* for details.

Figure 6-20 outlines the protocol when the GNT# (A) signal line is deasserted after IDLE ACHIEVED (FRAME# and IRDY# signal lines deasserted) at Point A has occurred for the last access cycle of the PCI bus master (A)(Circle A in Figure 6-20). Prior to the deassertion of the GNT# (A) signal line, the PCI bus master (A) owns the bus and must continue to drive the FRAME#, C/BE#, AD, PAR, PAR64 signal lines even if it does not intend to begin another access cycle. Thus, after the completion of the access cycle, the aforementioned signal lines are driven by the PCI bus master (A). In the case of C/BE#, A, PAR, and PAR64 signal lines this is totally invalid information. If the last access cycle read data, the PCI bus master (A) must wait until the IDLE PHASE, before driving the AD signal lines to prevent contention with the target. Similarly, the PAR and PAR64 signal lines are driven one CLK signal line period after the first IDLE PHASE period. When the GNT# (A) signal line is sampled deasserted, the PCI bus master (A) must immediately tri-state the FRAME#, IRDY#, C/BE#, and AD signal lines in anticipation that another PCI bus master will drive them. Similarly, the PAR and PAR64 signal lines are tri-stated one CLK signal line period later.

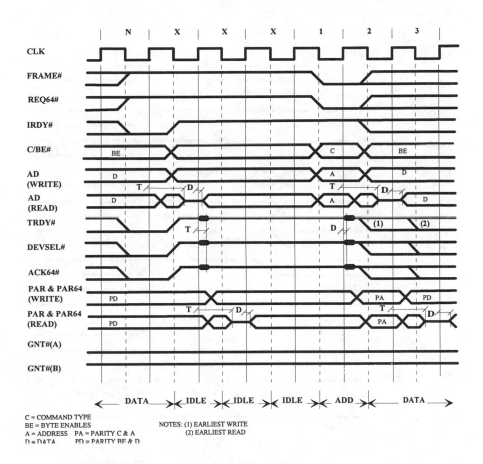

Figure 6-18: PCI Bus Master (A) to IDLE to PCI Bus Master (A)

261

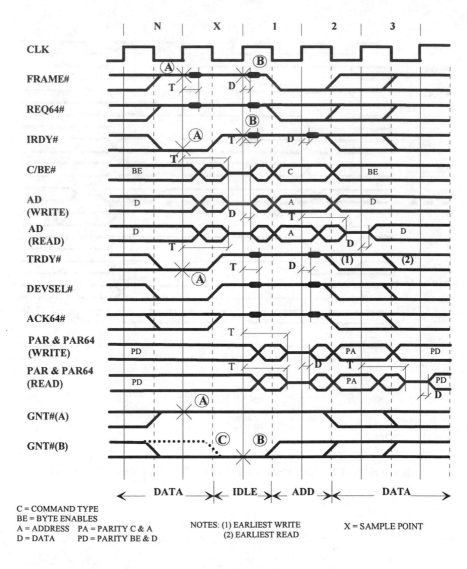

C = COMMAND TYPE
BE = BYTE ENABLES
A = ADDRESS   PA = PARITY C & A
D = DATA   PD = PARITY BE & D

NOTES: (1) EARLIEST WRITE
       (2) EARLIEST READ

X = SAMPLE POINT

Figure 6-19: PCI Bus Master (A) to IDLE to PCI Bus Master (B)

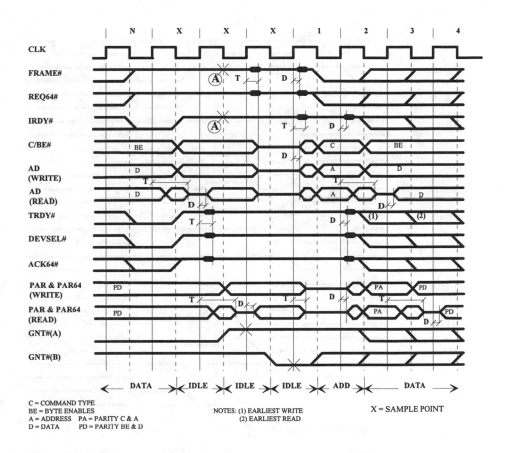

C = COMMAND TYPE
BE = BYTE ENABLES
A = ADDRESS   PA = PARITY C & A
D = DATA   PD = PARITY BE & D

NOTES: (1) EARLIEST WRITE
(2) EARLIEST READ

X = SAMPLE POINT

Figure 6-20: PCI Bus Master (A) to IDLE to PCI Bus Master (B)

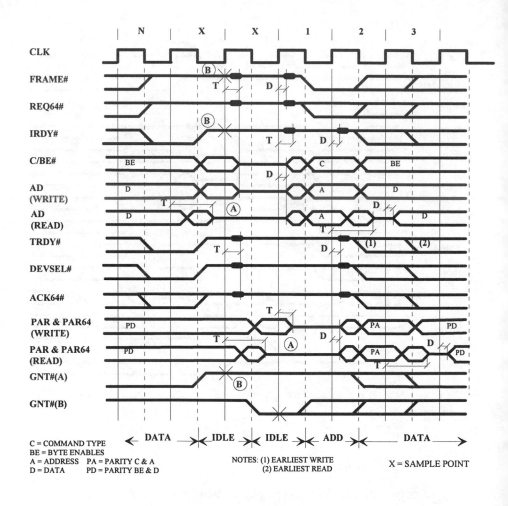

Figure 6-21: PCI Bus Master (A) to IDLE to PCI Bus Master (B)

The PCI bus master (B) uses the IDLE condition in conjunction with an asserted GNT# B signal line to begin driving the FRAME#, IRDY#, C/BE#, and AD signal lines. The PAR signal line is driven one CLK signal line period later. In that the IDLE PHASE was achieved when the GNT# (A) signal line was still asserted, the central arbiter will assert the GNT# (B) signal line one CLK signal line after it deasserts the GNT# (A) signal line. This protocol allows the PCI bus master (A) to tri-state the aforementioned signal lines without contention with the PCI bus master (B). The TRDY#, DEVSEL#, and STOP# signal lines are tri-stated and driven with the same protocol used when bus ownership has not changed. See *Chapter 9: Bus Ownership* for details.

Figure 6-21 outlines the protocol when the GNT# (A) signal line is deasserted simultaneously with IDLE ACHIEVED (FRAME# and IRDY# signal lines deasserted) at Point B for the last access cycle of the PCI bus master (A) (Circle B of Figure 6-21). PCI bus master (A) will immediately tri-state the signal lines it was driving. In other examples (Figures 6-19 and 6-20) the PCI bus master that just completed a read cycle will re-drive the AD, PAR, and PAR64 signal lines that had been driven by the target. In this example (Figure 6-21) the PCI bus master knows it must relinquish bus ownership at the completion of the bus cycle; consequently, it does not re-drive the AD, PAR, and PAR64 signal lines at Point A (Circle A in Figure 6-21) In that the IDLE PHASE was achieved simultaneously with the deassertion of the GNT# (A) signal line. The central arbiter will assert the GNT# (B) signal line one CLK signal line after it deasserts the GNT# (A) signal line. This protocol allows PCI bus master (A) to tri-state these signal lines without contention with PCI bus master (B). The TRDY#, DEVSEL#, and STOP# signal lines are tri-stated and driven with the same protocol whether or not bus ownership has not changed. See *Chapter 9: Bus Ownership* for details.

> Even though the examples use only SINGLE access cycle, the protocol also applies between BURST access cycles, and between SINGLE and BURST access cycles.

SPECIAL CYCLES

The access cycle to access cycle protocol outlined above applies to special cycle to special cycle, special cycle to access cycle or interrupt acknowledge cycle, and access cycle or interrupt acknowledge cycle to special cycle.

INTERRUPT ACKNOWLEDGE CYCLES

The access cycle to access cycle protocol outlined above applies to interrupt acknowledge cycle to interrupt acknowledge cycle, interrupt acknowledge cycle to access cycle or special cycle, and access cycle or special cycle to interrupt acknowledge cycle.

SIGNAL LINE DRIVING FAST BACK-TO-BACK

ACCESS CYCLE

The PCI bus has specific requirements for back-to-back access cycles by the same PCI bus master. As shown in Figure 6-19, the normal completion of a cycle includes achieving IDLE. By achieving IDLE, there is a minimum of one CLK signal line period between the DATA PHASE of the previous SINGLE access cycle and the ADDRESS PHASE of the next SINGLE access cycle. The achievement of IDLE would also occur between two BURST access cycles, SINGLE and BURST access cycles, and BURST and SINGLE access cycles. Under certain situations, the IDLE PHASE between two access cycles is not required. There are two situations where IDLE is not required: MASTER PROGRAMMED Fast Back-to-Back and Target Fast Back-to-Back. Either of these Fast Back-to-Back situations allow the DATA PHASE of the previous access cycle to be immediately followed by the ADDRESS PHASE of the present access cycle, provide higher bus performance.

Restrictions in the protocol of Fast Back-to-Back access cycles are to eliminate contention (buffer fights) on the signal lines. The FRAME#, IRDY#, C/BE#, PAR, and PAR64 signal lines are driven by the PCI bus master between back-to-back access cycles. The driving of these signal lines by the PCI bus master that owns the bus assures that no other resource is simultaneously driving these signal lines and causing contention between the back-to-back access cycles. Because the previous cycle of a back-to-back access cycle is always a write, there is no contention on the AD, PAR, or PAR64 signal lines. The TRDY#, DEVSEL#, and STOP# signal lines can be driven by different targets from one access cycle to another; consequently, these signal lines have a potential for contention. Contention on these signal lines is avoided by the protocol restrictions placed on Fast Back-to-Back access cycles.

The PAR and PAR64 signal lines can be driven by either the PCI bus master or the target. Except for a one CLK signal line period delay, the change of ownership for the PAR and PAR64 signal lines are patterned after the AD[31::0] and AD[63::32] signal lines, respectively. The requirement that the previous cycle must be a write access cycle insures that only one PCI bus master drives the PAR and PAR64 signal lines between access cycles.

> In order to prevent contention on some of the signal lines, an IDLE PHASE exists between the last access cycle of one PCI bus master and the first access cycle of the next PCI bus master. (IDLE is achieved with the FRAME# and IRDY# signal lines simultaneously deasserted.) For access cycles executed in a *non* Fast Back-to-Back fashion, the IDLE PHASE assures that there is no signal line contention.

> Target unlocking cannot occur between Fast Back-to-Back access cycles. See the *Lock* section.

A bus cycle that ends with a Retry, Disconnect, or Target Abort termination cannot be followed by a bus cycle in a Fast Back-to-Back fashion because the PCI bus master must deassert its REQ# signal line. One exception is when a Disconnect with data termination occurs when the IRDY# and FRAME# signal lines are asserted and deasserted, respectively. All of these terminations have the assertion of the STOP# signal line in common.

An IDLE PHASE must be placed between a snoop write-back access cycle and the subsequent bus cycle; consequently, the Fast Back-to-Back protocol cannot apply.

MASTER PROGRAMMED FAST BACK-TO-BACK

A MASTER PROGRAMMED Fast Back-to-Back (MP-Back/Back) can only occur when all of the following conditions are met:

■ The MP-Back/Back access cycles must be executed by the same PCI bus master.

■ The access cycles involved in the MP-Back/Back must be a write access cycle followed by a write or read access cycle. A read access cycle followed by a read or write access cycle is not allowed to be executed in a MP-Back/Back fashion.

■ The access cycles involved in MP-Back/Back must be to the same target.

■ The ASIC that drives the address onto the AD signal lines must be the same ASIC that drives the write data onto the AD signal lines.

■ The FRAME# signal line must be deasserted prior to the IRDY# and TRDY# signal lines are both asserted.

The concept of MP-Back/Back is that the PCI bus master knows prior to the completion of the previous access cycle the target and type of access of the present cycle. This knowledge, in conjunction with the requirements outlined in the bulleted items above, place the burden of preventing signal line contention on the PCI bus master.

The explanation and examples in Figures 6-22 and 6-23 use SINGLE access cycles. The protocol when BURST access cycles are involved is the same.

Figures 6-22 and 6-23 outline the protocol of MP-Back/Back. In Figure 6-22, the PCI bus master is first executing a STANDARD write access cycle. At the end of the previous access cycle, the FRAME# signal line is sampled deasserted, and the IRDY# and TRDY# signal lines are both asserted. Under the MP-Back/Back protocol, the aforementioned pattern of these signal lines qualifies as the completion of the previous access cycle and allows the PCI bus master to immediately assert the FRAME# signal line for the present access cycle without an IDLE PHASE if its associated GNT# signal line remains asserted. The completion of the present access cycle (READY WRITE) in Figure 6-22 also follows the MP-Back/Back protocol, and the next access cycle can begin as a Fast Back-to-Back access cycle.

Figure 6-23 exemplifies the MP-Back/Back for a STANDARD write access cycle followed by a STANDARD read access cycle. The protocol to complete the write access cycle and immediately begin the read access cycle is the same as outlined in Figure 6-22. The completion of the read access cycle clearly shows why a read access cycle cannot be followed by an access cycle under the MP-Back/Back protocol. The read data is driven onto the AD signal lines during the previous access cycle, and sufficient time for the target to tri-state the AD signal lines prior to the PCI bus master driving the address onto the AD signal lines for the next access cycle is required to prevent contention. Consequently, an extra CLK signal line clock period is needed which results in an IDLE PHASE.

> The MP-Back/Back protocol requires that ALL targets are designed to operate with this protocol. Targets do not know in advance if an MP-Back/Back is going to occur for the next access cycle unless the present access cycle is a read cycle, or a Retry, Disconnect, or Target Abort termination is executed. With a read cycle or the aforementioned terminations a Fast Back-to-Back will not occur. The aforementioned terminations require the PCI bus master to deassert its REQ# signal line. One exception is when a Disconnect with data termination occurs when the IRDY# and FRAME# signal lines are asserted and deasserted, respectively.

TARGET FAST BACK-TO-BACK

A Target Fast Back-to-Back (T-Back/Back) protocol removes the burden of preventing signal line contention from the PCI bus master and places it on the targets. All targets that potentially can be accessed by PCI bus master must be able to support T-Back/Back if the Fast Back-to-Back Capable bit is set in its Status Register. T-Back/Back can only occur when all of the following conditions are met:

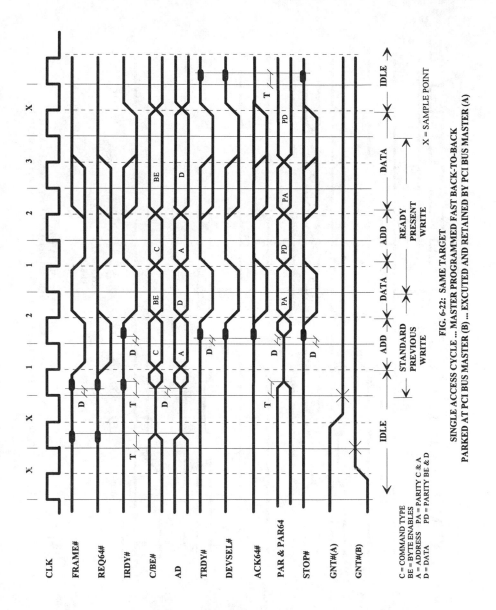

FIG. 6-22: SAME TARGET
SINGLE ACCESS CYCLE ... MASTER PROGRAMMED FAST BACK-TO-BACK
PARKED AT PCI BUS MASTER (B) ... EXCUTED AND RETAINED BY PCI BUS MASTER (A)

**Figure 6-22: Same Target—SINGLE Access Cycle , MASTER
PROGRAMMED Fast Back-to-Back Parked at PCI Bus Master (B),
Executed and Retained by PCI Bus Master (A)**

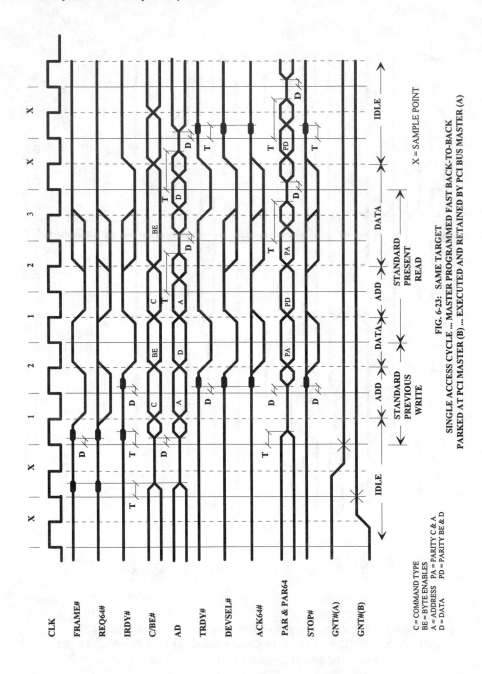

FIG. 6-23: SAME TARGET
SINGLE ACCESS CYCLE ... MASTER PROGRAMMED FAST BACK-TO-BACK
PARKED AT PCI MASTER (B) ... EXECUTED AND RETAINED BY PCI BUS MASTER (A)

**Figure 6-23: Same Target—SINGLE Access Cycle , MASTER
PROGRAMMED Fast Back-to-Back Parked at PCI Bus Master (B),
Executed and Retained by PCI Bus Master (A)**

■ The T-Back/Back allows the same PCI bus master to access different targets without IDLE PHASES.

■ In order for the PCI bus master to know that all potential targets can support the T-Back/Back protocol, the Fast Back-to-Back Enable bit must be set in the Command Register of the PCI bus master after the initialization software has determined that all potential targets have their respective Fast Back-to-Back Capable Status bit is set in its Status Register.

■ The Fast Back-to-Back capable bit in the Status Register of each target that will support T-Back/Back must be set (logical "1"). (To set the bit, the criteria outlined in the following two bullets must be met by the target).

■ All of the potential targets of the PCI bus master must be able to recognize the completion of the previous access cycle as indicated by a deasserted FRAME# signal line and the asserted TRDY# signal line. It must also be able to recognize when an IDLE PHASE does not occur (FRAME# and IRDY# signal lines both deasserted) prior to the assertion of the FRAME# signal line for the present access cycle.

■ The target of the present access cycle must delay the assertion of the DEVSEL#, TRDY#, STOP#, and ACK64# signal lines in the event that these signal lines are being asserted by the target of the previous access cycle. To meet this requirement ONE of the following conditions must be met:

⇒ If the fastest possible decode is not supported by the target (DEVSEL# signal line is not asserted at the end of the second CLK signal line period.), by definition the DEVSEL#, TRDY#, STOP#, and ACK64# signal lines will not be in contention with the previous access cycle. Point A (Circle A) in Figure 6-24 would be the earliest point for assertion of these signal lines would occur for the fastest decode. These signal lines must be asserted at or after Point B (Circle B). If a read access cycle was used in this example, the present access cycle would not have a contention on the TRDY# signal line for the fastest decode. There still remains a contention problem for the DEVSEL#, STOP#, and ACK64# signal lines.

OR

⇒ The target involved in the previous access cycle is the same target involved in the present access cycle. There is no contention with the DEVSEL#, TRDY#, STOP#, ACK64# signal lines in that these signal lines are driven by the same target. Under this condition, the fastest possible decode can be executed by the target. Point A

(Circle A) in Figure 6-25 would be the earliest place of assertion of these signal lines would occur for the fastest decode.

When a DUAL ADDRESS is executed, the ADDRESS PHASE is two CLK signal line periods in length. The earliest assertion point for the DEVSEL#, TRDY#, STOP#, and ACK64# signal lines for the fastest decode moves from the second to the third CLK signal line period (see Figures 6-1 A and B and 6-14-A and B). For a read access cycle, the earliest assertion point of the TRDY# signal line moves from the third to the fourth CLK signal line period. Consequently, the use of DUAL ADDRESS on the present access allows the use of the fastest decode and in essence removes the restrictions outlined in this item.

■ The previous bus cycle must be a write access cycle to allow a T-Back/Back to the present bus cycle

The concept of a T-Back/Back is that the burden to avoid contention on the signal lines when the IDLE PHASE is removed between back-to-back access cycles is placed on all potential targets of the PCI bus master. By placing the burden of signal line contention on the targets, the restrictions of the MP-Back/Back protocol to do Fast Back-to-Back access cycle to the same target is removed.

The design of a target should strive to support T-Back/Back to improve platform performance.

As will be explained in the following paragraphs, the T-Back/Back protocol prevents a Fast Back-to-Back situation following a read access cycle as did the MP-Back/Back protocol. Thus, even in the T-Back/Back protocol, the PCI bus master must be aware of read access cycles in the previous bus cycles.

The explanation and examples in Figures 6-24 to 6-25 use SINGLE access cycles. BURST access cycle protocol is the same.

Figure 6-24 outlines the protocol of the T-Back/Back situation when different targets are accessed in two access cycles. In Figure 6-24, the PCI bus master is executing a STANDARD write access cycle followed by a READY write access cycle. Simultaneously, the FRAME# signal line is deasserted, and the IRDY# and TRDY# signal lines are both asserted at the end of the access cycle. In this example, under the T-Back/Back protocol the sampled signal line pattern qualifies as the completion of the previous access cycle and allows the PCI bus master to immediately assert the FRAME# signal line for the present access cycle without an IDLE PHASE. In that the targets in the two access cycles are different, the target of the present access must delay driving the TRDY#, DEVSEL#, STOP#, and ACK64# signal lines until point B (Circle B). This delay reflects the fact that the target of the previous access cycle does not tri-state the TRDY#, DEVSEL#, and STOP# signal lines until point A (Circle A). Fig 6-25 outlines the T-Back/Back protocol when the target is the same for both access cycles. The only difference with the protocol outlined in Figure 6-24 is that the TRDY#, DEVSEL#, STOP#, ACK64# signal lines can be driven as early as point A (Circle A) in Figure 6-25. This is possible because the ownership of these signal lines do not change between the access cycles. The completion of the present access cycle in Figure 6-24 also follows the T-Back/Back protocol; consequently, at the discretion of the PCI bus master, the access cycle subsequent to the present cycle can also be a Fast Back-to-Back.

Figure 6-25 outlines the protocol of the T-Back/Back situation when the same target is accessed in the two access cycles. In Figure 6-25, the PCI bus master is executing a STANDARD write access cycle followed by a STANDARD read access cycle. The protocol to complete the write access cycle and immediately begin the read access cycle is the same as outlined in Figure 6-24. The completion of the read access cycle clearly shows why a read access cycle cannot be followed by a Fast Back-to-Back situation under the T-Back/Back protocol even when the target is the same. The read data is driven onto the AD signal lines during the present access cycle by the target and it must have sufficient time to tri-state the AD signal lines (Circle C in Figure 6-25) prior to the PCI bus master driving the address onto the AD signal lines (Circle D in Figure 6-25). Consequently, an extra CLK signal line clock period is needed which results in an IDLE PHASE.

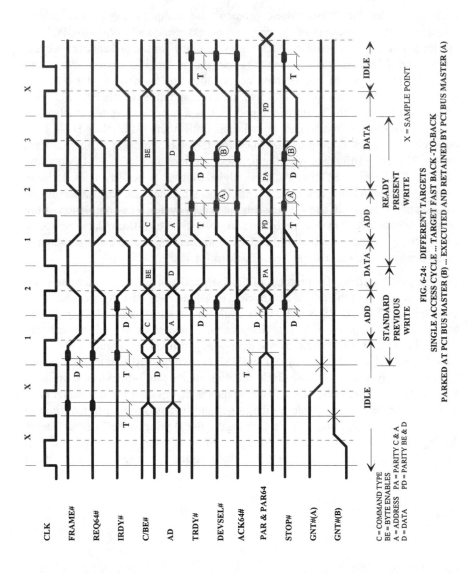

Figure 6-24: Different Targets—SINGLE Access Cycle , Target Fast Back-to-Back Parked at PCI Bus Master (B), Executed and Retained by PCI Bus Master (A)

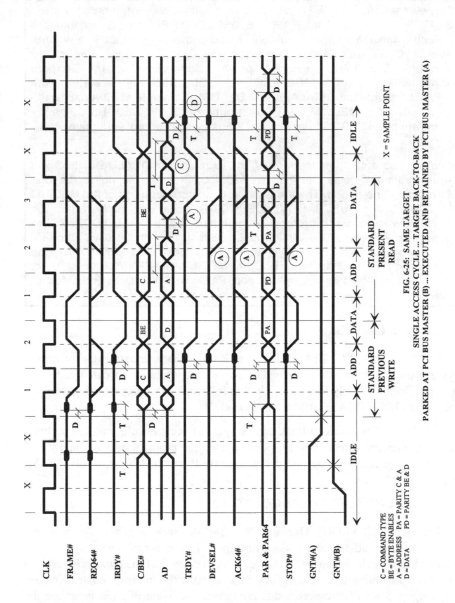

Figure 6-25: Same Target—SINGLE Access Cycle , Target Back-to-Back Parked at PCI Bus Master (B), Executed and Retained by PCI Bus Master (A)

Targets that support FAST decoding will indicate this information in their STATUS Registers. If all POSITIVE DECODING PCI resources that are potential targets support a FAST decode, the target that implements SUBTRACTIVE DECODING can assert the DEVSEL# signal line at the MEDIUM DECODING sample point. Consequently, the targets implementing "early" SUBTRACTIVE DECODING by asserting the DEVSEL# signal line at the MEDIUM DECODING sample point must "wait" (non-support of MEDIUM DECODING) until the SLOW DECODING sample point when the TARGET Back-to-Back bus cycle protocol is implemented.

Similarly, as previously mentioned, the execution of DUAL ADDRESS will "automatically" delay the POSITIVE DECODING sample points by one CLK signal line period. The aforementioned "non-support" of the MEDIUM DECODING for SUBTRACTIVE DECODING does not apply when the TARGET Back-to-Back protocol is executed with a DUAL ADDRESS. In other words, when a DUAL ADDRESS is executed with TARGET Back-to-Back protocol, a target implementing SUBTRACTIVE DECODING can assert the DEVSEL# signal line at the MEDIUM DECODING sample point when it and all other targets support FAST DECODING as indicated in their STATUS Registers.

SPECIAL CYCLES

The MASTER PROGRAMMED Fast Back-to-Back access cycle to access cycle protocol outlined above applies for access cycle to special cycle. The protocol does not apply to a bus cycle that follows a special cycle, because there must be an IDLE PHASE after a special cycle.

The Target Fast Back-to-Back access cycle to access cycle protocol outlined above applies for access cycle to special cycle. The protocol does not apply to a bus cycle that follows a special cycle, because there must be an IDLE PHASE after a special cycle.

INTERRUPT ACKNOWLEDGE CYCLES

The MASTER PROGRAMMED Fast Back-to-Back access cycle to access cycle protocol outlined above does not apply for an access cycle to interrupt acknowledge cycle, because the PCI resources (targets) of the two cycles are not the same (assuming the PCI resource that contains the interrupt controller does not support other PCI resources that are accessed). If the PCI resources are the same, the MASTER PROGRAMMED Fast Back-to-Back access cycle applies. The MASTER PROGRAMMED Fast Back-to-Back access cycle to access cycle protocol does not apply for interrupt acknowledge cycle to interrupt acknowledge cycles, or interrupt acknowledge cycle to access (or special) cycles, because the interrupt acknowledge cycle is a read cycle.

The Target Fast Back-to-Back access cycle to access cycle protocol outlined above can apply to access cycles and interrupt acknowledge cycles if the PCI resource that contains the interrupt controller supports this protocol. The Target Fast Back-to-Back protocol does not apply to interrupt acknowledge cycle to interrupt acknowledge cycle or interrupt acknowledge cycle to access (or special) cycles because the interrupt acknowledge cycle is a read cycle.

MASTER ABORT, RETRY, DISCONNECT, AND TARGET ABORT TERMINATION CONSIDERATIONS

Fast Back-to-Back protocol can be applied to the bus cycle subsequent to a cycle that completed with Master Abort termination with the exception of the special cycle. With the Master Abort termination, no PCI resource claimed the bus cycle; consequently, there is no bus contention with some of the signal lines. If the Master Abort is completing a special cycle, the Fast Back-to-Back protocol cannot apply.

The Fast Back-to-Back protocol cannot be applied to the bus cycle subsequent to a cycle that completed with a Retry, Disconnect, or Target Abort termination. When these terminations are executed, the PCI bus master must deassert its REQ# signal line; this results in the occurrence of an IDLE PHASE. One exception is when a Disconnect with data termination occurs when the IRDY# and FRAME# signal lines are asserted and deasserted, respectively.

CACHE SUPPORT ON PCI

This chapter consists of the following subchapters:

7.0 INTRODUCTION

The PCI bus allows special support of cache within the platform. There are many possible architectures and methods for supporting cache. The method chosen by PCI uses two signal lines (SDONE and SBO#), and assumes that only one cache resource is directly attached to the PCI bus.

In simplest terms, a cache is faster than DRAM, and more expensive. In a typical PC compatible architecture, DRAM caching is implemented only in memory address space. At certain times, portions of the DRAM are also stored in the cache for quick access. Independently of the HOST CPU, PCI bus master, or PCI data bus size; the minimum portions of DRAM stored in the cache are called *cache lines*. The size of the cache line will vary from platform to platform. For purposes of this discussion, the DRAM will be viewed as a collection of cache lines with a subset of these cache lines stored in the cache.

> To distinguish between the concept of faster and slower memory, the terms *cache* and *DRAM* will exemplify *fast* and *slow* memory, respectively.

The location of the cache relative to the HOST CPU and PCI bus master, and the type of cache (write-back versus write-through) determines how the cache controller operates. For the purposes of this discussion, the architecture in Figure 7-1 is assumed. The HOST CPU is on the same bus (HOST) as the cache and HOST DRAM. A similar architecture can be imagined with the PCI bus master containing its own local bus with local DRAM and local cache. For purposes of discussion it will be assumed that the platform cache will be on the HOST bus with the HOST CPU. There are two memory locations: the DRAM on the HOST bus (HDRAM) and the DRAM on the PCI bus (PDRAM). The cache on the HOST bus can cache either the HDRAM or PDRAM. Collectively, the HDRAM and PDRAM will be called DRAM. The cache controller is integrated into the HOST/PCI BRIDGE.

Another important consideration is the type of cache. In a write-through (WT) cache, whenever the cache is written to the same data is written to DRAM. Consequently, the data in a WT cache and DRAM *are always* the same. In a write-back (WB) cache, whenever data is written to the cache it *is not* immediately written to DRAM. Data in a WB cache and DRAM *are not* always the same.

The cache line in the cache can have four possible states:

Modified   DATA written to the cache by the HOST CPU has not yet been written to the DRAM. This term is defined for WB cache only.

Unmodified   The cache line in the cache is an exact copy of the cache line (per address) in the DRAM. This term is defined for WB cache only.

Valid   The cache line in the cache is an exact copy of the cache line (per address) in the DRAM. This term is defined for both WT and WB caches.

Invalid   The cache line is unused or contains old data compared to the new data contained in the DRAM. If the cache line had not been filled since RESET, a cache line marked invalid simply has never had data from the DRAM (unused). This term is defined for both WB and WT caches.

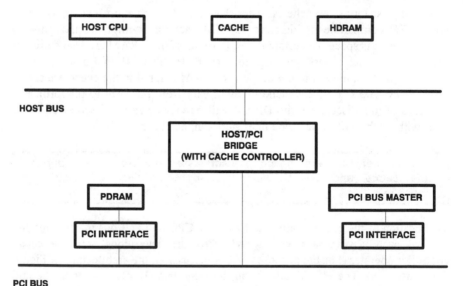

Figure 7-1: General Cache Architecture in the PCI Platform

> If the cache is flushed, all cache lines are marked invalid and the cache resembles its state immediately after RESET. If the cache is a WB, the data contained in modified/valid cache lines must be written to the DRAM when the cache is flushed. Cache flushing does not have direct bearing on the cache protocol of the PCI bus. To the PCI bus protocol, cache flushing is executed by the cache controller in the HOST/PCI BRIDGE and appears as a write access cycle. This chapter will not discuss flush protocol in detail because it is hidden behind the HOST/PCI BRIDGE on the HOST bus.

Other useful cache terms follow: A *cache hit* is defined as a memory access that addresses a valid cache line in the cache. A *cache miss* is defined as a memory access that does not address a valid cache line in the cache. A *snoop* is defined as the activity of the cache controller determining if the memory address matches addresses of the valid cache lines in the cache. A *snoop write-back* access cycle is defined as the activity of the cache controller in the HOST/PCI BRIDGE copying a cache line in the cache to the DRAM.

A basic concept of cache operation revolves around the retention of a DRAM cache line copy in the cache. Part of the cache protocol is to determine when a new cache line from the DRAM should replace an existing cache line in the cache. The cache lines in the cache marked invalid are the first to be replaced. The cache line replacement priority of valid cache lines in WT caches, and modified/valid and unmodified/valid cache lines in WB caches depends the on the architecture of the cache controller. The cache line replacement can be based on read and write protocols when a cache miss occurs. read replacement protocol is when a cache line in the cache is replaced by data read from the DRAM. write replacement protocol is when a cache line in the cache is replaced by data written to the DRAM.

> The discussion in this chapter assumes that the cache on the HOST bus is separate from the HOST CPU, and the HOST CPU has no internal cache. The PCI bus cache protocol for cache support when the cache is integrated into the HOST CPU is not affected because the cache and HOST CPU are behind the cache controller in the HOST/PCI BRIDGE.

Note: Subchapters 7.1 and 7.2 are general discussions of a typical cache operating in a platform with a PCI bus. The purpose of these two subchapters is to provide insight on how caches operate. Those readers that are very familiar with cache operation can skip directly to Subchapter 7.3.

7.1   BASIC CACHE PROTOCOL IN A PCI PLATFORM— WRITE THROUGH (WT) CACHE

The following discussion reviews platform operation when a WT cache is implemented on the HOST bus. The first part will explain platform operation when the HOST CPU makes a memory access that results in a cache hit. The second part will explain how the cache controller and PCI bus operate when the PCI bus master makes an access to a portion of DRAM (HDRAM or PDRAM) that is also in the cache. The third part will review the relationship of other WT cache operations and the PCI bus.

CACHE HIT TO WT CACHE

When the HOST CPU writes data to DRAM, a cache hit allows for the quick completion of the HOST bus access cycle. The data is also written to the DRAM that was cached. If the access addresses HDRAM, a PCI access cycle is not executed. If the access addresses PDRAM, a PCI write access cycle is executed by the cache controller in the HOST/PCI BRIDGE (see Figure 7-1). The HOST CPU will write to the cache and immediately complete the HOST access cycle. The HOST/PCI BRIDGE will also write the same data to PDRAM, but the PCI access cycle will not be completed as quickly as the HOST access cycle. It is assumed that the PCI write access cycle to PDRAM will be completed before the next access by the HOST CPU and thus improve HOST CPU performance. The cache controller in the HOST/PCI BRIDGE asserts the SDONE signal line to indicate to the PCI memory resources that snoop is complete.

> If the HOST/PCI BRIDGE had posted the data written to the cache in the PCI buffer but had not yet updated PDRAM, the completion of a subsequent PCI bus master access to PDRAM follows the WB cache protocol with the HOST/PCI BRIDGE acting as WB cache, that is, the SBO# signal line is used. See the WB Subchapter 7.2 for details.

If the PDRAM resource is locked by a PCI resource other than the HOST/PCI BRIDGE, the write access cycle by the cache controller in the HOST/PCI BRIDGE will complete with Retry termination (the SDONE and SBO# signal lines are not both asserted because the access was to the HDRAM.) Consequently, the cache controller in the HOST/PCI BRIDGE must execute the write access cycle as a snoop write-back access cycle to force the PDRAM to accept the cycle (the SDONE and SBO# signal lines are both asserted at the beginning of the write cycle.) If the write data had been posted in the HOST/PCI BRIDGE, the HOST/PCI BRIDGE must execute the write access cycle as a snoop write-back access cycle to force the PDRAM to accept the cycle.

If a HOST CPU executes a memory read access cycle and a cache hit occurs, the WT cache will provide the data from the cache. Under this cache hit condition no PCI or HOST bus read access cycle is executed to PDRAM or HDRAM, respectively.

When the PCI bus master executes a write access cycle to the PDRAM, the cache controller in the HOST/PCI BRIDGE snoops the cache. If a cache hit to a cache line in the cache marked invalid occurs, the SDONE signal line is asserted by the cache controller in the HOST/PCI BRIDGE to indicate to all PCI memory resources that snoop is complete. A cache miss does not affect the cache and the SDONE signal line is asserted by the cache controller in the HOST/PCI BRIDGE to indicate to all PCI memory resources that snoop is complete. The PCI bus master will complete the access by writing data to the PDRAM.

When the PCI bus master executes a write access cycle to the HDRAM, the cache controller in the HOST/PCI BRIDGE snoops the cache. The SDONE signal line is asserted by the cache controller in the HOST/PCI BRIDGE to indicate to the other PCI memory resources that snoop is complete. The assertion of the TRDY# signal line by the cache controller in the HOST/PCI BRIDGE represents the completion of the write cycle to HDRAM and invalidation of the cache line if a cache hit occurred.

When the PCI bus master executes a read access cycle to the PDRAM, the cache controller in the HOST/PCI BRIDGE snoops the cache and asserts the SDONE signal line to indicate to all PCI memory resources that snoop is complete. A WT cache always contains a correct copy of the contents at the same address of PDRAM and thus the PCI bus master only needs to complete a read access with data from the PDRAM.

When the PCI bus master executes a read access cycle to the HDRAM, the cache controller in the HOST/PCI BRIDGE snoops the cache. The SDONE signal line is asserted by the cache controller in the HOST/PCI BRIDGE to indicate to the other PCI memory resources that snoop is complete. The assertion of the TRDY# signal line by the cache controller in the HOST/PCI BRIDGE represents the completion of the read access cycle to HDRAM. The WT cache always contains a correct copy of the contents at the same address of the HDRAM, and thus the PCI bus master only needs to complete a read access with data from the HDRAM.

CACHE MISS OF WT CACHE

READ REPLACEMENT WHEN AN ENTIRE CACHE LINE IS ACCESSED BY HOST CPU

If the entire cache line in the DRAM (HDRAM or PDRAM) read by the HOST CPU results is a cache miss, the cache controller in the HOST/PCI BRIDGE replaces the cache line in the cache as the HOST CPU receives the data from the DRAM. The cache line in the cache being replaced is simply overwritten by the new cache line from DRAM and marked valid. If the access addresses PDRAM, a PCI read access cycle is executed by the cache controller in the HOST/PCI BRIDGE. The SDONE signal line is asserted by the cache controller in the HOST/PCI BRIDGE to indicate to all PCI memory resources that snoop is complete. If the access addresses HDRAM, a PCI access cycle is not executed.

Under the read replacement protocol, a cache miss during a write access cycle by the HOST CPU does not affect the cache. If the access addresses PDRAM, a PCI write access cycle is executed by the cache controller in the HOST/PCI BRIDGE. The SDONE signal line is asserted by the cache controller in the HOST/PCI BRIDGE to indicate to all PCI memory resources that snoop is complete. If the access addresses HDRAM, a PCI access cycle is not executed.

READ REPLACEMENT WHEN A PORTION OF THE CACHE LINE IS ACCESSED BY HOST CPU

If the portion of the cache line in the DRAM (HDRAM or PDRAM) read by the HOST CPU results is a cache miss, the HOST CPU will receive the data from the DRAM. The cache is not updated with the data read. If the access addresses PDRAM, a PCI read cycle is executed by the cache controller in the HOST/PCI BRIDGE. The SDONE signal line is asserted by the cache controller in the HOST/PCI BRIDGE to indicate to all PCI memory resources that snoop is complete. If the access addresses HDRAM, a PCI access cycle is not executed.

Depending on the platform architecture, the cache controller in the HOST/PCI BRIDGE can subsequently copy the associated cache line from the DRAM into the cache. If the access addressed PDRAM, a PCI read access cycle is executed. The SDONE signal line is asserted by the cache controller in the HOST/PCI BRIDGE to indicate to all PCI memory resources that snoop is complete. If the access addressed HDRAM, no PCI read access cycle is executed. This is at the option of the architect.

Under the read replacement protocol, a cache miss during a write access cycle by the HOST CPU does not affect the cache. If the access addresses PDRAM, a PCI write access cycle is executed by the cache controller in the HOST/PCI BRIDGE. The SDONE signal line is asserted by the cache controller in the HOST/PCI BRIDGE to indicate to all PCI memory resources that snoop is complete. If the access addresses HDRAM, a PCI access cycle is not executed.

WRITE REPLACEMENT WHEN AN ENTIRE *CACHE LINE IS ACCESSED BY HOST CPU*

If the entire cache line in the DRAM (HDRAM or PDRAM) written by the HOST CPU results in a cache miss, the cache controller replaces the cache line in the cache as the HOST CPU writes data to the DRAM. The cache line in the cache being replaced is simply overwritten by the new cache line written to the DRAM and marked valid. If the access addresses PDRAM, a PCI write cycle is executed by the cache controller in the HOST/PCI BRIDGE. The SDONE signal line is asserted by the cache controller in the HOST/PCI BRIDGE to indicate to all PCI memory resources that snoop is complete. If the access addresses HDRAM, a PCI access cycle is not executed.

Under the write replacement protocol, a cache miss during a read access cycle by the HOST CPU does not affect the cache. If the access addresses PDRAM, a PCI read cycle is executed by the cache controller in the HOST/PCI BRIDGE. The SDONE signal line is asserted by the cache controller in the HOST/PCI BRIDGE to indicate to all PCI memory resources that snoop is complete. If the access addresses HDRAM, a PCI access cycle is not executed.

WRITE REPLACEMENT WHEN A PORTION *OF THE CACHE LINE IS ACCESSED BY HOST CPU*

If a portion of the cache line in the DRAM (HDRAM or PDRAM) is written by the HOST CPU, the cache controller does not immediately replace an existing cache line and the HOST CPU writes to DRAM. If the access addresses PDRAM, a PCI read cycle is executed by the cache controller in the HOST/PCI BRIDGE. The SDONE signal line is asserted by the cache controller in the HOST/PCI BRIDGE to indicate to all PCI memory resources that snoop is complete. If the access addresses HDRAM, a PCI access cycle is not executed.

Depending on the platform architecture, the cache controller in the HOST/PCI BRIDGE can subsequently copy the associated cache line from the DRAM into the cache. If the access addressed PDRAM, a PCI read access cycle is executed. If the access addressed HDRAM, no PCI read access cycle is executed. This is at the option of the architecture.

Under the write replacement protocol, a cache miss during a read access cycle by the HOST CPU does not affect the cache. If the access addresses PDRAM, a PCI read cycle is executed by the cache controller in the HOST/PCI BRIDGE. The SDONE signal line is asserted by the cache controller in the HOST/PCI BRIDGE to indicate to all PCI memory resources that the snoop is complete. If the access addresses HDRAM, a PCI access cycle is not executed.

READ REPLACEMENT WHEN AN ENTIRE CACHE LINE IS ACCESSED BY PCI BUS MASTER

When a PCI Bus Master executes a read access cycle to the DRAM (PDRAM or HDRAM), the cache controller in the HOST/PCI BRIDGE asserts the SDONE signal line when the snoop is complete. The cache is part of the HOST CPU architecture; consequently, the cache is not updated for a PCI bus master access to DRAM.

When a PCI Bus Master executes a write access cycle to the DRAM (PDRAM or HDRAM), the cache controller in the HOST/PCI BRIDGE asserts the SDONE signal line when the snoop is complete. There is no subsequent update of the cache.

READ REPLACEMENT WHEN A PORTION OF THE CACHE LINE IS ACCESSED BY PCI BUS MASTER

When a PCI Bus Master executes a read or write access cycle to the DRAM (PDRAM or HDRAM), the cache controller in the HOST/PCI BRIDGE asserts the SDONE signal line when the snoop is complete. There is no subsequent update of the cache.

WRITE REPLACEMENT WHEN AN ENTIRE CACHE LINE IS ACCESSED BY PCI BUS MASTER

When a PCI Bus Master executes a write access cycle to the DRAM (PDRAM or HDRAM), the cache controller in the HOST/PCI BRIDGE asserts the SDONE signal line when the snoop is complete. The cache is part of the HOST CPU architecture; consequently, cache is not updated for a PCI bus master access to DRAM.

When a PCI Bus Master executes a read access cycle to the DRAM (PDRAM or HDRAM), the cache controller in the HOST/PCI BRIDGE asserts the SDONE signal line when the snoop is complete. There is no subsequent update of the cache.

*WRITE REPLACEMENT WHEN A PORTION OF THE CACHE LINE
IS ACCESSED BY A PCI BUS MASTER*

When a PCI Bus Master executes a read or write access cycle to the DRAM (PDRAM or HDRAM), the cache controller in the HOST/PCI BRIDGE asserts the SDONE signal line when the snoop is complete. There is no subsequent update of the cache.

OTHER WT CACHE PROTOCOL CONSIDERATIONS

All accesses to memory address space require the cache controller in the HOST/PCI BRIDGE to snoop the address and assert the SDONE signal line. In the protocol outlined above, the PDRAM waits until the SDONE signal line is asserted prior to asserting the TRDY# signal line. With a WT cache, it is possible for the PDRAM to assert the TRDY# signal line to complete the access prior to the cache controller in the HOST/PCI BRIDGE asserting the SDONE signal line. This latter protocol requires the PDRAM to know it is cached by a WT cache and to support ADDRESS STACKING. See *7.3: Protocol of the SDONE and SBO# Signal Lines* for details.

7.2 BASIC CACHE PROTOCOL IN A PCI PLATFORM WRITE BACK (WB) CACHE

The following discussion reviews the system operation when a WB cache is implemented on the HOST bus. The first part will explain platform operation when the HOST CPU makes a memory access that results in a cache hit. The second part will explain how the cache controller and PCI bus operate when a PCI Bus Master makes an access to a portion of DRAM (HDRAM or PDRAM) that is also in the cache. The third part will review the relationship of other WB cache operations and the PCI bus.

CACHE HIT TO WB CACHE

When a HOST CPU writes to DRAM and a cache hit occurs, the access cycle is executed only on the HOST bus. The data is written to the cache and not written to the DRAM; consequently, a PCI bus access cycle is not executed. The cache line in the cache is marked modified/valid by the cache controller in the HOST/PCI BRIDGE. Subsequent cache hits (read or write) by the HOST CPU to a modified/valid cache line are completed with an access executed to the cache without any change in the modified/valid state and without a PCI bus access cycle.

A cache hit by a HOST CPU during a read access to an unmodified/valid or modified/valid cache line does not change the cache state. The data is read from the cache and not from the DRAM; consequently, no PCI access cycle is executed.

When a PCI Bus Master executes a read access cycle to the PDRAM, the cache controller in the HOST/PCI BRIDGE snoops the cache. If the cache hit is to a cache line marked unmodified/valid, the data is provided to the PCI bus master by the PDRAM. The cache controller in the HOST/PCI BRIDGE will indicate an unmodified/valid cache line in the cache by the assertion and continued deassertion of the SDONE and SBO# signal lines, respectively. The assertion of the SDONE signal line indicates the completion of snoop and continued deassertion of the SBO# signal line indicates that the snooped cache line in the cache was unmodified/valid. Subsequently, the PDRAM asserts the TRDY# signal line to allow the access to be completed.

If the read access cycle results in a cache hit to a cache line marked modified/valid, the cache controller in the HOST/PCI BRIDGE will assert both the SDONE and SBO# signal lines. The WB cache and PDRAM contain different data at the same cache line address if it is marked modified/valid. The assertion of the SDONE signal line indicates the completion of snoop and the assertion of the SBO# signal line indicates that the cache line in the cache was modified/valid. Consequently, the PCI bus master will not be able to immediately complete the read access cycle to the PDRAM. The PDRAM must execute a Retry termination when it samples the SBO# and SDONE signal lines asserted. The cache controller in the HOST/PCI BRIDGE must subsequently arbitrate for the PCI bus and execute a snoop write-back access cycle to copy the modified/valid cache line in the cache to the PDRAM. The SBO# and SDONE signal lines remain asserted until the snoop write-back access cycle is executed.

It is assumed that the entire PDRAM can be potentially cached; consequently, all subsequent accesses to the PDRAM (except for the snoop write-back access cycle) by any PCI bus master results in a Retry termination, since the SDONE and SBO# signal lines are both asserted. After the snoop write-back access cycle is completed, the cache controller can mark the cache line in the cache unmodified/valid and the PDRAM allows accesses to complete without a Retry termination.

> The PDRAM must know that it is cached by a WB cache so it will not assert the TRDY# signal line until the SDONE and SBO# signal lines are asserted and deasserted, respectively. This protocol prevents the PCI bus master from reading invalid data. This is in contrast to a WT cache where the TRDY# signal line can be asserted prior to the assertion of the SDONE signal line.

If the PDRAM has portions that are not cached, subsequent accesses by the PCI bus master to these non-cacheable portions prior to a snoop write-back access cycle are allowed to complete without a Retry termination.

If other cacheable PCI memory resources (not the aforementioned PDRAM) are accessed prior to the snoop write-back access cycle, these memory resources must execute a Retry termination. The Retry termination must be executed because only one set of SDONE and SBO# signal lines are available to indicate snoops and write-backs. See *Subchapter 7.3: Protocol of the SDONE and SBO# Signal Lines* for details.

When the PCI bus master executes a write access cycle to the PDRAM, the cache controller in the HOST/PCI BRIDGE snoops the cache. If the cache hit is to a cache line marked unmodified/valid, the cache line in the cache is marked invalid, the SDONE signal line is asserted, and the SBO# signal line remains deasserted. The PCI bus master will complete the access by writing data to the PDRAM. The assertion of the SDONE signal line indicates the completion of snoop and continued deassertion of the SBO# signal line indicates that the snooped cache line in the cache was unmodified/valid. Subsequently, the PDRAM asserts the TRDY# signal line to allow the access to be completed.

If the write access cycle results in a cache hit to a cache line marked modified/valid, the cache controller in the HOST/PCI BRIDGE will assert both the SBO# and the SDONE signal lines. The WB cache and PDRAM contain different data at the same cache line address if the cache line is marked modified/valid. The assertion of the SDONE signal line indicates the completion of the snoop, and the assertion of the SBO# signal line indicates that the snooped cache line in the cache was modified/valid. Consequently, the PCI bus master will not be able to immediately complete the write access cycle to the PDRAM. The PDRAM must execute a Retry termination when it samples the SBO# and SDONE signal lines asserted. The cache controller in the HOST/PCI BRIDGE must subsequently arbitrate for the PCI bus and execute a snoop write-back access cycle to copy the modified/valid cache line in the cache to the PDRAM.

It is assumed that the entire PDRAM can potentially be cached; consequently, all subsequent accesses to the PDRAM (except for the snoop write-back access cycle) by any PCI bus master results in a Retry termination, since the SDONE and SBO# signal lines are both asserted. After the snoop write-back access cycle is completed, the cache controller can mark the cache line in the cache unmodified/valid and the PDRAM allows accesses to complete without a Retry termination.

There is a PDRAM design by which a write access cycle is completed WITHOUT Retry termination when a cache hit to a modified/valid WB cache line occurs. This PDRAM design employs the OVER WRITE protocol. See *Subchapter 7.3: Protocol of the SDONE and SBO# Signal Lines* for details.

When the memory write and invalidate command is executed, the assertion of the SBO# signal line is not required for a cache hit to a modified/valid cache line in a WB cache. The execution of the memory write and invalidate command results in the entire cache line being written in the DRAM. The cache controller in the HOST/PCI BRIDGE will mark the associated cache line in the cache as invalid. The protocol of the memory write and invalidate command insures that the entire cache line will be written to the DRAM in a single BURST access cycle.

If the PDRAM has portions that are not cached, subsequent accesses by the PCI bus master to these non-cached portions prior to a snoop write-back access cycle are allowed to complete WITHOUT Retry termination. Similarly, PCI bus master access cycles to PDRAM that is not cached are allowed to complete WITHOUT Retry termination prior to the execution of the snoop write-back access cycle.

If other cacheable PCI memory resources (not the aforementioned PDRAM) are accessed prior to the snoop write-back access cycle, these memory resources must execute a Retry termination. The Retry termination must be executed because only one set of SDONE and SBO# signal lines are available to indicate snoops and write-backs.

The following section outlines the WB cache activity when a PCI bus master accesses the HDRAM. This outline is provided to give insight on platform operation. As will be discussed, most of the HDRAM and cache activity is hidden from the PCI bus because the HOST bus is behind the HOST/PCI BRIDGE.

When the PCI bus master executes a read access to the HDRAM, the activity of the cache controller in the HOST/PCI BRIDGE will be hidden from the PCI bus master. The snoop activity that results in a cache hit will allow the cache controller in the HOST/PCI BRIDGE to complete the PCI access cycle by the assertion of the SDONE and TRDY# signal lines. The SDONE signal line is asserted to indicate to the other PCI memory resources that the snoop is complete. The SBO# signal line is not asserted because no snoop write-back access cycle will be executed on the PCI bus because the HDRAM and cache resources are on the same isolated bus (HOST). If the cache hit was to a unmodified/valid cache line in the cache, the data sent to the PCI bus can be from the HDRAM or the cache. If the cache hit was to a modified/valid cache line in the cache, the data sent to the PCI bus will be from the cache. The snoop write-back access cycle will be executed only on the HOST bus without any PCI bus activity. This can be performed simultaneously with the PCI read of the cache or performed subsequently. After the write-back access cycle has completed, the cache controller in the HOST/PCI BRIDGE will mark the cache line in the cache unmodified/valid.

When the PCI bus master executes a write access cycle to the HDRAM, the activity of the cache controller in the HOST/PCI BRIDGE will be hidden from the PCI bus master. The snoop activity that results in a cache hit will allow the cache controller in the HOST/PCI BRIDGE to complete the PCI access cycle by the assertion of the SDONE and TRDY# signal lines. The SDONE signal line is asserted to indicate to the other PCI memory resources that the snoop is complete. The SBO# signal line is not asserted because no snoop write-back access cycle will be executed on the PCI bus because the memory and cache resources are on the same isolated bus (HOST). The location of the cache and HDRAM on the same HOST bus behind the HOST/PCI BRIDGE allows the cycle to be completed in several ways depending on the condition of the cache line in the cache. The possibilities are as follows :

- Unmodified/Valid Cache Line:
    ⇒ If the cache hit was to an unmodified/valid cache line in the cache, the data from the PCI bus is written to the HDRAM and the cache line in the cache is marked unmodified/invalid.

OR

    ⇒ If the cache hit was to an unmodified/valid cache line in the cache, the data from the PCI bus is written simultaneously to the HDRAM and the cache. The cache line in the cache remains marked modified/valid.

OR

    ⇒ If the cache hit was to an unmodified/valid cache line in the cache, the data from the PCI bus is written only to the cache. The cache line in the cache is marked modified/valid.

- Modified/Valid Cache Line:
    ⇒ If the cache hit was to a modified/valid cache line in the cache, the data from the PCI bus is written to a buffer in the HOST/PCI BRIDGE to complete the PCI access cycle. The cache controller in the HOST/PCI BRIDGE will write-back data from the cache to the HDRAM and write the buffer in the HOST /PCI BRIDGE to the HDRAM. The cache line in the cache is marked invalid.

OR

⇒   If the cache hit was to a modified/valid cache line in the cache, the data from the PCI bus is written to a buffer in the HOST/PCI BRIDGE to complete the PCI access cycle. The cache controller in the HOST/PCI BRIDGE will write-back the buffer into the cache. The cache line in the cache is marked modified/valid.

> Other protocols are possible for a hit to a modified/valid cache line, but they are more complex than the above two and are highly dependent on the architecture of the cache controller.

CACHE MISS OF WB CACHE

READ REPLACEMENT WHEN ENTIRE CACHE LINE IS ACCESSED BY HOST CPU

If the entire cache line in the DRAM read by the HOST CPU results in a cache miss, the cache controller in the HOST/PCI BRIDGE can replace a cache line in the cache as the HOST CPU receives the data from the DRAM. If the cache line in the cache being replaced is marked invalid or unmodified/valid, the entire cache line is overwritten as the HOST CPU reads it and is marked unmodified/valid. If the access addresses PDRAM, a PCI read access cycle is executed by the cache controller in the HOST/PCI BRIDGE. The SDONE signal line is asserted by the cache controller in the HOST/PCI BRIDGE to indicate to all PCI memory resources that the snoop is complete. If the access addresses HDRAM, a PCI access cycle is not executed.

If the cache line being replaced is marked modified/valid, the cache controller in the HOST/PCI BRIDGE must first write-back the cache line in the cache to the DRAM. The HOST CPU is prevented from completing the access by ready or back off. The cache controller in the HOST/PCI BRIDGE will execute a PCI write access cycle if the DRAM is on the PCI bus (PDRAM). The SDONE signal line is asserted by the cache controller in the HOST/PCI BRIDGE to indicate to all PCI memory resources that the snoop is complete. If the DRAM is on the HOST bus (HDRAM), no PCI bus cycle is executed. The HOST CPU can now complete the access as outlined in the previous paragraph for a cache line in the cache marked invalid or unmodified/valid.

If the PDRAM resource is locked by a PCI resource other than the HOST/PCI BRIDGE, the write access cycle by the cache controller in the HOST/PCI BRIDGE will complete with Retry termination (the SDONE and SBO# signal lines are not both asserted because the access was to the HDRAM). Consequently, the cache controller in the HOST/PCI BRIDGE must execute the write access cycle as a snoop write-back access cycle to force the PDRAM to accept the cycle (the SDONE and SBO# signal lines are both asserted at the beginning of the write cycle).

Under the read replacement protocol, a cache miss during a write access cycle by the HOST CPU does not affect the cache. If the access addresses PDRAM, a PCI write cycle is executed by the cache controller in the HOST/PCI BRIDGE. The SDONE signal line is asserted by the cache controller in the HOST/PCI BRIDGE to indicate to all PCI memory resources that the snoop is complete. If the access addresses HDRAM, a PCI access cycle is not executed.

READ REPLACEMENT WHEN A PORTION OF THE CACHE LINE IS ACCESSED BY HOST CPU

If the portion of the cache line in the DRAM (HDRAM or PDRAM) read by the HOST CPU results is a cache miss, the HOST CPU will receive the data from the DRAM. The cache is not updated with the data read. If the access addresses PDRAM, a PCI read cycle is executed by the cache controller in the HOST/PCI BRIDGE. The SDONE signal line is asserted by the cache controller in the HOST/PCI BRIDGE to indicate to all PCI memory resources that snoop is complete. If the access addresses HDRAM, a PCI access cycle is not executed.

Depending on the platform architecture, the cache controller in the HOST/PCI BRIDGE can subsequently copy the associated cache line from the DRAM into the cache. If the cache line in the cache being replaced is marked invalid or unmodified/valid, the entire cache line is overwritten as the HOST CPU reads it and is marked unmodified/valid. If the access addressed PDRAM, a PCI read access cycle is executed. The SDONE signal line is asserted by the cache controller in the HOST/PCI BRIDGE to indicate to all PCI memory resources that snoop is complete. If the access addressed HDRAM, no PCI read access cycle is executed. This is at the option of the architecture.

If the cache line being replaced is marked modified/valid, the cache controller in the HOST/PCI BRIDGE must first write-back the cache line in the cache to the DRAM. The HOST CPU is prevented from completing the access by ready or back off. The cache controller in the HOST/PCI BRIDGE will execute a PCI write access cycle if the DRAM is on the PCI bus. The SDONE signal line is asserted by the cache controller in the HOST/PCI BRIDGE to indicate to all PCI memory resources that the snoop is complete. If the DRAM is on the HOST bus (HDRAM), no PCI bus cycle is executed. The HOST CPU can now complete the access as outlined in the previous paragraph for a cache line in the cache marked invalid or unmodified/valid.

Under the read replacement protocol, a cache miss during a write access cycle by the HOST CPU does not affect the cache. If the access addresses PDRAM, a PCI write access cycle is executed by the cache controller in the HOST/PCI BRIDGE. The SDONE signal line is asserted by the cache controller in the HOST/PCI BRIDGE to indicate to all PCI memory resources that snoop is complete. If the access addresses HDRAM, a PCI access cycle is not executed.

> If the PDRAM resource is locked by a PCI resource other than the HOST/PCI BRIDGE, the write access cycle by the cache controller in the HOST/PCI BRIDGE will complete with Retry termination. (The SDONE and SBO# signal lines are not both asserted because the access was to the HDRAM.) Consequently, the cache controller in the HOST/PCI BRIDGE must execute the write access cycle as a snoop write-back access cycle to force the PDRAM to accept the cycle. (The SDONE and SBO# signal lines are both asserted to at the beginning of the write cycle.)

WRITE REPLACEMENT WHEN ENTIRE CACHE LINE IS ACCESSED BY HOST CPU

If the entire cache line in the DRAM written by the HOST CPU results in a cache miss, and the cache line being replaced is marked invalid or unmodified/valid, it is overwritten and the new cache line is marked modified/valid. The DRAM is not accessed and no PCI bus cycles are executed.

If the cache line being replaced is marked modified/valid, the cache controller in the HOST/PCI BRIDGE must first write back the cache line in the cache to the DRAM. The HOST CPU is prevented from completing the access by ready or back off. The cache controller in the HOST/PCI BRIDGE will execute a PCI write access cycle if the DRAM is on the PCI bus. The SDONE signal line is asserted by the cache controller in the HOST/PCI BRIDGE to indicate to all PCI memory resources that the snoop is complete. If the DRAM is on the HOST bus (HDRAM), no PCI bus cycle is executed. The HOST CPU can now complete the access as outlined in the previous paragraph for a cache line in the cache marked invalid or unmodified/valid.

Under the write replacement protocol, a cache miss during a read access cycle does not affect the cache. If the access addressed PDRAM, a PCI read cycle is executed by the cache controller in the HOST/PCI BRIDGE. The SDONE signal line is asserted by the cache controller in the HOST/PCI BRIDGE to indicate to all PCI memory resources that the snoop is complete. If the access addresses HDRAM, a PCI access cycle is not executed.

WRITE REPLACEMENT WHEN A PORTION OF THE CACHE LINE HOST IS ACCESSED BY HOST CPU

If the portion of the cache line in the DRAM (HDRAM or PDRAM) written by the HOST CPU results is a cache miss, the cache controller does not overwrite a cache line in the cache and executes a write access cycle to the DRAM. If the access addresses PDRAM, a PCI read cycle is executed by the cache controller in the HOST/PCI BRIDGE. The SDONE signal line is asserted by the cache controller in the HOST/PCI BRIDGE to indicate to all PCI memory resources that snoop is complete. If the access addresses HDRAM, a PCI access cycle is not executed.

Depending on the platform architecture, the cache controller in the HOST/PCI BRIDGE can subsequently copy the associated cache line from the DRAM into the cache. If the cache line in the cache being replaced is marked invalid or unmodified/valid, the entire cache line is overwritten as the HOST CPU reads it and is marked unmodified/valid. If the access addressed PDRAM, a PCI read access cycle is executed. The SDONE signal line is asserted by the cache controller in the HOST/PCI BRIDGE to indicate to all PCI memory resources that snoop is complete. If the access addressed HDRAM, no PCI read access cycle is executed. This is at the option of the architecture.

If the cache line being replaced is marked modified/valid, the cache controller in the HOST/PCI BRIDGE must first write-back the cache line in the cache to the DRAM. The HOST CPU is prevented from completing the access by ready or back off. The cache controller in the HOST/PCI BRIDGE will execute a PCI write access cycle if the DRAM is on the PCI bus. The SDONE signal line is asserted by the cache controller in the HOST/PCI BRIDGE to indicate to all PCI memory resources that the snoop is complete. If the DRAM is on the HOST bus (HDRAM), no PCI bus cycle is executed. The HOST CPU can now complete the access as outlined in the previous paragraph for a cache line in the cache marked invalid or unmodified/valid.

Under the write replacement protocol, a cache miss during a read access cycle does not affect the cache. If the access addresses PDRAM, a PCI read access cycle is executed by the cache controller in the HOST/PCI BRIDGE. The SDONE signal line is asserted by the cache controller in the HOST/PCI BRIDGE to indicate to all PCI memory resources that snoop is complete. If the access addresses HDRAM, a PCI access cycle is not executed.

READ REPLACEMENT WHEN AN ENTIRE CACHE LINE IS ACCESSED BY A PCI BUS MASTER

When the PCI bus master executes a read access cycle to the DRAM (PDRAM or HDRAM), the cache controller in the HOST/PCI BRIDGE asserts the SDONE signal line when the snoop is complete. The cache is part of the HOST CPU architecture; consequently, cache is not updated for a PCI bus master access to DRAM.

When the PCI bus master executes a write access cycle to the DRAM (PDRAM or HDRAM), the cache controller in the HOST/PCI BRIDGE asserts the SDONE signal line when the snoop is complete. There is no subsequent update of the cache.

READ REPLACEMENT WHEN A PORTION OF THE CACHE LINE IS ACCESSED BY A PCI BUS MASTER

When the PCI bus master executes a read or write access cycle to the DRAM (PDRAM or HDRAM), the cache controller in the HOST/PCI BRIDGE asserts the SDONE signal line when the snoop is complete. There is no subsequent update of the cache.

WRITE REPLACEMENT WHEN AN ENTIRE CACHE LINE IS ACCESSED BY A PCI BUS MASTER

When the PCI bus master executes a write access cycle to the DRAM (PDRAM or HDRAM), the cache controller in the HOST/PCI BRIDGE asserts the SDONE signal line when the snoop is complete. The cache is part of the HOST CPU architecture; consequently, cache is not updated for a PCI bus master access to DRAM.

When the PCI bus master executes a read access cycle to the DRAM (PDRAM or HDRAM), the cache controller in the HOST/PCI BRIDGE asserts the SDONE signal line when the snoop is complete. There is no subsequent update of the cache.

WRITE REPLACEMENT WHEN A PORTION OF THE CACHE LINE IS ACCESSED BY A PCI BUS MASTER

When the PCI bus master executes a read or write access cycle to the DRAM (PDRAM or HDRAM), the cache controller in the HOST/PCI BRIDGE asserts the SDONE signal line when the snoop is complete. There is no subsequent update of the cache.

OTHER WB CACHE PROTOCOL CONSIDERATIONS

All accesses to memory address space require the cache controller in the HOST/PCI BRIDGE to snoop the address and assert the SDONE signal line. In the protocol outlined above, the PDRAM waits until the SDONE signal line is asserted prior to asserting the TRDY# signal line. The SBO# signal line is asserted when a cache hit occurs to modified/valid cache line.

With a WB cache, it is possible for the PDRAM to assert the TRDY# signal line to complete the access prior to the cache controller in the HOST/PCI BRIDGE asserting the SDONE signal line. This latter protocol requires the PDRAM to know it is cached by a WB cache and to support OVER WRITE and ADDRESS STACKING. See *Subchapter 7.3: Protocol of the SDONE and SBO# Signal Lines* for details.

7.3 PROTOCOL OF THE SDONE AND SBO# SIGNAL LINES

SDONE AND SBO# SIGNAL LINE OPERATION

The operation of cache in a PCI system that implements the SDONE and SBO# signal lines is based on the following assumptions:

- Only one cache resource resides on the PCI bus.

- The memory address is flat; that is, only one DRAM memory target (PDRAM) will respond to each address.

- The cache resource is linked to the PCI bus by a single LEVEL bridge to the PCI bus.

- Only the memory address space can be cached.

- The SDONE and SBO# signal lines are driven by the cache controller or the platform. (See the note below.) For purposes of this discussion, the cache controller is contained within the HOST/PCI BRIDGE.

- The SDONE and SBO# signal lines are monitored by all cacheable PCI memory resources, but are not monitored by the PCI bus master resources or non-cacheable PCI memory resources.

- PDRAM that is cacheable must know if it is cached and whether the cache resource is WT or WB for ADDRESS STACKING.

- The SDONE and SBO# signal lines are not monitored by the PCI bus masters.

- A PDRAM does not know the cacheable addresses of the other PCI memory resources.

- The PCI bus masters do not know the address ranges of the cacheable PCI memory resources.

- The HOST DRAM (HDRAM), in conjunction with the HOST/PCI BRIDGE, appear as a PDRAM to PCI bus masters.

- The HOST CPU, in conjunction with the HOST/PCI BRIDGE, appear as a PCI bus master to PDRAM.

- Immediately after reset the cacheable PCI memory resources must ignore the SDONE and SBO# signal lines until these resources are enabled to operate in the cacheable mode. Enabling the resource to operate in the cacheable mode is done by the initialization software via the configuration address space.

Under most implementations, the SDONE signal line is driven by the cache controller resource of the PCI bus. For proper operation of the PCI memory resources, the SDONE signal line must always be operational. If the cache is enabled, the cache controller will properly operate the SDONE signal line because an actual snoop is executed. If the cache is disabled, the cache controller must toggle the SDONE signal line as if an actual snoop was occurring. If the platform does not have a cache controller, the central resource must toggle the SDONE signal line as if an actual snoop is occurring. The toggling of the SDONE signal line for a PCI memory access cycle is required in order to simplify the PCI memory control circuitry. The PCI memory circuitry needs only to monitor the SDONE signal lines, does not need to know the cached address ranges within the platform, and does not need to know if the cache is enabled. The toggling of the SDONE signal line is not required if there is no cacheable PCI memory in the system. Under this condition, the SDONE may be held active continuously. Alternatively, the non-cacheable PCI memory resource may be programmed to the SDONE signal line.

Also consider the following: The configuration register for a cacheable PDRAM has not been defined, and at the time of this writing a PCI memory resource of this type has not been built. Any reader developing a cacheable PDRAM should contact the PCI Special Interest Committee to coordinate the architecture of this type of PCI resource.

Under most implementations, the SBO# signal line is driven by the cache controller resource of the PCI bus. The SBO# signal line is always deasserted by central resource or the cache controller if the cache is WT or if no cache is enabled. The SBO# signal line is only asserted by the controller of a WB cache under certain cache hit conditions.

Figure 7-2-A outlines a PCI read access cycle when one of the following occurs: a cache miss of a WB or WT cache, OR a cache hit of a valid cache line in a WT cache, OR a cache hit of an unmodified/valid cache line in a WB cache. The SDONE and SBO# signal lines, driven by the cache controller in the HOST/PCI BRIDGE, are deasserted during the ADDRESS PHASE to indicate that a snoop write-back access cycle is not pending. As the cycle progresses, the PDRAM will not assert the TRDY# signal line until the SDONE signal line is asserted and the SBO# signal line remains asserted. Figure 7-2-A shows that the snoop of a WB

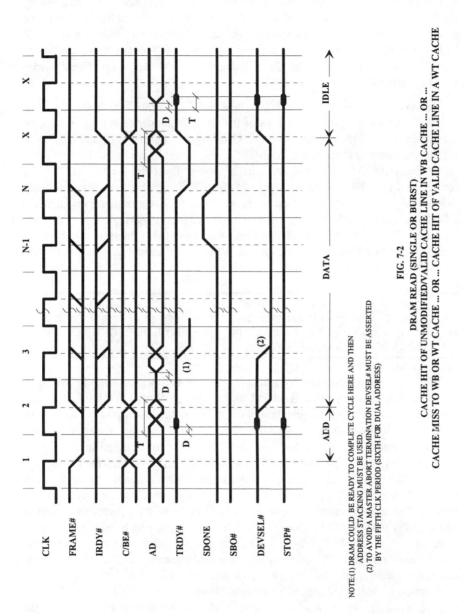

Figure 7-2-A: DRAM Read (Single or Burst) Cache Hit of Unmodified/Valid Cache Line in WB Cache, or Cache Miss to WB or WT Cache, or Cache Hit of Valid Cache Line in a WT Cache

or WT cache has been completed when the SDONE signal line is asserted during the DATA PHASE. If the cache was a WB type, the deasserted SBO# signal line when the SDONE signal line is asserted indicates that a cache miss or a cache hit to an unmodified/valid cache line occurred. For a WT cache type, the SBO# signal line is always deasserted. See *Chapter 4: Functional Interaction Between PCI Resources* for details.

The cycle shown in Figure 7-2-A is a SINGLE read access cycle. For a BURST access cycle, the first access of the BURST sequence is used to execute the snoop. If the snoop is complete (SDONE signal line asserted) and the SBO# signal line remains deasserted, the BURST access cycle continues to access the remaining data. The SDONE and SBO# signal lines are deasserted for the remainder of the BURST access cycle. If the SBO# signal line is deasserted, the SDONE signal line remains asserted for only one CLK signal line period. If the BURST access cycle crosses a cache boundary, the DRAM must immediately execute a Disconnect termination (without data version) if the next cache line is modified. With a Disconnect termination, all accesses executed prior to crossing the cache boundary will be valid.

> If the DRAM (HDRAM) and cache are on the same isolated bus (HOST) from the PCI bus, the Disconnect termination does not occur if the cache boundary is crossed. The cache controller in the HOST/PCI BRIDGE can independently manage cache coherency.

When the cache and memory resources are not behind the same BRIDGE or PCI interface circuitry (like HDRAM and cache on the HOST bus), it is still possible to cross a cache line boundary without the automatic execution of Disconnect without data termination. If the memory and cache controller resources "know" the cache line boundary, the protocol outlined in Fig. 7-2-B can apply. In Fig. 7-2-B the BURST memory access cycle has begun and the asserted SDONE signal line and the deasserted SBO# signal line at Point A (Circle A in Fig. 7-2-B) indicate that a snoop write-back access cycle is not needed. The access can continue until the last access of the present cache line is addressed at Point B (Circle B of Fig. 7-2-B). The cache line boundary is crossed at Point C (Circle C in Fig. 7-2-B), an event known to both the cache controller and memory resource. The memory resource will deassert the TRDY# signal line until the cache controller has asserted the SDONE signal to indicate the completion of address snoop. If the address snoop of this next cache line does not require a snoop write-back access cycle, the cache controller continues the deassertion of the SBO# signal line and the SDONE signal line is asserted only for one CLK signal line period. This results in the BURST access cycle continuing to pass the cache line boundary to access the next cache line. If the SDONE and SBO# signal lines are both asserted at Point D (Circle D in Fig. 7-2-

B), the result of the address snoops for the two cache lines are different. The address snoop of the first cache line indicated that the memory contained correct data and a snoop write-back access cycle was not needed; consequently, the access cycle can continue. The address snoop of the next cache line indicates that the memory does not contain correct data and a snoop write-back access cycle is needed. The cache controller will assert the SDONE and SBO# signal lines until the snoop write-back access cycle is executed. The memory must complete the present BURST access cycle with a Disconnect without data termination at Point E (Circle E in Fig. 7-2-B).

Figure 7-3 outlines a PCI read access cycle for a cache hit to a modified/valid cache line in WB cache. The SDONE and SBO# signal lines, driven by the cache controller in the HOST/PCI BRIDGE, are deasserted during the ADDRESS PHASE to indicate that a snoop and snoop write-back cache are not pending. As outlined in the description of Figure 7-2, the cycle progresses and the PDRAM will not assert the TRDY# signal line until the SDONE signal line is asserted and the SBO# signal line remains deasserted. Figure 7-3 shows that the snoop of a WB cache was completed. (The SDONE signal line is asserted during the DATA PHASE.) If the access addressed a modified/valid cache line of a WB cache, the SBO# signal line is asserted when SDONE signal line is asserted. The SBO# signal line can be asserted prior to or simultaneously with the assertion of the SDONE signal line. Once asserted, the SBO# and SDONE signal lines cannot be deasserted until the snoop write-back access cycle is executed (see Figure 7-4). The assertion of the TRDY# signal line by the DRAM does not occur because the data available from the PDRAM is invalid and a Retry termination is executed. When the memory write and invalidate command is executed, the SBO# signal line may remain deasserted even when the cache hit is to a modified/valid cache line in a WB cache.

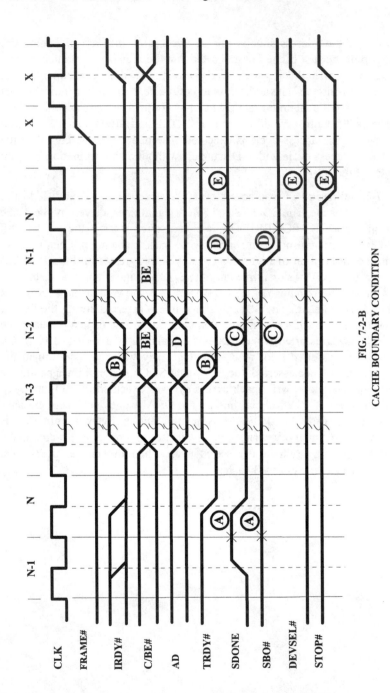

FIG. 7-2-B
CACHE BOUNDARY CONDITION

Figure 7-2-B: Cache Boundary Condition

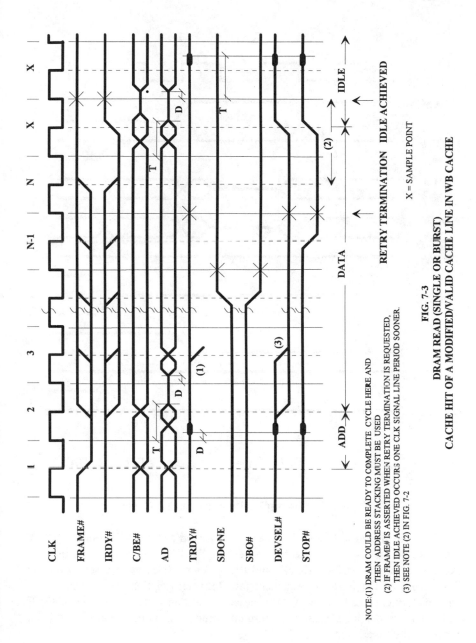

Figure 7-3: DRAM Read (Single or Burst) Cache Hit of a Modified/Valid Cache Line in WB Cache

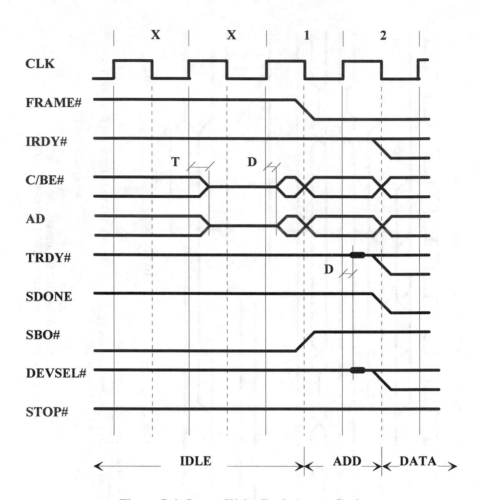

Figure 7-4: Snoop Write Back Access Cycle

The cycle shown in Figure 7-3 is a SINGLE read access cycle. For a BURST access cycle, the access to the first access of the BURST sequence is used to execute the snoop. If the SDONE and SBO# signal lines were asserted on the first access of the BURST sequence, the Retry termination would have been immediately executed and no valid accesses would have occurred. The SDONE and SBO# signal lines must both remain asserted until the snoop write-back access cycle is executed.

The above discussions are based on the PCI bus read access cycles, but a PCI bus write access cycle operates with the same protocol. For a WT and WB cache, an asserted SDONE signal line indicates that the snoop has completed. The continued deassertion of the SBO# signal line allows the cycle to continue. For a

WB cache, the asserted SDONE and SBO# signal lines indicate that the snoop has completed and the target must immediately execute a Retry termination. Subsequently, the cache controller in the HOST/PCI BRIDGE executes the snoop write-back access cycle.

The central arbiter does not have to immediately award the PCI bus to the cache controller in the HOST/PCI BRIDGE to execute the write-back of the modified/valid cache line in the WB cache to the PDRAM (snoop write-back access cycle). The cache controller in the HOST/PCI BRIDGE must arbitrate for PCI bus ownership like any other PCI bus master. As outlined in Figure 7-3, the SDONE and SBO# signal lines are asserted by the cache controller in the HOST/PCI BRIDGE when a cache hit to a modified/valid cache line in a WB cache occurs. The asserted SDONE and SBO# signal lines during IDLE and ADDRESS PHASES of subsequent access cycles to indicate a snoop write-back access cycle is pending. Accesses to any cacheable PDRAM when the snoop write-back access cycle is pending results in the PDRAM executing a Retry termination. A Retry termination does not occur if the access is to a non-cacheable PDRAM, or a PCI I/O or configuration resource.

Figure 7-4 outlines the snoop write-back access cycle that is executed by the cache controller in HOST/PCI BRIDGE. The access cycle is executed with the same protocol as other BURST write access cycles. Just prior to the ADDRESS PHASE of the snoop write-back access cycle, the SBO# signal line is deasserted. Thus, during the ADDRESS PHASE, the PDRAM resource knows that this is not an access from a PCI bus master that must end in a Retry termination. The deassertion of the SBO# signal line and the assertion of the SDONE signal line during the ADDRESS PHASE indicates to the PDRAM that a snoop write-back access cycle will be executed. If the SDONE and SBO# signal lines were asserted during the ADDRESS PHASE, the PDRAM knows this access is not a snoop write-back access cycle. Under the snoop write-back access cycle, the PDRAM will operate with the following protocol:

- The snoop write-back access cycle will not be terminated with Retry termination.

- If the target (PDRAM) of the snoop write-back access cycle is LOCKED, the access cycle is allowed to complete WITHOUT Retry termination. See *Chapter 6: Detailed Bus Cycle Operation* for details.

- The entire cache line must be written to the PDRAM. If the PDRAM is not able to immediately accept the data, it must deassert the TRDY# signal line as needed.

- During a snoop write-back access cycle, the IRDY# signal line is controlled by the cache controller in the HOST/PCI BRIDGE and the PDRAM controls the TRDY# signal line.

305

At the completion of a successful snoop write-back access cycle, the SDONE and SBO# signal lines are deasserted which indicate that no snoop or snoop write-back access cycle is pending. Notice that the SDONE and SBO# signal lines are both deasserted by the beginning of the DATA PHASE of the snoop write-back access cycle.

There is no Fast Back-to-Back situation between the PCI bus master and the cache controller in the HOST/PCI BRIDGE executing a snoop write-back access cycle. Thus there is always a minimum of one IDLE PHASE between the PCI bus master access cycle and the snoop write-back access cycle.

SPECIAL CONSIDERATIONS RELATIVE TO ADDRESS STACKING

As outlined in the above discussions, a snoop write-back access cycle is executed if a memory access cycle results in the assertion of both the SDONE and SBO# signal lines. The PDRAM does not assert the TRDY# signal line until it has determined if the SBO# signal would remain deasserted when the snoop is completed (SDONE signal line asserted). If the PDRAM knows that the SBO# signal line will not be asserted when the snoop is complete, the PDRAM can request the completion of the access cycle (TRDY# signal line asserted) prior to the completion of the snoop. If the PDRAM knows if it is cached by a WT cache, the SBO# signal line will remain deasserted. The SBO# signal line will also remain deasserted when a WB cache supports overwrite (see the subsequent section). The assurance that a snoop write-back access cycle (SBO# signal line remains deasserted) will not be executed allows the PDRAM to execute ADDRESS STACKING.

The memory access cycle protocol outlined to this point specifies that the SDONE signal line is asserted by the cache controller in the HOST/PCI BRIDGE prior to the PDRAM asserting the TRDY# signal line. This PCI bus protocol insures the completion of the memory access cycle (assertion of IRDY# and TRDY# signal lines) after the completion of the cache snoop (assertion of the SDONE signal line). Under the ADDRESS STACKING protocol, the SDONE signal line does not have to be asserted prior to the assertion of the TRDY# signal line during a SINGLE or BURST (initial microaccess cycle) memory access cycle. The assertion of the FRAME# signal line to access a cacheable or non-cacheable PDRAM indicates to all DRAM resources that a SDONE signal line must be asserted (even if a snoop is not executed). If the FRAME# signal line is deasserted and again asserted for a memory access cycle prior to the assertion of the SDONE signal line for the snoop associated with the first

FRAME# signal line assertion, the bus cycle associated with the second assertion of the FRAME# signal line can complete only under the one of the following :

- If the second access is to a *non-memory* resource (i.e., I/O), the cycle can be completed without the assertion of the SDONE signal line associated with the first assertion of the FRAME# signal line.

OR

- If the second access is to a non-cacheable PDRAM resource, the cycle can be completed without the assertion of the SDONE signal line associated with the first assertion of the FRAME# signal line.

OR

- If the second access is to a cacheable PDRAM resource, the cycle cannot be completed (TRDY# signal line remains deasserted) until the assertion of the SDONE signal line associated with the first assertion of the FRAME# signal line. The cacheable PDRAM inserts wait states because there is only one set of SDONE and SBO# signal lines. Thus, a maximum of two accesses to cacheable DRAM can be stacked (ADDRESS STACKING).

OVERWRITE PROTOCOL WITH WRITE-BACK CACHES

As outlined above, an access cycle to a PDRAM can be completed prior to the completion of snoop if the PDRAM knows that the SBO# signal line will not be asserted.

The write access protocol that does not implement ADDRESS STACKING assumes that potentially the SBO# signal line will be asserted when the snoop is complete. If the PDRAM allows the write access cycle to complete (IRDY# and TRDY# signal lines asserted) prior to snoop completion, the assertion of the SBO# signal line will cause the data written by the PCI bus master to be over written by the subsequent snoop write-back access cycle. The SBO# signal line will be asserted when the snoop results in cache hit to a modified/valid cache in a WB cache. The data that had been written by the PCI bus master will be replaced by older data from the cache when the snoop write-back access cycle is executed. Consequently, a PDRAM that does not support OVER WRITE and is cached by a WB cache will not complete a write access cycle until the SDONE signal line is asserted. As previously outlined, a deasserted or asserted SBO# signal line results in data written to PDRAM or execute a Retry termination, respectively. The PDRAM could be designed to complete the write access cycle and not execute a Retry termination when the snoop results in a cache hit to a modified/valid WB cache line (SDONE and SBO# signal lines both asserted). Such a protocol is defined as OVER WRITE. Consider the following: The PCI bus master does not monitor the SDONE or SBO# signal lines; consequently, it will complete the write access cycle to the PDRAM with the assertion of the TRDY# and IRDY# signal lines. The cache controller in the HOST/PCI BRIDGE will independently assert the SDONE and SBO# signal lines and begin arbitration for bus ownership to execute a snoop write-back access cycle. After the snoop write-back access cycle is executed, the PDRAM will OVER WRITE the associated cache line in PDRAM with the data that had be written earlier by the PCI bus master and stored in the overwrite buffer. Under this protocol, the PCI bus master is not required to wait until the snoop is complete before asserting the TRDY# signal line. Under this OVER WRITE protocol, ADDRESS STACKING is supported because the TRDY# signal line can be asserted prior to the assertion of the SDONE signal line. Also, PCI bus masters cannot complete an access to the aforementioned PDRAM (Retry termination will occur) between the access that caused a cache hit and the snoop write-back access cycle.

> The OVER WRITE protocol does not apply to PDRAM that is cached by WT cache; however, by definition of WT cache ADDRESS STACKING is supported.

SPECIAL CONSIDERATIONS RELATIVE TO THE MEMORY WRITE INVALIDATE COMMAND

One special consideration about cache snooping is when a memory write and invalidate (MWI) command is executed. When a normal non-MWI write access cycle is executed, a cache hit to a modified/valid WB cache line results in the assertion of both SBO# and SDONE signal lines and the termination of the access cycle (Retry termination). Subsequently, the cache controller in the HOST/PCI BRIDGE will execute a snoop write-back access cycle. A cache hit to a modified/valid WB cache line when an MWI command is executed may retain the SBO# signal line in the deasserted state when snoop is completed. The cache controller in the HOST/PCI BRIDGE will mark the associated WB cache line invalid according to the protocol of the MWI command. The invalidation of the cache line in the cache and the deasserted state of the SBO# signal line eliminates the need for the cache controller HOST/PCI BRIDGE to execute a snoop write-back access cycle. Under this protocol the SDONE signal line is still asserted to indicate the completion of the snoop. The elimination of the snoop write-back access cycle results in improved system performance.

At the option of the cache controller in the HOST/PCI BRIDGE, the SBO# signal line can be asserted for a Memory Write Invalidate command access that results in a cache hit to a modified/valid WB cache line. The cache line in the cache is marked invalid. The assertion of the SBO# signal line requires a Retry termination and the subsequent execution of the a snoop write-back access cycle. The cache controller in the HOST/PCI BRIDGE marks the associated cache line in the cache as unmodified/valid after the snoop write-back access cycle is completed. This situation may occur if the cache controller only supports the write access COMMAND and not memory write and invalidate.

CHAPTER 8

MASTER AND TARGET TERMINATION

This chapter consists of the following subchapters:

8.0   Introduction
8.1   Master Termination
8.2   Target Termination

8.0 INTRODUCTION

The PCI bus specification defines two types of termination: master and target. For master termination, the present PCI bus master determines when the bus cycle will be terminated. The three master termination protocols are: completion, Completion with Timeout, and Master Abort. For target termination, the current target determines when the bus cycle will be terminated. The three target terminations are: Retry, Disconnect, and Target Abort.

The PCI bus master must complete a terminated bus cycle in a orderly manner. All bus cycles that are terminated must be completed with a minimum of one CLK signal line period with the FRAME# signal line deasserted and the IRDY# signal line is asserted. Subsequently, when the DATA PHASE completes the FRAME# and IRDY# signal lines are both deasserted. When a bus cycle completes in a Fast Back-to-Back fashion, the FRAME# signal line is deasserted and the IRDY# signal line is asserted a minimum of one CLK signal line period. When the DATA PHASE subsequently completes, the IRDY# signal line is deasserted and the FRAME# signal line is asserted.

The majority of bus cycles complete with either Completion or Completion with Timeout terminations. Most targets should support requesting Retry termination, but the support of any target termination (Retry, Disconnect, and Target Abort terminations) is optional. PCI bus masters must support all of the master and target terminations. The operation and interpretation of the STOP#, DEVSEL#, SDONE, SBO#, SERR#, PERR#, PAR, and PAR64 signal lines vary for the different terminations. See details below.

In this chapter the phrase "PCI bus master is the HOST/PCI BRIDGE and the target is the PCI bus resource that contains the interrupt controller" will be used. As outlined in Chapter 2, the interrupt controller may also reside in a resource on the HOST bus not associated with the PCI bus (for example, the HOST/LEGACY BRIDGE, in the HOST/PCI BRIDGE, in the PCI/LEGACY BRIDGE, or the LEGACY bus). The interrupt controller which this phrase refers to is a resource on the PCI Bus 0, in the PCI/LEGACY BRIDGE, or in a resource on the LEGACY bus attached via the PCI/LEGACY BRIDGE.

When the interrupt controller resides in a resource on the HOST bus, in the HOST/PCI BRIDGE, or in a resource on the LEGACY bus attached by a HOST/LEGACY BRIDGE, no interrupt acknowledge cycle is executed on PCI bus 0.

8.1   MASTER TERMINATION

COMPLETION TERMINATION OF ACCESS CYCLES

A Completion termination of an access cycle occurs when the FRAME# signal line is deasserted and the IRDY# signal line is asserted simultaneously for one CLK signal line period. The other terminations to be discussed in this chapter must always incorporate Completion termination.

The assertion of the PERR# signal line during an access cycle does not require the PCI bus master to execute a Completion termination any sooner than it would if the PERR# signal line was not asserted. The assertion of the SERR# signal line during an access cycle does not require the PCI bus master to execute a Completion termination any sooner than it would if the SERR# signal line was not asserted.

COMPLETION TERMINATION OF SPECIAL CYCLES

The special cycle completes with Master Abort termination.

COMPLETION TERMINATION OF INTERRUPT ACKNOWLEDGE CYCLES

The protocol for a Completion termination of an interrupt acknowledge cycle is the same as a Completion termination for a read access cycle. The PCI bus master is the HOST/PCI BRIDGE and the target is the PCI bus resource that contains the interrupt controller.

COMPLETION WITH TIMEOUT TERMINATION OF ACCESS CYCLES

The request for Completion with Timeout termination occurs when the GNT# signal line for the current PCI bus master is deasserted and the internal Latency Timer has expired (see Figures 8-1-A to 8-6). For an access cycle, the data that has been accessed and is being accessed is valid, and the target can be accessed at a later time. The access cycle (or microaccess of a BURST access cycle) being executed when Completion with Timeout termination is requested is allowed to complete. The purpose of the Completion with Timeout termination is to terminate bus ownership by the present PCI bus master and provide a known latency to obtain bus ownership. See *Chapter 14: Latency and Performance* for details.

The Latency Timer is a programmable counter that counts (increments or decrements, depending on the timer) on each rising edge of the CLK signal line while the FRAME# signal line is asserted. The Latency Timer is reloaded with its count value at the beginning of the access cycle when the FRAME# signal line is first sampled asserted and expires after a count of 256 or less. The counter reload value can be a fixed (hardware) or a programmable value. Only the PCI bus master knows when the Latency Timer expires. The request occurs when the Latency Timer expires or has expired when the associated GNT# signal line is deasserted.

Latency Timer counting stops whenever the FRAME# signal line is deasserted because bus cycle completion is forthcoming (i.e. Completion termination).

If the Latency Timer is not programmable, it is hard coded with a count of 16 or less. If it is programmable, the count is programmable with counts of from 1 to 256. The Latency Timer is required when a PCI bus master executes a BURST access cycle containing more than two microaccesses. It is otherwise optional.

Figure 8-1-A and 8-1-B show the Completion with Timeout termination of a BURST access cycle. In Figure 8-1-A, the FRAME# signal line is asserted, and the GNT#, TRDY#, and IRDY# signal lines are deasserted prior to the expiration of the Latency Timer. When the Latency Timer expires at the CLK signal line rising edge, the access cycle must be terminated as soon as possible.

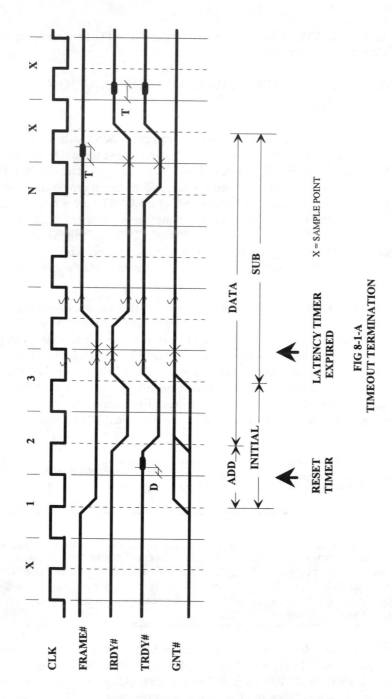

Figure 8-1-A: Timeout Termination

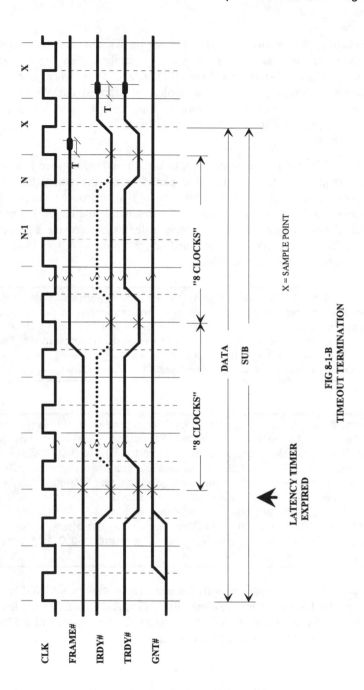

Figure 8-1-B: Timeout Termination

Consequently, the FRAME# signal line must be deasserted at the completion of the present microaccess, and only one more microaccess can be executed at this time. In Figure 8-1-B, the Latency Timer expires when one of the microaccesses is completed. In this example, the asserted IRDY# signal line signal line when the Latency Timer expires requires that two more microaccesses are executed in order for the FRAME# signal line to be deasserted correctly for the last microaccess.

Unless the PCI bus master must align to a cache boundary (see below), the worst case number of CLK signal line periods until the completion of the BURST access cycle is 16 periods. This reflects two microaccesses per the "8 clock" rule (see *Subchapter 14.0 : Latency* for details). If the target was not able to complete the microaccess per the "8 clock" rule, it must execute a Disconnect termination. The access cycle is completed under Completion termination (see *Completion termination* in this subchapter).

If the cycle is a memory write and invalidate (MWI) access cycle, the PCI bus master is allowed to complete all of the microaccesses of the BURST access cycle to a cache line boundary before honoring Completion with Timeout termination request. If the target requests a Disconnect, Target Abort, or Retry termination, these requests will force the PCI bus master to terminate the bus cycle prior to the cache line boundary.

In Figure 8-1-A and 8-1-B, the FRAME# signal line is immediately deasserted. Due to the protocol of the IRDY# and FRAME# signal lines, the FRAME# signal line cannot be deasserted until the IRDY# signal line is asserted. The IRDY# signal line cannot be asserted until the PCI bus master is ready to access the data; consequently, the FRAME# signal line may not be immediately deasserted. According to the PCI bus specification, IRDY# should be asserted within 2-3 CLK signal line periods after the Latency Timer expires. The execution of a Memory Write Invalidate BURST access cycle is exempted from the "2-3 CLK signal line period" rule.

Figure 8-2 shows the Completion with Timeout termination of a SINGLE access cycle. When the Latency Timer expires, the GNT#, and IRDY# signal lines are deasserted, and the FRAME# signal line is asserted. The protocol of a SINGLE access cycle allows it to complete a normal access.

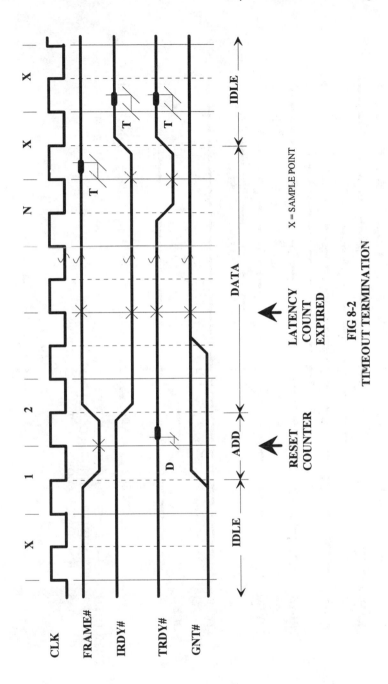

Figure 8-2: Timeout Termination

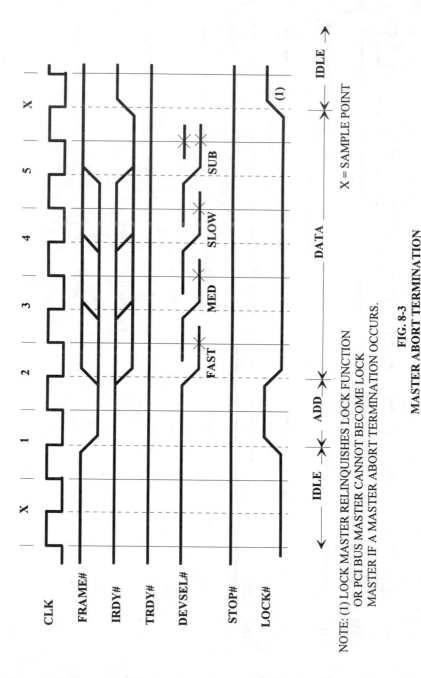

NOTE: (1) LOCK MASTER RELINQUISHES LOCK FUNCTION
OR PCI BUS MASTER CANNOT BECOME LOCK
MASTER IF A MASTER ABORT TERMINATION OCCURS.

X = SAMPLE POINT

FIG. 8-3
MASTER ABORT TERMINATION
(NO DUAL ADDRESS)

Figure 8-3: Master Abort Termination (No DUAL ADDRESS)

The Latency Timer is reloaded and counting starts at the beginning of each access cycle when the FRAME# signal line is first asserted. If the GNT# signal line of the present PCI bus master is asserted when the Latency Timer expires, the Completion with Timeout termination is not executed at that time. Subsequently, the PCI bus master can begin execution of another bus cycle if the GNT# signal line is asserted just prior to asserting the FRAME# signal line.

> Execution of Completion with Timeout termination has no effect on the central arbiter because only the PCI bus master knows that it has been requested. A Completion with Timeout termination does not force the PCI bus master to deassert the associated REQ# signal line.

> The request for Completion with Timeout termination (Latency Timer expires) is only known by the PCI bus master. The target termination requests (Retry, Disconnect, or Target Abort terminations) will take priority over the Completion with Timeout termination. When the Retry, Disconnect or Target Abort termination is requested, the access cycle is completed according to their respective protocols.

> A Completion with Timeout termination has no affect on a PCI bus master obtaining or retaining the Lock Function and locking or the lock of a target.

> The assertion of the PERR# signal line during an access cycle does not require the PCI bus master to execute a Completion termination any sooner than it would if the PERR# signal line was not asserted. The assertion of the SERR# signal line during an access cycle does not require the PCI bus master to execute a Completion termination any sooner than it would if the SERR# signal line was not asserted.

COMPLETION WITH TIMEOUT TERMINATION OF SPECIAL CYCLES OR INTERRUPT ACKNOWLEDGE CYCLES

This termination protocol does not apply to these bus cycles.

319

MASTER ABORT TERMINATION OF ACCESS CYCLES

The Master Abort termination of an access cycle occurs when there is no potential for a PCI resource to claim the access cycle and become the target. The cycle cannot be executed if not claimed by a target asserting the DEVSEL# signal line. The execution of a Master Abort termination requires a Completion termination; consequently, the IRDY# signal line must be asserted for a minimum of one CLK signal line period. As outlined in Figure 8-3, when the DEVSEL# signal line is sampled deasserted on the rising edge of the fourth CLK signal line period after the FRAME# signal line is first sampled asserted the Master Abort termination must be executed. The IRDY# signal line will be immediately deasserted if, prior to the sampling point of the deasserted DEVSEL# signal line, the FRAME# and IRDY# signal lines are deasserted and asserted, respectively. If the FRAME# and IRDY# signal lines are both asserted at the sample point of the deasserted DEVSEL# signal line, the FRAME# signal line is immediately deasserted and the IRDY# signal line is asserted one CLK signal line period later (see Figure 8-4). Finally, Figure 8-5 outlines a third scenario for the FRAME# and IRDY# signal line at the sampling point of the deasserted DEVSEL# signal line. When the FRAME# signal line is asserted and the IRDY# signal line is deasserted these, signal lines are immediately driven to the opposite state. Subsequently, the IRDY# signal line is deasserted. The three examples outlined above all complete with Completion termination. For one CLK signal line period, the FRAME# and IRDY# signal lines are deasserted and asserted, respectively. Subsequently, the FRAME# and IRDY# signal lines are both deasserted.

> In the above paragraph, the word *immediately* indicates the preferred protocol for the PCI bus master to complete the access cycle. However, the PCI bus master may complete the access cycle at a later time.

When the HOST/PCI BRIDGE is executing a PCI bus cycle, a Master Abort termination requires the BRIDGE to discard data for a write cycle and return all "1"s to the HOST bus for a read cycle. The BRIDGE must set the Master Abort Detected bit in the Status Register.

The Master Abort termination is appropriate for the following bus cycle situations (this is not a conclusive list ... other situations are possible.):

■ A target cannot claim a bus cycle by asserting the DEVSEL# signal line if a Reserve Command is encoded in the C/BE# signal lines in the ADDRESS PHASE.

■ A target cannot claim a bus cycle by asserting the DEVSEL# signal line if the DUAL ADDRESS is encoded in the C/BE# signal lines in the ADDRESS PHASE (the target does not decode 64 address bits).

■ A target may not claim a bus cycle by asserting the DEVSEL# signal line, if it detects an address parity error.

The above discussion and Figures 8-3 to 8-5 do not consider DUAL ADDRESS, ADDRESS/DATA STEPPING or PRE-DRIVE. If the access cycle is executing a DUAL ADDRESS, all of the sampling points for the DEVSEL# signal line are delayed by one CLK signal line period relative to when the FRAME# signal line is first sampled asserted. If an access or interrupt acknowledge cycle implements ADDRESS/DATA STEPPING or a configuration access cycle implements ADDRESS/DATA STEPPING or PRE-DRIVE, the sampling points are the same relative to when the FRAME# signal line is first sampled asserted. However, under the ADDRESS/DATA STEPPING or pre-drive protocols, the FRAME# signal line will be asserted later in the cycle (not at CLK signal line period #1) than shown in Figures 8-3 to 8-5.

If the target is not broken, it must claim the access cycle.

The PERR# signal line cannot be asserted when a Master Abort termination is executed because no PCI resource claimed the access cycle so no data was accessed. The PCI bus master can assert the SERR# signal line to report a Master Abort termination of an access cycle. The PCI bus master does not assert the SERR# signal line to report a Master Abort termination of a configuration access cycle during initialization.

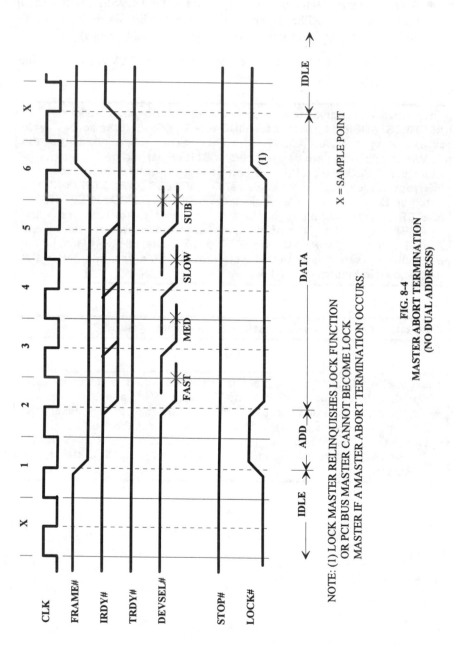

NOTE: (1) LOCK MASTER RELINQUISHES LOCK FUNCTION
OR PCI BUS MASTER CANNOT BECOME LOCK
MASTER IF A MASTER ABORT TERMINATION OCCURS.

X = SAMPLE POINT

FIG. 8-4
MASTER ABORT TERMINATION
(NO DUAL ADDRESS)

Figure 8-4: Master Abort Termination (No DUAL ADDRESS)

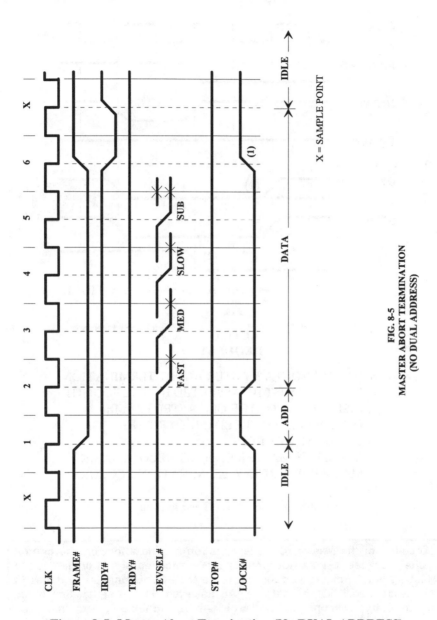

FIG. 8-5
MASTER ABORT TERMINATION
(NO DUAL ADDRESS)

Figure 8-5: Master Abort Termination (No DUAL ADDRESS)

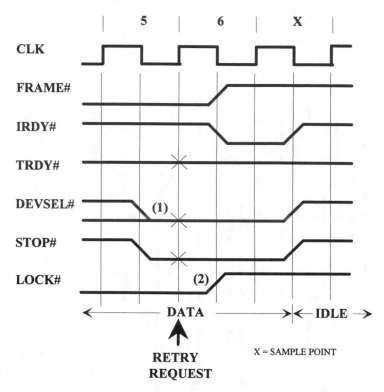

RETRY
REQUEST

X = SAMPLE POINT

NOTES: (1) TO AVOID A MASTER ABORT TERMINATION
DEVSEL# MUST BE ASSERTED BY THE FOURTH
RISING EDGE OF THE CLK AFTER FRAME#
IS SAMPLED ASSERTED (FIFTH RISING EDGE
FOR DUAL ADDRESS)
(2) PCI BUS MASTER CANNOT BECOME LOCK
MASTER IF A RETRY TERMINATION OCCCURS

Figure 8-6: Retry Termination

Execution of the Master Abort termination has no affect on the central
arbiter because it does not monitor the associated signal lines. Also, a
Master Abort termination does not force the PCI bus master to deassert
the associated REQ# signal line. An asserted STOP# signal line helps
define Retry, Disconnect, or Target Abort termination requests. The
STOP# signal line can only be asserted simultaneously with or after the
assertion of the DEVSEL# signal line; consequently, the Master Abort
termination has highest priority.

A PCI bus master cannot become Lock master and lock a target when a Master Abort termination is executed during the read access cycle that the PCI bus master is using to lock the target. The LOCK# signal line is immediately deasserted.

If the Lock master is accessing the locked target and a Master Abort termination occurs, the Lock master is required to relinquish the Lock Function. The LOCK# signal line is immediately deasserted and the target is immediately unlocked. If a non-Lock master accesses the locked target, the execution of a Master Abort termination does not force relinquishing of the Lock Function by the Lock master or the unlocking of the target.

MASTER ABORT TERMINATION OF SPECIAL CYCLES

The special cycle can only be terminated with the Master Abort termination in conjunction with the Completion termination as outlined above for access cycles. When the PCI bus master terminates an access cycle with a Master Abort termination, the Received Master Abort bit must be set in its Status Register. If the bus cycle is a special cycle the aforementioned bit is not set.

The PERR# signal line cannot be asserted when a Master Abort termination is executed, because no PCI resource claimed the access cycle so no data was accessed. The PCI bus master may assert the SERR# signal line to report a Master Abort termination of an access cycle if there is no other mechanism to do so. The PCI bus master does not assert the SERR# signal line to report a Master Abort termination of a configuration access cycle during initialization.

MASTER ABORT TERMINATION OF INTERRUPT ACKNOWLEDGE CYCLES

The protocol for a Master Abort termination of an interrupt acknowledge cycle is the same as a Master Abort termination for a read access cycle. The PCI bus master is the HOST/PCI BRIDGE and the target is the PCI bus resource that contains the interrupt controller.

8.2 TARGET TERMINATION

The rest of this chapter uses the phrase "forces the PCI bus master to deassert its associated REQ# signal line." The protocol for how long the REQ# signal line is deasserted is outlined in Subchapter 9.2.

RETRY TERMINATION OF ACCESS CYCLES

A Retry termination is requested when no data has been accessed in the cycle, the TRDY# signal line is deasserted, and the DEVSEL# signal line is asserted when the STOP# signal line is first asserted in the cycle (see Figures 8-6 to 8-7). Retry termination indicates that no cycle is possible at this time for whatever reason, but the target is not broken and can be accessed at a later time. For example, a Retry termination will occur for an access to a locked target by a PCI bus master that is not the Lock master. Once Retry termination is requested, no other termination occurs except for Completion termination.

The Retry termination is appropriate for the following bus cycle situations (this is not a conclusive list ... other situations are possible.):

■ A Retry termination must be executed when a locked target is accessed by a PCI bus master that is not the Lock master. An exception for an access by a PCI bus master that is not the Lock master is when a snoop write-back access cycle is executed.

■ A Retry termination must be executed per the "16 clock" rule (see the discussion below).

■ A Retry termination is executed whenever the target will not be able to immediately respond to the bus cycle; for example, as part of Delayed Transactions.

The Retry termination is NOT a response for an address or data parity error.

Retry termination must be executed by the target if it cannot complete a SINGLE access cycle or the initial microaccess of a BURST access cycle within sixteen CLK signal line periods ("16 clock" rule) from the assertion of the FRAME# signal line (STOP# signal line must be asserted on the seventeenth rising edge of the CLK signal line with the assertion of the FRAME# signal line at the first rising edge of the CLK signal line). For a write access cycle, the data is either accepted by the target (with or without posting) or a Retry termination is executed within the confines of the "16 clock" rule. For a read access cycle, the target must provide the data or execute Retry termination within the confines of the "16 clock" rule. A target that executes a Retry termination will have the data available when the access cycle is repeated. A method by which the target could have the data available for the repeated access is to latch the address, COMMAND type, byte enables, REQ64# signal line, etc., when it executed a Retry termination on the initial access (the latched information is to identify the repeat of the "exact same" access cycle). The target can proceed with the access independent of the PCI bus and prepare the data for a subsequent repeat of the access cycle as defined by the aforementioned latched information. The "16 clock" rule does not apply to the configuration access cycles during platform initialization, but is required during runtime. Also, the "16 clock" rule does not apply when an EEPROM is being copied to shadow DRAM. See Chapter 14 and Subchapters 4.0 and 8.2 for more information.

Rev. 2.0 of the PCI bus specification did not require Retry termination per the "16 clock" rule.

The posting of data for write access cycles or the latching of the address, COMMAND type, byte enables, REQ64# signal line, etc., for a read access cycle is highly recommended but not required provided the target can eventually provide the data without latching. Posted data for a write access cycle must be written in the order received. All of the posted data must be written before a read bus cycle is completed. If the latching of information for a read access cycle completed with Retry termination is supported, the target must not accept other bus cycles (must execute a Retry termination without latching the associated information) until the repeated access cycle ("exact same") is completed with a Completion (with or without timeout), Disconnect, Master Abort, or Target Abort termination. Also, the PCI bus master must repeat the "exact same" access cycle until it is completed with a Completion (with or without timeout), Disconnect, Master Abort, or Target Abort termination. See Subchapters 3.1 and 4.1 for more information.

As mentioned above, bus cycles executed between repeats of the "exact same" access cycle must also be completed (without latching of information) with Retry termination. One exception is the special bus cycle which cannot be completed with a Retry termination. When a special cycle is executed between the repeat of the "exact same cycle" it cannot be completed with Retry termination and must be accepted by the target. See Subchapter 3.1 for more information.

The execution of a Retry termination requires the IRDY# signal line to be asserted for a minimum of one CLK signal line period. In Figure 8-6, Retry termination is requested by the target when the FRAME# signal line is asserted. The Retry termination request causes the immediate deassertion of the FRAME# signal line and assertion of the IRDY# signal line (if not previously asserted). Subsequently, the IRDY#, DEVSEL#, and STOP# signal lines are deasserted and the cycle is completed when the FRAME# and IRDY# signal lines are both deasserted. In Figure 8-7 Retry termination is requested when the FRAME# signal line is deasserted. The Retry termination request causes the immediate deassertion of the IRDY#, DEVSEL#, and STOP# signal lines to complete the cycle. The assertion of the DEVSEL# signal line when a Retry termination is requested distinguishes it from a Target Abort termination.

> In the above paragraph, the word *immediate* indicates the preferred protocol for the PCI bus master to complete the access cycle. If a Retry termination is executed during a read or write access cycle, the PCI bus master is required to repeat the "exact same access" (same address, same addressing sequence, same C/BE# signal lines for byte lane enabling, etc.). The "exact same access" must be repeated until a Completion, Completion with Timeout, Target Abort, Master Abort, or Disconnect termination is executed. The assertion of the RST# signal line will also remove the requirement for the PCI bus master to repeat the "exact same access".
>
> The assertion of the SERR# signal line has no bearing on the aforementioned requirement to repeat the "exact same" access cycle that completed with Retry termination. Similarly, the requirement to continue repeating the "exact same" access cycle due to Retry termination is not affected by the assertion of the PERR# signal line.

> The PCI bus master may execute other bus cycles to the target that executed the Retry termination or other targets between repeating the "exact same" access cycle. Similarly, other PCI bus masters can execute bus cycles to the target that had executed a Retry termination. PCI bus masters that are executing the "exact same" access cycles must respond to accesses by other PCI bus masters if it also has target attributes.

> If the Lock master or a non-Lock master is accessing the locked target, the execution of a Retry termination does not force the Lock master to relinquish the Lock Function.

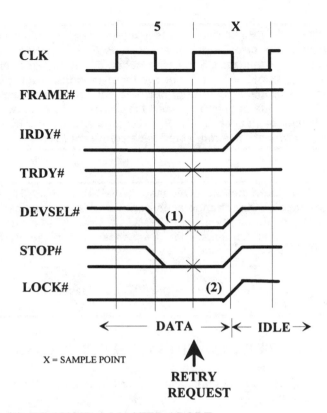

X = SAMPLE POINT

RETRY
REQUEST

NOTES: (1) TO AVOID A MASTER ABORT
TERMINATION DEVSEL# MUST BE
ASSERTED BY THE FOURTH RISING EDGE
OF THE CLK AFTER FRAME# IS SAMPLED
ASSERTED (FIFTH RISING EDGE FOR DUAL
ADDRESS)
(2) PCI BUS MASTER CANNOT BECOME LOCK
MASTER IF A RETRY TERMINATION OCCCURS

Figure 8-7: Retry Termination

When the SERR# signal line is asserted by the target to indicate an address parity error on the AD, C/BE#, PAR, and PAR64 signal lines, the target cannot request a Retry termination due to this address parity error. A Retry termination can occur for other reasons, such as the bus and target are properly operating, but data cannot be accessed at this time. The PCI bus master cannot assert the SERR# signal line to report a Retry termination of an access. The PERR# signal line cannot be asserted when a Retry termination is requested because no data was accessed.

Once Retry termination is requested, the TRDY#, DEVSEL#, and STOP# signal lines cannot change state until Completion termination occurs. At Completion termination, the DEVSEL# and STOP# signal lines are deasserted simultaneously with the deassertion of the IRDY# and TRDY# signal lines

A Retry termination requires the PCI bus master to deassert its REQ# signal line.

RETRY TERMINATION OF SPECIAL CYCLES

The special cycle does not address a specific target, so Retry termination does not apply to this cycle.

The "16 clock" rule as outlined in the previous section does not apply to the special cycle because the PCI bus master must assert the IRDY# signal line with valid data per the "PCI Master Latency rule" well within the sixteen clocks of the assertion of the FRAME# signal line. Also, because there is no specific target to claim the special cycle the STOP# signal line cannot be asserted to request a Retry termination. See Chapter 14 and Subchapter 3.1 for more information.

RETRY TERMINATION OF INTERRUPT ACKNOWLEDGE CYCLES

The protocol for a Retry termination of an interrupt acknowledge cycle is the same as a Retry termination for a read access cycle. The PCI bus master is the HOST/PCI BRIDGE and the target is the PCI bus resource that contains the interrupt controller.

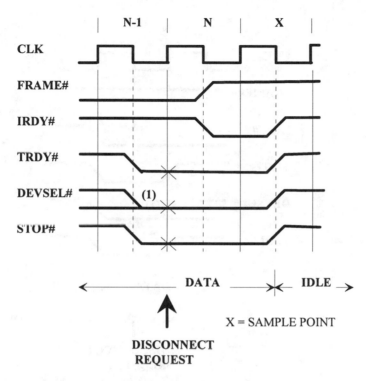

NOTE: (1) TO AVOID A MASTER ABORT TERMINATION
DEVSEL# MUST BE ASSERTED BY THE FOURTH
RISING EDGE OF THE CLK AFTER FRAME#
IS SAMPLED ASSERTED (FIFTH RISING EDGE
FOR DUAL ADDRESS)

Figure 8-8: Disconnect with Data Termination

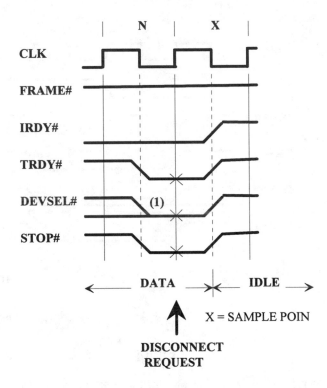

NOTES: (1) TO AVOID A MASTER ABORT TERMINATION
DEVSEL# MUST BE ASSERTED BY THE FOURTH
RISING EDGE OF THE CLK AFTER FRAME#
IS SAMPLED ASSERTED (FIFTH RISING EDGE
FOR DUAL ADDRESS)

Figure 8-9: Disconnect with Data Termination

DISCONNECT TERMINATION OF ACCESS CYCLES

The Disconnect termination is similar to the Retry termination in that the STOP#, DEVSEL#, and TRDY# signals lines are involved in the termination (see Figures 8-8 to 8-9). The only difference between a Retry and a Disconnect termination is that with a Disconnect termination data has been accessed in a microaccess (BURST access cycle) prior to the termination request or simultaneously with the access of data in a SINGLE access cycle or microaccess (BURST access cycle). The Retry termination simply means no data access for the cycle. The Disconnect termination provides whatever data access is available and indicates that the target cannot respond to further accesses in the cycle within a reasonable amount of time. The target is not broken and can be accessed at a later time.

The Disconnect termination is appropriate for the following bus cycle situations (this is not a conclusive list; other situations are possible:

- The target cannot provide data within eight CLK signal line periods from the beginning of the present subsequent microaccess during a BURST access cycle. The beginning of the microaccess is one CLK signal line period after the simultaneous assertion of the IRDY# and TRDY# signal lines of the previous microaccess. See "8 clock" rule in Chapter 14 for details.

- The target cannot support the burst cycle addressing sequence requested by the PCI bus master.

- The target can optionally execute a Disconnect termination when the PCI bus master attempts a 64 data bit access to a 32 data bit target.

- The BURST access cycle crosses a cache line boundary of the target (cacheable HOST or PCI memory resource).

> If the cache and cacheable memory resource are behind the same BRIDGE (isolated from the PCI bus master), Disconnect termination is not required when the cache boundary is crossed. Also, the executing of the Disconnect termination is not required if the crossing of the cache line boundary does not cause a no-op write-back access cycle to be required. See Chapter 7 for more information.

- The target may execute a Disconnect termination when a data parity occurred in a previous microaccess of a BURST bus cycle as part of the error reporting protocol. A target may execute a Disconnect with data termination when a data parity error occurs in the present microaccess.

> The Disconnect termination is NOT a response for an address parity error.

There are two types of Disconnect termination: *with* and *without* data. The Disconnect with data termination occurs when the last data of the present SINGLE access cycle or microaccess (BURST access cycle) is accessed. Disconnect without data termination occurs after data was accessed in previous microaccesses of the BURST access cycle but no additional data will be accessed during the present microaccess. Once a Disconnect termination is requested, no other termination occurs except for Completion termination.

> If the target termination request occurs without any data accessed (TRDY# signal line remains deasserted) for the SINGLE access cycle or the initial microaccess of a BURST access cycle, by definition it was a Retry termination.

> The execution of a Disconnect termination does not require the PCI bus master to repeat the "exact same access" (same address, same addressing sequence, same C/BE# signal lines for byte lane enabling, etc.).

> If the cycle is a memory write and invalidate (MWI) access cycle to a cacheable region, the BURST access cycle must be allowed to complete all of the microaccesses to a cache line boundary. Consequently, a Disconnect termination cannot be requested by a cacheable target during an MWI access cycle until a cache line boundary has been reached whether the cache is enabled or not. If the target is not cacheable, the MWI access cycle does not prevent the execution of Disconnect with termination at any time.

> The assertion of the SERR# or the PERR# signal line does not affect the execution of the Disconnect termination for other reasons.

Execution of *Disconnect termination* does not affect the central arbiter because it does not monitor the associated signal line. If the request for Disconnect with data termination occurs when the IRDY# signal line is asserted and the FRAME# signal line is deasserted (last access, see Figure 8-9), then data is accessed and the PCI bus master is not required to deassert the associated REQ# signal line. Otherwise, a request for Disconnect with data termination, when the FRAME# signal line is asserted (see Figure 8-8), or a Disconnect without data, requires the PCI bus master to deassert the associated REQ# signal line.

A Disconnect termination has no effect on a PCI bus master obtaining or retaining the Lock Function and therefore keeping a target locked.

Once Disconnect termination is requested, the TRDY#, DEVSEL#, and STOP# signal lines cannot change state until Completion termination occurs. At Completion termination, the DEVSEL# and STOP# (and TRDY# if Disconnect with data) signal lines are deasserted simultaneously with the deassertion of the IRDY# signal line.

DISCONNECT WITH DATA ACCESS

Figures 8-8 and 8-9 outline the different ways a Disconnect with data termination is executed. A Disconnect with data termination is requested when the STOP# signal line is first asserted in the access cycle in which the TRDY# signal line is asserted. The termination request indicates that the associated data is the last to be accessed at this time. After the STOP# signal line is asserted it remains asserted until the completion of the access cycle.

When the STOP# signal line is first asserted to request a Disconnect with data termination it must be simultaneous with the assertion of the TRDY# signal line. If the STOP# signal line is asserted prior to the assertion of the TRDY# signal line, either a retry or Disconnect without data termination is executed. (All of the above assume that the DEVSEL# signal line was asserted.)

In Figure 8-8, a Disconnect with data termination request occurs when the FRAME# signal line is asserted. The assertion of the TRDY# and STOP# signal lines indicates that the present access is the last access of data for this cycle. The Disconnect with data termination request causes the PCI bus master to immediately deassert the FRAME# signal line and asserts the IRDY# signal line (if not already asserted) when it is ready to complete the access. The deasserted

FRAME# signal line and asserted IRDY# signal line causes the IRDY#, TRDY#, STOP#, and DEVSEL# signal lines to be immediately deasserted. Data is accessed when the TRDY# and IRDY# signal line are both asserted. The access cycle is subsequently completed when the FRAME# and IRDY# signal lines are both deasserted.

In Figure 8-8, the FRAME# signal line was immediately deasserted. Due to the protocol of the IRDY# and FRAME# signal lines, the FRAME# signal line cannot be deasserted until the IRDY# signal line is asserted. The IRDY# signal line cannot be asserted until the PCI bus master is ready to access the data; consequently, the FRAME# signal line may not be immediately deasserted.

Figure 8-9 outlines Disconnect with data termination when the FRAME# signal line is deasserted prior to the assertion of the TRDY# and STOP# signal lines. By definition, the IRDY# signal line will have been asserted when the FRAME# signal line was deasserted. The deasserted FRAME# and asserted IRDY# signal lines cause the IRDY#, TRDY#, STOP#, and DEVSEL# signal lines to be immediately deasserted. Data is accessed when the TRDY# and IRDY# signal line are both asserted. The access cycle is completed when the FRAME# and IRDY# signal lines are both deasserted.

A Disconnect with data termination indicates that the bus and target are properly operating, but additional data cannot be accessed at this time.

If the 64 data bit access cycle (REQ64# signal line asserted) completes with Disconnect with data termination during the initial microaccess or Disconnect without data termination during the first subsequent microaccess, only the lower four bytes of the eight bytes (QWORD) of the 64 data bits has been accessed. The PCI bus master must subsequently execute an access cycle as a 32 data bit PCI bus master (REQ64# signal line deasserted) to access the upper four bytes of the "original" eight bytes (QWORD).

When the SERR# signal line is asserted by the target to indicate an address parity error on the AD, C/BE#, PAR, and PAR64 signal lines, the target cannot request a Disconnect with data termination due to this address parity error. A Disconnect with data termination can occur for other reasons, such as the bus and target are properly operating, but additional data cannot be accessed at this time. The PCI bus master cannot assert the SERR# signal line to report a Disconnect with data termination of an access cycle. The PERR# signal line can be asserted for a data parity error that occurs with a Disconnect with data termination because data was accessed. A target may execute a Disconnect with data termination for a data parity error occurring in the present or a previous microaccess.

DISCONNECT WITHOUT DATA ACCESS

As previously discussed, a Disconnect termination can occur without data being simultaneously accessed. For example, in a BURST access cycle data can be successfully accessed prior to the STOP# signal line being asserted. The cycle is terminated without the simultaneous access of data when the STOP# and DEVSEL# signal lines are both asserted, and the TRDY# signal line is deasserted. This type of cycle termination, Disconnect termination without data, completes in the same fashion as outlined for the Retry termination. The assertion of the DEVSEL# signal line when a Disconnect without data termination is requested distinguishes it from a Target Abort termination request.

A Disconnect without data termination indicates that the bus and target are operating properly, but data cannot be accessed at this time.

If the 64 data bit access cycle (REQ64# signal line asserted) completes with Disconnect with data termination during the initial microaccess or Disconnect without data termination during the first subsequent microaccess, only the lower four bytes of the eight bytes (QWORD) of the 64 data bits has been accessed. The PCI bus master must subsequently execute an access cycle as a 32 data bit PCI bus master (REQ64# signal line deasserted) to access the upper four bytes of the "original" eight bytes (QWORD).

When the SERR# signal line is asserted by the target to indicate an address parity error on the AD, C/BE#, PAR, and PAR64 signal lines, the target cannot request a Disconnect with data termination due to this address parity error. A Disconnect with data termination can occur for other reasons, such as the bus and target are properly operating, but additional data cannot be accessed at this time. The PCI bus master cannot assert the SERR# signal line to report a Disconnect with data termination of an access cycle. The PERR# signal line cannot be asserted for a data parity error that occurs with a Disconnect without data termination because no data was accessed. A target may execute a Disconnect without data termination for a data parity error occurring in the present or a previous microaccess.

DISCONNECT TERMINATION OF SPECIAL CYCLES

The special cycle does not address a specific target, so Disconnect termination does not apply to this cycle.

DISCONNECT TERMINATION OF INTERRUPT ACKNOWLEDGE CYCLES

The protocol for a Disconnect termination of an interrupt acknowledge cycle is the same as a Disconnect termination for a read access cycle. The PCI bus master is the HOST/BRIDGE and the target is the PCI bus resource that contains the interrupt controller.

TARGET ABORT TERMINATION OF ACCESS CYCLES

The Target Abort termination can only occur after the DEVSEL# signal line has been asserted for at least one CLK signal line period (see Figures 8-10 and 8-11). If the DEVSEL# signal line has not been asserted, a Master Abort termination will have occurred. Target Abort termination is requested by the target when the STOP# signal line is asserted and the DEVSEL# signal line is deasserted. Target Abort termination can be requested after data has or has not been accessed. Target Abort termination request occurs without the simultaneous access of data (i.e., the TRDY# signal line must be asserted). This type of termination also indicates to the PCI bus master that the target cannot support the access requested for the related address and *no* further accesses of the (command) type with the same address should be attempted by the present PCI bus master. In order to distinguish the Target Abort termination from a retry or Disconnect without data terminations, the DEVSEL# signal line must be deasserted when the STOP# signal line is asserted. Once Target Abort termination is requested, no other termination occurs except for Completion termination.

As discussed above, the present PCI bus master that was executing an access cycle when a Target Abort termination occurs should not repeat the access (same COMMAND type) to the same address (i.e. target). The present PCI bus master can access the target with the same address if a different COMMAND type is used Target Abort termination does not affect accesses to the same target by other PCI bus masters. Other PCI bus masters may access this address (i.e. target) because they may not have monitored the Target Abort termination.

The Target Abort termination is appropriate for the following bus cycle situations (this is not a conclusive list; other situations are possible):

- The target must execute a Target Abort termination if it is broken or it detected a fatal error.

- The target must execute a Target Abort termination when the byte lane pattern in the C/BE# signal line during the DATA PHASE (of a SINGLE access cycle or initial microaccess of a BURST access cycle) does not "match" the AD[01::00] signal lines during the ADDRESS PHASE.

- If the target cannot support the non-continuous byte lanes enabled by the PCI bus master, it must execute a Target Abort termination.

- A Target Abort termination may be executed as part of the reporting protocol for an address parity error.

- A Target Abort termination may be executed as part of the reporting protocol for a data parity error in a previous microaccess.

In Figure 8-10, the FRAME# signal is asserted when a Target Abort termination is requested by the target. The Target Abort termination request causes the FRAME# and IRDY# signal lines to be immediately deasserted and asserted (if not already asserted), respectively. The deasserted FRAME# and asserted IRDY# signal lines cause the IRDY# and STOP# signal lines to be deasserted. The cycle is completed when the FRAME# and IRDY# signal lines are both deasserted.

In Figure 8-11, the FRAME# signal line is deasserted and the IRDY# signal line is asserted when the Target Abort termination is requested. The IRDY#, and STOP# signal lines are subsequently deasserted. The cycle is completed when the FRAME# and IRDY# signal lines are both deasserted.

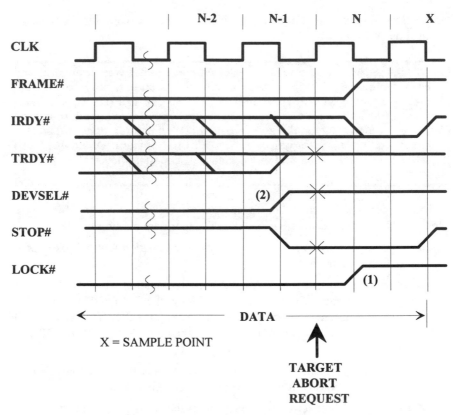

NOTE: (1) LOCK MASTER IS RELINGUISHES LOCK FUNCTION
         OR PCI BUS MASTER CANNOT BECOME LOCK
         MASTER IF A TARGET ABORT TERMINATION OCCURS
    (2) TO AVOID A MASTER ABORT TERMINATION DEVSEL#
         MUST BE ASSERTED BY THE FOURTH RISING EDGE OF CLK
         AFTER FRAME# IS SAMPLED ASSERTED (FIFTH RISING EDGE
         FOR DUAL ADDRESS)

Figure 8-10: Target Abort Termination

In both Figures 8-10 and 8-11, the TRDY# signal may be asserted, or may
not. The data is not considered valid. Consequently, the accessing of
data during a Target Abort termination is not important. The completion
of a bus cycle with Target Abort termination is dependent on the logical
states of DEVSEL#, STOP#, and IRDY# signal lines.

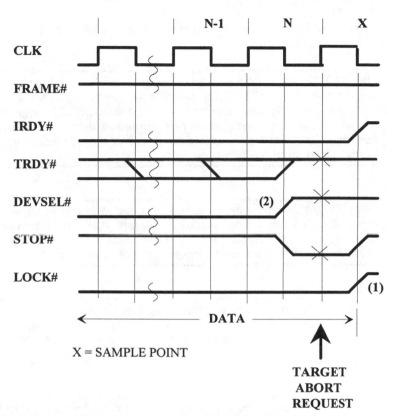

X = SAMPLE POINT

TARGET
ABORT
REQUEST

NOTE: (1) LOCK MASTER IS RELINGUISHES LOCK FUNCTION
OR PCI BUS MASTER CANNOT BECOME LOCK
MASTER IF A TARGET ABORT TERMINATION OCCURS
(2) TO AVOID A MASTER ABORT TERMINATION DEVSEL#
MUST BE ASSERTED BY THE FOURTH RISING EDGE OF CLK
AFTER FRAME# IS SAMPLED ASSERTED (FIFTH RISING EDGE
FOR DUAL ADDRESS)

Figure 8-11: Target Abort Termination

In the above paragraphs the word *immediate* indicates the preferred protocol for the PCI bus master to complete the access cycle. However, the PCI bus master may complete the access cycle later.

When a target terminates an access cycle with a Target Abort termination, the Signaled Target Abort bit must be set in its Status Register. When the PCI bus master detects a Target Abort termination, it must set the Received Target Abort bit in its Status Register.

The STOP# signal line can be asserted simultaneous or prior to the deassertion of the DEVSEL# signal line. If the STOP# signal line is asserted prior to the deassertion of the DEVSEL# signal line, a Disconnect or Retry termination is executed. If the STOP# signal line is asserted simultaneous with the deassertion of the DEVSEL# signal line, a Target Abort termination is executed.

Once Target Abort termination is requested, the DEVSEL# and STOP# signal lines cannot change state until Completion termination occurs. At Completion termination the STOP# signal line is deasserted simultaneously with the deassertion of the IRDY# signal line.

For a read access cycle, a Target Abort termination indicates that any data read (or interrupt acknowledge vector) may be invalid. For a write access it indicates that the data may not have been successfully written into the target.

Execution of Target Abort termination does not affect the central arbiter, because it does not monitor the associated signal lines. Target Abort termination forces the PCI bus master to deassert the associated REQ# signal line.

A PCI bus master cannot become Lock master and lock a target when a Target Abort termination is executed during the read access cycle which the PCI bus master is using to lock the target. The LOCK# signal line is immediately deasserted.

If the Lock master is accessing the locked target and a Target Abort termination occurs, the Lock master is required to relinquish the Lock Function. The LOCK# signal line is immediately deasserted and the target is immediately unlocked. If a non-Lock master accesses the locked target, the execution of a Target Abort termination does not force relinquishing of the Lock Function by the Lock master or the unlocking of the target.

When the SERR# signal line is asserted by the target to indicate an address parity error on the AD, C/BE#, PAR, and PAR64 signal lines, the target can request a Target Abort termination due to this address parity error. The PCI bus master may assert the SERR# signal line to report a Target Abort of an access cycle if there is no other mechanism to do so. The PERR# signal line cannot be asserted when a data parity occurs with a Target Abort termination because no data was accessed. A target may execute a Target Abort termination for a data parity error occurring in the present or a previous microaccess.

TARGET ABORT TERMINATION OF SPECIAL CYCLES

The special cycle does not address a specific target, so Target Abort termination does not apply to this cycle.

TARGET ABORT TERMINATION OF INTERRUPT ACKNOWLEDGE CYCLES

The protocol for a Target Abort termination of an interrupt acknowledge cycle is the same as a Target Abort termination for a read access cycle. The PCI bus master is the HOST/PCI BRIDGE and the target is the PCI bus resource that contains the interrupt controller.

CHAPTER 9

BUS OWNERSHIP

This chapter consists of the following subchapters:

9.0   Arbitration Protocol
9.1   Parking
9.2   Change of Bus Ownership

9.0   ARBITRATION PROTOCOL

INTRODUCTION

All PCI resources that can potentially own the bus are defined as PCI bus masters. Only one PCI bus master can own the bus at a time, controlling some of the signal lines during and between bus cycles that it is executing. Of special note is the LOCK# signal line, which can be owned by a PCI bus master that presently does not own the bus. Arbitration must occur among all of the PCI bus masters that want to own the bus through the use of the central arbiter. The potential PCI bus masters are individually linked to the central arbiter by individual Request (REQ#) and Grant (GNT#) signal lines. It is the responsibility of the central arbiter to determine which PCI resource will become the PCI bus master.

It must be noted that a PCI bus master only asserts its associated REQ# signal line when it is ready to immediately begin a bus cycle. Once its associated GNT# signal line is asserted the PCI bus master must assert the FRAME# signal line as soon as possible to begin the bus cycle. If the asserted GNT# signal line is deasserted prior to the assertion of the FRAME# signal line, the PCI bus master looses bus ownership and must rearbitrate.

The central arbiter must determine whether the present PCI bus master will retain the bus after the present bus cycle is completed, whether the bus will be awarded to another PCI resource, whether the Lock master will be awarded complete bus lock, and where the bus will be parked. See Chapters 4 and 6 for more Lock master information. See *Subchapter 9.1: Parking* for more park information.

The protocol for distinguishing the REQ# and GNT# signal lines of different PCI bus masters is to append a letter in parentheses. Example REQ#(A) is the request signal line for the PCI bus master labeled A.

The REQ# signal lines are individually routed point-to-point between a PCI resource and the central arbiter. The assertion and deassertion of a REQ# signal line is synchronized to the CLK signal line, and must follow the setup and hold times outlined in Chapter 12. The same considerations apply to the GNT# signal lines. The assertion and deassertion of the GNT# signal lines will be outlined in the figures in this chapter because of their relationship to bus cycle operation.

The PCI bus specification does not establish the exact protocol for the central arbiter to grant bus ownership. It does require the central arbiter to support a fairness algorithm in order to establish a known bus ownership latency for each PCI bus master (see Latency in Chapter 14 for more information).

General bus arbitration considerations have been documented in other texts and specifications for other buses. In its simplest form, the central arbiter should grant bus ownership on a rotating basis. For example, presume that the platform has three potential PCI bus masters (A, B, and C). The central arbiter will first grant the bus to (A) if it is requesting the bus. After (A) uses the bus or if (A) had not requested the bus, the central arbiter will grant it to (B). After (B) uses the bus or if (A) or (B) had not requested the bus, the central arbiter will grant it to (C). After the central arbiter has given each bus master the chance to own the bus the process begins again with (A).

Another simple arbitration protocol is for the bus masters to be assigned a priority. Whenever two bus masters simultaneously request the bus, the one with higher priority is granted the bus. To prevent always granting the bus to the bus master with higher priority and starving the other bus masters (almost no other bus grants), central arbiters that follow this protocol cannot again grant the bus to the highest priority bus master until all other bus masters have been serviced, or a minimum amount of time has elapsed.

There are many other protocols that can be implemented; the important considerations are: to not starve any bus master (excessively long latency), to establish a maximum time period from a bus request to bus grant for a specific bus master (latency guaranteed), and the granting of bus ownership to a specific PCI bus master (to support the previous two items) independent of other requests (fairness).

A central arbiter on a PCI bus must consider a few other things: first, if a low priority PCI bus master has locked a target that is also accessed by a high priority PCI bus master, accesses by the high priority PCI bus master will end with an excessive amount of Retry terminations. Second, if the cache controller in the HOST PCI/BRIDGE needs to write a cache line (cache hit to a modified/valid cache line in write-back cache) or a portion of a cache line (cache hit to a valid line in a write-through cache) to PCI memory, it should be given highest priority.

This is particularly true for a write due to a cache hit to a modified/valid cache line in a write-back cache. Until the write to PCI memory is completed, it must execute a Retry termination when accessed by other PCI bus masters. In order to improve platform performance, it is important to minimize Retry terminations.

A strict priority type of arbitration algorithm may lend to livelock conditions (see *Chapter 2: PCI System Architectural Overview*) which will decrease performance. Other arbitration protocols may lead to deadlock conditions (see Chapter 2) which are fatal to the system.

Other elements of the architecture must also be considered when determining an arbitration algorithm. For example, a pending snoop write-back access will cause a memory resource to issue Retry termination until the actual write-back occurs. Consequently, the cache controller should be given highest priority by the central arbiter.

The platform designer must select an algorithm that takes into consideration these lock situations.

9.1 PARKING

The PCI bus has an attribute that is unique relative to other buses. Other buses traditionally have not considered the secondary affects of floating signal lines. For example, the ISA bus traditionally lets the address signal lines float between bus cycles. Sometimes the address buffers have floated into unstable oscillations; consequently, some of the better ISA platforms have added pull-up resistors to the address signal lines. The PCI bus specification took a very proactive approach to this situation. Between PCI bus cycles the signal lines are either actively driven at all times by a single resource, are driven to a logical "1" by pull-up resistors on the platform, or are driven by a PCI bus master.

Chapter 6 explains the protocol for driving and tri-stating the signal lines during bus cycles. The information contained in the current section relates only to signal line protocol between the bus cycles.

Between bus cycles, the signal lines that are driven by a single resource or a pull-up resistor are not floating, by definition. The signal lines that can potentially float during the exchange of bus ownership are AD[31::0], C/BE#[3::0], and PAR signal lines. To limit the amount of float time, a PCI bus master drives these signal lines to a stable level.

At the completion of a bus cycle, the present PCI bus master will continue to drive the AD[31::0], C/BE#[3::0], FRAME#, IRDY#, and PAR signal lines if the associated GNT# signal line is asserted. If the associated REQ# signal line is asserted, by definition the PCI bus master is between bus cycles. If the associated REQ# signal line is deasserted, by definition the PCI bus master is defined as the Park master. If the central arbiter has deasserted all GNT# signal lines, it is the responsibility of the central arbiter to act as a Park master. A Park master is simply any resource that is actively driving the AD[31::0], C/BE#[3::0], and PAR signal lines to a stable level. The Park master will tri-state and rely on pull-up resistors to drive the FRAME# and IRDY# signal lines to logical "1". As outlined in Figure 9-3, a Park master will immediately tri-state the aforementioned signal lines when the associated GNT# signal line is deasserted.

A Park master is defined as only a 32 data bit resource; consequently, the signal lines associated with 64 data bits (AD[63::32], C/BE#[7::4], REQ64#, and PAR64 signal lines) are not driven by the Park master. These signal lines are driven to a logical "1" level by pull-up resistors when the bus is parked. The tri-stating and driving protocol of the 64 data bit signal lines AD[63::32], C/BE#[7::4], REQ64#, and PAR64 signal lines is the same as the AD[31::0], C/BE#[3::0], FRAME#, and PAR signal lines, respectively.

> A PCI resource must not request to become Park master by asserting its REQ# signal line. When a PCI resource asserts its REQ# signal line, it must have the intention to begin a bus cycle once OWNERSHIP ACHIEVED has occurred.

> When the central arbiter parks the bus at a PCI bus master, the latter must drive the AD[31::0] and C/BE#[3::0] signal lines to a stable level within eight (two to three is recommended) CLK signal line periods after the GNT# signal line is asserted. The PCI bus master must drive the PAR signal line to a stable level within nine (three to four is recommended) CLK signal line periods after the GNT# signal line is asserted.

> The central arbiter should park the bus with the present PCI bus master. This allows the present PCI bus master to continue with additional bus cycles without arbitration when no other PCI bus resource is requesting bus ownership.

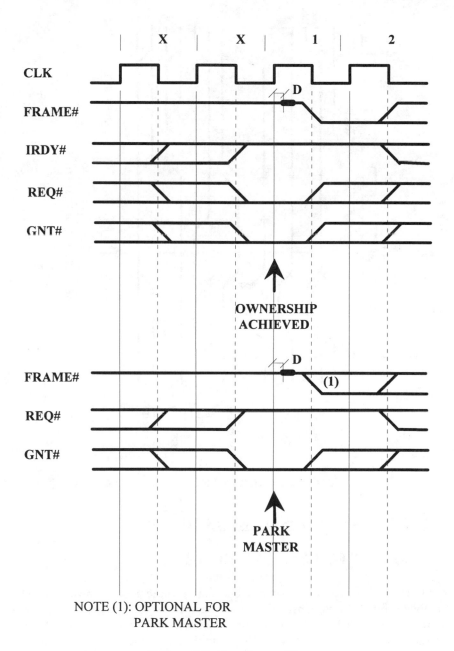

NOTE (1): OPTIONAL FOR
         PARK MASTER

Figure 9-1: Bus Ownership

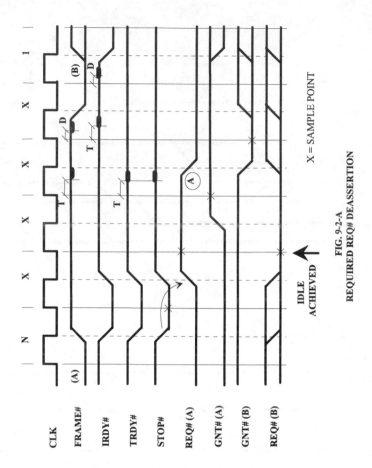

Figure 9-2-A: Required REQ# Deassertion

9.2   CHANGE OF BUS OWNERSHIP

REQUEST FOR BUS OWNERSHIP

There are two methods by which a bus master can request bus ownership. One method is for a PCI bus master to assert the associated REQ# signal line and wait until the associated GNT# signal line is asserted to become the next PCI bus master (new PCI Bus Master). The central arbiter must decide which PCI resource becomes the next PCI bus master. The second method is for the PCI bus master that has been parked (Park master) to simply begin the bus cycle. These two methods are outlined in the subsequent text.

Prior to the discussion of the new PCI Bus Master and Park master, other considerations about bus ownership must be reviewed. A PCI resource is considered a PCI bus master between bus cycles when FRAME# and IRDY# signal line are both deasserted and has its associated REQ# and GNT# signal lines are asserted. When the central arbiter wants to award the bus to another resource it must deassert the GNT# signal line of the present PCI bus master. If the PCI bus master has already asserted the FRAME# and is executing a bus cycle when its associated GNT# signal line is deasserted, the protocol outlined for a Completion with Timeout termination applies (see *Chapter 8: Master and Target Termination*, for details). If the PCI bus master is between bus cycles (IDLE PHASES) when the GNT# signal line is deasserted, the protocol outlined in Figure 9-3 for a Park master applies. The only difference is that some of the signal lines must be tri-stated by the PCI bus master when the associated GNT# signal line is deasserted. The FRAME# and IRDY# must be tri-stated by the PCI bus master; for a Park master, these signal lines are already tri-stated and are driven to logical "1" by pull-up resistors. Also, for a 64 data bit PCI bus master, the REQ64#, AD[63::32], C/BE#[7::4], and PAR64 signal lines must be tri-stated; for a Park master, these signal lines are already tri-stated and are driven to logical "1" by pull-up resistors.

Any PCI bus master can assert its REQ# signal line whenever it wishes to own the bus. It is the responsibility of the central arbiter to determine which PCI bus master is awarded the bus. Once the REQ# signal line is asserted, it can be deasserted at any time. When the REQ# and GNT# signal lines are both asserted, and FRAME# and IRDY# signal lines are both deasserted (OWNERSHIP ACHIEVED), the new PCI bus master can begin the bus cycle with the assertion of the FRAME# signal line (see Figure 9-1). After OWNERSHIP ACHIEVED has occurred, the GNT# and REQ# signal lines can be deasserted simultaneously with the assertion of the FRAME# signal line. The bus cycle completes according to the Completion with Timeout termination protocol if the GNT# signal line is deasserted during the bus cycle. After completion of the bus cycle, the continued assertion of the GNT# and REQ# signal lines allows the bus master to execute an additional cycle. After the completion of a bus cycle, the continued assertion of the GNT# signal line and deassertion of the REQ# signal line (during the bus cycle) simply turns the PCI bus master into a Park master.

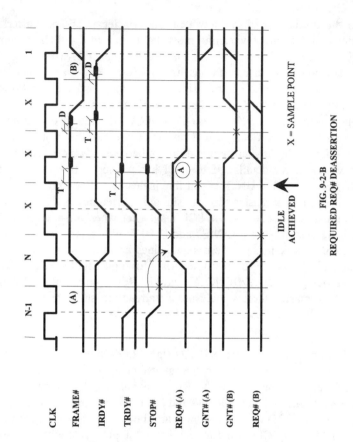

Figure 9-2-B: Required REQ# Deassertion

The determination of which PCI resource becomes PCI bus master or Park master is determined entirely by the central arbiter. The PCI bus specification does not specify a protocol for the central arbiter to award bus ownership.

The deassertion of the REQ# signal line does not require the associated GNT# signal line to be deasserted.

The PCI bus master can assert and deassert the REQ# signal line at any time. The only situation where an REQ# signal line *must* be deasserted is when a PCI bus master's cycle is terminated with a Retry, Disconnect, or Target Abort termination. These bus cycle terminations are all partly identified by the assertion of the STOP# signal line. The execution of one these terminations requires that the associated REQ# signal line to be deasserted, as outlined in the following section.

There is one exception to the protocol outlined in the above paragraph. The deassertion of the REQ# signal line is not required for a Disconnect termination if the FRAME# signal line is deasserted and the IRDY# signal line is asserted when the termination is requested. See Chapter 8 for more information.

The central arbiter does not monitor the PCI bus signal lines other than the REQ#, FRAME#, and IRDY# signal lines. There is no method for the central arbiter to determine that one of these terminations has been executed. In order to prevent a PCI bus master from continuing to access a target that caused the termination and provide bus ownership by other PCI bus masters, the bus must be granted to another PCI bus master that has requested the bus. In order to grant the bus to another PCI bus master the present PCI bus master must relinquish the bus. As shown in Figures 9-2-A to 9-2-C, the REQ#(A) is immediately deasserted when the STOP# signal line is sampled deasserted and the central arbiter responds with the deassertion of the GNT#(A) signal line. As explained later, when IDLE ACHIEVED occurs prior to or simultaneously with the deassertion of the GNT#(A) signal line, the GNT#(B) signal line cannot be asserted until one CLK signal line period later (see Figures 9-2-A and 9-2-B). As explained later, when IDLE ACHIEVED occurs after the deassertion of the GNT#(A) signal line the GNT#(B) signal line can be simultaneously asserted (see Figure 9-2-C). The protocol (Figures 9-2-A to 9-2-C) for the REQ# signal lines when a Retry, Disconnect or Target Abort Termination occurs is summarized as follows:

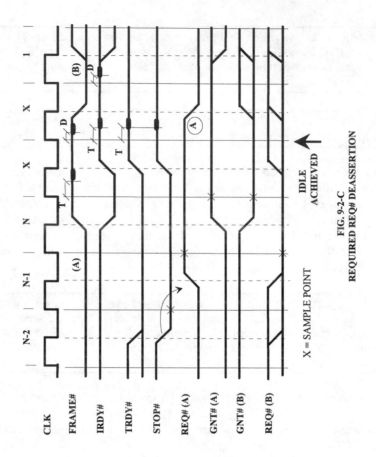

Figure 9-2-C: Required REQ# Deassertion

- REQ# signal line is asserted immediately when the STOP# signal line is sampled asserted.

- REQ# (A) signal line must remain deasserted for a minimum of two CLK signal line periods. If IDLE ACHIEVED has not occurred within the two CLK signal line periods, then the REQ# signal remains deasserted until IDLE Achieved has occurred (see Figure 9-2-C).

- PCI bus master (A) can reassert REQ# (A) after the conditions in the above bullet have been met as noted by Point A (Circle A in Figures 9-2-A to 9-2-C).

NEW PCI BUS MASTER

GRANT OF BUS OWNERSHIP

Once the arbiter has determined that another PCI resource will be awarded bus ownership, the termination of the present bus ownership must be accomplished. When the present bus owner is simply the a Park master that is not executing a bus cycle, termination of bus ownership is immediate. The GNT# signal line for the Park master is deasserted and the GNT# signal line for the new PCI bus owner is asserted one CLK signal line period later. If the present PCI bus master is executing a bus cycle, the central arbiter requests it to relinquish bus ownership at the end of the bus cycle by deasserting the associated GNT# signal line. The bus cycle completes with appropriate termination. See Chapter 8 for details.

Figure 9-3 outlines how PCI bus master (B) exchanges bus ownership with PCI bus master (A) (Park master) after IDLE ACHIEVED occurs (FRAME# and IRDY# signal lines both deasserted). To prevent signal line contention, the GNT# (A) signal line must be deasserted a minimum of one CLK signal line period prior to the assertion of the GNT# (B) signal line for new bus owner once IDLE is achieved. The deassertion of the GNT# (A) signal line forces the Park master to immediately tri-state the C/BE#[3::0], AD [31::0], and PAR signal lines. The assertion of the GNT# (B) signal line indicates to the PCI bus master (B) that it can begin a bus cycle.

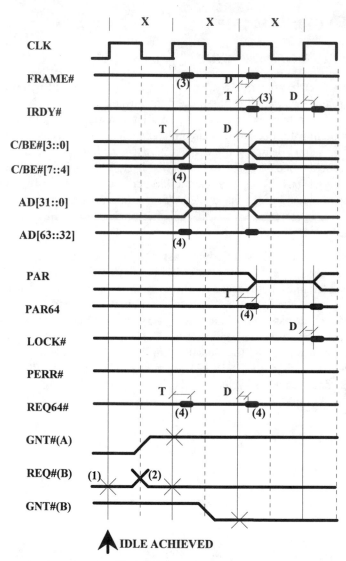

Figure 9-3: Bus Ownership Change

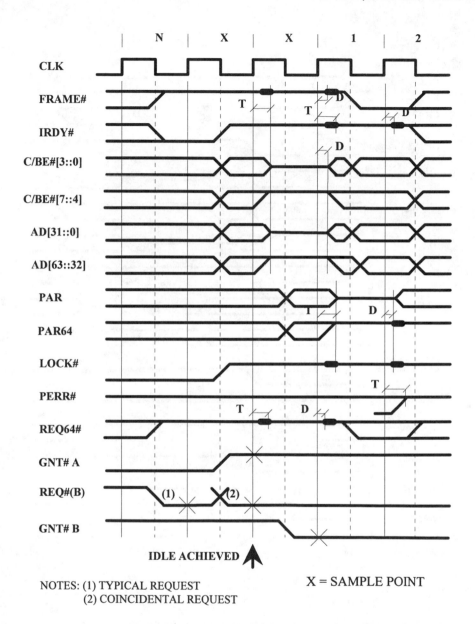

Figure 9-4: Bus Ownership Change, Previous Cycle Was a Write

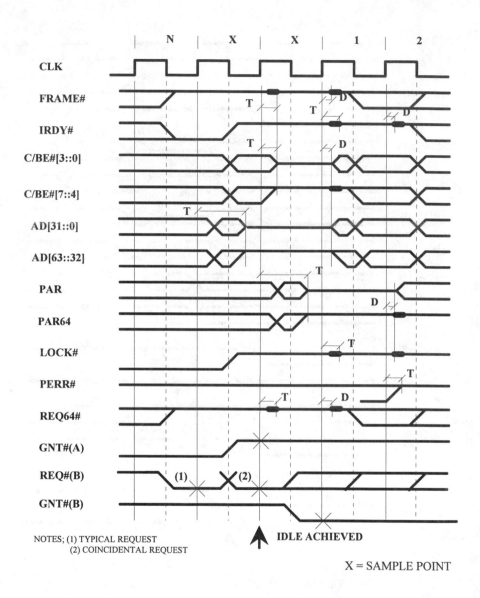

Figure 9-5: Bus Ownership Change, Previous Cycle Was a Read

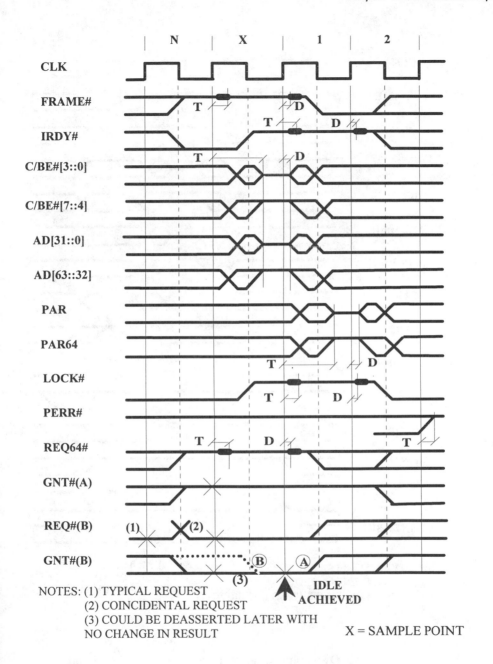

NOTES: (1) TYPICAL REQUEST
(2) COINCIDENTAL REQUEST
(3) COULD BE DEASSERTED LATER WITH
NO CHANGE IN RESULT

X = SAMPLE POINT

Figure 9-6: Bus Ownership Change, Previous Cycle Was a Write

359

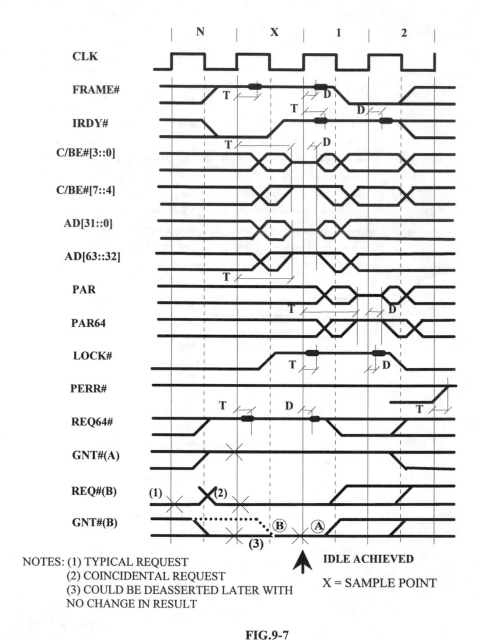

FIG.9-7

Figure 9-7: Bus Ownership Change, Previous Cycle Was a Read

The PCI bus master (B) is not required to immediately drive the C/BE#[3::0], AD[31::0], and PAR signal lines as outlined above, although PCI bus master (A) immediately floats them. PCI bus master (B) must assert the FRAME# signal line by the sixteenth CLK signal line rising edge after OWNERSHIP ACHIEVED (the appropriate REQ# and GNTx# signal lines both asserted) has occurred. See further information at the end of this section.

When the bus is parked at a 32 data bit Park master, the AD[63::32], C/BE#[7::4], and PAR64 signal lines are driven to a logical "1" by pull-up resistors. Similarly, when the bus is awarded to a new 32 data bit PCI bus master (PCI bus master (B) in this example), these signal lines remain at logical "1" by pull-up resistors. If the bus is awarded to a 64 data bit PCI bus master, these signal lines could optionally be driven to a logical "1" by the PCI bus master (B) as outlined in Figure 9-3.

The protocol outlined above for Figure 9-3 also applies when the central arbiter is simply changing the Park master from PCI bus master (A) to PCI bus master (B).

Figures 9-4 to 9-7 outline how PCI bus master (B) changes bus ownership with PCI bus master (A) immediately after PCI bus master (A) has completed a bus cycle. The protocol for signal line tri-stating and driving relative to the GNT# signal lines is the same as discussed for Figure 9-3. The distinction between Figures 9-4 and 9-5 and Figures 9-6 and 9-7 is the staggering of the deassertion and assertion of the GNT# (A) and GNT# (B) signal lines, respectively.

In Figures 9-4 and 9-5, bus ownership is removed (GNT# (A) signal line is deasserted) simultaneously when IDLE ACHIEVED has occurred (FRAME# and IRDY# signal lines both deasserted). To prevent signal line contention, the bus protocol requires the central arbiter to insert one CLK signal line period between the deassertion and assertion of the GNT# (A) and GNT# (B) signal lines, respectively. When the previous bus cycle is a write, the target tri-states the PERR# signal line indicating the completion of the access cycle; the line is not driven by PCI bus master (A) (see Figure 9-4). When the previous bus cycle is a read, the target will tri-state the AD, PAR, and PAR64 signal lines indicating the completion of the access cycle; the lines are not driven by PCI bus master (A) reflective of the change of bus ownership (see Figure 9-5). In both cases, the driving of the PERR# signal line by PCI bus master (B) or the target is reflective of the forthcoming cycle and not the change of bus ownership. The protocol for asserting the GNT# (B) signal line is the same if IDLE ACHIEVED (FRAME# and IRDY# signal lines deasserted) occurred prior to the deassertion of the GNT# (A) signal line.

In Figures 9-6 and 9-7 bus ownership is removed (GNT#(A) signal line is deasserted) prior to IDLE ACHIEVED (FRAME# and IRDY# signal lines deasserted) occurring In the situations outlined in Figures 9-4 to 9-5 the PCI bus master determines when to tri-state and drive the signal lines relative to IDLE ACHIEVED occurring and the value of the GNT# signal lines. The PCI bus master that is relinquishing bus ownership tri-states the signal lines when the associated GNT# signal line is deasserted and IDLE ACHIEVED has occurred. The PCI bus master that will become the new bus owner begins driving the signal lines when IDLE ACHIEVED occurs and the associated GNT# signal line is asserted. Fig. 9-6 and 9-7 outline situations when prior to IDLE ACHIEVED occurring the GNT#(A) and GNT#(B) signal lines are deasserted and asserted, respectively. PCI bus master (A) will implement a different protocol than in the situations outlined in Figures 9-4 to 9-5. The deassertion of the GNT#(A) prior to IDLE ACHIEVED occurring allows PCI bus master (A) to anticipate tri-stating the signal lines relative to the completion of the bus cycle. At the completion of the bus cycle PCI bus master (A) can begin tri-stating the signal lines a CLK signal line period earlier than in Figures 9-4 to 9-5. The central arbiter is aware that it deasserted GNT#(A) prior to IDLE ACHIEVED occurring; consequently, it will assert the GNT#(B) signal line prior to IDLE ACHIEVED occurring. The net result is that a one CLK signal line period between the deassertion of the GNT#(A) signal line and the assertion of the GNT# (B) signal line is not required; consequently, the change of bus ownership is quicker.

Figures 9-6 and 9-7 exemplify a couple of important protocols relative to the GNT# signal line. First, when the GNT# signal line is deasserted prior to IDLE ACHIEVED (FRAME# and IRDY# signal lines deasserted) occurring (GNT# (A) in this example) the GNT# signal line can be asserted (GNT# (B) in this example) immediately or at Point B (Circle B in Figures 9-6 and 9-7. The resulting bus cycle is the same for either point where the GNT# (B) signal line is asserted. Second, when the central arbiter has granted the PCI bus to a PCI resource it does not know, whether the PCI resource had begun a bus cycle until the FRAME# signal line is asserted. In Figures 9-6 and 9-7, the PCI resource samples the GNT# (B) signal line is asserted at Point A (Circle A) and IDLE ACHIEVED (FRAME# and IRDY# signal lines) occurred; subsequently, it becomes PCI bus master (B) by asserting the FRAME# signal line. The central arbiter can deassert the GNT# signal line at any time (At Point A - Circle A in Figures 9-6 and 9-7). If the central arbiter deasserts a GNT# signal line when the bus is in an IDLE PHASE, it must wait one CLK signal line period before asserting another GNT# signal line for another PCI bus master in case the FRAME# signal line is asserted. If the FRAME# signal line is asserted, the GNT# signal line can not grant the bus to another PCI bus master.

The new PCI bus master does not have to begin driving the signal lines or the bus cycle (FRAME# signal line asserted) immediately after OWNERSHIP ACHIEVED has occurred. The PCI bus master must drive the signal lines by the sixteenth CLK signal rising edge after OWNERSHIP ACHIEVED (the appropriate REQx# and GNTx# signal line is asserted) occurred. Otherwise, the central arbiter may declare the PCI bus master "dead" and never grant it the bus. Prior to the assertion of the FRAME# signal line, the output buffers of the PCI bus master can be enabled simultaneously or in a sequential fashion using ADDRESS/DATA STEPPING or pre-driving.

When the central arbiter grants the bus at a new PCI bus master that requested it, the latter must drive the AD[31..0] and C/BE#[3..0] signal lines to a stable level within eight (two to three is recommended) CLK signal line periods after the GNT# signal line is asserted. The PCI bus master must drive the PAR signal line to a stable level within nine (three to four is recommended) CLK signal line periods after the GNT# signal line is asserted.

Prior to the assertion of the FRAME# signal line, the output buffers of the PCI bus master can be enabled in a sequential fashion using ADDRESS/DATA STEPPING or PRE-DRIVING.

CONVERSION OF PARK MASTER TO NEW PCI BUS MASTER

The PCI bus master at which the central arbiter has parked the bus is not required to assert its REQ# signal line to execute a bus cycle. By definition, a Park master is a PCI resource with its REQ# and GNT# signal lines deasserted and asserted, respectively. Once the Park master begins the bus cycle while its REQ# signal line is deasserted, it executes with the same protocol used by a PCI bus master. If, during the bus cycle its associated REQ# signal line is asserted, the Park master becomes a normal PCI bus master by definition.

If the Park master is only executing one SINGLE or one BURST bus cycle, it should not assert the REQ# signal line.

CHAPTER 10

PARITY AND BUS ERRORS

This chapter consists of the following subchapters:

10.0 INTRODUCTION

The PCI bus specification supports a limited error structure. The C/BE# and AD signal lines are protected with even parity by the PAR and PAR64 signal lines. The PERR# and SERR# signal lines are used to report parity and other errors within a platform. The level of support of these error signal lines by various PCI resources varies widely. Error information is reported in registers that can be read by the BIOS, the operating system, and application software.

> This chapter uses the phrase "the PCI bus master is the HOST/PCI BRIDGE, and the target is the PCI bus resource that contains the interrupt controller." As outlined in Chapter 2, the interrupt controller may also reside in a resource on the HOST bus not associated with the PCI bus (the HOST/LEGACY BRIDGE, for example), in the HOST/PCI BRIDGE, in the PCI/LEGACY BRIDGE, or on the LEGACY bus. The use of this phrase represents an interrupt controller in a resource on the PCI Bus 0, in the PCI/LEGACY BRIDGE, or in a resource on the LEGACY bus attached via the PCI/LEGACY BRIDGE. When the interrupt controller resides in a resource on the HOST bus, in the HOST/PCI BRIDGE, or in a resource on the LEGACY bus attached by a HOST/LEGACY BRIDGE, no interrupt acknowledge cycle is executed on PCI bus 0.

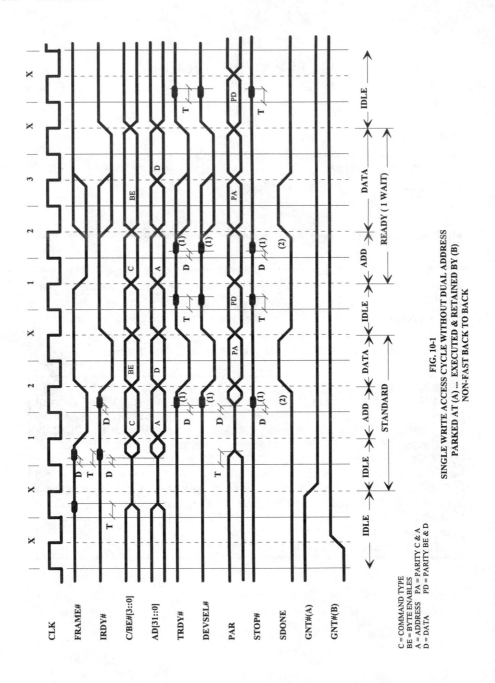

Figure 10-1: Single Write Access Cycle without DUAL ADDRESS Parked at (A), Executed and Retained by (B), Non-Fast Back-to-Back

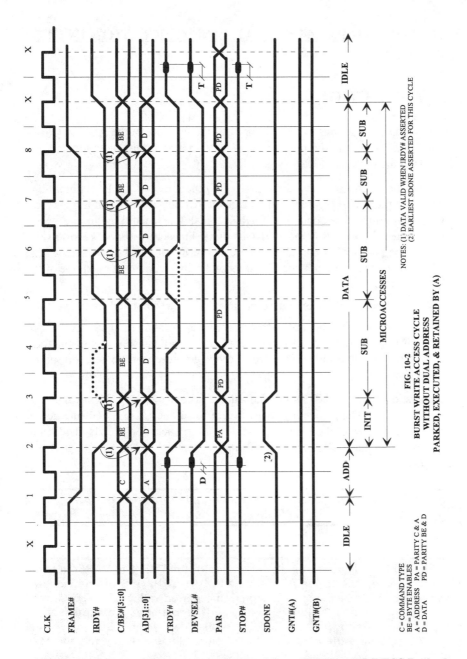

FIG. 10-2
BURST WRITE ACCESS CYCLE
WITHOUT DUAL ADDRESS
PARKED, EXECUTED, & RETAINED BY (A)

NOTES: (1) DATA VALID WHEN IRDY# ASSERTED
(2) EARLIEST SDONE ASSERTED FOR THIS CYCLE

C = COMMAND TYPE
BE = BYTE ENABLES
A = ADDRESS   PA = PARITY C & A
D = DATA   PD = PARITY BE & D

**Figure 10-2: Burst Write Access Cycle without DUAL ADDRESS Parked,
Executed, and Retained by (A)**

10.1   PAR AND PAR64 SIGNAL LINE OPERATION IN BUS CYCLES

INTRODUCTION

Parity is used on all bus cycles and protects the integrity of the AD and C/BE# signal lines. The generation of parity is not optional and must be computed and driven onto the PAR and PAR64 signal lines.

All PCI bus resources must drive parity information onto the PAR signal line according to the above protocol. All 64 data bit PCI bus masters and targets must drive parity information onto the PAR64 signal line according to the above protocol when the REQ64# and ACK64# signal lines are asserted, respectively. However, the parity does not have to be checked by all PCI bus resources. The PCI bus resources that do not check and report parity errors must meet one of the following conditions:

- Resources that are only used on the platform and not add-in cards.

- Resources that do not affect or process permanent data, e.g., video display. In other words, resources that will not cause a loss of platform integrity when a parity error occurs do not need to support parity checking.

The operation of the PAR signal line during access cycles is identical to the operation of the AD[31::0] signal lines except for a one CLK signal line period delay. The operation of the PAR64 signal line during access cycles is identical to the operation of the AD[63::32] signal lines except for a one CLK signal line period delay.

> Address parity error includes error in the address and COMMAND type. Data parity includes error in the data and byte enables.

> In the following discussions, the operation of the PAR and PAR64 signal lines are referenced to the ADDRESS and DATA PHASES. As previously mentioned, there is a one CLK signal line period delay of these signal lines relative to the AD signal lines. The AD signal lines are aligned with the ADDRESS and DATA PHASES; consequently, the use of these PHASES to define the PAR and PAR64 signal lines actually refer to the time line of the associated AD signal lines

PAR AND PAR64 SIGNAL LINE OPERATION IN ACCESS CYCLES

The PAR and PAR64 signal lines are driven by both the PCI bus master and the target. The C/BE#[3::0] and AD[31::0] signal lines are protected with even parity by the PAR signal line. Similarly, the C/BE#[7::4] and AD[63::32] signal lines are protected with even parity by the PAR64 signal line.

The existence of valid parity information on the PAR and PAR64 signal lines is dependent on the type of access cycle (read versus write) and the data size of the PCI bus master and target.

32 DATA BIT PCI BUS MASTER AND TARGET (REQ64# = DEASSERTED)

- During the ADDRESS PHASE, the PAR signal line contains valid parity information, and the target optionally checks the parity. During the DATA PHASE of a write access cycle, the PCI bus master drives valid parity onto the PAR signal line because the C/BE#[3::0] and AD[31::0] signal lines contain valid information (see Figures 10-1 and 10-2). The target optionally checks the parity. During the DATA PHASE of a read access, the PCI bus master drives the C/BE#[3::0] signal lines with byte enable information, and the target drives the AD[31::0] signal lines with valid data; consequently, it drives the PAR signal line with valid parity. The PCI bus master optionally checks parity (see Figures 10-3 and 10-4.).

> During the DATA PHASE of a read access cycle, the PCI bus master drives the byte enables onto the C/BE# [3::0] signal lines; consequently, the target generates parity for these signal lines, combines it with the parity of the AD[31::0] signal lines, and drives the PAR signal line.

- The operation of the PAR signal line between bus cycles also follows the operation of the AD[31::0] signal lines. If the PCI bus master is retaining bus ownership (REG# and GNT# both asserted) between bus cycles, it drives the PAR signal line to a stable level. If the PCI bus master does not retain bus ownership (REQ# and GNT# both deasserted), the Park master drives the PAR signal line to a stable level.

- Even parity is supported by the PAR signal line. The total number of "1"s on the AD[31::0], C/BE#[3::0], and PAR signal lines must be an even number.

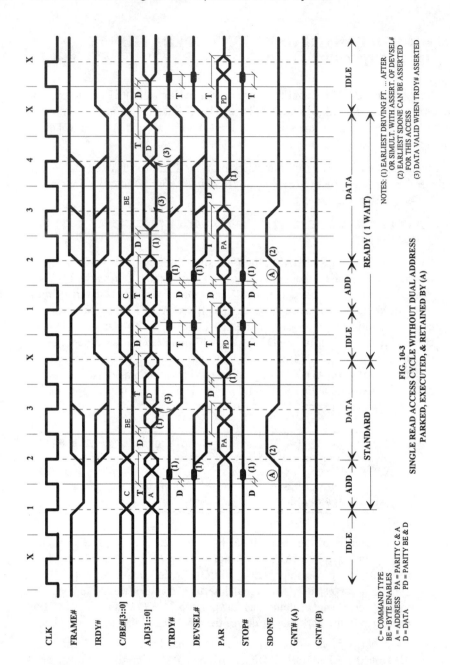

Figure 10-3: Single Read Access Cycle without DUAL ADDRESS Parked, Executed, and Retained by (A)

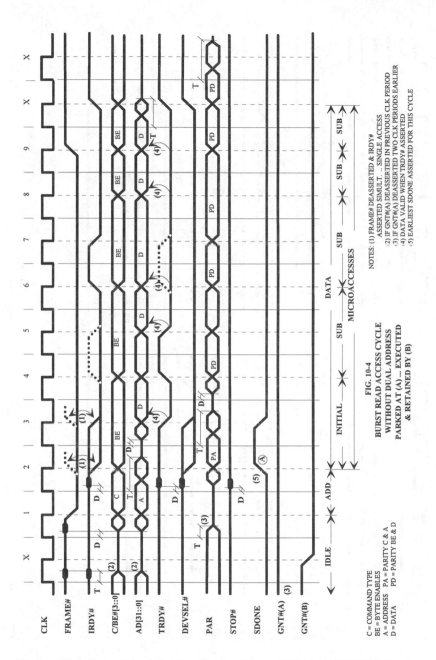

FIG. 10-4
BURST READ ACCESS CYCLE
WITHOUT DUAL ADDRESS
PARKED AT (A) ... EXECUTED
& RETAINED BY (B)

NOTES: (1) FRAME# DEASSERTED & IRDY#
ASSERTED SIMULT. ... SINGLE ACCESS
(2) IF GNT#(A) DEASSERTED IN PREVIOUS CLK PERIOD
(3) IF GNT#(A) DEASSERTED TWO CLK PERIODS EARLIER
(4) DATA VALID WHEN TRDY# ASSERTED
(5) EARLIEST SDONE ASSERTED FOR THIS CYCLE

C = COMMAND TYPE
BE = BYTE ENABLES
A = ADDRESS   PA = PARITY C & A
D = DATA   PD = PARITY BE & D

Figure 10-4: Burst Read Access Cycle without DUAL ADDRESS Parked at
(A), Executed, and Retained by (B)

371

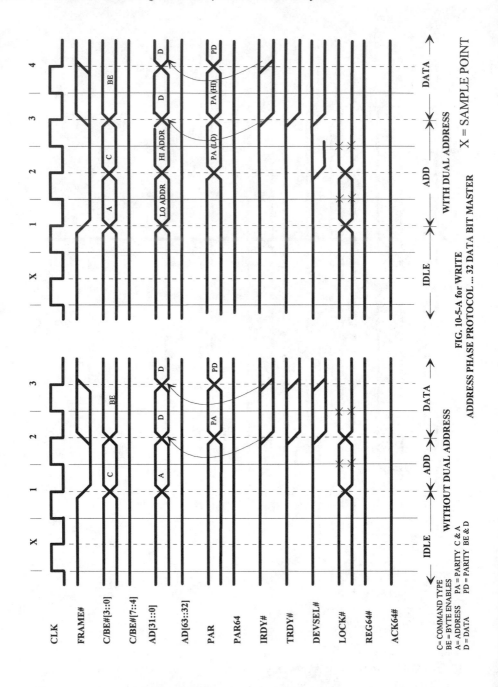

Figure 10-5-A: ADDRESS PHASE Protocol for Write, 32-Data Bit Master.

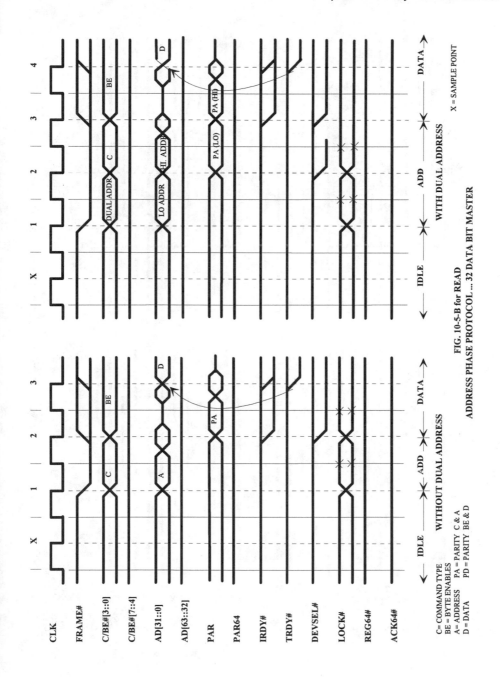

Figure 10-5-B: ADDRESS PHASE Protocol for Read, 64 Data Bit Master

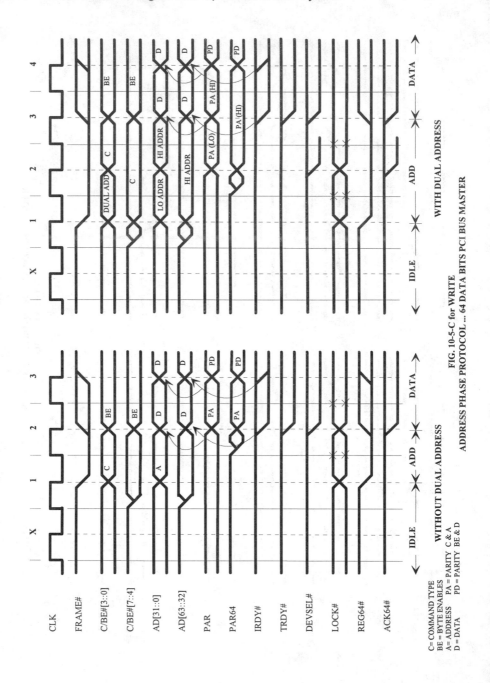

Figure 10-5-C: ADDRESS PHASE Protocol for Write, 64 Data Bit PCI Bus Master

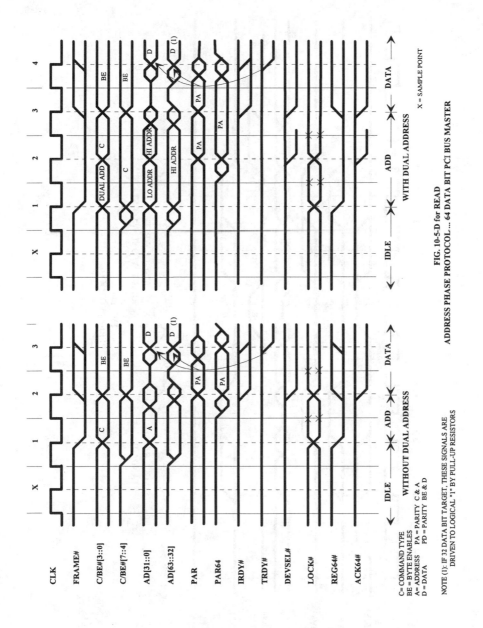

FIG. 10-5-D for READ
ADDRESS PHASE PROTOCOL.... 64 DATA BIT PCI BUS MASTER

X = SAMPLE POINT

C = COMMAND TYPE
BE = BYTE ENABLES   PA = PARITY   C & A
A = ADDRESS   PA = PARITY   C & A
D = DATA   PD = PARITY   BE & D

NOTE (1): IF 32 DATA BIT TARGET, THESE SIGNALS ARE
DRIVEN TO LOGICAL "1" BY PULL-UP RESISTORS

Figure 10-5-D: ADDRESS PHASE Protocol for Read, 64 Data Bit PCI Bus Master

375

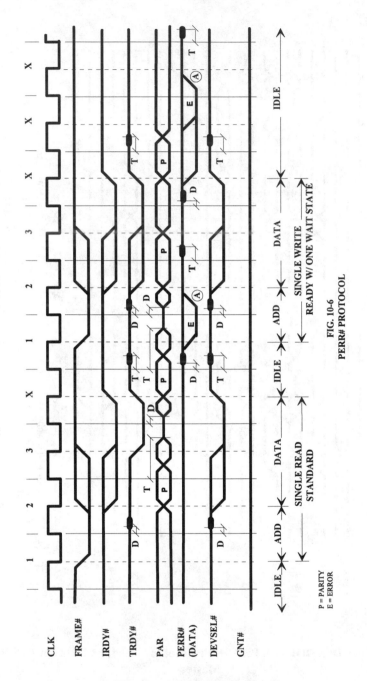

Figure 10-6: PERR# Protocol

- During the ADDRESS and DATA PHASES, all of the AD[31::0], C/BE#[3::0], PAR signal lines must contain valid information or be driven to a stable level. During the DATA PHASE, the C/BE#[3::0] signal lines indicate which AD[31::0] signal lines contain valid information. Parity is computed over both types of signal lines; those that are stable, and those that contain valid information.

> When the PCI bus master is requesting a 32 data bit access (REQ64# is deasserted), the AD[63::32], C/BE#[7::4], and PAR64 signal lines are driven to a logical "1" by pull-up resistors. The PAR64 signal line does not contain valid parity information. This is independent of the execution of DUAL ADDRESS (see Figures 10-5-A to 10-5-B).

64 DATA BIT PCI BUS MASTER AND
32 AND 64 DATA BIT TARGET (REQ64# = ASSERTED)

- The operation of the PAR signal line relative to the AD[31::0] and C/BE#[3::0] for a 64 data bit PCI bus master is the same as outlined for a 32 data bit PCI bus master. The operation of PAR64 signal line relative to the AD[63::32] and C/BE#[7::4] signal lines varies, depending on the execution of DUAL ADDRESS and the value of the ACK64# signal line as follows:

  ⇒ Dual address is not executed with a 32 data bit target (ACK64# is deasserted):

  During the ADDRESS PHASE, the PAR64 signal line contains valid parity because the C/BE#[7::4] and AD[63::32] signal lines contain valid information. The target is only 32 data bits; consequently, parity is not checked. However, other 64 data bit PCI resources can check the parity of these signal lines and assert the SERR# signal line if an error is detected. During the DATA PHASE of a SINGLE write access cycle and the initial microaccess of a BURST write access cycle, the PCI bus master drives valid parity onto the PAR64 signal line because the C/BE#[7::4] and AD[63::32] signal lines contain valid information. The target is only 32 data bits; consequently, parity is not checked. The PAR64 signal line may or may not contain valid parity information during the subsequent microaccesses of the BURST access cycle. During the DATA PHASE of a SINGLE read access cycle or the initial microaccess of a BURST read access cycle, the PCI bus master drives the C/BE#[7::4] signal lines with byte enable information but the AD[63::32] and PAR64 signal lines are driven to a logical "1" by pull-up resistors; consequently, the latter does not contain valid parity. The PAR64 signal line does not contain valid parity during the subsequent microaccesses of the BURST access cycle.

⇒ DUAL ADDRESS is executed with a 32 data bit target (ACK64# is deasserted):

During the ADDRESS PHASE, the PAR64 signal line contains valid parity because the C/BE#[7::4] and AD[63::32] signal lines contain valid information. The target is only 32 data bits; consequently, parity is not checked. However, other 64 data bit PCI resources can check the parity of these signal lines and assert the SERR# signal line if an error is detected. During the DATA PHASE of a SINGLE write access cycle and the initial microaccess of a BURST access cycle, the PCI bus master drives valid parity onto the PAR64 signal line because the C/BE#[7::4] and AD[63::32] signal lines contain valid information. The target is only 32 data bits; consequently, parity is not checked. During the DATA PHASE of a read access cycle, the PCI bus master drives the C/BE#[7::4] with byte enable information but the AD[63::32] and PAR64 signal lines are driven to a logical "1" by pull-up resistors; consequently, the latter does not contain valid parity. The PAR64 signal line does not contain valid parity during the subsequent microaccesses of the BURST access cycle.

⇒ Dual address is not executed with a 64 data bit target (ACK64# is asserted):

During the ADDRESS PHASE, the PAR64 signal line contains valid parity because the C/BE#[7::4] and AD[63::32] signal lines contain valid information. The target optionally checks the parity. During the DATA PHASE of a write access cycle, the PCI bus master drives valid parity onto the PAR64 signal line because the C/BE#[7::4] and AD[63::32] signal lines contain valid information. The target optionally checks the parity. During the DATA PHASE of a read access cycle, the PCI bus master drives the C/BE#[7::4] signal line with byte enable information, and the target drives the AD[63::32] signal lines with valid data; consequently, the PAR64 signal line is driven with valid parity. The PCI bus master optionally checks the parity.

⇒ DUAL ADDRESS is executed and 64 data bit target (ACK64# is asserted):

During the ADDRESS PHASE, the PAR64 signal line is valid because the C/BE#[7::4] and AD[63::32] signal lines contain valid information. The target optionally checks the parity. During the

DATA PHASE of a write access cycle, the PCI bus master drives valid parity onto the PAR64 signal line because the C/BE#[7::4] and AD[63::32] contain valid information. The target optionally checks the parity. During the DATA PHASE of a read access cycle, the PCI bus master drives the C/BE#[7::4] with byte enable information, and the target drives the AD[63::32] signal lines with valid data; consequently, the PAR64 signal line is driven with valid parity. The PCI bus master optionally checks the parity.

> During the DATA PHASE, the PCI bus master is driving the byte enables onto the C/BE# [7::4] signal lines during a read access cycle; consequently, the target must sample these signal lines and combine the parity with the AD[63::32] signal lines to drive the PAR64 signal line.

■ The operation of the PAR64 signal line between bus cycles also follows the operation of the AD[63::32] signal lines. If the PCI bus master is retaining bus ownership (REG# and GNT# both asserted) between bus cycles, it drives the PAR64 signal line to a stable level or tri-states it and a pull-up resistor drives the PAR64 signal line to a logical "1". If the PCI bus master does not retain bus ownership (GNT# signal line deasserted), the PAR64 signal line is driven to a logical "1" by a pull-up resistor. The Park master also does not drive the PAR64 signal line.

■ Even parity is supported by the PAR64 signal line. The total number of "1"s on the AD[63::32], C/BE#[7::4], and PAR64 signal lines must be an even number when valid.

■ During the ADDRESS and DATA PHASES, all of the AD[63::32], C/BE#[7::4], and PAR64 signal lines must contain valid information or be driven to a stable level. Parity is computed over both types of signal lines; those that are stable, and those that contain valid information.

PAR AND PAR64 SIGNAL LINE OPERATION IN SPECIAL CYCLES

The special cycle does not generate a valid address during the ADDRESS PHASE, but does provide a valid COMMAND type. The PCI bus master will drive the AD[31::0] to a stable level, the C/BE#[3::0] signal lines with valid COMMAND type, and the PAR signal with valid parity information. During the DATA PHASE, the PAR signal line will be driven by the PCI bus master and will contain the parity over the AD[31::0] and C/BE#[3::0] signal lines.

A special cycle is not defined for a 64 data bit bus cycle; consequently, the PAR64 signal line does not contain valid parity, is not checked, and is driven to a logical "1" by a pull-up resistor. The AD[63::32] and C/BE#[7::4] signal lines are driven to a logical "1" by pull-up resistors.

PAR AND PAR64 SIGNAL LINE OPERATION IN INTERRUPT ACKNOWLEDGE CYCLES

The interrupt acknowledge cycle does not generate a valid address during the ADDRESS PHASE, but does provide valid COMMAND type. The PCI bus master will drive the AD[31::0] to a stable level, the C/BE#[3::0] signal lines with valid COMMAND type, and the PAR signal with valid parity information. During the DATA PHASE, the PAR signal line will be driven by the target and will contain the parity over the AD[31::0] and C/BE#[3::0] signal lines. The PCI bus master is the HOST/PCI BRIDGE and the target is the PCI bus resource that contains the interrupt controller.

An interrupt acknowledge cycle is not defined for a 64 data bit bus cycle; consequently, the PAR64 signal line does not contain valid parity, is not checked, and is driven to a logical "1" by a pull-up resistor. The AD[63::32] and C/BE#[7::4] signal lines are driven to a logical "1" by pull-up resistors.

10.2   PERR# SIGNAL LINE OPERATION

INTRODUCTION

The parity error in the AD, C/BE#, PAR, and PAR64 signal lines during the ADDRESS and DATA PHASES is defined as address parity error and data parity error, respectively.

The PERR# signal line is driven by the PCI resource receiving data on the AD signal lines during an access cycle. It reflects the detection of a parity error on the AD, C/BE#, PAR, and PAR64 signal lines.

During a write, the PERR# signal line is asserted by the target to report a parity error first to the PCI bus master. If the PCI bus master cannot resolve the parity problem, the parity error can be reported to the device driver software via the SERR# signal line, an interrupt, etc. Similarly, if the device driver software cannot resolve the parity problem, the parity error can be reported to the device manager software. Finally, if the device manager software cannot resolve the parity problem, the parity error can be reported to the operating system. For a read bus cycle, the parity error reporting sequence is same except the assertion of the PERR# signal line is by the PCI bus master to indicate to the system that a data parity had occurred. The PCI bus master still retains the opportunity to resolve the parity problem before reporting to the device driver software.

Not all of the PCI bus resources must support the PERR# signal line. The PCI bus resources that do not support the PERR# signal line must meet one of the following conditions:

- Resources that are only used on the platform and not add-in cards

- Resources that do not affect permanent data; e.g., video display. In other words, resources that will not cause a loss of system integrity when the parity error occurs do not need to support parity checking.

> The term *data parity* includes parity in both data (AD signal lines) and byte enables (C/BE# signal lines).

PERR# SIGNAL LINE OPERATION DURING ACCESS CYCLES

The PERR# signal line is asserted with the detection of parity error during the DATA PHASE on the AD[31::0], C/BE#[3::0], and PAR signal lines. If it is a 64 data bit access cycle (REQ64# and ACK64# both asserted), the PERR# signal line also includes a parity error in the AD[63::32], C/BE#[7::4], and PAR64 signal lines.

The PERR# signal line is asserted only to report data parity errors. The PERR# signal line must be asserted by the resource receiving the data on the AD signal lines two CLK signal line periods after the data is accessed when a parity error occurs. For a write access cycle, the target drives the PERR# signal line (subsequent to the assertion of IRDY# and TRDY# signal lines) when a parity error is detected during the DATA PHASE. For a read access cycle, the PCI bus master drives the PERR# signal line (subsequent to the assertion of the IRDY# and TRDY# signal lines) when a parity error is detected during the DATA PHASE. When not driven by a PCI resource, the PERR# signal line is driven to a logical "1" by a pull-up resistor. Figure 10-6 outlines the operation of the PERR# signal line for SINGLE access cycles, and has the following protocol:

In the following discussion there is a difference between *drive* and *asserted*. When the PERR# signal line is *driven* it means that the signal line buffer is enabled but the signal line may remain deasserted. When the PERR# signal line is *asserted*, it is driven to a logical "0".

DATA PARITY ERROR DURING A READ ACCESS CYCLE:

- The PERR# signal line can be initially driven two CLK signal line periods after the FRAME# signal line is first sampled asserted at the beginning of the access cycle. The PERR# signal line can be driven at a later time prior to assertion for the valid sample point.

- The PERR# signal line can be asserted when a minimum of three CLK signal line periods after the FRAME# signal line is first sampled asserted at the beginning of the access cycle and after the TRDY# signal line is asserted.

- The PERR# signal line must be valid two CLK signal line periods after the IRDY# and TRDY# signal lines are both asserted.

- The PERR# signal line must be tri-stated three CLK signal line periods after the IRDY# and TRDY# signal lines are both asserted.

DATA PARITY ERROR DURING A WRITE ACCESS CYCLE:

- The PERR# signal line can be initially driven two CLK signal line periods after the FRAME# signal line is first sampled asserted at the beginning of the access cycle. The PERR# signal line is also driven until the second CLK signal line period after the FRAME# signal line is first sampled asserted when a target Fast Back-to-Back is occurring, with a minor buffer fight. The PERR# signal line can be driven at a later time prior to assertion for the valid sample point.

- The PERR# signal line can be asserted when a minimum of three CLK signal line periods after the FRAME# signal line is first sampled asserted at the beginning of the access cycle, after the DEVSEL# signal line is driven, and after the IRDY# signal line is asserted.

- The PERR# signal line must be valid two CLK signal line periods after the IRDY# and TRDY# signal lines are both asserted.

- The PERR# signal line must be tri-stated three CLK signal line periods after the IRDY# and TRDY# signal lines are both asserted for the last access of the bus cycle.

OTHER PROTOCOL CONSIDERATIONS:

- The above protocol relative to the assertion of the PERR# signal line applies to all bus cycles including Fast Back-to-Back. The ability to retain the same protocol during a Fast Back-to-Back reflects the fact that the PERR# signal line only reports data parity and does not have to be asserted during the ADDRESS PHASE.

■ Once the PERR# signal line is asserted, it cannot be deasserted until two CLK signal line periods after the IRDY# and TRDY# signal lines are both asserted (Circle A in Figure 10-6).

■ For a BURST access cycle, the PERR# signal line protocol is the same as that outlined above for the SINGLE access cycle. The only difference is the PERR# signal line protocol for each microaccess is relative to the individual assertion of the IRDY# and TRDY# signal line for each microaccess. If data is accessed with parity error on continuous rising edges of the CLK signal line, the PERR# signal line remains asserted for the associated continuous CLK signal lines.

> The above discussion uses only a 32 data bit access cycle as an example. The operation of the PERR# signal line relative to the PAR64 signal line uses the same protocol.

> The PCI bus master and target do not know that an access cycle was successful relative to errors until two CLK signal line periods after the data was accessed.

The PERR# signal line is asserted by the PCI bus master or the addressed target as follows:

■ During a write access cycle, the target asserts the PERR# signal line to report a data parity error to the PCI bus master. The target can assert the PERR# signal line and immediately terminate an access cycle (per normal bus cycle completion protocol) by executing a Disconnect or Target Abort termination if the access cycle hasn't already completed.

■ During a write access cycle, the most typical response is for the target to assert the PERR# signal line and the PCI bus master to execute a Completion or Completion with timeout termination as it would have if the PERR# signal had not been asserted.

■ During a read access cycle, the PCI bus master asserts the PERR# signal line to report a data parity error and can immediately terminate the access cycle (per normal bus cycle completion protocol) if the access cycle hasn't already completed.

■ During a read access cycle, the most typical response is for the PCI bus master to assert the PERR# signal line and execute a Completion or

Completion with timeout termination as it would have if the PERR# signal had not been asserted.

> The addressed target cannot assert the PERR# signal line for a data parity error detected with a Retry, Target Abort, or Disconnect without data termination because no data was accessed. A Disconnect without data, Disconnect with data, or Target Abort termination can be executed for a data parity error of an earlier microaccess.

For either read or write bus cycles the PCI bus master can attempt parity error recovery as outlined below.

When a data parity error occurs (provided data parity detection is enabled) the PCI bus master should repeat the access cycle provided no negative side effects will result. If the access cycle repeats without a data parity error, the PCI bus master does not have to report the occurrence of a data parity error to the system. If the repeated access cycle generates a parity error or if the PCI bus master cannot repeat the access cycle, the PCI bus master must report it to the system as follows:

- If the PCI bus master is supported by a device driver software, the device driver software is informed of the data parity error via an interrupt, Status Register information, flags, or other means. The device driver software can try other methods for recovering from a data parity error. If the device driver is successful without any negative side effects, no further action is required. If the device driver is unsuccessful or is unable to correct the parity error due to the negative side effects, it must report it to the device manager software.

- If the PCI bus master does not have device driver software support, it must report the data parity error by asserting the SERR# signal line as a method to report the error to the operating system.

- Once the data parity error has been reported to the operating system, the exact method for addressing it is operating system dependent.

> The platform designer can use the central resource to assert the SERR# signal line to reflect the assertion of the PERR# signal line for a data parity error.

When the PERR# signal line is asserted, the PCI bus master sets the Data Parity bit of the Status Register in its configuration space. The target cannot set the Data Parity bit of its Status Register when the PCI resources participating in the bus cycle (that do support data parity checking) have detected a data parity error on the AD, C/BE#, PAR, and PAR64 signal lines. The Detected Parity

Error bit in the Status Register must be set in its respective configuration space. This bit must be set even if the Parity Error Response bit is not set in the associated Command Register in the configuration space. The Parity Error Response bit must be supported by all PCI resources except for those resources defined in the Introduction of this Subchapter which do not support the PERR# signal line. When the Parity Error Response bit is set, the associated resource asserts the PERR# signal line when a data parity error is detected. When the Parity Error Response bit is not set, the associated resource does not assert the PERR# signal line and the data parity error is ignored.

PERR# SIGNAL LINE OPERATION DURING SPECIAL CYCLES

The PERR# signal line is not used during special cycles because data is broadcast (written by PCI bus master) to all PCI resources without a specific address. Resources that receive the data can check data parity on the AD[31::0], C/BE#[3::01], and PAR signal lines. However, the lack of a specific address does not allow a specific target to claim ownership of the PERR# signal line; consequently, the data parity error cannot be reported to the PCI bus master with this signal line. Any PCI resource that detects a parity error in the AD[31::0], C/BE#[3::0], and PAR signal lines during the DATA PHASE can report it by asserting the SERR# signal line.

> A special cycle is not defined as a 64 data bit bus cycle; consequently, the AD[63::32], C/BE#[7::4], and PAR64 signal lines are not checked for parity error, and are driven to a logical "1" by pull-up resistors.

PERR# SIGNAL LINE OPERATION DURING INTERRUPT ACKNOWLEDGE CYCLES

The PERR# signal line protocol for an interrupt acknowledge cycle is the same as a read access cycle. The PCI bus master is the HOST/PCI BRIDGE and the target is the PCI bus resource that contains the interrupt controller.

> An interrupt acknowledge cycle is not defined as a 64 data bit bus cycle; consequently, the AD[63::32], C/BE#[7::4], and PAR64 signal lines are not checked for parity error, and are driven to a logical "1" by pull-up resistors.

10.4   SERR# SIGNAL LINE OPERATION

INTRODUCTION

> The parity error in the AD, B/BE#, PAR, and PAR64 signal lines during the ADDRESS and DATA PHASES is defined as address parity error and data parity error, respectively.

The SERR# signal line can be asserted by any PCI resource independent of which PCI bus master or target is involved in the bus cycle or when the bus is parked. The SERR# signal line is an open collector signal line that is deasserted by a pull-up resistor and can be driven by multiple PCI resources. The SERR# signal line is used to directly report an address parity error during any bus cycle, a data parity error during special cycles, or report any error to the platform independent of the bus cycle.

Not all of the PCI bus resources are required to support the SERR# signal line. The PCI bus resources that are not required to support the SERR# signal line must meet one of the following conditions:

- Resources that are used only on the platform and never on add-in cards

- Resources that do not affect permanent data, i.e., video display. In other words, resources that do not support parity checking are those that will not cause a loss of system integrity when the parity error occurs.

There are no specific timing requirements for the assertion of the SERR# signal line. It should be asserted soon after the error is detected

> The SERR# signal line is asserted synchronously and deasserted asynchronously with the CLK signal line; consequently, once asserted the SERR# signal line is considered active until sampled deasserted for two consecutive CLK signal line periods. The SERR# signal line is asserted for one CLK signal line period and is then immediately tri-stated.

> The SERR# signal line can be asserted at any time; consequently, it has no relationship with the current bus cycle. A PCI resource can only assert the SERR# signal line if the SERR Enable bit in the Command Register is set. When a PCI resource asserts the SERR# signal line it must also set the Signaled System Error bit in its Status Register.

SERR# SIGNAL LINE OPERATION DURING ACCESS CYCLES

The SERR# signal line can be asserted by any PCI resource independently of which PCI bus master or target is involved in the access cycle. The SERR# is asserted after an address parity error is detected on the AD[31::0], C/BE#[3::0], and PAR signal lines during the ADDRESS PHASE. If it is a 64 data bit access (REQ64# signal line asserted) and a DUAL ADDRESS is executed, the SERR# is asserted for an address parity error in the AD[63::32], C/BE#[7::4], and PAR64 signal lines during the ADDRESS PHASE.

The SERR# signal line is asserted or not asserted during an access cycle by the PCI bus master or the addressed target as follows:

- The PCI bus master must assert the SERR# signal line when a Target Abort termination is executed if not reported to the system by other means.

- The PCI bus master can assert the SERR# signal line when a Master Abort termination is executed if not reported to the system by other means. A Master Abort termination is not an abnormal condition for a configuration access cycle during initialization, and the SERR# signal line should not be asserted.

- When an addressed target detects an address parity error it can claim the access cycle (assert DEVSEL# signal line) and assert the SERR# signal line, and allow a Disconnect, Retry, Completion termination, or Completion with timeout termination as if an address parity error had not occurred. Retry and Disconnect terminations are not executed as a response to detecting an address parity error. This is possible for FAST, MEDIUM, SLOW and SUBTRACTIVE DECODING.

- When an addressed target detects an address parity error it can claim the access cycle (assert DEVSEL# signal line), and execute a Target Abort termination. This will place the responsibility on the PCI bus master to assert the SERR# signal line. This is possible for FAST, MEDIUM, SLOW and SUBTRACTIVE DECODING.

- When an addressed target detects an address parity error it may not claim the access cycle (keep the DEVSEL# signal line deasserted); this will cause a Master Abort to occur and make it the responsibility of the PCI bus master to assert the SERR# signal line. However, the PCI bus master is not required to do so.

- Any PCI resource (PCI bus master or target) can assert the SERR# signal line to report a castastrophic error.

> The addressed target cannot execute a Retry or Disconnect termination because it detects an address parity error. Thus, if the target executes a Retry or Disconnect termination, it was independent of the address parity error.

SERR# SIGNAL LINE OPERATION DURING SPECIAL CYCLES

The SERR# signal line reports parity errors during the ADDRESS and DATA PHASES of special cycles. By definition the special cycle broadcasts data to all PCI resources without a specific address. During the ADDRESS PHASE of the special cycle, the PCI bus master drives the AD[31::0] signal lines to a stable level and valid information onto the C/BE#[3::0] signal lines. It also drives valid parity information onto the PAR signal line (one CLK signal line period later); consequently, the platform circuitry and PCI resources are able to check parity and assert the SERR# signal line if an error is detected. During the DATA PHASE, PCI resources that receive the data can check data parity on the AD[31::0], C/BE#[3::0], and PAR signal lines, but the lack of a specific address does not allow a specific PCI resource to claim ownership of the PERR# signal line. Consequently, parity can be checked by the platform circuitry or any PCI resource, and a data parity error can be reported by the assertion of the SERR# signal line.

The SERR# signal line is asserted or not asserted during a special cycle by the PCI bus master or the other PCI bus resources as follows:

- The PCI resource can assert the SERR# signal line to indicate an address or data parity error.

- The PCI bus master cannot assert the SERR# signal line to report a Master Abort termination to the system for a special cycle. A Master abort termination is not an abnormal condition for a special bus cycle.

- Any PCI resource (PCI bus master or target) can assert the SERR# signal line to report a castastrophic error.

> A special cycle is not defined as a 64 data bit bus cycle; consequently, the AD[63::32], C/BE#[7::4], and PAR64 signal lines are not checked for parity errors, and are driven to a logical "1" by pull-up resistors.

SERR# SIGNAL LINE OPERATION DURING INTERRUPT ACKNOWLEDGE CYCLES

The SERR# signal line protocol for an interrupt acknowledge cycle is the same as a read access cycle. An interrupt acknowledge cycle does not provide a valid address, but does drive the AD[31::0] signal lines stable and provides valid COMMAND type on the C/BE#[3::0] signal lines. The PCI bus master is the HOST/PCI BRIDGE and the target is the PCI bus resource that contains the interrupt controller.

> An interrupt acknowledge cycle is not defined as 64 data bit bus cycle; consequently, the AD[63::32], C/BE#[7::4], and PAR64 signal lines are not checked for parity errors, and are driven to a logical "1" by pull up resistors.

SERR# SIGNAL LINE OPERATION FOR NON BUS CYCLE RELATED ERRORS

The SERR# signal line can also be used to report any error; consequently, the SERR# signal line can be asserted at any time by any PCI resource. The use of the SERR# signal for errors other than parity during the ADDRESS PHASE is optional.

OTHER SERR# SIGNAL LINE CONSIDERATIONS

The platform circuitry may monitor the SERR# signal line to report errors to the operating system (i.e., the HOST CPU). The PCI bus specification does not specify how the system is to be informed. An interrupt, NMI, or a polled register are some of the probable solutions.

Any PCI resource can assert the SERR# signal line at any time for any platform error provided its respective SERR Enable bit is set in the Command Register of its respective configuration space. The assertion of the SERR# signal line requires the PCI resource to set the Signaled System Error bit in the Status Register of its respective configuration space.

If the error is due to an address parity error in an access cycle or a data parity error in a special bus cycle, the PCI resource that detected the error must set the Detected Parity Error bit in the Status Register of its configuration space. If the PCI resource is also going to assert the SERR# signal line, the two following conditions must be met:

■ Parity Error Response bit and SERR# Enable bit in the Command Register in its respective configuration space are enabled.

■ The error will not be reported by other methods.

When the SERR Enable bit is enabled in the Command Register, the PCI bus master can assert the SERR# signal line under the following conditions:

■ When the a PCI bus master is involved in a bus cycle that is terminated by a Target Abort termination, and it does not have application software to handle the situation.

■ When a PCI bus master (that is *not* executing a configuration access during initialization or special cycle) is involved in a bus cycle that is terminated by a Master Abort termination, and it does not have application software to handle the situation.

CHAPTER 11

RESET, POWER, AND SIGNAL LINE INITIALIZATION

This chapter consists of the following subchapters:

11.0   RESET
11.1   Power
11.2   Signal Line Initialization

11.0 RESET

The PCI bus defines a RESET protocol that is typical for most platforms. In addition, unlike other buses, the PCI bus requires a central resource to monitor certain PCI signal lines during RESET (see Figure 1-3).

RESET on the PCI bus occurs when the RST# signal line is asserted. This signal line changes states asynchronously to the CLK signal line, and must transition in a clean fashion without spikes between the minimum V_{ih} and maximum V_{il} (see *Chapter 12: Signal Line Timing and Electrical Requirements*, for more information). When the power good single line (PWR_GOOD# in Figure 11-1) from the power supply indicates the voltage levels above the minimum outlined in Table 11-1, the RST# signal line is asserted. The RST# signal line remains asserted until the following three events occur (see Figure 11-1):

- The RST# signal line is asserted a minimum of 1 millisecond (t_2).

- The CLK signal line has been oscillating a minimum of 100 microseconds (t_3).

- Voltage levels outlined in Table 11-1 have remained above the minimum levels (PWR_GOOD# asserted) for about 100 milliseconds (t_1).

VOLTAGE NAME	MINIMUM	MAXIMUM
5.0	4.75	5.25
3.3	3.00	3.60
12.0	11.40	12.60
−12.0	−11.80	−13.20

Table 11-1: Minimum and maximum voltage levels

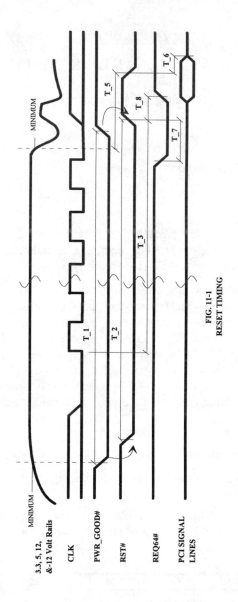

Figure 11-1: RESET Timing

The above figure is copied from *PCI Local Bus Specification Rev. 2.0*. Reprinted with the permission of the PCI Special Interest Group.

An important consideration is when the voltage levels fall below the minimum levels. For many power supplies, the PWR_GOOD# signal line may only reflect the status of the 5 volt supply. If the 3.3 or 5 volt power rails fail to meet the values listed in Table 11-1, the RST# signal line must be asserted. The criteria for RESET are as follows:

- The smaller t_5 of the following two conditions:
   - $\Rightarrow$ The RST# signal line must be asserted within 500 nanoseconds (t_5) (see Figure 11-1) from when 3.3 or 5 volts exceeds (by 500 millivolts) the minimum and maximum values in Table 11-1.

   OR

   - $\Rightarrow$ The RST# signal line must be asserted within 100 nanoseconds (t_5) (see Figure 11-1) from when the 5 volt rail falls below the 3.3 volt rail by 300 millivolts or more.
- The RST# signal line must be asserted during power up or during a power fail situation. The PCI components are not considered RESET until the times of both t_2 and t_3 have been met (see Figure 11-1).
- The assertion of the RST# signal lines require all PCI resources to tri-state the PCI signal lines within 40 nanoseconds (see Figure 11-1).

> When the RST# signal line is asserted, all of the output drivers (except for the CLK signal line) must be tri-stated.

> RST# signal line change of states do not have to be synchronous with the CLK signal line. Therefore, the 40 nanosecond requirement must be met independently of the CLK signal line.

11.1 POWER

There is no specification on the sequence of power rail activation or deactivation, or the rate of change. A platform that supports 3.3 volts signaling *must* also support the 5, 12 and -12 volts. A platform that supports 5 volt signaling is only required to support 12 and -12 volts. This type of platform should provide a field upgrade mechanism for support of 3.3 volt compliant add-in cards.

Each add-in card connector must be able to provide 500 milliamps at 12 volts and 100 milliamps at −12 volts. The power to be supplied to each connector will vary depending upon the value of the PRSNT1# and PRSNT2# pins on each connector according to the following protocol:

- No power—no add-in card attached.

- Maximum of 25 watts when PRSNT1# is grounded and PRSNT2# is open by add-in card.

- Maximum of 15 watts when PRSNT1# is open and PRSNT2# is grounded by add-in card.

- Maximum of 7.5 watts when PRSNT1# is grounded and PRSNT2# is grounded by add-in card.

> To indicate that an add-in card is installed it must ground either the PRSNT1# or PRSNT2# pins as outlined above.

The above wattages represent the maximum power from all power rails. In the worst case condition, the total wattage is drawn entirely from the 5 volt or the 3.3 volt rail. It may not be possible for the platform power supply to provide the maximum power to all connectors; consequently, PCI add-in cards that consume more that 10 watts under full operation should have a power-saving state. Such an add-in card should power up and RESET in the power-saving state. In the power-saving state, the PCI configuration space and bootstrap functions should be fully operational. Add-in cards installed in platforms with advance power management may be required to report (via registers) their respective power requirements before exiting the power-saving state. Power may also be reduced with lower CLK signal line frequencies.

> Maximum power for any PCI add-in card is 25 Watts.

11.2 SIGNAL LINE INITIALIZATION

Chapter 5 describes the value of the signal lines when the RST# signal line is asserted. Of special concern is the REQ64# signal line. For a PCI resource that becomes bus master to request a 64 data bit access cycle requires a 64 data bit bus. The REQ64# signal line is connected to all PCI resources and slots that are attached to a 64 data bit bus. Those PCI slots that are not attached to a 64 data bit bus have their respective REQ64# signal lines are driven to a logical "1" by a pull-up resistor. The central resource asserts the REQ64# signal lines relative to the rising edge of the RST# signal line. The sampling of the asserted REQ64# signal line during this period indicates to the PCI resource (bus master) that it can execute 64 data bit access cycles. The setup time (t7) is 10 x CLK signal line period. The hold time (t8) is a minimum of 0 nanoseconds and a maximum of 50 nanoseconds (see Figure 11-1).

64 data bit PCI resources that are attached only to a 32 data bit bus or slot must insure that the 64 data bit related signal lines do not oscillate (AD[63::32], C/BE#[7::4], PAR64, and ACK64# signal lines). Each PCI resource can drive these signal lines as outputs (stable level) or if an input, can be biased to a stable level. These and other solutions are allowed provided that the input leakage current specification is not violated. External resistors on an add-in card are not allowed. The PCI resources that are attached to a 64 data bit bus or slot rely on pull-up resistors in the central resource to drive the aforementioned signal lines to a logical "1".

CHAPTER 12

SIGNAL LINE TIMING AND ELECTRICAL REQUIREMENTS

This chapter consists of the following subchapters:

12.0 OVERVIEW

PCI has well-defined electrical specifications. Although some of these specifications may seem like an extra burden for the designer, these items are necessary for promoting interoperability between PCI components and PCI add-in cards. The PCI electrical specifications have been written with total system operation in mind.

The electrical specification has attempted to address a wide variety of potential market applications without placing too much burden for the user with just one solution in mind. This is demonstrated by the add on nature of the 64 bit extension or use of +3.3V logic. Although most I/O busses currently use +5V TTL-like logic signaling, PCI has anticipated (and promotes) a shift to +3.3V logic. Unfortunately, these two logic families do not mix well together and has inspired separate electrical specifications for PCI components.

For PCI components that are not part of the platform or motherboard, connectors are defined for both the platform and the pluggable add-in card. These are described in Chapter 13.

12.1 DISTINCTION BETWEEN ADD-IN CARD VOLTAGES

PCI bus has separate logic signaling levels: 3.3 volt and 5 volts. These names roughly follow the logic signaling levels used by logic families with 3.3 volt and 5 volt power supplies. It is important to understand that logic signaling levels refer only to the voltages used for communication on the PCI bus wires. The power supplies used for powering PCI resources may or may not correlate to the signaling levels on the bus. In fact, it is possible to have a PCI resource that requires a 3.3 volt power supply and produces the 5 volt signaling environment. The two signaling environments are not compatible with each other, therefore, all PCI resources in a system must be of the same type (all 3.3 volt or all 5 volt resources).

A PCI platform can be made for either the 5 volt signaling environment or the 3.3 volt signaling environment, but not both. To keep platforms distinct, the connectors for PCI add-in cards are keyed differently for 5 volt and 3.3 volt signaling environments.

The two types of platform connectors are:

- **5 Volt Connector:** Allows either a 5 Volt or Dual Voltage Add-in card to be inserted via a mechanical connector key.

- **3.3 Volt Connector:** Allows either a 3.3 Volt or Dual Voltage Add-in cards to be inserted via a mechanical connector key.

Add-in cards can be designed for either the 5 volt signaling environment, the 3.3 volt signaling environment, or both (a dual voltage or universal card). Each of these three add-in card possibilities has a connector that is keyed to fit into its appropriate PCI platform. The mechanical keying in the connector (see *Chapter 13: Connector, Platform and Add-in Card Design, and Mechanical Considerations*) insures that add-in cards can only be installed in an appropriate platform connector. The add-in cards can obtain power from either the 5 volt or 3.3 volt power supply pins on the connector.

The three types of add-in cards are:

- **5 Volt Add-In Card**: The I/O buffers of the component attached to the PCI signal lines adhere to the 5 volt signaling environment.

- **3.3 Volt Add-In Card**: The I/O buffers of the component attached to the PCI signal lines adhere to the 3.3 volt signaling environment.

- **Dual Voltage Add-In Card**: The I/O buffers of the components attached to the PCI signal lines assume the signaling environment of the platform. The dual voltage add-in card determines the signaling environment of the platform from connector-dependent power supply signals (defined as I/O Designated Power Pins). See *Chapter 13: Connector, Platform and Add-in Card Design, and Mechanical Considerations*.

> The I/O Designated Power Pins can be attached to either 3.3 volts or 5 volts (dependent on the platform); consequently, the I/O buffers of a dual voltage add-in card must be able to operate with either the 3 volt or the 5 volt signaling environment, and may use the 3.3 volt or the 5 volt power supplies.

12.2 5V COMPONENT ELECTRICAL SPECIFICATIONS

All electrical specifications and parameters assume packaged components. That is, measurements or simulations should not be obtained from an unpackaged die. All PCI electrical measurements (component and platform) are made at package pins.

For an overview of the specification philosophy, please see Appendix G.

5V SIGNALING ENVIRONMENT

The 5V signaling environment is basically industry standard TTL input thresholds with rail to rail output levels This environment is intended to be implemented with CMOS technology although any technology could be used that meets the specifications. Since the major current consumption of CMOS logic occurs during transitions, output drive capability is specified using V/I curves and AC specifications.

5V DC SPECIFICATIONS

The DC specifications are steady state parameters. That is, they do not contain any information about timing or switching. DC specifications are needed to insure that devices in the same logic family can reliably communicate with each other. The output voltage levels, input switching thresholds, and static parasitic electrical parameters (capacitance and inductance) are defined The following table outlines the DC parameters for 5V signaling:

5V DC SPECIFICATIONS

Symbol and Parameter	Conditions and (notes)	Min	Max	Units
V_{cc} Voltage Supply		4.75	5.25	V
V_{ih} Input High Voltage		2.0	V_{cc}+0.5	V
V_{il} Input Low Voltage		-0.5	0.8	V
V_{ipu} Input Pull-Up Voltage		2.7		V
I_{ih} Input High Leakage Current	V_{in} = 2.7 note (1)		70	µA
I_{il} Input Low Leakage Current	V_{in} = 0.5 note (1)		-70	µA
V_{oh} Output High Voltage	I_{out} = -2 mA	2.4		V
V_{ol} Output Low Voltage	I_{out} = 3 or 6 mA note (2)		0.55	V
C_{in} Input Pin Capacitance	note (3)		10 or 16	pF
C_{clk} CLK Pin Capacitance		5	12	pF
C_{idsel} IDSEL Pin Capacitance	note (4)		8	pF
L_{pin} Pin Inductance	note (5)		20	nH

NOTES:
(1) Includes all leakage currents associated with a bidirectional buffer including the tri-state condition.
(2) 3 milliamps for signal lines *without* pull-up resistors. 6 milliamps for signal lines *with* pull-up resistors. See section on pullups for specific signals.
(3) 10 pF for components mounted on add-in cards. Up to16 pF for components mounted on the platform. This precludes use of high capacitance packages on add-in cards.
(4) Lower capacitance allows for a non-resistive attachment of IDSEL to AD[xx].
(5) Recommended but not required. High inductance packages may produce undesirable signal integrity. See spec. sheet of component.
(6) Guaranteed by design. Minimum voltage used to calculate pull-up resistors values. Input buffer current is at the minimum value at this voltage when the application is sensitive to static power utilization.

Table 12-1: 5V DC Specifications

The above table is paraphrased from *PCI Local Bus Specification* Rev. 2.1, reprinted with permission of the PCI Special Interest Group.

5V AC SPECIFICATIONS

The PCI bus is designed to signal from one component to another with a *reflected wave* technique. When a signal is launched onto the bus, it is required to propagate to all extremes of the bus wire with only one half of the required logic threshold voltage amplitude. As the physical extremes of the bus wire are encountered, the signal *reflects* and propagates back to all points on the bus wire again. If the bus is implemented correctly, all points on the bus wire will obtain valid logic voltage threshold levels by the end of the second propagation. This system bus propagation parameter is defined as T_{prop} and will be described in greater detail in the timing section.

For this scheme to work properly, there must be enough instantaneous current from an output buffer to develop the initial half amplitude voltage step on a bus wire loaded with PCI components. On the other hand, too much current from the output buffer will create excessive reflections and may require too much time for the bus to settle. The AC table and the V/I curves shown in this section are the specification mechanisms used to constrain the output buffer currents.

In addition to developing the initial half amplitude voltage step without too little or too much current drive, a PCI output buffer must also meet these requirements:

- The minimum and maximum propagation time of the output buffer must be met. This parameter is defined as T_{val} and will be described further in the timing section.

- The slew rate (rate of output voltage change as a function of time), must be maintained within limits. This keeps the magnitude of any bus reflections under control. This parameter is defined as $slew_r$, $slew_f$ and is described in the AC table.

- Clamp devices to the lower voltage supply are required to limit excessive voltage excursions. These clamps are intended to absorb some of the reflected energy on the bus. The clamp parameters are defined in the 5V AC table.

The information contained in Tables 12-1 and 12-2 refers to the V/I curves in Figure 12-1

Symbol and Parameter	Conditions (notes)	Min	Max	Units
I_{oh} Switching Current High	$0<V_{out}<=1.4$ notes (1, 4)	-44		mA
	$1.4<V_{out}<2.4$ notes (1,2)	$-44+(V_{out}1.4)/0.024$		mA
	$3.1<V_{out}<V_{cc}$ notes (1,3)		EQ A on V/I curve	
I_{oh} Test Point	$V_{out} = 3.1$ note (3)		-142	mA
I_{ol} Switching Current Low	$V_{out}=>2.2$ notes (1, 4)	95		mA
	$2.2>V_{out}>0.55$ note (1)	$V_{out}/0.023$		mA
	$0.71>V_{out}>0$ notes (1,3)		EQ B on V/I curve	
I_{ol} Test point	$V_{out} = 0.71$ note (3)		206	mA
I_{cl} Low Clamp Current	$-5<V_{in} <= -1$	$-25+(Vin+1)/0.015$		mA
slew$_r$ Output Fall Slew Rate	0.4V to 2.4V note (5)	1	5	V/ns
slew$_f$ Output Rise Slew Rate	2.4V to 0.4V note (5)	1	5	V/ns

NOTES:

(1) Refer to the V/I curves in Figure 12-1. This parameter does not apply to the CLK and RST# signals. For the REQ# and GNT# signals, only half the specified output current is needed (since they are point to point signals). The I_{oh} specification does not apply to open drain outputs.

(2) This segment of the minimum portion of the V/I curve is drawn from the AC drive point directly to the DC drive point rather than to the voltage rail (Vcc). This allows for the possibility of an N-channel pull-up structure in the output buffer.

(3) Maximum current requirements must be met as drivers pull beyond the first step voltage (AC drive point). Equations defining these maximums (EQ A and EQ B) are provided with the respective V/I diagrams in Figure 12-1. The equation defined maximums should be met by design. In order to facilitate component testing, a maximum current test point is defined for the pull up and pull down V/I curve of the output driver.

(4) Refer to the V/I curves in Figure 12-1. This condition correlates to the **AC drive point** on the pullup or pulldown V/I curve.

(5) This parameter is the cumulative or average edge rate across the specified rise or fall voltage range. The rise slew rate does not apply to open drain outputs.

The minimum slew rate (slowest signal edge) and maximum slew rate (fastest signal edge) must be met by all PCI components. Note that in revision 2.0 of the PCI specification the max slew rate was optional. To determine the maximum slew rate, it is recommended that the test load shown below be used to determine compliance.

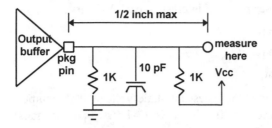

Max slew rate test load

Table 12-2: AC Specifications for 5 Volt Signaling

The above table is paraphrased from the PCI Local Bus Specification Rev. 2.1, reprinted with permission of the PCI Special Interest Group.

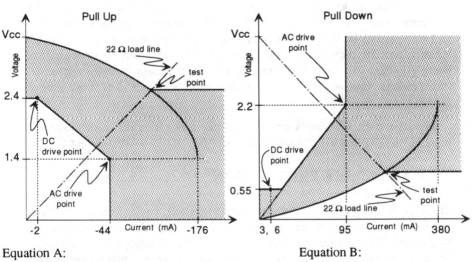

Equation A:

$$I_{oh} = 11.9*(V_{out}-5.25)*(V_{out}+2.45)$$

$$for\ Vcc > Vout > 3.1v$$

Equation B:

$$I_{ol} = 78.5*V_{out}*(4.4-V_{out})$$

$$for\ 0v < Vout < 0.71v$$

Figure 12-1: V/I Curves for 5V Signaling

The above figure is partly copied from *PCI Local Bus Specification Rev. 2.0 or 2.1*, reprinted with permission of the PCI Special Interest Group.

There are three particular points of interest on each V/I curve:

- The DC drive point
- The AC drive point
- The Test point

The **DC drive point** is the quiescent static voltage at the output of the PCI buffer. This point is also specified in Table 12-1 (DC Specifications) as V_{ol} and V_{oh}.

The **AC drive point** is the *minimum* instantaneous current needed to switch all points on the bus with one reflection. This parameter is specified in Table 12-2 (AC Specifications).

The **test point** is the *maximum* instantaneous current that any buffer is allowed to produce. Too much instantaneous current can create signal integrity problems (excessive ringing and slow settling times). This parameter is also specified in Table 12-2 (AC Specifications).

The V/I curves and associated parameters assume a bus configuration of six PCI components on the platform, and two PCI components in add-in slots, or two PCI components on the platform, and four PCI components in add-in slots. The 22 ohm load line shown on each V/I curve roughly represents the impedance of a heavily loaded PCI bus. Theoretically, if system busses actually appeared as resistive loads, buffers would not generate currents in excess of those shown at the load line.

Note that each V/I curve current axis is not drawn to scale. If plotted to scale, the 22 ohm load line will fall on the opposite side of the AC drive point.

5V AC DEVICE PROTECTION

Since the PCI bus is a reflected wave non-terminated environment, it is possible that voltage excursions at the input of devices may exceed the power supply rails. Some logic technologies have intrinsic immunity to large voltage excursions, while others can incur device damage. Because it is known that reflecting signal voltages on a PCI bus wire can exceed the power rails (both positive and negative excursions), the PCI specification recommends an overvoltage test for PCI devices. This overvoltage test environment is shown in Figure 12-2.

The purpose of the test is to help determine long term reliability. The conditions of the test are defined as follows:

- A zero impedance voltage source must provide the waveforms shown as an open circuit voltage.

■ The appropriate resistor is inserted between the voltage source and the device under test (DUT).

All PCI input, bi-directional, and tri-state pins should be able withstand continuous exposure to the test conditions.

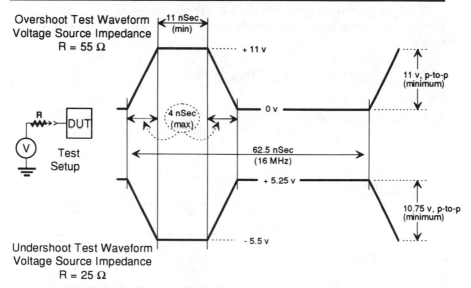

Figure 12–2: Test Waveform for 5V Signaling

The above figure is partly copied from *PCI Local Bus Specification Rev. 2.1*, reprinted with permission of the PCI Special Interest Group.

Note that the test waveform is not applied directly to the device under test. The resistor is always between the voltage source and the DUT. Well implemented clamp devices (as specified in *5V AC Specifications* ,Table 12-2) can greatly reduce undershoot voltages. An upper rail clamp is optional for the 5V environment, but if implemented, the supply clamp must always connect to +5V.

12.3 3.3V COMPONENT ELECTRICAL SPECIFICATIONS

The 3.3V signaling environment not only differs from the 5V environment in voltage levels, but also in the way the voltages are specified. A scheme is used that specifies all important voltages as being proportional to the power supply voltage. This V_{cc} *-relative* scheme is applied to all DC and AC voltage specifications in the 3.3V environment. This environment is intended to be implemented exclusively with CMOS technology.

Like the 5V signaling environment, output drive capability is specified using an AC drive point and the test point on V/I curves. Unlike the 5V environment, the 3V environment requires both upper and lower power rail clamp devices. These clamps are one important reason why the 5V and 3V signaling environments are incompatible.

3V signaling environment specifications are presented here, but without the specification explanations. See the 5V signaling environment section for these details.

3.3V DC SPECIFICATIONS

The following table outlines the important DC parameters for 3V signaling. Note that the switching thresholds (V_{ih}, and V_{il}), have changed from the 2.0 revision of the PCI specification:

3.3V DC SPECIFICATIONS

Symbol and Parameter	Conditions and (notes)	Min	Max	Units
V_{cc} Voltage Supply		3.0	3.6	V
V_{ih} Input High Voltage		$0.5V_{cc}$	$V_{cc}+0.5$	V
V_{il} Input Low Voltage		-0.5	$0.3V_{cc}$	V
V_{ipu} Input Pull-Up	note (1)	$0.7V_{cc}$		V
I_{il} Input Low Leakage Current	$0 < V_{in} < V_{cc}$		±10	µA
V_{oh} Output High Voltage	I_{out} = -500 µA	$0.9V_{cc}$		V
V_{ol} Output Low Voltage	I_{out} = 1500 µA		$0.1V_{cc}$	V
C_{in} Input Pin Capacitance	note (3)		10 or 16	pF
C_{clk} CLK Pin Capacitance		5	12	pF
C_{idsel} IDSEL Pin Capacitance	note (4)		8	pF
L_{pin} Pin Inductance	note (5)		20	nH

NOTES:
(1) Guaranteed by design. The minimum voltage to which pull-up resistors are calculated to pull a floated network. Input buffers sensitive to static power consumption should assure minimum conducting current at this input voltage.

(2) Includes all leakage currents associated with a bidirectional buffer including the tri-state condition.

(3) 10 pF for components mounted on add-in cards. Up to 16 pF for components mounted on the platform motherboard. This precludes use of high capacitance packages on add-in cards.

(4) Lower capacitance allows for a non-resistive attachment of IDSEL to AD[xx].

(5) Recommended but not required. High inductance packages may produce undesirable signal integrity. See spec. sheet of component.

Table 12-3: 3.3V DC Specifications

The above table is paraphrased from *PCI Local Bus Specification* Rev. 2.1, reprinted with permission of the PCI Special Interest Group.

3.3V AC SPECIFICATIONS

For an overview discussion of AC specifications, see the section *5V AC Specifications*. The AC table and the V/I curves shown in this section are the specification mechanisms used to constrain the 3.3V output buffer currents.

In addition to developing the initial half amplitude voltage step without too little or too much current drive, a PCI output must also meet these requirements:

- The minimum and maximum propagation time of the output buffer must be met. This parameter is defined as T_{val} and will be described further in the timing section.

- The slew rate (rate of output voltage change as a function of time), must be maintained within limits. This keeps the magnitude of any bus reflections under control. This parameter is defined as $slew_r$, $slew_f$ and is described in the AC table.

- Input clamp devices are required on both the upper and lower voltage supply rails to limit excessive voltage excursions. These clamps are intended to absorb some of the reflected energy on the bus. The clamp parameters are defined in the 3.3V AC table.

The information contained in Tables 12-3 and 12-4 refers to the V/I curves in Figure 12-3.

407

Symbol and Parameter	Conditions (notes)	Min	Max	Units
I_{oh}	$0 < V_{out} \le 0.3V_{cc}$ notes (1, 3)	$-12V_{cc}$		mA
	$0.3V_{cc} < V_{out} < 0.9V_{cc}$ note (1)	$-17.1(V_{cc} - V_{out})$		mA
Switching Current High	$0.7V_{cc} < V_{out} < V_{cc}$ notes (1, 2)		EQ C on V/I curve	
I_{oh} Test Point	$V_{out} = 0.7V_{cc}$ note (2)		$-32V_{cc}$	mA
I_{ol}	$V_{cc} > V_{out} => 0.6V_{cc}$ notes (1, 3)	$16V_{cc}$		mA
	$0.6V_{cc} > V_{out} > 0.1V_{cc}$ note (1)	$26.7/V_{out}$		mA
Switching Current Low	$0.18V_{cc} > V_{out} > 0$ notes (1, 2)		EQ C on V/I curve	
I_{ol} Test point	$V_{out} = 0.18V_{cc}$ note (2)		$38V_{cc}$	mA
I_{cl} Low Clamp Current	$-3 < V_{in} \le -1$	$-25 + (V_{in}+1)/0.015$		mA
I_{ch} High Clamp Current	$V_{cc}+4 > V_{in} => V_{cc}+1$	$25 + (V_{in}-V_{cc}-1)/0.015$		mA
$slew_r$ Output Fall Slew Rate	$0.2V_{cc} - 0.6V_{cc}$ note (4)	1	4	V/ns
$slew_f$ Output Rise Slew Rate	$0.6V_{cc} - 0.2V_{cc}$ note (4)	1	4	V/ns

NOTES:
(1) Refer to the V/I curves in Figure 12-3. This parameter does not apply to the CLK and RST# signals. For the REQ# and GNT# signals, only half the specified output current is needed.

The I_{oh} specification does not apply to open drain outputs.

(2) Maximum current requirements must be met as drivers pull beyond the initial first step voltage (AC drive point). Equations defining these maximums (EQ C and EQ D) are provided with the respective V/I diagrams in Figure 12-3. The equation defined maximums should be met by design. In order to facilitate component testing, a maximum current test point is defined for the pull up and pull down V/I curve of the output driver.

(3) Refer to the V/I curves in Figure 12-3. This condition correlates to the **AC drive point** on the pullup or pulldown V/I curve.

(4) This parameter is the cumulative or average edge rate across the specified rise or fall voltage range. The rise slew rate does not apply to open drain outputs.

The minimum slew rate (slowest signal edge) and maximum slew rate (fastest signal edge) must be met by all PCI components. To determine the maximum slew rate, it is recommended that the test load shown below be used to determine compliance.

408

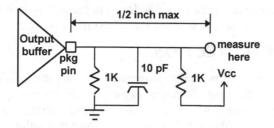

Max slew rate test load

Table 12-4: AC Specifications for 3.3 Volt Signaling

The above table is paraphrased from the *PCI Local Bus Specification Rev. 2.1*, reprinted with permission of the PCI Special Interest Group.

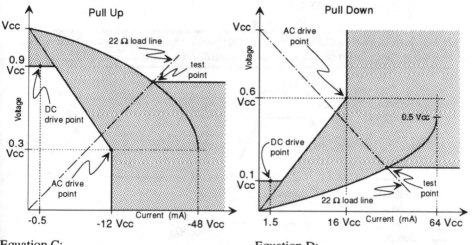

Equation C:

$$I_{oh} = (98.0/V_{cc})*(V_{out}-V_{cc})*(V_{out}+0.4V_{cc})$$

$$for\ V_{cc} > V_{out} > 0.7\ V_{cc}$$

Equation D:

$$I_{ol} = (256/V_{cc})*V_{out}*(V_{cc}-V_{out})$$

$$for\ 0v < V_{out} < 0.18\ V_{cc}$$

Figure 12-3: V/I Curves for 3.3V Signaling

The above figure is partly copied from *PCI Local Bus Specification Rev. 2.1*, reprinted with permission of the PCI Special Interest Group.

Note that each V/I curve current axis is not drawn to scale. If plotted to scale, the 22 ohm load line will fall on the opposite side of the AC drive point.

3V AC DEVICE PROTECTION

Since the PCI bus is a reflected wave non-terminated environment, it is possible that voltage excursions at the input of devices may exceed the power supply rails. Some logic technologies have intrinsic immunity to large voltage excursions, while others may incur device damage. Because it is known that reflecting signal voltages on a PCI bus wire can exceed the power rails (both positive and negative excursions), the PCI specification recommends an overvoltage test for PCI devices. This overvoltage test environment is shown in Figure 12-4.

The purpose of the test is to help determine long term reliability. The conditions of the test are defined as follows:

- A zero impedance voltage source must provide the waveforms shown as an open circuit voltage.
- The appropriate resistor is inserted between the voltage source and the device under test (DUT).

All PCI input, bi-directional, and tri-state pins should be able withstand continuous exposure to the above test conditions.

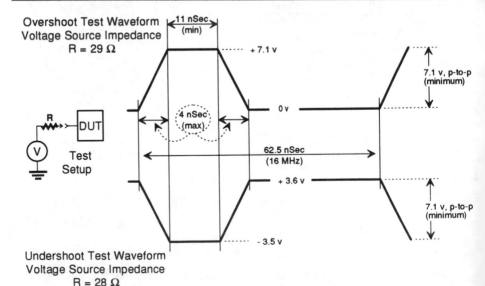

Figure 12-4: Test Waveform for 3.3V Signaling

The above figure is partly copied from *PCI Local Bus Specification Rev. 2.1*, reprinted with permission of the PCI Special Interest Group.

Note that the test waveform is not applied to the device under test. The resistor is always between the voltage source and the DUT. Well implemented clamp devices (as specified in *3V AC Specifications* ,Table 12-4) can greatly reduce overshoot and undershoot voltages. The upper rail voltage supply clamp must always connect to +3.3V.

12.4 CLOCK TIMING

All PCI signals are synchronized to the rising edge of CLK except for RST#, SERR#, and INTx#

A 33 MHz PCI system will have a clock period of 30 ns. The PCI specification requires that PCI components operate from a frequency DC up to 33 MHz.

> All PCI resources must operate with a CLK signal line frequency from DC to 33 MHz. The CLK signal line frequency may be changed at any time provided the minimum t_{cyc}, t_{high}, and t_{low} times are maintained. The CLK signal line edges must be clean and complete transitions at all times. PCI resources that will only be installed on the platform (not an add-in card) can be designed to operate at only one fixed frequency without supporting changes in the CLK signal line frequency.

The duty cycle of the clock waveform is specified as having a minimum high time ($T_{\_high}$) of 11 ns, and a minimum low time ($T_{\_low}$) of 11 ns. Systems that operate at frequencies slower that 33 MHz, can have larger values of $T_{\_high}$ and $T_{\_low}$.

The PCI clock must be generated and distributed carefully on the platform and on add-in cards to maintain low clock skew (t_{skew}). As seen in Figure 12-5, all PCI components must obtain a copy of the PCI clock within 2 ns of any other PCI component. Clock skew is measured at the package pins of components.

Symbol	5V Signaling	3.3V Signaling	Units
V_{TEST}	1.5	$0.4\ V_{CC}$	V
t_{SKEW}	2 (max)	2 (max)	ns

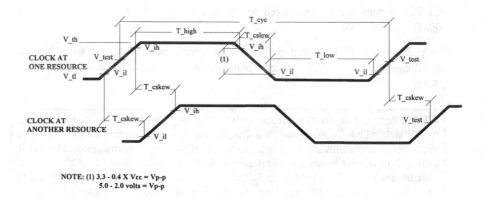

NOTE: (1) 3.3 - 0.4 X Vcc = Vp-p
5.0 - 2.0 volts = Vp-p

Figure 12-5: Clock Skew

The above table is copied from *PCI Local Bus Specification Rev. 2.1*, reprinted with permission of the PCI Special Interest Group.

For a detailed description of clock waveforms and measurement definitions, see Appendix G, from the PCI Bus Specification Rev. 2.1 (section 4.2.3.1), reprinted with permission of the PCI Special Interest Group.

12-5 SYSTEM TIMING

PCI bus electrical communication is a conventional synchronous register to register scheme. Some important parameters for specifying a PCI register to register transfer are:

- Cycle time (T_cyc). The period of one clock cycle; the total amount of time available to complete a transfer.

- Clock to data valid time (T_{val}). CLK and data measured at component pins.

- Clock skew (t_{skew}). The uncertainty of the rising edge of the clock at any PCI component package pin. clock skew subtracts directly from the cycle time.

- Bus propagation time (T_{prop}). This is the time needed for the electrical signal to propagate from one PCI component to all other PCI components.

- Input setup time (t_{su}). The time data must arrive at the receiving register before the PCI clock arrives.

- Input hold time (t_h). The time data must remain at the receiving register after the PCI clock arrives.

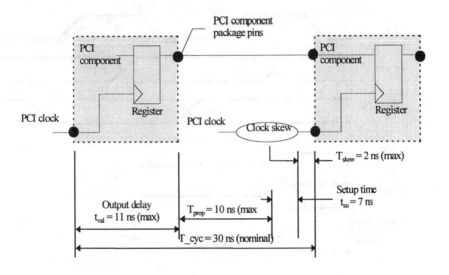

Figure 12-6: System Timing Parameters

For more detailed specifications of all system timing parameters, see Appendix G, from the PCI Bus Specification Rev. 2.1 (sections 4.2.3.2 and 4.2.3.3), reprinted with permission of the PCI Special Interest Group

TRI-STATE SIGNALS

At times, the signal lines are not always driven and are tri-stated. Refer to Figure 12-7. The Driving event t_4 (t_on) and Tri-stating event t_5 (t_off) of the signal line are also referenced to the rising edge of the CLK signal line.

> Throughout the book, the driving and tri-stating of signal lines are identified by *D* and *T*, respectively. In Figure 12-1-A, *D* is $t_4(t_{on})$ and *T* is $t_5(t_{off})$. The FRAME#, IRDY#, TRDY#, DEVSEL#, REQ64#, ACK64#, STOP#, PERR#, and LOCK# signal lines (specified as bi-directional drive tri-state in Chapter 5) must be driven by an active driver for one CLK signal line period before it is tri-stated, as shown in Figure 12-5-B.

The timing requirements are summarized in Table 12-7. (All entries are in nanoseconds, except as noted.)

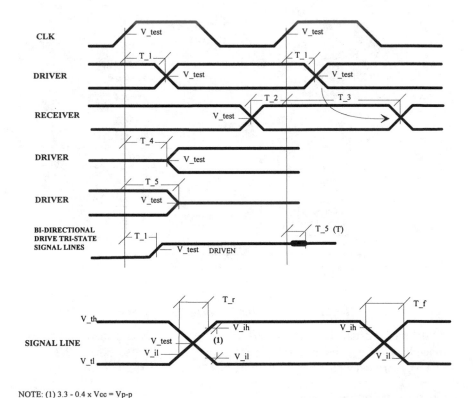

NOTE: (1) 3.3 - 0.4 x Vcc = Vp-p
        5.0 - 2.0 volts = Vp-p

Figure 12-7: Signal-Line Timing Relationships

The above figure is partly copied from PCI Local Bus Specification Rev. 2.1, reprinted with permission of the PCI Special Interest Group.

The timing parameters assume certain test conditions and voltage levels which are listed in Table 12-5 and referenced in Figure 12-7.

SYMBOL	5 Volt Signaling (Volts)	3.3 Volt Signaling (Volts)
V_{th} (1)	2.4	$0.6 \times V_{cc}$
V_{tl} (1)	0.4	$0.2 \times V_{cc}$
V_{test}	1.5	$0.4 \times V_{cc}$
V_{max} (1)	2.0	$0.4 \times V_{cc}$
V_{ih}	2.0	$0.5 \times V_{cc}$
V_{il}	.8	$0.3 \times V_{cc}$
Test Edge Rate	1 V/ns	1 V/ns

NOTES:
(1) Input test for 5 volt signaling is performed with input swing of 400 millivolts + $(V_{ih}-V_{il})$
(2) Input test for 3.3 volt signaling is performed with input swing of 0.1 x V_{cc} + $(V_{ih}-V_{il})$

Table 12-5: Test and Measurement Conditions

The above table is paraphrased from *PCI Local Bus Specification Rev. 2.1*, reprinted with permission of the PCI Special Interest Group.

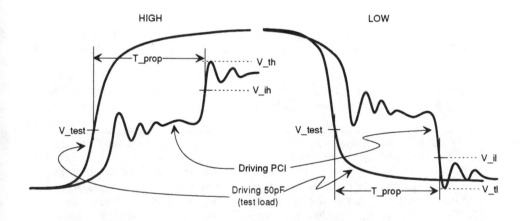

Figure 12-8: Measurement of T$_{prop}$ for 5V signaling

The above figure is copied from *PCI Local Bus Specification Rev. 2.0*, reprinted with permission of the PCI Special Interest Group.

T$_{prop}$ is the actual "flight time" of a signal on the bus. That is, the time a signal leaves the driving pin to when a full amplitude signal arrives at all receivers. The platform design must insure the T$_{prop}$ time as follows:

- The T$_{prop}$ time must be less than 10 nanoseconds for systems operating at 33 MHz. If slower clock rates are used, more time can be allocated to T$_{prop}$.

■ When calculating minimum bus transfer scenarios, assume T_{prop} to be 0
ns. In this case, T_{val} (min) will just cover the clock skew.

12.6 PULL-UP RESISTORS

As outlined in Chapter 5, some of the signal lines have pull-up resistors. The
value of these resistors are summarized in Table 12-6.

SIGNALING VOLTAGE	MIN. OHMS (1)	MAX. OHMS
5	963	$[(V_{cc}\text{- min})\text{-}2.7]/[\#loads \times I_{ih}]$
3.3	2.42K	$[(V_{cc}\text{- min})\text{-}(0.7 \times V_{cc})]/[\#loads \times I_{ih}]$

Notes:
Min pullup resistance = $[(V_{cc} \text{max})\text{-}V_{ol}]/[I_{ol} +(16 \times I_{il})]$ Where the max # loads=16

Table 12-6: Pull-Up Resistor Values

The above table is paraphrased from *PCI Local Bus Specification Rev. 2.1*, reprinted with
permission of the PCI Special Interest Group.

PCI signals that require pull-ups are: FRAME#, TRDX#, IRDY# DEVSEL#,
STOP#, SERR#, PERR#, LOCK#. If implemented, AD[63::32], C/BE[7::4]#,
PAR64#, REQ64#, ACK64.

The central resource in the platform may need pull-ups on REQ# signals. The
specification for REQ# pull-ups is platform independent.

> A PCI bus resource that supports 64 data bit accesses may be attached
> to a PCI bus that only supports 32 data bits. Consequently, the AD[63::32]
> C/BE#[7::4], and PAR64 signal lines will not be attached to pull-up
> resistors on the platform. In order to prevent these signal lines from
> floating and possibly oscillating, the component must drive these signal
> lines as outputs or, if in the input state, they must be biased. Solutions
> that violate the input leakage current specification, or, in the case of add-
> in cards external pull-up resistors, are *not* allowed.

12.7 CLAMP ISSUES

Clamps are specified on PCI input pins to help maintain good bus signal
integrity. Care must be taken when connecting devices that operate at different
supply voltages to prevent parasitic DC current paths.

Input pins of a PCI integrated circuit operating in the 5V signaling environment must be diode clamped to ground. Inputs to circuits operating in the 3.3C signaling environment must be diode clamped to both the 3.3V rail and ground.. The requirements for diode clamping to 5 or 3.3 volts and associated I/O buffer issues are as follows:

- Diode clamping of the 5 volt signaling I/O buffers to the 3.3 volt power rail is not allowed under any conditions.

- If 3.3 volt PCI integrated circuit components are 5 volt tolerant and are mounted on a Dual Voltage Add-in Card, the I/O buffers can optionally be connected to either the I/O Designated Power pads or the 3.3 volt power pads.

- Diode clamps and pull-up devices must be able to withstand a short-circuit condition due to power failure during the smaller, t_5 (t_{off}), of the following two conditions. See *Chapter 11: RESET, Power, and Signal Line Initialization* for details.

  ⇒ The RST# signal line must be asserted within 500 nanoseconds (t_5,t_{off}) from when 3.3V or 5 volts exceeds the minimum and maximum values in Table 11-1 by 500 millivolts. See Figure 11-1.

  or

  ⇒ The RST# signal line must be asserted within 100 nanoseconds (t_5,t_{off}). from when the 5 volt rail falls below the 3.3 volt rail by 300 millivolts or more. See Figure 11-1

  ⇒ The above minimum time must be increased by 40 nanoseconds to account for the signal lines to tri-state after the RST# signal line is asserted. See Figure 11-1.

CHAPTER 13

CONNECTOR, PLATFORM, AND ADD-IN CARD DESIGN

This chapter consists of the following subchapters:

13.0 CONNECTOR PINS AND PADS

INTRODUCTION

As outlined in Chapter 12, there are three types of add-in cards (5 Volt, 3.3 Volt, and Dual Voltage) and two types of connectors (5 volt and 3.3 volt). As shown in Figure 13-1, the specific type of add-in card that can be inserted into a specific connector type is controlled by the keying of the add-in card and connector. Also, as outlined in earlier chapters, the PCI bus specification supports 32 and 64 data bit resources. The connector assignments are outlined in Table 13-1 for the two types of connectors. Pins 1 to 62 define the two types of connectors that support 32 data bit PCI resources. The additional pins (63 to 94) support the 64 data bit extension of the PCI bus.

The PCI add-in card pinout is the same as the connector (Table 13-1) except for the "connector key" is the "keyway". Also, the "connector pins" defined for the connector on the platform are specified as "connector pads" on the add-in card.

There are several connector pins and pads that deserve particular note:

- On the platform, pins labeled +5V(I/O) and +3.3V(I/O) are the I/O Designated Power Pins. If the platform supports 3.3 volt signaling, the +3.3V(I/O) pins are attached to the 3.3 volt power plane. If the platform supports 5 volt signaling, the +5V(I/O) pins are attached to the 5 volt power plane. This is how A Dual Voltage Add-in Card "knows" what type of system it is plugged into. A Dual Voltage Add-in Card can power the I/O buffers from the I/O Designated Power Pins. The 5 Volt and 3.3 Volt Add-in Card can attach the I/O buffers of its components to the +V(I/O) connector pins and be sure to obtain the proper signaling environment power supply.

Pin	5V System Side B	5V System Side A	3.3V System Side B	3.3V System Side A
	5V System		**3.3V System**	
Pin	**Side B**	**Side A**	**Side B**	**Side A**
	32-Bit Connector Start			
1	-12V	TRST#	-12V	TRST#
2	TCK	+12V	TCK	+12V
3	GND	TMS	GND	TMS
4	TDO	TDI	TDO	TDI
5	+5V	+5V	+5V	+5V
6	+5V	INTA#	+5V	INTA#
7	INTB#	INTC#	INTB#	INTC#
8	INTD#	+5V	INTD#	+5V
9	PRSNT1#	RSVD	PRSNT1#	RSVD
10	RSVD	+5V (I/O)	RSVD	+3.3V (I/O)
11	PRSNT2#	RSVD	PRSNT2#	RSVD
12	GND	GND	KEY	KEY
13	GND	GND	KEY	KEY
14	RSVD	RSVD	RSVD	RSVD
15	GND	RST#	GND	RST#
16	CLK	+5V (I/O)	CLK	+3.3V (I/O)
17	GND	GNT#	GND	GNT#
18	REQ#	GND	REQ#	GND
19	+5V (I/O)	RSVD	+3.3V (I/O)	RSVD
20	AD[31]	AD[30]	AD[31]	AD[30]
21	AD[29]	+3.3V	AD[29]	+3.3V
22	GND	AD[28]	GND	AD[28]
23	AD[27]	AD[26]	AD[27]	AD[26]
24	AD[25]	GND	AD[25]	GND
25	+3.3V	AD[24]	+3.3V	AD[24]
26	C/BE[3]#	IDSEL	C/BE[3]#	IDSEL
27	AD[23]	+3.3V	AD[23]	+3.3V
28	GND	AD[22]	GND	AD[22]
29	AD[21]	AD[20]	AD[21]	AD[20]
30	AD[19]	GND	AD[19]	GND
31	+3.3V	AD[18]	+3.3V	AD[18]
32	AD[17]	AD[16]	AD[17]	AD[16]
33	C/BE[2]#	+3.3V	C/BE[2]#	+3.3V
34	GND	FRAME#	GND	FRAME#
35	IRDY#	GND	IRDY#	GND

Table 13-1: PCI Connector Pinout.

36	+3.3V	TRDY#	+3.3V	TRDY#
37	DEVSEL#	GND	DEVSEL#	GND
38	GND	STOP#	GND	STOP#
39	LOCK#	+3.3V	LOCK#	+3.3V
40	PERR#	SDONE	PERR#	SDONE
41	+3.3V	SBO#	+3.3V	SBO#
42	SERR#	GND	SERR#	GND
43	+3.3V	PAR	+3.3V	PAR
44	C/BE[1]#	AD[15]	C/BE[1]#	AD[15]
45	AD[14]	+3.3V	AD[14]	+3.3V
46	GND	AD[13]	GND	AD[13]
47	AD[12]	AD[11]	AD[12]	AD[11]
48	AD[10]	GND	AD[10]	GND
49	M66EN	AD[09]	M66EN	AD[09]
50	Key	Key	GND	GND
51	Key	Key	GND	GND
52	AD[08]	C/BE[0]#	AD[08]	C/BE[0]#
53	AD[07]	+3.3V	AD[07]	+3.3V
54	+3.3V	AD[06]	+3.3V	AD[06]
55	AD[05]	AD[04]	AD[05]	AD[04]
56	AD[03]	GND	AD[03]	GND
57	GND	AD[02]	GND	AD[02]
58	AD[01]	AD[00]	AD[01]	AD[00]
59	+5V (I/O)	+5V (I/O)	+3.3V (I/O)	+3.3V (I/O)
60	ACK64#	REQ64#	ACK64#	REQ64#
61	+5V	+5V	+5V	+5V
62	+5V	+5V	+5V	+5V
	32-Bit Connector End			
	Key	Key	Key	Key
	Key	Key	Key	Key
	64-Bit Connector Start			
63	RSVD	GND	RSVD	GND
64	GND	C/BE[7]#	GND	C/BE[7]#
65	C/BE[6]#	C/BE[5]#	C/BE[6]#	C/BE[5]#
66	C/BE[4]#	+5V (I/O)	C/BE[4]#	+3.3V (I/O)
67	GND	PAR64	GND	PAR64
68	AD[63]	AD[62]	AD[63]	AD[62]
69	AD[61]	GND	AD[61]	GND

Table 13-1: PCI Connector Pinout (continued)

70	+5V (I/O)	AD[60]	+3.3V (I/O)	AD[60]
71	AD[59]	AD[58]	AD[59]	AD[58]
72	AD[57]	GND	AD[57]	GND
73	GND	AD[56]	GND	AD[56]
74	AD[55]	AD[54]	AD[55]	AD[54]
75	AD[53]	+5V (I/O)	AD[53]	+3.3V (I/O)
76	GND	AD[52]	GND	AD[52]
77	AD[51]	AD[50]	AD[51]	AD[50]
78	AD[49]	GND	AD[49]	GND
79	+5V (I/O)	AD[48]	+3.3V (I/O)	AD[48]
80	AD[47]	AD[46]	AD[47]	AD[46]
81	AD[45]	GND	AD[45]	GND
82	GND	AD[44]	GND	AD[44]
83	AD[43]	AD[42]	AD[43]	AD[42]
84	AD[41]	+5V (I/O)	AD[41]	+3.3V (I/O)
85	GND	AD[40]	GND	AD[40]
86	AD[39]	AD[38]	AD[39]	AD[38]
87	AD[37]	GND	AD[37]	GND
88	+5V (I/O)	AD[36]	+3.3V (I/O)	AD[36]
89	AD[35]	AD[34]	AD[35]	AD[34]
90	AD[33]	GND	AD[33]	GND
91	GND	AD[32]	GND	AD[32]
92	RSVD	RSVD	RSVD	RSVD
93	RSVD	GND	RSVD	GND
94	GND	RSVD	GND	RSVD
64-Bit Connector End				

NOTE:

1.   Pins marked '+5V (I/O)' or '+3.3V (I/O)' on the system board are connected to 'V (I/O)' (3.3V or 5V) on the expansion (universal) board.

Table 13-1: PCI Connector Pinout (continued)

The table and figure are copied from PCI Local Bus Specification Rev. 2.0, reprinted with permission of the PCI Special Interest Group.

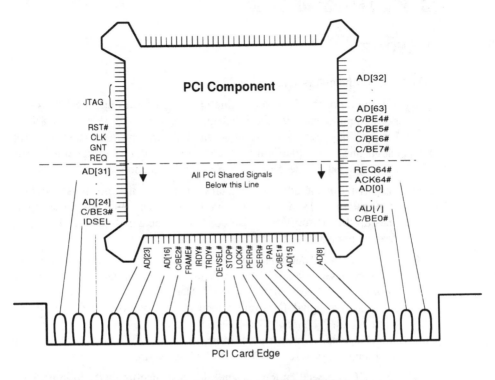

Figure 13-1: Suggested Pinout for PQFP PCI Component

■   The REQ64# and ACK64# pins on the connector are attached to pull-up
    resistors on the platform (no pull-up resistors are allowed on the add-in
    card) and are defined as part of the 32 data bit connector. On a platform
    that supports a 64 data bit (including connector) PCI bus, all of the
    REQ64# pins are attached to a single pull-up resistor. Similarly, all of
    the ACK64# pins are attached to a single pull-up resistor. On a platform
    that supports only a 32 data bit PCI bus, these pins must be individually
    attached to separate pull-up resistors and nothing else. On the add-in
    cards, the REQ64# and ACK64# pins are attached to the REQ64# and
    ACK64# signal lines, respectively.

■   The PRSNT1# and PRSNT2# pins identify the power (wattage)
    requirements of the add-in card and are grounded or left open by the
    add-in card. Please see *Chapter 11: RESET, Power, and Signal Line
    Initialization* for details.

■   To support the J-TAG boundary scan, the TDI and TDO signal lines are
    available on the connector. If the add-in card does not support J-TAG,
    the add-in card must connect these two pins together.

13.1 PLATFORM DESIGN

LAYOUT

The layout of the platform has several requirements:

- The layout of the CLK signal line on the platform must meet the clock skew requirements defined in Chapter 12. The clock skew is measured between any two PCI resources on the platform. The layout of this signal line on the platform must also consider the CLK signal traces on the add-in card as described in the following section.

- The layout of the other PCI signal lines on the platform must meet the propagation delay defined in Chapter 12. The layout of these signal lines on the platform must also consider associated traces on the add-in card as described in the following section.

- Any PCI signal line that can be shared by other PCI resources on the bus can have several PCI-compliant loads (*Chapter 2: PCI System Architectural Overview* for details). The pull-up resistors required for some of the signal lines are placed on the platform with the values outlined in *Chapter 12: Signal Line Timing and Electrical Requirements*. Consideration must be made to include add-in card requirements as described in the following section.

- The PCI bus specification does not define a specific platform impedance for the signal line traces. The platform impedance and layout must support a round trip time within the propagation delay defined in Chapter 12. The loaded impedance on the platform must allow the PCI output driver to meet the V/I curves in Figures 12-1 and 12-4 (roughly 22 ohms or greater). Consideration must be made to include add-in card requirements as described in the following section. To accommodate components and platform layouts that do not comply with these requirements, the CLK signal line frequency can be reduced. It is the responsibility of the platform designer to insure proper operation of all PCI resources under this consideration.

- Ideally, the platform should have six layers: one for 3.3 volts, one for 5 volts, one for ground, and three for non-power signal lines. For cost considerations, however, a four layer board may be more practical. In this case, two layers can be used for non-power signal lines (usually the outer layers), one layer for ground, and one layer (power plane) for either 5 or 3.3 volts. If both 3.3 and 5 volts are required, the power plane must be split. When the power plane is split, the non-power signal lines should be routed on the layer adjacent to the ground layer. If non-power signal lines are routed on the layer adjacent to the split power plane layer, care must be taken to keep the signal lines entirely on the 3.3 or the 5 volt section of the split power plane. If the non-power signal line must cross between the 3.3 and 5 volt sections, the two sections must be coupled by a 0.01 uF high-speed capacitor for every four non-power signal lines. This capacitor must be within 0.25 inches of the point where the non-power signal lines cross the split. These requirements reflect the concern that the split in the plane disrupts the AC return path for the non-power signal lines, creating an impedance discontinuity.

■

The preceding text is copied from PCI Local Bus Specification Rev. 2.0, and is reprinted with permission of the PCI Special Interest Group.

> The 12 and -12 volt power supply lines must be distributed as large traces, usually on the non-power signal line layers.

DECOUPLING CAPACITORS

In addition to the capacitors to connect split power planes, there are other capacitor requirements:

- The use of decoupling capacitors between the 3.3v, 5v, and ground layers is dependent on the platform and is not stated by the PCI bus specification. However, the PCI bus specification does state that twelve 0.01 uF high speed capacitors must be evenly spaced between the 3.3 volt and ground layers.

- The PRSNT1# and PRSNT2# pins on the connector must be individually decoupled to ground with 0.01 µF high speed capacitors.

13.2 ADD-IN CARD DESIGN

LAYOUT

The layout of the add-in card has several requirements:

- Maximum trace length of 1.5 inches from a connector pad to a component for all signal lines. Three exceptions are :
  ⇒ Maximum trace length of 2.0 inches from the connector pad to the component for the AD[63::32], C/BE#[7::4], PAR64, REQ64#, and the ACK64# signal lines.

⇒ The CLK signal line can only have a trace length of 2.5 inches +/- 0.1 inches from connector pad to a component and may be attached to only one load.

⇒ System Pins, Interrupt Pins, and JTAG Pins are not constrained by length requirements.

⇒ Maximum trace length (at 20 milli-inch thickness) of 0.25 inches from the connector pad to the 3.3 or 5 volt power planes.

■ Any PCI signal line that can be shared by other PCI resources on the bus can only have one PCI-compliant load (see Chapter 2: *PCI System Architectural Overview* for details). No pull-up resistors, other discrete devices, or non-compliant PCI components may be attached. A PCI/PCI bridge component must be used as a buffer if the add-in card requires circuitry that would violate these restrictions. The one exception to these requirements is the use of a resistor between the AD and IDSEL signal lines. Pre-driving of the address during configuration cycles is recommended to allow more time for a resistively coupled AD line to settle.

■ The unloaded characteristic impedance (Z_0) if the shared PCI signal line traces on the add-in card shall be controlled to be in the 60 to 100 ohm range. The signal velocity on the trace must be between 150 to 190 picoseconds per inch.

■ Ideally, the add-in card should be six layers: one for 3.3 volts, one for 5 volts, one for ground, and three for non-power signal lines. For cost considerations, a four layer board may be more practical. In this case, two layers may be used for non-power signal lines (usually the outer layers), one layer for ground, and one layer (power plane) for 5 or 3.3 volts.

If both 3.3 and 5 volts must be available, the power plane must be split. When the power plane is split, the non-power signal lines should be routed on the layer adjacent to the ground layer. If non-power signal lines are routed on the layer adjacent to the split power plane layer, care must be taken to keep the signal lines entirely on 3.3 to the 5 volt section of the split power plane. If the non-power signal line must cross between the 3.3 and 5 volt sections, the two sections must be coupled by a 0.01 uF high-speed capacitor for every four non-power signal lines. This capacitor must be within 0.25 inches of point where the non-power signal lines cross the split. These requirements reflect the concern that the split in the plane disrupts the AC return path for the non-power signal lines, creating an impedance discontinuity.

The above two bullets are copied from PCI Local Bus Specification Rev. 2.1, reprinted with permission of the PCI Special Interest Group.

> **The 12 and -12 volt power supply lines must be distributed as large traces, usually on the non-power signal line layers.**

- Figure 13-1 outlines the trace layout for a PCI component relative to the connector pads. Please note the following:

  ⇒ Idcally, no resistor should be placed between the individual AD and IDSEL signal lines; consequently, the IDSEL pin should be placed close to its respective AD pins.

  ⇒ The order of component pin assignments is the same order as specified in the connector pin assignments.

DECOUPLING CAPACITORS

In addition to the capacitors required to connect split power planes, there are other capacitor requirements as follows:

- For the Dual Voltage Add-in Card, the V(I/O) connector pads (I/O Designated Power Pins) must individually decouple to the ground layer with one 0.047 uF capacitor per connector pad. Several 0.047 uF capacitors may be combined into a larger capacitor.

- All unused 3.3 volt and 5 volt connector pads must be individually attached to a 0.01 uF high speed capacitor by a trace with a minimum width of 0.02 inches and a maximum length of 0.25 inches. Several connector pads can share a capacitor if trace requirements are met.

CHAPTER 14

LATENCY AND PERFORMANCE

This chapter consists of the following subchapters:

14.0   Latency
14.1   Performance

14.0 LATENCY

INTRODUCTION

There are three basic elements relative to latency for a PCI resource to become PCI bus master: Arbitration Latency, Acquisition Latency, and Target Latency.

ARBITRATION LATENCY

The Arbitration Latency is dependent on the arbitration algorithm of the central arbiter, the priority of the PCI resource requesting bus ownership, and the present bus cycle. It reflects the time required for the central arbiter to assert the GNT# signal line of a PCI resource that asserted its REQ# signal line to request bus ownership. The algorithm and priority components of the Arbitration Latency vary according to the PCI resource and platform. The length of time attributed to the present bus cycle component is controlled by two elements of the PCI bus protocol: Latency Timer and Disconnect termination. The Latency Timer prevents a PCI bus master from executing an infinitely long BURST access cycle when another PCI bus master with higher priority wants to own the bus. The Disconnect termination (as applied according to the "8 clock" rule) prevents a slow target from excessively extending an access cycle.

The Latency Timer is a programmable timer for each PCI bus master that reloads with the assertion of the FRAME# signal line. The timer counts each rising edge of the CLK signal line when the FRAME# signal line is asserted and expires within 256 or fewer CLK signal lines periods. The Latency Timer insures that each PCI bus master has a minimum time slot for it to own the bus, but places an upper limit on how long a PCI bus master will own the bus. Under the above protocol, the PCI bus master is not required to deassert its associated REQ# signal line. See *Completion with Timeout Termination of Access Cycles* for details. The Latency timer protocol is as follows:

- If the associated GNT# signal line is deasserted prior to the expiration of the timer, there are two possible protocols: (1) The PCI bus master is allowed to retain bus ownership until the present SINGLE bus cycle is complete, or (2) The PCI bus master is allowed to retain bus ownership and execute subsequent microaccesses of a BURST bus cycle until the burst is complete or the Latency Timer expires ... whichever occurs first. The expiration of the Latency Timer with the GNT# signal line deasserted requires the BURST bus cycle to be immediately completed with some exceptions relative to cache line boundaries. Also, an additional microaccess of a BURST cycle is allowed to be executed if the FRAME# and IRDY# signal line are both asserted when the GNT# signal line is deasserted and the Latency Timer expires.

- If the associated GNT# signal line is asserted when the Latency Timer expires, the PCI bus master is allowed to complete the bus cycle without any requirement to complete it "immediately" When the bus cycle completes the PCI bus master can reload the Latency Timer and begin another bus cycle if the associated GNT# signal line is still asserted.

> The Latency Timer does not apply to the completion of interrupt acknowledge or special cycles.

There are three rules related to how quickly a SINGLE bus cycle or a microaccess of a BURST cycle is completed: "Master Latency", "16 clock", and the "8 clock".

The "Master Latency" rule requires that the PCI bus master assert the IRDY# signal line within eight CLK signal line periods from when the FRAME# signal line was first asserted. That is, the IRDY# signal line will be sampled asserted on the ninth rising edge of the CLK signal line relative to the first rising edge of the CLK signal line when the FRAME# signal line was asserted. "Master latency" also requires that during subsequent microaccesses of a BURST bus cycle asserted the IRDY# signal line will be sampled asserted on the ninth rising edge of the CLK signal line relative to the first rising edge of the CLK signal line when the IRDY# and TRDY# signal lines are both asserted in the previous microaccess.

The target must implement the "16 clock" rule for a SINGLE bus cycle or the initial microaccess of a BURST bus cycle or execute a Retry termination. See Subchapter 8.1 for more information on the "16 clock" rule.

The target must implement the "8 clock" rule with the subsequent microaccesses of a BURST access cycle. The net effect of the "8 clock" rule is to place limits on the length of a BURST access cycle. The restrictions do not apply to a SINGLE access cycle or to the initial microaccess of a BURST access cycle. The "8 clock" rule simply forces the target to execute a Disconnect termination request under all of the following conditions.

■ All subsequent microaccesses of a BURST access cycle are governed by the "8 clock" rule.

■ The initial microaccess is completed when the IRDY# and TRDY# signal lines are both asserted at a CLK signal line rising edge. The target will begin counting on the subsequent CLK rising edge until one of the following occurs:

⇒ If the TRDY# signal line is asserted simultaneous with a count value of eight or less, the access cycle is allowed to complete with Completion termination whenever the IRDY# signal line is asserted

OR

⇒ If the TRDY# signal line is not asserted when the count reaches eight, the STOP# signal line must be asserted (the TRDY# or STOP# signal line will be sampled asserted on the ninth rising edge of the CLK signal line relative to the first rising edge of the CLK signal line when the IRDY# and TRDY# signal lines are both asserted in the previous microaccess). The assertion of the STOP# signal line results in a Disconnect termination without data.

■ See Figure 8-1-B in Subchapter 8.1 for an example of the "8 clock" rule.

> If the present Park master and the new PCI bus master are different PCI resources, the Arbitration Latency is two CLK signal line periods. If the present Park master and the new PCI bus master are the same PCI resource, the Arbitration Latency is zero CLK signal line periods. A Park master can begin a bus cycle without arbitration for bus ownership, without asserting its REQ# signal line, and without waiting for the assertion of its GNT# signal line (which is already asserted).

> The above "16 clock" and "8 clock" protocol rules apply to interrupt acknowledge cycles but does not apply to the special cycles. The special cycle does not have a specific target to claim the cycle and thereby own the STOP# signal line.

The Latency Timer does not restrict the number of CLK signal line periods relative to the DATA PHASE of a SINGLE access cycle or the initial microaccess of a BURST access cycle. When the FRAME# signal line is asserted at the beginning of the access cycle, the timer is reloaded and the counting begins. When the FRAME# signal line is deasserted, the completion of the access cycle is forthcoming; consequently, the timer counting is stopped. When the Latency Timer has expired and the associated GNT# signal line is deasserted, the access is allowed to complete. For a SINGLE access cycle, the FRAME# signal line is deasserted when the IRDY# signal line is asserted. If the IRDY# signal line remains deasserted until the timer has expired, the protocol still allows the access cycle to complete. For a BURST access cycle, the FRAME# signal line is asserted for the entire initial microaccess. If the IRDY# signal line remains deasserted during the initial microaccess until the timer has expired, the protocol still allows the access cycle to complete. The PCI bus master is the only resource that knows that a timer has expired. For a BURST access cycle, the PCI bus master can deassert the FRAME# signal line when the IRDY# signal line is asserted after the timer has expired and thus turn the BURST access cycle into a SINGLE access cycle. However, in some cases the PCI bus master must ignore the expiration of the timer. For example, a Memory Write Invalidate (MWI) must access an entire cache line. A 64 data bit PCI bus master may have to turn a SINGLE access cycle into a BURST access cycle to access a 32 data bit target.

For Disconnect terminations, the "8 clock" rule does not apply to a SINGLE access or the initial microaccess of a BURST access cycle. The "8 clock" rule applies only to the subsequent microaccesses of the BURST access cycle and interrupt acknowledge cycles.

ACQUISITION LATENCY

Once the central arbiter determines the next PCI bus master and the completion of the present bus cycle, it will award bus ownership by asserting the appropriate GNT# signal line. The delay between a PCI resource sampling the asserted GNT# signal line on the rising edge of the CLK signal line and the target sampling the asserted FRAME# signal line on the rising edge of the CLK signal line defines Acquisition Latency. As outlined in Chapter 9, there are three considerations about Acquisition Latency:

- As shown in Figures 9-6 and 9-7, the minimum Acquisition Latency delay is one CLK signal line period if the previous PCI bus master is just then completing a bus cycle. Similarly, if the new PCI bus master was the present Park master, the Acquisition Latency is one CLK signal line period.

■ As shown in Figures 9-4 and 9-5, the Acquisition Latency can be two CLK signal line periods when one PCI bus was in the IDLE PHASE and the present PCI bus master or Park master is not the new PCI bus master.

> The central arbiter should park the bus at the PCI resource that has the greatest need for the shortest latency.

TARGET LATENCY

Once the FRAME# signal is sampled asserted, the remaining latency component is Target Latency. As outlined above, the "16 clock" rule applies to the latency for the first data access and the "8 clock" rule applies to the subsequent data accesses (if a BURST cycle is executed). The time associated with the "Master Latency" rule falls within the confines of the two "8 clock" and "16 clock" rules.

TOTAL LATENCY

The total latency of a PCI bus master accessing a target is the total of the aforementioned three latencies. Consider the following four examples:

1. Assume that the new PCI bus master is also the present Park master and that the first access to a target is the fastest possible write. The total latency is equal to arbitration + acquisition + target = 0 + 1 + 1 = 2 CLK signal line periods (60 nanoseconds at a 33 MHz CLK).

2. Assume that the new PCI bus master is *not* the present Park master and that the first access to a target is the fastest possible write. The total latency is equal to arbitration + acquisition + target = 1 + 2 + 1 = 5 CLK signal line periods (150 nanoseconds at a 33 MHz CLK).

3. Assume that the present PCI bus master has just begun executing a subsequent microaccess in a BURST access cycle and the Latency Timer has expired when a new PCI bus master requests the bus (with the highest priority), and that the first access by the new PCI bus master to the a target is the fastest possible write. The total latency is equal to arbitration + acquisition + target = 17 + 1 + 1 = 19 CLK signal line periods (396 nanoseconds with a 33 MHz CLK).

4. Assume that the present PCI bus master has just asserted the FRAME# signal line for a SINGLE access cycle and reloaded the Latency Timer with a full count of 256 when a new PCI bus master requests the bus (with the highest priority), and that the first access by the new PCI bus master to the a target is the fastest possible write. The total latency is equal to arbitration + acquisition + target = 256 + 1 + 1 = 258 CLK signal line periods (7740 nanoseconds at a 33 MHz CLK).

> In example number 4, it is assumed that the assertion of the IRDY# and TRDY# signal lines of the last access of the present PCI bus master coincides with reaching the count of 256.

The total latency of a given bus on a platform depends on the number of PCI bus masters, the type of bus cycles executed, and several other factors. For PCI bus masters that rely on low total latency may want to implement a buffer to support 30 microsecond total latency delay. The typical total latency should be approximately 2-4 microseconds.

If one considers that the latency timer is programmable and due to bus loading five PCI bus masters seems practical, it is possible to determine a reasonable number to program into the latency timer. Rev. 2.1 of the PCI bus specification shows the calculation of 3.84 microseconds, with five PCI bus masters and a latency timer value of 24. The bus specification also recommends that PCI resources design for 10 microseconds.

> In that the worst case total latency cannot be guaranteed, all PCI resources should be able to gracefully recover if the total latency they were not designed for was not achieved.

LATENCY PROTOCOL

As outlined above, the PCI bus has latency protocols that allow some level of predictability of the maximum latency. Of particular concern is when an ISA bus master accesses a PCI resource through a PCI/LEGACY BRIDGE. The protocol of an ISA bus master allows it to retain ownership of the ISA bus (and thus the PCI bus) indefinitely. Also, there is no ISA bus master preemption protocol or ability for the BRIDGE to terminate an ISA bus cycle. The EISA bus also prevents the BRIDGE from terminating an EISA cycle, but it does have a preemption protocol that restricts an EISA access cycle to 64 BCLK signal line periods (7680 nanoseconds at a CLK = 8.33 MHz). The ability to predict a maximum latency requires that the aforementioned issues related to LEGACY buses are not considered for the remainder of this discussion.

It is the responsibility of the platform designer and integrator to carefully identify the protocol of the elements allowed in the platform to achieve a specific arbitration and Acquisition Latency time. Following are the latency-related guidelines:

■ The target of a SINGLE bus cycle should limit the number of CLK signal line periods for the DATA PHASE to 16 or less. The target of a BURST bus cycle should limit the initial microaccess to 16 or less CLK signal line periods. The PCI bus master associated with the BURST bus cycle should be ready (IRDY# signal line asserted) to complete the initial microaccess in 16 or less CLK signal line periods.

■ PCI bus masters must complete the DATA PHASE per the "Master Latency" rule. A PCI bus master that will not be able to meet the requirements of the "Master Latency" rule for a given DATA PHASE must not begin that particular DATA PHASE. (This requirement is new in PCI bus specification Rev. 2.1.)

■ Targets not able to complete the DATA PHASE per the "16 clock" rule (due to a defect or internal conflict) of a SINGLE bus cycle, or the initial microaccess of a BURST cycle, must execute a Retry termination. (Recommended in Rev. 2.0, required in Rev. 2.1.)

■ Targets not able to complete the DATA PHASE per the "8 clock" rule (due to a defect or internal conflict) of a subsequent microaccess of a BURST bus cycle must execute a Disconnect termination.

■ The posting of write data in BRIDGEs should be performed very carefully. In most architectures a strong data ordering is required; consequently, all of the posted writes must be completed before a read access cycle can be executed. The read access cycle may become exceptionally long while waiting for the posted write buffers to be emptied.

■ A BRIDGE should execute a Retry termination when the destination bus is owned by another bus master.

Interrupt acknowledge and special cycles adhere to the latency protocol outlined above. The "16 clock" and "8 clock" rules do not apply to special cycles because no specific target can claim the special cycle.

14.1 PERFORMANCE

The previous subchapter outlined the amount of time required to obtain ownership of the bus. Once a PCI bus master owns the bus and begins a cycle, the number of bytes accessed per unit time is a measure of performance. The PCI protocol defines several different types of bus cycles, some of which can be executed with the Fast Back-to-Back protocol (see *Chapter 6: Detailed Bus Cycle Operation* for details).

The maximum access rates for a 33 MHz CLK signal line are as follows:

NON FAST BACK-TO-BACK

- **Serial SINGLE reads**—33 Megabytes/sec at 32 data bits or 66 Megabytes/sec at 64 data bits
- **Serial SINGLE writes**—44 Megabytes/sec at 32 data bits or 88 Megabytes/sec at 64 data bits
- **BURST reads and writes**—132 Megabytes/sec at 32 data bits or 264 Megabytes/sec at 64 data bits

FAST BACK-TO-BACK

- **Serial SINGLE writes**—66 Megabytes/sec at 32 data bits or 132 Megabytes/sec at 64 data bits

The maximum access rates for a 66 MHz CLK signal line are as follows:

NON FAST BACK-TO-BACK

- **Serial SINGLE reads**—66 Megabytes/sec at 32 data bits or 128 Megabytes/sec at 64 data bits
- **Serial SINGLE writes**—88 Megabytes/sec at 32 data bits or 176 Megabytes/sec at 64 data bits
- **BURST reads and writes**—264 Megabytes/sec at 32 data bits or 528 Megabytes/sec at 64 data bits

FAST BACK-TO-BACK

- **Serial SINGLE writes**—132 Megabytes/sec at 32 data bits or 264 Megabytes/sec at 64 data bits

I/O and configuration access cycles and special and interrupt acknowledge cycles are only defined for 32 data bits.

64 data bit I/O targets can be implemented, but there is no benefit to requiring the increased complexity. Thus it is strongly recommended that 64 data bit I/O targets are not implemented. For the purposes of this book, I/O targets are only 32 data bits in size. If a 64 data bit I/O target is implemented, the 64 data bit protocol applied to memory targets would also apply to I/O targets.

CHAPTER 15

MECHANICAL SPECIFICATION

This chapter consists of the following subchapters:

15.1 Overview
15.2 Expansion Card Physical Dimensions and Tolerances

Text and figures in this chapter are copied from PCI Local Bus Specification Rev. 2.0, and is reprinted with permission of the PCI Special Interest Group.

15.1 OVERVIEW

The PCI expansion card is based on a raw card design (see Figures 15-1 and 15-2) that is easily implemented in existing designs from multiple manufacturers. The card design adapts to ISA, EISA, and MC systems. PCI expansion cards have two basic form factors: standard length and short length. The standard length card provides 49 square inches of real estate. The short card was chosen for panel optimization to provide the lowest cost for a function. The short card also provides the lowest cost to implement in a system, the lowest energy consumption, and allows the design of smaller systems. The interconnect for the expansion card has been defined for both the 32-bit and 64-bit interfaces.

PCI cards and connectors are keyed to manage the 5 volt to 3.3 volt transition. The basic 32-bit connector contains 120 pins. The logical numbering of pins, shows 124 pin identification numbers, but four pins are not present and are replaced by the keying location. In one orientation, the connector is keyed to accept 5 volt system signaling environment boards; turned 180° the key is located to accept 3.3 volt system signaling environment boards. Universal add-in cards, cards built to work in both 5 volt and 3.3 volt system signaling environments, have two key slots so that they can plug into either connector. A 64-bit extension, built onto the same connector molding, extends the total number of pins to 184. The 32-bit connector subset defines the system signaling environment. 32-bit cards and 64-bit cards are inter-operable within the system's signaling voltage classes defined by the keying in the 32-bit connector subset. A 32-bit card identifies itself for 32-bit transfers on the 64-bit connector. A 64-bit card in a 32-bit connector will configure for 32-bit transfers.

Maximum card power dissipation is encoded on the PRSNT1# and PRSNT2# pins of the expansion card. This hard encoding can be read by system software upon initialization. The system's software can then make a determination whether adequate cooling and supply current is available in that system for reliable operation at start-up and initialization time. Supported power levels and their encoding are defined in *Chapter 12: Signal Line Timing and Electrical Requirements*.

The PCI expansion card includes a mounting bracket for card location and retention. The backplate is the interface between the card and the system that provides for cable escapement. The card has been designed to accommodate PCI brackets for both ISA/EISA and MC systems. See Figures 15-4 and 15-5 for the ISA/EISA assemblies and Figure 15-6 and 15-7 for the MC assemblies. Bracket kits for each card type must be furnished with the PCI card so that end users may configure the card for their systems. The ISA/EISA kit contains a PCI bracket, four 4-40 screws, and a card extender. The assembled length of the PCI expansion board is that of an MC card. The extender fastens to the front edge of the PCI card to provide support via a standard ISA card guide. The MC bracket kit contains an MC bracket, four pan head 4-40 screws, and a bracket brace.

The component side of a PCI expansion card is the opposite of ISA/EISA and MC cards. The PCI card is a mirror image of ISA/EISA and MC cards. A goal of PCI is to enable its implementation in systems with a limited number of expansion card slots. In these systems, the PCI expansion board connector can coexist, within a single slot, with an ISA/EISA or MC card. However, only one expansion board can be installed in a shared slot at a time. For example, shared slots in PCI systems with an ISA expansion bus can accommodate an ISA or PCI expansion board; shared slots in PCI systems with an MC expansion bus can accommodate an MC or PCI expansion board; etc.

15.2   EXPANSION CARD PHYSICAL DIMENSIONS AND TOLERANCES

The maximum component height on the primary component side of the PCI expansion card is not to exceed 0.570 inches (14.48 mm). The maximum component height of the back side of the card is not to exceed 0.105 inches (2.67 mm). Datum A on the illustrations is used to locate the PCI card to the planar and to the frame interfaces; the back of the frame and the card guide. Datum A is carried through the locating key on the connector.

See Figures 15-1 through 15-10 for PCI expansion card physical dimensions.

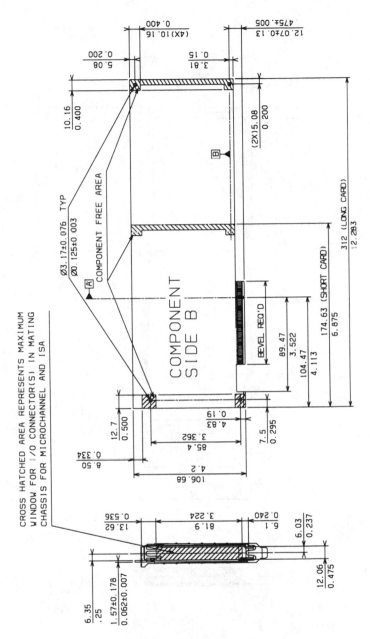

Figure 15-1: PCI Raw Card (5 volt)

441

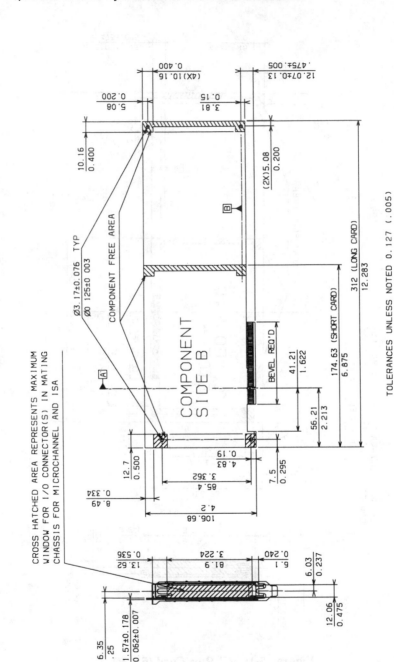

Figure 15-2: PCI Raw Card (3.3 volt)

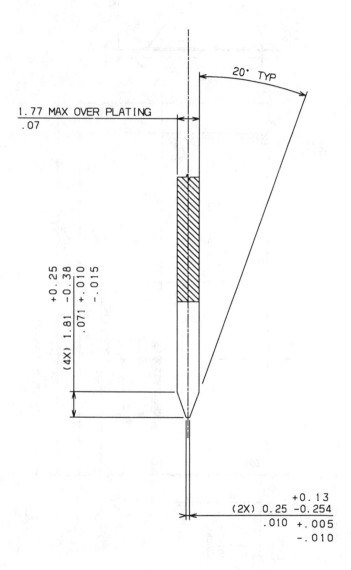

Figure 15-3: PCI Card Edge Connector Bevel

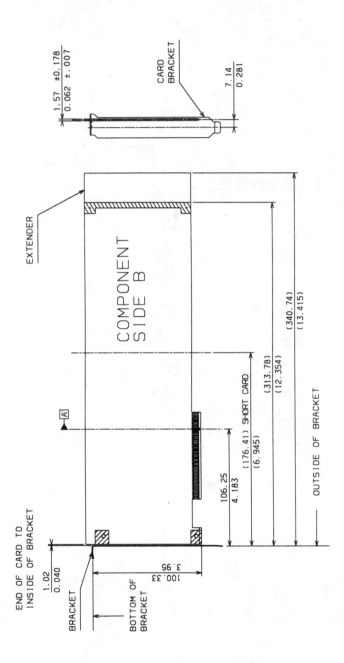

Figure 15-4: ISA Assembly (5 volt)

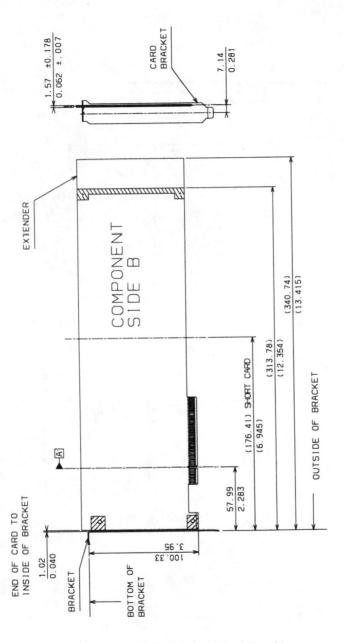

Figure 15-5: ISA Assembly (3.3 volt)

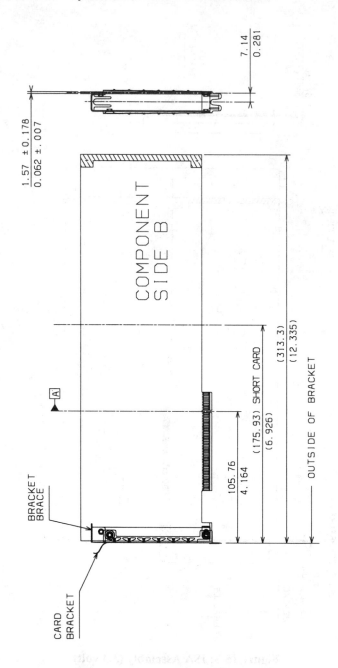

Figure 15-6: MC Assembly (5 volt)

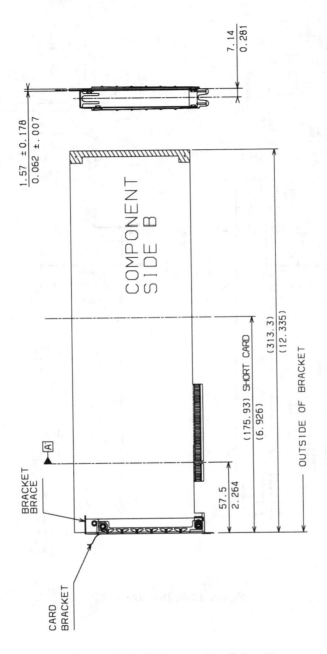

Figure 15-7: MC Assembly (3.3 volt)

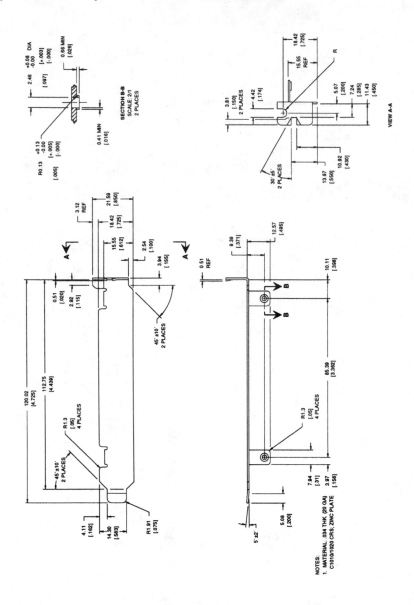

Figure 15-8: ISA Bracket

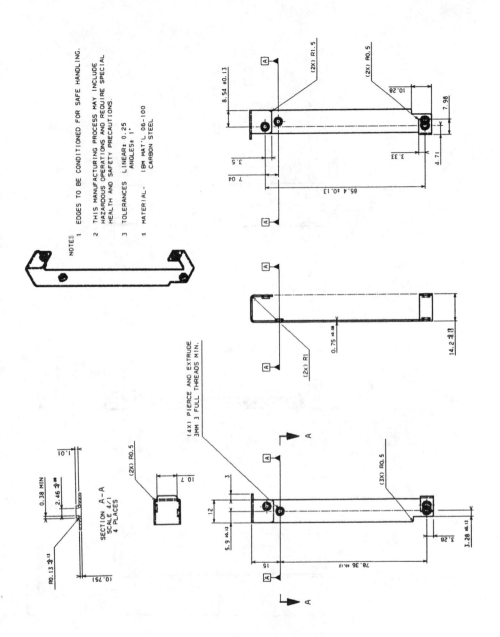

Figure 15-9: MC Bracket Brace

449

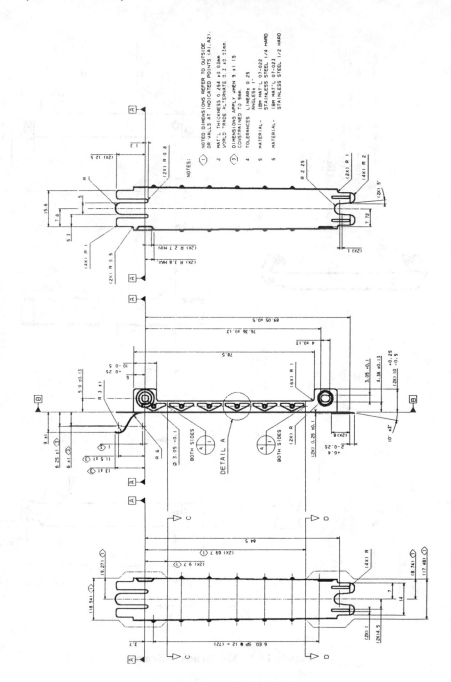

Figure 15-10: MC Bracket

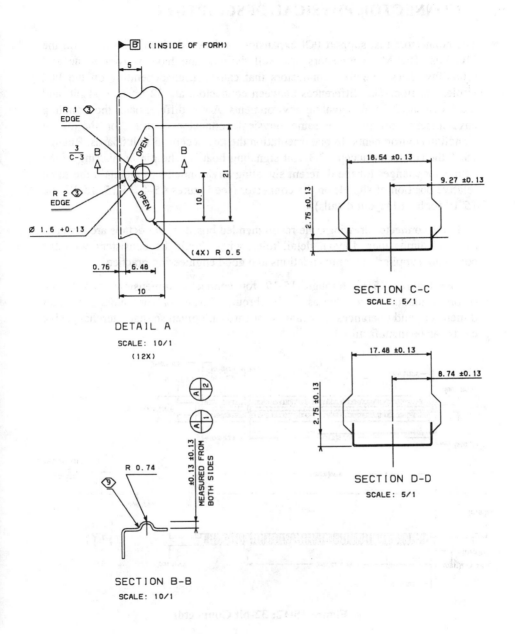

Figure 15-11: MC Bracket Details

451

CONNECTOR PHYSICAL DESCRIPTION

The connectors that support PCI expansion cards are derived from those on the MC bus. The MC connectors are well defined and have proven value and reliability. These are four connectors that can be used depending on the PCI implementation. The differences between connectors are 32 bit and 64 bit, and the 5 volt and 3.3 volt signaling environments. A key differentiates the signaling environment voltages. The same physical connector is used for the 32-bit signaling environments. In one orientation the key accepts 5 volt boards. Rotated 180°, the connector accepts 3.3 volt signaling boards. The pin numbering of the connector changes for the different signaling environments to maintain the same relative position of signals on the connector (see Figures 15-4, 15-15, 15-17 and 15-19 for board layout details).

In the connector drawings, the recommended board layout details are given as nominal dimensions. Layout detail tolerancing should be consistent with the connector supplier's recommendations and good engineering practice.

See Figures 15-13 through 15-19 for connector dimensions and layout recommendations. See Figures 15-20 through 15-26 for card edge connector dimensions and tolerances. Tolerances for cards are given so that interchangeable cards can be manufactured.

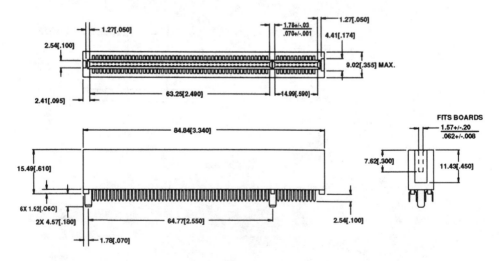

Figure 15-12: 32-bit Connector

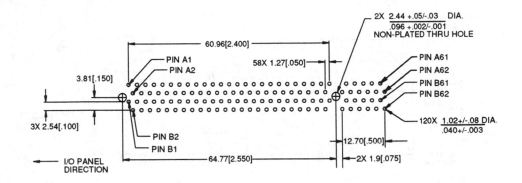

Figure 15-13: 5 Volt/32-bit Connector Layout Recommendation

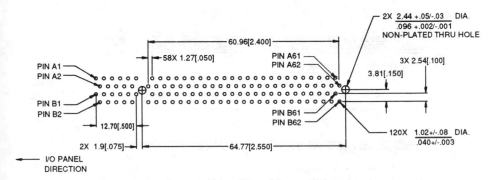

Figure 15-14: 3.3 Volt/32-bit Connector Layout Recommendation

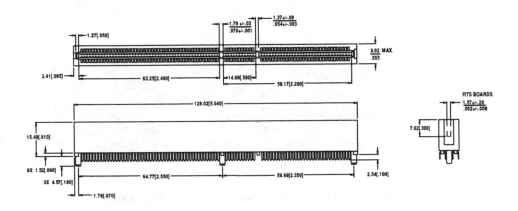

Figure 15-15: 5V/64-Bit Connector

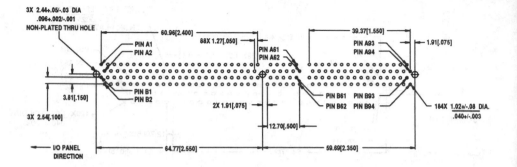

Figure 15-16: 5 Volt/64-Bit Connector Layout Recommendation

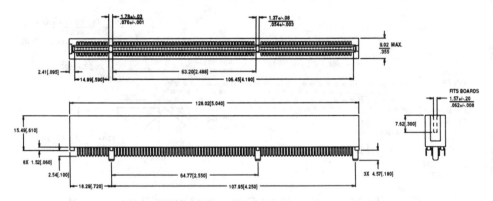

Figure 15-17: 3.3 Volt/64-Bit Connector

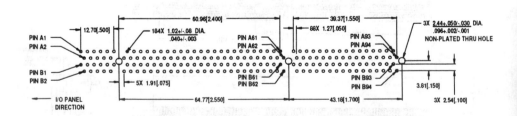

Figure 15-18: 3.3 Volt/64-Bit Connector Layout Recommendation

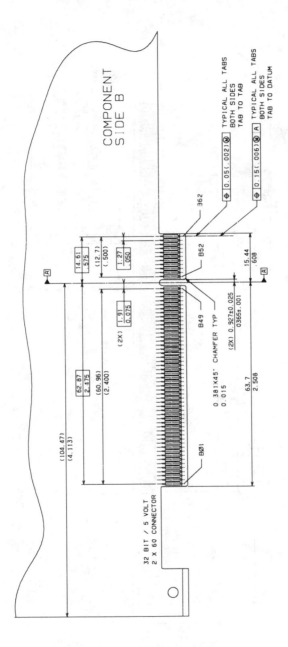

Figure 15-19: 5 Volt/32-Bit Card Edge Connector Dimensions and Tolerances

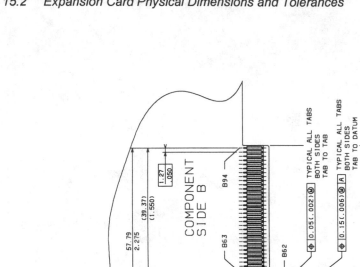

Figure 15-20: 5 Volt/64-Bit Card Edge Connector Dimensions and Tolerances

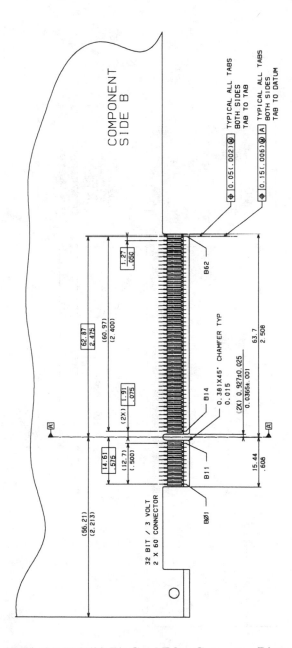

Figure 15-21: 3.3 Volt/32-Bit Card Edge Connector Dimensions and Tolerances

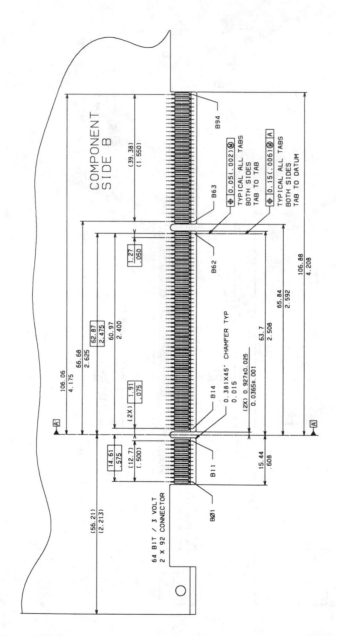

Figure 15-22: 3.3 Volt/64-Bit Card Edge Connector Dimensions and Tolerances

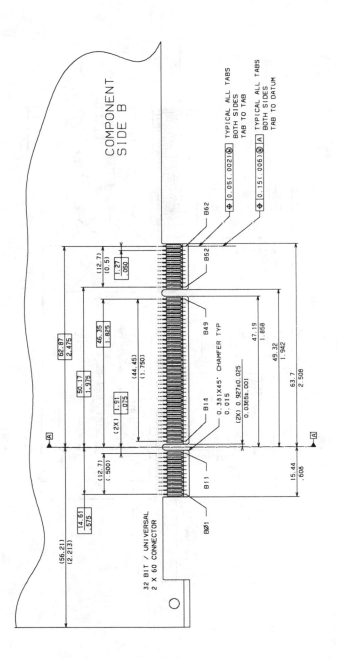

Figure 15-23: Universal 32-Bit Card Edge Connector Dimensions and Tolerances

459

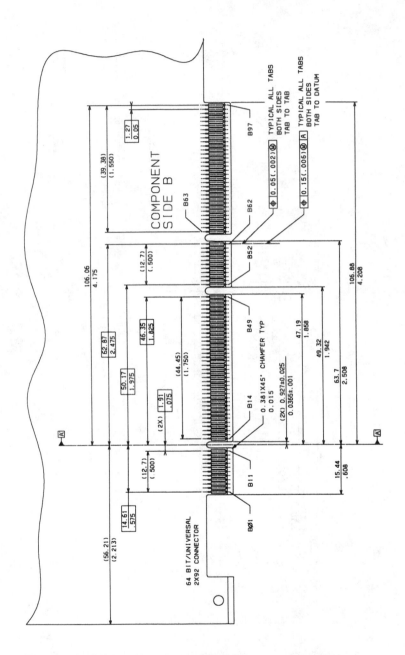

Figure 15-24: Universal 64-Bit Card Edge Connector Dimensions and Tolerances

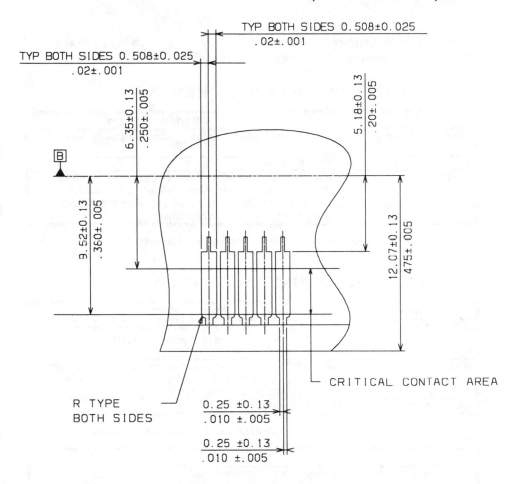

TYP BOTH SIDES

Figure 15-25: PCI Card Edge Connector Contacts

The vendors listed in Table 15-1 supply PCI expansion connectors. Other connectors may be used as long as they meet the specification in this document.

Description	AMP P/N	Burndy P/N	Foxconn P/N
32-bit, 5 volt	646255–1	CEE2X60SV3Z14W	TBD
32-bit 3.3 volt	6462551	CEE2X60SV3Z14W	TBD
64-bit, 5 volt	TBD	TBD	TBD
64-bit, 3.3 volt	TBD	TBD	TBD

Table 15-1: PCI Connectors

461

This specification makes no recommendation about the suitability of parts from these or any other vendors for a particular application.

CONNECTOR PHYSICAL REQUIREMENTS

Part	Materials
Connector Housing	Polyphenylene Sulfide, UL flammability rating 94V0, color; white.
Contacts	Phosphor Bronze
Contact Finish	0.000030 inch minimum gold over 0.000050 inch minimum nickel in the contact area. Alternate finish: gold flash over 0.000040 inch (1 micron) minimum palladium or palladium-nickel over nickel in the contact area.

Table 15-2: Connector Physical Requirements

CONNECTOR PERFORMANCE SPECIFICATION

Parameter	Specification
Durability	100 mating cycles without physical damage or exceeding low-level contact resistance requirement when mated with the recommended card cage.
Mating Force	Average 6 oz (1.7N) maximum per opposing contact pair using MIL-STD-1344, Method 2013.1 and gauge per MIL-C-21097 with profile as shown in add-in board specification.
Contact Normal Force	75 grams minimum

Table 15-3: Connector Mechanical Performance Requirements

Parameter	Specification
Contact Resistance	(low signal level) 30 milliohms maximum initial, 10 milliohms maximum increase through testing. Contact resistance, texted per MIL-STD-1344, Method 3002.1.
Insulation Resistance	1000 Megohms minimum per MIL-STD-202, Method 302, Condition B.
Dielectric Withstand Voltage	500 VAC RMS per MIL-STD-1344, Method D3001.1, Condition 1.
Capacitance	2 pF maximum, at 1 MHz.
Current Rating	1 A, 30° C rise above ambient.
Voltage Rating	125 volts.
Certification	UL Recognition and CSA Certification required.

Table 15-4: Connector Electrical Performance Requirements

Parameter	Specification
Operating Temperature	–40° C to +105° C
Thermal Shock	55° C to +85° C, 5 cycles per MIL-STD-1344, Method 1003.1.
Flowing Mixed Gas Test	Battelle, Class II. Connector mated with board and tested per Battelle method.

Table 15-5: Connector Environmental Performance Requirements

PLANAR IMPLEMENTATION

Two types of planar implementations are supported by the PCI expansion card design: expansion connectors mounted on the planar and expansion connectors mounted on a riser card. For illustrative purposes, only the planar mounted expansion connectors are detailed here. The basic principles may be applied to riser card designs. See Figures 15-27, 15-28, and 15-29 for planar details for ISA, EISA, and MC cards, respectively. The planar drawings show the relative locations of the PCI 5 volt and 3.3 volt connector datums to the ISA, EISA, and MC connector datums. Both 5 volt and 3.3 volt connectors are shown on the planar to concisely convey the dimensional information. Normally, a given system would incorporate either the 5 volt or the 3.3 volt PCI connector, but not both. Standard card spacing of 0.8 inches for ISA/EISA and 0.85 inches for MC allows for only one shared slot per system. If more PCI expansion slots are required, while using existing card spacing, additional slots must be dedicated to PCI. Viewing the planar from the back of the system, the shared slot is located so that dedicated ISA, EISA, or MC slots are located to the right and dedicated PCI slots are located to the left.

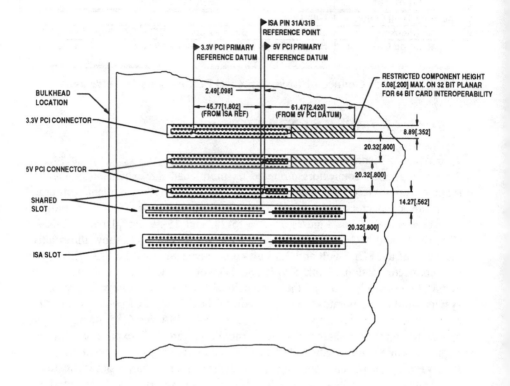

**Figure 15-26: PCI Connector Location on Planar Relative to Datum on the
ISA Connector**

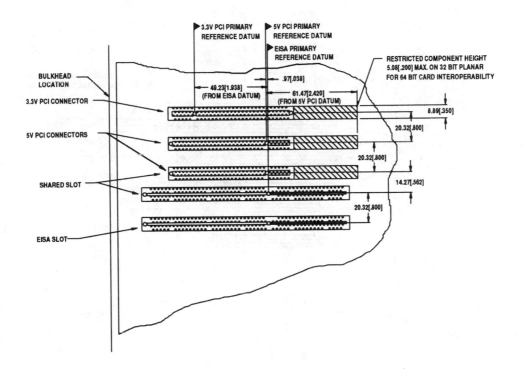

Figure 15-27: PCI Connector Location on Planar Relative to Datum on the EISA Connector

465

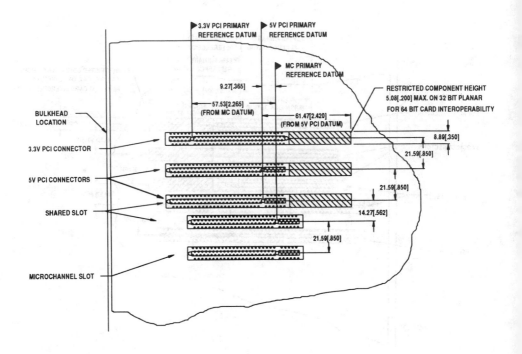

Figure 15-28: PCI Connector Location on Planar Relative to Datum on the MC Connector

CHAPTER 16

SYSTEM RESOURCES

This chapter consists of the following subchapters:

16.0 OVERVIEW OF SYSTEM RESOURCES

Computer systems contain hardware peripherals and unique components that provide the individual functions of the system. These peripherals and components are usually either mounted directly onto the platform or are added to the system by inserting an add-in card into one of the platform's expansion slots. In the case of peripherals such as the speaker, serial port, floppy diskette, fixed disk, and keyboard, each peripheral has at least one individual hardware device that manages the configuration and control of the peripheral. For example, the Intel 8254 Programmable Timer chip is normally integrated on the system platform. This integrated circuit includes three independent timers. Traditionally, each of the timer circuits supplies the ISA compatible system with a different function: Timer 0 initiates the system time-of-day update sequence, Timer 1 is used for dynamic RAM refresh, and Timer 2 can be used to generate sounds via the speaker peripheral connected to the system.

It is not enough, however, to electrically connect the 8254 Programmable Timer (or for that matter any other device) to its associated circuitry on the system platform in order to obtain the chip's functions. Devices such as the 8254 Programmable Timer must be programmed by software to configure each of the timers individually to provide the specified functionality.

A software program consists of a set of instructions that are executed by the microprocessor. Programs that configure and manage the operation of peripherals instruct the microprocessor to send and/or receive data from the controller devices. Consequently, the microprocessor, and in certain cases the devices independent of the microprocessor, must have a way of communicating with each other. It is through the use of the system resources that this communication is accomplished.

System resources are segregated into four distinct classes. The division of these system resource classes is based on the type of hardware functions provided as well as the global interface requirements each class must adhere to in order to be considered ISA compatible. The four system resource classifications are memory address space, input/output (I/O) ports, interrupts, and direct memory access (DMA).

Software programs use memory address space and I/O ports to communicate with hardware devices. In contrast, devices that control peripherals generate hardware interrupts to communicate to the microprocessor that the peripheral needs to send or receive data to the system. Finally, DMA resources permit the direct transfer of large data streams between system components while consuming very little microprocessor bandwidth.

> Most devices do not require all four system resource types. Rather, a subset of the four types is used. For example, ISA compatible system serial ports are assigned an interrupt and a range of eight contiguous I/O port addresses. They do not use the memory address space or DMA channel resources.

To function properly, each device in the computer system must have a unique set of system resources dedicated to it. Typically, when two or more devices are assigned the same system resources, one or more of the devices will not function properly. Erroneously assigning two or more devices the same system resource is referred to as a system resource conflict. The result of a system resource conflict is usually a loss of functionality and/or reliability within the system. In some instances the entire system's operation is impaired.

> Typically, unique system resources are assigned to individual devices. However, in some instances system resources such as IRQs can be shared.

Older system platforms and add-in cards are assigned system resources by either moving jumpers or modifying switch settings. Newer system platforms and add-in cards have replaced these manual operations with software programs that configure the hardware for operation. Plug and Play devices such as PCI devices take the system device configuration and management process to a new level. The fundamental premise of Plug and Play devices is that the user is only required to add the device to the system. The System BIOS, device drivers and/or operating system will automatically detect and configure the Plug and Play devices in the system while avoiding any system resource conflicts. To achieve this goal it is imperative to have an understanding of system resources.

To this end, this chapter addresses:

- The four classes of system resources: memory address space, Input/Output ports, interrupts, and DMA channels.
- How system resources are accessed by the system hardware.

This information will also aid the reader in understanding the constraints the system power-up initialization software has in attempting to determine which system resources are being utilized during the current system initialization sequence. In addition, by understanding the basics of system resources, the reader will be able to grasp the concepts behind assigning unused system resources to PCI devices during the initialization of the system. Both of these topics are addressed in Chapter 20, *PCI Device Configuration*.

16.1 MEMORY ADDRESS SPACE

In a computer system, Random Access Memory (RAM), and Read-Only Memory (ROM), are devices which provide the storage space for software program code and data. In an ISA compatible system, the placement of ROM and RAM devices within the four gigabyte address space is pre-defined. This division of memory address locations between ROM and RAM is due in part to the inherent characteristics of the Intel microprocessors. In addition, system designers chose to maintain backward compatibility to the original PC in order to support IBM PC compatible software. The way ROM and RAM address space is partitioned in an ISA compatible system has a great impact on PCI based systems, as will be seen in the discussion on PCI ROM initialization.

Table 16.1 shows the memory address space in a typical ISA compatible system with an Intel 80386 or higher microprocessor.

> Observe that while the microprocessor can access every address in this memory map, there is no guarantee that a physical ROM or RAM device exists behind every address, except where noted.

THE SYSTEM BIOS ROM AND THE RESTART VECTOR

Notice in Table 16-1 that the System BIOS ROM is accessible to the microprocessor just below the fourth gigabyte memory address region immediately after a system power-up or after a hard RESET to the microprocessor occurs. This is because address lines A20 through A31 in Intel 32 bit microprocessors are driven high for code fetches immediately after one of these resets occurs. In addition, Intel microprocessors set the 16 bit Instruction Pointer (IP) to a fixed starting value of FFF0h. This forces the microprocessor to fetch its first instruction from physical address FFFFFFF0h.

Memory Address	Length	Contents
FFFF0000–FFFFFFFF	64K	System BIOS ROM (system initialization and boot code) when decoded immediately after power-up or hard RESET to the microprocessor
100000–FFFF0000	4G–1.06M	System RAM from 1M to 4 Gigabytes minus 64K
F0000–FFFFF	64K	System BIOS ROM (system initialization and boot code) when decoded in Real Mode
E0000–EFFFF	64K	System ROM BIOS (system initialization and boot code) or Available for adapter ROM BIOS, device drivers, memory managers
C8000–DFFFF	96K	Available for adapter BIOS ROMs, device drivers, memory managers
C0000–C7FFF	32K	Available for adapter BIOS ROMs (typically EGA/VGA Video BIOS ROM), device drivers, memory managers
B8000–BFFFF	32K	CGA Video RAM
B0000–B7FFF	32K	Monochrome Video RAM
A0000–BFFFF	128K	EGA/VGA Video RAM
80000–9FFFF	128K	System RAM from 512K to 640K or available to ISA compatible add-in cards. This functionality is device dependent.
00000–7FFFF	512K	System RAM from 0K to 512K

Table 16-1: ISA System Memory Layout

Placing the code start vector at a fixed address is very advantageous to both System BIOS ROM programmers and hardware designers. For System BIOS ROM programmers, the address of the first instruction to be executed after a system power-up or hard RESET to the microprocessor occurs is a known constant. This permits start-up code specifically designed to handle these two events to be located at a known location. Hardware designers have the advantage of decoding the System BIOS ROM device at the extreme high end of memory address space. This is a key factor in keeping the memory address space between addresses 1M and 4G unobstructed.

Due to the design of the system hardware, the top 64K of system ROM can be decoded starting at both memory address F0000h and FFFF0000h. The first iAPX intersegment control transfer instruction executed by the Intel microprocessor will disable address lines A20 through A31 from being driven during code fetches. This will place the microprocessor into true x86 Real Mode where only the first twenty bits of memory address space (zero to one megabyte) are accessible to the microprocessor. To permit the system ROM code to initially execute in Real Mode, the first instruction executed in an ISA compatible System BIOS ROM is always a FAR JMP instruction. This maintains backward compatibility to the Intel 8088 (PC) and 8086 (PC/XT) microprocessors that are only capable of decoding the first twenty bits of memory address space.

Below is a partial display of the System BIOS ROM code which shows the FAR JMP instruction that the microprocessor fetches from system ROM code start vector at memory address FFFFFFF0h. The data was obtained by running the DEBUG.EXE program under DOS Version 6.0 on an PS/ValuePoint computer system. By typing d F000:FFF0 L 5 the program displays the five bytes located in ROM at physical memory address FFFF0h. The data obtained from running the DEBUG.EXE program has been transposed to the figure below for greater readability.

OFFSET:	0	1	2	3	4	5	6	7	8	9	A	B	C	D	E	F
F000:FFF0	EA	5B	E0	00	F0											

Figure 16-1: Code Bytes at the System Start Vector

All ISA compatible systems contain the identical bytes of code shown. The five-byte instruction executed by the microprocessor is:

```
JMP FAR F000:E05B
```

Once the first far jump has been executed, the microprocessor is placed in the Real ADDRESS mode compatible with the Intel 8088 and 8086 microprocessor based IBM compatible PC and XT computer series. The microprocessor can only access the first megabyte of system memory address space. Instead of fetching and executing its code instructions from the 64K memory address block at FFFF0000h, the microprocessor begins fetching and executing instructions from the 64K memory address block starting at F0000h. The code segment (CS) register value after the first far jump is F000h. The instruction pointer (IP) register value at this point is E05Bh. All instructions executed after this CS:IP pair are System BIOS dependent. What the System BIOS does after this initial jump instruction is also discussed in Chapter 20, *PCI Device Configuration.*

SYSTEM RAM

System RAM is divided into three categories that are discussed below. The categories are *conventional RAM, shadow RAM,* and *extended RAM.* These categories are defined by which memory address region within the four gigabyte address range the RAM occupies.

Intel microprocessors support several instructions that software programs can use to read data from or write data to system memory. These include bit manipulation instructions such as BTR (Bit Test and RESET), data transfer instructions such as PUSHA (Push All registers onto stack) and string manipulation instructions such as MOVSB (Move String Byte-by-Byte). Figure 16-2 shows a sample program that will copy the System BIOS ROM date from its fixed memory vector at 0FFFF5h to a RAM buffer in conventional memory using the MOVSB, PUSH and POP instructions. The INT software instruction is explained later in this chapter during the discussion on interrupts.

```
        TITLE copydate.asm
        DOSSEG
        .MODEL medium
        .STACK 100H

        .CODE
START:  PUSH  DS          ; Copy microprocessor DS and ES
                          ;register
        PUSH  ES          ; contents to RAM based stack
        CLD               ; Set Direction flag to increment mode
        MOV AX, 0F000H    ;Set DS:SI to base of date string located
        MOV DS, AX        ; in System BIOS ROM
        MOV SI, 0FFF5H ;
        MOV AX, 0000H     ; Set ES:DI to base of RAM buffer
        MOV ES, AX        ; located in RAM
        MOV DI, 8000H     ;
        MOV CX, 8H        ; Use CX register as loop counter for
                          ; the copy
DATE_LP: MOVSB            ; Copy one byte at a time
        LOOP DATE_LP      ; Repeat until done

        POP  ES           ; Restore original DS and ES register
        POP  DS           ; contents using RAM based stack data

        MOV AX, 4C00H     ; Call DOS
        INT 21H           ; with the exit function
        END  START
```

Figure 16-2: Software Program Memory Manipulation Example

SYSTEM CONVENTIONAL RAM

Once the first far jump instruction is completed, the System BIOS code begins its Power-On Self Test, or POST. It is during POST that the system is tested and initialized in preparation for bootstrapping an operating system. A key component of POST is the test and initialization of the RAM physically present in the system. ISA compatible systems that use the INTEL 80286 microprocessor or one of its successors are always guaranteed a minimum of 512K of RAM. This RAM is based at physical memory address 00000h. In addition, the next 128K address space above 512K is normally assigned to the RAM address space. Enabling the decode of this memory address region as RAM is a function of the system memory controller. The RAM that constitutes the first 640K of system memory is known as conventional memory. The System BIOS reserves a portion of conventional memory for POST and run-time operation. Figure 16-3 shows the standard memory address regions used by the System BIOS and DOS level programs in the conventional memory address space.

Memory Address	Length	Contents
9FC00–9FFFF	1K Bytes	System Extended BIOS Data Segment
00500–9FBFF	637.75K Bytes	Used by DOS, device drivers, terminate and stay ready (TSR) programs and DOS applications
00400–004FF	256 Bytes	System BIOS Data Segment
00300–003FF	256 Bytes	System BIOS Stack
00000–002FF	768 Bytes	BIOS Interrupt Vector Table

Figure 16–3: Standard ISA Conventional RAM Map

SYSTEM SHADOW RAM

Because of component and manufacturing costs, it is common to include RAM which spans the entire first megabyte of system memory instead of just the first 640K of address space. System RAM above 640K and below one megabyte is typically ignored for two reasons: (1) because the memory region from A0000h through BFFFFh is assigned to video memory, and (2) because the memory region from C0000h through FFFFFh is assigned to adapter BIOS ROMs and the System BIOS ROM. However, many system memory controllers contain the capability to decode either the system RAM or ROM devices between memory addresses C0000h and FFFFFh. Physical RAM within this range of addresses is known as *shadow RAM*.

System BIOSs often copy the software programs contained in the system and adapter ROMs to shadow RAM. This is done to improve system performance because the microprocessor can access system RAM significantly faster than it can ROM devices that reside on a slower bus and that have a slower access time than dynamic RAM. A System BIOS will usually shadow itself in RAM from address F0000h to FFFFFh to speed up the Power–On Self Test and bootstrap process. In addition, the System BIOS will typically shadow the video BIOS from ROM to shadow memory starting at location C0000h as well to improve video output performance.

Figure 16–4 illustrates the system memory address space relationship between the system shadow RAM and the ISA ROM region in relationship to the microprocessor.

Special commands specific to the system memory controller permit the microprocessor to perform the following tasks:

- Read from ROM, Write to ROM (shadowing disabled)
- Read from ROM, Write to RAM (ROM to RAM copy mode enabled)
- Read from RAM, Write to ROM (shadowing enabled and RAM write protected)

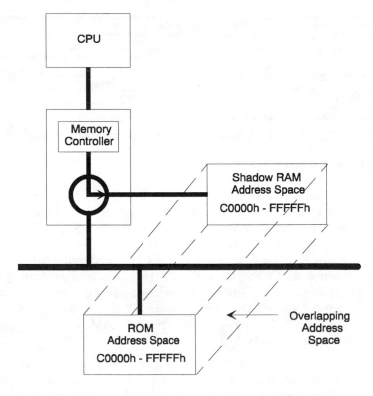

Figure 16–4: Overlapping Shadow RAM and ROM Memory Space

PCI based systems must incorporate a memory controller with the above capabilities. The reason for this is because expansion BIOSs located in ROMs mounted on compliant PCI add–in boards do not directly map into the memory address region between C0000h and F0000h. However, PCI adapter BIOSs can only execute out of this memory address region in an ISA compatible system. It is the responsibility of the System BIOS to copy PCI adapter BIOSs to shadow RAM.

There are two common methods used to shadow a PCI BIOS. The first method involves copying the PCI BIOS from ROM directly to the ISA Compatibility Region address space. Not all memory controllers support reading from ROM and writing to shadow RAM at the same time. It is, however, the fastest and most code efficient.

The second method uses a method known as buffering. The PCI option ROM code is read from ROM and written to system RAM. The option ROM code is then read from system RAM and written to shadow RAM. While not as fast or efficient as the first method, this method is system memory controller device independent.

For an example of how the shadow RAM functions are controlled by a PCI device, see the discussion on the Programmable Attribute Map registers (address offset 59h–5Fh) of the 82434LX PCI device in the Intel 82430 PCIset Cache/Memory Subsystem manual.

SYSTEM EXTENDED RAM

Memory addresses above FFFFFh, or one megabyte, are not accessible to the microprocessor in Real ADDRESS mode. RAM in this region is known as Extended memory because it extends beyond the one megabyte boundary. Extended memory is required for programs which need more RAM than the 640K of conventional memory to execute.

The microprocessor must be programmed to operate in Protected mode in order to use extended memory. Once this is done the microprocessor can access memory anywhere within the entire four gigabyte region.

The System BIOS will begin testing and initializing extended memory at memory address 100000h. It will continue until it either detects a failure during the testing or finds the last byte of contiguous memory. The System BIOS maintains the size of the extended memory it validates in the system. This is important because DOS and typical extended memory drivers will only use the amount of contiguous extended RAM memory reported by the System BIOS.

It is possible and sometimes desirable to have non–contiguous extended memory within a DOS based system. For example, video frame buffers consist of RAM. If this memory is appended to the top of the system extended RAM it might be interpreted as additional extended memory by the System BIOS during system RAM testing and initialization. Other run–time programs which size memory would also make the same determination.

For PCI device initialization, it is extremely important to identify where all the extended RAM is located within the system. The reason is two–fold. First, the top of the physical extended memory located on the platform must be identified in order to append extended memory located on the PCI Bus to it. Second, a contiguous region of memory address space above one megabyte that contains no physical ROM or RAM must be identified for the purpose of shadowing PCI expansion BIOSs. This is explained in greater detail in Chapter 20, *PCI Device Configuration*.

16.2 INPUT/OUTPUT PORTS

Input/Output (I/O) ports are used in ISA compatible systems to enable the microprocessor to communicate with and control other system hardware. Starting with the Intel 80386 microprocessor family software programs can read or write I/O Ports via 8-, 16-, or 32-bit accesses. The individual devices along with the hardware implementation determines which type of accesses are permitted. See Appendix D for a discussion of ISA Aliasing and Appendix E for a discussion of the effects of ISA Aliasing on the PCI architecture.

Note that certain other hardware devices such as the 8237 DMA controller chip have the ability to communicate with other devices via I/O Ports independent of the microprocessor.

Intel microprocessors support two instructions that software programs can use to read data from or write data to an I/O Port. The IN software instruction moves data from an I/O Port into the microprocessor. The OUT software instruction transfers data from the microprocessor to the I/O Port. Figure 16–5 shows a sample program which will transfer the byte–wide seconds value from the system Real–Time Clock to the microprocessor. The INT software instruction is explained later in the discussion on interrupts.

```
        TITLE readrtc.asm
        DOSSEG
        .MODEL medium
        .STACK 100H

        .CODE
START:  OUT 70H, 00H   ; I/O Port 70H is the index register for the RTC
                       ; Select RTC offset 00H, the Seconds field
        IN    AL, 71H  ; I/O Port 71H is the data register for the RTC
                       ; Transfer the Seconds count to the CPU
        MOV AX, 4C00H  ; Call DOS
        INT 21H        ; with the exit function
        END START
```

Figure 16–5: Software Program I/O Port Manipulation Example

Table 16.2 illustrates the standard implementation of I/O Ports for ISA compatible systems. Note that I/O Ports 0000h through 00FFh are used to address devices mounted on the platform. I/O Ports 0100h through 03FFh typically address devices mounted on add–in cards. These add–in cards become part of the system when they are installed in expansion slots on the platform.

16.3 INTERRUPTS

ISA compatible systems support exception, hardware, and software interrupts. The purpose of interrupts is to suspend the execution of the software program that the microprocessor is currently executing and execute an interrupt handler. An interrupt handler is simply a software routine that services the function identified by the interrupt type or number. During system initialization and the subsequent bootstrapping/execution of a Real Mode operating system, 256 individual interrupt types are supported. These interrupts are numbered 0 through 255 (FFh). Each interrupt type may have an associated software program that is executed each time the interrupt is invoked. The starting address, or vector, of each of the interrupt routines is stored in a table in RAM. This table is called the interrupt vector table.

Address	Description
000–01F	DMA Controller #1 (8237)
020–03F	Master Interrupt Controller (8259)
040–05F	Programmable Interrupt Timer (8254)
060–06F	Keyboard (8042)
070–07F	Real Time Clock (MC146818)
080–09F	DMA Page Register
0A0–0BF	Slave Interrupt Controller (8259)
0C0–0DF	DMA Controller #2 (8237)
0F0–0F1	Math Coprocessor
0F8–0FF	Math Coprocessor
170–177	Fixed Disk Controller #2
1F0–1F8	Fixed Disk Controller #1
200–207	Game Port
278–27F	Parallel Port
2F8–2FF	Serial Communications
300–31F	Prototype Card
360–36F	Network
370–377	Floppy Diskette Controller #2
378–37F	Parallel Port
3B0–3BF	Monochrome Display Adapter and parallel Port
3C0–3CF	VGA EGA Video
3D0–3DF	Color Graphics Adapter
3F0–3F7	Floppy Diskette Controller #1
3F8–3FF	Serial Communications

Table 16–2: Standard ISA Compatible I/O ADDRESS Ports

The interrupt vector table stores the starting address of each interrupt in a 4–byte table entry. The lower word of each vector contains the value for instruction pointer (IP) and the upper word contains the code segment (CS) for its associated routine. The total length of the interrupt vector table is 1024 bytes (256 vectors x 4 bytes). The table is based at physical offset 0000:0000 in system memory. The last entry in the table is at address 0000:03FC. Table 16–3 illustrates the standard implementation of the interrupt vector table during the Real Mode operation of DOS. All values in the table are in hexadecimal notation except for the IRQ numbers, which are in decimal notation. Also, notice that vectors 1Dh, 1Eh, 1Fh, 41h and 46h are not pointers to interrupt handlers. They are pointers to tables to various tables of information used by the System BIOS and the operating system.

Refer to the Intel data books and sheets for a description on how to process interrupts in microprocessor modes other than Real Mode.

PROCESSING INTERRUPTS

Servicing hardware and software interrupts is a two–stage process when the microprocessor type is within the 80x86 family of microprocessors:

STAGE 1

Stage 1 is performed under complete control of the microprocessor. A programmer has no control of the microprocessor's actions at this time. The purpose of Stage 1 is to ensure that the software program which was interrupted can continue once the interrupt has been serviced.

1. The execution of the current software program by the CPU is temporarily suspended.

2. The current state of the microprocessor flags register is pushed onto the stack. This allows the interrupt handler to modify the microprocessor flags freely without affecting the interrupted software program.

3. The code segment (CS) of the interrupted program is pushed onto the stack.

4. The address of the next instruction (IP) to be executed by the interrupted program is pushed onto the stack.

5. Hardware interrupts are disabled to ensure that the interrupt handler has the opportunity to service the current interrupt.

6. The microprocessor jumps to the memory location specified by the segment: offset values obtained from the interrupt vector table. The vector loaded is determined by the interrupt type. Because each vector in the table is four bytes in length, the microprocessor automatically multiplies the interrupt type by four to obtain the correct index into the interrupt vector table for the required vector.

STAGE 2

Stage 2 is the responsibility of the programmer. Once the microprocessor loads the CS:IP pair of the interrupt handler, the next instruction it executes is the first instruction of the interrupt handler. The purpose of Stage 2 is to perform the function requested by the interrupt.

INT	Vector Address	Function	Type
00	000–003	Divide by Zero or Divide Overflow	Exception
01	004–007	Single Step	Exception
02	008–00B	Nonmaskable (NMI)	Exception
03	00C–00F	Breakpoint	Exception
04	010–013	Numeric Overflow	Exception
05	014–017	Print Screen	Software
06	018–01B	Reserved	Software
07	01C–01F	Reserved	Software
08	020–023	IRQ0: System Time–of–Day	IRQ 0
09	024–027	IRQ1: Kbd Controller Output Buffer Full	IRQ 1
0A	028–02B	IRQ2: Cascade Input from slave 8259	IRQ 2
0B	02C–02F	IRQ3: Serial Communications	IRQ 3
0C	030–033	IRQ4: Serial Communications	IRQ 4
0D	034–037	IRQ7: Parallel Port	IRQ 7
0E	038–03B	IRQ6: Diskette Controller	IRQ 6
0F	03C–03F	IRQ5: Parallel Port	IRQ 5
10	040–043	Video	Software
11	044–047	Equipment Check	Software
12	048–04B	Determine System RAM Size	Software
13	04C–04F	Diskette/Fixed Disk	Software
14	050–053	Serial Communications	Software
15	054–057	Cassette/Miscellaneous Extended Functions	Software
16	058–05B	Keyboard	Software
17	05C–05F	Printer	Software
18	060–063	Resident ROM BASIC/Bootstrap Failure	Software
19	064–067	Bootstrap System	Software
1A	068–06B	Time of Day/PCI	Software
1B	06C–06F	Keyboard Break Key	Software
1C	070–073	Timer Tick (called after each INT 08)	Software
1D	074–077	Pointer to Video parameter Table	Table
1E	078–07B	Pointer to Diskette parameter Table	Table
1F	07C–07F	Pointer to Graphic Characters Table	Table
20	080–083	Exit program running under DOS	Software
21	084–087	DOS Functions	Software
22	088–08B	Pointer to DOS Exit Program Routine	Software
23	08C–08F	Pointer to DOS Control–Break Routine	Software
24	090–093	Pointer to DOS Fatal Error Function	Software
25	094–097	Read Diskette/Fixed Disk	Software

Table 16–3: BIOS/DOS Interrupt Vector Table

26	098–09B	Write Diskette/Fixed Disk	Software
27	09C–09F	Terminate and Stay Resident	Software
28–32	0A0–0CB	Reserved	Software
33	0CC–0CF	Mouse Driver Functions	Software
34–40	0D0–0FF	Reserved	Software
41	104–107	Pointer to Fixed Disk Table 1	Software
42–45	108–117	Reserved	Software
46	118–11B	Pointer to Fixed Disk Table 2	Software
47–49	11C–127	Available to Programs	Software
4A	128–12B	Alarm	Software
4B–5B	12C–16F	Available to Programs	Software
5C	170–17C	NETBIOS	Software
5D–66	174–19B	Available to Programs	Software
67	19C–19F	EMS Functions	Software
68–6F	1A0–1BF	Available to Programs	Software
70	1C0–1C3	IRQ8: Real Time Clock	IRQ 8
71	1C4–1C7	IRQ9: IRQ2 Redirect	IRQ 9
72	1C8–1CB	IRQ10: Available to the system	IRQ 10
73	1CC–1CF	IRQ11: Available to the system	IRQ 11
74	1D0–1D3	IRQ12: Mouse or Available to the system	IRQ 12
75	1D4–1D7	IRQ13: Math Coprocessor	IRQ 13
76	1D8–1DB	IRQ14: AT Fixed Disk Controller	IRQ 14
77	1DC–1DF	IRQ15: Available to the system	IRQ 15
78–7F	1E0–1FF	Reserved	Software
80–85	200–217	BASIC	Software
86–F0	218–3C3	BASIC Interpreter (When BASIC is running)	Software
F1–FF	3C4–3CF	Reserved	Software

Table 16–3: BIOS/DOS Interrupt Vector Table (Continued)

1. The current state of the microprocessor registers used by the interrupt handler, except for registers that will contain output parameters, is pushed onto the stack. This ensures that the interrupted software program will resume with the exact microprocessor state it had when it was interrupted.

2. The interrupt handler can service the call. Note that hardware interrupts should be enabled as soon as possible using the iAPX STI instruction. This will ensure that time critical events, such as the timer interrupt (IRQ0) which occurs 18.2 times a second, can transpire normally. Output parameters, if any, are loaded into the microprocessor registers at this time.

3. The entry state of the microprocessor registers that were saved by the interrupt handler are restored from the stack.

4. The interrupt handler executes the IRET instruction. This instruction will restore the microprocessor flags register to the value it contained on

entry to the interrupt handler. In addition, it also forces a FAR return to the CS:IP address pushed onto the stack by the microprocessor when the interrupt occurred.

5. The execution of the previously suspended software program by the CPU is resumed.

INTERRUPT CHAINING

Note that the system initialization software is responsible for programming the interrupt vector table with its vectors first. However, because the interrupt vector table is in system RAM, other programs such as expansion ROM programs, operating systems, TSRs and device drivers are allowed to replace the current interrupt vector entries with addresses which point to their own routines. The program that replaces or "hooks" an interrupt vector is responsible for preserving the previous interrupt vector data. Each time a hooked interrupt routine is invoked, the interrupt handler should check to ensure that the interrupt function or device is one which it services. If not, the current interrupt handler has the responsibility of invoking the previous interrupt handler via the preserved vector.

This methodology allows several different programs to hook one specific interrupt during system operation. For example, this capability allows a video expansion ROM BIOS to take over the INT 10H vector from the System BIOS during the system initialization in order to manipulate its video controller properly when video function requests are serviced. In turn, a video driver has the capability of replacing the video expansion ROM BIOS with its vector in order to increase the video capabilities of the system.

The figure below contains a partial example of a Real Mode interrupt vector table's data. The data was obtained by running the DEBUG.EXE program under DOS Version 6.0 on an IBM PS/ValuePoint computer system. By typing d 0:0 the program displays the interrupt vector data starting with interrupt type 00, the divide by zero exception interrupt handler. The data obtained from running the DEBUG.EXE program has been transposed to the figure below for greater readability.

Observe the vector data for interrupt type 11h, the Equipment Check interrupt. Located at bytes 44–47 in the table, the vector contains F000:F84D. The segment address of F000 indicates that this interrupt is serviced by the system ROM BIOS code, which is always located in system memory from address F0000h to FFFFFh. In contrast, note that the two–byte segment address at memory location 0000:0002 is 0116, not F000. This indicates that at least one other program has hooked the type 00 interrupt's vector because the code segment value is not F000. Such is the case for the majority of the interrupt vectors.

OFFSET:	0	1	2	3	4	5	6	7	8	9	A	B	C	D	E	F
0000:0000	8A	10	16	01	F4	06	70	00	16	00	96	09	F4	06	70	00
0000:0010	F4	06	70	00	FB	07	6A	1C	43	EB	00	F0	EB	EA	00	F0
0000:0020	00	00	F1	1E	25	0D	6A	1C	97	EA	00	F0	6F	00	96	09
0000:0030	97	EA	00	F0	97	EA	00	F0	B7	00	96	09	F4	06	70	00
0000:0040	0F	00	FC	1E	4D	F8	00	F0	41	F8	00	F0	BA	02	6A	1C
0000:0050	39	E7	00	F0	00	00	B3	1E	F8	02	6A	1C	2B	06	6A	1C
0000:0060	00	E0	00	F0	C7	18	06	15	6E	FE	00	F0	EE	06	70	00
0000:0070	98	01	F1	1E	A4	F0	00	F0	22	05	00	00	D6	29	00	C0

Figure 16–6: Interrupt Vector DATA Example

EXCEPTION INTERRUPTS

Exception interrupts occur automatically when the system detects an error condition. Intel defined this class of interrupts to handle the class of events which are not controlled by the programmer via software interrupts or by the hardware designer via hardware interrupts. Consequently, any computer system that incorporates an Intel 80x86 microprocessor should provide interrupt handlers for exception interrupts.

An example of a Real Mode exception is the Divide by Zero error. This exception occurs when (a) the microprocessor detects a division operation with a divisor of 0 or (b) the result of a legal division operation cannot fit into the accumulator register (AL, AX, EAX). A type 00 interrupt is invoked when either of these events occurs.

SOFTWARE INTERRUPTS

Software interrupts are under the control of the programmer. In addition, software interrupts do not actually interrupt the microprocessor because they are intentionally included in software programs. From a programming viewpoint, software interrupts simply permit a caller to invoke a subroutine without knowing the address of the function called. The invocation is accomplished using the iAPX INT instruction. The caller specifies the interrupt type with the INT instruction. In addition to specifying the interrupt type, the caller also has the advantage of specifying input parameters required by the routine called. These parameters are passed to the interrupt handler via the x86 microprocessor registers. As stated above, during Stage 1 of processing the interrupt the microprocessor automatically multiplies the interrupt type by four to obtain the correct index into the interrupt vector table for the required vector. The microprocessor then performs the tasks outlined in Stage 2.

Figure 16–7 below is a sample program to illustrate the use of software interrupts under DOS. It will set the system time to 9:30 A.M.

```
            TITLE settime.asm
            DOSSEG
            .MODEL medium
            .STACK 100h

            .CODE
START:  MOV  AH, 2DH    ; AH <= DOS INT 21H set time function
        MOV  CH, 09     ; CH <= hour
        MOV  CL, 30     ; CL <= minutes
        MOV  DH, 00     ; DH <= seconds
        MOV  DL, 00     ; DL <= hundredths of seconds
        INT  21H        ; Call the DOS set system time function
        MOV  AX, 4C00H  ; Call DOS
        INT  21H        ;  with the exit function
        END  START
```

Figure 16–7: Software Interrupt Programming Example

The advantage of software interrupts within the ISA compatible system architecture is readily apparent. There is a standard set of interrupts along with their associated interrupt handlers defined for both the ISA compatible System BIOS and DOS. In most instances, these interrupt handlers relieve the applications programmer from having to know about the low level hardware implementation of a particular system. For example, in the sample program above, the caller does not need to know what underlying system hardware is used to maintain the system time to be able to set the time. In addition, the caller is not required to know how to program the hardware to set the correct time. Finally, the code size of the application is greatly reduced because interrupt handlers bear the code burden that services each function.

HARDWARE INTERRUPTS

Hardware interrupts are initiated by physical devices within the system. These devices may be located physically on the platform or located on an add–in board. In both cases, a special signal from the device is connected to an interrupt request (IRQ) line of a system interrupt controller. The primary function of hardware interrupts is to relieve the CPU from having to poll devices waiting for hardware events to happen. In other words, microprocessor bandwidth to process external hardware events is consumed only when the hardware interrupt is detected and serviced.

Unlike software interrupts which are under programmer control, hardware interrupts may be generated by system events in a random fashion. For instance, when a key is pressed on the keyboard or when a mouse is moved, a hardware interrupt request is generated. Multiple hardware interrupts may occur simultaneously. The system interrupt controllers are responsible for detecting that a device has requested service, prioritizing the interrupt, and generating a request to the CPU to execute the interrupt handler specific to the interrupt request. The only control the programmer has over an interrupt generated by hardware is what the system does when the interrupt occurs.

Beginning with the implementation of the Intel 80286 microprocessor, ISA compatible systems use two 8259 programmable interrupt controllers or their equivalent to manage hardware interrupts. These controllers serve as priority arbiters for the devices connected to them. During system initialization, the system ROM BIOS code will initialize the 8259 controllers. This code sets the priority of the interrupt inputs as well as the interrupt vectors which will be used by the microprocessor in response to a hardware interrupt.

Each 8259 has input pins to support up to eight hardware interrupt sources. The master (or primary) 8259 inputs are labeled IRQ0 through IRQ7. The slave (or secondary) 8259 inputs are labeled IRQ8 through IRQ15. This would seem to indicate that 16 hardware interrupts are available to the system. However, the slave 8259 is cascaded to the master 8259 via the master's IRQ2 input line. This reduces the number of available hardware interrupts to fifteen because IRQ2 is not used by external devices to generate an interrupt request. It also gives higher priority to all devices connected to the slave 8259 than IRQ3 through IRQ7 of the master 8259. This is because the master 8259 is programmed so that IRQ0 has the highest priority and IRQ7 has the lowest. Similarly, IRQ8 on the slave 8259 has the highest priority and IRQ15 has the lowest.

When two or more hardware interrupts occur simultaneously, priority is arbitrated. The IRQ with the highest priority level is serviced first by the microprocessor. Processing of any pending lower level IRQ is delayed until all higher IRQ levels serviced.

The master 8259 is programmed so that IRQ0 will generate an interrupt type 08. This base interrupt type value forces IRQ1 through IRQ7 to generate interrupt types 09 through 0F respectively. The slave 8259 is programmed so that IRQ8 will generate an interrupt type 70. This base interrupt type value forces IRQ9 through IRQ15 to generate interrupt types 71 through 77 respectively.

When a hardware interrupt request is being serviced by the microprocessor, the interrupt type is placed on the microprocessor's data bus by the 8259. This value is read by the microprocessor. As stated above, during Stage 1 of processing the interrupt the microprocessor automatically multiplies the interrupt type by four to obtain the correct index into the interrupt vector table for the required vector. The microprocessor then performs the tasks outlined in Stage 2.

Processing slave 8259 interrupt requests is more complex than servicing the master's. When an interrupt request is detected by the slave 8259 it in turn generates an IRQ2 interrupt request to the master 8259. The master 8259 then checks to see if either an IRQ0 (Timer Interrupt) or IRQ1 (Keyboard Interrupt) request is pending. If not, the IRQ2 request for servicing is granted by the master 8259. The master then issues a hardware–generated command to the slave 8259 to place the interrupt type associated with the IRQ line being serviced onto the microprocessors data bus. The microprocessor then completes the interrupt servicing.

The table below presents the typical use of the hardware IRQs. The priority level of each IRQ (IRQ0 has the highest, IRQ7 has the lowest), its interrupt type, the physical address of its vector table entry and the function of the hardware interrupt are shown.

DIRECT INVOCATION OF REAL MODE INTERRUPTS

The system ROMs in ISA compatible systems contain fixed memory addresses that point to certain interrupt handlers, specific System BIOS code and System BIOS–specific tables. These entry points are used to maintain backward compatibility to the PC and XT computer systems. Table 16–5, The System ROM Compatibility Table, contains a list of the compatible fixed entry points.

| IRQs | | Type | Vector Address | Function |
Master	Slave			
0		08	020–023	Timer
1		09	024–023	Keyboard
2		0A	028–02B	Cascade Input from slave 8259
	8	70	1C0–1C3	Real Time Clock
	9	71	1C4–1C7	IRQ2 Redirect
	10	72	1C8–1CB	Available to the system
	11	73	1CC–1CF	Available to the system
	12	74	1D0–1D3	Mouse or Available to the system
	13	75	1D4–1D7	Math Coprocessor
	14	76	1D8–1DB	Fixed Disk Controller
	15	77	1DC–1DF	Available to the system
3		0B	02C–02F	Serial Communications
4		0C	030–033	Serial Communications
5		0D	034–037	Parallel Port
6		0E	038–03B	Diskette Controller
7		0F	03C–03F	Parallel Port

Table 16–4: Hardware Interrupts Priority Levels

INT 1AH FIXED MEMORY ADDRESS

One fixed memory address, the INT 1Ah entry point, is critical to the successful implementation of a PCI–based system. The reason is that the INT 1Ah interrupt handler was selected to be used as the System BIOS interface between the PCI based hardware and software. See *Chapter 19: PCI System BIOS Software Interface* for an in–depth discussion of the PCI INT 1Ah interface. The INT 1Ah interrupt handler is the PCI BIOS interface for both Real Mode and 16 bit Protected Mode microprocessor operation. The 32 bit Protected Mode PCI BIOS interface is a separate entity, mainly because of its 32 bit attributes. It does not use the INT 1Ah interrupt handler routine. See *Chapter 19: PCI System BIOS Software Interface* for the discussion on the 32 bit Protected Mode PCI BIOS interface.

Because the INT 1Ah instruction is native to 8086 Real Mode operation, the software programmer can choose to use the INT 1Ah instruction or call the entry point directly to access the PCI/Time of Day interrupt services. However, executing Real Mode interrupt handlers using the iAPX INT instruction in 16 bit Protected Mode is not possible when the Real Mode interrupt descriptor table is in use. Note Table 16–6. In Real Mode, the microprocessor's segment registers contain 16 bit paragraph addresses, ranging from 0000h to FFFFh. In Protected Mode, each segment register holds a selector. Selectors are 16 bit values that specify a segment descriptor. Segment descriptors specify the segment's base address, size and usage attributes. Recall that Real Mode interrupt vectors contain a 16 bit segment address and a 16 bit offset address. Consequently, a protection fault would be generated if a 16 bit Protected Mode program executed a Real Mode interrupt handler using the iAPX INT instruction because the microprocessor would attempt to load an invalid selector into the code segment register.

Fixed Address	System BIOS Function	Type
FE05Bh	System BIOS POST entry point	BIOS Code
FE2C3h	NMI handler entry point	Handler
FE3FEh	INT 13h Fixed Disk Service entry point	Handler
FE401h	Fixed Disk Drive parameter Table	Table
FE6F2h	INT 19h Boot Strap Service entry point	Handler
FE6F5h	Configuration DATA Table	Table
FE729h	DATA Transmission Rate generator Table	Table
FE739h	INT 14h Serial Communications Service entry point	Handler
FE82Eh	INT 16h Keyboard Service entry point	Handler
FE987h	INT 09h Keyboard Service entry point	Handler
FEC59h	INT 13h Floppy Disk Service entry point	Handler
FEFC7h	Floppy Disk Controller parameter Table	Table
FEFD2h	INT 17h parallel Printer Service entry point	Handler
FF045h	INT 10h Video Service Functions 00 through 0Fh entry point	Handler
FF065h	INT 10h Video Service entry point	Handler
FF0A4h	MDA and CGA Video parameter Table	Table
FF841h	INT 12h Memory Size Service entry point	Handler
FF84Dh	INT 11h Equipment List Service entry point	Handler
FF859h	INT 15h Systems Service entry point	Handler
FFA6Eh	Low order 128 of the 300x200 and 640x200 graphics fonts	Table
FFE6Eh	INT 1Ah Time of Day/PCI entry point	Handler
FFEA5h	INT 08h System Timer Interrupt Handler entry point	Handler
FFEF3h	Initial Interrupt Vector offsets loaded by POST	BIOS Code
FFF53h	IRET Instruction for Dummy Interrupt Handler	BIOS Code
FFF54h	INT 05h Print Screen Service entry point	Handler
FFFF0h	Power–On entry point	BIOS Code
FFFF5h	ROM Date (ASCII). Eight characters in mm/dd/yy format	BIOS Code
FFFFEh	System Model ID	BIOS Code

Table 16–5: System ROM Compatibility Table

There is, however, a method to execute the INT 1Ah interrupt handler without using the iAPX INT instruction in 16 bit Protected Mode. As Table 16–6 illustrates, the register size for both Real Mode and 16 bit Protected Mode is 16 bits. This means that in both modes the IP (Code Instruction Pointer) and SP (Stack Pointer) registers are used.

Attribute	Real Mode	16–Bit Protected Mode
Reference 16 bit Segment	Yes	No
Reference 16 bit Selector	No	Yes
Segment Base Address Limit	16 bit (1Mb)	24 bit (16Mb)
Segment Size Limit (64K)	16 bit (64K)	16 bit (64K)
Operand and Address Size	16 bit	16 bit
Interrupt Descriptor Table (IDT)	Fixed at 00000h	Protected Mode IDT

Table 16–6: Addressing Attributes for Real Mode and 16-Bit Protected Mode.

Because the two modes use 16 bit code and stack references, the 16 bit Protected Mode code can call the INT 1Ah entry point directly. When doing so, the following should be taken into account (assume that the code is currently executing in protected mode):

1. The 16 bit Protected Mode calling routine is required to place the contents of the Flags Register onto the stack prior to executing the call. The PUSHF iAPX instruction is typically used to accomplish this.

2. The call to the System BIOS INT 1Ah PCI interrupt handler at physical address FFE6Eh must be typed FAR.

3. The code segment descriptor should have a base of F0000h and a limit of 64k.

4. The System BIOS INT 1Ah PCI interrupt handler will use the caller's stack.

5. If the INT 1Ah interrupt handler was hooked by an application prior to the 16 bit protected mode call, the hooked code will not be executed.

6. The INT 1Ah interrupt handler will execute a FAR return to the caller by using the iAPX IRET instruction. This instruction automatically restores the contents of the Flags Register.

16.4 DMA CHANNELS

DMA is currently not implemented by the PCI Specification. This discussion is included in this section on system resources for completeness.

Beginning with the implementation of the Intel 80286 microprocessor, ISA compatible systems use two 8237 Direct Memory Access (DMA) controller chips or their equivalent. These controllers can transfer large amounts of data directly between physical I/O devices such as the floppy diskette or hard disk and main memory without the assistance of the CPU.

The figure below displays the function and type of each DMA channel.

Channel	Function	Type
0	Memory refresh. This function recharges RAM cells.	8–Bit
1	Available to the system.	8–Bit
2	Diskette operations.	8–Bit
3	Available to the system.	8 bit
4	DMA controller cascade line. Not available to the system.	
5	Available to the system.	16– Bit
6	Available to the system.	16–Bit
7	Available to the system.	16–Bit

Figure 16–8: DMA Channels

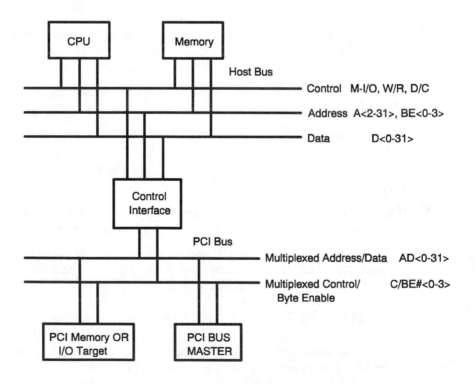

Figure 16–9: General Architecture of PC/AT with PCI bus

16.5 ACCESSING SYSTEM RESOURCES

The microprocessor controls most of the computer system through software programs. This control is made possible by the implementation of three distinct buses in the ISA architecture. These three buses are the control bus, address bus and data bus. These buses provide the communication path between the microprocessor and the individual devices in the system. Figure 16–9 shows a simple diagram of the bus connections between the system microprocessor and hardware devices.

CONTROL BUS

Starting with the Intel 80386 microprocessor family, software programs can access of up to four gigabytes of system memory. This memory consists of Read–Only Memory (ROM) and Random–Access Memory (RAM). ROM and RAM system memory address values range from 0 to FFFFFFFFh, or 4,294,967,295 unique byte–wide addresses.

I/O port address values range from 0 to FFFFh, or 65,535 unique byte–wide addresses.

Notice that the address region assigned to the I/O port memory address space is also assigned to the lowest sixty–four kilobyte address region of RAM in ISA compatible systems. However, because of the signals generated on the control bus, the four gigabytes of system memory address space and the 64 kilobytes of I/O port memory address space are not affiliated. When the microprocessor communicates with an I/O port, it generates a unique pattern of signals on the control bus which are recognized by hardware devices that implement I/O ports. For RAM or ROM device accesses, a different set of control signals are generated. It is the responsibility of both the computer system's hardware along with the individual devices accessible to the microprocessor to decode the control bus signals.

ADDRESS BUS

While the decode of the control bus signals directs the memory access to either RAM, ROM or an I/O port, it is the address bus that communicates to the system hardware which unique address is to be either read or written. The memory addresses that the microprocessor can physically access are determined by the address decoding logic hardware. Each time a memory address is read or written, this decode logic routes the access to the selected device. Because of the address decoding in conjunction with the operation of the control bus, system

RAM, ROM and I/O are made exclusive and cannot be accessed at the same time.

DATA BUS

During a memory read cycle, the data bus holds the information, or data, retrieved from the memory. RAM, ROM and I/O ports may be read. During a memory write cycle, the data bus holds the data to write to memory. However, only RAM and I/O ports (that are designated writeable) may be written. ROM devices are read–only. Attempts to write read–only memory should not adversely affect system operation.

16.6 SYSTEM RESOURCES EXAMPLE

To complete the discussion on system resources, an example of how they are used in the system as well as the interaction between the individual components is now presented. The sequence required to update the System BIOS Time–of–Day count was chosen for this example because it demonstrates the connectivity between different system resources as well as the System BIOS and operating system level software. Refer to Figure 16–10 as the example is explained.

SYSTEM CLOCK

The System Clock provides the 8254 Programmable Timer with a fixed input clock rate of 1.9318 MHz. This frequency is the same on all ISA compatible systems. The microprocessor frequency, which is considerably higher, has no effect on the clock rate of the 8254 Timer chip. The System Clock is unique in that the device does not consume any system resources. It also does not require any special programming. Once system power is applied, this device starts oscillating at the correct frequency. The output of the System Clock is continuously fed to the 8254 Programmable Timer's clock input signal.

8254 PROGRAMMABLE TIMER

The 8254 Programmable Timer chip contains three independent timer circuits, or channels. The three timers are identical. However, each timer is used to supply a different function. This discussion is limited to Timer 0.

The 8254 Timer is uninitialized when power is applied to the system. The System BIOS must program the 8254 Timer for correct operation. Each channel of the 8254 Timer can be programmed to operate in one of six modes. The microprocessor uses four I/O ports to communicate with the 8254 Timer. These

I/O port resources are not shareable with any other device in the system. In addition, they should never be assigned to any other device in the system. The I/O port addresses assigned to the 8254 Timer are as follows:

I/O Port	Function
40h	Timer 0
41h	Timer 1
42h	Timer 2
43h	8254 Timer Command Register

Recall that I/O port addresses in the range 00h through 00FFh are used to address devices mounted on the platform, which is where the 8254 Timer is located.

The microprocessor uses I/O ports 40h and 43h to program the 8254 Timer to pulse its output line 18.2 times per second. The 8254 will run continuously in this mode without any further intervention on the part of the microprocessor. The output line of Timer 0 is connected directly to the IRQ0 input line of the 8259 Interrupt Controller chip. Each time the Timer 0 output is pulsed, it generates a hardware interrupt request to the 8259 chip.

8259 INTERRUPT CONTROLLER

As explained in Subchapter 16–3, there are two 8259 Interrupt Controllers in an ISA compatible system. These are referred to as the master and slave interrupt controllers. Their purpose is to manage the system's hardware interrupts.

Both 8259 Interrupt Controllers are also initialized when power is applied to the system. The System BIOS must program each interrupt controller for correct operation. The microprocessor uses I/O ports 20h and 21h to communicate with the master 8259 Interrupt Controller. It uses I/O ports A0h and A1h to communicate with the slave 8259 Interrupt Controller. These I/O port resources are not shareable. In addition, they should never be assigned to any other device in the system. Once each interrupt controller is programmed for ISA compatible operation, it will run continuously in this mode without any further intervention on the part of the microprocessor.

When the 8254 Timer 0 output is pulsed, it generates a hardware interrupt request to the 8259 master 8259 Interrupt Controller via its IRQ0 input line. This is the highest priority hardware interrupt in the system. If a different hardware interrupt is currently being serviced, IRQ0 will be serviced next. This is regardless of any other pending hardware interrupts such as the keyboard or fixed disk types. In addition, this hardware interrupt resource is not shareable.

Hardware system designers should never use IRQ0 for any other purpose than to generate the time–of–day interrupt request.

> Recall that hardware interrupts can be disabled using the iAPX CLI instruction or via the 8259 Interrupt Controller's interrupt mask register. Be careful not to disable interrupts for a long period of time in your software or the system time–of–day will become invalid.

The master 8259 Interrupt Controller will execute a series of hand–shakes with the microprocessor while the IRQ0 interrupt is being processed. During this time the microprocessor is instructed by the master 8259 Interrupt Controller to fetch the interrupt vector that services IRQ0.

FETCH INTERRUPT VECTOR

Fetching the interrupt vector that services IRQ0 is important for two reasons. First, because the microprocessor was asynchronously interrupted by a device in the system. In this case, the microprocessor is being requested to halt its current process and provide software support for the system time–of–day function. Second, because up until this point, only I/O port and hardware interrupt system resources have been used. Fetching the interrupt vector requires the utilization of a third type of system resource, system RAM.

Recall that the Real Mode interrupt vector table is located in system RAM from physical address 0000:0000 through 0000:03FF. Also remember that the master 8259 Interrupt Controller is programmed to request service from the Type 8 interrupt handler when an IRQ0 is generated. The vector for this handler is at physical address 0000:0020. Once the microprocessor fetches the vector from the interrupt vector table, the INT 8h interrupt handler is called.

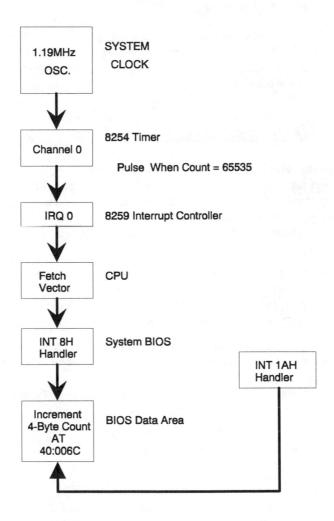

Figure 16–10: BIOS Time-of Day Count; Update Sequence

INT 8H INTERRUPT HANDLER

The INT 8h interrupt handler is responsible for registering the number of times the output of Timer 0 of the 8254 Programmable Timer pulses while the system power is on. Each time this routine is invoked, the value contained in the four–byte system memory resource located at physical address 0040:006C is incremented by one. This is the system time-of-day-count.

495

INT 1AH INTERRUPT HANDLER

The INT 1Ah interrupt handler is responsible for servicing the system Real Time Clock Lock Functions. Software programs can use the INT 1Ah interrupt handler to read (function 0) and set (function 1) the system time–of–day count at physical address 0040:006C.

16.7 CHAPTER SUMMARY

The system resources example just presented reinforces several concepts that have been introduced in this chapter. First, communication between the devices in the system rarely occurs without the use of system resources. System memory and I/O port resources are used to transfer data between devices. Hardware interrupts relieve the CPU from having to poll devices waiting for hardware events to occur.

In addition, the management of system resources is of primary importance. In the example, there is a seamless interaction between several devices despite the fact that certain devices use only I/O ports while others use memory, etc. Assign system resources judiciously to guarantee that the desired results are achieved.

System resources that are assigned to standard ISA devices such as the 8254 Programmable Timer should be protected. These type of resources are usually non-shareable. When the system resources have been assigned, avoid using them for anything else in the system or catastrophic system failures may occur.

CHAPTER 17

PCI CONFIGURATION ADDRESS SPACE

This chapter consists of the following subchapters:

17.0 OVERVIEW OF PCI CONFIGURATION ADDRESS SPACE

PCI configuration register space permits software to access PCI devices in order to perform Plug and Play operations. It is through this space that PCI devices are detected and their functions are identified. In addition, the PCI configuration space contains the requests for system resources required by each device. Finally, to complete the automatic configuration process, it is through the PCI configuration register space that system resources are assigned to each PCI device.

The three major functions of PCI configuration space are summarized as follows:

- To permit device detection and automatic configuration of PCI devices.

- To initialize PCI devices.

- To support catastrophic error handling functions.

The PCI configuration register space is designed to accommodate many different types of computer systems. These include RISC architectures as well as Intel x86 implementations.

> The architects of the PCI configuration space used a template approach for ease of use. This template consists of a block of 256-byte-wide contiguous addresses into which all of the PCI configuration registers are mapped. The block of addresses is divided into a Configuration Space Header region and a Device Dependent region. PCI device vendors need support only those registers that are applicable within each region of the PCI configuration space. Note that all PCI Configuration Space Registers must be readable.

17.1 RULES FOR ACCESSING PCI CONFIGURATION SPACE

READING PCI CONFIGURATION SPACE

The following rules pertain to reading PCI configuration space:

- PCI devices are required to return data when their configuration space is read.

- Read accesses of reserved or unused configuration registers must terminate normally.

- Reserved bit values are undefined.

- Data values read are the values the device is actually using.

- A value of zero must be returned for read accesses of reserved or unused Configuration Space Register bits.

> Software should not rely on any bits being a particular value when reading these reserved or unused register bits.

WRITING PCI CONFIGURATION SPACE

The following rules pertain to writing PCI configuration space:

- PCI devices must treat write operations to Reserved Registers in configuration space as NO–OPs. The data must not be written to the device. The transaction must complete normally.

- Reserved bit states must be preserved when writing PCI configuration registers. Use a Read/Modify/Write implementation when writing registers with reserved bits.

17.2 OVERVIEW OF THE PCI CONFIGURATION SPACE HEADER REGION

Every PCI compliant device must support a predefined PCI Configuration Space Header Region and strictly adhere to its organization. The purpose of the PCI Configuration Space Header registers is two–fold:

1. To uniquely identify the PCI device.

2. To permit generic control of all PCI compliant devices.

The PCI Configuration Space Header Region is subdivided into two regions: the PCI Device Independent Region and the PCI Device Header Type Region.

Note that the PCI Local Bus Specification treats the predefined header as a monolithic 64 byte structure. This structure is examined in two parts in this subchapter. The first part to be examined is the first 16 bytes of the predefined PCI Configuration Space Header Region. The layout of this region must be the same for all PCI devices. The second part to be examined is the remaining portion of the predefined PCI Configuration Space Header region. This part of the structure has a layout and size determined by the Header Type register value.

Also note that while many registers in the predefined PCI Configuration Space Header region must be supported, programmer control over the individual bits in the registers is not required to be implemented. For example, the Bus Master Control bit (bit 3 of the Command Register), does not have to be programmable for devices that are not bus masters. In this case it is recommended that:

1. The bit attribute is read only; writes should have no affect on the bit.

2. The state of the bit is set to the value (0 or 1) which is optimum for the PCI device. In most instances, this will be the disable state.

RESERVED, REQUIRED AND OPTIONAL REGISTERS AND BITS

A PCI device is required to implement the entire PCI configuration space. The reason is that PCI devices must respond (i.e., assert DEVSEL) on any access to all 256 bytes of its configuration space. Within this 256 byte region there can be reserved, required, and optional registers and bits.

> On write operations, a PCI device can choose to throw away the data. On read operations, a PCI device can return any value, subject to the Required and Reserved Register rules.

RESERVED REGISTERS AND BITS

Reserved Registers and bits do not perform any function. Reserved Registers and bits are reserved for future PCI Special Interest Group use. Because of this they cannot be used for any other purpose. Reserved Registers and bits must not be writeable, and must always return zero when read.

REQUIRED REGISTERS AND BITS

When the PCI Local Bus Specification states that a register is required, it means that it cannot be treated as a Reserved Register. Required registers or bits must have the capability or encoding provided in the specification.

In some cases this can make a register or bit behave exactly like a Reserved Register or bit (i.e. not writeable, returns zero on reads). For example, in most devices the Header Type register is hard–coded to zero because zero is the correct value for the device. Also, older PCI devices may return a Base Class Code of zero, which was a valid value at the time the device was implemented.

OPTIONAL REGISTERS AND BITS

When the PCI Local Bus Specification states that a register or bit is optional it means that the device designer can choose to implement the register as reserved or to implement it with the capability/encoding defined in the PCI Local Bus Specification.

In some cases optional registers become required if the device has a certain capability. For instance, any device that needs to generate interrupts must implement the Interrupt Line register as an eight bit Read/Write register. If a device does not generate interrupts, the Interrupt Line register can be treated as reserved (i.e., not writeable, returns zero when read).

SUMMARY

In summary, Reserved Registers or bits must be read–only and return zero when read. Required registers or bits must be implemented to the capabilities/encoding defined in the PCI Local Bus Specification. Optional registers or bits must follow the capability/encoding defined in the specification or be treated as reserved.

PCI DEVICE INDEPENDENT REGION

The PCI Device Independent Region occupies the first 16 bytes of the PCI Configuration Space Header Region. This region is identical in function and layout for all PCI devices. The purpose for this region is device identification and generic control. Of these first 16 bytes, the PCI Local Bus Specification states that the Vendor ID, Device ID, Command, Status, Revision ID, Class Code and Header Type registers are required to be supported by all PCI compliant devices. All other PCI Device Independent registers can be implemented as Reserved Registers. Remember that Reserved Registers must return a value of zero when read.

PCI DEVICE HEADER TYPE REGION

The layout and use of the remaining bytes (starting at offset 10H) in the PCI Configuration Space Header Region are defined according to the value encoded in the lower seven bits of the PCI Header Type register. This register is located at offset 0EH within the PCI Device Independent Region. Currently Type 00h and Type 01h are the only two defined PCI device header types. Note that all device dependent registers must be located after the predefined header in the PCI configuration space.

17.3 TYPE 00H PCI CONFIGURATION SPACE HEADER REGION

A Type 00h PCI Configuration Space Header Region consists of sixty-four bytes. The first 16 bytes are the PCI Device Independent Region. The remaining 48 bytes are assigned to the PCI Device Header Type Region. Consequently, 64 bytes are assigned to the predefined PCI Configuration Space Header Region and 192 bytes to the Device Dependent region of the PCI configuration register space. For details about the device header types, refer to the description of the PCI Header Type register, found later in this chapter. In addition, refer to Table 17.1 and Figure 17.1 for pictorial representations of the Type 00h PCI Device Header Region.

> A Type 00h PCI Device Header Type Register (offset 0EH) specifies that the PCI Device Header Type Region consists of 48 bytes. When defined, other header types may specify more or fewer registers for this region.

Note that individual PCI devices need only implement the registers required to support their functionality. For example, Intel Corporation's 82434 PCI device is a Host/PCI BRIDGE. This device does not support an expansion ROM.

501

Consequently, the Expansion ROM Base Address Register (DWORD at offset 30H), of the PCI Configuration Header Region is not implemented. In this case the register is treated as reserved. As specified by rule four listed in the section *Reading PCI Configuration Space,* all bits in this register are hardwired to zero.

Table 17.1 contains a list of the Type 00h PCI Configuration Space Header Region registers with their corresponding offset from the base of the structure.

Figure 17.1 is a pictorial view of the 64 byte register layout of Type 00h PCI Configuration Space Header. All PCI compliant devices that implement a Type 00h header must support this layout. Fields that utilize more than one byte follow little–endian ordering. The least significant portion of a field is contained in the lowest byte of the field.

TYPE 00H HEADER REGION REGISTER DEFINITIONS

The remainder of this section contains a description of each register in a Type 00h PCI Configuration Header region. Each register description contains the name of the register, the address location within the PCI device of the register, the byte width of the register, the read/write attribute assigned to the register, the valid value range of the register, the register's global function definition, and the individual bit definitions of the register. Default values for each register are vendor and device specific and therefore are not specified.

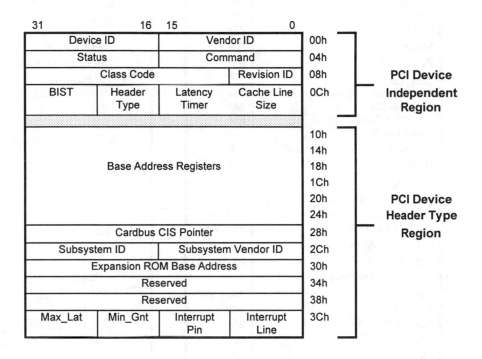

Figure 17–1: Type 00h PCI Configuration Space Header Region

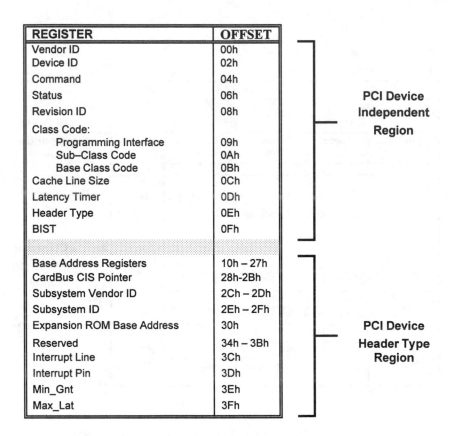

REGISTER	OFFSET
Vendor ID	00h
Device ID	02h
Command	04h
Status	06h
Revision ID	08h
Class Code:	
Programming Interface	09h
Sub–Class Code	0Ah
Base Class Code	0Bh
Cache Line Size	0Ch
Latency Timer	0Dh
Header Type	0Eh
BIST	0Fh
Base Address Registers	10h – 27h
CardBus CIS Pointer	28h-2Bh
Subsystem Vendor ID	2Ch – 2Dh
Subsystem ID	2Eh – 2Fh
Expansion ROM Base Address	30h
Reserved	34h – 3Bh
Interrupt Line	3Ch
Interrupt Pin	3Dh
Min_Gnt	3Eh
Max_Lat	3Fh

PCI Device Independent Region

PCI Device Header Type Region

Table 17–1: Type 00h PCI Configuration Space Header Region

Vendor ID	
Offset:	00h
Width:	2 Bytes
Valid Values:	0000h–FFFEh
Description:	This register is used to identify the manufacturer of the device. The PCI Special Interest Group assigns vendor identifiers to ensure uniqueness. For example, a value of 8086h will always be read from the Vendor ID register of any PCI device manufactured by Intel Corporation.

Bit	Type	Function
15:0	RO	Vendor ID
		This register contains a unique 16 bit value assigned to each vendor. This number enables each PCI device's manufacturer to be identified.

Table 17–2: Vendor Identification Register

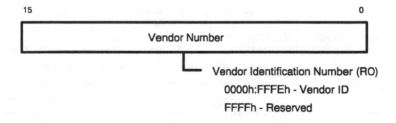

Figure 17–2: Vendor Identification Register

The platform hardware is responsible for ensuring that a value of FFFFH is returned when an attempt is made to read the vendor identifier of a non–existent PCI device. Consequently, the Vendor ID register is the one that should be used when attempting to determine whether a PCI device exists in a system. Because FFFFh is an invalid value for Vendor ID, that value will be returned only when no device is present.

Device ID	
Offset:	02h
Width:	2 Bytes
Valid Values:	0000h–FFFFh
Description:	This register identifies the device with a unique number. The value is assigned by the vendor of the device.
	Vendors may choose to assign device IDs such that devices in one family that are backward compatible with earlier members of the family are easily recognized by software device drivers. For instance, assume a vendor built a SCSI device with some base functionality and assigned an identification number of 0AA0h to the device. Later the vendor develops the next generation part which has all the capabilities of the first part, but has extensions that make it perform better if they are used. The vendor assigned an identification number of 0AA1h to this device.
	A device driver for the original part would continue to work for the new part if the driver looked for an identification number of 0AAxh when trying to locate its device. The current device driver wouldn't take advantage of new features. However, the problem of immediately providing a new driver for the latest device would be solved.

Avoid assigning a Device ID of either 0000h or FFFFh, because zero indicates a Reserved Register and FFFF a *no response.*

Bit	Type	Function
15:0	RO	Device ID
		The value in this register is the vendors' device identifier.

Table 17–3: Device Identification Register

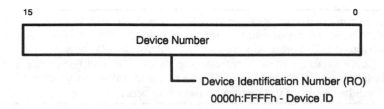

Figure 17–3: Device Identification Register

Command	
Offset:	04h
Width:	2 Bytes
Valid Values:	N/A. This field is a collection of bits, not a range of values. The register should not be viewed as values, but as individual bits.
Description:	This register controls the device's ability to generate and respond to PCI bus accesses. Note that a value of zero in this register logically disconnects the device from the PCI bus.

All PCI devices are required to respond to PCI configuration accesses, even when bits 2:0 are set to zero.

Bit	Type		Function
0	RW		**I/O Space Control**
		0	Disables a device's response to I/O space accesses (**RST#** state).
		1	Enables a device's response to I/O space accesses.
			This bit must be implemented if the device wants to consume I/O space.
1	RW		**Memory Space Control**
		0	Disables a device's response to memory space accesses (**RST#** state).
		1	Enables a device's response to memory space accesses.
			This bit must be implemented if the device wants to consume memory space.
2	RW		**Bus Master Control**
		0	Disables a device's ability to generate PCI bus accesses (**RST#** state).
		1	Enables a device's ability to generate PCI bus accesses.
			Any device that can be a master (i.e. asserts **FRAME#**) must implement this bit.
3	RW		**Special Cycles Control**
		0	Device ignores all Special Cycle operations (**RST#** state).
		1	Device monitors Special Cycle operations.
			Devices that always ignore Special Cycle's are not required to implement this bit.
4	RW		**Memory Write and Invalidate Control**
		0	Device will use Memory Write (**RST#** state).
		1	Bus master devices can generate the Memory Write and Invalidate command.
			Devices that can never generate Memory Write and Invalidate commands are not required to implement this bit.

Table 17–4: Command Register

5	RW		**VGA Palette Snoop Control**
		0	Positively respond to write accesses to the palette registers. VGA compatible and graphics devices should initialize this bit to this state on RESET.
		1	Snoop write accesses to the palette registers. The device does not respond to palette register writes. Non–VGA graphics controllers that need palette information should initialize this bit to this state on RESET.
			This bit is required for VGA compatible devices. Other devices are not required to implement this bit. See Appendix C for details.
6	RW		**Parity Error Response**
		0	Device ignores detected parity errors (**RST#** state).
		1	Device responds to detected parity errors.
			1 Devices that implement parity checking are required to support this bit.
			2 Devices will generate parity even if parity checking is disabled.
			3 Any device that doesn't check parity (and as a result will never get a parity error) can hardwire the bit to zero.
7	RW		**Wait Cycle Control**
		0	Disable ADDRESS/DATA STEPPING. Hardwire this bit to zero if ADDRESS/DATA STEPPING is not implemented.
		1	Enable ADDRESS/DATA STEPPING. Hardwire this bit to one if ADDRESS/DATA STEPPING is always performed.
			Bit 7 must be read/writeable if the device can either enable or disable ADDRESS/DATA STEPPING. The RST# state of this bit is one.
8	RW		**System Error Control**
		0	Disable the **SERR#** output driver (**RST#** state).
		1	Enable the **SERR#** output driver.
			1 Devices which implement SERR# must support this bit.
			2 This bit and bit 6 must be set to one to report address parity errors.
9	RW		**Fast Back–to–Back Control**
		0	Fast back–to–back transactions are only allowed to the same agent (**RST#** state).
		1	Enable fast back–to–back transactions.
			1 This bit is optional. It has the read/write attribute when implemented.
			2 Software (typically the System BIOS) may set this bit to one only if all targets are capable of fast back–to–back transactions.
15:10	RO		**Reserved**

Table 17–4: Command Register (cont.)

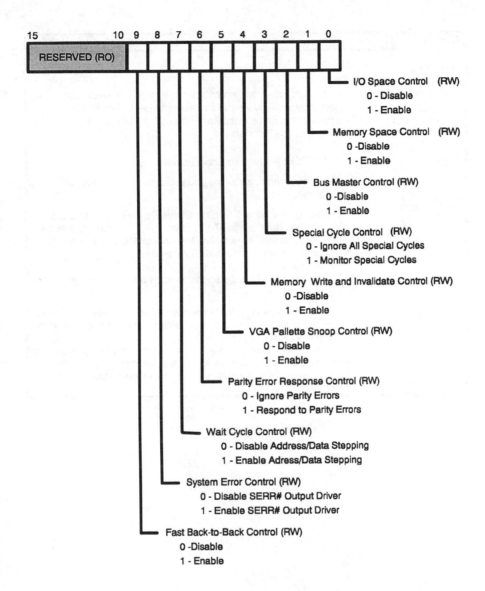

Figure 17–4: Command Register

Status

Offset:	**06h**
Width:	**2 Bytes**
Valid Values:	N/A. This field is a collection of bits, not a range of values. The register should not be viewed as values, but as individual bits.
Description:	This register records events that occur on the PCI bus. The following rules apply to this register:

1   Reads of this register occur normally.

2   Writes to this register may clear bits to zero but never set them to one.

3   There are several bits in the Status Register Table below bits with the attribute type RWC. These are individual bits that are cleared to zero if the bit has the write attribute and its bit location is written with a data value of one.

4   The function of the device determines which bits will be implemented.

The Status Register is typically not used by device drivers. Rather, it is intended to record events that (a) tend to be catastrophic and (b) are not part of normal operation.

System monitoring software can use the Status Register to determine precisely what happened if a catastrophic error occurs. In addition, the system monitoring software can keep statistics on PCI specific events.

Table 17–5: Status Register

Bit	Type	Function
4:0	RO	**Reserved**
5	RO	**66MHz Capable Status** 0 The device is capable of running at 33MHz. 1 The device is capable of running at 66MHz. This bit is optional.
6	RO	**User Definable Features Status** 0 The device supports User Definable Features. 1 The device does not support User Definable Features. This bit is optional. It is required to be set when a device function has device specific configuration selections that must be presented to the user. See Appendix B for a complete decripton of requirements for setting this bit.
7	RO	**Fast Back–to–Back Status** 0 The target is not capable accepting fast–back–to–back transactions. 1 The target is capable accepting fast–back–to–back transactions. This bit is optional.
8	RWC	**Data Parity Status** 0 No data parity errors have occurred. (**RST#** state). 1 All three of the following conditions must be met: a. **PERR#** was asserted by the bus master or the bus master observed **PERR#** asserted. b. The agent which set the bit was the bus master during the transaction when the error occurred. c. Parity Error Response (bit 6 of the bus master's Command Register) is enabled. This bit is only implemented by Bus Masters.
10:9	RO	**Device Select Timing Status** 00 Device asserts **DEVSEL#** in the *fast* timing mode for any bus command. 01 Device asserts **DEVSEL#** in the *medium* timing mode for any bus command. 10 Device asserts **DEVSEL#** in the *slow* timing mode for any bus command. 11 Reserved. Configuration read and write cycles do not apply to the above definition. For example, if a device performs FAST decode for all memory and I/O accesses, but *medium* decode for configuration accesses, the device should set this register to fast.
11	RWC	**Signaled Target Abort Status** 0 Target device did not terminate a transaction with a Target Abort (**RST#** state). 1 Target device terminated a transaction with a Target Abort. Devices incapable of terminating a transaction with a target are not required to implement this bit.

Table 17–5: Status Register

Bit	Type	Function
12	RWC	**Received Target Abort Status** 0 – A Target Abort did not terminate a bus master's transaction (**RST#** state). 1 – A Target Abort terminated a bus master's transaction. All bus master devices are required to implement this bit.
13	RWC	**Received Master Abort Status** 0 – A bus Master Abort did not terminate a bus master's transaction (**RST#** state). 1 – Set by a bus master whose transaction was terminated by a bus Master Abort. 1 All bus master devices are required to implement this bit. 2 A Master Abort on a Special Cycle transaction should not cause this bit to be set.
14	RWC	**Signaled System Error Status** 0 – Device did not generate a system error on the **SERR#** line. 1 – Device generated a system error on the **SERR#** line. Devices which cannot assert **SERR#** are not required to implement this bit.
15	RWC	**Detected Parity Error Status** 0 – Device did not detect a parity error (**RST#** state). 1 – Device detected a parity error. Devices will set this bit regardless of the state of Parity Error Response (bit 6 of the Command Register).

Table 17–5: Status Register (cont.)

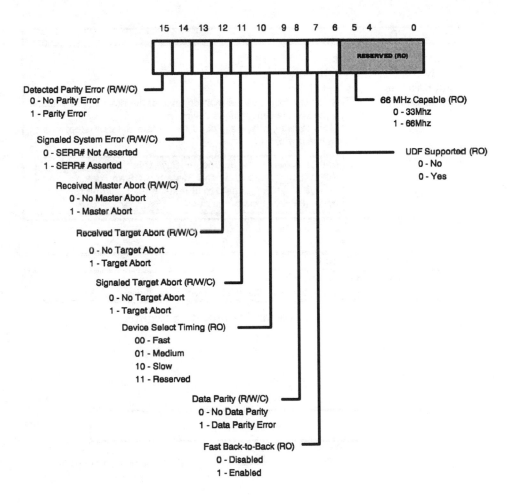

Figure 17–5: Status Register

Revision ID

Offset:	08h
Width:	1 Byte
Valid Values:	00h–FFh
Description:	This register identifies the revision level of the device. The value is assigned by the vendor of the device.
	This register is typically used to indicate different steppings of the same device.

> Plug and Play software does not use this field for device identification purposes. The System BIOS and device drivers can use this field to isolate code execution to particular revisions of the device.

Bit	Type	Function
7:0	RO	**Revision ID** This value reflects the version level of the device.

Table 17–6: Vendor Identification Register

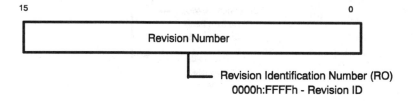

Figure 17–6: Revision Identification Register

Figure 17–6: Revision Identification Register

Class Code

Offset:	09h
Width:	3 Bytes
Valid Values:	Programming Interface (09h): Base Class specific
	Sub–Class Code (0Ah): Base Class specific
	Base Class Code (0Bh): 00h–0Ch, FFh
Description:	This register identifies the generic function of the device and the register level programming interface of the device (if applicable to the class of the device). The figure below show the current definitions for the Base Class field of this register. **See Appendix A for a complete definition of this register.**

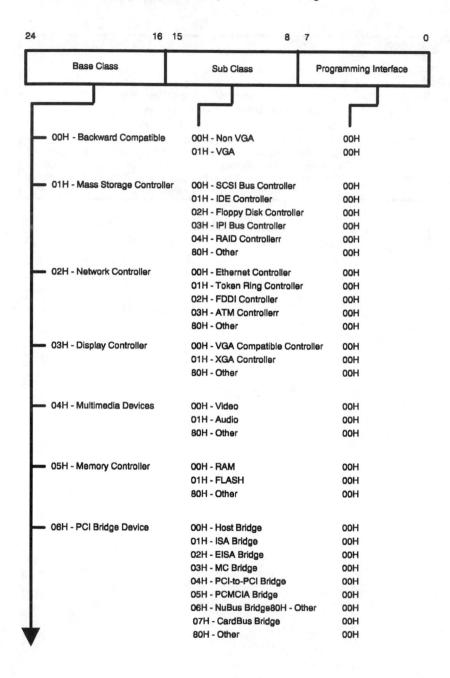

Figure 17–7: Class Code Register

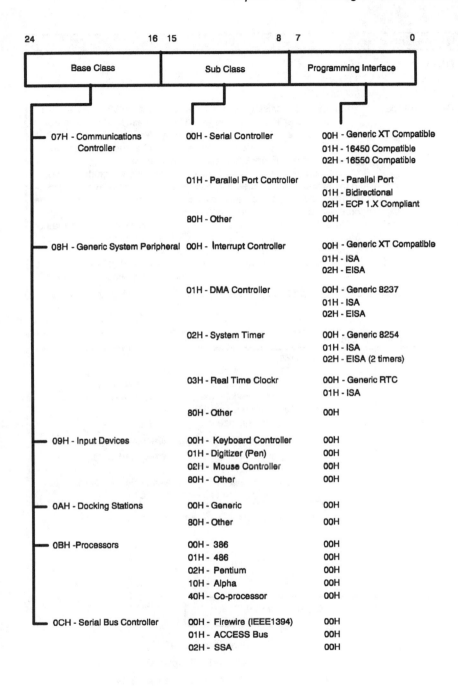

Figure 17–7: Class Code Register (cont.)

Cache Line Size

Offset:	0Ch
Width:	1 Byte
Valid Values:	0000h–FFFFh
Description:	This register specifies the system cacheline size in 32 bit words.

This register is required in two different cases. The first case is any device that can generate a Memory Write and Invalidate bus cycle. These devices need to know the cache line size in order to generate valid Memory Write and Invalidate cycles.

The second case is any device that provides cacheable memory to the system. In this case the register is used to know when to break BURST accesses to the cacheable memory (at cache line boundaries) so that cache snoops can occur.

In both cases, the value 00h has a special meaning. For master devices it indicates that the Memory Write and Invalidate command should not be used. Instead use Memory Write.

For cacheable memory devices, the value 00H indicates that the system cache (if it exists) is not caching that device's memory and therefore the **SBO#** and **SDONE** signals may be ignored.

Bit	Type	Function
7:0	RW	**Cache Line Size**
		00h – Memory target is configured as non–cacheable. Ignore PCI support lines **SDONE** and **SBO#**. Master devices use Memory Write transactions to update memory. (**RST#** state).
		01H:0FFh – Cache line size in 32 bit words.
		1 Bus Masters that generate the Memory Write and Invalidate command are required to implement this register.
		2 Devices that provide cacheable memory are required to implement this register.

Table 17–8: Cache Line Size Register

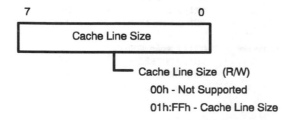

Cache Line Size (R/W)
00h - Not Supported
01h:FFh - Cache Line Size

Figure 17–8: Cache Line Size Register

Latency Timer	
Offset:	0DH
Width:	1 Byte
Valid Values:	00h–FFh
Description:	This register specifies the Master Latency Timer value for a PCI Master when the device is on the PCI bus. A reasonable implementation of this register is to only implement the top five bits. This means that field can only be modified in increments of 8, but this is acceptable. A typical way for a System BIOS to configure this register is to just choose an appropriate value and use that value for all devices. 32 (approximately 1 μsec) is a reasonable value. Higher level software, i.e. an OS heuristic, can use the knowledge of how the system is being used (server, desktop, multimedia) as well as MIN_GNT and MAX_LAT values to adjust the timers appropriately.

Bit	Function
7:0	**Read Only Implementation:** Bus Masters incapable of bursting for more than two DATA PHASES may implement this register with a Read Only attribute. The register must contain a fixed value of 16 or less.
	Read/Write Implementation: Bus Masters capable of bursting for more than two DATA PHASES must implement this register with a Read/Write attribute. **RST#** should clear this register.

Table 17–9: Latency Timer Register

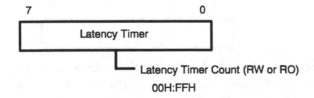

Figure 17–9: Latency Timer Size Register

Header Type

Offset:	0Eh
Width:	1 Byte
Valid Values:	00h or 80h
Description:	This register identifies the layout of bytes beginning at offset 10h in the PCI configuration space. In addition, this register specifies whether the device is a single or multi-function device. Configuration software such as a System BIOS should validate this register's value prior to doing anything with the device.

> If configuration software finds a header type that it does not know about, it should disable the device. This is done by setting the bottom three bits in the Command Register to zero. Leave the device alone once this is done.

Bit	Type	Function
6:0	RO	**Header**
		000000B Device supports the layout of configuration registers 10h through 3FH as defined in Figure 17-XX.
		000001B Device supports the layout of PCI to PCI Bridge configuration registers 10h through 3FH as defined in Figure 17-XX.
		02h-7Fh Reserved.
7	RO	**Multi-Function Status**
		0 Device has one function.
		1 Device contains between two and eight functions.

Table 17–10: Header Type Register

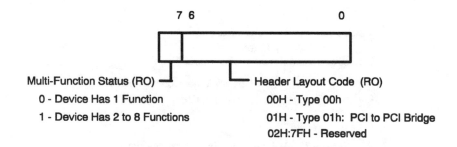

Figure 17–10: Header Type Register

BIST (Built-In Self Test)		
Offset:	0Fh	
Width:	1 Byte	
Valid Values:	Device dependent. See description below.	
Description:	This register is used to control the invocation of a PCI device's BIST and to report the status of the BIST. Devices that do not support BIST must return a value of 00H when this register is read.	

POST code may choose to run a device's BIST at cold boot. When a device is running its BIST it should not generate any cycles to the PCI bus.

Bit	Type	Function
3:0	RO	**BIST Completion Status** 00h Device test passed. 01h:0Fh Device test failed. Vendors may define up to 15 device specific failure codes in these bits.
5:4	RO	**Reserved** Device must return zero in these two bit fields.
6	RW	**BIST Start Control Bit** 0 Device resets this bit after BIST completes. 1 Invoke the device's BIST. Software should fail the device if this bit is not RESET to zero within two seconds after the BIST is invoked. Hard code this bit to 0, RO, if BIST is not implemented.
7	RO	**BIST Support Status** 0 Device does not support BIST. 1 Device supports BIST.

Table 17–11: BIST Register

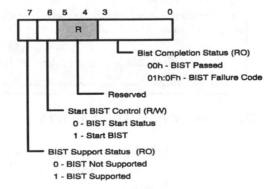

Figure 17–11: BIST Register

521

I/O and Memory Base Address Registers

Offset:	10h (first register location)
Width:	I/O: 32 bit word length
	Memory: 32 bit or 64 bit word length
Valid Values:	Device dependent
Description:	

This register set allows a PCI device's I/O and memory functions to be dynamically mapped into a system's memory and I/O address spaces. Depending on the system implementation, this dynamic mapping may be accomplished by the System ROM BIOS during POST or later by other system software such as a device driver or operating system.

PCI devices with a Type 00h configuration space header contain twenty-four bytes dedicated for memory and I/O base address assignments. Because the first base address register location is 10h, the second base address register may either be located at 14h or 18h. The offset location of the any base address register other than zero depends on the size of the previous one. In other words, the word length of preceding base address register determines the offset addresses of the remaining base address registers.

PCI devices with a Type 01h configuration space header contain 8 bytes dedicated for memory and I/O base address. The rules stated in the previous paragraph also apply to devices with Type 01h configuration space Headers.

> Note that there is no specification for the order in which registers request blocks of I/O or memory. Any combination is permissible. For example, a device may request a block of memory followed by a request for two blocks of I/O, followed by another request for a block of memory.
>
> There may also be gaps in the register implementations. For instance, in a Type 00h configuration space header a device may implement a register at offset 10h, leave the registers at offsets 14h and 18h unimplemented, and implement another register at offset 1Ch.
>
> These registers do not provide a mechanism that allows the device to request specific addresses in the address space.
>
> PCI devices should always allow control functions to be mapped into memory space.

I/O BASE ADDRESS IMPLEMENTATION

For I/O base address registers, there are two ways to decrease the number of bits in the address decoder. The first method is to claim more address space than is actually needed. For example, a device that has 16 bytes of registers may decide to claim 128 bytes of address space, thus saving three bits in the decoder.

The second way to decrease the number of bits in the address decoder is to take advantage of the Intel x86 architecture. This architecture only has a 64K I/O space. Hence, there is no need to implement the top 16 bits of the 32 bit I/O base register. These bits can be hardwired to zero. However, a full 32 bit decode must still be performed. Note that the decode for the top 16 bits can be accomplished using a simple NAND gate.

The first method should be avoided since I/O space is typically tight. In no case should a PCI device designed to operate in a ISA compatible system request more than 256 bytes of I/O space per each I/O base address register. The major reason is the ISA aliasing issue, which is discussed in Appendices E and F.

To assign a value to an I/O base address register, software should do the following:

1. Write a value of 1 to all bits within this register.

2. Confirm that bit 0 of this register contains a value of 1, indicating an I/O request.

3. Starting at bit location 2, search for the first bit set to a value of 1. This bit is the binary weighted size of the total contiguous block of I/O address space requested. For example, if bit 8 is the first bit set, the device is requesting a 256 byte block of I/O address space.

4. Write the start address of the I/O space block assigned to this register.

Bit	Type	Function
0	RO	**Address Space Indicator** 0　　N/A for I/O—see Memory Base Address Implementation. 1　　Base address register is requesting I/O space.
1	RO	**Reserved** This bit must return zero when read.
31:2	RW	**I/O Base Address** Start address of an I/O space region assigned to this device.

Table 17–12: I/O Base Address Register

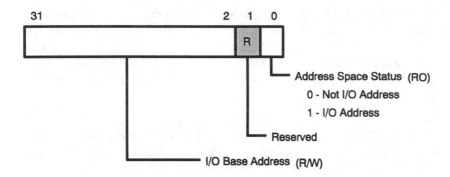

Figure 17–12: I/O Base Address Register

MEMORY BASE ADDRESS IMPLEMENTATION

Memory base address decoders can decrease the number of address bits by claiming more space than is needed. Hardwiring upper order address bits is not allowed (unless the device is requesting space at an address below one megabyte - see the definition for Base Address Memory Type bits in Table 17-13).

If a device takes advantage of decreasing the number of address bits by claiming more space than is needed to minimize decode bits, the device must decode down to at least a 4K region. For example, if a device has 256 bytes that it wants to map to memory, the base address register can be implemented with sizes of 256, 512, 1K, 2K or 4K. Sizes larger than that are illegal.

To assign a value to a memory base address register software should do the following:

1. Write a value of 1 to all bits within this register.

2. Confirm that bit 0 of this register contains a value of 0, indicating a memory request.

3. Starting at bit location 4, search upwards for the first bit set to a value of 1. This bit is the binary weighted size of the total contiguous block of memory requested. For example, if bit 15 is the first bit set, the device is requesting a 32 kilobyte block of memory.

4. Write the start address of the memory block assigned to this register. This memory address region must not conflict with any other memory space utilized within the system. In addition, it must comply with the definition contained in bits 1 and 2 of this register.

Bit	Type	Function
0	RO	**Address Space Indicator** 0 Base address register is requesting memory space. 1 N/A for Memory—see I/O Base ADDRESS Implementation.
2:1	RO	**Memory Type** 00 Base address is 32 bits wide. Set the base address anywhere within the 32 bit memory space. 01 Base address is 32 bits wide. Set the base address below 1Mb in memory space. The upper 12 bits in this register can be hardwired to zero, but must still participate in address decode. Auto configuration software must handle this case. 10 Base address is 64 bits wide. Set the base address anywhere within the 64 bit memory space. 11 Reserved.
3	RO	**Prefetchable** 0 Memory is not prefetchable. 1 A device can mark its memory range as prefetchable if the following conditions are met: 1 The device returns all bytes on reads regardless of the byte enables. 2 Reads to this memory space create no side effects. 3 Host BRIDGEs can merge CPU writes (i.e. take multiple byte and/or word accesses from the CPU and merge them into single DWORD writes on PCI) into this range without errors. Linear frame buffers on graphics devices are an example of prefetchable memory. They behave like system memory. However, linear frame buffers do not participate in PCI's caching protocol. Host BRIDGEs can make performance optimizations on memory ranges that support prefetching.
31:4	RW	**32–Bit Memory Base Address** 32 bit start address of a memory space region assigned to this device. Bits 2:1 must be set to a value of either 00 or 01.
63:4	RW	**64–Bit Memory Base Address** 64 bit start address of a memory space region assigned to this device. Bits 2:1 must be set to a value of 10 Bits

Table 17–13: Memory Base Address Register

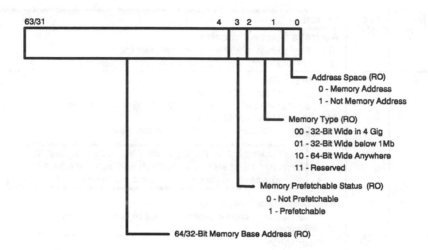

Figure 17–13: Memory Base Address Register

MEMORY AND I/O BASE ADDRESS REGISTER GUIDELINES

Power-up system software such as the PC/AT compatible System BIOS is responsible for initializing memory and I/O base address registers with system resources in a resource conflict free manner. However, depending on the system configuration, certain system resources (most likely I/O) may be depleted before all base address registers have been initialized. Base address registers that do not get a system resource assigned will be initialized with a value zero. In addition, depending on the type of resource that failed to be assigned, the associated memory or I/O control bit in the PCI function's Command Register will be set to disabled (zero). This gives device specific software two quick methods for determining what memory and I/O system resource allocations failed for their device.

Device specific executables such as device drivers and add-in card BIOSs should never assign system resources to their device. System resource conflicts could result, rendering the system inoperable. Allocating system resources is the task of power-up system software and operating systems.

When a resource allocation fails for a given PCI device, the power-up system software should attempt to allocate memory and I/O system resources to the

526

remaining base address registers that have requested resources. This permits PCI devices that map their control functions into both memory and I/O spaces at the same time to use the space that was successfully assigned. The other space should remain disabled and unused.

> The Command Register control bit for either the memory or I/O address space that is disabled by the power-up system software or an operating system should not be enabled by device specific software. This could result in system resource conflicts, depending on the programmed values of the control bit's associated base address registers.

If a device uses the "claim more than needed" technique for minimizing decoder bits (in either memory or I/O), there is no requirement for how the device should behave if it is accessed in the "unused" portion of a claimed range. As an example, take a device that has 256 bytes of registers mapped to memory but claims 4K of memory space. When software accesses any of the 256 bytes, the device is expected to respond appropriately for those bytes. Accesses to any other part of the 4K range can behave anyway the device finds appropriate. For instance, it may be easiest to alias the 256 bytes throughout the 4K range. Another possibility is to just return garbage whenever the "unused" portion is accessed.

CardBus CIS Pointer

Offset:	28h
Width:	4 Bytes
Valid Values:	See Below
Description:	This register is optional. It is also read-only.

This register is used by devices that want to share silicon between CardBus and PCI. CardBus cards use the Card Information Structure (CIS). This structure contains specific information about the card. The information contained in this register identifies the location of the CIS start address in the system.

The Card Information Structure can be located in one of the following address spaces:

Configuration Space
The CIS must be located in the device dependent region of the PCI device; that is, after the PCI device's predefined header.
Memory Space
The CIS can be accessed using the value of one of the memory Base Address registers.
Expansion ROM
The CIS is stored in an expansion ROM image.

Each configuration space of a multi-function card must have its own CIS. The CIS will be pointed to by the CIS Pointer located in its own configuration space.

Bit	Type	Function
31	RO	**Reserved**
30:28	RO	**Address Space Indicator** This 3-bit field identifies the address space in which the Card Information Structure is located.
		0 The Card Information Structure resides in device-dependent PCI configuration space.
		1 The Card Information Structure resides in the memory space addressed by the Memory Base Address register located at offset 10h in the predefined header.
		2 The Card Information Structure resides in the memory space addressed by the Memory Base Address register located at offset 14h in the predefined header.
		3 The Card Information Structure resides in the memory space addressed by the Memory Base Address register located at offset 18h in the predefined header.
		4 The Card Information Structure resides in the memory space addressed by the Memory Base Address register located at offset 1Ch in the predefined header.

528

		5 The Card Information Structure resides in the memory space addressed by the Memory Base Address register located at offset 20h in the predefined header. 6 The Card Information Structure resides in the memory space addressed by the Memory Base Address register located at offset 24h in the predefined header. 7 The Card Information Structure resides in an expansion ROM.
27:0	RO	**Address Space Offset Value** This value specifies the offset into the address space indicated by the Address Space Indicator field at which the CIS begins.

Space Indicator	Address Space Offset Value
0	The CIS start address is located in PCI device dependent configuration space. Valid values are: 40h <= Offset Value <= 0ffh
1 thru 6	The CIS start address is located in the system memory address space addressable by the selected Base Address Register. Add the value in bits 0::27 of this register to the Base Address Register to obtain the CIS start address. Valid values are: 0h <= Offset Value <= 0fffffffh
7	The CIS is located in an expansion ROMs address space. PCI expansion ROMS may contain multiple images. Bits 27::24 of this register contains the image number within the expansion ROM that contains the CIS. Valid values are: 0h <= image <= 0fh The value programmed into the PCI device's Expansion ROM Base Address register plus the offset of the specified image within the ROM is added to the value contained in bits 23::0 of this register. This value is the start address of the CIS within the ROM. Valid values are: 0h <= offset value <= 0fffffh

Table 17–14: CardBus CIS Pointer Register

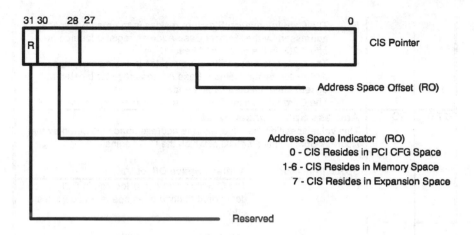

Figure 17–14: CardBus CIS Pointer Register

Expansion ROM Base Address Register	
Offset:	30h
Width:	4 Bytes
Valid Values:	Device dependent
Description:	This register allows a PCI device's expansion ROM to be mapped into a system's physical address space. Depending on the system implementation, this dynamic mapping may be accomplished by the System ROM BIOS during POST or later by other system software such as a device driver or operating system.
	See Chapter 20 for a description of how this register is implemented in a system.

Bit	Type	Function
0	RW	**Expansion ROM Decode Enable**
		0 Disable decode the Expansion ROM within System memory address space.
		1 Enable decode of the Expansion ROM within System memory address space.
		Bit 1 of this device's Command Register, the Memory Space Control bit, has precedence over this bit. It must be set to a value of 1 for this bit to enable the expansion ROM address decode.
10:1	RO	**Reserved**
31:11	RW	**Expansion ROM Base Address**
		Start address of the expansion ROM memory space region assigned to this device. This is where the expansion ROM code will appear in system memory when bit 0 of this register contains a value of 1 and bit 1 of this device's Command Register contains a value of 1.
		Because the Expansion ROM Base Address may share a decoder with the I/O and Memory Base Address Register, device independent software *should not* access any other base address register of this device while the expansion ROM decode for this device is enabled.

Table 17–15: Expansion ROM Base Address Register

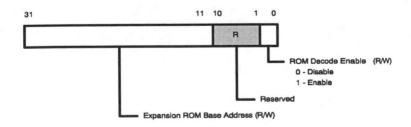

Figure 17–15: Expansion ROM Base Address Register

To assign an expansion ROM base address to this register software should do the following:

1. Write a value of 1 to bits 11 through 31 of this register.

2. Starting at bit location 11, search upward for the first bit set to a value of 1. This bit is the binary weighted size of the total contiguous block of memory address space requested. For example, if bit 16 is the first bit set, the device is requesting a 64 kilobyte block of memory address space.

3. Write the start address of the memory space block assigned to this register. This memory space region must not conflict with any other memory address space utilized within the system. Otherwise, data reads from the ROM may be corrupted.

Expansion ROM Base Address registers may share an address decoder with other Base Address registers. This reduces the number of address decoders on a device. While this feature permits each base address register to hold a unique value at the same time, it does place constraints on software:

A device-independent software program should only set Bit 0, the Expansion ROM Decode Enable bit, to 1 when it is copying the expansion ROM code to the shadow memory. For example, when a PC/AT System BIOS copies a PCI ROM image to the ISA compatibility region between C0000h and EFFFFh. Also POST code should RESET Bit 0 to zero before calling the initialization function of any relocated expansion ROM code. This is because the option ROM code may try to access the device using the allocation in the standard base address registers, which may be non-functional if the expansion ROM register is left enabled.

Device specific code, (i.e. a device driver) may set this bit to one (after locating a non-conflicting address space and doing the appropriate mapping) to obtain some device specific information out of the ROM.

Interrupt Line	
Offset:	3Ch
Width:	1 Byte
Valid Values:	00h–FFh
Description:	This register identifies which interrupt request line of a system interrupt controller the PCI device's interrupt line is connected to. Device drivers as well as other device dependent software query this register to determine the interrupt request line assigned to their device.

This value is system architecture specific. For ISA compatible systems, valid encodings are shown below. The PCI Specification does not provide encodings for other system architectures.

00h = IRQ0
01h = IRQ1
—

0Eh = IRQ14
0Fh = IRQ15

Note that these encodings specify the physical pin on the system interrupt controller that the interrupt line is connected to. These encodings do not specify the interrupt vector that is generated by the interrupt controller. Other values are reserved.

Bit	Type	Function	
7:0	RW	**Interrupt Line Value**	
		00h:FEh	Interrupt line number that the device is connected to.
		FFh	Device interrupt line is not connected to a system interrupt controller.

Table 17–16: Interrupt Line Register

POST software is responsible for routing the device's interrupt line to a system interrupt controller. This routing is dependent upon the specific hardware implementation. In addition, POST code will update this register with the interrupt line value assigned to the device. Software other than POST may read this register to determine which interrupt line the PCI device is connected.

Device specific executables such as device drivers and add-in card BIOSs should never assign system resources to their device. System resource conflicts could result, rendering the system inoperable. Allocating system resources is the task of power-up system software and operating systems.

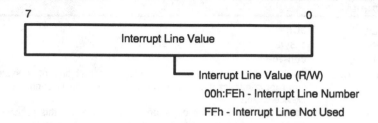

Figure 17–16: Interrupt Line Register

Interrupt Pin

Offset:	3Dh
Width:	1 Byte
Valid Values:	00h–04h
Description:	This register identifies which interrupt pin, **INTA#** through **INTD#**, a device function uses. This register assists in the proper initialization of the Interrupt Line register. Once initialization software knows which interrupt pin(s) the device uses, the Interrupt Line register(s) can be initialized appropriately.

Bit	Type	Function
7:0	RO	**Interrupt Pin Value**

00h	Interrupt pin is not used by the device.
01h	Device function uses interrupt pin **INTA#**.
02h	Device function uses interrupt pin **INTB#**.
03h	Device function uses interrupt pin **INTC#**.
04h	Device function uses interrupt pin **INTD#**.
05h:FFh	Reserved

Table 17–17-A: Interrupt Pin Register

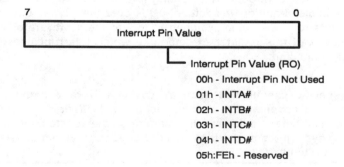

Figure 17–17: Interrupt Pin Register

SINGLE-FUNCTION DEVICE

A Single-Function Device can have only one interrupt pin. If the device has an interrupt pin it must be connected to the INTA# of the add–in board connector (if the device is on an add–in board).

MULTI–FUNCTION DEVICE

A multi–function device can have zero, one, or more interrupt pins. If it has one interrupt pin and both functions use it, both functions must have 01h in their Interrupt Pin registers. The interrupt pin must be connected to the INTA# of the add–in board connector (if the device is on an add–in board).

If the multi–function device has two interrupt pins, function 0 should have 01h in its Interrupt Pin register, and function 1 should have 02h in its interrupt pin register. If the device is located on an add–in card, the two interrupt pins must be connected to INTA# and INTB#, respectively, of the card connector. Vendors of devices with multiple interrupt pins must clearly label these pins so that integrators can properly connect them to the pins on the add–in board connector. Table 17-17-B below lists the valid interrupt pin encodings.

Number of Interrupt Pins	Number of Functions	Valid Interrupt Pin Encodings	Comments
0	1 to 8	00h	Interrupt line register in all functions should have the value 00h, indicating that no interrupt pins are used.
1	1 to 8	00h	Use this encoding in any functions that don't use the interrupt pin.
		01h	Use this encoding in any functions that use the interrupt pin.
2	2 to 8	00h	Use this encoding in any functions that don't use the interrupt pin.
		01h	Use this encoding in any functions that use the interrupt pin corresponding to **INTA#**.
		02h	Use this encoding in any functions that use the interrupt pin corresponding to **INTB#**.
3	3 to 8	00h	Use this encoding in any functions that don't use the interrupt pin.
		01h	Use this encoding in any functions that use the interrupt pin corresponding to **INTA#**.
		02h	Use this encoding in any functions that use the interrupt pin corresponding to **INTB#**.
		03h	Use this encoding in any functions that use the interrupt pin corresponding to **INTC#**.
4	4 to 8	00h	Use this encoding in any functions that don't use the interrupt pin.
		01h	Use this encoding in any functions that use the interrupt pin corresponding to **INTA#**.
		02h	Use this encoding in any functions that use the interrupt pin corresponding to **INTB#**.
		03h	Use this encoding in any functions that use the interrupt pin corresponding to **INTC#**.
		04h	Use this encoding in any functions that use the interrupt pin corresponding to **INTD#**.

Table 17–17-B: Interrupt Pin Register: Valid Encodings

From the table above, devices must have at least as many functions as interrupt pins. Functions in a device can share an interrupt pin allowing fewer interrupt pins than functions in the device.

Note that each function in a device can use at most one interrupt.

MIN_GNT	
Offset:	3Eh
Width:	1 Byte
Valid Values:	00h–FFh
Description:	This register specifies the burst period (assuming a clock rate of 33MHz) required by the device. The value is specified in 250 nanoseconds (1/4 microsecond) increments. This value is used to determine Latency Timer values.

Bit	Type	Function
7:0	RO	**Min_Gnt Value**
		00h Do not use this register for calculating Latency Timer values.
		01h:FFh Number of 250 nanosecond units required for a burst period.

Table 17–189: Min_Gnt Register

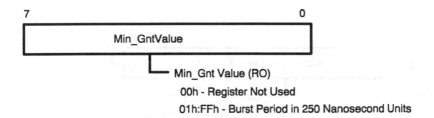

Figure 17–18: Min_Gnt Register

MAX_LAT	
Offset:	3Eh
Width:	1 Byte
Valid Values:	00h–FFh
Description:	This register specifies how often (assuming a clock rate of 33MHz) the device needs to gain access to the PCI Bus. The value is specified in 250 nanoseconds (1/4 microsecond) increments. This value is used to determine Latency Timer values.

Bit	Type	Function	
7:0	RO	**Max_Lat Value**	
		00h	Do not use this register for calculating Latency Timer values.
		01h:FFh	How often the device needs to gain access to the PCI Bus in 250 nanosecond units.

Table 17–19: Max_Lat Register

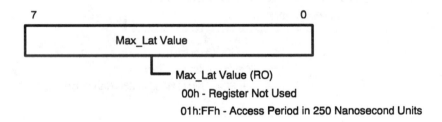

Figure 17–19: Max_Lat Register

The MIN_GNT and MAX_LAT registers are used to help tune the performance of the system. This tuning is accomplished by adjusting Latency Timer values throughout the system. The values in these registers provide a measure of how much of the PCI bus bandwidth the device requires. As an example, consider a device whose MIN_GNT value is 02h (0.5 µsecs) and whose MAX_LAT value is 14h (5 µsecs). These values say that for every 5 µsecs, the device needs .5 µsecs on the bus, or 10% of the bus bandwidth (at 33 MHz).

538

17.4: TYPE 01H PCI CONFIGURATION SPACE HEADER REGION

The primary function of a PCI to PCI Bridge device is to permit transactions to occur between a PCI master on one PCI bus and a PCI target on another PCI bus. As with all compliant PCI devices, PCI to PCI Bridge devices must support the 256 byte configuration space requirement of the PCI Local Bus Specification.

The Type 01h PCI Configuration Space Header Region is the predefined header format for PCI to PCI Bridge devices. A Type 01h PCI Configuration Space Header Region consists of 64 bytes. The first 16 bytes are the PCI Device Independent Region. The remaining 48 bytes are assigned to the PCI Device Header Type Region. Consequently, 64 bytes are assigned to the predefined PCI Configuration Space Header Region and 192 bytes to the Device Dependent region of the PCI configuration register space. For additional details about PCI configuration space device header types, refer to the description of the PCI Header Type register, found later in this section. In addition, refer to Table 17-20 and Figure 17-20 for pictorial representations of the Type 01h PCI Device Header Region.

> A Type 01h PCI Device Header Type Register (offset 0EH) specifies that the PCI Device Header Type Region consists of 48 bytes. When defined, other header types may specify more or fewer registers for this region.

Note that individual PCI devices need only implement the registers required to support their functionality. For example, some PCI to PCI Bridge devices may not support an expansion ROM. Consequently, the Expansion ROM Base Address Register (DWORD at offset 38H), of the PCI Configuration Header Region is not implemented. In this case, the register is treated as reserved. As specified by rule five listed in Section 17.1, all bits in this register must be hardwired to zero.

Table 17-20 contains a list of the Type 01h PCI Configuration Space Header Region registers with their corresponding offset from the base of the structure.

Figure 17-20 is a pictorial view of the 64 byte register layout of Type 01h PCI Configuration Space Header. All PCI compliant devices that implement a Type 01h header must support this layout. Fields that utilize more than one byte in this structure follow little–endian ordering. The least significant portion of a field is contained in the lowest byte of the field.

TYPE 01H HEADER REGION REGISTER DEFINITIONS

The remainder of this section contains a description of each register in a Type 01h PCI Configuration Header region. Each register description contains the name of the register, the address location within the PCI device of the register, the byte width of the register, the read/write attribute assigned to the register, the valid value range of the register, the register's global function definition, and the individual bit definitions of the register. Default values for each register are vendor and device specific and therefore are not specified.

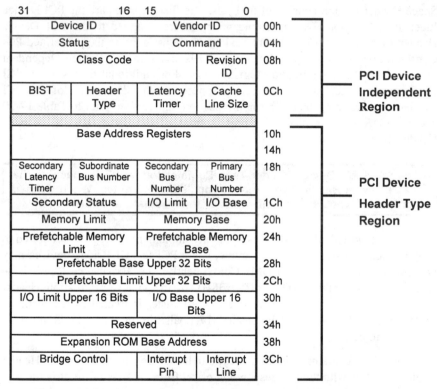

Figure 17-20: Type 01h PCI Configuration Space Header Region

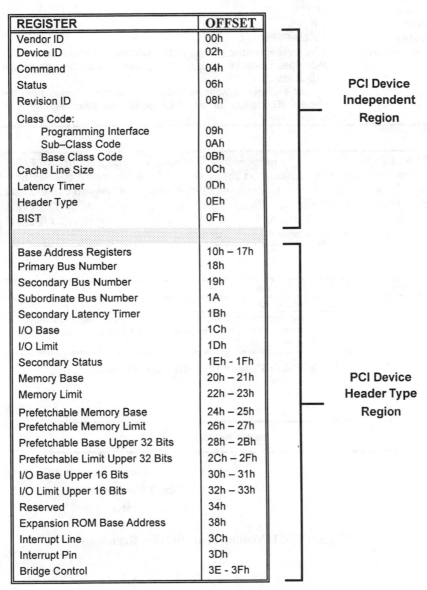

REGISTER	OFFSET	
Vendor ID	00h	
Device ID	02h	
Command	04h	
Status	06h	**PCI Device**
Revision ID	08h	**Independent**
Class Code:		**Region**
Programming Interface	09h	
Sub–Class Code	0Ah	
Base Class Code	0Bh	
Cache Line Size	0Ch	
Latency Timer	0Dh	
Header Type	0Eh	
BIST	0Fh	
Base Address Registers	10h – 17h	
Primary Bus Number	18h	
Secondary Bus Number	19h	
Subordinate Bus Number	1A	
Secondary Latency Timer	1Bh	
I/O Base	1Ch	
I/O Limit	1Dh	
Secondary Status	1Eh - 1Fh	
Memory Base	20h – 21h	**PCI Device**
Memory Limit	22h – 23h	**Header Type**
Prefetchable Memory Base	24h – 25h	**Region**
Prefetchable Memory Limit	26h – 27h	
Prefetchable Base Upper 32 Bits	28h – 2Bh	
Prefetchable Limit Upper 32 Bits	2Ch – 2Fh	
I/O Base Upper 16 Bits	30h – 31h	
I/O Limit Upper 16 Bits	32h – 33h	
Reserved	34h	
Expansion ROM Base Address	38h	
Interrupt Line	3Ch	
Interrupt Pin	3Dh	
Bridge Control	3E - 3Fh	

Table 17-20: Type 01h PCI Configuration Space Header Region

Vendor ID	
Offset:	00h
Width:	2 Bytes
Valid Values:	0000h–FFFEh
Description:	This register is used to identify the manufacturer of the device. The PCI Special Interest Group assigns vendor identifiers to ensure uniqueness. For example, a value of 8086H will always be read from the Vendor ID register of any PCI device manufactured by Intel Corporation.

The platform hardware is responsible for ensuring that a value of FFFFH is returned when an attempt is made to read the vendor identifier of a non–existent PCI device. Consequently, the Vendor ID register is the one that should be used when attempting to determine whether a PCI device exists in a system. Because FFFFh is an invalid value for Vendor ID, that value will be returned only when no device is present.

Bit	Type	Function
15:0	RO	Vendor ID
		This register contains a unique 16 bit value assigned to each vendor. This number enables each PCI device's manufacturer to be identified.

Table 17-21: Vendor Identification Register

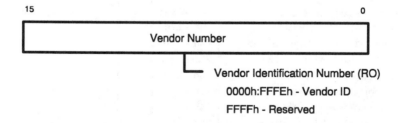

Figure 17-21: Vendor Identification Register

Device ID

Offset:	02h
Width:	2 Bytes
Valid Values:	0000h–FFFFh
Description:	This register identifies the device with a unique number. The value is assigned by the vendor of the device.

Vendors may choose to assign device IDs such that devices in one family that are backward compatible with earlier members of the family are easily recognized by software device drivers. For instance, assume a vendor built a SCSI device with some base functionality and assigned an identification number of 0AA0h to the device. Later the vendor develops the next generation part which has all the capabilities of the first part, but has extensions that make it perform better if they are used. The vendor assigned an identification number of 0AA1h to this device.

A device driver for the original part would continue to work for the new part if the driver looked for an identification number of 0AAxh when trying to locate its device. The current device driver wouldn't take advantage of new features. However, the problem of immediately providing a new driver for the latest device would be solved.

Bit	Type	Function
15:0	RO	Device ID
		The value in this register is the vendors' device identifier.

Table 17-22: Device Identification Register

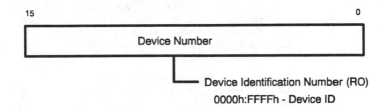

Device Identification Number (RO)
0000h:FFFFh - Device ID

Figure 17-22: Device Identification Register

Avoid assigning a Device ID of either 0000h or FFFFh, because zero indicates a Reserved Register and FFFF a *no response*.

543

Command	
Offset:	**04h**
Width:	**2 Bytes**
Valid Values:	N/A. This field is a collection of bits, not a range of values. The register should not be viewed as values, but as individual bits.
Description:	This register controls the device's ability to generate and respond to PCI bus accesses. Note that a value of zero in this register logically disconnects the device from the PCI bus.

All PCI devices are required to respond to PCI configuration accesses, even when bits 2:0 are set to zero.

Bit	Type		Function
0	RW		**I/O Space Control** This bit controls the bridge's response to accesses on the primary interface.
		0	Ignore I/O transactions on the primary interface (RST# state).
		1	Enable response to I/O transactions on the primary interface.
1	RW		**Memory Space Control** This bit controls the bridge's response to memory accesses for both memory mapped I/O and prefetchable memory ranges.
		0	Ignore all memory transactions on the primary interface (RST# state).
		1	Enable response to memory transactions on the primary interface
2	RW		**Bus Master Control** This bit controls the bridge's ability to operate as a bus master on the primary interface on behalf of a bus master on the secondary interface for memory or I/O transactions. Configuration commands that are either forwarded or converted by the PCI bridge device are not affected by this bit.
		0	Do not initiate transactions on the primary interface. Also disable all resonses to memory or I/O on the secondary interface. (**RST#** state).
		1	Enables the bridge to operate as a master on the primary interface.

Table 17-23: Type 01h Command Register

3	RO		**Special Cycles Control**
		0	PCI to PCI bridge devices cannot respond as a target to special cycles tranactions. Consequently, this bit is read only and must return a zero read. (**RST#** state).
4	RW		**Memory Write and Invalidate Control**
		0	PCI to PCI bridge devices cannot initiate a memory write and invalidate command unless it is operating on behalf of another master whose transaction has crossed the bridge. The initiating master has the control to determine which memory write command to use. Consequently, this bit is read only and must return a zero read. (**RST#** state).
5	RW		**VGA Palette Snoop Control** This bit is optional. It controls the bridge's response to VGA palette accesses. The definition of this bit for PCI to PCI bridges is different from the the PCI Local Bus Specification. **Read Only Implementation:**
		0	VGA palette snooping is not supported. **Read/Write Implementation:**
		0	Ignore VGA paleete accesses on the primary bridge (**RST#** state).
		1	Enable response to VGA palette writes on the primary interface. I/O writes with address bits AD<9::0> = 3C6h, 3C8h and 3C9h (inclusive of ISA aliases - AD<15::10> are not decoded) must be positively decoded on the primary side and forwarded to the secondary interface. Note that the bridge on the secondary interface must not respond to these three addresses.
6	RW		**Parity Error Response** This bit controls the bridge's response to parity errors.
		0	Device ignores detected parity errors (**RST#** state).
		1	Device responds to detected parity errors.
		1	Devices that implement parity checking are required to support this bit.
		2	Devices will generate parity even if parity checking is disabled.
		3	Any device that doesn't check parity (and as a result will never get a parity error) can hardwire the bit to zero.

Table 17-23: Type 01h Command Register (cont.)

7	RW		**Wait Cycle Control** This bit controls address/data stepping by the bridge. The primary and secondary interfaces are affected.
		0	Disable ADDRESS/DATA STEPPING. Hardwire this bit to zero if ADDRESS/DATA STEPPING is not implemented.
		1	Enable ADDRESS/DATA STEPPING. Hardwire this bit to one if ADDRESS/DATA STEPPING is always performed.
			Bit 7 must be read/writeable if the device can either enable or disable ADDRESS/DATA STEPPING. The **RST#** state of this bit is one.
8	RW		**System Error Control** This bit controls the enable for the SERR# driver on the primary interface.
		0	Disable the **SERR#** output driver (**RST#** state).
		1	Enable the **SERR#** output driver.
			1 Devices which implement **SERR#** must support this bit. 2 This bit and bit 6 must be set to one to report address parity errors.
9	RW		**Fast Back–to–Back Control** This bit controls the ability of the bridge to generate fast back to back transactions to different devices on the primary interface.
		0	Fast back–to–back transactions are only allowed to the same agent (**RST#** state).
		1	Enable fast back–to–back transactions.
			1 This bit is optional. It has the read/write attribute when implemented. 2 Software (typically the System BIOS) may set this bit to one only if all targets are capable of fast back–to–back transactions.
15:10	RO		**Reserved**

Table 17-23: Type 01h Command Register (cont.)

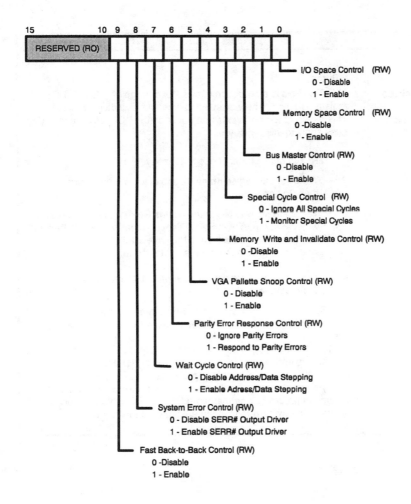

Figure 17-23: Type 01h Command Register

Status

Offset:	**06h**
Width:	**2 Bytes**
Valid Values:	N/A. This field is a collection of bits, not a range of values. The register should not be viewed as values, but as individual bits.
Description:	This register records events that occur on the PCI bus. The following rules apply to this register:

1   Reads of this register occur normally.

2   Writes to this register may clear bits to zero but never set them to one.

3   There are several bits in the Status Register Table below bits with the attribute type RWC. These are individual bits that are cleared to zero if the bit has the write attribute and its bit location is written with a data value of one.

4   The function of the device determines which bits will be implemented.

The Status register bit definitions are compliant with the PCI Local Bus Specification. However, these bits only apply to the primary interface of a PCI to PCI bridge.

The Status Register is typically not used by device drivers. Rather, it is intended to record events that (a) tend to be catastrophic and (b) are not part of normal operation.

System monitoring software can use the Status Register to determine precisely what happened if a catastrophic error occurs. In addition, the system monitoring software can keep statistics on PCI specific events.

Bit	Type	Function
4:0	RO	**Reserved**
5	RO	**66MHz Capable Status** 0 The device is capable of running at 33MHz. 1 The device is capable of running at 66MHz.. This bit is optional.
6	RO	**User Definable Features Status** 0 The device supports User Definable Features. 1 The device does not support User Definable Features. This bit is optional. It is required to be set when a device function has device specific configuration selections that must be presented to the user. See Appendix B for a complete docripton of requirements for setting this bit.
7	RO	**Fast Back–to–Back Status** 0 The target is not capable accepting fast–back–to–back transactions. 1 The target is capable accepting fast–back–to–back transactions. This bit is optional.
8	RWC	**Data Parity Status** 0 No data parity errors have occurred. (**RST#** state). 1 All three of the following conditions must be met: a. **PERR#** was asserted by the bus master or the bus master observed **PERR#** asserted. b. The agent which set the bit was the bus master during the transactioin when the error occurred. c. Parity Error Response (bit 6 of the bus master's Command Register is enabled). This bit is only implemented by Bus Masters.
10:9	RO	**Device Select Timing Status** 00 Device asserts **DEVSEL#** in the *fast* timing mode for any bus command. 01 Device asserts **DEVSEL#** in the *medium* timing mode for any bus command. 10 Device asserts **DEVSEL#** in the *slow* timing mode for any bus command. 11 Reserved. Configuration read and write cycles do not apply to the above definition. For example, if a device performs FAST decode for all memory and I/O accesses, but *medium* decode for configuration accesses, the device should set this register to *fast*.

Table 17-24: Status Register

11	RWC	**Signaled Target Abort Status**
		0 Target device did not terminate a transaction with a Target Abort (**RST#** state). 1 Target device terminated a transaction with a Target Abort. Devices incapable of terminating a transaction with a target are not required to implement this bit.
12	RWC	**Received Target Abort Status**
		0 – A Target Abort did not terminate a bus master's transaction (**RST#** state). 1 – A Target Abort terminated a bus master's transaction. All bus master devices are required to implement this bit.
13	RWC	**Received Master Abort Status**
		0 – A bus Master Abort did not terminate a bus master's transaction (**RST#** state). 1 – Set by a bus master whose transaction was terminated by a bus Master Abort. 1 All bus master devices are required to implement this bit. 2 A Master Abort on a Special Cycle transaction should not cause this bit to be set.
14	RWC	**Signaled System Error Status**
		0 – Device did not generate a system error on the **SERR#** line. 1 – Device generated a system error on the **SERR#** line. Devices which cannot assert **SERR#** are not required to implement this bit.
15	RWC	**Detected Parity Error Status**
		0 – Device did not detect a parity error (**RST#** state). 1 – Device detected a parity error. Devices will set this bit regardless of the state of Parity Error Response (bit 6 of the Command Register).

Table 17-24: Status Register (cont.)

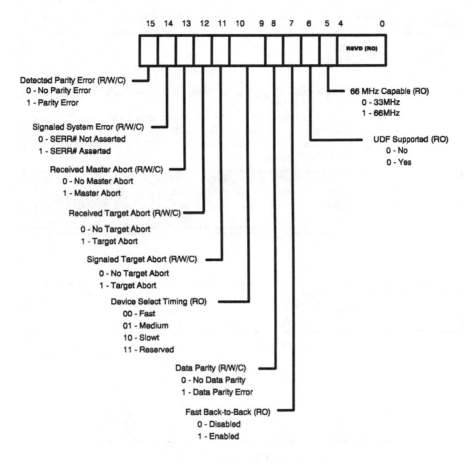

Figure 17-24: Status Register

Revision ID

Offset:	08h
Width:	1 Byte
Valid Values:	00h–FFh
Description:	The Revision ID register definition is compliant with the PCI Local Bus Specification.

This register identifies the revision level of the device. The value is assigned by the vendor of the device.

This register is typically used to indicate different steppings of the same device.

> Plug and Play software does not use this field for device identification purposes. The System BIOS and device drivers can use this field to isolate code execution to particular revisions of the device.

Bit	Type	Function
7:0	RO	**Revision ID** This value reflects the version level of the device.

Table 17-25: Revision Identification Register

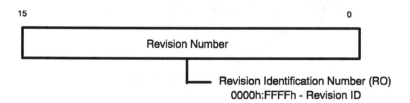

Figure 17-25: Revision Identification Register

Class Code	
Offset:	09h
Width:	3 Bytes
Valid Values:	Programming Interface (09h): 00h
	Sub–Class Code (0Ah): 04h PCI to PCI Bridge
	Base Class Code (0Bh): 60h Bridge Device
Description:	The Class Code register definition is compliant with the PCI Local Bus Specification.
	This register identifies the generic function of the device and the register level programming interface of the device (if applicable to the class of the device). **See Appendix A for a complete definition of the Class Code register.**

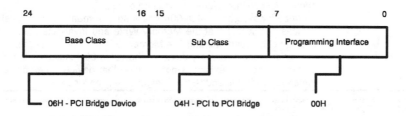

Figure 17-26: Class Code Register

Cache Line Size	
Offset:	0Ch
Width:	1 Byte
Valid Values:	0000h–FFFFh
Description:	The Cache Line Size register definition is compliant with the PCI Local Bus Specification. This register is applicabler to the primary and secondary interfaces of a PCI to PCI bridge.
	This register specifies the system Cache Line Size in 32 bit words.
	This register is required in two different cases. The first case is any device that can generate a Memory Write and Invalidate bus cycle. These devices need to know the cache line size in order to generate valid Memory Write and Invalidate cycles.
	The second case is any device that provides cacheable memory to the system. In this case the register is used to know when to break BURST accesses to the cacheable memory (at cache line boundaries) so that cache snoops can occur.
	In both cases, the value 00h has a special meaning. For master devices it indicates that the Memory Write and Invalidate command should not be used. Instead use Memory Write.
	For cacheable memory devices, the value 00H indicates that the system cache (if it exists) is not caching that device's memory and therefore the **SBO#** and **SDONE** signals may be ignored.

Bit	Type	Function
7:0	RW	**Cache Line** Size 00h – Memory target is configured as non–cacheable. Ignore PCI support lines **SDONE** and **SBO#**. Master devices use Memory Write transactions to update memory. (**RST#** state). 01H:0FFh – Cache line size in 32 bit words. 1 Bus Masters that generate the Memory Write and Invalidate command are required to implement this register. 2 Devices that provide cacheable memory are required to implement this register.

Table 17-27: Cache Line Size Register

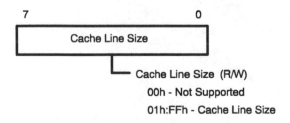

Cache Line Size (R/W)
00h - Not Supported
01h:FFh - Cache Line Size

Figure 17-27: Cache Line Size Register

Latency Timer	
Offset:	**0DH**
Width:	**1 Byte**
Valid Values:	**00h–FFh**
Description:	The Latency Timer register definition is compliant with the PCI Local Bus Specification. This register is applicabler only to the primary interface of a PCI to PCI bridge.
	This register specifies the Master Latency Timer value for a PCI Master when the device is on the PCI bus.
	A reasonable implementation of this register is to only implement the top five bits. This means that field can only be modified in increments of 8, but this is acceptable.
	A typical way for a System BIOS to configure this register is to just choose an appropriate value and use that value for all devices. 32 (approximately 1 μsec) is a reasonable value. Higher level software, i.e. an OS heuristic, can use the knowledge of how the system is being used (server, desktop, multimedia) as well as MIN_GNT and MAX_LAT values to adjust the timers appropriately.

Bit	Function
7:0	**Read Only Implementation:** Bus Masters incapable of bursting for more than two DATA PHASES may implement this register with a Read Only attribute. The register must contain a fixed value of 16 or less.
	Read/Write Implementation: Bus Masters capable of bursting for more than two DATA PHASES must implement this register with a Read/Write attribute. **RST#** should clear this register.

Table 17-28: Latency Timer Register

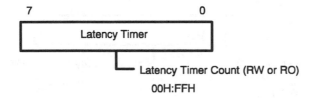

Figure 17-28: Latency Timer Register

Header Type

Offset:	0Eh
Width:	1 Byte
Valid Values:	00h or 80h
Description:	The Header Type register definition is compliant with the PCI Local Bus Specification.

> This register identifies the layout of bytes beginning at offset 10h in the PCI configuration space. In addition, this register specifies whether the device is a single or multi–function device. Configuration software such as a System BIOS should validate this register's value prior to doing anything with the device.

> If configuration software finds a header type that it does not know about, it should disable the device. This is done by setting the bottom three bits in the Command Register to zero. Leave the device alone once this is done.

Bit	Type	Function
6:0	RO	**Header Layout Code**
		000000B Device supports the layout of configuration registers 10h through 3FH as defined in Figure 17-XX.
		000001B Device supports the layout of PCI to PCI Bridge configuration registers 10h through 3FH as defined in Figure 17-XX.
		02h-7Fh Reserved.
7	RO	**Multi–Function Status**
		0 Device has one function.
		1 Device contains between two and eight functions.

Table 17-29: Header Type Register

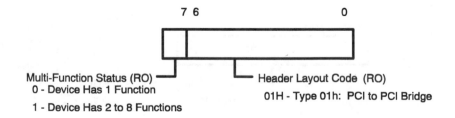

Figure 17-29: Header Type Register

BIST (Built-In Self Test)	
Offset:	0Fh
Width:	1 Byte
Valid Values:	Device dependent. See description below.
Description:	The BIST register definition is compliant with the PCI Local Bus Specification.
	This register is used to control the invocation of a PCI device's BIST and to report the status of the BIST. Devices that do not support BIST must return a value of 00H when this register is read.
	POST code may choose to run a device's BIST at cold boot. When a device is running its BIST it should not generate any cycles to the PCI bus.

Bit	Type	Function
3:0	RO	**BIST Completion Status**
		00h Device test passed.
		01h:0Fh Device test failed. Vendors may define up to 15 device specific failure codes in these bits.
5:4	RO	**Reserved**
		Device must return zero in these two bit fields.
6	RW	**BIST Start Control Bit**
		0 Device resets this bit after BIST completes.
		1 Invoke the device's BIST. Software should fail the device if this bit is not RESET to zero within two seconds after the BIST is invoked.
		Hard code this bit to 0, RO, if BIST is not implemented.
7	RO	**BIST Support Status**
		0 Device does not support BIST.
		1 Device supports BIST.

Table 17-30: BIST Register

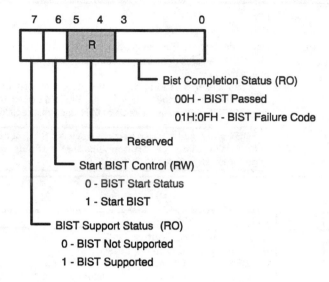

Figure 17-30: BIST Register

I/O and Memory Base Address Registers

Offset:	10h (first register location)
Width:	I/O: 32 bit word length
	Memory: 32 bit or 64 bit word length
Valid Values:	Device dependent
Description:	The Base Address register bit definitions are compliant with the PCI Local Bus Specification.

This register set allows a PCI to PCI bridge device's internal (device specific) bridge registers to be dynamically mapped into I/O and memory space. Depending on the system implementation, this dynamic mapping may be accomplished by the System ROM BIOS during POST or later by other system software such as a device driver or operating system.

PCI devices with a Type 01h configuration space header contain 8 bytes dedicated for memory and I/O base address. This means that a PCI to PCI Bridge can implement either one or two Base Address Registers, depending on the word length and type of the register.

> Note that there is no specification for the order in which registers request blocks of I/O or memory. Any combination is permissible.
>
> These registers do not provide a mechanism that allows the device to request specific addresses in the address space.
>
> PCI devices should always allow control functions to be mapped into memory space.

I/O BASE ADDRESS IMPLEMENTATION

For I/O base address registers, there are two ways to decrease the number of bits in the address decoder. The first method is to claim more address space than is actually needed. For example, a device that has 16 bytes of registers may decide to claim 128 bytes of address space, thus saving three bits in the decoder.

The second way to decrease the number of bits in the address decoder is to take advantage of the Intel x86 architecture. This architecture only has a 64K I/O space. Hence, there is no need to implement the top 16 bits of the 32 bit I/O base register. These bits can be hardwired to zero. However, a full 32 bit decode must still be performed. Note that the decode for the top 16 bits can be accomplished using a simple NAND gate.

The first method should be avoided since I/O space is typically tight. In no case should a PCI device designed to operate in a ISA compatible system request more than 256 bytes of I/O space per each I/O base address register. The major reason is the ISA aliasing issue, which is discussed in Appendices E and F.

To assign a value to an I/O base address register, software should do the following:

1. Write a value of 1 to all bits within this register.

2. Confirm that bit 0 of this register contains a value of 1, indicating an I/O request.

3. Starting at bit location 2, search for the first bit set to a value of 1. This bit is the binary weighted size of the total contiguous block of I/O address space requested. For example, if bit 8 is the first bit set, the device is requesting a 256 byte block of I/O address space.

4. Write the start address of the I/O space block assigned to this register.

Bit	Type	Function
0	RO	**Address Space Indicator** 0 N/A for I/O—see Memory Base Address Implementation. 1 Base address register is requesting I/O space.
1	RO	**Reserved** This bit must return zero when read.
31:2	RW	**I/O Base Address** Start address of an I/O space region assigned to this device.

Table 17-31: I/O Base Address Register

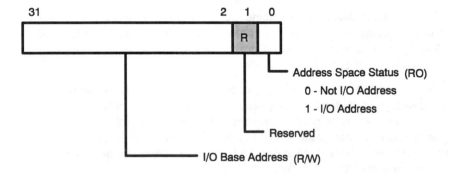

Figure 17-31: I/O Base Address Register

MEMORY BASE ADDRESS IMPLEMENTATION

Memory base address decoders can decrease the number of address bits by claiming more space than is needed. Hardwiring upper order address bits is not allowed (unless the device is requesting space at an address below 1 megabytes - see the definition for Base Address Memory Type bits in Table 17-14B).

If a device takes advantage of decreasing the number of address bits by claiming more space than is needed to minimize decode bits, the device must decode down to at least a 4K region. For example, if a device has 256 bytes that it wants to map to memory, the base address register can be implemented with sizes of 256, 512, 1K, 2K or 4K. Sizes larger than that are illegal.

Bit	Type	Function
0	RO	**Address Space Indicator** 0 Base address register is requesting memory space. 1 N/A for Memory—see I/O Base ADDRESS Implementation.
2:1	RO	**Memory Type** 00 Base address is 32 bits wide. Set the base address anywhere within the 32 bit memory space. 01 Base address is 32 bits wide. Set the base address below 1Mb in memory space. The upper 12 bits in this register can be hardwired to zero, but must still participate in address decode. Auto configuration software must handle this case. 10 Base address is 64 bits wide. Set the base address anywhere within the 64 bit memory space. 11 Reserved.
3	RO	**Prefetchable** 0 Memory is not prefetchable. 1 A device can mark its memory range as prefetchable if the following conditions are met: 1 The device returns all bytes on reads regardless of the byte enables. 2 Reads to this memory space create no side effects. 3 Host BRIDGEs can merge CPU writes (i.e. take multiple byte and/or word accesses from the CPU and merge them into single DWORD writes on PCI) into this range without errors. Linear frame buffers on graphics devices are an example of prefetchable memory. They behave like system memory. However, linear frame buffers do not participate in PCI's caching protocol. Host BRIDGEs can make performance optimizations on memory ranges that support prefetching.
31:4	RW	**32–Bit Memory Base Address** 32 bit start address of a memory space region assigned to this device. Bits 2:1 must be set to a value of either 00 or 01.
63:4	RW	**64–Bit Memory Base Address** 64 bit start address of a memory space region assigned to this device. Bits 2:1 must be set to a value of 10 Bits

Table 17-32: Memory Base Address Register

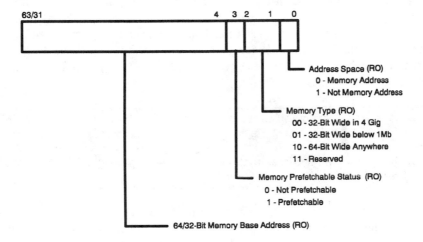

Figure 17-32: Memory Base Address Register

To assign a value to a memory base address register software should do the following:

1. Write a value of 1 to all bits within this register.

2. Confirm that bit 0 of this register contains a value of 0, indicating a memory request.

3. Starting at bit location 4, search upwards for the first bit set to a value of 1. This bit is the binary weighted size of the total contiguous block of memory requested. For example, if bit 15 is the first bit set, the device is requesting a 32 kilobyte block of memory.

4. Write the start address of the memory block assigned to this register. This memory address region must not conflict with any other memory space utilized within the system. In addition, it must comply with the definition contained in bits 1 and 2 of this register.

MEMORY AND I/O BASE ADDRESS REGISTER GUIDELINES

Power-up system software such as the PC/AT compatible System BIOS is responsible for initializing memory and I/O base address registers with system resources in a resource conflict free manner. However, depending on the system configuration, certain system resources (most likely I/O) may be depleted before all base address registers have been initialized. Base address registers that do not get a system resource assigned will be initialized with a value zero. In addition, depending on the type of resource that failed to be assigned, the associated memory or I/O control bit in the PCI function's Command Register will be set to disabled (zero). This gives device specific software two quick methods for determining what memory and I/O system resource allocations failed for their device.

> Device specific executables such as device drivers and add-in card BIOSs should never assign system resources to their device. System resource conflicts could result, rendering the system inoperable. Allocating system resources is the task of power-up system software and operating systems.

When a resource allocation fails for a given PCI device, the power-up system software should attempt to allocate memory and I/O system resources to the remaining base address registers that have requested resources. This permits PCI devices that map their control functions into both memory and I/O spaces at the same time to use the space that was successfully assigned. The other space should remain disabled and unused.

> The Command Register control bit for either the memory or I/O address space that is disabled by the power-up system software or an operating system should not be enabled by device specific software. This could result in system resource conflicts, depending on the programmed values of the control bit's associated base address registers.

If a device uses the "claim more than needed" technique for minimizing decoder bits (in either memory or I/O), there is no requirement for how the device should behave if it is accessed in the "unused" portion of a claimed range. As an example, take a device that has 256 bytes of registers mapped to memory but claims 4K of memory space. When software accesses any of the 256 bytes, the device is expected to respond appropriately for those bytes. Accesses to any other part of the 4K range can behave any way the device finds appropriate. For instance, it may be easiest to alias the 256 bytes throughout the 4K range. Another possibility is to just return garbage whenever the "unused" portion is accessed.

Primary Bus Number	
Offset:	18h
Width:	1 Byte
Valid Values:	See Below
Description:	The Primary Bus Number register is a read/write register. Configuration software programs this register with the number of the PCI bus that the primary interface of the bridge is connected to. The PCI bridge uses this register to decode type 1 configuration transactions on the secondary interface that should be converted to Special Cycle transactions on the primary interface.

Bit	Type	Function
7:0	RW	**Primary Bus Number** The number of the PCI bus that the primary interface of the bridge is connected to.
		The value of this register after reset must be 00h.

Table 17-33: Primary Bus Number Register

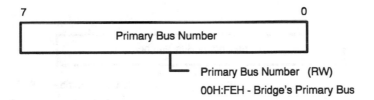

Figure 17-33: Primary Bus Number Register

Secondary Bus Number	
Offset:	19h
Width:	1 Byte
Valid Values:	See Below
Description:	The Secondary Bus Number register is a read/write register. Configuration software programs this register with the number of the PCI bus that the secondary interface of the bridge is connected to. Configuration software programs the value in this register. The bridge uses this register to determine when to respond to type 1 configuration transactions on the secondary interface

Bit	Type	Function
7:0	RW	**Secondary Bus Number** The number of the PCI bus that the secondary interface of the bridge is connected to. The value of this register after reset must be 00h.

Table 17-34: Secondary Bus Number Register

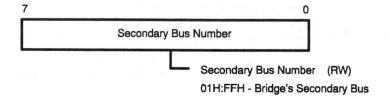

Figure 17-34: Secondary Bus Number Register

Subordinate Bus Number	
Offset:	1Ah
Width:	1 Byte
Valid Values:	See Below
Description:	The Subordinate Bus Number register is a read/write register. Configuration software programs this register with the number of the highest numbered PCI bus that is behind (or subordinate to) a bridge. The bridge uses this register to determine when to respond to type 1 configuration transactions on the primary interface and to pass them on to the secondary interface.

Bit	Type	Function
7:0	RW	**Subordinate Bus Number** Contains the highest numbered PCI bus that is behind (or subordinate to) a bridge. The value of this register after reset must be 00h.

Table 17-35: Subordinate Bus Number Register

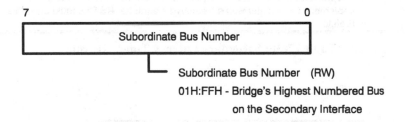

Figure 17-35: Subordinate Bus Number Register

Secondary Latency Timer	
Offset:	1Bh
Width:	1 Byte
Valid Values:	00h–FFh
Description:	The Secondary Latency Timer register definition is compliant with the PCI Local Bus Specification. Its definition is the same as the Latency Timer register at offset 0Dh in the predefined header region. The Latency Timer at offset 0Dh is only applicable to the primary interface of a PCI bridge. The Secondary Latency Timer register is only applicable to the secondary interface.
	This register specifies the Master Latency Timer value for a PCI Master when the device is on the PCI bus.
	A reasonable implementation of this register is to only implement the top five bits. This means that field can only be modified in increments of 8, but this is acceptable.
	A typical way for a System BIOS to configure this register is to just choose an appropriate value and use that value for all devices. 32 (approximately 1 μsec) is a reasonable value. Higher level software, i.e. an OS heuristic, can use the knowledge of how the system is being used (server, desktop, multimedia) as well as MIN_GNT and MAX_LAT values to adjust the timers appropriately.

Bit	Function
7:0	**Read Only Implementation:** Bus Masters incapable of bursting for more than two DATA PHASES may implement this register with a Read Only attribute. The register must contain a fixed value of 16 or less.
	Read/Write Implementation: Bus Masters capable of bursting for more than two DATA PHASES must implement this register with a Read/Write attribute. **RST#** should clear this register.

Table 17-36: Secondary Latency Timer Register

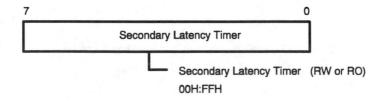

Figure 17-36: Secondary Latency Timer Register

I/O Base		
Offset:	1Ch	
Width:	1 Byte	
Valid Values:	See Below	
Description:	The I/O Base register defines the bottom address (inclusive) of an I/O address range. This range is used by the PCI to PCI bridge to determine when to forward I/O transactions from one interface to the other. This register is optional. Consequently, the I/O Base register can be either a read/write or read only register. If a bridge supports an I/O address range then this register must be initialized by configuration software.	

Bits	Type	Function
7:0	RO	**Read Only Implementation:** The register must return a value of zero.
3:0	RO	**Read/Write Implementation:** These bits encode the I/O addressing capability of the PCI to PCI Bridge as follows: 0h 16 Bit I/O addressing 01h 32 Bit I/O addressing 02h-Fh Reserved
7:4	RW	0h-0Fh These bits correspond to address bits AD<15::12> for I/O address decoding. The lower 12 address bits, AD<11::0>, are not implemented in the I/O Base register. The bridge always assumes that these bits are zero. Consequently, PCI to PCI bridge devices consume a minimum of 4K of I/O address space when the I/O Base register is implemented.

Table 17-37: I/O Base Register

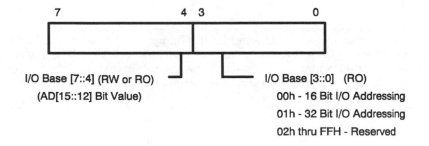

Figure 17-37: I/O Base Register

569

PCI TO PCI BRIDGE I/O BASE REGISTER

Configuration software such as a System BIOS or operating system is responsible for allocating system resources. When initializing PCI to PCI bridges, the resource allocation algorithm must account for the I/O address space that the bridge itself consumes, as well as the I/O resources that are requested by devices below (on the secondary interface) of the bridge. These devices may be other bridges as well as single and multifunction PCI devices such as LAN, and SCSI.

> With only 64K of I/O address space, it is easy to see how this resource can be depleted in a fully loaded system. This is a major reason of why PCI devices should implement memory base address registers that support memory mapped I/O.

Once the configuration software has determined how much I/O address space is required for a bridge and its secondary interface components, it will allocate a previously unassigned amount of contiguous I/O address space to the bridge device. The base of the allocated I/O address space is the value programmed into the I/O Base Register. The base address for this register will always be aligned on a 4K boundary. The reason is because the bridge assumes that the lower 12 address bits, AD<11::0>, of the I/O Base Address are zero. When assigning I/O address resources to the bridge and its secondary interface components, the configuration software will use the range of I/O addresses between the values contained in the I/O Base registers and the I/O Limit registers.

16 BIT I/O ADDRESSING

PCI to PCI bridges support 16 bit I/O address decoding when I/O Base register bits <3::0> contain a value of 0h. The bridge assumes that that the upper 16 address bits, AD[31::16], of the I/O base are 0000h. The I/O Base Upper 16 Bits and the I/O Limit Upper 16 Bits registers are implemented as read only and return zero when read

> The I/O address range supported by the bridge will be restricted to the first 64 Kbytes of PCI I/O address space (0000 0000h to 0000 FFFFh) when using 16 Bit I/O addressing. However, the bridge must still perform a full 32 bit decode of the I/O address as required by the PCI Local Bus Specification (i.e., check that AD[31::16] = 0).

570

32 BIT I/O ADDRESSING

PCI to PCI bridges support 32 bit I/O address decoding when I/O Base register bits <3::0> contain a value of 01h. The upper 16 bits of the 32 bit I/O Base address, corresponding to AD[31::16], are contained in the I/O Base Upper 16 Bits register. The I/O address range supported by the bridge may be located anywhere in the 4 Gigabyte PCI I/O address space.

Note that the 4 Kbyte alignment and granularity restrictions still apply.

I/O Limit	
Offset:	**1Dh**
Width:	**2 Bytes**
Valid Values:	**See Below**
Description:	The I/O Limit register defines the top address (inclusive) of an I/O address range. This range is used by the PCI to PCI bridge to determine when to forward I/O transactions from one interface to the other. This register is optional. Consequently, the I/O Limit register can be either a read/write or read only register. If a bridge supports an I/O address range then this register must be initialized by configuration software.

Bits	Type	Function
7:0	RO	**Read Only Implementation:** The register must return a value of zero.
3:0	RO	**Read/Write Implementation:** These bits encode the I/O addressing capability of the PCI to PCI Bridge as follows: 0h 16 Bit I/O addressing 01h 32 Bit I/O addressing 02h-Fh Reserved
7:4	RW	0h-0Fh These bits correspond to address bits AD<15::12> for I/O address decoding. The lower 12 address bits, AD<11::0>, are not implemented in the I/O Limit register. The bridge always assumes that these bits are FFFh. Consequently, the top of anPCI to PCI bridge device's I/O address range will be at the top of a 4K aligned address block when the I/O Limit register is implemented.

Table 17-38: I/O Limit Register

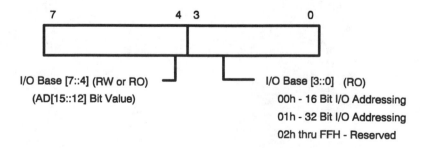

I/O Base [7::4] (RW or RO)   I/O Base [3::0] (RO)
(AD[15::12] Bit Value)   00h - 16 Bit I/O Addressing
                                 01h - 32 Bit I/O Addressing
                                 02h thru FFH - Reserved

Figure 17-38: I/O Limit Register

Secondary Status

Offset:	1Eh
Width:	2 Bytes
Valid Values:	N/A. This field is a collection of bits, not a range of values. The register should not be viewed as values, but as individual bits.
Description:	This register records events that occur on the PCI bus. The following rules apply to this register:

1   Reads of this register occur normally.

2   Writes to this register may clear bits to zero but never set them to one.

3   There are several bits in the Status Register Table below bits with the attribute type RWC. These are individual bits that are cleared to zero if the bit has the write attribute and its bit location is written with a data value of one.

4   The function of the device determines which bits will be implemented.

The Secondary Status register bit definitions are compliant with the PCI Local Bus Specification. However, these bits only apply to the secondary interface of a PCI to PCI bridge.

The Secondary Status Register is typically not used by device drivers. Rather, it is intended to record events that (a) tend to be catastrophic and (b) are not part of normal operation.

Bit 14 of the Status register, offset 06h in the PCI to PCI bridge' configuration space, is the Signaled System Error bit. In the Secondary Status register, the bit is defined as the Received System Error bit. This is the major difference between the two status registers.

A PCI to PCI bridge never asserts SERR# on thesecondary interface. The bridge will assert SERR# on the primary interface if SERR# is asserted on the secondary interface. Note that the SERR# Enable bit in the Command register, offset 04h, and the Secondary SERR# bit in the Bridge Control register, offset 3Eh, must be enabled to allow the secondary interface SERR# to be reported.

Bit	Type	Function
4:0	RO	**Reserved**
5	RO	**66MHz Capable Status** 0 The device is capable of running at 33MHz. 1 The device is capable of running at 66MHz.. This bit is optional.
6	RO	**User Definable Features Status** 0 The device supports User Definable Features. 1 The device does not support User Definable Features. This bit is optional. It is required to be set when a device function has device specific configuration selections that must be presented to the user. See Appendix B for a complete decripton of requirements for setting this bit.
7	RO	**Fast Back–to–Back Status** 0 The target is not capable accepting fast–back–to–back transactions. 1 The target is capable accepting fast–back–to–back transactions. This bit is optional.
8	RWC	**Data Parity Status** 0 No data parity errors have occurred. (**RST#** state). 1 All three of the following conditions must be met: a. **PERR#** was asserted by the bus master or the bus master observed **PERR#** asserted. b. The agent which set the bit was the bus master during the transaction when the error occurred. c. Parity Error Response (bit 6 of the bus master's Command Register) is enabled. This bit is only implemented by Bus Masters.
10:9	RO	**Device Select Timing Status** 00 Device asserts **DEVSEL#** in the *fast* timing mode for any bus command. 01 Device asserts **DEVSEL#** in the *medium* timing mode for any bus command. 10 Device asserts **DEVSEL#** in the *slow* timing mode for any bus command. 11 Reserved. Configuration read and write cycles do not apply to the above definition. For example, if a device performs FAST decode for all memory and I/O accesses, but *medium* decode for configuration accesses, the device should set this register to *fast.*

Table 17-39: Secondary Status Register

11	RWC	**Signaled Target Abort Status**
		0 Target device did not terminate a transaction with a Target Abort (**RST#** state).
		1 Target device terminated a transaction with a Target Abort.
		Devices incapable of terminating a transaction with a target are not required to implement this bit.
12	RWC	**Received Target Abort Status**
		0 – A Target Abort did not terminate a bus master's transaction (**RST#** state).
		1 – A Target Abort terminated a bus master's transaction.
		All bus master devices are required to implement this bit.
13	RWC	**Received Master Abort Status**
		0 – A bus Master Abort did not terminate a bus master's transaction (**RST#** state).
		1 – Set by a bus master whose transaction was terminated by a bus Master Abort.
		1 All bus master devices are required to implement this bit.
		2 A Master Abort on a Special Cycle transaction should not cause this bit to be set.
14	RWC	**Received System Error Status**
		0 – SERR# assertion not detected on the secondary interface.
		1 – SERR# assertion detected on the secondary interface.
		Devices which cannot assert **SERR#** are not required to implement this bit
15	RWC	**Detected Parity Error Status**
		0 – Device did not detect a parity error (**RST#** state).
		1 – Device detected a parity error.
		Devices will set this bit regardless of the state of Parity Error Response (bit 6 of the Command Register).

Table 17-39: Secondary Status Register (cont.)

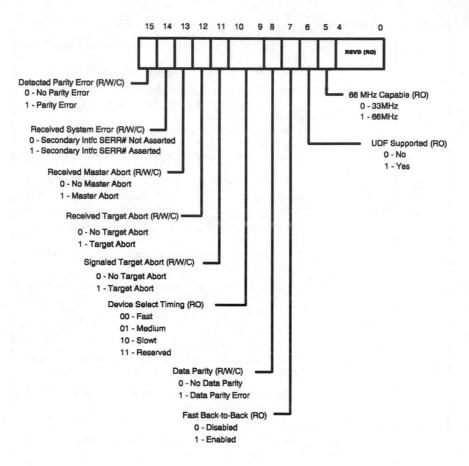

Figure 17-39: Secondary Status Register

Memory Base	
Offset:	20h
Width:	2 Bytes
Valid Values:	See Below
Description:	The Memory Base register defines the base address of a memory mapped I/O address range. This range is used by the PCI to PCI bridge to determine when to forward I/O transactions from one interface to the other.

Bits	Type	Function
15:4	RW	These bits correspond to address bits AD<31::20> for decoding a 32 bit address.
		The bridge does not implement AD<19::0> in the Memory Base register. The bridge assumes that these lower 20 bits are zero. This aligns the Memory Base register value on a 1 Megabyte boundary.
3:0	RO	These bits return zero when read.

Table 17-40: Memory Base Register

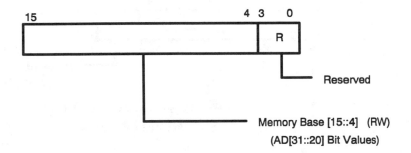

Figure 17-40: Memory Base Register

577

Memory Limit	
Offset:	22h
Width:	2 Bytes
Valid Values:	See Below
Description:	The Memory Limit register defines the top address (inclusive) of a memory mapped I/O address range. This range is used by the PCI to PCI bridge to determine when to forward I/O transactions from one interface to the other.

Bits	Type	Function
15:4	RW	These bits correspond to address bits AD<31::20> for decoding a 32 bit address.
		The bridge does not implement AD<19::0> in the Memory Limit register. The bridge assumes that these lower 20 bits are FFFFh. This aligns the top of the memory address range at the top of a 1 Megabyte aligned address block.
3:0	RO	These bits return zero when read.

Table 17-41: Memory Limit Register

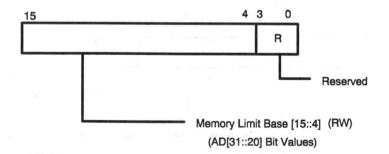

Reserved

Memory Limit Base [15::4] (RW)
(AD[31::20] Bit Values)

Figure 17-41: Memory Limit Register

Prefetchable Memory Base	
Offset:	24h
Width:	2 Bytes
Valid Values:	See Below
Description:	The Prefetchable Memory Base register defines the base address of a prefetchable memory address range. This range is used by the PCI to PCI bridge to determine when to forward memory transactions from one interface to the other. This register is optional. Consequently, the Prefetchable Memory Base register can be either a read/write or read only register. If a bridge supports a prefetchable memory address range, then this register must be initialized by configuration software.

Bits	Type	Function
15.0	RO	**Read Only Implementation:** The register must return a value of zero.
3:0	RO	**Read/Write Implementation:** These bits encode the prefetchable memory addressing capability of the PCI to PCI Bridge as follows: 0h — 32 Bit addressing 01h — 64 Bit addressing 02h-Fh — Reserved If bits <3::0> contain 01h, the bridge supprts 64 bit addresses. The upper 32 bits of the Prefetchable Memory Base register are contained in the Prefetchable Base Upper 32 Bits register.
15:0	RW	0h- FFF0h — These bits correspond to address bits AD<31::20> of a 32 bit address. The bridge does not implement AD<19::0> in the Prefetchable Memory Base register. The bridge assumes that these lower 20 bits are zero. This aligns the Prefetchable Memory Base register value on a 1 Megabyte boundary.

Table 17-42: Prefetchable Memory Base Register

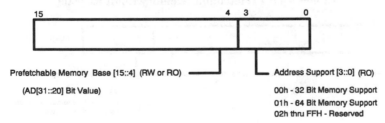

Prefetchable Memory Base [15::4] (RW or RO)

(AD[31::20] Bit Value)

Address Support [3::0] (RO)

00h - 32 Bit Memory Support
01h - 64 Bit Memory Support
02h thru FFH - Reserved

Figure 17-42: Prefetchable Memory Base Register

Prefetchable Memory Limit	
Offset:	26h
Width:	2 Bytes
Valid Values:	See Below
Description:	The Prefetchable Memory Limit register defines the top address (inclusive) of a prefetchable memory address range. This range is used by the PCI to PCI bridge to determine when to forward memory transactions from one interface to the other. This register is optional. Consequently, the Prefetchable Memory Limit register can be either a read/write or read only register. If a bridge supports a prefetchable memory address range, then this register must be initialized by configuration software

Bits	Type	Function
15:0	RO	**Read Only Implementation:** The register must return a value of zero.
3:0	RO	**Read/Write Implementation:** These bits encode the prefetchable memory addressing capability of the PCI to PCI Bridge as follows: 0h 32 Bit addressing 01h 64 Bit addressing 02h-Fh Reserved If bits <3::0> contain 01h, the bridge supprts 64 bit addresses. The upper 32 bits of the Prefetchable Memory Limit register are contained in the Prefetchable Limit Upper 32 Bits register.
15:0	RW	0h- FFF0h	These bits correspond to address bits AD<31::20> of a 32 bit address. The bridge does not implement AD<19::0> in the Prefetchable Memory Limit register. The bridge assumes that these lower 20 bits are FFFFFh. This aligns the top of the Prefetchable Memory Limit register at the top of a 1 Megabyte aligned address block.

Table 17-43: Prefetchable Memory Limit Register

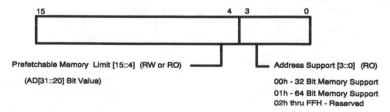

Figure 17-43: Prefetchable Memory Limit Register

Prefetchable Base Upper 32 Bits	
Offset:	28h
Width:	4 Bytes
Valid Values:	See Below
Description:	The Prefetchable Base Upper 32 Bits register defines the upper 32 bits of the base of a prefetchable 64 bit memory address range. This range is used by the PCI to PCI bridge to determine when to forward memory transactions from one interface to the other. This register is optional. Consequently, the Prefetchable Base Upper 32 Bits register can be either a read/write or read only register. If a bridge supports a 64 bit prefetchable memory address range, then this register must be initialized by configuration software.

Bits	Type	Function
31:0	RO	**Read Only Implementation:** Configured as read only if the bridge does not implement a Prefetchable Memory Base register or the Prefetchable Memory Base register indicates support for 32 bit addressing. The register must return a value of zero.
31:0	RO	**Read/Write Implementation:** Specifies the upper 32 bits of a 64 bit Prefetchable Memory Base address. The bit in this register correspond to AD<63::32>.

Table 17-44: Prefetchable Base Upper 32 Bits Register

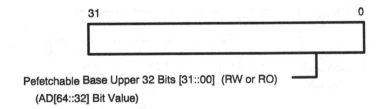

Pefetchable Base Upper 32 Bits [31::00] (RW or RO)
(AD[64::32] Bit Value)

Figure 17-44: Prefetchable Base Upper 32 Bits Register

581

Prefetchable Limit Upper 32 Bits	
Offset:	2Ch
Width:	4 Bytes
Valid Values:	See Below
Description:	The Prefetchable Limit Upper 32 Bits register defines the top address (inclusive) of a prefetchable 64 bit memory address range. This range is used by the PCI to PCI bridge to determine when to forward memory transactions from one interface to the other. This register is optional. Consequently, the Prefetchable Limit Upper 32 Bits register can be either a read/write or read only register. If a bridge supports a 64 bit prefetchable memory address range, then this register must be initialized by configuration software

Bits	Type	Function
31:0	RO	**Read Only Implementation:** Configured f the bridge does not implement a Prefetchable Memory Base register or the Prefetchable Memory Base register indicate s support for 32 bit addressing. The register must return a value of zero.
31:0	RO	**Read/Write Implementation:** Specifies the upper 32 bits of a 64 bit Prefetchable Memory Limit address. The bits in this register correspond to AD<63::32>.

Table 17-45: Prefetchable Limit Upper 32 Bits Register

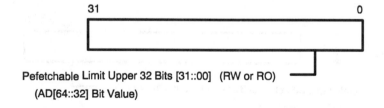

Pefetchable Limit Upper 32 Bits [31::00]   (RW or RO)

(AD[64::32] Bit Value)

Figure 17-45: Prefetchable Limit Upper 32 Bits Register

I/O Base Upper 16 Bits	
Offset:	30h
Width:	2 Bytes
Valid Values:	See Below
Description:	The I/O Base Upper 16 Bits register defines the upper 16 bits of the base of a 32 bit I/O address range. This range is used by the PCI to PCI bridge to determine when to forward I/O transactions from one interface to the other. This register is optional. Consequently, the I/O Base Upper 16 Bits register can be either a read/write or read only register. If a bridge supports a 32 bit I/O address range, then this register must be initialized by configuration software

Bits	Type	Function
15:0	RO	**Read Only Implementation:** Configured as read only if the bridge does not implement an I/O Base register or the I/O Base register indicates support for 16 bit addressing. The register must return a value of zero.
15:0	RO	**Read/Write Implementation:** Specifies the upper 16 bits of a 32 bit I/O Base address. The bits in this register correspond to AD<31::16>.

Table 17-46: I/O Base Upper 16 Bits Register

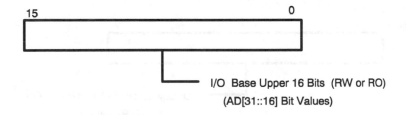

I/O Base Upper 16 Bits (RW or RO)

(AD[31::16] Bit Values)

Figure 17-46: I/O Base Upper 16 Bits Register

583

I/O Limit Upper 16 Bits	
Offset:	**32h**
Width:	**2 Bytes**
Valid Values:	**See Below**
Description:	The I/O Limit Upper 16 Bits register defines the top address (inclusive) of a 16 bit I/O address range. This range is used by the PCI to PCI bridge to determine when to forward memory transactions from one interface to the other. This register is optional. Consequently, the I/O Limit Upper 16 Bits register can be either a read/write or read only register. If a bridge supports a 32 bit I/O address range, then this register must be initialized by configuration software

Bits	Type	Function
15:0	RO	**Read Only Implementation:** Configured as read only if the bridge does not implement an I/O Base register or the I/O Base register indicates support for 16 bit addressing. The register must return a value of zero.
15:0	RO	**Read/Write Implementation:** Specifies the upper 16 bits of a 32 bit I/O Limit address. The bits in this register correspond to AD<31::16>.

Table 17-47: I/O Limit Upper 16 Bits Register

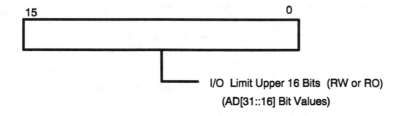

I/O Limit Upper 16 Bits (RW or RO)
(AD[31::16] Bit Values)

Figure17-47: I/O Limit Upper 16 Bits Register

Expansion ROM Base Address Register		
Offset:	38h	
Width:	4 Bytes	
Valid Values:	Device dependent	
Description:	The Expansion ROM Base Address register bit definitions are compliant with the PCI Local Bus Specification.	
	This register allows a PCI device's expansion ROM to be mapped into a system's physical address space. Depending on the system implementation, this dynamic mapping may be accomplished by the System ROM BIOS during POST or later by other system software such as a device driver or operating system.	
	See Chapter Twenty for a description of how this register is implemented in a system.	

Bit	Type	Function
0	RW	**Expansion ROM Decode Enable**
		0 Disable decode the Expansion ROM within System memory address space.
		1 Enable decode of the Expansion ROM within System memory address space.
		Bit 1 of this device's Command Register, the Memory Space Control bit, has precedence over this bit. It must be set to a value of 1 for this bit to enable the expansion ROM address decode.
10:1	RO	**Reserved**
31:11	RW	**Expansion ROM Base Address**
		Start address of the expansion ROM memory space region assigned to this device. This is where the expansion ROM code will appear in system memory when bit 0 of this register contains a value of 1 and bit 1 of this device's Command Register contains a value of 1.
		Because the Expansion ROM Base Address may share a decoder with the I/O and Memory Base Address Register, device independent software *should not* access any other base address register of this device while the expansion ROM decode for this device is enabled.

Table 17-48: Expansion ROM Base Address Register

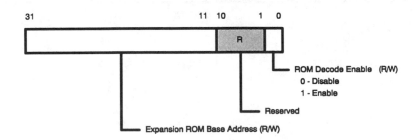

Figure 17-48: Expansion ROM Base Address Register

585

To assign an expansion ROM base address to this register, software should do the following:

1. Write a value of 1 to bits 11 through 31 of this register.

2. Starting at bit location 11, search upward for the first bit set to a value of 1. This bit is the binary weighted size of the total contiguous block of memory address space requested. For example, if bit 16 is the first bit set, the device is requesting a 64 kilobyte block of memory address space.

3. Write the start address of the memory space block assigned to this register. This memory space region must not conflict with any other memory address space utilized within the system. Otherwise, data reads from the ROM may be corrupted.

Expansion ROM Base Address registers may share an address decoder with other Base Address registers. This reduces the number of address decoders on a device. While this feature permits each base address register to hold a unique value at the same time, it does place constraints on software:

A device-independent software program should only set Bit 0, the Expansion ROM Decode Enable bit, to 1 when it is copying the expansion ROM code to the shadow memory. For example, when a PC/AT System BIOS copies a PCI ROM image to the ISA compatibility region between C0000h and EFFFFh. Also, POST code should RESET Bit 0 to zero before calling the initialization function of any relocated expansion ROM code. This is because the option ROM code may try to access the device using the allocation in the standard base address registers, which may be non-functional if the expansion ROM register is left enabled.

Device specific code, (i.e. a device driver) may set this bit to one (after locating a non-conflicting address space and doing the appropriate mapping) to obtain some device specific information out of the ROM.

Interrupt Line	
Offset:	3Ch
Width:	1 Byte
Valid Values:	00h–FFh
Description:	This register identifies which interrupt request line of a system interrupt controller the PCI device's interrupt line is connected to. Device drivers as well as other device dependent software query this register to determine the interrupt request line assigned to their device.
	This value is system architecture specific. For ISA compatible systems, valid encodings are shown below.
	00h = IRQ0
	01h = IRQ1
	—
	0Eh = IRQ14
	0Fh = IRQ15
	Note that these encodings specify the physical pin on the system interrupt controller that the interrupt line is connected to. These encodings do not specify the interrupt vector that is generated by the interrupt controller. Other values are reserved.

Bit	Type	Function	
7:0	RW	**Interrupt Line Value**	
		00h:FEh	Interrupt line number that the device is connected to.
		FFh	Device interrupt line is not connected to a system interrupt controller.

Table 17-49: Interrupt Line Register

POST software is responsible for routing the device's interrupt line to a system interrupt controller. This routing is dependent upon the specific hardware implementation. In addition, POST code will update this register with the interrupt line value assigned to the device. Software other than POST may read this register to determine which interrupt line the PCI device is connected.

Device specific executables such as device drivers and add-in card BIOSs should never assign system resources to their device. System resource conflicts could result, rendering the system inoperable. Allocating system resources is the task of power-up system software and operating systems.

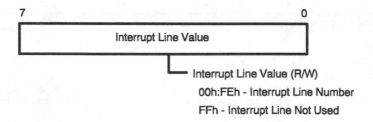

Figure 17-49: Interrupt Line Register

Interrupt Pin

Offset:	3Dh
Width:	1 Byte
Valid Values:	00h–04h
Description:	The Interrupt Pin register bit definitions are compliant with the PCI Local Bus Specification.

This register identifies which interrupt pin, **INTA#** through **INTD#**, a device function uses. This register assists in the proper initialization of the Interrupt Line register. Once initialization software knows which interrupt pin(s) the device uses, the Interrupt Line register(s) can be initialized appropriately.

Bit	Type	Function
7:0	RO	**Interrupt Pin Value**

00h	Interrupt pin is not used by the device.
01h	Device function uses interrupt pin **INTA#**.
02h	Device function uses interrupt pin **INTB#**.
03h	Device function uses interrupt pin **INTC#**.
04h	Device function uses interrupt pin **INTD#**.
05h:FFh	Reserved

Table 17-50: Interrupt Pin Register

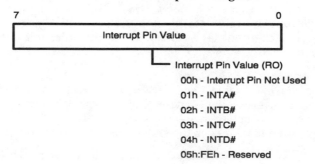

Figure 17-50: Interrupt Pin Register

Bridge Control	
Offset:	3Eh
Width:	2 Bytes
Valid Values:	N/A. This field is a collection of bits, not a range of values. The register should not be viewed as values, but as individual bits.
Description:	This register provides extensions to the Command register, offset 04h, that are specific to PCI to PCI bridges. Certain bits within this register affect the operation of both the primary and secondary interfaces of PCI to PCI bridges; other bits are applicable only to the secondary interface. These bits provide the same controls to the secondary interface as the Command register provides for the primary interface.

Bit	Type	Function
0	RW	**Parity Error Response Enable** Controls the bridge's response to parity detected on the secondary interface. 0 Ignore address and data parity errors on the secondary interface. (**RST#** state) 1 Enable parity error reporting and detection on the secondary interface.
1	RO	**SERR# Enable** Controls the forwarding of secondary interface SERR# assertions to the primary interface 0 Disable forwarding secondary SERR# to primary interface's SERR#(**RST#** state) 1 Disable forwarding secondary SERR# to primary interface's SERR#(**RST#** state) The bridge can only detect the assertion of SERR# on the secondary interface if the SERR# Enable bit in Command register is set.
2	RW	**ISA Enable** 0 Forward all I/O addresses in the address range as defined by the I/O Base and I/O Limit registers. 1 Block forwarding of the top 768 bytes of each 1K I/O in the address range as defined by the I/O Base and I/O Limit registers. This applies to the first 64k of PCI I/O address space. I/O addresses in the defined range will not be forwarded to the secondary interface if this bit is set. Conversely, the secondary interface can forward I/O addresses in the top 768 bytes of each 1K to the primary interface.

Table 17-51: Bridge Control Register

3	RW	**VGA Enable** This bit modifies the PCI to PCI bridge's response to VGA compatible addresses. 0 Do not forward VGA compatible I/O and Memory addresses from the primary interface to the secondary interface. (**RST#** state) 1 Forward VGA compatible I/O and Memory addresses from the primary interface to the secondary interface. This will be done regardless of the state of the ISA Enable bit and the bridge's I/O and memory address ranges.
4	RO	**Reserved**
5	RW	**Master Abort Mode** 0 Do not report master aborts. The bridge will return FFFF FFFFh on reads. Data is discarderd on writes. (**RST#** state). 1 Report master aborts. SERR# will be detected if enabled. Target abort will be signalled if possible.
6	RW	**Secondary Bus Reset** Assert the RST# signal pin on the secondary interface. 0 Do not assert the secondary interface RST# signal pin. (**RST#** state). 1 assert the secondary interface RST# signal pin.
7		**Fast Back to Back Enable** Controls ability of the bridge to generate Fast Back to Back transactions to different devices on the secondary interface.
	RO	**Read Only Implementation:** 0 Fast Back to Back transactions not supported. Return 0 when this bit is read.
	RW	**Read/Write Implementation:** 0 Disable Fast Back to Back transactions on the secondary interface. (RST# state). 1 Enable Fast Back to Back transactions on the secondary interface. Bridges capable of generating Fast Back to Back cycles must implement this as a read/write bit. Configuration software should only set this bit if all devices on the secondary interface are capable of Fast Back to Back operation.
15:8	RO	**Reserved**

Table 17-51: Bridge Control Register (cont.)

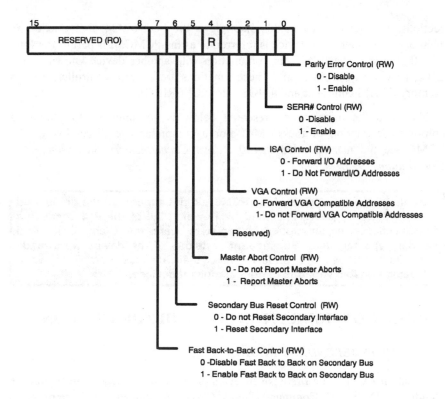

Figure 17-51: Bridge Control Register

17.5 PCI CONFIGURATION SPACE DEVICE DEPENDENT REGION

The PCI configuration space Device Dependent region consists of the last 192 bytes of the PCI configuration space. PCI device vendors are only permitted to place device specific information in the registers of this region.

This area of PCI configuration space can be used for any device functionality that is not typically accessed during runtime. The most likely use of this region is device specific configuration. PCI device designers should avoid placing run–time control and status in this area because of the longer access times.

17.6 PCI CONFIGURATION SPACE EXAMPLE

In this subchapter an actual implementation of the PCI configuration space is presented to demonstrate the principles of design discussed in the previous sections. The device used in this example is the Intel 82434, PCI Cache and Memory Controller. This device is referred to as the PCMC. It is part of the Intel 82430 chip set. The PCMC, in conjunction with another device known as the LBX, provides three functions. These functions are a cache controller, a main memory DRAM controller and a HOST–to–PCI BRIDGE.

Note that the information presented below is not intended to provide a complete description of the PCMC. For a comprehensive discussion of the PCMC see the manual titled *82430 PCIset Cache/Memory Subsystem, Intel Corporation, 1993.*

Note that the first revision of the PCMC did not support all the predefined header region registers specified by Revision 2.0 of the PCI Local Bus Specification. The unsupported registers were the Class Code and Header Type registers. Subsequent revisions of the device were made compliant. All vendors should make their devices compliant when releasing updated versions of non–compliant devices.

PCMC CONFIGURATION SPACE HEADER REGION

DEVICE INDEPENDENT REGION

Recall that within the first sixteen bytes of the device independent region the Vendor ID, Device ID, Command, Status, Class Code and Header Type registers must be supported by all PCI compliant devices. All other PCI Device Independent registers can be implemented as Reserved Registers. Remember that Reserved Registers must return a value of zero when read.

OFFSET	REGISTER
00h	Vendor ID The vendor identification number. This value is 8086h. All Intel devices, not just the PCMC, contain a vendor ID of 8086.
02h	Device ID The device identification number. This value is 04A3h. Intel assigned this number according to the company's internal numbering scheme. This number is unique to the PCMC. No matter how many times this device is revised, this value will not change.
04h	Command Provides control over the PCMC's ability to respond to PCI cycles. Of particular importance are bits zero, one and two: Bit Comments 0 I/O Access Enable bit: PCI accesses to HOST I/O space is always disabled (0). Consequently, this bit is hard–coded to zero. Bit–0 is read–only. 1 Memory Access Enable bit: PCI master access to main memory is enabled/disabled with this bit. This bit is set to one at power–on. 2 Bus Master Enable bit: This bit is always enabled (1). This setting ensures that the PCMC bus master on the PCI bus can never be disabled. Writes to this bit will have no effect.
06h	Status Event notification
08h	Revision ID The revision of the PCMC. 00h was the original value. Later revisions will contain a different value, depending on the stepping.
09h 0Ah 0Bh	Class Code: Programming Interface Sub–Class Code Base Class Code This device contains a Programming Interface value of 00h, a Sub–Class code of 00h, and a Base Class code of 06h, indicating that this is a Host Bridge device. (060000h).
0Ch	Cache Line Size Not required for the PCMC. Reads of this register return a value of zero.
0Dh	Latency Timer Controls the amount of time the PCMC, acting as a bus master, can burst data on the PCI bus.
0Eh	Header Type Identifies the layout of bytes 10h through 3Fh in the PCMC configuration space. The value is 00h. See figure 17–1 for the layout description.
0Fh	BIST Built–In Self Test. This register was supported in the first revision of the device, although the BIST functions were not supported. Later revisions of the PCMC now reserve this register. Reads of this register return a value of zero.

PCI DEVICE HEADER TYPE REGION

A description of the PCI Device Header Type Region is shown below. The PCMC does not require any of these registers to support its functionality. Hence all registers are reserved and should return a value of zero when read. The guideline here is simple: only implement the registers required to reduce complexity, programming requirements and device costs.

OFFSET	REGISTER
10h – 27h	Base Address Registers
28h – 2Bh	Reserved
30h	Expansion ROM Base Address
34h – 3Bh	Reserved
3Ch	Interrupt Line
3Dh	Interrupt Pin
3Eh	Min_Gnt
3Fh	Max_Lat

17.7 PCI DEVICE DETECTION

To determine if a device is present on the PCI bus do the following:

1. Read the Vendor ID register of Function 0. If a value other than FFFFh is read, the device is present.

2. Determine if the device is a single function or multi–function device: Read the Header Type register, located at offset 0Eh of the PCI configuration space Header. If bit seven is not set it is a Single-Function Device; otherwise it is a multi–function device.

3. If the device is a multi–function device, for each function, one through seven,

4. Read the Vendor ID register of Function [1, 7]. If a value other than FFFFh is read, the function is present.

Note that Single-Function Devices may not decode AD10::AD8. This will force all 8 functions of the device to return the same values.

17.8 MULTI-FUNCTION DEVICES

Each PCI device may contain between one and eight functions. For example, a device may contain functions that provide a SCSI connection and an Ethernet connection. Each individual function must implement a separate set of PCI Configuration Space Registers.

Multi–function devices should not respond to configuration space accesses to functions that are not implemented. For instance, a device with two functions, 0 and 4, should not respond (i.e. assert DEVSEL) when functions 1, 2, 3, 5, 6, and 7 are accessed. It is important that when the Vendor ID field of an unimplemented function is read the value returned is 0FFFFh.

SHARING CONFIGURATION SPACE REGISTERS

Certain Configuration Space Registers can be shared when implementing multifunction devices. For instance, Vendor IDs are typically (but not always) the same for different functions in a device. When a register is read–only and has the same value in multiple functions, the register can be shared by the two functions. This sharing reduces the number of silicon gates required to implement the device.

Registers that have writeable bits must not be shared. For instance, all functions must implement unique Command Registers so that they can be individually controlled. Two exceptions to this rule are allowed. The Cache Line Size register and the Expansion ROM Base Address Register can be shared between multiple functions in a device. Cache Line Size can be shared because this is a fixed value throughout the system. Expansion ROM Base ADDRESS can be shared because device independent software will only enable and copy one ROM image at a time.

17.9 CHAPTER SUMMARY

In this chapter rules for reading and writing PCI configuration address space were introduced. A detailed description of the PCI configuration space header region was presented. This region is divided into two partitions: the PCI device independent region and the PCI header type region. The size of the PCI device independent region is 16 bytes. The size of the PCI header type region is defined by the header type register. Support of certain registers within the PCI device independent region is required by all PCI devices. On the other hand, support of PCI header type region registers is optional.

CHAPTER 18

OVERVIEW OF SYSTEM BIOS

This chapter consists of the following subchapters:

18.0 INTRODUCTION

As stated in Chapters 1 and 2, the ROM–based system initialization and run–time software contained in all personal computers must be modified to manage the automatic configuration of PCI devices. To aid in the comprehension of the required modifications (these are discussed in Chapters 19 and 20), this chapter presents an overview of an unmodified System BIOS program.

THE SYSTEM BIOS ROM

The System BIOS ROM is the only ROM device required in all ISA–compatible systems. This ROM contains a minimum of two software components. The first component is a software program called Power On Self Test, or POST. This is executed first each time the computer is turned on or RESET. The second required component of an ISA compatible System ROM BIOS is known as System BIOS.

POST OVERVIEW

While there are many System BIOS vendors such as AMI, Phoenix Technologies, Award Software, and Annabooks, the fundamental tasks performed by each POST software program remains the same. The POST software is responsible for checking for the presence or absence of devices within the system, initializing those devices that require software initialization, testing the system hardware, reporting the system configuration and diagnostic status, and finally loading (or bootstrapping) an operating system.

SYSTEM BIOS OVERVIEW

The ISA Compatible System BIOS is the portion of code in a system ROM BIOS that contains software programs that are available during POST and the operating system run-time. This is in contrast to the POST, which is not used during run-time operations.

> The System BIOS ROM may contain other software programs such as a Setup or Configuration Utility. These software programs are beyond the scope of this discussion. In addition, the System BIOS may be implemented in more than one ROM memory device.

18.1 INVOKING POST

POST is typically invoked by one of four methods:

1. Applying power to the computer system will automatically invoke the POST. This is accomplished by the microprocessor jumping to the address located at the RESET vector, which is located at physical address FFFF0h. Refer to Chapter 16, the section entitled *The System BIOS ROM and the Restart Vector,* for additional information.

2. Many computers have a RESET button or switch. It is normally located on the front panel of the computer. When activated, the POST is invoked as described in method one.

3. Simultaneously pressing the <CTRL> <ALT> <DEL> keys on the keyboard in the DOS environment will halt execution of the current software program and transfer control to the start of the POST program. This is known as a *warm* RESET. Multi–tasking software may trap warm resets and handle them without invoking the System BIOS POST.

4. Software programs can jump to the microprocessor RESET vector located at physical address FFFF0h. When this method is used, the POST is invoked as described in method one.

18.2 POST DEVICE INITIALIZATION AND TESTING

In ISA compatible systems the initialization and testing of the various system components is not a simple two–stage process wherein all components are first initialized and then tested. Rather, it is a sequence of individual component initialization and testing processes.

The early component tests and initializations involve those system components that are mission–critical to the operation of the computer system. If a failure is detected during this stage of the POST it is considered fatal and code execution is halted. For example, if the system ROM BIOS checksum test fails, the System BIOS code is considered unreliable. In this case, code execution is halted instead of risking the possibility of damaging any system component by executing faulty code.

The later POST component tests and initializations involve those system components that, while perhaps are critical to the overall operation of the computer system, do not warrant terminating the code execution process. For instance, should the system cache memory fail to pass its initialization and test process the overall system performance would be degraded. However, the operation of the system would not be hindered.

POST ERROR HANDLING

The POST errors that occur prior to video initialization are reported via the system speaker. A unique sequence of beeps is output, usually through Channel 2 of the 8254 Programmable Timer chip, for each type of failure. Each System BIOS vendor documents their own beep code sequences.

The POST errors that occur after video initialization are reported via the computer CRT. Some System BIOSs print failure numbers that have to be referenced via documentation to determine the failure. Other System BIOSs may go so far as to place exhaustive failure and help screen messages on the CRT. A sequence of beeps may also be output to the system speaker when a failure occurs. Each System BIOS vendor documents their own failure reporting codes and messages.

POST TESTS

Below is a description of typical Power–On Self Tests performed by an ISA System BIOS. Note that the sequence of the tests, and the test descriptions themselves, may vary among System BIOS vendors. While perhaps not exhaustive, this will provide helpful insight into the POST initialization and testing phase.

POST TEST	DESCRIPTION
Microprocessor	The microprocessor built–in self–test status is examined for pass/fail. The individual microprocessor registers are tested by writing various values to them. These values are read back and verified. A minimal set of iAPX instructions may be executed and their operations verified.
System BIOS Checksum	A checksum is performed on the System BIOS ROM contents.
CMOS RAM	The CMOS RAM battery is checked for operational status. A checksum test of the standard CMOS RAM is performed. If a system has greater than 64 bytes of CMOS RAM, the extended CMOS RAM may be tested.
DMA Controller	The DMA controller registers are tested, then initialized.
Keyboard Controller	The keyboard controller has a self–test command. The System BIOS issues this command and then checks the result.
Interrupt Controller	The two interrupt controllers are tested, then initialized.
System Timer	Each timer channel is tested for proper operation. Upon test completion, each timer channel is initialized to its standard run–time operating mode.
Memory Refresh	Ensures that the system RAM is being refreshed properly. This usually includes testing timer channel 1.
First 64K	The first 64K of system RAM is tested. This typically includes a parity test for this region. The System BIOS will set up a stack in this region after the test passes.
Video	The system video device is identified, tested and initialized.
Cache Memory	The cache memory subsystem is tested. A failure results in the cache being disabled.
Protected Mode	The ability to switch into and out of Protected Mode is tested.
Address Lines	All system memory address lines are tested.
System RAM	All of system RAM is tested with various data patterns. This test also checks the system data lines.
Parallel and Serial Ports	Each port detected is tested and initialized.
Keyboard	The keyboard has a self–test command. The System BIOS issues this command and then checks the result. The keyboard interface is also tested.
Floppy	Usually a Seek is executed and verified. This also tests and initializes the Floppy controller.
Hard Disk	Usually a Seek is executed and verified. This also tests and initializes the Hard Disk controller.

Table 18–1: System BIOS POST Tests

18.3   POST STACK AND DATA INITIALIZATION

The System BIOS reserves a portion of the system RAM for itself. This dynamic memory is used for a stack, storing information about the system, and the Real Mode interrupt vector table. These areas are initialized after the first 64K system

RAM test is performed by the System BIOS. See *Chapter 16: System Resources* for additional information.

STACK

The microprocessor stack segment register [SS] is usually initialized to 30h. The stack pointer register [SP] is initialized to 100h. This sets the top of stack to physical address 400h. This translates into 256 bytes of stack space available for program execution. Because the System BIOS executes in Real Mode (except for the Protected Mode and Extended Memory tests), each time 16 bits of data are placed (pushed) on the stack the [SP] register is decremented by two bytes. For instance, a near call would place the contents of the 16 bit instruction pointer [IP] register onto the stack. If [SP] contained the top of stack value prior to the call, the [SP] register value after the call would be 3FEh.

> In Chapter 16, System Resources, the Real Mode interrupt vector table was described as having a physical memory base address of 0000:0000. Its length is 1K, or 400 hex bytes. The ISA–compatible system Real Mode stack uses the top 256 bytes (100h) of the interrupt vector table for its stack region. By convention, the highest interrupt vector implemented will never extend into the stack region. This reduces the actual number of available interrupt vectors to 192.

INTERRUPT VECTOR TABLE

Shortly after the first 64K of RAM is tested, the System BIOS will initialize the Real Mode Interrupt Vector Table with segment:offset address pairs that point to System BIOS service routines. The base of the Real Mode Interrupt Vector Table is always located at physical address 0000h in system RAM. There are 256 Real Mode interrupt vectors. Each segment:offset address pair is four bytes. Thus, the first 1K of system RAM, or 0000h–03FFh, is allocated to Interrupt Vector Table. Notice that the location of the standard System BIOS stack overlaps the Interrupt Vector Table.

SYSTEM BIOS DATA AREA

During the testing and initialization phase of the POST, the System BIOS stores information about the system environment in an area referred to as the BIOS Data Area. The structure of this area is predefined. This area is based at physical address 400h. Every ISA compatible System BIOS reserves 256 bytes (400h–4FFh) for the BIOS Data Area. The data stored in this region is used to control the operation of the system.

> **Because this information is stored in system RAM, any program can access and modify the contents of the BIOS Data Area.**

It is beyond the scope of this book to list the structure of the entire BIOS Data Area. However, to demonstrate how this area is used, included below is a partial display containing data stored in the first sixteen bytes of the BIOS Data Area and their System BIOS usage. The data shown in Figure 18–1-A was obtained by running the DEBUG.EXE program under DOS Version 6.0 on an IBM PS/ValuePoint computer. The first sixteen bytes are displayed by typing *d 40: 0 L F*. The data obtained from running the DEBUG.EXE program has been transposed to the figure below for greater readability. Note that, depending on the system configuration, the values displayed below may change.

OFFSET:	0	1	2	3	4	5	6	7	8	9	A	B	C	D	E	F
40:0	F8	03	00	00	00	00	00	00	78	03	00	00	00	00	5F	03

Figure 18–1-A: Partial Contents of the System BIOS Data Area

Figure 18–1-B shows the structure definition and use of the first sixteen bytes of the BIOS Data Area. The BIOS interrupt service routine for the system serial ports is INT 14h. For the system parallel ports, the BIOS interrupt service routine is INT 17h. Note that only one serial port and one parallel port were detected, tested and initialized by the System BIOS. In addition, the contents of the serial and parallel ports structure elements are I/O port addresses. The contents of the Extended BIOS Data Area Segment contain a system RAM address. Also, there is no BIOS interrupt service routine associated with the Extended BIOS Data Area Segment.

18.4   POST EXPANSION ROM BIOS INITIALIZATION

Expansion ROM BIOSs are software programs typically located on add–in cards. They may sometimes be integrated into the System BIOS ROM. The purpose of these software programs is to either augment or replace the System BIOS service routines. For example, VGA video add–in cards always contain a ROM BIOS. During its initialization, the VGA ROM BIOS software will usually replace the System BIOS INT 10h interrupt vector with a segment:offset pair pointing to the VGA ROM BIOS INT 10h service routine.

Offset (from 40:0)	BIOS Service	Description	Contents
00h	INT 14h	Serial Port 1 (LSB)	03F8h (I/O address):
01h	INT 14h	Serial Port 1 (MSB)	Serial Port 1 present
02h	INT 14h	Serial Port 2 (LSB)	0000h:
03h	INT 14h	Serial Port 2 (MSB)	No Serial Port 2
04h	INT 14h	Serial Port 3 (LSB)	0000h:
05h	INT 14h	Serial Port 3 (MSB)	No Serial Port 3
06h	INT 14h	Serial Port 4 (LSB)	0000h:
07h	INT 14h	Serial Port 4 (MSB)	No Serial Port 4
08h	INT 17h	Parallel Port 1 (LSB)	0378h: (I/O address):
09h	INT 17h	Parallel Port 1 (MSB)	Parallel Port 1 present
0Ah	INT 17h	Parallel Port 2 (LSB)	0000h:
0Bh	INT 17h	Parallel Port 2 (MSB)	No Parallel Port 2
0Ch	INT 17h	Parallel Port 3 (LSB)	0000h:
0Dh	INT 17h	Parallel Port 3 (MSB)	No parallel Port 3
0Eh	POST	Ext. BIOS Data Area Segment (LSB)	035Fh (memory address)
0Fh	POST	Ext. BIOS Data Area Segment (MSB)	Ext. BIOS segment

Figure 18–1-B: Partial Contents of the System BIOS Data Area

EXPANSION ROM BIOS DETECTION

Expansion ROM BIOSs may appear on any even 2K boundary between physical addresses C0000h and EF800h.

This allows 64K of code space for System BIOS run–time operation. The actual top of memory where an expansion ROM BIOS could reside is system dependent. For example, some System BIOSs have a size of 128K. In this case the last even 2K boundary an expansion ROM could reside at is DF800h.

The address that the POST starts searching for expansion ROM BIOSs depends on whether a video device with a ROM BIOS is detected and initialized during the Post Device Initialization And Testing phase. If such a device is initialized by the POST during this time, the search for other ROM extensions will usually commence at physical address C8000h. This is because ISA video expansion BIOSs typically consume 32K of address space at run–time. Depending on the System BIOS implementation, the search for non–video ROM extensions will commence at physical address C0000h or C8000h if no video device is detected in the system.

603

The POST detects an expansion ROM BIOS by searching for a predefined header that all ISA compatible system expansion ROMs must support. A partial structure definition of the expansion ROM header is as follows:

Offset	Description	Value	Size
00h	Expansion ROM identification byte #1	55h	1 Byte
01h	Expansion ROM identification byte #2	AAh	1 Byte
02h	Size of expansion ROM BIOS code in 512–byte blocks.		1 Byte
03h	Start of the expansion ROM BIOS initialization code. Normally contains a FAR return or 3–byte JMP instruction.		4 Bytes

Figure 18–2: Partial Expansion BIOS Header

EXPANSION ROM BIOS VERIFICATION

Once an expansion ROM BIOS signature has been detected, the System BIOS must verify the expansion ROM BIOS is valid. It does this by reading the contents of offset three of the Expansion ROM BIOS Header. The System BIOS will perform a byte–wide checksum of the expansion ROM BIOS starting at offset zero and ending with the last byte of the last 512–byte block of the BIOS. The expansion ROM BIOS is considered to be valid if the checksummed value equals zero.

EXPANSION ROM BIOS INITIALIZATION

When a valid expansion ROM BIOS is located, the System BIOS executes a FAR CALL to offset three of the expansion ROM BIOS. For example, in the case of a video expansion BIOS detected at physical address C0000h, the System BIOS would call address C000:0003.

Once invoked, the expansion ROM BIOS initialization routine will test and initialize the devices that it manages. It also has the option of hooking the existing interrupt vector(s) that service its device type. The expansion ROM BIOS will execute a FAR return to the System BIOS when it is done initializing.

Some expansion ROM BIOSs use the microprocessor [BP] register to return completion status to the System BIOS. A status of [BP]=0000h indicates success. A non–zero status indicates failure. This information is System BIOS dependent. Because not all expansion ROM BIOS vendors use this completion status mechanism, the status indicator is generally useless. As a caution, if your software calls expansion ROM, remember to preserve the [BP] register prior to the call.

18.5 BOOTSTRAPPING AN OPERATING SYSTEM

The last function performed by the POST is to load an operating system. Note that the operating system type is not relevant to the boot process. It can be a non–DOS type.

INT 19H BOOTSTRAP LOADER

The POST will execute the INT 19h software interrupt. This service routine will attempt to load an operating system from a floppy diskette or hard disk or network device. If the boot sequence passes, the operating system will assume control of the computer system. If the INT 19h boot process fails (usually due to a no–disk or non bootable disk condition), the INT 18h software interrupt service routine is invoked.

INT 18H SERVICE ROUTINE

Network expansion ROM BIOSs may also hook the INT 18h interrupt vector when the system is configured to boot from a network. If this is the case, an attempt will be made to boot from the network. If the network boot fails or if the INT 18h interrupt vector was not hooked by a bootable device, a message will be displayed on the CRT and/or a beep code is issued. These will inform the user that the boot process failed and may also contain a request for a bootable device.

18.6 SYSTEM BIOS

> The System BIOS ROM may contain other software programs such as a Setup or Configuration Utility. These software programs are beyond the scope of this discussion. In addition, the System BIOS may be implemented in more than one ROM memory device.

The BIOS provides a system-independent programming interface for the upper layers of software to easily access and control the system hardware. All of the system ROM BIOS level interrupt service routines and device drivers described in Chapter 16 are part of the System BIOS. POST and operating system level software use the functions of the System BIOS that communicate with the system components such as hard disks, floppy drives, parallel and serial ports to perform their hardware related tasks.

The majority of the System BIOS software interfaces to the system hardware were originally specified by IBM Corporation in its PC, XT, and AT technical reference manuals. All ISA compatible System BIOSs provide the software interfaces for the machine class as defined in these reference manuals. In addition, various System BIOS vendors often define private software interfaces that are not made available for public use. For example, manufacturing and test software use private software interfaces for production reliability testing of subsystems such as the cache, memory and communication ports. This allows system independent software (in this example, test software that can be reused on various types of systems without modifying the software) to access system dependent hardware.

18.7   CHAPTER SUMMARY

The basic functions of the System BIOS, particularly the POST functions, are presented in this chapter. A description of non-PCI device testing and initialization is given that will be used as a reference in the following chapters when PCI device initialization and testing are discussed.

In addition, the initialization of reserved segments of system memory was given. PCI device initialization has a direct impact on these reserved memory segments.

Also, expansion ROM BIOS initialization of non-PCI devices was covered. While there are some similarities between LEGACY type expansion ROM BIOSs and PCI expansion ROM BIOSs, there are differences that require major reconstruction of the System BIOS, expansion ROM BIOS detection, and initialization code.

Finally, the ISA compatible System BIOS method for loading an operating system was presented. This is one area where little has changed between a LEGACY style System BIOS and a PCI–aware System BIOS.

With an understanding of the information presented in this and the previous chapters, the reader is now prepared to delve into the intricacies surrounding the implementation of a PCI–aware System BIOS.

CHAPTER 19

PCI SYSTEM BIOS SOFTWARE INTERFACE

This chapter consists of the following subchapters:

19.0 INTRODUCTION TO THE PCI SYSTEM BIOS SOFTWARE INTERFACE

Chapter 2, *PCI System Architectural Overview,* presented a high–level design of a Plug–and–Play system. Within the System BIOS section of the design is a partition entitled Plug–and–Play Device Services. Each Plug–and–Play device class such as PCI will have an associated set of device service routines. These services are similar to the ones described in Chapter 16, *System Resources,* in the section on software interrupts.

As with the services described in Chapter 16, the major function of the Plug–and–Play Device Services is to provide a hardware independent programming interface that allows software to manipulate the computer's hardware. These device services are used by the System BIOS during the POST. They are also used by the System BIOS and operating system level software at run–time. The PCI software interface supports multiple microprocessor operating and addressing modes. This chapter describes the Plug–and–Play device service routines specific to the PCI device class.

PCI SYSTEM BIOS INTEGRATION

Accessing PCI configuration space and generating Special Cycles at the lowest hardware level is typically platform dependent. This is due in part to the hardware dependencies associated with individual PCI chip sets and in part to an individual platform's PCI hardware implementation. For example, some chip sets only support PCI Configuration Mechanism #1 while others only support PCI Configuration Mechanism #2. Because of hardware dependencies as well as the requirement to allow system level PCI based software to be platform independent, the computer's System BIOS is the most sensible location to install

PCI software support. Placing PCI software support in the System BIOS minimizes code size and coding effort in the following three programming areas:

■ The computer's System BIOS itself can use the PCI BIOS extensions when detecting and initializing PCI devices. The defined extensions are also portable from product to product because once written and debugged, they require no further modifications. Only the code that interfaces directly with the hardware needs to be modified to accommodate the specific PCI hardware implementation.

■ PCI based adapter BIOSs can utilize the PCI BIOS extensions during the Power–On Self Test (POST) phase of the system to correctly identify and initialize their PCI hardware. By using the PCI BIOS extensions, this initialization code remains platform independent. This ensures that the add–in board will work in a variety of manufacturer's systems.

■ PCI based system level software can utilize the PCI BIOS extensions during the run–time phase of the system to correctly identify and initialize their PCI hardware. Like the PCI add–in boards, this initialization code remains platform independent, thus ensuring that the application software will also work in a variety of manufacturer's systems.

> PCI configuration registers can always be accessed directly by software programs. Programmers should be cautious when using direct access programming because software transparency may be reduced between PCI based systems.

X86 OPERATING MODE SUPPORT OVERVIEW

The PCI BIOS software extensions support the 16 bit Real Mode, 16 bit Protected Mode and 32 bit Protected Mode operating modes of the x86 architecture. This represents a major departure from the standard ISA System BIOS.

REAL MODE PCI SYSTEM BIOS

Standard ISA computer System BIOSs traditionally only support system level software with a 16 bit Real Mode interface that utilizes the software interrupt method described in Chapter 16. To maintain compatibility with this implementation and to provide ease of use, the PCI BIOS software interface includes support for 16 bit Real Mode extensions that are also invoked using the software interrupt process.

16 BIT PROTECTED MODE PCI SYSTEM BIOS

16 bit Protected Mode is also supported by the PCI System BIOS. The System BIOS code that supplies the Real Mode PCI System BIOS support is the same code that is executed when 16 bit Protected Mode extensions are invoked. The only difference is how the extensions are invoked. The Real Mode extensions are typically invoked using the iAPX software interrupt mechanism. However, due to the nature of 16 bit Protected Mode users must call the INT 1AH entry point directly, as described in Chapter 16.

> Real Mode users have the option of using the software interrupt method or calling the INT 1AH fixed entry point directly.

32 BIT PROTECTED MODE PCI SYSTEM BIOS

The PCI System BIOS supports 32 bit Protected Mode software extensions. Because of the nature of the 32 bit Protected Mode, these extensions are supported by a different set of code than its 16 bit counterparts. In addition, a different software interface is supplied to specifically support the 32 bit Protected Mode callers.

The PCI–specific System BIOS software extensions and the different methodologies used to access them are discussed in the remainder of this chapter.

19.1 PCI SYSTEM BIOS SOFTWARE EXTENSIONS

INTRODUCTION

The PCI BIOS software extensions consist of a limited set of routines that allow software programmers to access and manage PCI based hardware in a platform independent manner. These software extensions include services for locating a PCI device, support for PCI special cycles, and methods for accessing the configuration space. This subchapter describes the defined PCI BIOS extensions and their microprocessor register usage. Note that the description of each function applies to both the 16 bit and 32 bit PCI software extensions.

PCI FUNCTION IDENTIFIER

PCI has been assigned a software function identifier that is used with the system INT 1Ah interrupt service routine. Its value is B1h. When invoking PCI software functions this value will always be passed to the PCI BIOS services 16 bit or 32 bit entry point in the x86 [AH] register.

32 bit Protected Mode users must use a special 32 bit calling interface to access PCI System BIOS extensions. This calling interface does not require the [AH] microprocessor register to contain B1h upon invocation. However, System BIOSs may validate [AH] = B1h for 32 bit calls. Therefore, to be safe, initialize the [AH] Register prior to making 32 bit calls.

PCI SUBFUNCTION IDENTIFIERS

In addition, each of the defined PCI software functions has been assigned a unique subfunction identifier. These subfunction identifiers are always passed in the x86 [AL] register. The System BIOS uses both the PCI function and subfunction identifier when a PCI software function request is made in order to fully qualify the function request and to invoke the correct System BIOS code to properly service the request.

CLASS DEFINITIONS FOR PCI EXTENSIONS

Currently there are twelve defined PCI BIOS extensions. These extensions are divided into one of three classes, depending on their specific purpose. These classes are:

- PCI Resource Identification Extensions
- PCI Support Extensions
- PCI configuration space Access Extensions

PCI EXTENSIONS LIST

The table below is a list of the PCI BIOS software functions along with their respective subfunction code and class type. For completeness, the PCI software function identifier is also included in the table.

PCI EXTENSIONS COMPLETION STATUS

All routines use the Carry Flag (bit 0 of the Flags register), and the microprocessor [AH] Registers to return status to the caller. The routine was successful if the Carry Flag bit and the [AH] Register equal zero upon return to the caller. Note that some of the System BIOS extensions, such as the GENERATE A PCI SPECIAL CYCLE, return extended status ([AH] will be non-zero in these instances) in the [AH] Register.

PCI Function	AH	AL	Class
PCI Function ID	B1h		
Get PCI BIOS Present Status		01h	Resource Identification
Find a PCI Device		02h	Resource Identification
Find a PCI Class Code		03h	Resource Identification
Generate A PCI Special Cycle		06h	PCI Support
Read a PCI Configuration Byte		08h	Configuration space
Read a PCI Configuration Word		09h	Configuration space
Read a PCI Configuration Dword		0Ah	Configuration space
Write a PCI Configuration Byte		0Bh	Configuration space
Write a PCI Configuration Word		0Ch	Configuration space
Write a PCI Configuration Dword		0Dh	Configuration space
GET PCI Interrupt Routing Options		0Eh	PCI Support
SET PCI Hardware Interrupt		0Fh	PCI Support

Table 19–1: PCI Software Function List

Callers can optimize their status check code by using either the microprocessor [AH] Register or the Carry Flag bit after the execution of a specific extension; typically both do not have to be checked to verify the completion status.

PCI EXTENSIONS COMPLETION CODE LIST

The table below is a list of the predefined completion codes for PCI BIOS software functions. These codes will be returned to the caller in the [AH] microprocessor register. These codes will be referenced in all the PCI functions described below.

PCI Function Return Code	AH
SUCCESSFUL	00h
FUNCTION_NOT_SUPPORTED	81h
BAD_VENDOR_ID	83h
DEVICE_NOT_FOUND	86h
BAD_REGISTER_NUMBER	87h
SET_FAILED	88h
BUFFER_TOO_SMALL	89h

Table 19–2: PCI Function Return Code List

Get PCI BIOS Present Status		
PURPOSE:	This function returns the following information to the caller:	
	1	Existence of a PCI BUS and PCI System BIOS Services.
	2	PCI BIOS interface level.
	3	Hardware mechanism type used to access PCI configuration space.
	4	PCI Special Cycles support status.

ENTRY:	[AH]	0B1h
	[AL]	01h

EXIT:

[AH]   Return Code:

00h =   Successful. PCI BIOS Services are present. This field must be qualified by the contents of [EDX].

[AL]   Hardware mechanism type to access PCI configuration space.

Bits	Value	Description
0	0	Configuration Mechanism #1 not supported
	1	Configuration Mechanism #1 supported
1	0	Configuration Mechanism #2 not supported
	1	Configuration Mechanism #2 supported
3:2	0	Reserved (return value is always zero)
4	0	Special Cycle not supported via Config. Mechanism #1
	1	Special Cycle supported via Config. Mechanism #1
5	0	Special Cycle not supported via Config. Mechanism #2
	1	Special Cycle supported via Config. Mechanism #2
7:6	0	Reserved (return value is always zero)

[BH]   PCI BIOS Interface Level Major Version Number in BCD format

[BL]   PCI BIOS Interface Level Minor Version Number in BCD format

[CL]   Number of the last PCI bus in the system

[EDX]   PCI signature string in ASCII. The value of each byte is as follows:

Bits	Hex Value	ASCII Value
7:0	50h	'P'
15:8	43h	'C'
23:16	49h	'I'
31:24	20h	'∧'

[CF]   PCI BIOS Services present status.
This bit is qualified by the contents of [EDX].
0 =   PCI BIOS Services are present.
1 =   PCI BIOS Services are not present.

SPECIAL NOTES

1. This routine will indicate that a PCI BUS and PCI System BIOS Services exist if:

    1. [AH] = 00h AND [EDX] = 'PCI∧'

    OR

    2. [CF] = 00h AND [EDX] = 'PCI∧'

    OR

    3. [CF] = 00h AND [AH] = 00h AND [EDX] = 'PCI∧'

2. PCI configuration space can be accessed by two separate hardware mechanisms. These are referred to as Configuration Mechanism #1 and Configuration Mechanism #2. Platforms typically only support one of the two mechanisms. Note that both mechanisms can be supported on the same platform. To ensure robust software in either environment, it is recommended that the PCI BIOS software functions always be used to access configuration space.

3. Each PCI bus in the system is assigned a number. The BUS Numbers start at zero. For example, if three PCI buses are detected by the System BIOS POST, a value of 02h will be returned in the [CL] register.

4. The PCI BIOS software interface described in this chapter is Version 2.0. System BIOSs written to this function specification will return a of 02h in the [BH] register and 00h in the [BL] register.

PCI RESOURCE IDENTIFICATION EXTENSIONS

There are three PCI Resource Identification Extensions. This class of PCI subfunctions permits the caller to determine if the platform System BIOS contains PCI BIOS software support and to query the system for the presence of specific PCI devices.

Find a PCI Device		
PURPOSE:		This function returns the location of a PCI device that has a specific Device Identifier and Vendor Identifier.
ENTRY:	[AH]	0B1h
	[AL]	02h
	[CX]	PCI Device Identifier (0.65535)
	[DX]	PCI Vendor Identifier (0.65534)
	[SI]	Index (0.N) i.e., which instance of the device to search for
EXIT:	[AH]	Return Code:
		00h = Successful. A PCI device was found
		83h = Routine was called with a Bad_Vendor_ID
		86h = A PCI Device_Not_Found
	[BH]	PCI Bus number (0.255) where device is located
	[BL]	PCI Device/Function Numbers in the following format:
		Bits Description
		2:0 Function Number
		7:3 Device Number
	[CF]	Function Completion Status
		0 = Successful
		1 = Error

SPECIAL NOTES

1. Although the Carry Flag will contain completion status, do not use it. Instead, interpret the [AH] microprocessor register for the routine's actual return status.

2. Return Code 83h, BAD_VENDOR_ID, will only be returned if the caller invoked this function with a value of FFFFh in the [DX] register.

3. This function is extremely useful for callers that wish to quickly locate all devices in the system that contain the same Device ID and Vendor ID. See the suggested algorithm below:

    1. Set the [SI] register to zero to search for the first device.
    2. Call this function. If return code in [AH] equals 86h, then no more devices. Go to Step 5.
    3. Increment the Index input parameter, [SI] register. At least one device found.
    4. Go to Step 2.
    5. Done.

Find a PCI Class Code

PURPOSE:	This function returns the location of a PCI device that has a specific Class Code.	

ENTRY:	[AH]	0B1h
	[AL]	03h
	[ECX]	PCI Device Class Code (Bits 0.23)
	[SI]	Index (0.N) i.e., which iteration of the Class Code to search for

EXIT:	[AH]	Return Code:
		00h = Successful. A PCI device was found.
		86h= A PCI Device_Not_Found with the specified Class Code
	[BH]	PCI Bus number (0.255) where device is located
	[BL]	PCI Device/Function Numbers in the following format:
		Bits Description
		2:0 Function Number
		7:3 Device Number
	[CF]	Function Completion Status
		0 = Successful
		1 = Error

SPECIAL NOTES

1.   This function is extremely useful for callers that wish to quickly locate all devices in the system that contain the same Class Code. See the suggested algorithm below:

    1.   Set the [SI] register to zero to search for the first device with the specified Class Code.

    2.   Call this function. If return code in [AH] equals 86h then no more devices. Go to Step 5.

    3.   Increment the Index input parameter, [SI] register. At least one device found.

    4.   Go to Step 2.

    5.   Done.

PCI SUPPORT EXTENSIONS

There are three PCI Support Extensions. This class of PCI subfunctions permits the caller to generate PCI bus specific operations.

615

Generate a PCI Special Cycle	
PURPOSE:	This function allows the caller to broadcast PCI Special Cycle data to a specified bus in the system.
ENTRY:	[AH] 0B1h [AL] 06h [BH] PCI Bus number (0.255) to broadcast data to [EDX] Special Cycle DATA.

EXIT:	[AH] Return Code:
	        00h = Successful.
	        81h = This PCI Function_Not_Supported
	
	[CF] Function Completion Status
	        0 = Successful
	        1 = Error

SPECIAL NOTES:

1. PCI Configuration Mechanism #2 cannot generate a Special Cycle on any PCI bus except Bus zero.

2. This function should return successful if the operation was done. Otherwise the [AH] Register will contain 81h indicating that the function is not supported.

Offset	Size	Description
0	Byte	PCI bus number
1	Byte	PCI Device number (in upper 5 bits)
2	Byte	Link Value for **INTA#**
3	Word	IRQ Bit–Map for **INTA#**
5	Byte	Link Value for **INTB#**
6	Word	IRQ Bit–Map for **INTB#**
8	Byte	Link Value for **INTC#**
9	Word	IRQ Bit–Map for **INTC#**
11	Byte	Link Value for **INTD#**
12	Word	IRQ Bit–Map for **INTD#**
14	Byte	Slot Number
15	Byte	Reserved

Table 19–3: IRQ Routing Table Entry Structure Definition

Get PCI Interrupt Routing Options

PURPOSE:	This function returns the PCI interrupt routing options available on the platform. The PCI interrupt routing options define how the platform is able to route individual hardware interrupt lines to PCI devices and PCI Slots.
	This function also returns a bit–map containing the current hardware interrupt line (IRQ) assignments that are exclusive to PCI devices.

ENTRY:	[AH]	0B1h
	[AL]	0Eh
	[BX]	0000h

16–Bit Real Mode parameters:

[DS]	Segment for BIOS data. The base address value in [DS] must resolve to F0000h. The limit value for [DS] must equal 64K.
[ES]	Segment to caller's data structure.
[DI]	16 bit offset address to caller's data structure.

16–Bit Protected Mode parameters:

[DS]	Selector for BIOS data. The base address value in [DS] must resolve to F0000h. The limit value for [DS] must equal 64K.
[ES]	Selector to caller's data structure.
[DI]	16 bit offset address to caller's data structure.

32–Bit Protected Mode parameters:

NOTE: For 32 bit code, see section 19.3.

[DS]	Selector for BIOS data.
[ES]	Selector to caller's data structure.
[EDI]	32 bit offset offset address to caller's data structure.

EXIT:	[AH]	Return Code:
		00h = Successful.
		81h = This PCI Function_Not_Supported
		89h = Buffer too small.
	[BX]	IRQ bitmap. Indicates which IRQs are exclusively dedicated to PCI devices.
	[CF]	Function Completion Status
		0 = Successful
		1 = Error

617

SPECIAL NOTES

1.   Description of the caller's data structure:

Get PCI Interrupt Routing Options is called with a FAR pointer to a data structure. The base of this data structure will be pointed to by ES:DI for 16 bit callers and ES:EDI for 32 bit callers. The caller will use this structure to pass information to this function. The data structure contains two fields. These fields are defined as follows:

Buffer Size (Offset 00)

■   On entry, this field contains size of the caller's buffer. This is a 2–byte value.

■   If the caller's buffer size is greater than or equal to the actual table size, the System BIOS will update this field with the actual size in bytes of the IRQ routing table.

■   If the System BIOS returns a size of zero in this field then the system does not have any PCI add–in card slots or any integrated PCI devices that use an IRQ.

> If the system has at least one PCI add–in card slot then the returned data structure will contain the IRQ routing information for that slot.

■   The System BIOS must update this field with the required buffer size if the caller's buffer is too small to contain the IRQ routing data.

> A buffer size of 256 bytes should avoid this problem. This value assumes: 16 devices times the length of one IRQ routing table entry, which is 16 bytes.

DATA Buffer (Offset 02)

■   This field contains a far pointer to the caller's buffer. Upon successful completion, this buffer will hold the system IRQ hardware routing information for each PCI device and PCI add–in card slot in the system.

For each of the microprocessor operating modes, the structure elements will be as follows:

Structure Field	Mode		
	16 Bit Real	**16 Bit Protected**	**32 Bit Protected**
Buffer Size	2 Bytes	2 Bytes	2 Bytes
DATA Buffer Segment/Selector	2 Byte Segment	2 Byte Selector	2 Byte Selector
DATA Buffer Offset	2 Bytes	2 Bytes	4 Bytes

2. Description of the System BIOS PCI IRQ Routing Table:

The System BIOS knows the PCI IRQ routing options for the integrated PCI devices and add–in card slots. The routing options are returned to the caller in table format via the buffer pointed to by the caller's data structure. The data in the table consists of individual IRQ routing table entries. Each entry describes how the platform is able to route hardware interrupt lines to individual PCI devices and PCI add–in card slots. One IRQ routing table entry is required for every integrated PCI device that uses an IRQ and for every PCI add–in card slot. See Table 19–3 on the next page for the structure definition of an IRQ routing table entry.

> Note that the information in this table is static because it reflects platform capabilities. The table contents will always be the same.

The fields within an IRQ routing table entry are defined as follows:

PCI bus number

- PCI bus that the device or slot resides on.

PCI Device Number

- PCI Device Number (upper 5 bits) of the integrated device or slot.

Link Values

- The Link Value field provides a way of specifying which PCI Interrupt Pins are wire–ORed together on the platform.

- Interrupt Pins that are wired together must have the same 'link' value in their table entries.

- Values for the 'link' field are arbitrary except for a value of zero.

> A value of zero indicates that the PCI Interrupt Pin has no connection to the interrupt controller. This is typically used for integrated devices that have an INTA# pin and not an INTB#, INTC#, or INTD# pin.

IRQ Bit–Map

- This field defines (in a bit– map format) which of the standard PC/AT IRQs the associated PCI interrupt pin can be routed to. Note that entries with the same 'link' value must have the same IRQ Bit–Map value.

    #### Bit–Map Definition:

    Bit 0 corresponds to IRQ0, bit 1 to IRQ1, bit 15 to IRQ15.

>   0 –   indicates no routing is possible
>   1 –   indicates a routing is possible

Slot Number

■   This field indicates if the table entry is for an integrated PCI device or a PCI add–in card slot:

Zero   – Integrated PCI device

Non–Zero   – PCI add–in card slot number.

See Figure 19–1 for an example of how to number platform add–in card slots.

> Add–in slot numbering is vendor specific. Slot numbers should correspond to the physical placement of the slots on the platform. It is recommended that add–in card slot numbers be silk–screened onto the platform for ease of identification and reference.

3.   Description of the IRQ Bit–Map return value:

This parameter is contained in the microprocessor [BX] register. The caller must initialize this input parameter to 0000h prior to invoking this routine. Upon return [BX] will contain a 16 bit word that indicates which IRQs are solely dedicated to PCI. These IRQs are not available for use by devices on other device class buses such as the ISA bus.

> Any IRQs that can be used by both PCI and other buses should not appear in this value. This value reflects the *current* state of interrupt routings. It may change from one call to the next if any routings change.

Bit–Map Definition:

Bit 0 corresponds to IRQ0, bit 1 to IRQ1, bit 15 to IRQ15.

0 – IRQ can be routed to both PCI and non-PCI devices in the system

1 – IRQ can only be routed to PCI devices in the system

IRQ ROUTING TABLE EXAMPLE

A PCI based system can contain a maximum of 256 PCI buses. Each PCI bus can contain between 1 and 32 unique devices. Each PCI device or slot on a given PCI bus is assigned a unique Device Number. This unique PCI Device Number is an encoded number assigned to each device by tying the device's Initialization Device Select line (IDSEL) to one of the AD<31:0> system address lines. An IDSEL line is used as a device select line during PCI configuration read and write transactions. See *Chapter 4: Functional Interaction Between PCI Resources* for details on the IDSEL signal.

For purposes of this example, assume that the first (lowest) system address line assigned to a PCI device's IDSEL line is system address line AD<16>. The corresponding Device number would be 0. The maximum number of devices on this particular bus is 16 because only AD<31:16> are used as shown in Table 19-4.

Table 19–4 contains an example of physical PCI Device Number assignments for a single PCI bus system. Note that the 82430 HOST/PCI BRIDGE and the SIO ISA BRIDGE are used in this example. Also, the slot numbers are defined according to Figure 19–1.

Address Line	Device Number	Integrated PCI Device/Slot
16	00h	82434 (PCMC)
17	01h	On–board IDE controller
18	02h	82378IB (SIO)
19	03h	N/C
20	04h	N/C
21	05h	N/C
22	06h	PCI/System Slot 2
23	07h	N/C
24	08h	N/C
25	09h	N/C
26	0Ah	N/C
27	0Bh	N/C
28	0Ch	PCI/System Slot 4
29	0Dh	N/C
30	0Eh	PCI/System Slot 3
31	0Fh	N/C

Table 19–4: Physical PCI Device Number Assignment Example

Notice that the Single PCI platform mounted and three PCI slot assignments are not assigned contiguous PCI device numbers. Also, since PCMC and SIO PCI devices do not require an IRQ resource, the IRQ Routing Table will not contain entries for these devices.

PCI INTERRUPT PIN ROUTING

Before the IRQ Routing Table structure entry for each PCI device can be filled in, the specific routing for each interrupt pin to the PCI mappable IRQ lines must be determined. Figure 19–2 is an example of how a platform can route PCI interrupt pins to hardware interrupt request lines. Note that the actual routing of PCI interrupt pins is platform dependent. The major components of the interrupt pin routing in this example are the Hardware Interrupt Lines, the IRQ Router and the Interrupt Pin Routes.

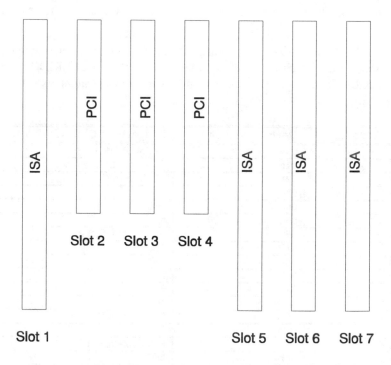

Figure 19–1: Slot Numbering Example

HARDWARE INTERRUPT LINES

The Hardware Interrupt Line (or IRQ) signals are outputs of the IRQ Router. They are inputs to the 8259–compatible hardware interrupt controllers. In this example, five IRQ lines are available for mapping to PCI devices. When a device requires servicing, it will signal the request to one of the hardware interrupt lines. See *Chapter 16: System Resources*, page **Error! Bookmark not defined.**, for details on interrupt requests and servicing.

Note that the IRQ numbers and quantity of Hardware Interrupt Lines available for mapping to PCI devices is platform dependent. It is recommended that this number should be three or greater.

IRQ ROUTER

The IRQ Router may be either a single device or group of hardware components. The function of the IRQ Router is to connect an interrupt pin of a PCI device to a specific hardware interrupt line. Once the connection is made and interrupts are enabled, the device can request servicing by generating a hardware interrupt. The inputs to the IRQ Router are called Interrupt Pin Routes. The IRQ Router allows the Interrupt Pin Routes to be mapped to any of its outputs.

> IRQ Routers vary in complexity from full crossbar switches to hardwired connections. The IRQ router should always allow selection from at least three Hardware Interrupt Lines.

INTERRUPT PIN ROUTES

Each PCI slot supports four interrupt pin signals. These signals are INTA#, INTB#, INTC#, and INTD#. Each of these four signals on each slot should be routed to an input of the IRQ Router in order to permit the connection to a hardware interrupt line. The physical paths of the various interrupt pin signals to the IRQ Router are the Interrupt Pin Routes.

> Note that the number of Interrupt Pin Routes available for mapping to PCI devices to Hardware Interrupt Line signals is platform dependent. This number ranges from one to as many interrupt pins as there are in the system. A reasonable number of Interrupt Pin Routes for a desktop system is four.

Figure 19–2 illustrates the concept of interrupt line balancing of PCI add–in card slots. In the IRQ Routing Table example there are three physical add–in card slots. These slots are associated with PCI device numbers 06h (Slot 2), 0Ch (Slot 4) and 0Eh (Slot 3). Notice that there is not a straight 1–to–1 connection of the interrupt pins between these slots. In other words, all interrupt pin A#s are not connected together, interrupt pin B#s are not connected together, and so forth. Interrupt Pin Route 0 consists of a connection of interrupt pin C# of Slot 2, interrupt pin B# of Slot 3, and interrupt pin A# of Slot 4 Wiring the individual Interrupt Pin Routes in this way allows the IRQ line load to be distributed to prevent the possibility of one IRQ line servicing all of the slots.

For example, consider the case where:

- All slot interrupt pin A#s are wired together on one Interrupt Pin Route, all INTB#s from another Interrupt Pin Route, all INTC#s, etc.

- Each PCI slot contains an add–in card

- Each add–in card uses its INTA#

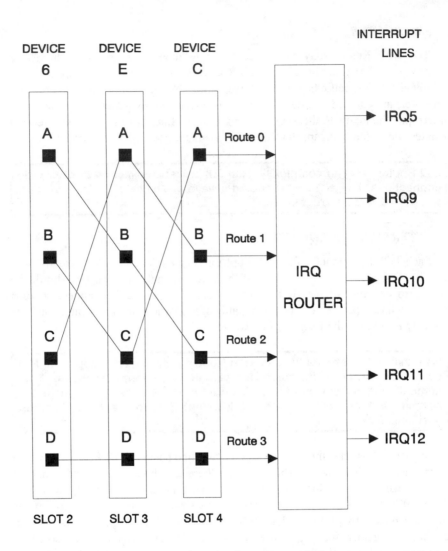

Figure 19–2: Interrupt Pin Routing Example

In this case, even though the platform supports multiple Interrupt Pin Routes, the add–in cards are forced to share one interrupt line because of the way the Interrupt Routes were wired. This would place an unnecessary latency factor on servicing the interrupts of the PCI add–in devices.

In Figure 19–2, Interrupt Pin Routes 1 and 2 are wired in a manner similar to Interrupt Pin Route 0. However, for purposes of illustration, note how Interrupt Pin Route 3 has the interrupt pin D# signal of all three add–in slots wired together. The impact to interrupt servicing to a system with this configuration depends on the number and types of multi–function devices inserted into the PCI add–in card slots at any given time.

INTERRUPT LINE MAPPING

Ultimately, either POST or operating system level software is responsible for mapping each Interrupt Pin Route to a specific Hardware Interrupt Line. Factors that influence the decision of which IRQ line to use for a specific Interrupt Pin Route are whether a LEGACY device already consumes a specific IRQ line that can be mapped to a PCI as well as IRQ line priority levels.

Offset	Size	Value	Description	Comments
0	Byte	00h	PCI bus number	PCI Bus #0
1	Byte	08h	PCI Device number (in upper 5 bits)	IDSEL connected to AD<17> Bus Device = 1
2	Byte	0FFh	Link Value for INTA#	Unique Link ID
3	Word	0100000000000000b	IRQ Bit–Map for INTA#	Route to IRQ 14 only
5	Byte	00h	Link Value for INTB#	No routing possible
6	Word	0000h	IRQ Bit–Map for INTB#	N/A
8	Byte	00h	Link Value for INTC#	No routing possible
9	Word	0000h	IRQ Bit–Map for INTC#	N/A
11	Byte	00h	Link Value for INTD#	No routing possible
12	Word	0000h	IRQ Bit–Map for INTD#	N/A
14	Byte	00h	Slot Number	00h = platform device
15	Byte	00h	Reserved	Not used

Table 19–5-A: IRQ Routing Table Example

SINGLE ROUTED PCI DEVICE

Table 19–5 is one of four IRQ routing entries in the IRQ Routing Table that would be returned for the system shown in Figure 19–2. Table 19–5 is an example of how to define the IRQ routing table structure for a device that does not have a link to any other PCI device. This means that no other PCI interrupt pins are wire–ORed with this device's interrupt pin.

> Note that the order of IRQ routing entries in an IRQ Routing Table is arbitrary.

MULTIPLE ROUTED PCI DEVICE

Table 19–4 shows that the example system also has three PCI add–in card slots. These PCI slots are labeled Slot 2, Slot 3, and Slot 4 as shown in Figure 19–1. The IRQ Routing Table entries for these three slots are shown in Tables 19–5-B through 19–5-D below. These tables are a continuation of the IRQ Routing Table example started in Table 19–5-A.

PCI DEVICE 06H:

Offset	Size	Value	Description	Comments
0	Byte	00h	PCI bus number	PCI Bus #0
1	Byte	30h	PCI Device Number (in upper 5 bits)	**IDSEL** connected to **AD<22>** Device Number = 6h
2	Byte	012h	Link Value for INTA#	Wired to Interrupt Pin Route 2
3	Word	1000111000100000b	IRQ Bit–Map for INTA#	Route to IRQ 5, 9, 10, 11, or 15
5	Byte	11h	Link Value for INTB#	Wired to Interrupt Pin Route 1
6	Word	1000111000100000b	IRQ Bit–Map for INTB#	Route to IRQ 5, 9, 10, 11, or 15
8	Byte	10h	Link Value for INTC#	Wired to Interrupt Pin Route 0
9	Word	1000111000100000b	IRQ Bit–Map for INTC#	Route to IRQ 5, 9, 10, 11, or 15
11	Byte	13h	Link Value for INTD#	Wired to Interrupt Pin Route 3
12	Word	1000111000100000b	IRQ Bit–Map for INTD#	Route to IRQ 5, 9, 10, 11, or 15
14	Byte	02h	Slot Number	Slot = 2
15	Byte	00h	Reserved	Not used

Table 19–5-B: IRQ Routing Table Example

Recall that, except for a value of zero, values for the link fields are arbitrary. The values used in Tables 19–5-B through 19–5-D were selected based on the Interrupt Pin Route numbers shown in Figure 19–2 as follows:

Link Value	Represents
10h	Interrupt Pin Route 0
11h	Interrupt Pin Route 1
12h	Interrupt Pin Route 2
13h	Interrupt Pin Route 3

This method makes it easy to identify specific link values of each slot. Example: to assign the link value of interrupt pin A# of PCI slot 1 (PCI Device Number 06h) determine which Interrupt Pin Route slot 1's interrupt pin A# signal is wired to. As Figure 19–2 shows, the Interrupt Pin Route for this case is 2. Thus, the assigned link value for the INTA# signal of slot 1 is 12h. Similarly, INTB# of slot 1 is wired to Interrupt Pin Route 1. Its assigned link value is 11h. And so on.

PCI DEVICE 0EH:

Offset	Size	Value	Description	Comments
0	Byte	00h	PCI bus number	PCI Bus #0
1	Byte	70h	PCI Device Number (in upper 5 bits)	**IDSEL** connected to **AD<30>** Device Number = 0Eh
2	Byte	011h	Link Value for INTA#	Wired to Interrupt Pin Route 1
3	Word	1000111000100000b	IRQ Bit–Map for INTA#	Route to IRQ 5, 9, 10, 11, or 15
5	Byte	10h	Link Value for INTB#	Wired to Interrupt Pin Route 0
6	Word	1000111000100000b	IRQ Bit–Map for INTB#	Route to IRQ 5, 9, 10, 11, or 15
8	Byte	12h	Link Value for INTC#	Wired to Interrupt Pin Route 2
9	Word	1000111000100000b	IRQ Bit–Map for INTC#	Route to IRQ 5, 9, 10, 11, or 15
11	Byte	13h	Link Value for INTD#	Wired to Interrupt Pin Route 3
12	Word	1000111000100000b	IRQ Bit–Map for INTD#	Route to IRQ 5, 9, 10, 11, or 15
14	Byte	03h	Slot Number	Slot = 3
15	Byte	00h	Reserved	Not used

Table 19–5-C: IRQ Routing Table Example

PCI DEVICE 0CH:

Offset	Size	Value	Description	Comments
0	Byte	00h	PCI bus number	PCI Bus #0
1	Byte	60h	PCI Device Number (in upper 5 bits)	IDSEL connected to AD<28> Device Number = 0Ch
2	Byte	010h	Link Value for INTA#	Wired to Interrupt Pin Route 0
3	Word	1000111000100000b	IRQ Bit–Map for INTA#	Route to IRQ 5, 9, 10, 11, or 15
5	Byte	12h	Link Value for INTB#	Wired to Interrupt Pin Route 2
6	Word	1000111000100000b	IRQ Bit–Map for INTB#	Route to IRQ 5, 9, 10, 11, or 15
8	Byte	11h	Link Value for INTC#	Wired to Interrupt Pin Route 1
9	Word	1000111000100000b	IRQ Bit–Map for INTC#	Route to IRQ 5, 9, 10, 11, or 15
11	Byte	13h	Link Value for INTD#	Wired to Interrupt Pin Route 3
12	Word	1000111000100000b	IRQ Bit–Map for INTD#	Route to IRQ 5, 9, 10, 11, or 15
14	Byte	04h	Slot Number	Slot = 4
15	Byte	00h	Reserved	Not used

Table 19–5-D: IRQ Routing Table—Routing Example

IRQ BIT–MAP RETURN VALUE

To illustrate what the Get IRQ Routing Options function would return for the IRQ Bit–Map value (in the microprocessor [BX] register) assume that the system is configured such that:

- Interrupt Route 0 is connected to IRQ9
- Interrupt Route 1 is connected to IRQ15
- Interrupt Route 2 is connected to IRQ9
- Interrupt Route 3 is not connected to any IRQ

In this case the value returned for IRQ Bit–Map is 1000000100000000b. This indicates that IRQ9 and IRQ15 are the only IRQs that can be used exclusively by PCI. All other IRQs can be used by other devices in the system.

Set PCI Hardware Interrupt		
PURPOSE:	This function allows the caller to request that a specific hardware interrupt line (IRQ) be connected to a specified interrupt pin of a PCI device.	

ENTRY:	[AH]	0B1h
	[AL]	0Fh
	[BH]	PCI bus number (0.255) where device is located
	[BL]	PCI Device/Function Numbers in the following format:

Bits   Description
2:0   Function Number
7:3   Device Number

[CL]   PCI device's Interrupt Pin Number to connect to IRQ line. Values are:

0AH =   INTA#
0BH =   INTB#
0CH =   INTC#
0DH =   INTD#

[CH]   Interrupt Line number (0–15), to connect to PCI device Interrupt Pin. This value corresponds directly to IRQ0–IRQ15 (i.e., 0 = IRQ0, 1 = IRQ1,..15 = IRQ15.).

16–Bit Real Mode parameters:

[DS]   Segment for BIOS data. The base address value in [DS] must resolve to F0000h. The limit value for [DS] must equal 64K.

16–Bit Protected Mode parameters:

[DS]   Selector for BIOS data. The base address value in [DS] must resolve to F0000h. The limit value for [DS] must equal 64K.

32–Bit Protected Mode parameters:

NOTE: For 32 bit code, see section 19.3.

[DS]   Selector for BIOS data.

EXIT:	[AH]	Return Code:
		00h = Successful
		81h = This PCI Function_Not_Supported
		88h = The set hardware interrupt operation failed
	[CF]	Function Completion Status
		0 = Successful
		1 = Error

SPECIAL NOTES

1.   The caller is responsible for:

- All error checking. No resource conflict should exist between the specific hardware interrupt line assigned to the PCI device and any other hardware interrupt resource in the system.

- Ensuring that the specified interrupt is configured properly (level triggered) in the interrupt controller.

- Updating PCI configuration space (i.e. Interrupt Line register at offset 3Ch) for all affected devices.

> The return status of this function should be verified for a successful completion prior to updating any Interrupt Line register.

2.   This function returns the SET_FAILED status if the requested interrupt cannot be assigned to the specified PCI device.

3.   This function will set the platform hardware to comply with the caller's request prior to returning to the caller if the requested interrupt can be assigned to the specified PCI device.

4.   Changing the IRQ routing for one device will also change the IRQ routing for other devices whose INTx# pins are WIRE–ORed together (i.e. they have the same 'link' field. See the Get PCI Interrupt Routing Options call).

5.   The IRQ line mapping affected by this routine has no affect on the PCI interrupt mapping of next system boot. No routing information is stored by this function for later use.

PCI CONFIGURATION SPACE ACCESS EXTENSIONS

There are six PCI configuration space Access Extensions. This class of PCI subfunctions permits the caller to perform read and write operations in PCI configuration space.

Read A PCI Configuration Register Byte

PURPOSE:		This function allows the caller to read a single byte from the configuration space of a specified PCI device.
ENTRY:	[AH]	0B1h
	[AL]	08h
	[BH]	PCI bus number (0.255) where device is located
	[BL]	PCI Device/Function Numbers in the following format:

Bits   Description
2:0   Function Number
7:3   Device Number

	[DI]	Configuration Space Register Number to read (0.255)
EXIT:	[AH]	Return Code:
		00h = Successful
	[CL]	Byte Value read from the PCI Configuration space Register
	[CF]	Function Completion Status
		0 = Successful
		1 = Error

SPECIAL NOTE

The PCI BIOS Specification, Revision 2.0, incorrectly states that return code 87h, Bad_Register_Number, is a valid return code. This is not the case for byte–wide read operations in the PCI configuration space. Each byte can be individually read.

Read a PCI Configuration Register Word

PURPOSE: This function allows the caller to read two contiguous bytes from the configuration space of a specified PCI device.

ENTRY:

[Ah]	0B1h
[AL]	09h
[BH]	PCI bus number (0.255) where device is located
[BL]	PCI Device/Function Numbers in the following format:

Bits	Description
2:0	Function Number
7:3	Device Number

[DI]	Configuration Space Register Number to read (0, 2, 4,.. 254)

EXIT:

[AH]	Return Code:
	00h = Successful
	87h = Function called with Bad_Register_Number
[CX]	Word Value read from the PCI configuration space
[CF]	Function Completion Status
	0 = Successful
	1 = Error

SPECIAL NOTE

The Register Number parameter, [DI], must be a multiple of two (i.e., bit 0 must be set to 0). The PCI BIOS function should return a value of 87h in the [AH] register and set the Carry Flag if this condition is not met.

Read A PCI Configuration Register Dword

PURPOSE:		This function allows the caller to read four contiguous bytes from the configuration space of a specified PCI device.

ENTRY:	[AH]	0B1h
	[AL]	0Ah
	[BH]	PCI bus number (0.255) where device is located
	[BL]	PCI Device/Function Numbers in the following format:

Bits	Description
2:0	Function Number
7:3	Device Number

	[DI]	Configuration Space Register Number to read (0, 4, 8,.. 252)

EXIT:	[AH]	Return Code:
		00h = Successful
		87h = Function called with Bad_Register_Number
	[ECX]	Dword Value read from the PCI configuration space
	[CF]	Function Completion Status
		0 = Successful
		1 = Error

SPECIAL NOTE

The Register Number parameter, [DI], must be a multiple of four (i.e., bits 0 and 1 must be set to 0). The PCI BIOS function should return a value of 87h in the [AH] register and set the Carry Flag if this condition is not met.

Write a PCI Conrfiguration Register Byte

PURPOSE:	This function allows the caller to write a single byte value to the Configuration Space Register of a specified PCI device.	

ENTRY:	[AH]	0B1h
	[AL]	0Bh
	[BH]	PCI bus number (0.255) where device is located
	[BL]	PCI Device/Function Numbers in the following format:

Bits	Description
2:0	Function Number
7:3	Device Number

	[CL]	Byte Value to Write
	[DI]	Configuration Space Register Number to Write (0.255)

EXIT:	[AH]	Return Code:
		00h = Successful
	[CF]	Function Completion Status
		0 = Successful
		1 = Error

SPECIAL NOTE:

The PCI BIOS Specification, Revision 2.0, incorrectly states that return code 87h, Bad_Register_Number, is a valid return code. This is not the case for byte–wide write operations in the PCI configuration space. Each byte can be individually written.

Write a PCI Configuration Register Word		
PURPOSE:	This function allows the caller to write a word value to two contiguous bytes of configuration space of a specified PCI device.	
ENTRY:	[AH]	0B1h
	[AL]	0Ch
	[BH]	PCI bus number (0.255) where device is located
	[BL]	PCI Device/Function Numbers in the following format:
		Bits Description
		2:0 Function Number
		7:3 Device Number
	[CX]	Word Value to Write
	[DI]	Configuration Space Register Number to Write (0, 2, 4,.. 254)
EXIT:	[AH]	Return Code
		00h = Successful.
		87h = Function called with Bad_Register_Number
	[CF]	Function Completion Status
		0 = Successful
		1 = Error

SPECIAL NOTE:

The Register Number parameter must be a multiple of two (i.e., bit 0 must be set to 0). The PCI BIOS function should return a value of 87h in the [AH] Register and set the Carry Flag if this condition is not met.

Write a PCI Configuration Register DWORD		
PURPOSE:	This function allows the caller to write a DWORD value to four contiguous bytes of configuration space of a specified PCI device.	
ENTRY:	[AH]	0B1h
	[AL]	0Ch
	[BH]	PCI bus number (0.255) where device is located
	[BL]	PCI Device/Function Numbers in the following format:
		Bits Description
		2:0 Function Number
		7:3 Device Number
	[ECX]	Dword Value to Write
	[DI]	Configuration Space Register Number to Write (0, 4, 6.. 252)
EXIT:	[AH]	Return Code
		00h = Successful.
		87h = Function called with Bad_Register_Number
	[CF]	Function Completion Status
		0 = Successful
		1 = Error

SPECIAL NOTE:

The Register Number parameter must be a multiple of four (i.e., bits 0 and 1 must be set to 0). The PCI BIOS function should return a value of 87h in the [AH] Register and set the Carry Flag if this condition is not met.

19.2 16–BIT PCI SYSTEM BIOS SOFTWARE INTERFACE

The 16 bit PCI BIOS Software Interface is provided through extensions added to the ISA compatible INT 1AH software interrupt handler. The initial function of this interrupt handler was to provide time–of–day services. However, a new function identifier, B1h, has been assigned to the System BIOS to identify requests for PCI BIOS services when an iAPX INT 1Ah instruction is executed. The individual PCI BIOS subfunctions have also been assigned unique identifiers in order to allow the caller to specify which PCI BIOS function is to be serviced.

> Using the INT 1Ah handler to service PCI based software also represents a major departure from the standard ISA System BIOS. Traditionally, all programming extensions to the ISA System BIOS have been serviced through the INT 15h Miscellaneous Extended Functions software interrupt handler.

The 16 bit PCI BIOS Software extensions operate in either the real mode, virtual–86 mode or 16:16 protected mode of the microprocessor. The PCI System BIOS extensions are under all the conditions and restraints of the ISA software interrupt mechanism that is discussed in Chapter 16. In addition, other restrictions apply. The requirements for invoking and returning from 16 bit PCI BIOS functions are listed below:

- The caller must pass parameters to the interrupt handler in the microprocessor's registers.

- Return parameters are placed in the microprocessor's registers. All other registers are preserved.

- Both the microprocessor [AH] Register and the Carry Flag (bit zero of the microprocessor Flags register) indicate the PCI BIOS function interrupt handler completion status.

- The PCI BIOS function interrupt handler will not enable hardware interrupts. The Interrupt Enable bit (bit nine of the microprocessor Flags register) is not modified.

- All PCI BIOS functions are re–entrant.

- The caller to the PCI System BIOS function must provide a minimum of 1024 bytes of stack.

- The caller must ensure that microprocessor privilege levels are set so that the PCI BIOS functions can access I/O address space without generating a protection fault.

- 16 bit Protected Mode users must invoke Real Mode PCI System BIOS extensions by simulating an iAPX INT 1Ah instruction. This is performed by pushing the Flags Register onto the stack and calling the System BIOS fixed entry point at physical address FFE6Eh. See *Chapter 16: System Resources* for details.

The microprocessor Code Segment [CS] and Data Segment [DS] should be set as follows prior to calling the INT 1Ah entry point:

[CS] Must have a base of F0000h
    Segment size must be at least 64K
    May be execute only

[DS] Should have a base of F0000h
    Segment size must be at least 64K
    May be read only

- Real Mode users have the option of using the software interrupt method or simulating the call the INT 1Ah interrupt handler.

The figure below is a partial sample program that illustrates the invocation of a 16 bit PCI BIOS function using the INT 1Ah software interrupt handler. It will request the ISA/PCI System BIOS to find an 82378IB System I/O (SIO) PCI device in the system.

```
        .
        .
        .
MOV   AH, 0B1h    ; AH <= PCI Function ID
MOV   AL, 02h     ; AL <= Find PCI Device identifier
MOV   CX, 0484h   ; CX <= SIO Device ID
MOV   DX, 8086h   ; DX <= SIO Vendor ID
MOV   SI, 00      ; SI <= command to find first SIO device
INT   1Ah         ; Call the PCI BIOS function
        .
        .
```

Figure 19–3: 16 Bit PCI BIOS Software Interrupt Programming Example

19.3 32 BIT PCI SYSTEM BIOS SOFTWARE INTERFACE

The 32 bit PCI BIOS Software Interface is more complicated than its 16 bit counterpart. The reason is that the microprocessor is in 32 bit protected mode. The Interrupt Descriptor Table that was based at physical memory address zero is no longer valid because it relies upon the microprocessor's 16 bit operating mode to compute the physical address of an interrupt vector's entry point. In addition, recall that a typical ISA System BIOS does not support a 32 bit software interface for application programs. Consequently, the 32 bit PCI BIOS support had to be developed from scratch.

BIOS32 SERVICE DIRECTORY

As Intel Architecture microprocessors become more and more powerful, operating systems running on those microprocessors are evolving into full–featured 32 bit operating systems. These operating systems still need to access System BIOS functions. However, doing this in the traditional Real Mode manner is often not realistic. The BIOS32 Service Directory was defined to allow 32 bit operating systems to determine what 32 bit BIOS functions are supported by the System BIOS. The BIOS32 Service Directory is a routine that maintains a database of all 32 bit BIOS software service types, such as PCI, supported by the platform's System BIOS.

Finding and using a specific 32 bit BIOS service involves three steps which are further defined below:

1. Determine the existence of the BIOS32 Service Directory

2. Determine the existence of a specific 32–Bit BIOS Service

3. 32–Bit BIOS Service Invocation

BIOS32 SERVICE DIRECTORY INSTALLATION CHECK

Standard ISA System BIOSs typically do not support a 32 bit software interface. Therefore, applications which require 32 bit BIOS function support must first ascertain whether this support is present in the System BIOS of the machine they are currently running on. This will allow application programs the ability to gracefully handle the 32–bit–BIOS–support–not–present condition. The verification process also prevents unpredictable results from occurring if an attempt is made to access a 32 bit BIOS service when it is not supported by the System BIOS.

In Chapter 16 it was shown that a standard ISA system ROM is allocated the physical address space from E0000h through FFFFFh. An ISA/PCI based System BIOS will contain a contiguous 16 byte data structure within this address range. This data structure must be aligned on a 16 byte boundary. Embedded in this data structure is all of the information an application program requires to verify the existence of a System BIOS that supports 32 bit BIOS services. The fields of the data structure are defined in Table 19–7 below.

> The software application is responsible for handling the condition "BIOS32 Service Directory structure not found".

Offset	Size	Description
00h	4 bytes	BIOS32 signature string in ASCII. The value of each byte follows: **Offset Hex Value ASCII Value** 0 5Fh '_' 1 33h '3' 2 32h '2' 3 5Fh '_'
04h	4 bytes	Entry point for the BIOS32 Service Directory. This is a 32 bit physical address.
08h	1 byte	Revision level of the BIOS32 Service Directory data structure. This version has revision level 00h.
09h	1 byte	The length of this data structure in 16–byte units. This data structure is 16–bytes long so this field contains 01h.
0Ah	1 byte	Checksum byte. The contents of this field forces the checksum of the complete data structure to add up to 0.
0Bh	5 bytes	Reserved. Must be zero.

Table 19–7: BIOS32 Service Directory Structure

> This data structure only confirms the existence of the BIOS32 Service Directory. It does not confirm the existence of 32 bit software services such as the 32 bit PCI BIOS extensions.

Below is a suggested algorithm for a procedure that applications can implement to verify the existence of the BIOS32 Service Directory:

1. Save registers.

2. Scan physical address E0000h for the BIOS32 signature string "_32_".

3. If found go to Step 10.

4. Add 16 to the last physical address that did not contain "_32_".

5. Compare the physical address obtained in Step 3 with FFFF0h.

6. If the physical address obtained in Step 4 equals FFFF0h then 32 bit BIOS support is not available. Save status and go to step 13.

    Stop here because the last 16 bytes of the System BIOS cannot contain the structure. This is because physical address FFFF0h contains a hard coded jump instruction to the start of the platform System BIOS code.

7. Scan the current physical address for "_32_".

8. If found go to Step 10.

9. Go to Step 4.

10. Perform a byte–wide checksum of the 16 bytes beginning at the current physical address (i.e., add the contents of bytes E0000h through byte E000Fh if you get here from Step 3)

11. If the byte checksum value obtained in Step 10 is 00h then 32 bit BIOS support is available in the platform System BIOS. Save status and go to Step 13.

12. Go to Step 4.

13. Done. Restore registers and return status to the caller.

> There may be more than one occurrence of the BIOS32 signature string " 32 " in the E0000h – FFFFFFh region. Verify the that the data checksums correctly to ensure that this is indeed the BIOS32 Service Directory data structure.

32–BIT BIOS SERVICES INSTALLATION CHECK

Offset 4 of the BIOS32 Service Directory Structure contains the entry point to the BIOS32 Service Directory routine. Support for specific 32 bit services such as PCI can be determined by calling the BIOS32 Service Directory. The BIOS32 Service Directory is invoked by doing a CALL FAR to the entry point provided in the BIOS32 Service Directory data structure. All parameters to the BIOS32 Service Directory routine are passed in registers.

Each 32 bit BIOS software service type is assigned a unique Service Identifier. This Service Identifier is a parameter passed in a microprocessor register to the BIOS32 Service Directory routine. The routine compares this value against valid Service Identifiers in its data base and returns an exist status to the caller. If the exist status is true for the specific Service Identifier, the caller is also returned information about the physical location and entry point of the service. The Service Identifier for PCI is the ASCII string "$PCI", or 49435024h. Note that the "$" is the least significant byte in the string.

> Software programs should check the System BIOS for 32 bit PCI software support only if the existence of the BIOS32 Service Directory has first been confirmed.

On the next page is the definition of the BIOS32 Service Directory routine software interface:

CALLER REQUIREMENTS

There are specific requirements for invoking the BIOS32 Service Directory routine. These are listed below:

- The caller must pass parameters to the BIOS32 Service Directory routine in the microprocessor's registers.

- The System BIOS implementor must assume that the microprocessor [CS] (Code Segment) is execute–only.

- The System BIOS implementor must assume that the microprocessor [DS] (Data Segment) is read–only.

- As a minimum, the microprocessor [CS] and [DS] descriptors must be set up to encompass the 4K physical page that contains the BIOS32 Service Directory entry point as well as the next contiguous 4K physical page.

- The microprocessor [CS] and [DS] selectors must be assigned the same base address.

BIOS32 Directory Service		
PURPOSE		Verify if 32-bit service routines are present in the System BIOS for a specific class of devices such as PCI
ENTRY:	[EAX]	Service Identifier. This is a four character string used to specifically identify which 32 bit BIOS Service is being sought.
	[EBX]	The low order byte ([BL]) is the BIOS32 Service Directory function selector. Currently only one function is defined (with the encoding of zero) which returns the values provided below
		The upper three bytes of [EBX] are reserved and must be zero on entry.
EXIT:	[AL]	Return code:
		00h = Service corresponding to Service Identifier is present.
		80h = Service corresponding to Service Identifier is not present
		81h = Unimplemented function for BIOS Service Directory (i.e. BL has an unrecognized value).
	[EBX]	Physical address of the base of the BIOS service.
	[ECX]	Length of the BIOS service.
	[EDX]	Entry point into BIOS service. This is an offset from the base provided in EBX.

- The caller must provide the BIOS32 Service Directory routine with at least 1024 bytes of stack space.

- Return parameters are placed in the microprocessor's registers. All other registers are preserved.

■ The caller must ensure that microprocessor privilege levels are set so that the BIOS32 Service Directory routine can access I/O address space without generating a protection fault.

■ The caller must execute an iAPX FAR CALL to the BIOS32 Service Directory entry point.

As an example, assume that the following BIOS32 Service Directory Structure exists in a System BIOS:

BIOS32 Service Directory Structure				Offset
'_'	'2'	'3'	'_'	00
00	0E	00	00	04
00	CE	01	00	08
00	00	00	00	0C

This structure indicates:

■ The 32 bit PCI software support is present in the platform System BIOS.

■ The physical address of the BIOS32 Directory Service is E0000h.

At this point, the presence of 32 bit BIOS software services has been determined. The next step is to access the BIOS32 Service Directory with a query for whether 32 bit PCI BIOS services are present in the System BIOS. The figure below is a partial sample program that illustrates the invocation of the BIOS32 Service Directory routine. Assume that the CS and DS descriptor 32 bit base addresses are set to 00000000h and their segment limits are set to one megabyte. This permits code and data accesses from physical address 00000000h through 000FFFFFh.

```
; Assume EDX contains the value 000E0000h
            .
            .
            .
       MOV  EAX, 49435024h   ; EAX <= PCI Service Identifier
       MOV  EBX, 0000h       ; EBX <= Function selector 0
       CALL FAR PTR EDX      ; FAR CALL to Directory Service
                             ;  entry address
            .
            .
            .
```

Figure 19–4: Partial BIOS32 Service Directory Programming Example

Assume that the return values after making this call are as shown in the table below.

Reg	Value	Description
[AL]	00h	32–Bit PCI Service is present.
[EBX]	E0000h	Physical address of the base of the 32 bit PCI BIOS service.
[ECX]	10000h	Length of the 32 bit PCI BIOS service.
[EDX]	8000h	The entry point to the 32 bit PCI BIOS service. This value is an offset from the base of the PCI service.

These return values provide the following information:

- The physical address of the base of the 32 bit PCI BIOS service is E0000h.

- The length of the 32 bit PCI BIOS service is specified as 64K or 10000h. Although the actual code length is not this great, it makes it easier for the caller to set up the protected mode descriptors for accessing the services.

- The 32 bit PCI BIOS service entry point is located at physical address E8000h.

32–BIT PCI BIOS SERVICE INVOCATION

The caller can use the returned values in the EBX and ECX registers to easily create both the CS and DS segment descriptors These descriptors contain the proper base address and segment limit that permit calls to the 32 bit PCI BIOS functions. To invoke a 32 bit PCI BIOS function after the descriptors and segment registers have been initialized, simply set up the microprocessor registers in the same manner as was for the 16 bit PCI BIOS functions. Then execute an iAPX FAR CALL to the entry point of the 32 bit PCI BIOS software services to execute the desired PCI software function.

CALLER REQUIREMENTS

The specific requirements for invoking the 32 bit PCI BIOS routines are listed below:

- At a minimum, the microprocessor [CS] and [DS] descriptors must be set up to encompass the physical ranges specified by return values in the BIOS32 Service Directory Call.

- The microprocessor [CS] and [DS] selectors must be assigned the same base address.

- The System BIOS implementor must assume that the microprocessor [CS] (Code Segment) is execute–only.

- The System BIOS implementor must assume that the microprocessor [DS] (Data Segment) is read–only.

- The caller must provide the PCI BIOS routines with at least 1024 bytes of stack space.

- The caller must ensure that microprocessor privilege levels are set so that the PCI BIOS routines can access I/O address space without generating a protection fault.

- The caller must execute an iAPX FAR CALL to the PCI BIOS entry point.

19.4 CHAPTER SUMMARY

In this chapter PCI System BIOS extensions were introduced. These software extensions allow software programmers to access and manage PCI based hardware in a platform independent manner. Each routine's purpose and register usage was described. In addition, the specific calling interfaces for both 16 bit Real Mode and 16/32 bit Protected Mode were discussed.

Several important guidelines and restrictions for invoking the PCI System BIOS extensions were introduced. These will aid the reader in producing more robust software when implementing System BIOS or higher level software.

Be aware that the BIOS32 Directory Service implementation that is described has not been adopted as an industry standard yet. However, several major System BIOS vendors are implementing it. Perform all the checks described in this chapter prior to attempting 32 bit Protected Mode accesses to PCI System BIOS functions.

CHAPTER 20

PCI DEVICE CONFIGURATION

This chapter consists of the following subchapters:

20.0 INTRODUCTION

Chapter 19 discusses the System BIOS section of the Plug–and–Play system architecture that deals with PCI Plug–and–Play Device Services. These services are used by both the System BIOS during POST and run–time as well as by the operating system level software at run–time to access the PCI hardware within the system.

In this chapter the remainder of the Plug–and–Play System BIOS software architecture as it pertains to the PCI Bus is discussed. The concepts required for dynamically configuring PCI devices during the power–up system initialization sequence are addressed. In addition, operating system level software concepts will be addressed when applicable. Note that to make the discussion more practical and to reinforce concepts discussed in the previous chapters, an ISA bus is assumed to be integrated in the system along with a single PCI bus. In addition, the discussion will assume a single microprocessor system. Although the x86/ISA bus architecture is used in the following examples, the discussion is broad enough to adapt to any computer system architecture.

For ease of understanding, this discussion is aligned with the basic program flow that an ISA compatible system's BIOS follows to initialize the system components in preparation for bootstrapping an operating system:

- System RESET
- Before–Video System Initialization

- Video Sub–System Initialization
- After–Video Initialization
- System Boot

In addition to the above, PCI Expansion ROM BIOS Initialization is also discussed in this chapter. This topic is directly related to PCI device configuration. Because of its complexity and the desire to position this information in one easy to reference location, this topic is contained in a separate subchapter.

> Note that throughout this chapter the PCI Configuration Manager, which is described in Chapter 2, is said to perform certain functions. Keep in mind that while only the PCI Configuration Manager may only be referenced, the functions described may be carried out as a result of the PCI Configuration Manager calling the PCI Device Initialization Functions, etc.

20.1 SYSTEM RESET

As we wrote in Chapter 18, *Overview of the System BIOS*, there are four typical ways to force the microprocessor to execute code starting at the system restart vector:

- Applying power to the computer system.
- Depressing the system front panel RESET button or switch (if installed).
- Simultaneously pressing the <CTRL> <ALT> <DEL> keys on the keyboard in the DOS environment.
- Jumping to the microprocessor RESET vector located at physical address FFFF0h via software instructions.

Once at the RESET vector, certain conditions must be met by the different BRIDGEs in a PCI–based system.

1. After a hard RESET, all BRIDGEs except the compatibility BRIDGE and the LEGACY bus BRIDGE must be in the disabled state. The disable state includes:

    a. The BRIDGE does not respond to I/O space accesses.

    b. The BRIDGE does not respond to memory space accesses.

    c. The BRIDGE does respond to Configuration space accesses.

2. After any type of RESET the compatibility BRIDGE must be in a state that permits the System BOOT ROM to be accessed.

3. When main memory is the only type of device on the HOST bus, the compatibility BRIDGE must respond to all accesses in I/O address space and to the memory address space between 000A0000h and 000FFFFFh. This ensures that the microprocessor is able to fetch code from the System BIOS ROM. This ROM resides on the LEGACY bus.

NOTES

A compatibility BRIDGE is a HOST BRIDGE that supports PC–compatible functionality by controlling the read/write attributes of the system memory between addresses 000800000h and 000FFFFFFh. This region is referred to as the ISA Compatibility Region.

> This BRIDGE is used to enable the shadow RAM mapping of expansion ROMs and the system ROM in the memory address region between 000C0000h and 000FFFFFh.

A LEGACY bus BRIDGE is one that actually provides the PC–compatible functionality.

> This BRIDGE incorporates PC–compatible functions compatible with devices such as the 8259 interrupt controllers, the 8254 timers, and 8237 DMA controllers.

PCIRST#

PCIRST# is an asynchronous signal on the PCI bus. Its function is to generate a hard RESET to each device on the PCI bus(s). The result is that the sequencer of each PCI device is forced to a known, power–up type state.

PCIRST# can be activated in several ways. First, the signal is always asserted during the system power–up sequence. Second, a HOST compatibility BRIDGE can and should provide a way for software to assert PCIRST#. Finally, specific hardware capable of asserting PCIRST# can be incorporated onto the platform. This circuitry is under software control.

Asserting PCIRST# after any type of RESET is required for proper system operation. This action will halt all PCI device operations that were in progress at the time of the RESET. These operations include networking device data transfer cycles and PCI video output. Asserting PCIRST# guarantees that these type of operations will not commence until after the PCI devices have been initialized, either by the System BIOS or a device driver. IF PCIRST# is not asserted after a RESET occurs the system could become inoperable. For example, if the PCI networking device was not RESET, it would attempt to continue its previous data transfer operations once the device was enabled. This could lead to data corruption in the system address space.

Some PCI based systems do not have the ability to control PCIRST# through any of the methods described above except for the system power–up RESET. Because of this the following is recommended for all System BIOS and add–in card vendors:

- The System BIOS must RESET the bus master (bit 2), memory space (bit 1) and I/O space (bit 0) control bits of each PCI device's Command Register as early in POST as possible. This will disable the PCI device functions. This includes the Command Register of each function within a multi–function device.

- If a device has an associated option ROM, the option ROM code (when it's INIT function is called) must RESET its device(s) in a device specific manner.

- If a device has an associated option ROM, the option ROM code (when its INIT function is called) may enable its bus master (bit 2) bit by setting it to 1.

- If a device does not have an associated option ROM, the device's device driver must RESET its device(s) in a device specific manner.

- The device's device driver may enable its bus master (bit 2) bit by setting it to 1 after resetting its associated PCI device(s).

PCI DEVICE BIST OPERATIONS

The Built–In Self Test (BIST) register is located at offset 0Fh of the PCI configuration space predefined header. This register is optional. The purpose of the BIST register is to control the testing of a PCI device and perform status checking on the BIST operation. To date, PCI device vendors have not implemented this register. In addition, it is not known how the individual System BIOS vendors treat this register. The usefulness of this register is questionable. For example, if the device was inoperative it is doubtful that its configuration space could be written to even initiate the BIST.

If both the System BIOS and the PCI device support the PCI configuration space BIST register, invoke the BIST after PCIRST# and before the video device initialization occurs. The following are guidelines for testing a PCI device via its BIST register:

1. The System BIOS should test all devices that support the BIST register, regardless of whether they are boot devices or not.

2. The System BIOS should wait a minimum of two seconds for BIST completion to occur.

3. The System BIOS should guarantee that the lower three bits (bus master, memory space and I/O space control bits)of the Command Register in PCI configuration space are disabled for any PCI device that fails its BIST.

4. The System BIOS should not attempt to initialize any PCI device that fails its BIST.

5. The System BIOS should not call the associate option ROM of a PCI device that fails its BIST.

6. The System BIOS should report failed devices to the user during POST any time after the video device has been initialized (assuming the video device does not fail its BIST).

7. Device drivers, applications software and the operating system should not attempt to configure and use a PCI device that fails its BIST.

20.2 BEFORE–VIDEO PCI DEVICE INITIALIZATION

OVERVIEW

Typically, only components required to enable the operation of video are initialized at this time. This includes testing and initializing the first 64K bytes of system memory in order to set up a stack. The stack is required for calling the video BIOS. If a fatal error occurs prior to video device initialization, beep codes are issued to the system speaker to identify the failure. It is at this point that any PCI bus(s) and register initialization must take place in preparation for the possible configuration of a PCI video device.

Figure 2–4 shows the design of a Plug–and–Play system that encompasses both the System BIOS and the operating system. Note in Figure 2–4 that the entry point for all Plug–and–Play device class configuration is the POST Global Device Class Configuration Manager. All Plug–and–Play device initialization in this model is accomplished by the System BIOS calling the POST Global Device Class Configuration Manager with a specific initialization request. Notice how easy it is in Figure 2–4 for the System BIOS to bypass any and all Plug–and–Play device initialization code. As will be seen, this is a very important feature of a Plug–and–Play enabled System BIOS.

EARLY PCI INITIALIZATION

One of the tasks performed by the System BIOS before video initialization occurs is to call the POST Global Device Class Configuration Manager with the *Early Plug–and–Play Device Initialization* request. This permits the POST Global Device Class Configuration Manager to invoke the early device initialization code for each Plug–and–Play device class. In the case of PCI, the POST Global Device Class Configuration Manager will call the PCI Configuration Manager with the *Early PCI Device Initialization* request. The PCI Configuration Manager will call PCI Device Initialization functions to accomplish the early PCI device initialization. Note that the PCI 16/32–bit Functions are available because the system stack is initialized at this point. However, depending on the implementation, the System Resource Manager may or may not be functional this early in POST. The System BIOS must accommodate either scenario.

PCI BUS COUNT

One of the PCI initialization tasks that should be performed early is to determine how many PCI buses exist in the system. The number of the last PCI bus must be stored by the System BIOS for both POST and run–time reference. For example, this is one of the parameters returned to the caller when INT 1Ah, function B101, Get_PCI_Bios_Present_Status, is invoked. See *Chapter 19: PCI System BIOS Software Interface* for a description of this function.

CONFIGURATION SPACE

Depending on the hardware implementation, certain PCI registers located in the 64–byte predefined Configuration Space Header may require early POST time initialization. The System Resource Manager does not need to be functional at the time these specific PCI registers and bits are initialized because specific system resources are not required. Consequently, this initialization can be accomplished early in POST. Some of the registers that may need to be initialized at this time are:

Offset	Register
06h	Status
0Ch	Cache line Size
0Dh	Latency Timer

STATUS REGISTER

The Status Register is located at offset 06h of the predefined PCI Configuration Space Header. The Status Register records system wide events that occur on the PCI bus. This register is a collection of bits. Several bits in the Status Register have the attribute type RWC. These are individual bits that are cleared to zero if the bit has the write attribute and its bit location is written with a data value of one. It is recommended (but not required) that the System BIOS clear any set status bits in this register prior to booting an operating system. The Status Register may be initialized by writing the value FFFFh to it.

CACHE LINE SIZE REGISTER

The Cache Line Size register is located at offset 0Ch of the predefined Configuration Space Header. This register specifies the system cache line size in 32 bit words. This value is fixed by the hardware implementation. System BIOS vendors can specify this value with an equate.

> For Intel 80486 class machines the value programmed into this register is 04h (16 byte–cache line size). For Intel Pentium class machines the value programmed into this register is 08h (32 byte–cache line size).

This register is implemented in any device that can generate a Memory Write and Invalidate bus cycle or in any device that provides cacheable memory to the system.

> A cache line size value of 00h has a special meaning. For master devices it indicates that the Memory Write and Invalidate command should not be used. Instead use Memory Write.
>
> For cacheable memory devices, the value 00h indicates that the system cache (if it exists) is not caching that devices memory and therefore the SBO# and SDONE signals may be ignored.

LATENCY TIMER REGISTER

The Latency Timer register is located at offset 0Dh of the predefined Configuration Space Header. The Latency Timer register specifies the Master Latency Timer value for a PCI Master when the device is on the PCI bus. A typical way for a System BIOS to configure this register is to just choose an appropriate value and use that value for all devices. 32 (approximately 1 μsec at 33 MHz) is a reasonable value.

> Higher level software, i.e. an OS heuristic, can use the knowledge of how the system is being used (server, desktop, multimedia) as well as MIN_GNT and MAX_LAT values to adjust the Latency Timer appropriately.

20.3 GENERIC PCI EXPANSION BIOS INITIALIZATION

A PCI device may have an expansion BIOS associated with it. For example, devices such as video and SCSI usually have an associate expansion BIOS either integrated on an add–in card or on the platform itself. The actual expansion BIOS code is stored in a ROM device. The expansion BIOS code is responsible for the initialization of the specific device it is associated with. In addition, some expansion BIOSs contain a system boot function. Understanding the initialization process of PCI expansion BIOSs is essential to understanding PCI device initialization.

PCI EXPANSION ROM

In Chapter 18, *Overview of the System BIOS*, the structure of an ISA compatible expansion ROM BIOS was presented. PCI has extended the ISA definition to increase the functionality of the expansion ROM contents to support new requirements and features. Below is a comparison of the ISA expansion ROM definitions.

EXPANSION ROM ACCESSES

ISA

ISA expansion ROMs can be accessed with either a byte (8–bit) or word (16–bit) access. The ISA expansion BIOS must reside in the ISA Compatibility Region within the physical address range C0000h and EFFFFh. All ISA expansion BIOSs must be visible to the microprocessor at initialization time. In addition, each ISA expansion BIOS must begin on a 2K boundary.

PCI

PCI expansion ROMs must be accessible with any combination of byte– enables. This includes byte (8–bit), word (16–bit), and DWORD (32–bit) accesses. PCI expansion BIOSs that reside within a PCI add–in card ROM device are never executed in place. They are copied from the PCI ROM to shadow RAM within the ISA Compatibility Region.

> The reason that the PCI expansion BIOS must always be copied to system RAM is because of the PCI device ROM decoder implementation. The decoder that is used to make the PCI expansion BIOS appear in the system address space may also be used for one of the other PCI configuration space Base Address Registers. If the PCI expansion BIOS were executed in place the other Base Address Register could not be accessed. PCI expansion BIOS initialization code must have access to all of its device's Base Address Registers (not including the Expansion ROM Base Address Register.

PCI expansion BIOSs that are integrated on the platform itself are typically stored in the System BIOS ROM. When the PCI expansion BIOS is integrated on the platform the System BIOS is responsible for preventing system conflicts.

> The System BIOS is still required to copy the PCI expansion BIOS to shadow RAM and to invoke the expansion BIOS initialization code.

> PCI add-in card expansion BIOSs should never be hardwired to a fixed address. There is no guarantee that an ISA LEGACY BIOS does not map to the same address space. For example, PCI and ISA video BIOSs that are based at physical address C0000h would cause a system conflict.

MULTIPLE IMAGE SUPPORT

ISA

ISA expansion ROMs contain only one expansion BIOS. There is no mechanism for supporting an ISA expansion ROM with multiple images. The ISA image must start on a 2K boundary in order for the System BIOS to detect its presence.

PCI

PCI expansion ROMs may contain several different code images. Each code image can be designed to support a specific platform, a different microprocessor, or a different function within a multifunction device. This allows add-in card manufacturers to support different hardware architectures with a single version of a physical expansion ROM. See Figure 20-1 for a description.

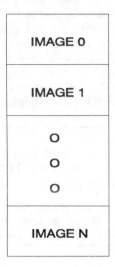

Figure 20-1: PCI Expansion ROM Structure

The first image in a PCI add-in card ROM must start at offset 00h in the ROM. Subsequent images (if any) must start on a 512-byte boundary.

PCI expansion BIOSs that are integrated on the platform itself are typically stored in the System BIOS ROM. There are no boundary requirements for integrated PCI expansion BIOSs.

PCI EXPANSION BIOS LAYOUT

As shown above, the PCI expansion ROM may contain multiple expansion BIOS images. This section discusses the contents and organization of a single generic PCI image. The data contained in each PCI expansion BIOS ROM includes two PCI device class specific sections. The first section is the PCI Expansion ROM header. This header is designed for compatibility with existing expansion BIOS headers such as the one used by ISA expansion BIOSs. The second section is the PCI data structure. This structure contains information specific to the PCI expansion BIOS as well as to the PCI device that is supported by the expansion BIOS.

EXPANSION ROM HEADER

ISA

In Chapter 18, *Overview of the System BIOS*, the structure of an ISA compatible expansion BIOS header was discussed. This structure has the format shown in Figure 20–2. See Chapter 18 for details.

Offset	Description	Value	Length
00h	Expansion ROM identification byte #0	55h	1 Byte
01h	Expansion ROM identification byte #1	AAh	1 Byte
02h	Size of expansion ROM BIOS code in 512–byte blocks.	xx	1 Byte
03h	Start of the expansion ROM BIOS initialization code. Normally contains a 3–byte JMP instruction.	xx	3 Bytes

Figure 20–2: Partial ISA Expansion BIOS Header

PCI

The structure of a PCI expansion ROM header is defined to permit compatibility with existing expansion BIOS header structures. The PCI expansion ROM header must be located at the beginning of the PCI expansion BIOS image. That is, the image begins with Expansion ROM identification byte #0. Figure 20–3 shows the format of the PCI expansion ROM header.

Offset	Description	Value	Length
00h	Expansion ROM identification byte #0	55h	1 Byte
01h	Expansion ROM identification byte #1	AAh	1 Byte
02h–17h	Reserved (processor architecture unique data)	xx	16h Bytes
018h–19h	Pointer to PCI data structure	xx	2h Bytes

Figure 20–3: Partial PCI Expansion ROM BIOS Header

IDENTIFICATION BYTES (BYTES 00H–01H)

The Expansion ROM identification bytes identify the start of an expansion BIOS. The value at byte 00h is always 55h. The value at byte 01h is always AAh.

RESERVED BYTES (BYTES 02H–17H)

This region is reserved for extensions to the standard PCI ROM header. The architecture of the system in which the PCI expansion BIOS will function determines the specific extensions that may be added. For an example, see the discussion on PC Compatible PCI Expansion ROMs later in this chapter.

POINTER TO PCI DATA STRUCTURE (BYTES 18H–19H)

This is the offset address of the PCI data structure within the current expansion BIOS image. The offset is calculated from Expansion ROM identification byte #0 of the current PCI expansion BIOS image. The address is in little endian format. For example, if the offset address of the structure is 4300h, byte 18h will contain 00h and byte 19h will contain 43h.

> The PCI data structure must be located within the first 64K of the PCI expansion BIOS image.

PCI DATA STRUCTURE

The PCI data structure contains information specific to the PCI expansion BIOS and the device it supports. Figure 20–4 shows the format of the PCI data Structure. The offset values are from the beginning of the data structure. The length values are the number of bytes each field is assigned.

> The PCI data structure must be aligned on a DWORD boundary (0000h, 0004h, 0008h, etc.).

Offset	Length	Description
0	4	Data structure signature, the string "PCIR"
4	2	Vendor Identification
6	2	Device Identification
8	2	Pointer to Vital Product DATA
A	2	PCI data structure Length
C	1	PCI data structure Revision
D	3	Class Code
10	2	Image Length
12	2	Revision Level of Code/DATA
14	1	Code Type
15	1	Indicator
16	2	Reserved.

Figure 20–4: Partial Expansion ROM BIOS Header

SIGNATURE STRING

The signature string is used to identify and validate the PCI data structure. It is used instead of a checksum. The signature string "PCIR". "P" is inserted at offset 0 of the structure, "C" at offset 1, "I" at offset 2 and "R" at offset 3.

VENDOR IDENTIFICATION

This field contains the Vendor ID of the PCI device that the image is to be used for. This field (along with the Device Identification field) is one of the criteria for selecting the proper image.

DEVICE IDENTIFICATION

This field contains the Device ID of the PCI device that the image is to be used for. This field (along with the Vendor Identification field) is one of the criteria for selecting the proper image.

POINTER TO VITAL PRODUCT DATA

This is the offset address of the Vital Product DATA (VPD) structure within the current expansion BIOS image. The offset is calculated from Expansion ROM identification byte #0 of the current PCI expansion BIOS image. The address is in little endian format. For example, if the VPD structure is at offset 4300h in the image, byte 18h will contain 00h and byte 19h will contain 43h. A value of 0000h in bytes 8 and 9 of the PCI data structure indicates that no Vital Product DATA is contained in the expansion BIOS image.

Vital Product DATA must be within the first 64K of the PCI expansion BIOS image. The content of the Vital Product DATA structure has not been defined. Until it is, ensure that bytes 8 and 9 of the PCI data structure contain 00h.

PCI DATA STRUCTURE LENGTH

The PCI data structure Length declares the length of the PCI data structure. The length of the structure is calculated from offset 0 of the structure, which is the first byte of the Signature field. This field is in little endian format and is in units of bytes.

PCI DATA STRUCTURE REVISION

The PCI Data Structure Revision identifies the revision level of the PCI Data Structure definition. The current revision level is 00h. This value should be placed at offset 0Ch of the PCI Data Structure.

CLASS CODE

Each PCI device contains an 24–bit device class code field. This device identification field is located at offset 09h of the PCI device's configuration space. The values in this field are placed into the PCI Data Structure at offset 0Dh (device programming interface), 0Eh (sub–class code), and 0Fh (base class code) of the PCI Data Structure. This information permits software to easily identify the function(s) supported by the expansion BIOS image.

IMAGE LENGTH

The Image Length declares the length of the current expansion BIOS image. This field is in little endian format and is in units of 512 bytes. This information is used to calculate the address of the next PCI expansion BIOS image (if any) in the PCI expansion ROM device.

REVISION LEVEL

The Revision Level field contains the revision level of the expansion BIOS code in the current image. Layout and interpretation of this field is vendor specific.

CODE TYPE

The Code Type field identifies the type of code contained in the current image of the PCI expansion ROM device. This field is used as part of the selection criteria for finding the proper image for a device. The following code types have been assigned:

Type	Description
0	Intel x86, PC–AT compatible
1	OPENBOOT standard for PCI

OPENBOOT is a processor architecture and system architecture independent standard. This standard addresses the implementation of device specific option ROM code. OPENBOOT is documented in IEEE Draft Std P1275/D7, January 4, 1993.

INDICATOR

Bit	Description
6:0	Reserved for future use
7	0—Another PCI expansion BIOS image follows the current image
	1—This is the last PCI expansion BIOS image in the ROM device

PCI expansion BIOSs that are integrated with the platform instead of the with PCI device (as in the case of add–in cards) will typically set bit 7 of the indicator field. It is permissible to integrate an expansion ROM BIOS that contains more than one expansion BIOS image in it on a platform. However, the System BIOS will require additional code to handle this type of implementation. This implementation is beyond the scope of this discussion.

PCI EXPANSION BIOS INVOCATION

PCI Expansion BIOSs may either be located in a PCI add–in card ROM device or integrated in a ROM device on the Platform. Each of these implementations requires special, yet distinct handling. The PCI add–in card and integrated expansion BIOS initialization functions may be performed as two distinct operations, or combined.

All system resources requested by a PCI device must be assigned prior to invoking the PCI device's expansion BIOS code. The only exception to this rule is in the case of PCI video device initialization. See Subchapter *20.5 Video Sub–System Initialization*, page 674, for details.

In addition, the device must have both the I/O (bit–0) and Memory (Bit 1) of the configuration space Command Register set to 1 (if possible, some devices do not implement read/write capability for these bits) prior to the PCI expansion BIOS invocation phase.

ADD–IN CARD PCI EXPANSION BIOS DETECTION AND SELECTION

The PCI Configuration Manager (see Figure 2–4) is responsible for locating and invoking the PCI expansion BIOS associated with a device on a PCI add–in card. The steps below describe the generic process for detecting and selecting a PCI expansion BIOS image. Specific details on this subject for PC compatibles are found in the *PC Compatible PCI Expansion ROM* section later in this chapter. Note that the System Resource Manager must be functional at this time. The steps for locating and invoking a PCI expansion BIOS associated with a device on a PCI add–in card are as follows:

1. Test the PCI device to determine if the Expansion ROM Base Address Register at offset 30h of the device's configuration space has been implemented. Do this by:

    a.   Writing FFFFFFFEh to the register. (Use PCI BIOS function B10Ch.)

    b.   Reading the DWORD contents of the register. (Use PCI BIOS, function B10Ah.)

    c.   If the value read is 00000000h, the register is not implemented. Go to DONE.

2.   The upper 21–bits read from the Expansion ROM Base Address Register indicate the address range required for mapping the PCI expansion ROM code into the system's physical address space.

The PCI Configuration Manager makes a request to the System Resource Manager for an unused contiguous memory space within the memory address map that will accommodate the PCI device's expansion ROM address requirement. The address allocated by the System Resource Manager is written to the Expansion ROM Base Address Register .

This process ensures that no system resource conflict occurs when the PCI device's expansion ROM is mapped into the system memory address space.

> A device's Expansion ROM Base Address Register should never request more than a 16 Megabyte memory area. Systems may not be able to satisfy requests larger than this.

3.   The PCI Configuration Manager turns on the Memory Space bit (bit 0) of the PCI device's configuration space Command Register (offset 4).

> The Memory Space bit in the Command Register has precedence over the expansion ROM's address decode Enable bit. PCI devices must only respond to expansion ROM accesses when the Memory Space bit and the expansion ROM's address decode enable bit are both set to 1.

4.   The PCI Configuration Manager enables the PCI device's expansion ROM address decode enable bit. This is bit 0 of the Expansion ROM Base Address Register. The PCI expansion ROM is now physically mapped to the system address space obtained in Step 2.

> PCI devices are permitted to share a decoder between the
> Expansion ROM Base Address Register and a Base
> Address Register. When the expansion ROM address
> decode is enabled the decoder is used to access the PCI
> ROM expansion BIOS. The Base Address Register is
> disabled. For this reason, device independent software
> should never access any other Base Address Register of a
> PCI device whose expansion ROM address decode is
> enabled.

5. The PCI Configuration Manager checks the first two bytes contained in the expansion ROM image for the expansion ROM identification signature, AA55h.

   If the value read is not AA55h, the PCI expansion ROM is not present. Go to Step 14, UNMAP ROM.

> This will occur if a PCI device is integrated on a platform
> and the device implemented the Expansion ROM Base
> Address Register .

6. The expansion ROM is present. The PCI Configuration Manager obtains the Pointer to the PCI Data Structure from bytes 18h and 19h of the current expansion BIOS image.

7. The PCI Configuration Manager checks the first four bytes contained in the PCI Data Structure for the PCI Data Structure Signature, the string "PCIR".

   If the value read is not *PCIR*, the PCI expansion ROM image is invalid. Go to Step 14, UNMAP ROM.

8. The PCI Configuration Manager compares the value of the Vendor Identification field in the PCI device's configuration space with the Vendor Identification field in the expansion BIOS's PCI Data Structure. If the values do not match, the expansion BIOS does not match the PCI device. Go to Step 12, NEXT IMAGE.

9. The PCI Configuration Manager compares the value of the Device Identification field in the PCI device's configuration space with the Device Identification field in the expansion BIOS's PCI Data Structure. If the values do not match, the expansion BIOS does not match the PCI device. Go to Step 12, NEXT IMAGE.

10. The PCI Configuration Manager verifies that the expansion BIOS's PCI data structure code type value is appropriate for the system. If the value is not appropriate, the expansion BIOS does not match the PCI system. Go to Step 12, NEXT IMAGE.

11. At this point a valid PCI expansion BIOS image has been found. The PCI Configuration Manager PCI copies the expansion BIOS image to system RAM. In the case of PC compatibles, the image is copied to shadow RAM in the ISA Compatibility Region.

    Go to Step 14, UNMAP ROM

12. **NEXT IMAGE**—The PCI Configuration Manager vectors here if an expansion BIOS image is detected in the PCI expansion ROM that does not match the PCI device to be initialized. The PCI Configuration Manager reads the Indicator field of the expansion BIOS's PCI data structure. If bit 7 is set to 1 there are no more expansion BIOS images in the expansion ROM. Go to Step 14, UNMAP ROM.

13. The PCI Configuration Manager reads the Image Length field of the expansion BIOS's PCI data structure. This value is multiplied by 512 to obtain the length in bytes of the current expansion BIOS image. The result of the multiplication operation is added to the base address value of the current expansion BIOS image. The result of the addition operation is the base address of the next expansion BIOS image within the PCI expansion ROM. Go to Step 5 and repeat the search for a valid image.

14. **UNMAP ROM**—The PCI Configuration Manager disables the PCI device's expansion ROM address decode by writing a DWORD value of 00000000h to the Expansion ROM Base Address Register. The PCI expansion ROM is no longer physically mapped to the system address space obtained in Step 2. If no valid image was found go to Step 16, DONE.

15. The PCI Configuration Manager PCI calls the expansion BIOS initialization code. The PCI expansion BIOS initialization code will return to the PCI Configuration Manager when the device initialization is complete.

> This step assumes that the PCI device has been allocated system resources prior to the invocation of the expansion BIOS initialization code.

16. DONE.

INTEGRATED PCI EXPANSION BIOS INVOCATION

PCI devices may be integrated on platforms. An integrated PCI device may require expansion BIOS initialization. To satisfy this configuration, a PCI expansion BIOS can be integrated in a ROM device on the platform. The System BIOS contains the information on which PCI devices have been integrated with the platform as well as the location of any integrated PCI expansion BIOSs.

The PCI Configuration Manager (see Figure 2–4) is responsible for invoking PCI expansion BIOSs associated with PCI devices that are integrated on a platform. The PCI Configuration Manager skips this section if there are no integrated PCI expansion BIOSs to be initialized. Note that the System Resource Manager must be functional at this time. The steps for invoking PCI expansion BIOSs associated with PCI devices that are integrated on a platform are as follows:

1. For the First/Next integrated PCI expansion BIOS in the system, the PCI Configuration Manager obtains the following information from the System BIOS device specific code:

    a. The location of the integrated PCI expansion BIOS.

    b. The Vendor Identification number that corresponds to the PCI expansion BIOS.

    c. The Device Identification number that corresponds to the PCI expansion BIOS.

    d. The Device/Function number of the device that corresponds to the PCI expansion BIOS.

    e. The Bus number of the device that corresponds to the PCI expansion BIOS.

2. The PCI Configuration Manager copies the PCI expansion BIOS image to system RAM. In the case of PC compatibles, the image is copied to shadow RAM in the ISA Compatibility Region.

3. The PCI Configuration Manager PCI calls the expansion BIOS initialization code. The PCI expansion BIOS initialization code will return to the PCI Configuration Manager when the device initialization is complete.

4. Go to Step 1 and repeat until no more integrated PCI BIOSs to initialize.

20.4 PC COMPATIBLE PCI EXPANSION BIOS INITIALIZATION

PCI expansion ROM images that are used in PC compatible systems require extensions to both the PCI ROM Header and to the PCI Configuration Manager ROM initialization code. These extensions apply to any image that specifies Intel x86, PC–AT compatible in the Code Type field of the PCI data structure and to any platform that is PC compatible.

PC COMPATIBLE PCI EXPANSION BIOS IMAGE

Figure 20–5 is a pictorial representation of a PC compatible PCI Expansion BIOS Image. The layout of the image incorporates an extended PCI Expansion ROM Header (discussed below) in addition to the standard PCI data structure. The image also has three lengths associated with it. These lengths are the Image Length, Initialization Length and Run-Time Length. These features are combined to make the PC compatible PCI Expansion BIOS highly optimized for PC compatible system architectures.

IMAGE LENGTH

The Image Length is the total length of the PCI expansion BIOS image. The Image Length must be greater than or equal to the Initialization Length. The Image Length is contained in the 'Image Length' field of the PCI data structure.

> The total length of the PCI expansion BIOS image is not required to be checksummed.

INITIALIZATION LENGTH

The Initialization Length is the portion of the image that contains both the PCI expansion BIOS initialization code and run–time code. The PCI Configuration Manager copies this portion of the image from the ROM device to shadow RAM in the ISA Compatibility Region. The shadow RAM is left writeable after the copy to allow the PCI expansion BIOS to have a scratch pad and to permit the initialization code to update the Run-Time checksum. The PCI Configuration Manager will then call the entry point to the PCI expansion BIOS initialization code that is located at offset 3 of the PC Compatible PCI ROM Header of the image.

The Initialization Length must be greater than or equal to the Run-Time Length of the PCI expansion BIOS image. The expansion ROM vendor must include in the image a byte–wide checksum of the PCI expansion BIOS. The checksum is calculated by adding all bytes in the Initialization Length. The checksummed value must equal 00h.

Minimize the size of the Initialization Length. This increases the possibility of fitting the PCI expansion BIOS into the unused address space of the ISA Compatible Region.

RUN-TIME LENGTH

The Run-Time Length is the portion of the image that contains the PCI expansion BIOS run–time code. This is the amount of code that will be used after the system is booted with an operating system.

PCI Expansion BIOSs should always adjust their Run-Time Size down to the smallest value possible. This consumes as little as possible of the ISA Compatibility Region (a very limited system resource). The Run-Time Length must be less than or equal to the Initialization length of the PCI expansion BIOS image. If the PCI expansion BIOS initialization code does adjust its Run-Time Size, the Run-Time Length checksum must equal zero. The checksum must be stored in the Run-Time portion of the image.

PCI DATA STRUCTURE LOCATION

The PCI expansion BIOS run–time image must contain the PCI data structure. However, if the PCI expansion BIOS image only contains initialization code, then the initialization image must contain the PCI data structure.

PC COMPATIBLE PCI ROM HEADER EXTENSIONS

Two fields, highlighted in Figure 20–6, are added to the PCI Expansion ROM Header to make it PC compatible. At offset 02h a field is added to declare the initialization size for the PCI expansion BIOS image. Offset 03h contains the entry point for the PCI expansion BIOS initialization code.

Offset	Description	Value	Length
00h	Expansion ROM identification byte #0	55h	1 Byte
01h	Expansion ROM identification byte #1	AAh	1 Byte
02h	Initialization size of the PCI expansion ROM BIOS code in 512–byte blocks.	xx	1 Byte
03h	Start of the PCI expansion ROM BIOS initialization code. Normally contains a 3–byte JMP instruction.	xx	4 Bytes
06h–17h	Reserved (processor architecture unique data)	xx	12h Bytes
018h–19h	Pointer to PCI data structure	xx	2h Bytes

Figure 20–6: PC Compatible PCI Expansion BIOS Header

PCI ADD–IN CARD EXPANSION BIOS INVOCATION

The actions that the PCI Configuration Manager takes to initialize a PC compatible add–in card PCI expansion BIOS are divided into three areas. These areas deal with the activities that take place before the PCI expansion BIOS is invoked, during the PCI expansion BIOS initialization, and after the PCI expansion BIOS initialization completes. These areas are discussed below.

Note that all system resources requested by a PCI device must be assigned prior to invoking the PCI device's expansion BIOS code. The only exception to this rule is in the case of PCI video device initialization. See Subchapter *20.5Video Sub–System Initialization*, page 674, for details.

In addition, the device must have both the I/O (bit–0) and Memory (Bit 1) of the configuration space Command Register set to 1 (if possible, some devices do not implement read/write capability for these bits) prior to the PCI expansion BIOS invocation phase.

BEFORE THE EXPANSION BIOS IS INVOKED

The PCI Configuration Manager performs the following steps before invoking each PC compatible PCI expansion BIOS integrated within the ROM device of a PCI add–in card:

1.   If the PCI expansion BIOS image is contained in a PCI add–in card ROM device, this step assumes that Steps 1 through 10 of the *Add–In Card PCI Expansion BIOS Invocation* section of this chapter have been performed.

2.   The PCI Configuration Manager asks the System Resource Manager to allocate a region of memory address space within the ISA Compatibility

Region large enough to hold the Initialization image of the PCI expansion BIOS.

If the request is denied, the PCI expansion BIOS Initialization image is too large to fit into the unused ISA Compatibility Region memory address space. A message may be printed to the CRT to notify the user.

> The device is NOT disabled in this case. The reason is that another expansion BIOS may have already initialized the device.

If the image is too large to copy into shadow RAM, go to the DONE (Step 5) in the *After the Expansion BIOS Is Called* section.

3. The PCI Configuration Manager asks the System Resource Manager to allocate an unused region of memory within the 4 gigabyte address space large enough to satisfy the alignment request of the PCI device's Expansion ROM Base Address Register.

    If the request is denied, the PCI Device requested a block of memory that cannot be granted by the System Resource Manager. A message may be printed to the CRT to notify the user. In this case, go to the DONE (Step 5) in the *After the Expansion BIOS Is Invoked* section.

> A device's Expansion ROM Base Address Register should never request more than a 16 Megabyte memory area. Systems may not be able to satisfy requests larger than this.

4. The PCI Configuration Manager checksums the expansion BIOS Initialization image within the PCI expansion ROM using the method described for ISA expansion BIOSs in Chapter 18. The length of the Initialization image is stored in the byte at offset 2 of the PCI compatible PCI Expansion ROM Header. The value at offset 2 is the number of 512 byte blocks in the initialization image.

    If the Initialization portion of the PCI expansion BIOS image fails to checksum to zero the expansion BIOS initialization code will not be invoked. Go to the DONE (Step 5) in the *After The Expansion BIOS Is Called* section if the expansion BIOS fails to checksum.

> The System Resource Manager may have allocated an extended memory address region to the PCI Device's Expansion ROM Base Address Register. The x86 microprocessor must be in either Protected Mode or Flat Mode to read the PCI add-in card expansion BIOS.

5. The PCI Configuration Manager configures the system memory controller to make the shadow RAM region allocated in Step 3 writeable. The code required for this operation is device dependent and specific to a given platform.

6. The PCI Configuration Manager copies the PCI expansion BIOS image from the PCI add-in card ROM device to the shadow RAM region allocated in Step 3.

> For efficiency, the PCI Configuration Manager may use DWORD reads of the PCI ROM device during the copy.

7. The PCI Configuration Manager checksums the expansion BIOS Initialization image within the shadow RAM using the method described for ISA expansion BIOSs in Chapter 18. The length of the Initialization image is stored in the byte at offset 2 of the PCI compatible PCI Expansion ROM Header.

IF THE CHECKSUM OPERATION FAILS:

The PCI Configuration Manager either removes the entire image from shadow RAM or erase the Expansion ROM identification byte #0 and #1 signature from the shadowed image. The address space is either allocated to a different expansion PCI BIOS or made available to the operating system after boot.

The PCI Configuration Manager configures the system memory controller to make the shadow RAM region allocated in Step 3 non-readable and non-writeable.

Set ERROR status and go to Step 8.

8. Unmap ROM

The PCI Configuration Manager disables the PCI device's expansion ROM address decode by writing a DWORD value of 00000000h to the Expansion ROM Base Address Register. The PCI expansion ROM is no longer physically mapped to the system address space.

If ERROR, go to the DONE (Step 5) in the *After the Expansion BIOS Is Called* section.

9. The PCI Configuration Manager calls the PCI expansion BIOS initialization code at offset 3 of the PCI compatible PCI Expansion ROM Header. The PCI Configuration Manager must pass the PCI expansion BIOS initialization code three parameters:

[AH]—*Number* of the PCI Bus where the device to be initialized resides.

[AL]—*Device Number* (upper 5–bits) and *Function Number* (lower 3–bits) of the device to be initialized.

EXPANSION BIOS INITIALIZATION

The Initialization function of a PCI expansion BIOS is responsible for initializing an I/O device(s) and preparing the expansion BIOS for Run-Time operation. The PCI Configuration Manager copies the PCI expansion BIOS initialization image to shadow RAM within the ISA Compatibility Region. This region ranges from C0000h to EFFFFh.

A key element in the PCI expansion initialization is that the PCI Configuration Manager must leave the shadow RAM where the expansion BIOS has been copied to writeable while the BIOS initialization function is executing. This opens up a range of possibilities to PCI expansion BIOS vendors. Single parameters as well as tables can be created/adjusted on the fly. This and other information may be stored for use by the BIOS or device drivers at run–time. This data will not be destroyed because the shadow regions where PCI BIOSs are installed are write–protected after the initialization function returns to the PCI Configuration Manager.

> PCI expansion BIOSs often hook real mode interrupt vectors. It is recommended that the Segment Offset address pairs of the hooked vectors be stored within the shadow RAM region to which the PCI expansion BIOS is assigned.

The PCI expansion BIOS initialization code must never attempt to use shadow RAM that was not allocated to it. For example, assume that an expansion BIOS is 8K, and that it will be based at C8000h–C9FFFh (8K). However, the memory controller is only capable of manipulating shadow RAM on a 16K granularity. When the expansion BIOS initialization function is invoked the shadow RAM region between C8000h and CBFFFh (16K) is writeable. Another expansion BIOS may be based at CA000h–CBFFFh (8K). If the BIOS based at C8000h wrote any data into an address between CA000h–CBFFFh, that BIOS would be corrupted. There is a high probability that the system will crash when the code between CA000h–CBFFFh is attempted to be executed.

Another feature of the PCI initialization function is that the expansion BIOS can adjust its size field. This will conserve memory in the ISA Compatibility Region. This is possible because the shadow RAM is writeable at initialization time. This means that the Initialization Size and Run-Time Size can be different. There are three requirements that must be met when the expansion BIOS size is adjusted:

1. The size field at offset 2 of the PCI expansion BIOS Header must be updated to reflect the Run-Time image size.

2. The Run-Time size must be less than (or equal to) the Initialization Size.

There is no requirement that the Run-Time size of a PCI expansion BIOS be adjusted down from the Initialization Size. However, the Run-Time Size should never be set greater than the Initialization Size. A Run-Time size that equals 00h indicates that the PCI expansion BIOS did not install a run–time image. This is the only mechanism that PCI expansion BIOS vendors should use to declare that there is no Run-Time BIOS image for the device. When a Run-Time Size is set to 00h, the expansion BIOS does not have to checksum its BIOS.

3. The Run-Time BIOS must checksum to zero as described in Chapter 18.

As an example of a PCI expansion BIOS initialization, consider the case where there are two of the same PCI device, in the system. These are the only PCI devices in the system. Each device has an identical expansion ROM BIOS associated with it. The initialization size of the expansion BIOS is 16K. The first expansion BIOS is copied to shadow RAM based at C8000h–CC000h (16K). The PCI Configuration Manager passes the bus location and device/FUNCTION Number of the device to its expansion BIOS. The expansion BIOS can determine the device associated with it. The expansion BIOS can then use the FIND_DEVICE PCI routine to locate all of the other devices in the system that it can support. The expansion BIOS can then initialize its own device as well as all other devices in the system that it can service. The expansion BIOS can build a table of its device system configuration table in shadow RAM. This table can be used at run–time. Finally, the expansion BIOS can adjust its size, say to 8K, for run–time operation. This makes the first expansion BIOSs run–time size address region from C8000h–C9FFFh (8K). The expansion BIOS returns to the PCI Manager when its initialization function is complete.

The PCI Configuration Manager adjusts the system memory map to account for the change in the expansion BIOSs size (how this is accomplished is explained in the *After the Expansion BIOS Is Called* section). Now assume that the next BIOS to be initialized is the second PCI expansion BIOS. The second 16K BIOS image will be copied to address region CA000h–CDFFFh (16K). The PCI Configuration Manager passes the bus location and device/FUNCTION Number of the device to its expansion BIOS. By using a device specific mechanism, the second PCI expansion BIOS detects that its device has already been initialized. The BIOS initialization code understands that only one image of itself has to be in shadow RAM. The second expansion BIOS therefore sets its Run-Time Size to 00h and simply returns to the PCI Configuration Manager. The PCI Configuration Manager adjusts the system memory map to account for the disappearance of the second expansion BIOS. The next BIOS that fits would be copied to shadow RAM at CA000h.

AFTER THE EXPANSION BIOS IS CALLED

The PCI Configuration Manager performs the following steps after invoking each PC compatible PCI expansion BIOS initialization code integrated within the ROM device of a PCI add–in card:

1. When the device initialization is complete, the PCI expansion BIOS initialization code returns to the PCI Configuration Manager.

2. The PCI Configuration Manager configures the system memory controller to make the shadow RAM region allocated in Step 3 read–only. The code required for this operation is device dependent and specific to a given platform.

3. The PCI Configuration Manager checks the byte value of the Run-Time Length at offset 2 of the shadowed PCI expansion BIOS image:

    A. If the Run-Time Length equals 00h, the PCI expansion BIOS did not install a run–time image. This is the **only** mechanism

671

that PCI expansion BIOS vendors should use to declare that there is no Run-Time BIOS image for the device.

> A typical example of this is when a SCSI BIOS only detects a CD ROM device. Current SCSI BIOSs do not support CD ROM devices. Consequently, there is no reason for the SCSI BIOS to remain in system memory.

The PCI Configuration Manager:

1.   Asks the System Resource Manager to deallocate the memory address space that the PCI expansion BIOS was allocated.

2.   Configures the system memory controller to make the shadow RAM region allocated in Step 3 writeable.

3.   Then either removes the entire image from shadow RAM or erases the Expansion ROM identification byte #0 and #1 signature, AA55h, from the shadowed image. The freed address space is either allocated to a different expansion PCI BIOS or made available to the operating system after boot.

4.   Configures the system memory controller to make the shadow RAM region allocated in Step 3 non–readable and non–writeable.

5.   Go to Step 5 DONE.

B.   If the Run-Time Length is greater than the Initialization Length the system is unstable.

> This is considered a CATASTROPHIC error. It should NEVER happen. One reason is because the PCI expansion BIOS code may have overwritten a previously installed expansion BIOS. An error message will be printed. In addition, the System BIOS vendor can take one of several actions if this occurs: Halt, Continue–on–error, etc.

4.   The Run-Time image is checksummed.

If the checksum operation fails:

The PCI Configuration Manager either removes the entire image from shadow RAM or erases the Expansion ROM identification byte #0 and #1 signature from the shadowed image. The address space is either allocated to a different expansion PCI BIOS or made available to the operating system after boot.

The PCI Configuration Manager configures the system memory controller to make the shadow RAM region allocated in Step 3 non–readable and non–writeable only if the region is not used by another device.

Set ERROR status and go to Step 5.

5.   DONE.

Print error message if error occurred.

PCI INTEGRATED EXPANSION BIOS INITIALIZATION

The PCI Configuration Manager performs the following when invoking the initialization code of a PCI expansion BIOS integrated with the platform:

1.   If the PCI expansion BIOS image is integrated on the platform, this step corresponds to Step 3 of the *Integrated PCI Expansion BIOS Invocation* section of this chapter.

2.   The PCI Configuration Manager asks the System Resource Manager to allocate a region of memory address space within the ISA Compatibility Region large enough to hold the Initialization image of the PCI expansion BIOS. If the request is denied, the PCI expansion BIOS Initialization image is too large to fit into the unused ISA Compatibility Region memory address space. A message may be printed to the CRT to notify the user. In this case go to Step 9, Done.

3.   The PCI Configuration Manager configures the system memory controller to make the shadow RAM region allocated in Step 3 writeable. The code required for this operation is device dependent and specific to a given platform.

4.   The PCI Configuration Manager copies the PCI expansion BIOS image from the memory location specified by the System BIOS to the shadow RAM region allocated in Step 2.

5.   The PCI Configuration Manager checksums the expansion BIOS Initialization image within the shadow RAM using the method described for ISA expansion BIOSs in Chapter 18. The length of the Initialization image is stored in the byte at offset 2 of the PCI

compatible PCI Expansion ROM Header. If the checksum operation fails:

The PCI Configuration Manager either removes the entire image from shadow RAM or erases the Expansion ROM identification byte #0 and #1 signature from the shadowed image. The address space is allocated to a different expansion PCI BIOS or made available to the operating system after boot.

The PCI Configuration Manager configures the system memory controller to make the shadow RAM region allocated in Step 3 non–readable and non–writeable.

Set error status and go to step 9, Done.

6. The PCI Configuration Manager calls the PCI expansion BIOS initialization code at offset 3 of the PCI compatible PCI Expansion ROM Header. The PCI Configuration Manager must pass the PCI expansion BIOS initialization code three parameters:

    [AH]—BUS Number of the PCI device to be initialized.

    [AL]—Device Number (upper 5–bits) and Function Number (lower 3–bits) of the device to be initialized.

7. The PCI expansion BIOS initialization code is executed as described in the Expansion BIOS Initialization section

8. The remainder of the PCI integrated expansion BIOS initialization is the same as the After the Expansion BIOS Is Called section. Reference it for details.

9. DONE

    Print error message if error occurred.

20.5   VIDEO SUB–SYSTEM INITIALIZATION

OVERVIEW

The power–up video device is detected and initialized during the Video Sub–System Initialization. As a minimum the system may have a monochrome device, VGA compatible device or combination of both. In a system that supports more than one type of bus, such as the ISA and PCI combination used in this discussion, the initialization sequence for video is more complex because the System BIOS must determine which video device to enable. An initialization sequence that handles both PCI and non-PCI video devices is presented. This initialization sequence gives precedence to video devices on the ISA bus. This is because LEGACY ISA add–in cards do not come up disabled at power–up, while all PCI compliant devices (except the compatibility BRIDGE and the LEGACY bus BRIDGE) power–up in a disabled state.

VIDEO DEVICE LOCATIONS

Video devices can be located in several different areas in an ISA/PCI based system as follows:

1. ISA add–in card slot: Monochrome device installed.

2. ISA add–in card slot: VGA compatible device installed.

3. Integrated on the ISA bus on the platform: VGA compatible device installed.

4. One or more PCI add–in card slots: VGA compatible device installed.

5. Integrated on the PCI bus on the platform: VGA compatible device installed.

6. A combination of one ISA monochrome add–in video card, one ISA VGA compatible add–in video card along with one or more PCI VGA compatible video devices. The PCI video devices may be integrated on the platform, installed in add–in card slots, or a combination of both.

The fundamental question is: Which VGA compatible video device should the system use?

VIDEO DEVICE SELECTION

The System BIOS is responsible for the selection and initialization of the VGA compatible video device that the system will use during the POST and bootstrapping process. A precisely defined method for the video device selection is required. This method must handle LEGACY (a standard ISA VGA compatible device in this example) and Plug–and–Play video devices. The video device selection algorithm presented in this section uses the following assumptions.

1. VGA compatible video devices always have precedence over monochrome video devices. Except for implementations such as serial port video redirection, monochrome video devices are the POST and bootstrapping video device only if a VGA device is not detected in the system.

> The video device used for the POST and bootstrapping video is referred to as the primary video device.

2. LEGACY video devices (such as ISA VGA compatible video devices) always have precedence over Plug–and–Play video devices. This is because the best way to avoid system resource conflicts is to give precedence to those devices which cannot be programmatically disabled and whose exact system resource consumption cannot be determined.

3. Add–in video devices always have precedence over video devices integrated onto the platform. The reason is that it requires special effort to add a video card to the system when video is available from the platform. Under normal circumstances a user would not install a video card in this situation unless its video output was desired.

> Because of the dynamic configuration capabilities of PCI devices, the Setup Utility can have an option that permits the user to select off–board vs. on–board PCI video as the default power–up video device.

4. The System BIOS previously RESET the bus master (bit–2), memory space (bit–1) and I/O space (bit–0) control bits of each PCI video device's Command Register to 0 prior to the video device check. This ensures that no PCI video device is active on a PCI bus.

5. The System BIOS only searches for a Plug–and–Play VGA compatible video device if it determines that no LEGACY VGA compatible video device is present in the system.

6. The System BIOS will attempt to initialize and use the first Plug–and–Play VGA compatible video device detected in the system. All other Plug–and–Play VGA compatible video devices in the system remain uninitialized until the time when non–Plug–and–Play video devices are initialized. At that time, non–boot video devices are initialized along with non–video devices. This ensures that system resources are properly allocated to all non–boot PCI video devices found in the system. This is performed to allow video device drivers to function with non–video boot devices after boot.

7. The expansion BIOS of the primary Plug–and–Play VGA compatible video device such as PCI is always based at physical address C0000h.

In some systems the active VGA video BIOS can be located at either physical address C0000h or E0000h. In regard to Plug–and–Play VGA compatible video devices such as PCI, this capability extends beyond the scope of this discussion.

8.   The LEGACY ISA expansion ROM BIOS never exceeds a size of 32K.

The manner in which platform PCI slots are assigned is key to achieving a clean video solution. Hardware designers that integrate PCI video onto the platform should assign the device select lines so that the PCI add–in slots are assigned to either all higher or all lower device selects than the integrated PCI video device. The integrated PCI video device select line should never be interleaved with the PCI add–in card select lines.

By assigning the PCI device select lines in this manner the System BIOS can easily search up from the lowest device found on the bus or search down from the highest device found on the bus for the first video PCI device found. By using this method, the System BIOS can handle on–board and add–in PCI video devices with little or no special casing software.

It is recommended that integrated devices be placed on PCI Bus 0 with a device select line lower than the one assigned to the first PCI add–in card slot. This will avoid potential problems on both single PCI bus systems as well as multiple PCI bus implementations.

ADD–IN ISA VIDEO DEVICE DETECTION AND INITIALIZATION

It is relatively easy to detect whether an ISA VGA compatible device is present in the system when all other VGA compatible devices are disabled. The standard ISA video expansion ROM BIOS is assumed to always be based at physical address C0000h.

The System BIOS can verify that a valid expansion ROM is present at this address by following the guidelines in *Chapter 18: Overview of System BIOS.* See the *Post Expansion* section entitled *Expansion ROM BIOS Detection.*

If a valid expansion ROM BIOS is found at physical address C0000h, the System BIOS will assume that it is an ISA VGA compatible video BIOS. The System BIOS will invoke the initialization code of the video BIOS. For an expansion of how this is performed, see Chapter 18, the *POST Expansion ROM BIOS Initialization* section.

Once the video BIOS has completed its initialization sequence, the system will have video output from the ISA VGA compatible device. INT 10h video requests will be serviced by the ISA Video BIOS instead of the System BIOS from this point on.

INTEGRATED ISA VIDEO DEVICE INITIALIZATION

Some platforms have an integrated ISA VGA compatible video device. If this device is enabled, then it will be the one selected by the System BIOS to provide video output to the system CRT. The location of an integrated video expansion ROM BIOS that supports the on–board ISA video device complicate matters.

The location of the video expansion ROM BIOS that supports the integrated LEGACY ISA video device is system dependent. Special handling may be required by the System BIOS in order to locate and initialize an integrated LEGACY ISA video BIOS. Below is a list of some of the different methods that platform designers use to integrate the ISA video device onto the platform. Note that the System BIOS should give precedence to an ISA add–in video card. In this case the integrated video device should be disabled and the integrated video BIOS should not be invoked.

1. The system platform incorporates a ROM device that contains the ISA video BIOS code. This ROM device is decoded beginning at physical address C0000h. The System BIOS invokes the LEGACY ISA VGA BIOS initialization code at address C0000h.

2. The video BIOS code is integrated into the ROM device(s) that also contains the System BIOS code. The system platform incorporates a chip set capable of mapping the section of the System BIOS ROM that contains the video BIOS code directly to physical address C0000h. The System BIOS invokes the LEGACY ISA VGA BIOS initialization code at address C0000h after the mapping has been enabled.

3. The video BIOS code is integrated into the ROM device(s) that also contains the System BIOS code. However, the system platform does not incorporate a chip set capable of mapping the section of the System BIOS ROM that contains the video BIOS code directly to physical address C0000h. The System BIOS copies the video BIOS code from the System ROM to the 32K of shadow RAM based at physical address C0000h. The System BIOS invokes the LEGACY ISA VGA BIOS initialization code at address C0000h after the shadow function is completed.

4. The video BIOS code is integrated into the ROM device(s) that also contains the System BIOS code. This code is located at a fixed location

that is visible at all times to the microprocessor. (e.g.; physical address E0000h). The System BIOS special cases this implementation and invokes the LEGACY ISA VGA BIOS initialization code at E0000h instead of C0000h.

There are deviations on the above methods. However, regardless of the implementation, the System BIOS is responsible for locating the LEGACY ISA video device and calling the video BIOS initialization code.

Finally, the System BIOS must bypass the code that detects and initializes a Plug–and–Play video device as the POST and bootstrapping video device whenever a LEGACY video device is detected and initialized first.

ADD–IN PCI VIDEO DEVICE DETECTION AND INITIALIZATION

In the case of Plug–and–Play video device initialization, the System BIOS first determines that no LEGACY video device is installed in the system. Once the determination is made that no LEGACY video device is installed, it is valid for the System BIOS to request that a Plug–and–Play video device be searched for and, if found, initialized as the primary video device.

In the example system, only LEGACY ISA and PCI video devices can be installed in the system. Note that if more than one class of Plug–and–Play devices is integrated into the system (and both device classes support video devices) the video device detection and initialization algorithm requires a slight modification. The System BIOS vendor must extend the example hierarchical video device detection and initialization scheme so that each Plug–and–Play device class in turn has the opportunity to install its video device. Figure 20–7 shows a flow chart of an implementation that supports two Plug–and–Play device classes.

The PCI primary video device initialization code will likely be performed separately from all other PCI device initialization code. The reason is that it is highly desirable to have screen output operational prior to any non–video PCI device initialization. This is because configuration information and error reporting are infinitely easier when screen output is functional.

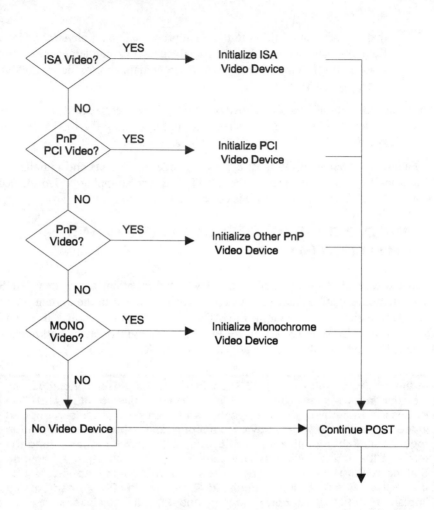

Figure 20–7: Video Selection Heirarchy

This discussion assumes that in all cases the PCI video device BIOS size is 32K. Like all PCI expansion BIOSs, the PCI video BIOS must be copied to shadow RAM. In most PCI based systems the shadowed PCI video BIOS will be absolutely located at physical address C0000h–C7FFFh.

To locate and initialize a PCI video add–in card in an ISA/PCI only based system according to Figure 2–4 the following will be performed:

1. The System BIOS calls the POST Global Device Class Configuration Manager with the POST Global Device Class Configuration Manager.

2. The POST Global Device Class Configuration Manager calls the PCI Configuration Manager with the *Initialize PCI Video Device* request.

3. The PCI Configuration Manager calls the PCI Device Initialization Function that is responsible for PCI video initialization.

4. By invoking the Get_PCI_Bios_Present_Status INT 1Ah PCI Function, the PCI Video Device Initialization Function can obtain the number of the last PCI Bus to search. This function returns the number of the last PCI bus in the system. In this example, the value returned will be 00h, indicating that the system contains one PCI bus.

5. Depending on the system implementation, the PCI Video Device Initialization Function will either begin its scan for a video device at the highest PCI bus number and PCI Device Number or at the lowest PCI bus number and PCI Device Number. This search includes multi-function devices.

> **The Find Device and/or Find PCI Class Code INT 1Ah PCI Functions can be used to quickly locate a PCI video device.**

6. Once an add–in card PCI video device has been found, its BIOS will be installed as described in the subchapter PCI Expansion ROM BIOS Initialization of this chapter.

> **Plug–and–Play video devices are guaranteed the use of standard VGA system resources at video BIOS initialization time. Other system resources such as a video frame buffer address or interrupt line may not be assigned until later and thus are not guaranteed at this time.**

7. The PCI Video Device Initialization Function returns status to the System BIOS declaring that PCI software has initialized the primary video device. The System BIOS then knows to halt the search for the primary video device.

INTEGRATED PCI VIDEO DEVICE INITIALIZATION

PCI based platforms may include an integrated PCI VGA compatible video device. Like the integrated ISA video device, the System BIOS must incorporate special software to handle this configuration. Again, note that the System BIOS will typically give precedence to an ISA or PCI add–in video card over an integrated video device for the reasons described earlier in this chapter.

INTEGRATED PCI VIDEO BIOS LOCATION

The physical location of the video expansion BIOS that supports the integrated PCI video device is system dependent. The most common implementations place the PCI video BIOS in the System ROM device along with the System BIOS code. The address space the System ROM device consumes is either 64K in size at physical address F0000h–FFFFFh or 128K in size at physical address E0000h–FFFFFh. The latter size is typical in platforms that integrate device expansion BIOSs.

VIDEO DEVICE INITIALIZATION

The process used to locate and initialize an integrated PCI device is identical to steps 1 through 5 that are used to locate and initialize a PCI video add–in card. In fact, when the PCI Video Device Initialization Function locates a video device, it does not know if the device even has a BIOS that can be manipulated via PCI configuration space. If the first PCI video device located is the integrated device, the PCI Video Device Initialization Function will discover that there is no video BIOS associated with the device. In this case PCI Video Device Initialization Function will query the device dependent code for the location of an integrated PCI video BIOS. The query is carried out by comparing the PCI video device vendor identification number and device identification number against the vendor identification number and device identification number associated with the integrated PCI video BIOS. If the compare is positive, the integrated PCI video BIOS will be installed as described in the subchapter PCI Expansion ROM BIOS Initialization of this chapter that discusses integrated BIOSs. The PCI Video Device Initialization Function will return status to the System BIOS declaring that PCI software has initialized the primary video device.

HANDLING A NO–BIOS CONDITION

In the event that there is not a match between the PCI video device and the integrated PCI video BIOS the PCI Video Device Initialization Function will still return status to the System BIOS declaring that PCI software has initialized the primary video device. This is because the System BIOS cannot determine what the user's intentions are. For instance, the user may have inserted a PCI video add–in card into the system that does not have a video BIOS associated with it. In any case, the assumption is made that a run–time device driver will initialize the PCI video device during the operating system boot sequence.

> The no match algorithm presented above may vary among System BIOS vendors. This situation might be a good candidate for a Setup Utility option that would allow the user to stop the search in this event or continue looking for another video device.

20.6 SYSTEM RESOURCE REGISTRATION

SYSTEM RESOURCE MAP

Figure 2–4 contains an element called the System Resource Map. The System Resource Map is a list of all allocated (assigned) system resources in a given system. This information is used to allocate the remaining system resources to devices that have not been assigned resources. The System Resource Map data is stored in non–volatile system memory. This memory is typically either CMOS RAM or a Flash ROM device. The format of the data as well as how the storage devices are programmed with the data is beyond the scope of this document. As Figure 2–4 shows, both the System Resource Manager (System BIOS Level—POST) and Disk Based Configuration Utilities (Operating System Level—Run-Time) access the System Resource Map for the purpose of allocating system resources. To ensure a system that is free of resource conflicts, a System Resource Map that is stored in non–volatile memory must be implemented in the system.

SYSTEM RESOURCE MANAGER

In a Plug–and–Play environment, the System BIOS is responsible for resource management during POST. Figure 2–4 contains an element called the System Resource Manager. The System Resource Manager is responsible for allocating (assigning) and deallocating (removing) system resource assignments to/from devices in the system. During POST, the System Resource Manager maintains the list of all currently allocated system resources in the System Resource Map.

ALLOCATION REQUEST PHASE

System resource allocation requests can be one of two types. The first type of request is non–specific. When this type of request is used, the device requiring the resource does not care which resource is assigned. The second type of request is a specific request. The device requiring the resource needs a specific resource assigned to it.

During the request phase of a resource allocation cycle the System Resource Manager executes extensive error checking on the request. An error will occur if the resource is not available (the System Resource Map indicates that the resource is assigned to another device or the resource type is exhausted beyond the device's requirement) or if the request is non–compliant (the system resource request is not within the bounds of acceptable limits for the specific device class—for example, a PCI device requesting more than 256 contiguous bytes of I/O space with one request).

ALLOCATION GRANT PHASE

During the grant phase of a resource allocation cycle the System Resource Manager updates its list (registers the system resource assigned to a device in the System Resource Map) of allocated resources to account for the resource assignment. The System Resource Manager then returns the resource allocation to the caller.

DEALLOCATION REQUEST PHASE

System resource de–allocation requests must be specific requests. This means that the caller must provide the correct type of the resource to deallocate, the exact base address (if I/O, DMA, or Memory) and amount (size) of the assigned resource, or, as in the case of IRQs, the reference value of the assigned resource. If the parameters are correct, the System Resource Manager will remove the resource from the System Resource Map This 'frees' the resource. Depending on the hardware implementation the freed resource may be assigned to other devices within the system.

MANAGING SYSTEM RESOURCES

To successfully manage system resources, the System BIOS must be aware of three things:

- What are the actual system resources available in the system. These include hardware interrupts, I/O ports, system memory and DMA channels.

- What are the different types and attributes of the system resources. For example, some interrupts in a PC compatible system may be shareable while others are not.

- At a given moment, which system resources have been allocated (assigned to devices).

RESOURCE TYPES

The System BIOS is aware of all system resources that are or may be consumed by the platform. This awareness encompasses both LEGACY and Plug–and–Play devices integrated on the platform. These resources are divided into two categories: fixed and dynamic.

IXED RESOURCES

PC Compatible platforms contain several fixed resources that are consumed by the platform. These resources are not configurable and must be assigned to the platform for successful operation. The System BIOS is aware of all fixed system resources that must be allocated to the platform. For example, in a PC compatible system IRQ0 and IRQ2 are always consumed by the platform. These and other fixed platform resources may not be assigned to any other device in the system. During POST the System BIOS must ask the System Resource Manager to allocate (assign and register) all fixed system resources to the platform (see figure 2–4). This activity occurs prior to assigning dynamic system resources to any PCI device. In addition, platform fixed resource requests are always specific system resource requests. Note that in a properly configured system, no resource conflicts should occur when performing fixed system resource allocations.

DYNAMIC RESOURCES

Dynamic system resources are resources that may or may not be consumed by the system. For example, the platform may contain an integrated device that provides a serial port function. This serial port may be assigned one of several I/O port ranges as well as one of several IRQs. Depending on the implementation, the System BIOS can execute either a specific or non–specific request for each resource allocation.

Note that devices such as serial ports are typically configurable when it comes to assigning system resources to them. These devices may be enabled or disabled, depending on the system configuration. The System BIOS is responsible for determining if the various devices (serial ports, parallel ports, IDE controllers, etc.) are enabled. If the devices are enabled, the System BIOS, in conjunction with the System Resource Manager, must assign system resources to the devices for successful operation. Again, the System Resource Manager must maintain a list of allocated system resources.

LEGACY VS. PLUG AND PLAY DEVICES

The System BIOS is aware of all system resources that are requested by Plug–and–Play devices. The geographical location of Plug–and–Play devices (platform vs. add–in card) is not relevant. The reason is that the System BIOS can identify each Plug–and–Play device in the system as well as identify the device's system resource requirements.

In contrast, identifying add–in card LEGACY devices and their system resource requirements is, in most instances, beyond the capability of the System BIOS. To avoid system resource conflicts, an operating system level application such as a Disk Based Configuration Utility (shown in Figure 2–4), should be used to allocate system resources to LEGACY devices. This utility is capable of accessing the System Resource Map to obtain the system resource allocation data. The Disk Based Configuration Utility uses this information to recommend specific system resource assignments for the various LEGACY devices. If the recommendations are accepted, the System Resource Map is updated to reflect the resource consumption.

SUMMARY

System resources used by both the platform and LEGACY add–in cards should be registered in the System Resource Map. This should be performed prior to the dynamic configuration of Plug–and–Play devices. Proper system resource registration ensures that no conflicts will occur when allocating the remaining system resources to Plug–and–Play devices.

20.7 AFTER–VIDEO PCI DEVICE INITIALIZATION

OVERVIEW

The remainder of system memory is tested and initialized. Device initialization continues. If a device has an associated ROM, the ROM will be called by the System BIOS to permit the ROM to configure the system for its device. In a PCI based system all non-PCI devices should be configured and initialized first. This ensures that no resource conflicts will occur when PCI devices are assigned their system resources. A method for initializing PCI devices while avoiding system resource conflicts is presented. Again, only one PCI Bus is assumed. In addition, this discussion assumes that the PCI Configuration Manager is responsible for initializing all PCI devices in the system.

PCI DEVICE INITIALIZATION

There are several steps involved in initializing a PCI device. First, the device has to be detected. Then its resource requirements must be determined. System resources must be allocated to the device. Finally, the device must be enabled for system operation. This section discusses how to initialize one PCI device.

VENDOR ID CHECK

The first requirement for initializing a PCI device is to locate the device. To determine if a PCI device is present on the PCI bus do the following:

1. Read the Vendor ID register of Function 0. If a value other than FFFFh is read, then the device is present.

2. Determine if the device is a single function or multi–function device: Read the Header Type register, located at offset 0Eh of the PCI

Configuration Space Header. If bit seven is not set it is a Single-Function Device; otherwise it is a multi–function device.

3. If the device is a multi–function device, for each function, one through seven: Read the Vendor ID register of Function [1...,. 7]. If a value other than FFFFh is read, then the function is present.

ASSIGN SYSTEM RESOURCES

See *Chapter 17: PCI Configuration ADDRESS Space* for an in–depth discussion of each of the PCI Configuration Space Registers mentioned below. In addition, only valid system resource request are assumed for this discussion.

ALGORITHM

The PCI device has been located on Bus 0. The PCI Configuration Manager now performs a three-step process to assign system resources to the device in a device independent manner:

1. Determine the system resource requirements.

2. Request the System Resource Manager to allocate the required resources.

3. Program the PCI device with the allocated system resources.

In the event that a PCI device cannot be assigned all of the resources it requests, the PCI Configuration Manager will attempt to assign as many resources as possible. However, the PCI Configuration Manager will leave the device disabled. An expansion BIOS or device driver associated with the PCI devices may be able to function with the resource that were assigned. However, the expansion BIOS or devices driver must first initialize their device.

HARDWARE INTERRUPT LINE

The PCI Configuration Manager reads the PCI device's Interrupt Pin register. If the value of the register is zero the PCI device does not request a hardware interrupt. If the value of the register is between one and four the PCI device is requesting that a hardware interrupt be assigned to one of its interrupt pin lines.

1. The interrupt pin mappings are as follows:

    1   INTA#

    2   INTB#

    3   INTC#

    4   INTD#

2. The PCI Configuration Manager calls the System Resource Manager with a request for an IRQ line. The PCI Configuration Manager passes the Interrupt Pin register value to the System Resource manager along with the BUS Number and device/FUNCTION Number of the device.

3. The System Resource Manager determines which hardware interrupt line to assign to the device based on the capabilities of the platform's IRQ line mapping functions.

4. The System Resource Manager calls a PCI Device Initialization Function to perform the actual hardware mapping of the IRQ line to the PCI device.

5. The System Resource Manager returns a value between 0 and 15 to the PCI Configuration Manager. This value indicates which of the 15 PC compatible IRQ lines the PCI device is now mapped to.

6. This assumes that the system reserves at least one hardware interrupt line for PCI device initialization.

   The PCI Configuration Manager programs the PCI device's Interrupt Line register.

7. DONE.

BASE ADDRESS REGISTERS

For each Base Address Registers starting at offset 10h of the PCI configuration space:

1. Per Chapter 17, the PCI Configuration Manager determines if the PCI device is requesting I/O or Memory Space, how many bytes of the resource are requested, and in the case of memory, which system memory address space the request is for.

2. The PCI Configuration Manager calls the System Resource Manager with a request for the system resource that the device requires. The PCI Configuration Manager passes the memory or I/O type, and length requested value to the System Resource Manager along with the BUS Number and device/FUNCTION Number of the device.

3. The PCI Configuration Manager programs the PCI device's Base Address Register with the value returned by the System Resource Manager.

4. DONE.

LATENCY TIMER

This register specifies the Master Latency Timer value for a PCI Master when the device is on the PCI bus. A typical way for PCI Configuration Manager to configure this register is to just choose an appropriate value and use that value for all devices. 32 (approximately 1 μsec) is a reasonable value.

PRIMARY VGA DEVICE CHECK

The PCI Configuration Manager checks each PCI video device it encounters in the system to determine if the device is the primary VGA device. It does this by reading the Class Code Register. If the byte value in the Base Class register (offset 0Bh of configuration space) is either 03h or 00h (with a Sub–Class register, offset 0Ah, value of 01h), the device is a video device. If the device is the primary VGA device, the PCI Configuration Manager leaves the device enabled. If the device is not the primary VGA device, the PCI Configuration Manager ensures that the device is disabled. Note that all non–primary PCI VGA devices are assigned the system resources they requested.

COMMAND REGISTER

For each control bit in the PCI device's configuration space Command Register:

Bit	Action
0	I/O Space Access bit is set to 1.
	Some devices hardwire this bit to 0 if the device does not utilize I/O address space.
1	Memory Space Access bit is set to 1.
	Some devices hardwire this bit to 0 if the device does not utilize memory address space.
2	The Master Enable bit is set to 0. A PCI device expansion BIOS or device driver is responsible for enabling Bus Master capabilities.
3	Special Cycles Operation is set to 1. This allows the device to monitor special cycle operations.
4	Memory Write and Invalidate may be set. This function is supported by some bus master devices. The System BIOS is responsible for the enable/disable of Memory Write and Invalidate.
5	VGA Palette Snoop may be set. VGA devices must support this bit. See Appendix C.
6	Parity Error Response may be set. This permits the device to respond to parity errors. The System BIOS is responsible for the enable/disable of Parity Error Response.
7	Wait Cycle control may be set. The System BIOS is responsible for the enable/disable of Wait Cycle control
8	SERR# Enable may be set to 1. The System BIOS is responsible for the enable/disable of SERR#.
9	Fast Back–to–Back Enable is set to 1 if all targets can do fast back–to–back transactions to different devices. A value of 0 indicates that fast back–to–back transactions are only allowed to the same agent. Bit 7 of a PCI device's Status Register indicates if the device is capable of Fast back–to–Back transactions.

STATUS REGISTER

The PCI device's Status Register is written with all 1's. This action clears all pending status flags.

20.8   BOOT-DEVICE-ONLY INITIALIZATION

Plug–and–Play operating systems will have the capability of determining the type and number of devices within the system. To a large extent, the Plug–and–Play operating systems will have the capability of initializing all non–primary boot devices in the system. These devices include serial ports, parallel ports and so on. This means that the System BIOS only needs to configure the primary boot device prior to bootstrapping the operating system.

> The primary video device will typically be initialized by the System BIOS as well.

The major problem for the System BIOS when bootstrapping the operating system is that there is no way for the System BIOS to determine which type of operating system will be loaded—Plug–and–Play or non–Plug–and–Play. The System BIOS is responsible for the platform and add–in card initialization in the case of a non–Plug–and–Play BIOS.

It is recommended that a user option in the Setup Utility program be installed for handling both scenarios. This option would give the user the choice of which method to use for device initialization.

20.9 PCI DEVICE DRIVERS

PCI device drivers have two requirements that extend beyond standard or existing device drivers. First, PCI device drivers must be able to use any system resource assigned to their devices. This is because PCI devices are not assigned hardwired resources. For example, a LEGACY ISA SCSI device may only be able to use either IRQ9 or IRQ11. The selection of which IRQ to use is typically based on a jumper setting or configuration utility option setting. The corresponding PCI device can be assigned any IRQ that the system hardware is capable of mapping to the PCI device. PCI device drivers are required to read their Configuration Space Registers to obtain their device's system resource mapping information. PCI device drivers must use the resources assigned to their devices.

> A PCI device driver should never attempt to assign resources to its device. This could cause the system to become unstable or crash.
>
> In a non–Plug–and–Play boot scenario the System BIOS Resource Manager is responsible for allocating all system resources to PCI devices.
>
> In a Plug–and–Play boot scenario the Operating System Device Class Configuration Manager is responsible for allocating all system resources to PCI devices.

The second requirement that PCI device drivers have that extends beyond standard or existing device drivers is that they must support shareable hardware interrupts. This is because a single hardware interrupt can be assigned to more than one PCI device at a time.

20.10 CHAPTER SUMMARY

This chapter presents several different aspects concerning the detection and initialization of PCI devices. PCI devices are capable of true Plug–and–Play operation. This chapter referenced Figure 2–4, the system Plug–and–Play pictorial figure, very heavily. Keep in mind that the device and system initialization algorithms presented here are designed to give the reader a working understanding of PCI device initialization from the System BIOS, operating system, and device driver points of view. In an actual implementation some concepts presented in this chapter, such as how the video sub–system is implemented, may be performed differently.

GLOSSARY

KEY TERMS AND ABBREVIATIONS

Access Cycle. A bus cycle where data is written to an addressed resource or read from an addressed resource.

Add–in Card. A plug–in board that is inserted into an expansion bus slot (connector) on the platform. The add–in board contains at least one device that adds one or more functions to the computer system.

ADDRESS PHASE. The portion of the PCI bus cycle when address and the COMMAND type are present on the bus.

Automatic Configuration. The automatic software detection of configurable hardware in a computer system and the subsequent assignment of system resources to this hardware. Human intervention such as adjusting switches or jumpers is not required. No resource conflicts will exist when the configuration process is performed. See Configuration.

BIOS. Basic Input/Output System. This is a firmware program that is responsible for the power–on testing and initialization of a computer. In addition, it may provide run–time services for operating systems.

Bits. The smallest binary unit of a byte, word, DWORD, or QWORD.

Bridge. A component that connects two independent buses together. This device permits a bus master on the source bus to interact with a resource on the destination bus.

Burst Cycle. A bus cycle where only one address is provided and multiple blocks of data at other associated addresses are accessed.

Bus. A collection of signal lines that interconnects resources.

Bus Cycle. The time dependent sequencing of the signal lines levels.

Bus Identification Number. A number in the range 0 to 255. This number permits the selection of individual PCI buses within the computer system.

Bus Level. The buses on a platform are interconnected with BRIDGEs. From the view point of HOST CPU every BRIDGE and PCI bus that is transcended to access a PCI or LEGACY bus resource represents a level.

Byte. A block of data with a width of 8 bits.

Cache Coherency. The protocol that insures that both the cache and DRAM have a correct copy of the data. It prevents an access to the cache or DRAM by a bus master if the data is not the same for the addressed cache line.

Command Type. The encoding in the C/BE# signal lines during the ADDRESS PHASE which specifies if the bus cycle is reading or writing, with memory, I/O, configuration etc.

Configuration. The allocation of resources to individual devices within the computer system. See *System Resource and Automatic Configuration.*

Configuration address space. PCI devices are required to support a record structure of 256 bytes of configuration registers. The configuration space is divided into two sections: (1) a 64 byte header region which all PCI devices must support and (2) a 192 byte device dependent region. Access to the PCI register set is accomplished via a physical address space unique to PCI buses. Software can always access the PCI configuration address space to identify and configure PCI devices.

DATA PHASE. The portion of the PCI bus cycle when data and the byte enable information are present on the bus.

Destination Bus. The bus on which the resource resides that is being accessed by the BRIDGE on behalf of a bus master on another bus.

DOS Compatibility Hole. The memory address range from 80000h to 0FFFFFh on an IBM AT or compatible personal computer. The typical (but not restricted) use of this memory address space is as follows:

80000H – 09FFFFH		Conventional read/writeable memory.
0A0000H – 0BFFFFH		Address space assigned to video memory.
0C0000H – 0C7FFFH		Address space assigned to video ROM.
0C8000H – 0DFFFFH		Address space used for expansion ROMs.
0E0000H – 0EFFFFH		Address space allocated for expansion ROMs or system ROM.
0F0000H – 0FFFFFH		Address space allocated for the system ROM.

DWORD. A block of Standard Architecture. This is an expansion bus which supports 32 bits of address and data with an extension to 64 bits of data.

Firmware. A software program which executes out of ROM. The computer's system ROM as well as ROMs contained on add–in cards are examples of firmware.

Function Number. A number in the range 0 to 7. A physical PCI component may contain between one and eight individual PCI devices. Each device provides a single function such as a disk drive controller or LAN. This number, along with the PCI bus and Device Number, permits the selection of an individual function within a PCI device.

HOST Bus. The bus that contains the HOST CPU, cache, and the platform memory (DRAM).

Host/PCI BRIDGE. A device which permits transactions between a HOST CPU bus and a PCI bus. The source side of the Bridge is connected to the HOST CPU and the destination side is connected to the PCI bus.

Host/LEGACY BRIDGE. A device which permits transactions between the HOST CPU bus and a LEGACY bus. The source side of the Bridge is connected to the HOST CPU while the destination side is connected to the LEGACY bus.

IDLE PHASE. The portion of the PCI bus cycle when no address, COMMAND type, data, or byte enable information is on the bus.

Interrupt Acknowledge Cycle. A bus cycle executed to retrieve the interrupt number from the interrupt controller.

I/O Address Space. A unique physical address space that contains ports to hardware functions. CPUs such as the Intel x86 processors contain special commands for accessing this address space.

IRQ. Interrupt Request Level. In an IBM AT or compatible personal computer this level dictates the priority in which the processor will service the interrupt request.

ISA. Industry Standard Architecture. This is the LEGACY expansion bus incorporated into all IBM AT or compatible personal computers.

LEGACY Bus. This is one of the non-PCI buses commonly used. Some LEGACY buses are ISA, EISA, and MC.

Lock. The protocol by which a PCI bus master can only access a specific target and the specific target can only be accessed by the aforementioned PCI bus master.

Memory Address Space. A unique physical address space that typically contains DRAM or other memory elements. It usually contains instruction code and general data.

Micro–Channel. Micro–Channel Architecture. This is the expansion bus which IBM designed and incorporated into its PS/2 line of computers.

Park. The protocol by which signal lines on a non active bus (during IDLE PHASE) are driven to a stable level.

PCI/PCI BRIDGE. A device which permits transactions between the PCI bus and a PCI bus. The source side of the BRIDGE is connected to the PCI bus master while the destination is connected to another PCI bus.

PCI Bus. Peripheral Component Interconnect bus.

PCI Bus Master. An integrated circuit or add–in card that can own the PCI bus. A BRIDGE can be a PCI bus master of one bus on behalf of another PCI bus master on another bus.

PCI Device. A device (electrical component) that conforms to the specification for operation in a PCI Local Bus environment.

PCI Device ID. A required field in PCI configuration space. Combined with the Vendor ID, it permits the unique identification of a PCI device in the system. Vendors define their own device identifiers.

PCI/LEGACY BRIDGE. A device which permits transactions between the PCI bus and a LEGACY bus. The source side of the BRIDGE is connected to the PCI bus master while the destination side is connected to the LEGACY bus.

PCI Resource. Any integrated circuit or add–in card that contains a PCI bus master, target, or BRIDGE

Peer BRIDGES. Two or more BRIDGEs which share a common source bus in the system.

Platform. Hardware that contains the HOST CPU, memory, cache, central arbiter, central resources some of the PCI buses, and connectors for add–in cards.

Plug and Play. The ability to install an add–in card in a system and have it automatically configured by software. See Automatic Configuration.

QWORD. A block of data with a width of 64 bits.

Revision ID. A required field in PCI configuration space. Vendors specify the revision of their device in this field. Zero is a valid value for this field.

Signal Lines. The collection of traces on the platform and add–in card that interconnect the PCI resources

Single Cycle. A bus cycle where only one address is provided and one accessed of data occurs.

Source Bus. The bus on which the a bus master is executing a bus cycle that will be ported by the BRIDGE to another bus

Special Cycle. The PCI bus command used to broadcast to all PCI devices in the system.

Stable Level. A state of the signal lines where they are held at a constant high or low logical voltage.

System Resource. IRQs, DMA channels. I/O address space, and memory address space.

System Software. This term refers to the BIOS, operating system, and software device drivers. See BIOS.

Target. A PCI resource that does not own the bus. It responds to bus cycles executed by the PCI bus master.

Vendor ID. A required field in PCI configuration space. Combined with the Device ID, it permits the unique identification of a PCI device in the system. The manufacturer identifier of the PCI device is contained in this field. The PCI Special Interest Group assigns each manufacturer their vendor identifier. 0FFFFH is an invalid value for this field.

Word. A block of data with a width of 16 bits.

PCI CLASS CODE REGISTER ENCODING

The PCI Class Code Register is segregated into three contiguous byte wide fields starting at offset 09H of the PCI Configuration Header region.

This Class Code Register has two uses. The first is to generically identify the function that the device performs or provides. The second use is to allow generic device drivers to work with devices from multiple vendors. For instance, a standard VGA device driver will work with any device whose Class Code indicates it is VGA.

> Be aware that the PCI Special Interest Group will define new values for the Class Code Register as the need arises. This register is currently read only. However, its use will probably be extended to have some writeable bits for specific encodings.

The definition of each byte is as follows:

Offset 0B	**Base Class Code** PCI devices are classified according to the function they perform. This value identifies the functional class of the device.
Offset 0Ah	**Sub–Class Code** This value identifies the specific function of a device within its Class Code.
Offset 09h	**Programming Interface** This value specifies a register level programming interface. This interface allows device independent software to interact with the device. Note that currently most devices do not support a register level programming interface.

Table A-1: Class Code Register Definitions

BASE CLASS DEFINITIONS

The following table describes the current definitions for the Base Class Code field (offset 0BH) of the Class Code Register:

Base Class	Description
00h	Backward Compatible Base Class
01h	Mass Storage Controller
02h	Network Controller
03h	Display Controller
04h	Multimedia Device
05h	Memory Controller
06h	Bridge Device
07h	Simple Communication Controllers
08h	Base System Peripherals
09h	Input Devices
0Ah	Docking Stations
0Bh	Processors
0Ch	Serial Bus controllers
0Dh – FEh	Reserved
FFh	Undefined Base Class

Table A-2: Base Class Register Definitions

SUB CLASS AND PROGRAMMING INTERFACE DEFINITIONS

The following sections describe the current definitions for the Sub–Class field and Programming Interface field for each Base Class value. Values not defined are reserved for future use.

BACKWARD COMPATIBLE BASE CLASS

Devices built prior to when the Class Code field was defined have a value of 00h. New devices will use Base Class Codes 01h through 06h or 0FFh. It is recommended that existing devices with a Base Class code of 00h switch to the value which correctly identifies the device's function.

Base Class	Sub– Class	Prog. Intfc.	Description
00h	00h	00h	All non–VGA compatible devices with a Base Class value of 00h will contain these values.
	01h	00h	All VGA compatible devices with a Base Class value of 00h will contain these values.

Table A-3-A: Base Class 00h

MASS STORAGE CONTROLLER BASE CLASS

Use this Base Class for all mass storage controller devices. Note that no standard programming interfaces are defined. Refer to the PCI SIG document *PCI IDE Controller Specification* and the document *Programming Interface for Bus Master IDE Controller* for more information on the IDE sub-class.

Base Class	Sub–Class	Prog. Intfc.	Description
01h	00h	00h	SCSI Bus Controller
	01h	00h	IDE Controller
	02h	00h	Floppy Disk Controller
	03h	00h	IPI Bus Controller
	04h	00h	RAID Controller
	80h	00h	Other Mass Storage Controller

Table A-3-B: Base Class 01h

NETWORK CONTROLLER BASE CLASS

Use this Base Class for all network controller devices. Note that no standard programming interfaces are defined.

Base Class	Sub–Class	Prog. Intfc.	Description
02h	00h	00h	Ethernet Controller
	01h	00h	Token Ring Controller
	02h	00h	FDDI Controller
	03h	00h	ATM Controller
	80h	00h	Other Network Controller

Table A-3-C: Base Class 02h

DISPLAY CONTROLLER BASE CLASS

Use this Base Class for all display controller devices. The VGA code (030000h) indicates that the device is VGA compatible. A device with this class code will work with any generic VGA device driver. The programming interface field is used to describe the video controller's compatibility modes. Devices can support multiple video interfaces. The bit map defines which interfaces are supported by the controller.

Base Class	Sub–Class	Prog. Intfc.	Description
03h	00h	00000000b	VGA Compatible Controller. Memory addresses A00000h-BFFFFFh. I/O addresses 3B0h-3BBh, 3C0h-3DFh and all aliases of these addresses.
		00000001b	8514 Compatible Controller. I/O addresses 2E8hand its aliases, 2EAh-2EFh.
	01h	00h	XGA Controller
	80h	00h	Other Display Controller

Table A-3-D: Base Class 03h

MULTIMEDIA DEVICE BASE CLASS

Use this Base Class for all multimedia devices such as video capture devices and video codecs.

Base Class	Sub–Class	Prog. Intfc.	Description
04h	00h	00h	Video Device
	01h	00h	Audio Device
	80h	00h	Other Multimedia Device

Table A-3-E: Base Class 04h

MEMORY CONTROLLER BASE CLASS

Use this Base Class for all memory controller devices. PCI add-in memory will be defined in the future. Note that no standard programming interfaces are defined.

Base Class	Sub–Class	Prog. Intfc.	Description
05h	00h	00h	RAM
	01h	00h	Flash
	80h	00h	Other Memory Device

Table A-3-F: Base Class 05h

BRIDGE DEVICE BASE CLASS

Use this Base Class for all PCI BRIDGE devices. Note that no standard programming interfaces are defined.

Base Class	Sub–Class	Prog. Intfc.	Description
06h	00h	00h	Host Bridge
	01h	00h	ISA Bridge
	02h	00h	EISA Bridge
	03h	00h	MC Bridge
	04h	00h	PCI to PCI Bridge
	05h	00h	PCMCIA Bridge
	06h	00h	NuBus Bridge
	07h	00h	CardBus Bridge
	80h	00h	Other Bridge Device

Table A-3-G: Base Class 06h

BASE CLASS 07H

Use this Base Class for all types of simple communication controllers. Several sub-class values are defined, some of these having specific well-known register-level programming interfaces.

Base Class	Sub–Class	Prog. Intfc.	Description
07h	00h	00h	Generic XT Compatible Serial Controller
		01h	16450 Compatible Serial Controller
		02h	16550 Compatible Serial Controller
	01h	00h	Parallel Port
		01h	Bidirectional Parallel Port
		02h	ECP 1.X Compliant Parallel Port
	80h	00h	Other Communications

Table A-3-H: Base Class 07h

BASE CLASS 08H

Use this Base Class for all types of generic system peripherals. Note that each of the defined sub-class values has a specific well-known register-level programming interface.

Base Class	Sub–Class	Prog. Intfc.	Description
08h	00h	00h	Generic 8259 PIC
		01h	ISA PIC
		02h	EISA PIC
	01h	00h	Generic 8237 DMA Controller
		01h	ISA DMA Controller
		02h	EISA DMA Controller
	02h	00h	Generic 8254 System Timer
		01h	ISA System Timer
		02h	EISA System Timers (2 Timers)
	03h	00h	Generic RTC Controller
		01h	ISA RTC Controller
	80h	00h	Other System Peripheral

Table A-3-I: Base Class 08h

BASE CLASS 09H

Use this Base Class for all types of input devices. Several sub-class values are defined. Note that no specific register-level programming interfaces are defined.

Base Class	Sub–Class	Prog. Intfc.	Description
09h	00h	00h	Keyboard Controller
	01h	00h	Digitizer (Pen)
	02h	00h	Mouse Controller
	80h	00h	Other Input Controller

Table A-3-J: Base Class 09h

BASE CLASS 0AH

Use this base class for all types of docking stations. Note that no specific register-level programming interfaces are defined.

Base Class	Sub–Class	Prog. Intfc.	Description
0Ah	00h	00h	Generic Docking Station
	80h	00h	Other Type of Docking Station

Table A-3-K: Base Class 0Ah

BASE CLASS 0BH

Use this base class for all types of processors. Several sub-class values are defined corresponding to different processor types or instruction sets. Note that no specific register-level programming interfaces defined.

Base Class	Sub–Class	Prog. Intfc.	Description
0Bh	00h	00h	386
	01h	00h	486
	02h	00h	Pentium
	10h	00h	Alpha
	40h	00h	Co-processor

Table A-3-L: Base Class 0Bh

BASE CLASS 0CH

Use this base class for all types of serial bus controllers. Note that no specific register-level programming interfaces defined.

Base Class	Sub–Class	Prog. Intfc.	Description
0Ch	00h	00h	Firewire (IEEE 1394)
	01h	00h	ACCESS.bus
	02h	00h	SSA

Table A-3-M: Base Class 0Ch

UNDEFINED BASE CLASS

Specific device class not defined.

Vendors should NOT arbitrarily use this class if a device does not correspond to one of the defined device classes. When in doubt, contact the PCI Special Interest Group for aid in determining the proper Base Class to use for a new device. A new Base Class code may be created if needed.

Base Class	Sub–Class	Prog. Intfc.	Description
FFh	00h	00h	Undefined Class

Table A-3-N: Base Class FFh

USER DEFINABLE CONFIGURATION ITEMS

This appendix (reprinted from the PCI specification with permission) describes the mechanism to support the configuring of PCI adapters that have User Definable Features (UDFs) using system configuration mechanisms (such as the EISA Configuration Utility). UDFs are defined to be device configuration items that are dependent on the environment into which the device is installed and whose settings can not be automatically determined by hardware or system software. For example, the token ring speed setting for token ring network devices will be dependent on the specific token ring network into which the device is installed. Therefore, the default value of these configuration items may prevent successful system boot given the environment in which it is installed and the user may be required to insure a proper configuration. UDFs do not apply to devices that have a common compatible default configuration, such as VGA compatible graphics adapters, since a successful system boot can be achieved using the device's default configuration.

OVERVIEW

Device UDFs are described in a text based file that is supplied with an adapter. This file will be referred to as a PCI Configuration File, or PCF. The PCF will specify to the system configuration mechanism the device specific user definable features (UDFs). Adapters that do not support device specific UDFs are not required to supply a PCF. Adapter vendors are required to supply a separate PCF for each adapter function that supports device specific UDFs.

The PCF can be supplied with an adapter via a 1.44 MB diskette formatted with the PC/MS-DOS File Allocation Table (FAT) format. The filename for the file containing the PCF should be XXXXYYYY.PCF, where XXXX is the two byte Vendor Id as specified in the device's configuration space header (represented as hexadecimal digits), and YYYY is the two byte Device Id as specified in the device's configuration space header (represented as hexadecimal digits). The file must be in the root directory on the diskette.

A function on an adapter is required to indicate that it has user definable features via the UDF_Supported bit. This read only UDF_Supported bit resides in the Status Register and will be set when a device function has device specific configuration selections that must be presented to the user. Functions that do not support user selectable configuration items would not implement this bit, and therefore return a 0 when read.

For devices where the UDF_Supported bit is set, system startup and/or configuration software will then recognize the function on the adapter as one that supports user definable features. Systems are not required to be capable of interpreting a PCF. For such systems, the user will need to rely on a vendor supplied device specific configuration utility if the user requires the ability to alter user definable features of that device.

Systems that choose to support interpreting PCFs are also responsible for supplying non-volatile storage (NVS) to hold the device specific configuration selected by the user. In this scenario, system Power-On-Self-Test (POST) software will at system boot time copy the appropriate values for each PCI adapter from the non-volatile storage to the appropriate configuration space registers for each function. The mechanism for interpreting a PCF, presenting the information to the user and storing the selections in the non-volatile storage is system specific. Note that when sizing NVS for a given system, the number of adapters supported, the number of functions per adapter, and the number of bytes of configuration information per function must be analyzed. In addition, the system will need to store enough overhead information such that POST knows what address of which device/function each configuration byte will be written to, masked appropriately as specified in the PCF. It is recommended that system non-volatile storage be sized such that an average of 32 bytes of configuration data (potentially non-contiguous) will be written to each adapter device function. In addition, vendors should design adapters such that they do not require more than 32 bytes of configuration information per function as a result of PCF specified configuration options.

PCF DEFINITION

NOTATIONAL CONVENTION

The PCF contains ISO Standard 8859-1 character set text, commonly referred to as Code Page 850. The text includes keywords that aid the system configuration mechanism's interpretation of the PCF information, as well as provides generic text representing device specific information. All text is case insensitive, unless otherwise noted. White space, including spaces, tabs, carriage returns, and linefeeds, is ignored outside of quoted strings. All PCF selections must be for device specific configuration options and be targeted for the device specific portion (192 bytes) of the function's configuration space. The PCF can not be used for requesting allocation of system level resources such as interrupt assignments, or memory, I/O or expansion ROM address allocations. The PCF can not request writes to the PCI Configuration Space Header (addresses less than 40h). This must be enforced by the system configuration mechanism.

System configuration software will use the PCF to present to the user the device specific configuration options. User selections will be stored in system non-volatile storage, presumably as values to be written to device specific configuration space addresses. POST software will use the information stored in non-volatile memory to write appropriate configuration settings into each device's configuration space. The device's logic can use the information as loaded in configuration space, or require their expansion ROM logic or device driver SW to copy the device specific configuration space values into appropriate I/O or memory based device registers at system initialization. In addition, the device can choose to alias the device specific configuration space registers into appropriate I/O or memory based device registers if needed. Any configuration information required to be accessible after device initialization should not be accessible exclusively via configuration space.

VALUES AND ADDRESSES

A *value* or *address* can be given in hexadecimal, decimal, or binary format. The radix, or base identifier, is specified by attaching one of the following characters to the end of the *value* or *address*:

H or h - Hexadecimal

D or d - Decimal

B or b - Binary

The radix character must be placed immediately after the value, with no space in between. If no radix is specified, decimal is assumed.

Example: 1FOOh

Hexadecimal numbers beginning with a letter must have a leading zero.

Example: 0C000h

TEXT

Text fields contain information that is to be presented to the user. These fields are free form and are enclosed in quotation marks. These text fields can be tailored to a specific international market by using the Code Page 850 character set to support international languages (see the LANG statement description below). Text field maximum lengths are given for each instance. Text fields can contain embedded tabs, denoted by \t, and embedded linefeeds, denoted by \n. Quotation marks and backslashes can also be placed in the text using \" and \\ respectively.

Embedded tabs are expanded to the next tab stop. Tab length is eight characters (tab stops are located at 9, 17, 25, etc.).

INTERNAL COMMENTS

Comments can be embedded in the PCF for annotational purposes. Comments are not presented to the user. Comments can be placed on separate lines, or they can follow other PCF statements. Comments begin with a semi-colon (;) and are terminated with a carriage return.

SYMBOLS USED IN SYNTAX DESCRIPTION

This description of the PCF syntax uses the following special symbols:

[ ]   The item or statement is optional.

x|y   Either x or y is allowed.

PCI CONFIGURATION FILE OUTLINE

A PCF is structured as follows:
  Device Identification Block

Function Statement Block(s)

[Device Identification Block

Function Statement Block(s)]

The Device Identification Block identifies the device by name, manufacturer, and ID. The PCF must begin with this block.

The Function Statement Blocks define the user presentable configuration items associated with the device.

The Device Identification Block and Function Statement Block set can optionally be repeated within the PCF file to support multiple languages.

DEVICE IDENTIFICATION BLOCK

The Device Identification Block within the PCF is defined as follows:
        BOARD
        ID="XXXXYYYY"
        NAME="*text*"
        MFR="*text*"
        SLOT=PCI
        [VERSION=value]
        [LANG=XXX]

The BOARD statement appears at the beginning of each PCF. This statement, along with the other required statements, must appear before the optional statements contained in brackets [ ]. The statements should occur in the order shown.

ID is a required statement containing the vendor and device IDs, XXXXYYYY, where XXXX is the two byte vendor ID as specified in the device's configuration space header (represented as hex digits), and YYYY is the two byte device ID as specified in the device's configuration header (represented as hex digits). The ID must contain eight characters and must be placed in quotation marks.

NAME is a required statement that identifies the device. Vendor and product name should be included. A maximum length of 90 characters is allowed. The first 55 characters are considered significant (that is, only the first 55 characters will be shown if truncation or horizontal scrolling is required).

MFR is a required statement that specifies the board manufacturer. A maximum length of 30 characters is allowed.

SLOT=PCI is a required statement that identifies the device as PCI. This is included to assist configuration utilities that must also parse EISA or ISA CFG files.

VERSION is an optional statement that specifies the PCF standard that this PCF was implemented to. The syntax described by this appendix represents version 0. This statement allows future revisions of the PCF syntax and format to be recognized and processed accordingly by configuration utilities. Version 0 will be assumed when the VERSION statement is not found in the Device Identification Block.

LANG is an optional statement that specifies the language used within the quote enclosed text found within the given Device Identification Block/Function Statement Block set. When no LANG statement is included, then the default language is English. XXX can have the following values:

CZE	Czech
DAN	Danish
DUT	Dutch
ENG	English (default)
FIN	Finnish
FRE	French
GER	German
HUN	Hungarian
ITA	Italian
NOR	Norwegian
POL	Polish
POR	Portuguese
SLO	Slovak
SPA	Spanish
SWE	Swedish

FUNCTION STATEMENT BLOCK

Function Statement Blocks define specific configuration choices to be presented to the use. A Function Statement Block is defined as follows:

FUNCTION="*text*"
[HELP="*text*"]
Choice Statement Block

.

.

.

[Choice Statement Block]

The FUNCTION statement names a function of the device for which configuration alternatives will be presented to the user. A maximum of 100 characters is allowed for the function name.

HELP is an optional text field containing additional information that will be displayed to the user if the user requests help while configuring the function. This text field can contain a maximum of 600 characters.

Each Choice Statement Block names a configuration alternative for the function, and lists the register addresses, sizes, and values needed to initialize that alternative. Each Function Statement Block must contain at least one Choice Statement Block. The first choice listed for a given function will be the default choice used for automatic configuration.

CHOICE STATEMENT BLOCK

CHOICE = "*text*"
[HELP="*text*"]
INIT Statement

.

.

.

[INIT Statement]

CHOICE statements are used to indicate configuration alternatives for the function. Each FUNCTION must have at least one CHOICE statement, and can have as many as necessary. A maximum of 90 characters is allowed for the choice name.

HELP is an optional text field containing additional information that will be displayed to the user if the user requests help with the CHOICE. This text field can contain a maximum of 600 characters.

A Choice Statement Block can contain one or more INIT statements. INIT statements give the register addresses and values needed to initialize the configuration alternative named by the CHOICE statement.

INIT STATEMENTS

INIT=PCI(*address*) [BYTE|WORD|DWORD] *value*

INIT statements provide the register addresses and values needed to initialize the device's vendor specific registers.

The PCI keyword is used to indicate that this is a PCI INIT statement. This is included to assist configuration utilities that must also parse EISA or ISA CFG files.

Address is the register's offset in the PCI configuration space. This address value must be within the 192 bytes of device specific configuration space (offsets 64-255).

An optional BYTE, WORD, or DWORD qualifier can be used to indicate the size of the register. The default is BYTE.

Value gives the value to be output to the register. Bit positions marked with an 'r' indicate that the value in that position is to be preserved. The 'r' can only be used as a bit position in a binary value, or as a hex digit (4 bit positions) in a hex value. The length of the value must be the same as the data width of the port: 8, 16, or 32 bits.

Examples:
INIT = PCI(58h) 11110000b

```
INIT = PCI(5Ah) 0000rr11b
INIT = PCI(0A6h) WORD R8CDh
INIT = PCI(48h) WORD RR0000001111RR11b
```

SAMPLE PCF

```
BOARD
ID="56781234"    ; Vendor is 5678h, Device is
1234h
       ; Filename would be "56781234.PCF"
NAME=         "Super Cool Widget PCI Device"
MFR=          "ABC Company"
SLOT=         PCI
VERSION=      0

FUNCTION="Type of Widget Communications"
HELP="This choice lets you select which type of
communication you want this device to use."
  CHOICE="Serial"
   INIT=PCI(45h)         rrr000rrb  ;Default size
is BYTE
   INIT=PCI(8Ch)         DWORD       0ABCDRRRRh
  CHOICE="Parallel"
    INIT=PCI(45h)        rrr010rrb
    INIT=PCI(8Ch)        DWORD       1234abcdh
  CHOICE="Cellular"
    INIT=PCI(45h)        rrr100rrb
    INIT=PCI(8Ch)        DWORD       5678abcdh

FUNCTION="Communication Speed"
  CHOICE="4 Mbit/Sec"  INIT=PCI(56h) WORD R12Rh
  CHOICE="16 Mbit/Sec"  INIT=PCI(56h) WORD R4CRh
  CHOICE="64 Gbit/Sec"  INIT=PCI(56h) WORD R00Rh

FUNCTION="Enable Super Hyper Turbo Mode"
HELP="Enable Super Hyper Turbo Mode only if the
64 Gbit Speed has been selected."
  CHOICE="No"    INIT=PCI(49h)        rrrrr0rrb
  CHOICE="Yes"   INIT=PCI(49h)        rrrrr1rrb

FUNCTION="Widget Host ID"
  CHOICE="7"     INIT=PCI (9Ah)       rrrrr000b
  CHOICE="6"     INIT=PCI (9Ah)       rrrrr001b
```

```
CHOICE="5"        INIT=PCI (9Ah)        rrrrr010b
CHOICE="4"        INIT=PCI (9Ah)        rrrrr011b
```

APPENDIX C

VGA PALETTE SNOOPING

Some graphics controllers that are not VGA compatible, take the output from a VGA controller and map it onto their display as a way to provide boot information and VGA compatibility. However, the color information coming from the VGA controller references the palette table inside the VGA controller. In order for the graphics controller to generate the proper colors, it has to know what is in the VGA controller's palette. To do this the non–VGA graphics controller watches for write accesses to the VGA palette registers, and snoops the data.

In PCI based systems where the VGA controller is on the PCI bus and a non–VGA graphics controller is on the ISA bus, write accesses to the palette will not show up on the ISA bus if the PCI VGA controller responds to the writes. In this case the PCI VGA controller should not respond to the write (does not assert DEVSEL#), should only snoop the data, and should permit the access to be forwarded to the ISA bus. The non–VGA ISA graphics controller can then snoop the data on the ISA bus.

The value of bit 5 in the command register of the PCI VGA device determines whether or not the PCI VGA controller responds to the palette write, or whether it just snoops the data. Non–VGA PCI graphics controllers that need to have VGA palette information must also implement bit 5 in the Command Register to control whether or not to respond or snoop the palette access.

Table C–1 shows how to interpret the Snoop Enable bit in the command register. The table applies to both PCI VGA controllers and non–VGA graphics controllers that need to have VGA palette information. This bit only affects the behavior on <u>write</u> accesses to the palette registers. PCI VGA controllers always respond to read accesses to the palette; non–VGA graphics controllers always ignore read accesses to the palette.

Snoop Enable (Bit 5 in Command)	Description
0	Positively respond to write accesses to the palette registers. VGA controllers should initialize this bit to this state on RESET.
1	Snoop write accesses to the palette registers. Non–VGA graphics controllers that need palette information should initialize this bit to this state on RESET.

Table C–1: Snoop Enable Bit

ISA ALIASING

IBM PC AND COMPATIBLES

Intel x86 microprocessors support a 64K I/O address space. However, the original IBM PC platform design only routed ten address lines, SA<0–9>, to the expansion slots for decoding I/O address space. For I/O address space the upper five address lines SA<10–15> were not connected and were treated as "don't cares" by add–in cards. This effectively limited the I/O address space to 1K (ten address bits). The I/O address range for ten address bits is 0000h to 03FFh.

The result of limiting the I/O address space decode to the first ten address lines is that this 1K block of I/O address space is repeated 64 times in the address space. This is because the upper five address lines are ignored by add-in devices during I/O bus cycles. Aliasing SA<10–15> are ignored by add–in devices during I/O bus cycles. For example, an add–in device located at I/O address 300h (address lines SA<8–9> are active) that only decodes address lines SA<0–9> will respond to I/O addresses 300h, 1300h, 2300h, 700h, 1700h, 2700h, 0B00h, 1B00h, 2B00h, 0F00h, 1F00h, 2F00h, and so on for a total of sixty–four combinations within the I/O address space. In each instance, address lines SA<8–9> are active, regardless of the state of address lines SA<10–15>. The device assigned I/O port address 300h will respond to any of these addresses. Therefore, I/O port addresses are said to be aliased because devices assigned to an I/O port address between 0000h and 03FFh, or the first 1K of I/O port address space, will respond to multiple addresses above that range.

Of the first 1K of I/O port address space IBM reserved the first 256 bytes of I/O address space (0000h–00FFh) were for platform devices such as interrupt and DMA controllers. The upper 768 bytes (0100h–03FFh) were left free to assign to add–on devices. The defacto standard in the PC industry is to only make a combination of address lines SA<0–7> active when accessing platform devices. The figure below shows how the original IBM PC platform decoded I/O port addresses.

IBM XT AND COMPATIBLES

When IBM introduced their XT model, they increased the number of I/O address lines routed to the expansion slots to 16 allowing access to the full 64K I/O address space. This was largely to overcome the problem of only having 1K of address space in which to map devices. But unfortunately there were (and still are) a large number of add–in cards that only decoded 10 bits. Using the example above, the device that claimed the 10–bit address 300h would continue to claim all the 16–bit aliases of that address making them useless for other devices. Also, platform devices were still doing a 10–bit decode. So even though the number of address lines was increased, the usable address space remained the same.

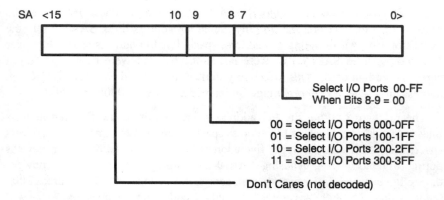

Figure D–1: PC Ten-Bit I/O Decode

To overcome the limited address space, add–in card vendors started claiming some address in the first 1K, and then using that addresses aliases for unique registers in the device. For example a device may claim the address 0300h for one of it's registers and then use the address 1300h (an alias) for another register with a different function. The register at address 300h could be used as an address register, while the register at 1300h may be a data register. Using this technique a device could claim one byte in the 10–bit address space, and implement up to 63 others in the aliases of that address. Many high–function add–in cards use this technique to provide more registers, while consuming small amounts of the 10–bit address space.

IBM AT AND COMPATIBLES

When IBM introduced the AT model, ISA aliasing was once again affected. A full 16–bit I/O address space decode of platform devices was implemented. This means that aliases of platform devices (i.e., addresses where SA<8–9> = 00) can be used for add–in cards. In fact in EISA machines these aliases are used to uniquely address cards in add–in slots.

PRESENT DAY IMPLEMENTATIONS

As a result of this history, the currently defined I/O address map of AT–class machines is such that in each of the unique sixty–four 1K segments the upper 768 bytes of each segment are used by ISA devices (including their aliases) and the lower 256 bytes of each segment are available for use. Effectively, this means that 3/4 of the *total* I/O address space is consumed by ISA devices.

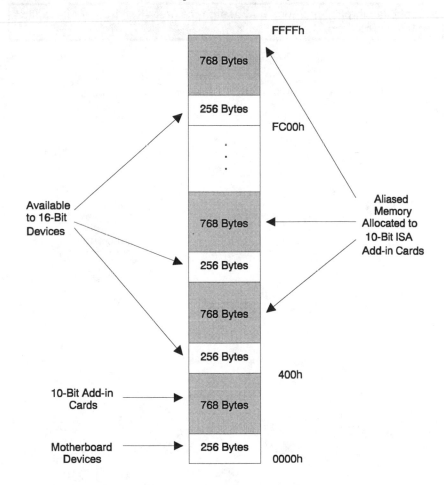

Figure D–2: 64K I/O Decode Map

However, 10–bit add–in cards still assume that an I/O address is for a platform device whenever an I/O address is on the bus with address lines SA<8–9> set to zero. This leaves the upper sixty–three 1K segments for assigning unique I/O addresses to add–in devices in a manner that will not conflict with add–in cards that only decode the first ten address lines. In all cases this requires that address lines SA<8–9> =00 and at least one address line in the range SA<10–15> is set to one. As the following figure illustrates, this means that only the lower 256–bytes of each 1K segment are available in order to avoid I/O address space conflicts.

Present day implementations now assign the first 4K of I/O address space to platform devices.

PCI AND ISA ALIASING

The typical PCI system architecture has an interesting impact on the ISA address aliasing problem. I/O addresses emitted by the processor first go to the PCI bus where a PCI device can claim the access. If no PCI device claims the access, the access is then forwarded (using subtractive decode) to the expansion bus (i.e. ISA). If configuration software places a PCI device at the same address as an ISA device *(or any of the ISA aliases),* the ISA device will never see I/O accesses to it. The device on the expansion bus will appear to be broken. As a result, both the design of the PCI device as well as PCI configuration software must account for ISA aliasing to permit the computer system to be configured with no conflicts.

PCI DEVICE DESIGN

PCI devices should never request more than 256 bytes of contiguous I/O address space in one base address register. If more than 256 bytes is requested, it is impossible to assign an address that won't conflict with a possible ISA alias.

> A PCI BIOS is responsible for ensuring that the system resources are assigned in a conflict free manner. Therefore, assume that a PCI BIOS will disable any PCI device requesting more than 256 contiguous bytes of I/O address space.

CONFIGURATION SOFTWARE DESIGN

Configuration software should configure PCI devices such that no conflicts exist. This can be performed in one of two ways. In the first method the configuration software can explicitly know what ISA devices are in the system, what addresses and aliases those devices use, and then configure PCI devices so that no conflicts occur. The major problem with this method is that the automatic detection of ISA devices as well as determining what resources they consume is very difficult. Typically this method can only be accomplished with user input.

The second method is to pre–allocate 3/4 of the address space to ISA devices and their aliases. PCI devices are placed in the remaining spaces. Essentially any I/O address that is greater the 4K (to avoid platform ISA devices) and where $SA<8–9> = 00$ (to avoid ISA aliases) is a valid address for PCI devices. This technique provides for sixty 256 byte–wide addresses where PCI devices can be mapped without conflicting with platform or ISA devices. This is the preferred method for allocating I/O address space in a PCI based system.

Figure E–1 is an illustration of the I/O port address line assignments for PCI devices.

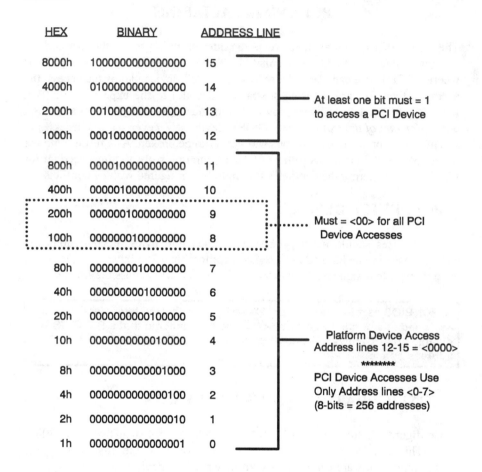

Figure E–1: PCI I/O Address Line Map

PCI AND I/O PORTS 0000H THROUGH 03FFH

The effects of assigning a given range of I/O ports within the 0000h through 03FFh range to the PCI bus in an ISA/PCI based system are as follows:

1. If PCI devices are assigned some of the I/O port addresses between 0000h and 00FFh, the ISA bus will never see the addresses. Some system platform devices may not respond. This may result in a non–functional system.

2. If PCI devices are assigned all of the I/O port addresses between 0000h and 00FFh, the ISA bus will never see the addresses. No system platform devices will respond. This will result in a non–functional system.

3. If PCI devices are assigned some of the I/O port addresses between 0100h and 03FFh, the ISA bus will never see the addresses. Some add–in ISA devices may not respond. How the system will react cannot be determined.

4. If PCI devices are assigned all of the I/O port addresses between 0100h and 03FFh, the ISA bus will never see the addresses. No add–in ISA devices will respond. How the system will react cannot be determined.

5. If PCI devices are assigned all I/O port addresses between 0000h and 03FFh, the ISA bus will never see this range of addresses. The system platform and all add–in ISA devices will never respond. This will result in a non–functional system.

GUIDELINES FOR PCI AND ISA ALIASING

To avoid the effects of ISA Aliasing in a PCI based system, do the following:

1. Follow the current PC/AT compatible defacto standard. Recognize that the first 4K of I/O address space should only be decoded by the platform ISA bus.

2. Remember that ISA add–in devices only decode the first ten address lines of I/O port address space. Do not assign the I/O address space between 0100h and 03FFh to any PCI device. An ISA bus device assigned to the same I/O port address space as a PCI Device will not respond if you do.

3. Because of items one and two, never assign I/O port address space 0000h through 0FFFFH to the PCI bus. Do not assign this I/O port address space to anything but the ISA bus.

4. The PCI bus should never respond to an aliased I/O port address that would prevent any device on the platform ISA bus from responding to I/O port address space 0100h through 03FFh. This means that address lines SA<8–9> will never be active when the PCI bus claims an I/O port access. In effect, this limits the size of the I/O port address space for any PCI device to 256 contiguous bytes. Only I/O port address bits SA<0–7> and SA<10–15> may be active during an I/O port access claimed by the PCI bus. For example, the first valid 256 byte range of I/O address space that can be assigned to the PCI bus is 1000h through 10FFh. In

this instance address line SA<12> is active for all I/O port accesses in this region. The next valid 256 byte range of I/O address space that can be assigned to PCI is 1400h through 14FF. For this region address lines SA<10> and SA<12> are active for all I/O port accesses. Because there are 64K of I/O port addresses, decoding the lower 256 bytes of I/O port address space within a specific 1K block can be repeated 63 times; once for each 1K block of I/O address space above the first 1K block. However, the first 4K are assigned to the platform; this leaves only [60 times 256] byte–wide I/O ports that can be assigned to PCI devices.

5. To summarize, the base address of any PCI device's I/O port region is defined by the contents of address lines SA<0–7> combined with SA<10–15>. At least one of the SA<12–15> address lines should be active for a PCI device to claim the I/O port access. If none of the SA<10–15> address lines is active, then the I/O port access should be forwarded to the ISA bus. In addition, a PCI device should never be assigned more than 256 contiguous bytes of I/O port address space. There is a possibility of preventing an ISA add–in device from functioning if this occurs because at least one of the SA<8–9> address lines will be active.

COMMON PROBLEMS TO AVOID

This appendix lists some of the common problems that have been observed in early versions of PCI devices. Component designers and add–in card vendors should take care to avoid these problems.

DEVICE ASKS FOR MORE THAN 256 BYTES OF I/O SPACE.

A PCI device should never request more than 256 bytes of I/O space. This is because of the address aliasing characteristics of ISA add–in cards (see Appendix D). A PCI device that does request more that 256 bytes will likely be left disabled in any system that contains ISA devices.

EXPANSION ROM IS NOT RELOCATABLE.

One of the key features of PCI that enables Play and Play behavior is the ability to relocate Expansion ROM code (so the user doesn't have to make any decisions) and to tightly pack the code for optimum use of the Expansion ROM area (0C0000h–0E8FFFh). VGA devices must also provide relocatable Expansion ROMs even though the code will eventually be relocated to 0C0000h. This is to allow easy detection of VGA devices on other buses, as well as allowing multiple display devices on PCI (two–headed graphics system).

EXPANSION ROM PUTS SECOND LOAD ON BUS.

The PCI Specification is very clear that add–in cards can have only one electrical load on each PCI signal pin. And yet designs appear where the controller device is attached to the AD lines, and an Expansion ROM is also attached to the AD lines. Designs like this cause subtle timing problems in the system and are very difficult to isolate.

DEVICE'S CONFIGURATION SPACE IS NOT ACCESSIBLE AS BYTES OR WORDS.

Configuration space must be accessible as bytes, words, and dwords. Many POST code algorithms depend on this when accessing the predefined header portion of configuration space. For instance, when POST wants to clear the Status Register (at offset 06h) it does a word write with all bits set. If the device only supports DWORD accesses, this operation will cause the

Command byte (at offset 04h) to be modified as well. Similarly in the Expansion ROM Base address register, the address is written in one operation (typically DWORD) and then the enable is modified with a byte operation. If the device only supports DWORD accesses to config space, this byte write will corrupt the address information.

DEVICE COMES UP ENABLED.

All add–in devices on PCI must power–up in the disabled state. There are no exceptions for any class of devices. Even devices that are used in the boot process must come up disabled, and the BIOS will enable them after resources have been assigned and the device has been selected to perform the boot operation.

UNIMPLEMENTED FUNCTIONS IN MULTIFUNCTION DEVICE RESPOND TO CONFIG ACCESSES.

Most PCI multifunction devices do not implement a complete set of eight functions. Typically the number of functions implemented is less than four. When the System BIOS is checking to see how many functions the device contains, it is important that the device not respond when reads are made to unimplemented functions config space. If the device does respond the BIOS will falsely detect functions, operating systems will start unnecessary and incorrect drivers and system behavior will become erratic.

BASE ADDRESS REGISTERS NOT FULLY WRITABLE.

The PCI Specification requires PCI devices to be fully relocatable in the address spaces. Devices cannot decode fixed addresses. Similarly when a Base Address Register is implemented, all bits in the upper part of the register (down to some alignment and size) must be writeable. A device should never hardwire any address bits in a Base Address Register to one. For instance, it is not correct for a device designer to decide that the device operates best when assigned to I/O addresses 3F0h or 1F0h, hardwire bits 8::4 in the Base Address Register to 1, make bit 9 writeable and hardwire all other address bits to 0. This will have the effect of mapping the device to 3F0h when all 1's are written to the Base Address Register and mapping the device to 1F0h when all 0's are written to the register. However, virtually all BIOSs will break when their POST code tries to determine the size and alignment requirements for this device.

USING RESERVED PINS ON THE CONNECTOR.

Reserved pins on the PCI connector are off limits. Platform designs should never use these pins, and add–in cards should never use these pins. Both platform designs and add–in card designs should leave these pins as "no–

connects". The PCI Special Interest Group controls these pins and will decide when and if these pins are assigned a specific function.

3.3V PINS NOT TIED TOGETHER AND DECOUPLED.

The PCI Specification requires that 5V only add–in cards decouple the unused 3.3V pins to the ground plane. Decoupling should average at least 0.01 ʋF per 3.3V pin, and should occur within 0.25 inches of the pin pad. More details on the decoupling requirements can be found in Section 13.2, Add-in Card Design.

EXPANSION BIOS CODE GOES DIRECTLY TO HARDWARE TO ACCESS CONFIG SPACE.

Expansion BIOS code should always use the PCI BIOS functions to access PCI configuration space. Expansion BIOS code should not assume, or try to determine, which config space access mechanism is implemented and then manipulate the hardware directly to access configuration space. Direct access of the hardware mechanism increases the code size of the expansion BIOS (because both mechanisms have to be supported) and may also cause problems if the hardware mechanism is not truly compliant.

EXPANSION BIOS CODE CHANGES OTHER DEVICE'S CONFIGURATION SETTINGS.

Some devices that have problems with certain PCI features (e.g.; bursting) have their expansion ROM code disable the feature in the platform chip set. This should not be done. Add–in boards that do this will cause systems to mysteriously have lower performance. Also more and more chip sets are appearing in systems and each of these have a device specific method for enabling/disabling platform features. It is impossible for expansion BIOS code to be aware of all chip sets so eventually the card will be added into a system where the feature is not disabled and the card will cause the system to fail. Bottom line is that Expansion ROM code should only modify the specific device that was added in.

TARGET INSERTS TOO MANY WAIT STATES BEFORE RETURNING FIRST DATA.

The PCI Specification is rather lenient about (in fact it doesn't specify) how many wait states the target (or the master) is allowed to insert between the ADDRESS PHASE and the first DATA PHASE of a bus transaction. Some devices abuse this leniency by inserting fifty or more wait states. While this is not technically illegal it is clearly ill behaved especially when there are protocol mechanisms where this bus hogging can be eliminated. target devices that cannot deliver data within a reasonable amount of time (16 clocks) after the ADDRESS PHASE should retry the access by asserting the STOP# signal. This allows the bus to be used by other PCI agents while the target clears up the condition that was causing the large number of wait states. The master will retry the transaction when it gets granted the bus). Note that some targets (if they are inherently slow on reads) may choose to automatically retry the access while they go fetch the read data. When the master tries the access again the target can then deliver the data with few wait states.

VGA DEVICES DON'T IMPLEMENT PALETTE SNOOP BIT CORRECTLY.

Some VGA devices operate correctly only when the Palette Snoop bit (bit 5 in the Command Register) is in a certain state. This is not the correct behavior in that VGA devices should continue to function no matter what the state of the Palette Snoop bit. See Appendix C for more details on the meaning and usage of the Palette Snoop bit.

ELECTRICAL SPECIFICATION NOTES

This appendix contains selected quotations from the PCI Local Bus Specification 2.1, reprinted with permission. Most of the references to this appendix will be found in Chapter 12.

DYNAMIC VS. STATIC DRIVE SPECIFICATION

The PCI bus has two electrical characteristics that motivate a different approach to specifying I/O buffer characteristics. First, PCI is a CMOS bus, which means that steady state currents (after switching transients have died out) are very minimal. In fact, the majority of the DC drive current is spent on pull-up resitors. Second, PCI is based on reflected wave rather than incident wave signaling. This means that bus drivers are sized to only switch the bus half way to the required high or low voltage. The electrical wave propagates down the bus, reflects off the unterminated end and back to the point of origin, thereby doubling the initial voltage excursion to achieve the required voltage level. The bus driver is actually in the middle of its switching range during this propagatioin time, which lasts up to 10 ns, one third of the bus cycle time at 33 MHz.

PCI bus drivers spend this relatively large proportion of time in transient switching, and thc DC current is minimal, so the typical approach of specifying buffers based on their DC current sourcing capability is not useful. PCI bus drivers are specified in terms of their AC switching characteristics, rather than DC drive. Specifically, the voltage to current relationship (V/I curve) of the driver through its active switching range is the primary means of specification. These V/I curves are targeted at achieving acceptable switching behavior in typical configurations of six loads on the motherboard and two expansion connectors, or two loads on the motherboard and four expansion connectors. However, it is possible to achieve different or larger configurations depending on the actual equipment practice, layout arrangement, loaded impedance of the motherboard, and so forth.

COMPONENT SPECIFICATION

This section specifies the electrical and timing parameters for PCI components, i.e., integrated circuit devices. Both 5V and 3.3V rail-to-rail signaling environments are defined. The 5V environment is based on absolute switching voltages in order to be compatible with TTL switching levels. The 3.3V environment, on the other hand, is based on V_{cc}-relative switching voltages, and is an optimized CMOS approach. The intent of the electrical specification is that components connect directly together, whether on the planar on an expansion board, without any external buffers or other "glue".

These specifications are intended to provide a design definition of PCI component electrical compliance and are not, in general, intended as actual test specifications. Some of the elements of this design definition cannot be tested in any practical way, but must be guaranteed by design characterization. It is the responsibility of component designers and ASIC vendors to devise an appropriate combination of device characterization and production tests, correlated to the parameters herein, in order to guarantee the PCI component complies with this design definition. All component specifications have reference to a packaged component, and therefore include package parasitics. Unless specifically stated otherwise, component parameters apply at the package pins; not at the bare silicon pads nor at card edge connectors.

The intent of this specification is that components operate within the "commerical" range of environmental parameters. However, this does not preclude the option of other operating environments at the vendor's discretion.

PCI output buffers are specified in terms of their V/I curves. Limits on acceptable V/I curves provide for a maximum output impedance that can achieve an acceptable first step voltage in typical configurations, and for a minimum output impedance that keeps the reflected wave within reasonable bounds. Pull-up and pull-down sides of the buffer have separate V/I curves, which are provided with the parametric specification. The effective buffer strength is primarily specified by an AC drive pint, which defines an acceptable first step voltage, both high going and low going, together with required currents to achieve that voltage in typical configurations. The DC drive point specifies steady state conditions that must be maintained, but in a CMOS environment these are minimal, and do not indicate real output drive strength. The shaded areas on the V/I curves shown in Figures 12-1 and 12-3 define the allowable range for output characteristics.

It is possible to use weaker output drivers that don't comply with the V/I curves or meet the timing parameters in this book, if they are set up to do continuous stepping as described in Section 3.6.3 of the PCI specification. However, this practice is strongly discouraged as it creates violations of the input setup time at all inputs, as well as having significant negative performance impacts. In any case, all output drivers must meet the turn off (float) timing specification.

DC parameters must be sustainable under steady state (DC) conditions. AC parameters must be guaranteed under transient switching (AC) conditions, which may represent up to 33% of the clock cycle. The sign on all current parameters (direction of current flow) is referenced to a ground *inside* the component; that is, positive currents flow into the component while negative currents flow out of the component. The behavior of reset is described in Section 4.3.2 of the specification rather than in this section.

CLOCK SPECIFICATION

The clock waveform must be delivered to each PCI component in the system. In the case of expansion boards, compliance with the clock specification is measured at the expansion board component, not at the connector slot. Figure G-1 shows the clock waveform and required measurement points for both 5V and 3.3V signaling environments. Table G-1 summarizes the clock specifications.

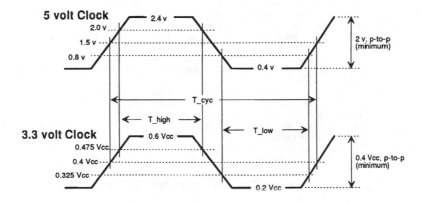

Figure G-1: Clock Waveforms

Symbol	Parameter	Min	Max	Units	Notes
t$_{CYC}$	CLK Cycle Time	30	∞	ns	1
t$_{HIGH}$	CLK High Time	11		ns	
t$_{LOW}$	CLK Low Time	11		ns	
-	CLK Slew Rate	1	4	V / ns	2
-	RST# Slew Rate	50		mV/n s	3

Notes:
1. In general, all PCI components must work with any clock frequency between nominal DC and 33 MHz. Device operational parameters at frequencies under 16 MHz may be guaranteed by design rather than by testing. The clock frequency may be changed at any time during the operation of the system so long as the clock edges remain 'clean' (monotonic) and the minimum cycle and high and low times are not violated. The clock may only be stopped in a low state. A variance on this specification is allowed for components designed for use on the system motherboard only. These components may operate at any single fixed frequency up to 33 MHz, and may enforce a policy of no frequency changes.
2. Rise and fall times are specified in terms of the edge rate measured in V/ns. This slew rate must be met across the minimum peak-to-peak portion of the clock waveform.
3. The minimum RST# slew rate applies only to the rising (deassertion) edge of the reset signal, and ensures that system noise cannot render an otherwise monotonic signal to appear to bounce in the switching range.

Table G-1: Clock and Reset Specifications

TIMING PARAMETERS

Table G-2 provides the timing parameters for 5V and 3.3V signaling environments.

5V AND 3.3V

Symbol	Parameter	Min	Max	Units	Notes
t_{VAL}	CLK to Signal Valid Delay-bussed signals	2	11	ns	1, 2, 3
t_{VAL}(ptp)	CLK to Signal Valid Delay-point to point	2	12	ns	1, 2, 3
t_{ON}	Float to Active Delay	2		ns	1,7
t_{OFF}	Active to Float Delay		28	ns	1,7
t_{SU}	Input Set Up Time to CLK-bussed signals	7		ns	7, 10
t_{SU}(ptp)	Input Set Up Time to CLK-point to point	10, 12		ns	3, 4
t_H	Input Hold Time from CLK	0		ns	4
t_{RST}	Reset Active Time After Power Stable	1		ms	5
$t_{RST-CLK}$	Reset Active Time After CLK Stable	100		µs	5
$t_{RST-OFF}$	Reset Active to Output Float Delay		40	ns	5, 6,7
t_{RRSU}	REQ64# to RST# setup time	10 * t_{CYC}		ns	
t_{RRH}	RST# to REQ64# hold time	0	50	ns	

NOTES:
1. See timing measurement conditions.
2. For 5V: Minimum times are measured with 0 pF equivalent load; maximum times are measured with 50 pF equivalent load. Actual test capacitance may vary, but results should be correlated to these specifications. Note that faster buffers may exhibit some ring back when attached to a 50 pF equivalent load, which should be of no consequence as long as the output buffers are in full compliance with slew rate and V/I curve specs. For 3.3V: Minimum times are evaluated with same load used for slew rate measurement; maximum times are evaluated with the load circuits shown in Rev. 2.1.
3. REQ# and GNT# are point-to-point signals, and have different output valid delay and input setup times than do bussed signals. GNT# has a setup of 10; REQ# has a setup of 12. All other signals are bussed.
4. See timing measurement conditions.
5. RST# is asserted and deasserted asynchronously with respect to CLK.
6. All output drivers must be floated when RST# is active.
7. For purposes of Active/Float timing measurements, the Hi-Z or "off" state is defined to be when the total current delivered through the component pin is less than or equal to the leakage current specification.

Table G-2: Timing Parameters

MEASUREMENT AND TEST CONDITIONS

Figures G-2 and G-3 define the conditions under which timing measurements are made. The component test guarantees that all timings are met with minimum clock slew rate (slowest edge) and voltage swing. The design must guarantee that minimum timings are also met with maximum clock slew rate (fastest edge) and voltage swing. In addition, the design must guarantee proper input operation for input voltage swings and slew rates that exceed the specified test conditions.

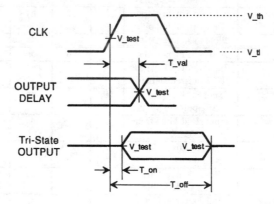

Figure G-2: Output Timing Measurement Conditions

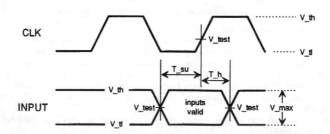

Figure G-3: Input Timing Measurement Conditions

Symbol	5V Signaling	3.3V Signaling	Units
V_{TH}	2.4	$0.6\ V_{CC}$	V (note)
V_{TL}	0.4	$0.2\ V_{CC}$	V (note)
V_{TEST}	1.5	$0.4\ V_{CC}$	V
V_{MAX}	2.0	$0.4\ V_{CC}$	V (note)
V_{STEP} rising edge	n/a	$0.285\ V_{CC}$	V
V_{STEP} falling edge	n/a	$0.615\ V_{CC}$	V
Input Signal Edge Rate	1 V/ns		

NOTE:
1. The input test for the 5V environment is done with 400 mV of overdrve (over V_{IH} and V_{IL}); the test for the 3.3V environment is done with $0.1\ *V_{CC}$ of overdrive. Timing parameters must be met with no more overdrive than this. V_{MAX} specifies the maximum peak-to-peak waveform allowed for testing input timing.

Table G-3: Measure and Test Condition Parameters

VENDOR PROVIDED SPECIFICATION

In the time frame of PCI, many system vendors will do board-level electrical simulation of PCI components. This will ensure that system implementations are manufacturable and that components are used correctly. To help facilitate this effort, as well as provide complete information, component vendors should make the following information available. It is recommended that component vendors make this information electronically available in the IBIS model format.

- Pin capacitance for all pins
- Pin inductance for all pins
- Output V/I curves under switching conditions. Two curves should be given for each output type used: one for driving high, the other for driving low. Both should show best-typical-worst curves. Also, "beyond-the-rail" response is critical, so the voltage range should span -5 to 10V for 5V signaling and -3 to 7V for 3.3V signaling.
- Input V/I curves under switching conditions. A V/I curve of the input structure when the output is tri-stated is also important. This plot should also show best-typical-worst curves over the range of 0 to V_{CC}.

- Rise/fall slew rates for each output type
- Complete absolute maximum data, including operating and non-operating temperature, DC maximums, etc.

In addition to this component information, connector vendors should make available accurate simulation models of PCI connectors.

Index

A

You are welcome to send us comments or questions concerning this or other Annabooks products, or to request a catalog of our other products and seminars.

Annabooks
11838 Bernardo Plaza Court
San Diego, CA 92128-2414

800-462-1042

619-673-0870

619-673-1432 FAX

73204.3405 @ compuserve.com